Strategy in the Contemporary World

New to this edition

- Updated chapters take account of the significant changes that have been taking place in global politics, including the geopolitical events and conflicts associated with the 'Arab Spring', the rise of China and the strategic adjustments to US security policies, and the exit strategies associated with the wars in Iraq and Afghanistan.

- A new chapter looks at cyberpower as a strategic instrument and discusses the future of warfare in light of the phenomenal pace of innovation in electronics and computer systems.

- Substantial updating throughout ensures that material is contemporary and relevant.

Strategy in the Contemporary World

An Introduction to Strategic Studies

FOURTH EDITION

Edited by

John Baylis

James J. Wirtz

Colin S. Gray

OXFORD
UNIVERSITY PRESS

OXFORD
UNIVERSITY PRESS

Great Clarendon Street, Oxford OX2 6DP,
United Kingdom

Oxford University Press is a department of the University of Oxford.
It furthers the University's objective of excellence in research, scholarship,
and education by publishing worldwide. Oxford is a registered trade mark of
Oxford University Press in the UK and in certain other countries

First Edition Published 2002
Second Edition Published 2007
Third Edition Published 2010

Impression: 2

British Library Cataloguing in Publication Data

Data available

ISBN 978-0-19-969478-5

Printed in Great Britain by
Ashford Colour Press Ltd, Gosport, Hampshire

To Leo and Connie Jo
And to Daniel and Andrew

Brief Contents

Detailed Contents ix

Acknowledgements xiv

List of Contributors xv

Preface to the Fourth Edition xix

Guided Tour of Learning Features xxii

Guided Tour of the Online Resource Centre xxiv

Strategy in the Contemporary World: Strategy after 9/11 1
John Baylis and James J. Wirtz

PART ONE **Enduring Issues of Strategy**

1   **The Causes of War and the Conditions of Peace** 19
     John Garnett

2   **The Evolution of Modern Warfare** 39
     Michael Sheehan

3   **Strategic Theory** 60
     Thomas G. Mahnken

4   **Strategic Culture** 76
     Jeffrey S. Lantis and Darryl Howlett

5   **Law, Politics, and the Use of Force** 96
     Justin Morris

6   **Geography and Strategy** 115
     Daniel Moran

7   **Technology and Warfare** 132
     Eliot Cohen

8   **Intelligence and Strategy** 151
     Roger George

PART TWO **Contemporary Problems**

9   **Irregular Warfare: Terrorism and Insurgency** 173
     James D. Kiras

10   **The Second Nuclear Age: Nuclear Weapons in the Twenty-first Century** 195
     C. Dale Walton

11 **The Control of Weapons of Mass Destruction**   213
John Baylis

12 **Conventional Power and Contemporary Warfare**   230
John Ferris

13 **Iraq, Afghanistan, and American Military Transformation**   247
Stephen Biddle

14 **Homeland Security: A New Strategic Paradigm?**   267
Jacob N. Shapiro and Rudolph P. Darken

15 **Humanitarian Intervention and Peace Operations**   286
Sheena Chestnut Greitens and Theo Farrell

16 **The Rise of Cyberpower**   303
John B. Sheldon

PART THREE **The Future of Strategy**

17 **A New Agenda for Security and Strategy?**   323
James J. Wirtz

18 **Strategic Studies and its Critics**   341
Columba Peoples

19 **The Practice of Strategy**   358
Colin S. Gray and Jeannie L. Johnson

20 **Does Strategic Studies have a Future?**   377
Lawrence Freedman

Notes   393
Bibliography   395
Index   415

Detailed Contents

Acknowledgements   xiv

List of Contributors   xv

Preface to the Fourth Edition   xix

Guided Tour of Learning Features   xxii

Guided Tour of the Online Resource Centre   xxiv

Strategy in the Contemporary World: Strategy after 9/11   **1**
John Baylis and James J. Wirtz

PART ONE Enduring Issues of Strategy

1   The Causes of War and the Conditions of Peace   **19**
John Garnett
Introduction   20
The Study of War   21
Human Nature Explanations of War   28
Wars 'Within' and 'Beyond' States   34
Conclusion   37

2   The Evolution of Modern Warfare   **39**
Michael Sheehan
Introduction   40
The Napoleonic Legacy   40
The Industrialization of War   44
Naval Warfare   47
Total War   49
Nuclear Weapons and Revolutionary Warfare   55
Conclusion: Postmodern War   56

3   Strategic Theory   **60**
Thomas G. Mahnken
Introduction   61
The Logic of Strategy   61
Clausewitz's *On War*   65
Sun Tzu, Mao, and the Jihadists   70
The Enduring Relevance of Strategy   72
Conclusion   74

4 Strategic Culture   **76**
Jeffrey S. Lantis and Darryl Howlett

Introduction   77
Thinking about Culture and Strategy   77
Sources of Strategic Culture   80
Constructivism and Strategic Culture   83
Continuing Issues   84
Delineating Non-state, State, and Multi-state Strategic Cultures   88
Strategic Culture and Weapons of Mass Destruction   90
Conclusion   93

5 Law, Politics, and the Use of Force   **96**
Justin Morris

Introduction: The Efficacy of International Law   97
Why States Obey the Law   98
International Law and the Use of Force   102
Jus ad Bellum   105
Jus in Bello   109
Conclusion   112

6 Geography and Strategy   **115**
Daniel Moran

Introduction: The Lay of the Land   116
Land Warfare: The Quest for Victory   117
Maritime Strategy   121
Airpower   124
The Final Frontier: Space War   128
War by Other Means: Cyberspace   129
Conclusion   130

7 Technology and Warfare   **132**
Eliot Cohen

Introduction: Technophiles and Technophobes   133
Some Ways of Thinking about Military Technology   133
Mapping Military Technology   136
The Revolution in Military Affairs Debate   138
Challenges of the New Technology   146
Conclusion: The Future of Military Technology   147

8   Intelligence and Strategy   **151**
Roger George

Introduction   152
What is Intelligence?   153
Intelligence as Enabler of US Strategy   157
Strategic Surprise: Causes and Correctives   160
The Post-9/11 World of Intelligence   164
Conclusion   168

PART TWO **Contemporary Problems**

9   Irregular Warfare: Terrorism and Insurgency   **173**
James D. Kiras

Introduction   174
Subverting the System: The Theory and Practice of Irregular Warfare   176
Protecting the System: Counterinsurgency and Counterterrorism
in Theory and Practice   184
Irregular Warfare Now and in the Future   189
Conclusion   192

10   The Second Nuclear Age: Nuclear Weapons in the Twenty-first Century **195**
C. Dale Walton

Introduction   196
The First Nuclear Age   197
Risks in the Second Nuclear Age   200
Adapting to the Second Nuclear Age   205
Conclusion: Looking Towards the Third Nuclear Age?   209

11   The Control of Weapons of Mass Destruction   **213**
John Baylis

Introduction   214
Arms Control during the Cold War   214
The Residual Role of Arms Control in the Post-Cold War Era   218
From Arms Control to Counterproliferation   220
The Challenges of Counterproliferation   222
The Diplomatic Option: Strategic Responses Withheld?   223
The Return of Arms Control: Attempts to Reduce the Saliency of Nuclear Weapons 224
Conclusion   227

12   Conventional Power and Contemporary Warfare   **230**
John Ferris

Introduction: Power and War—A History   231
New World Orders: 1945, 1989, 2001   232
Power and Hyperpower   234
Military Affairs: Revolution and Counter-Revolution   235
Arts of War   237
Military Balances   239
World on the Scales   241
War, What is It Good For?   242
Conclusion   245

13   Iraq, Afghanistan, and American Military Transformation   **247**
Stephen Biddle

Introduction   248
Afghanistan and the Transformation Thesis   249
Iraq 2003 and the Transformation Thesis   255
An Alternative View   259
Conclusion   263

14   Homeland Security: A New Strategic Paradigm?   **267**
Jacob N. Shapiro and Rudolph P. Darken

Introduction   268
A New Threat?   268
What Should Preparations Look Like?: Dealing with the Small-N Problem 273
What is the United States Preparing For?   274
Conclusion   282

15   Humanitarian Intervention and Peace Operations   **286**
Sheena Chestnut Greitens and Theo Farrell

Introduction   287
The Changing Face of Peacekeeping   287
The Politics of Humanitarian Intervention   292
The Military Character of Peace Operations   295
Conclusion: Problems and Prospects   300

16   The Rise of Cyberpower   **303**
John B. Sheldon

Introduction   304
Terms and Definitions   304
Cyberspace, Cyberpower, and the Infosphere   308
A New Dimension for Conflict   311
A Twenty-first Century Revolution in Military Affairs?   315
Conclusion   317

PART THREE **The Future of Strategy**

17 A New Agenda for Security and Strategy?   323
James J. Wirtz
Introduction   324
The Need for a Conceptual Framework   325
Population: The Demographics of Global Politics   327
Commons Issues   329
Direct Environmental Damage   332
Disease   334
Sensitivities and Vulnerabilities   338
Conclusion   339

18 Strategic Studies and its Critics   341
Columba Peoples
Introduction   342
Strategy and its Critics in the 'Golden Age'   342
Strategic Studies Strikes Back   345
Critical Approaches to Strategic Studies   348
A Continuing Debate?   355
Conclusion   356

19 The Practice of Strategy   358
Colin S. Gray and Jeannie L. Johnson
Introduction: Strategic Expertise   359
Improving a Strategic Education   359
The General Theory of Strategy   363
A Call for Consummate (Re)Assessing   373
Conclusion   374

20 Does Strategic Studies have a Future?   377
Lawrence Freedman
Introduction: The Development of Strategic Studies   378
In and Out of the Cold War   379
Strategy and the Crisis in Social Science   382
The Academic and Policy Worlds   384
Realism: Old and New   386
The Study of Armed Force   388
Conclusion: Does Strategic Studies Have a Future?   390

Notes   393
Bibliography   395
Index   415

Acknowledgements

We would like to thank the Naval Postgraduate School for providing a venue for our discussions on contemporary strategic issues and all those who participated in the Monterey Strategy Seminar. As in past editions, we are grateful to the US Advanced Systems Concepts Office, Defense Threat Reduction Agency, and especially David Hamon, for supporting our project. Sheena Chestnut Greitens of Harvard University deserves special mention for all her expertise and hard work in the administration and production of the final manuscript. The Editors would also like to thank Martha Skipper of Oxford University Press for her support and valuable advice during the production of the new edition.

List of Contributors

John Baylis is Emeritus Professor of Politics and International Relations and a former Pro-Vice Chancellor at Swansea University. Prior to that he had been Professor of International Politics and Dean of Social Sciences at Aberystwyth University. He has published more than twenty books and over a hundred chapters and articles. His books include *Anglo-American Defence Relations 1939–1984* (Macmillan, 1984); *Anglo-American Relations since 1939: The Enduring Alliance* (Manchester University Press, 1997); *Alternative Nuclear Futures: The Role of Nuclear Weapons in the Post-Cold War World*, with Robert O'Neill (Oxford University Press, 2000); *The Makers of Nuclear Strategy*, with John Garnett (Pinter, 1991). The *Globalization of World Politics*, with Steve Smith and Patricia Owens (5th edn, Oxford University Press, 2010); and *An Introduction to Global Politics*, with Steven Lamy, Steve Smith, and Patricia Owens (Oxford University Press, 2010). He has a BA, MSc (Econ), PhD and DLitt, from Swansea and Aberystwyth Universities.

Stephen Biddle is the Roger Hertog Senior Fellow for Defense Policy at the Council on Foreign Relations (CFR). Before joining CFR in January 2006, he held the Elihu Root Chair in military studies at the US Amy War College Strategic Studies Institute (SSI) and has held teaching and research posts at the University of North Carolina at Chapel Hill; the Institute for Defense Analyses (IDA); Harvard University's Belfer Center for Science and International Affairs (BCSIA); and the Harvard Kennedy School of Government's Office of National Security Programs. He is the author of *Military Power: Explaining Victory and Defeat in Modern Battle* (Princeton University Press, 2004), and is working on a book project examining the military methods of non-state actors.

Eliot A. Cohen is Robert E. Osgood Professor of Strategic Studies at Johns Hopkins University's School of Advanced International Studies. His books include *Supreme Command: Soldiers, Statesmen, and Leadership in Wartime* (2002) and, most recently, *Conquered into Liberty: Two Centuries of Battles Along the Great Warpath that made the American Way of War* (2011). From 2007 to 2009 he served as Counselor of the Department of State.

Rudolph Darken is Professor of Computer Science at the Naval Postgraduate School in Monterey, California. He also serves as Academic Chair for the Center for Homeland Defense and Security (CHDS) and is a past Director of the Modeling, Virtual Environments, and Simulation (MOVES) Institute. His research has been focused on training technologies and methodologies.

Theo Farrell is Professor of War in the Modern World in the Department of War Studies at King's College London, and Vice Chair of the British International Studies Association. He holds a three-year research fellowship (2009–2012) funded under the UK Research Council's 'Global Uncertainties Programme'. His most recent books, both as co-editor, are *A Transformation Gap? American Innovations and European Military Change* (Stanford University Press, 2010), and a forthcoming book on *Military Adaptation in the Afghanistan War*. Professor Farrell is currently writing a history of the British war in Afghanistan, 2001–2012.

John Ferris is Professor of History at The University of Calgary; Honorary Professor at The Department of International Politics, The University of Wales, Aberystwyth; and Adjunct Professor at The Department of War Studies, The Royal Military College of Canada. He publishes widely in military, international, strategic and intelligence history, and strategic studies.

Sir Lawrence Freedman has been Professor of War Studies at King's College London since 1982, and Vice-Principal since 2003. Elected a Fellow of the British Academy in 1995 and awarded the CBE in 1996, he was appointed Official Historian of the Falklands Campaign in 1997. He was awarded the KCMG in 2003. In June 2009 he was appointed to serve as a member of the official inquiry into Britain and the 2003 Iraq War. Professor Freedman has written extensively on nuclear strategy and the cold war, as well as commentating regularly on contemporary security issues. His most recent book, *A Choice of Enemies: America confronts the Middle East*, won the 2009 Lionel Gelber Prize and Duke of Westminster Medal for Military Literature.

John Garnett was formerly Woodrow Wilson Professor of International Politics at the University of Wales, Aberystwyth, and, until his retirement, Chairman of the Centre for Defence Studies at King's College London. He was educated at the London School of Economics where he received a first-class honours degree and master's in International Relations. He is the author of numerous books on International Relations and Strategic Studies, including *Contemporary Strategy* (Croom Helm, 1975) with John Baylis, Ken Booth, and Phil Williams; and *Makers of Nuclear Strategy* (Pinter, 1991) with John Baylis.

Roger Z. George is Professor at the National War College. He was a career CIA intelligence analyst who served at the State and Defense departments and has been the National Intelligence Officer for Europe. He is co-editor (with James B. Bruce) of *Analyzing Intelligence: Origins, Obstacles, and Innovations* (2008) and co-editor (with Harvey Rishikof) of *The National Security Enterprise: Navigating The Labyrinth* (2011).

Colin S. Gray is Professor of International Politics and Strategic Studies at the University of Reading. He worked for many years in the United States as well as in Britain, and has long been an advisor to the US and British Governments. The subjects of his professional concerns and writings span most of the domain of strategy. His books include *Modern Strategy* (Oxford University Press, 1999); *Another Bloody Century: Future Warfare* (Phoenix, 2006); *The Strategy Bridge: Theory for Practice* (Oxford University Press, 2010); (with John Andreas Olsen) eds., *The Practice of Strategy: From Alexander the Great to the Present* (Oxford University Press, 2011); *War, Peace, and International Relations: An Introduction to Strategic History*, 2nd edn (Routledge, 2011); and *Airpower for Strategic Effect* (Maxwell AFB: Air University Press, 2012), this next book, *Perspectives on Strategy*, a follow-on to *The Strategy Bridge*, will be published by Oxford University Press.

Sheena Chestnut Greitens is a doctoral candidate in the Department of Government at Harvard University and a Fellow at the United States Institute of Peace and the University of Virginia's Miller Center for Public Affairs. Her most recent publication is 'The People's Republic of China at Sixty: Is it Rising?' in William C. Kirby, ed., *The People's Republic of China at 60: An International Assessment* (Harvard University Press, 2011, with Alastair Iain Johnston), which has also been published, in Chinese, in the *China International Strategy Review*.

Darryl Howlett obtained his master's degree from Lancaster University and his PhD from Southampton University. He teaches at Southampton University. His most recent publications include 'The Emergence of Stability: Deterrence-in-Motion and Deterrence Reconstructed', in Ian R. Kenyon and John Simpson, eds., *Deterrence and the Changing Security Environment* (Routledge, 2006).

Jeannie L. Johnson is a Lecturer in the Political Science Department at Utah State University. She is a former intelligence officer and is co-editor of *Strategic Culture and Weapons of Mass Destruction: Culturally Based Insights into Comparative National Security Policymaking* (New York: Palgrave Macmillan, 2009).

James D. Kiras is an Associate Professor and Director of International Programs at the School of Advanced Air and Space Studies, Air University, Maxwell Air Force Base, Alabama, where he directs the course on irregular warfare and also teaches on military theory and defence policy. He received his PhD from the University of Reading (UK) and is a Senior Associate Fellow of the Joint Special Operations University, United States Special Operations Command, Tampa, Florida. Dr Kiras co-authored *Understanding Modern Warfare* (Cambridge University Press, 2008) and his first book was *Special Operations and Strategy: From World War II to the War on Terrorism* (Routledge, 2006).

Jeffrey S. Lantis is Professor of Political Science/International Relations at The College of Wooster. He earned a PhD in Political Science from The Ohio State University. A former Fulbright Senior Scholar in Australia, he is an expert on strategic culture, international security, and nuclear non-proliferation. Among his many books and academic journal articles, Lantis is author of *The Life and Death of International Treaties* (Oxford University Press, 2009) and co-editor of *Foreign Policy in Comparative Perspective: Domestic and International Influences on State Behavior* (CQ Press, 2012).

Thomas G. Mahnken is currently Jerome E. Levy Chair of Economic Geography and National Security at the US Naval War College and a Visiting Scholar at the Philip Merrill Center for Strategic Studies at The Johns Hopkins University's Paul H. Nitze School of Advanced International Studies (SAIS). His books include *Competitive Strategies for the 21st Century* (Stanford University Press, 2012); *Technology and the American Way of War Since 1945* (Columbia University Press, 2008); and *Uncovering Ways of War: US Intelligence and Foreign Military Innovation, 1918–1941* (Cornell University Press, 2002). He is editor of *The Journal of Strategic Studies*.

Daniel Moran is a Professor in the Department of National Security Affairs at the Naval Postgraduate School, Monterey, California.

Justin Morris is Head of the Department of Politics and International Studies at the University of Hull, UK. His primary research interests include international organizations, particularly the United Nations Security Council, humanitarian intervention, the relationship between power and responsibility, and the role of international law in international politics. He is co-author (with the late Professor Hilaire McCoubrey) of *Regional Peacekeeping in the Post-Cold War Era* (Kluwer, 2000) and co-editor (with Dr Richard Burchill and Professor Nigel White) of *International Conflict and Security Law: Essays in Memory of Hilaire McCoubrey* (Cambridge University Press, 2005). He is currently working on a project on great powers and international hierarchy.

Columba Peoples is Lecturer in International Relations in the School of Sociology, Politics, and International Studies at the University of Bristol. He received his PhD in International Politics from the University of Wales, Aberystwyth in 2007, and is the author of *Justifying Ballistic Missile Defence: Technology, Security, and Culture* (Cambridge University Press, 2010).

Jacob N. Shapiro is Assistant Professor of Politics and International Affairs at Princeton University and co-directs the Empirical Studies of Conflict Project. His research focuses on political violence, the uses of development assistance, and security policy.

Michael Sheehan is Professor of International Relations at Swansea University. He is a graduate of Aberystwyth University (BSc in International Politics 1976, PhD 1985). He was formerly Director of the Scottish Centre for International Security at Aberdeen University. He is the author of 11 books on security, the most recent being *International Security: An Analytical Survey* (Lynne Rienner, 2005); *The International Politics of Space* (Routledge, 2007); and *Securing Outer Space*, (Routledge, 2009, co-edited with Natalie Bormann). His next book is *The Ethics and Law of War in Space*, (Continuum, forthcoming, with Michel Bourbonnière).

John B. Sheldon has a PhD from Reading (UK) and is Assistant Professor of Space and Cyberspace Strategic Studies at the School of Advanced Air and Space Studies (SAASS), Maxwell AFB, Alabama, where he directs the Information and Cyberspace course.

C. Dale Walton is an Assistant Professor in International Relations and Strategic Studies Lindenwood University, St. Louis. His previous career experience includes serving on the faculty of Defense and Strategic Studies Department at Missouri State University and as a Senior Analyst with the National Institute for Public Policy. His works include *Grand Strategy and the Presidency: Foreign Policy, War, and the American Role in the World*; *Geopolitics and the Great Powers in the Twenty-first Century: Multipolarity and Revolution in Strategic Perspective*; and *The Myth of Inevitable U.S. Defeat in Vietnam*. He is also a co-author of *Understanding Modern Warfare*.

James J. Wirtz is the Dean of the School of International Graduate Studies, Naval Postgraduate School, Monterey, California. He is the co-editor of *Over The Horizon Proliferation Threats* (Stanford University Press, 2012).

Preface to the Fourth Edition

The first edition of *Strategy in the Contemporary World* reflected the notion that security studies had given too much emphasis to non-military issues. This situation reflected the euphoria that followed the relatively peaceful end of the cold war, a mood that cast the first Gulf War, the conflicts associated with the disintegration of Yugoslavia, and tribal wars in Africa as aberrations that highlighted the positive trends in world politics. The first edition asserted that there was room for scholarship that focused on the sad reality that military power remained a significant feature of the world in which we live. It evaluated many of the theories, which had been developed during the cold war, by testing their relevance in the new post-cold war environment. The aim of the first edition was to show what insights from this era remained relevant, which ones needed to be redefined, and what new ideas might be incorporated into strategic studies.

The attacks on the World Trade Center and the Pentagon in September 2001 occurred just as the first edition was near completion. It was now clear that ideas of 'perpetual peace' were not going to be realized anytime soon. In the aftermath of the attacks, the relevance and significance of the first edition changed. There was now an increased need to address issues of war and peace that were of immediate concern, especially terrorism, irregular warfare, the spread of weapons of mass destruction, and the revolution in military affairs. Strategy had returned.

Our second edition contained a more specific set of reflections on the role of military power in the contemporary world. It offered analyses of the recent conflicts in Afghanistan and the Iraq War and the ongoing debates about the lessons that can be learnt from these wars. Attention was also given to the strategic implications of the changing structure of global politics and the role of American military power in a unipolar world. At a broader conceptual level, the second edition went further than the first volume by analysing the continuing relevance of various theories of peace and security in a world that is vastly different from the cold war era when these concepts were central to most thinking about strategic studies. There was also considerably more emphasis in the second edition on the implications of 9/11 and the war on terrorism, as well as on the prospects for further proliferation of weapons of mass destruction, not only by states but also by non-state actors.

Our third edition offered an update on a host of topics that had come into sharper focus since the middle of the decade. 'Homeland Security', a topic that was not even addressed by the first edition, had emerged further as a distinct area of study. Strategists, it was argued, had to deal with a set of policy concerns focused on intragovernmental relations, finding a balance between privacy and security and devising credible measures of effectiveness when it came to preventing domestic terrorism. We also added a new chapter on the contribution of intelligence in the formulation of strategy—an issue that is often at the centre of national debates about politics and policy. In response to several requests from users of our earlier editions, we also gave critics of strategic studies their say, which added an important part of the 'story' of strategic studies to our text. And for the twenty-first century strategists using the volume, we gave some advice on how they might go about doing a better job at strategy than those scholars and practitioners who were centre stage at the time.

For this fourth edition we have again listened carefully to the comments of a wide range of reviewers from a number of different countries. We have updated the chapters to take account of the significant changes that have been taking place in global politics, especially the geopolitical events (and conflicts) associated with the 'Arab Spring', the rise of China and the strategic adjustments to US security policies, the exit strategies associated with the wars in Iraq and Afghanistan, as well as important technological changes affecting security policies. In the latter case, this has required a new chapter on cyberpower and cyber warfare, which have become increasingly important in the period since the last edition was written. Important questions arise about whether cyberpower represents a form of warfare and whether it affects the nature of war in the sense that we have traditionally known it. In order to respond to criticisms of what some reviewers saw as the narrowness of the theoretical approaches adopted across the various contributions we have also added to the 'Critique' chapter by discussing alternative theoretical approaches to the traditional realist perspectives that have tended to dominate strategic studies.

We trust that our readers, the future strategists and policymakers of tomorrow, will benefit from our efforts to place the enduring concepts of strategy into a contemporary context. We have written these essays with you in mind.

Guided Tour of Learning Features

This book is enriched with a range of learning tools to help you navigate the text and reinforce your knowledge of Strategic Studies. This guided tour shows you how to get the most out of your textbook package and do better in your studies.

Reader's Guide

Recent years have seen the rapid spread of info
gies around the world, creating a globally con
Every aspect of modern society, from how we
can now be said to be cyberdependent. Nearly
enabled by cyberspace. This is both an advantag

Reader's Guides

Reader's Guides at the beginning of every chapter set the scene for upcoming themes and issues to be discussed, and indicate the scope of coverage within each chapter topic.

BOX 15.3 The CNN Effect as a Double-ed

The fact that the USA pulled the plug on its Somali in
firefight in October 1993 indicates how capricious pu
dying Somalis had persuaded the outgoing [George H
humanitarian rescue mission, but once the US public
Americans being dragged through the streets of Mo

Boxes

A number of topics benefit from further explanation or exploration in a manner that does not disrupt the flow of the main text. Throughout the book, boxes provide you with extra information on particular topics that complement your understanding of the main chapter text.

Key points

- The idea that war is endemic in the human conditi nevertheless be true. Even if human nature cannot behaviour so that wars are less frequent.
- Since there are many different kinds of war, it is not su

Key Points

Each main chapter section ends with a set of Key points that summarize the most important arguments developed within each chapter topic.

Questions

1. What were the key characteristics of the Firs the two nuclear ages differ?

2. Why might the cold war model of nuclear de In what respects might it still be relevant?

3. Does the horizontal proliferation of nuclear

Questions

A set of carefully devised questions has been provided to help you assess your comprehension of core themes, and may also be used as the basis of seminar discussion and coursework.

Further Reading

John Glenn, Darryl A. Howlett, Stuart Poore (eds
UK: Ashgate, 2004).
A recent classic, this book addresses head-on the
cultural and ideational models versus the more p

A. Hyde-Price, 'European Security, Strategic C

 Web Links

Atlantic Council's *Cyber Statecraft Initiative* **http:/**
site provides excellent analysis of cyberpower
statecraft, and international politics.

The Citizen Lab **http://citizenlab.org/** Hosted by
of Toronto, this innovative outfit stands at the

Further Reading

To take your learning further, reading lists have
been provided as a guide to find out more about
the issues raised within each chapter topic and
to help you locate the key academic literature in
the field.

Web Links

At the end of every chapter you will find an
annotated summary of useful web sites that
are central to Strategic Studies and that will
be instrumental in further research.

Guided Tour of the Online Resource Centre

The Online Resource Centre that accompanies this book provides students and instructors with ready-to-use teaching and learning materials. These resources are free of charge and designed to maximize the learning experience.

www.oxfordtextbooks.co.uk/orc/baylis4e/

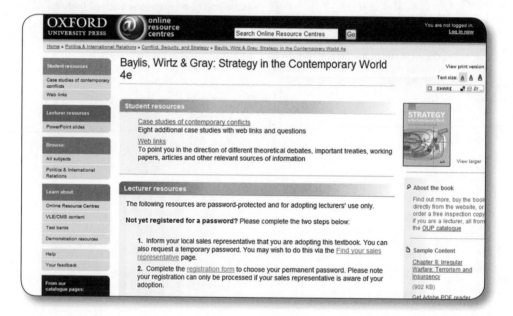

For students:

Case Studies

Eight additional case studies with web links and questions on the following conflicts:

1. Afghanistan
2. Israel's invasion of Lebanon and action in Gaza
3. The South Ossetian war
4. The US—Coalition invasion and occupation of Iraq
5. The conflict in the Congo
6. The Russian war in Chechnya
7. The Israel—Palestinian struggle from the Oslo Accords to the present day
8. The Iran—Iraq War

Web Links

Web links have been provided to point you in the direction of different theoretical debates, important treaties, working papers, articles, and other relevant sources of information.

For instructors:

Password protected to ensure only lecturers can access these resources, each registration is personally checked to ensure the security of the site.

Registering is easy: click on 'Lecturer Resources' on the Online Resource Centre, complete a simple registration form which allows you to choose your own username and password, and access will be granted within three working days (subject to verification).

PowerPoint Slides

These complement each chapter of the book and are a useful resource for preparing lectures and handouts. They allow you to guide students through the key concepts and can be fully customized to meet the needs of the course.

Strategy in the Contemporary World: Strategy after 9/11

JOHN BAYLIS AND JAMES J. WIRTZ

 Chapter Contents

Introduction to the Fourth Edition   2

What is Strategic Studies?   4

Strategic Studies and the Classical Realist Tradition   7

What Criticisms are made of Strategic Studies?   9

What is the Relationship between Strategic Studies and Security Studies?   13

Introduction to the Fourth Edition

Books often reflect a specific historical context, shaped by the hopes, fears, and problems that preoccupy authors and policymakers alike. This is especially true of books on strategy, security studies, and public policy because contemporary issues are of paramount importance to authors in these fields. Our efforts also reflect contemporary threats and opportunities. When we gathered in September 2000 to present chapters for the first edition of this volume, we wanted to create a textbook that demonstrated the continued relevance of strategy and strategic studies and to interpret contemporary issues using insights gained from the classic works on strategy. Little did we know that less than a year later, the 'New World Order', would be shattered by the al-Qaeda attacks on the Pentagon and the World Trade Center. The wars in Afghanistan and Iraq, the terrorist bombings in Madrid in 2004 and London in 2005, and the proliferation of nuclear weapons to North Korea, erased any lingering doubts about the relevance of strategy when it came time to produce the second and third editions of this volume. By the time we gathered again in September 2011 to discuss our contributions to our ongoing project, the 'al-Qaeda' decade had come to an end. But as we scanned the strategic horizon, we began to consider the possibility of a renewal of balance of power politics along the Pacific Rim, a showdown between the West and Iran over its nuclear weapons programme, and the potential threat posed by cyberwar. In the nearly 15 years since we started this project, the 'New World Order' had been superseded by the 'war against transnational terror', which has in turn been replaced by concerns about the emergence of new forms of warfare and a return of Great Power rivalry.

It is clear that interest in strategic studies is cyclical and reflects the times. Strategic studies emerged during the early years of the cold war when political leaders, government officials, and academics interested in security issues wrestled with the problems of how to survive and prosper in the nuclear age, when Armageddon might be just minutes away. Given the experiences of the 1930s, when appeasement and 'utopian' ideas of collective security had largely failed to ensure peace, the prevailing mindset during the cold war was one of 'realism'. It was believed that in a world characterized by anarchy and unending competition, states inevitably exercised power to secure their national interests. For nuclear age realists, however, power had to be exercised in a way that promoted the interests of the state, while at the same time avoiding a conflict, which would lead to the destruction not only of the states involved but of civilization as a whole. This predicament gave rise to theories of deterrence, limited war, and arms control that dominated the literature of strategic studies (and indeed international relations) during the period from the 1950s to the 1980s. Writings by Herman Kahn, Bernard Brodie, Henry Kissinger, Albert Wohlstetter, and Thomas Schelling became classics in the field.

Did the key assumptions inherent in the strategic studies literature lead to the adoption of particular security policies or did policy itself drive the writing on the subject? The answer to these questions remains a matter of debate. Some believed that the literature reflected existing realities, others believed that the writings themselves helped to generate a particular way of looking at the world and legitimized the use of military power. An iterative process was probably at work, however, as theory and practice modified and reinforced each other.

The great strength of the literature on strategic studies was that it reflected the harsh realities of a world in which military power was (regardless of utopian ideals) an instrument of state policy. One of its weaknesses, however, was the inherent conservatism in realist thinking that implied that the contemporary world was the best of all possible worlds. For good theoretical and practical reasons, realists hoped that the cold war, with its magisterial confrontation between the United States and the Soviet Union, would continue into the indefinite future. Significant change, because it raised the spectre of nuclear Armageddon, was a prospect that was nearly too horrific to contemplate and too risky to act upon.

With the relatively peaceful collapse of the Soviet Union, realism came under suspicion and the ideas and policies of disarmament advocates and utopian thinkers began to hold greater sway in policy circles. The 1990s was the decade of the 'peace dividend' and 'dot.com' mania as the information revolution entered consumer and business culture. The preoccupation of strategists with the state, and its use of military power, was viewed by a new generation of 'utopian' scholars as part of the problem of international security itself. Strategists were often seen as 'dinosaurs'. Preoccupied with 'old think', they appeared unwilling to come to terms with the fact that force was apparently fading as a factor in world politics. The traditional emphasis on the military aspects of security was challenged by scholars who believed that the concept should be broadened and deepened. According to this view, there were political, economic, societal, and environmental aspects of security that had been ignored. Some scholars asserted that 'security' as a concept had been used by elites to push issues to the top of the political agenda or to secure additional resources for particular policies and government organizations and military programmes. In the view of some critics, official policy was pushed along by armies of military contractors and manufacturers, government workers, and members of the military who had a vested interest in keeping war alive to preserve their careers and livelihoods.

By the mid-1990s, these criticisms of traditional realist thinking were transformed into mainstream scholarship. Security studies emerged as an area of intellectual enquiry that increasingly eclipsed strategic studies. Researchers came to focus on the nature of security itself and how greater security might be achieved at the individual, societal, and even global levels, compared with the cold war preoccupation with state security, defined only in military terms. Although security studies reflected a wider range of theoretical positions than had characterized strategic studies in the past, there was a strong normative (realists would say utopian) dimension to much of the writing, especially from those of a post-positivist persuasion. The end of the cold war fundamentally challenged the conservative tendency in realism (and the strategic studies literature). Peaceful change was now a reality and military power was no longer seen by many as the predominant prerequisite for security. The balance of terror between East and West had not simply been mitigated (in line with the theories proposed in the strategic studies literature) but had now been transcended, opening up the prospects for a new more peaceful world.

Although the post-cold war euphoria and the literature that followed in its wake was very much a product of its time, there were warning signs in the years leading up to the millennium that the emergence of peace, or as Francis Fukuyama put it 'an end of history' (meaning an end of major conflicts), might have been premature. The first Gulf War, the conflicts associated with the disintegration of Yugoslavia, and tribal wars in Africa demonstrated all too clearly that military force remained a ubiquitous feature of the contemporary world. It was at this point, just as the attacks on the Twin Towers and the Pentagon took place in September 2001, that the first edition of this book was published. The book reflected a growing feeling that perhaps too much emphasis in security studies literature had been given to non-military security. The argument contained in the book was that, useful as this new literature was, there was still room for writing and scholarship that focused on the sad, but continuing, reality that military power remained a significant feature of world politics. The book was very much a product of its time, and things changed on the morning of 11 September 2001.

Although the first edition had much to say about our present circumstances, the second and third editions reflected a more mature set of reflections on the role of military power in the contemporary world and the changes that have occurred over the last decade. Our fourth volume reflects analyses of the recent conflicts including Afghanistan, the Iraq War, and Libya, following the Arab Spring, Georgia, Lebanon, and Gaza, as well as the ongoing debates about the lessons that can be learned from these conflicts. We also explore the debates about whether there has been a revolution in military affairs and the future of warfare, given the phenomenal pace of innovation in electronics and computer systems, which is often referred to as cyberwar. Attention is also given to the strategic implications of the changing structure of global politics and the role of American military power in a world in transition. At a broader conceptual level this edition also explores the continuing relevance of various theories of peace and security in a world that is vastly different from the cold war era when these concepts were central to most thinking about strategic studies. Looking back from the perspective of the fourth edition, it is illustrative to note that issues that barely received mention at the turn of the last century—cyber warfare, transnational terrorism, homeland security—now seem to be enduring issues for consideration by strategists. To set the scene for the chapters that follow, this introduction answers three questions: (1) What is strategic studies? (2) What criticisms are made of strategic studies? and (3) What is the relationship of strategic studies to security studies?

What is Strategic Studies?

The definitions of 'strategy' contained in Box 1 display some common features but also significant differences. The definitions by Carl von Clausewitz, Field Marshal Count H. Von Moltke, B. H. Liddell Hart, and Andre Beaufre all focus on a fairly narrow definition, which relates military force to the objectives of war. This reflects the origins of the word strategy, which is derived from the ancient Greek term for 'generalship'. The definitions from Gregory Foster and Robert Osgood, however, draw attention to the broader focus on 'power', while Williamson Murray and Mark Grimslay highlight the dynamic quality of 'process' inherent in the formulation of strategy. Recently, writers have emphasized that strategy (particularly in the nuclear age) has a peacetime as well as a wartime application. Strategy embodies more than just the study of wars and military campaigns. Strategy is the application of military power to achieve political objectives, or more specifically 'the theory and practice of the use, and threat of use, of organized force for political purposes' (Gray 1999a). Broader still is the concept of Grand Strategy, which involves the coordination and direction of 'all the resources of a nation, a band of nations, towards the attainment of the political objectives' sought (Liddell Hart 1967).

BOX 1 Definitions of Strategy

Strategy (is) the use of engagements for the object of war.

Carl von Clausewitz

Strategy is the practical adaptation of the means placed at a general's disposal to the attainment of the object in War.

Von Moltke

Strategy is the art of distributing and applying military means to fulfill the ends of policy.

Liddell Hart

Strategy is . . . the art of the dialectic of force or, more precisely, the art of the dialectic of two opposing wills using force to resolve their dispute.

Andre Beaufre

Strategy is ultimately about effectively exercising power.

Gregory D. Foster

Strategy is a plan of action designed in order to achieve some end; a purpose together with a system of measures for its accomplishment.

J. C. Wylie

Strategy is a process, a constant adaptation to the shifting conditions and circumstances in a world where chance, uncertainty, and ambiguity dominate.

W. Murray and M. Grimslay

Strategy must now be understood as nothing less than the overall plan for utilizing the capacity for armed coercion—in conjunction with economic, diplomatic, and psychological instruments of power—to support foreign policy most effectively by overt, covert, and tacit means.

Robert Osgood

Because strategy provides the bridge between military means and political goals, students of strategy require knowledge of both politics and military operations. Strategy deals with the difficult problems of national policy, the areas where political, economic, psychological, and military factors overlap. There is no such thing as purely military advice when it comes to issues of strategy. This point has also been made in a different way by Henry Kissinger, who stated that

> the separation of strategy and policy can only be achieved to the detriment of both. It causes military power to become identified with the most absolute application of power and it tempts diplomacy into an over-concern with finesse.
>
> Kissinger (1957)

Strategy is best studied from an interdisciplinary perspective. To understand the dimensions of strategy, it is necessary to know something about politics, economics, psychology, sociology, and geography, as well as technology, force structure, and tactics.

Strategy is also essentially a pragmatic and practical activity. This is summed up in Bernard Brodie's comment that 'Strategic theory is a theory of action'. It is a 'how to do it' study, a guide to accomplishing objectives and attaining them efficiently. As in many other branches of politics, the question that matters in strategy is: will the idea work? As such, in some ways strategic studies is 'policy relevant'. It can be an intellectual aid to official performance. At the same time, however, it can also be pursued as 'an idle academic pursuit for its own sake' (Brodie 1973).

Strategic studies, however, cannot be regarded as a discipline in its own right. It is a subject with a sharp focus—the role of military power—but no clear parameters, and it is relies upon arts, sciences, and social science subjects for ideas and concepts. Scholars who have contributed to the literature on the subject have come from very different fields. Herman Kahn was a physicist, Thomas Schelling was an economist, Albert Wohlstetter was a mathematician, Henry Kissinger was a historian, and Bernard Brodie was a political scientist.

Given the different academic backgrounds of strategic thinkers, it is not surprising that strategic studies has witnessed an ongoing debate about methodology (i.e. how to study the subject). Bernard Brodie, who more than anyone else helped to establish strategic studies as a subject in the aftermath of the Second World War, initially argued that strategy should be studied 'scientifically'. He was concerned that strategy was 'not receiving the scientific treatment it deserves either in the armed services or, certainly, outside them'. In his 1949 article entitled 'Strategy as Science', Brodie called for a methodological approach to the study of strategy similar to the one adopted by economics. Strategy, he argued, should be seen as 'an instrumental science for solving practical problems'. What he wanted was a more rigorous, systematic form of analysis of strategic issues compared with the rather narrow approach to security problems adopted by the military, who were preoccupied with tactics and technology.

As Brodie himself was later to recognize, however, the enthusiasm for science, which he had helped to promote, meant that strategic studies in the 1950s 'developed a scientistic strain and overreached itself'. By the 1960s, Brodie was calling for a 'mid-course correction'. The conceptualization of strategy using economic models and theories had been taken further than he had expected. Brodie was concerned about the 'astonishing lack of political sense' and the 'ignorance of diplomatic and military history' that seemed to be evident among those writing about strategy. Brodie's worries were heeded. From the 1970s onwards, more comparative historical analysis was introduced into strategic studies.

The academic approach to the study of strategy also raised concerns about the neglect of operational military issues. For Brodie (echoing Clemenceau) strategy was too serious a business to be left to the generals. As strategic studies developed in the late 1940s, civilian analysts came to dominate the field. By the 1980s, however, there was a growing feeling that many of the civilian strategists in their university departments and academic think tanks were ignoring the capabilities and limitations of military units and operations in their analyses and theorizing. For a new breed of strategists, the reality of operational issues had to be brought back into their studies. Military science had become the 'missing discipline'. Writing in 1997, Richard K. Betts suggested that: 'if strategy is to integrate policy and operations, it must be devised not just by politically sensitive soldiers but by military sensitive civilians'. Just as Brodie had been concerned about the overly narrow approach of the military in 1949, so Betts was concerned that the pendulum had swung too far in the opposite direction. Although as Stephen Biddle has demonstrated in his volume entitled *Military Power*, in the end it was left to a civilian strategist to make headway in understanding the changes unfolding on the modern battlefield (Biddle 2004).

This concern with operational issues helped to revive an interest among strategists with the different 'elements' or 'dimensions' of strategy. In his study *On War*, Clausewitz argued that 'everything in strategy is very simple, but that does not mean that everything is very easy'. Reflecting this sentiment, Clausewitz pointed out that strategy consisted of moral, physical, mathematical, geographical, and statistical elements. Michael Howard, in a similar vein, refers to the social, logistical, operational, and technological dimensions of strategy. This notion of strategy consisting of a broad, complex, pervasive, and interpenetrating set of dimensions is also explored in Colin Gray's study, entitled *Modern Strategy*. Gray identifies three main categories ('People and politics'; 'Preparation for war'; and 'War proper') and seventeen dimensions of strategy. Under the 'People and politics' heading he focuses on people, society, culture, politics, and ethics. 'Preparations for war' includes economics and logistics, organization, military administration, information and intelligence, strategic theory and doctrine, and technology. The dimensions of 'War proper' consist of military operations, command, geography, friction, the adversary, and time. Echoing Clausewitz, Gray argues that the study of strategy is incomplete if it is considered in the absence of any one of these (interrelated) dimensions.

Strategic Studies and the Classical Realist Tradition

What are the traditional philosophical underpinnings or assumptions of the scholars, soldiers, and policymakers who have written about strategy? Most contemporary strategists in the Western world belong to the same intellectual tradition. They share a set of assumptions about the nature of international political life, and the kind of reasoning that can best handle political–military problems. This set of assumptions is often referred to by the term 'realism'.

Although there are differences between 'realists', there are certain views and assumptions that most would agree upon. These can be best illustrated under the headings of human nature; anarchy and power; and international law, morality, and institutions.

Human Nature

Most traditional realists are pessimistic about human nature. Reflecting the views of philosophers like Thomas Hobbes, people are seen as 'inherently destructive, selfish, competitive, and aggressive'. Hobbes accepted that human beings are capable of generosity, kindness, and cooperation but the pride and egoism, which is inherent in human nature, means that mankind is also prone to conflict, violence, and great evil. For realist writers, one of the great tragedies of the human condition is that these destructive traits can never be eradicated. Reflecting this view, Herbert Butterfield argued that 'behind the great conflicts of mankind is a terrible human predicament which lies at the heart of the story' (in Butterfield and Wight, 1966). Thus, realism is not a normative theory in the sense that it purports to offer a way to eliminate violence from the world. Instead, it offers a way to cope with the ever-present threat of conflict by the use of strategy to minimize the likelihood and severity of international violence. Realists tend to stress what they see as the harsh realities of world politics and are somewhat contemptuous of Kantian approaches that highlight the possibility of 'permanent peace'. As Gordon Harland has argued:

Realism is a clear recognition of the limits of reason in politics: the acceptance of the fact that political realities are power realities and that power must be countered with power; that self-interest is the primary datum in the action of all groups and nations.
Herzog (1963)

In an anarchical system, power is the only currency of value when security is threatened.

Anarchy and Power

Given this rather dark view of the human condition, realists tend to view international relations in similarly pessimistic terms. Conflict and war are seen as endemic in world politics and the future is likely to be much like the past. States (upon which realists focus their attention) are engaged in a relentless competitive struggle. In contrast to the way in which conflicts are dealt with in domestic society, however, the clash between states is more difficult to resolve because there is no authoritative government to create justice and the rule of law. In the absence of world government, realists note that states have adopted a 'self-help' approach to their interests and especially their security. In other words, they reserve the right to use lethal force to achieve their objectives, a right that individuals living in civil society have given up to the state. Who wins in international relations does not depend on who is right according to some moral or legal ruling. As Thucydides demonstrated in his account of the Peloponnesian wars, power determines who gets their way. In international relations, *might* makes *right*.

International Law, Morality, and Institutions

Realists see a limited role for 'reason', law, morality, and institutions in world politics. In a domestic context, law can be an effective way for societies to deal with competing selfish interests. In an international system without effective government, states will agree to laws when it suits them, but will disregard them when their interests are threatened. When states want to break the rules, there is very little to stop them from doing it apart from countervailing force.

Similarly, realists do not believe that moral considerations can significantly constrain the behaviour of states. Some realists believe that very little attention should be given to moralizing about the state of world politics. They point to the absence of a universal moral code and to the disregard of constraining moral principles by policymakers, especially when they believe their vital interests are threatened. This is not to argue that realists are wholly insensitive to moral questions. Great realist thinkers, including Rheinhold Niebuhr and Hans Morgenthau, agonized about the human condition. Most realist writers, however, attempt to explain the way the world is, rather than how it ought to be. Realists view international institutions (e.g. the United Nations or the Nuclear Nonproliferation Treaty) in much the same light as they view law and morality. Just as law and morality are unable to constrain state behaviour significantly when important state interests are threatened, international institutions can also only play a limited role in preventing conflict. Realists do not dismiss the opportunities created by institutions for greater cooperation. They see these institutions, however, not as truly independent actors but as agents set up by states to serve their national interests. As long as they do this, the member states will support the institution, but when support for the institution threatens national interests, nations tend to abandon or ignore them. Realists point to the inability of the League of Nations in the interwar period to stop aggression, or the way the United Nations became a hostage to the cold war as evidence of the limited utility of these organizations. When it really mattered, international institutions could not act against the interests of their member states (see Chapter 5).

What Criticisms are made of Strategic Studies?

Although the shared philosophical underpinnings of strategists have helped to give the subject intellectual coherence, many realist assumptions have been subjected to fierce criticism. This critique has been discussed in detail elsewhere (Gray 1982 and Chapter 18), but our purpose here is to give a flavour of the concern expressed by critics of strategic studies. Strategists are said to be:

- obsessed with conflict and force,
- insufficiently concerned with ethical issues,
- not scholarly in their approach,
- part of the problem, not the solution,
- state-centric,
- liable to adopt a narrow theoretical approach.

Many critics argue that because strategists focus on the role of military power, they tend to be preoccupied by violence and war. Because their view of the world is conflict-oriented they tend to ignore the more cooperative, peaceful aspects of world politics. This leads critics to claim that strategists have a distorted, rather than realistic, view of the world. Some critics have gone so far as to suggest that strategists are fascinated by violence, and even take grim satisfaction in describing the darker side of the human condition.

For their part, strategists accept that they are interested in violence and conflict. In their own defence, however, they point out that just as a doctor of heart disease does not claim to deal with all aspects of health, so they do not claim to be studying every aspect of international relations. They reject the view that they have a distorted view of the world, and that they are fascinated in an unhealthy sense by violence.

The claim to moral neutrality, sometimes made by strategists, is another shortcoming identified by critics. Strategists are depicted as clinical, cool, and unemotional in the way they approach the study of war, despite the fact that, in the nuclear age, millions of lives are at risk in the calculations that take place about strategic policies. Emphasizing the moral outrage felt by some, J. R. Newman described Herman Kahn's book, *On Thermonuclear War*, as 'a moral tract on mass murder, how to commit it, how to get away with it, how to justify it'. Philip Green, in his study of *Deadly Logic* (1966), also accused strategists who wrote about nuclear deterrence as being 'egregiously guilty of avoiding the moral issue altogether, or misrepresenting it'.

Although many strategists have justified the moral neutrality of their approach in terms of scholarly detachment, some have been sensitive to this criticism. As a result, a number of studies of ethical issues have been written. These include Joseph Nye's book on *Nuclear Ethics*, Michael Walzer's *Just and Unjust Wars*, and Steven P. Lee's study of *Morality, Prudence and Nuclear Weapons*. These books (together with the more critical studies by writers like Green) now form an important part of the literature on strategic studies.

Another important criticism levelled against strategic studies is that it represents 'a fundamental challenge to the values of liberal, humane scholarship, that define a university'. The implication is that strategy is not a scholarly subject and should not be taught at a university. This criticism has a number of related parts. First, according to Philip Green, it is pseudoscientific, using apparent scientific method to give it a spurious air of legitimacy. Second, because strategists often advise governments on a paid basis they are operating 'in a manner incompatible with the integrity of scholarship'. E. P. Thornton described the cosy relationship between strategists and government officials as 'suspect, corrupt and at enmity with the universal principles of humane scholarship'. Third, critics charge that strategists not only provide advice to governments, but they are also involved in policy advocacy—which is not part of scholarship. Critics claim that strategists are a vestige of government and spend their time either providing advice on how to achieve or justify dubious international objectives.

With a qualification on the issue of policy advocacy, strategists reject the view that their subject should not be found in a university (see Box 2). They would argue that war cannot be made to disappear simply by ignoring it (Leon Trotsky, a leading figure in the Bolshevik revolution, put it best: 'You might not have an interest in war, but war has an interest in you.'). They argue that the study of war and peace are issues of profound importance that can, and should be, studied in a scholarly way. There have been attempts at developing a scientific approach to strategy (and as Brodie recognized, some writers might have taken this too far) but the debate about methodology is not confined to strategic studies. The nature of science in a social science context remains a lively, ongoing debate.

BOX 2 Strategic Studies in the Academy

The study of strategy in universities may be defended on several different, yet complementary, grounds. In strictly academic terms, the subject poses sufficient intellectual challenge as to merit inclusion in, or even as, a course of study fully adequate to stretch mental resources. In, and of itself, that argument is sufficient to justify the inclusion of strategic studies in university curricula, but one can, and should, proceed to argue that the study of strategy is socially useful . . . Many views are defensible concerning the proper and appropriate duties of a university. This author chooses a liberal, permissive perspective. He sees value in a field of study that seeks truth and may have relevance to contemporary policy and, as a consequence, may contribute to the general wellbeing.

C. S. Gray

In strategic studies the ability to argue logically and to follow a piece of strategic reasoning is very important, but even more important is the elusive, almost indefinable quality of political judgement which enables a man to evaluate a piece of analysis and locate it in a wider political framework.

J. C. Garnett

In general, strategists recognize the dangers of developing too cosy a relationship with officials when they advise governments on a paid basis. Like many other experts, (e.g. economists), however, they see no necessary inconsistency between scholarship and advice. Because it is a practical subject, there are some benefits from analysing strategic issues at close hand, providing that a detached approach is adopted. Policy advocacy, however, is a different matter. Some strategists do drift into the realm of advocating specific policies, but when they do so they slowly but surely lose their credibility. People who make a career out of arguing for the adoption of specific policies or weapons systems gain a reputation for knowing the 'answer' regardless of the question that is posed.

Another forceful criticism of strategic studies is that it is part of the problem, not the solution. What opponents mean by this is that the Clausewitzian perspective of strategists, which sees military power as a legitimate instrument of policy, helps to perpetuate a particular mindset among national leaders and the public that encourages the use of force. It is this realist thinking, critics argue, which lies behind the development of theories of deterrence, limited war, and crisis management that were especially dangerous during the cold war. Anatol Rapoport is one writer who charges strategists with a direct responsibility for promoting a framework of thinking about security, which is largely hostile to what he regards as the proper solution to global conflict, namely disarmament. In a stinging attack he argues that

> the most formidable obstacles to disarmament are created by the strategists who place their strategic considerations above the needs of humanity as a whole, and who create or help maintain an intellectual climate in which disarmament appears to be unrealistic.
> **Rapoport (1965)**

Instead of spending their time thinking about how better to justify and conduct mass murder, critics suggest that strategists should spend their time devising disarmament strategies, cooperative security arrangements, and global campaigns to denounce violence.

Linked to this criticism is the view that because strategists are so pessimistic about human nature and the chances of significant improvements in the conduct of international politics, they *ignore the opportunities that exist for peaceful change*. It is suggested that to see the past as a history of constant conflict and to suggest that the future will be the same is to help create a fatalistic impression that plans for human progress will always fail. By emphasizing mistrust, self-help, and the importance of military power in an anarchic international system, their advice becomes self-fulfilling. In other words, if policymakers take strategists' advice to heart, deterrent threats and defence preparations would lead to a spiral of hostility and mistrust as leaders respond to the defence policies of their competitors. Given this 'socially constructed' view of the world, it is not surprising that states will constantly find themselves in conflict with each other.

Once again, strategists vigorously contest these criticisms. They argue that their ideas reflect (rather than create) the 'reality' of world politics. The fact that most policymakers and elected officials tend to share their realist assumptions is not due to an intellectual climate 'socially constructed' by academic strategists but by the challenges and threats presented to them by international relations. The notion that strategic studies as a subject is 'a monstrous crime committed by self-interested strategists against the general public' is seen as absurd.

Of course, throughout history, various observers have championed war as a preferred instrument of statecraft. Often they depict war in romantic or heroic terms; today's romantic image of war found in movies and video games is simply a technologically embellished version of this traditional imagery. Enthusiasts see war as a relatively bloodless contest in which technically adept professionals use their superior skills and equipment to paralyse the opponent's military command, leading to quick and humane victories. Strategic studies, however, stands as a major impediment to those who claim to have found a quick and easy path to guaranteed victory. Because they recognize the true nature of war, most strategists consider armed conflict to be a tragedy, an activity unfit for human beings that must be limited to the greatest extent possible.

On the question of peaceful change, strategists do not dismiss the fact that there are opportunities for periods of peaceful coexistence. They are, however, very sceptical about the prospects for 'perpetual peace' based on a radical transformation of world politics. They believe that conflict can be mitigated through effective strategy, but it is highly unlikely that it can be transcended completely. In such a context, it is impossible to abolish the need for strategic studies.

The fact that strategists focus on the task of creating effective national strategies or international initiatives creates the basis for another criticism of the enterprise. Strategic studies incorporates a state-centric approach to world politics. According to this critique, strategists are so preoccupied by threats to the interests of states that they ignore security issues within the state or new phenomenon such as transnational terrorist networks. Many observers argue that the state is not the most appropriate referent for studying security. Rather, attention should be focused on the individual whose security is often threatened, rather than protected by the state. Other writers, who perceive the growing erosion of the state, prefer to focus on 'societal security' or even 'global security' issues.

Strategists would argue that while they have stressed the role of the state, they have not neglected intra-state conflict. Clausewitz himself dealt with people's war and a considerable part of the strategic studies literature addresses revolutionary warfare. As wars of national disintegration (Bosnia, Kosovo, Chechnya) have become more prevalent, more attention has been given in the literature to the problem of ethnic conflict. The emergence of al-Qaeda has led to an explosion of research and writing on the origins, objectives, strategies, and tactics of violent non-state actors with an eye towards destroying international terrorist networks and other criminal organizations. Despite the prevalence of intra-state violence or the rise of important non-state actors, strategists continue to argue that, even with all the contemporary challenges to the modern state, it continues to be the major actor in world politics. In fact the importance of the state, with its access to a myriad of resources and instruments of control and surveillance, has only been highlighted by the emergence of 'super-empowered individuals' and transnational terrorism. Strategists offer no apologies for their continuing interest in issues of state security.

Another criticism often levelled against strategic studies is that the traditional dominant realist approach is theoretically too narrow, closing off insights that can be gained from other theories of peace and security. In a study of *Strategic Studies and World Order*, written in 1994, Bradley S. Klein argued that it 'was important to take seriously the realist tradition's emphasis upon power in world affairs, and there can be no escaping a sustained engagement with the primary texts that demarcate that tradition'. Nevertheless, he argues that it was important 'to see that tradition not as some fixed map of the yellow brick road to modern realism or its 'neo' variants for contemporary articulations of the genre have tended to sever the tradition from its roots in political theory.' In their *Evolution of International Security Studies*, Buzan and Hansen highlight the limitations of realist thinking which gave rise to a range of new theoretical approaches to the study of security in the 1990s, including Constructivism, Critical Security Studies, Feminism, and Poststructuralism (2009).

These are criticisms which have some merit. Bradley S. Klein's own study and Peter J. Katzenstein's study of *The Culture of National Security Studies*, to name but two, have attempted to broaden the theoretical basis of Strategic Studies. We have also included two chapters in this book (Chapters 4 and 18), which reflect alternative perspectives on strategic studies. This said realism remains the dominant approach to the subject, which is one factor that distinguishes the study of strategy from the broader field of Security Studies (see Chapter 20).

What is the Relationship between Strategic Studies and Security Studies?

One of the main challenges to strategic studies since the end of the cold war has come from those who argue that attention should be shifted away from the study of strategy to the study of security. According to this view security, defined in terms of 'freedom from threats to core values', is a more appropriate concept for analysis. The problem with strategy, it is argued, is that it is too narrow and increasingly less relevant at a time when major wars are declining and threats to political, economic, social, and environmental security interests are increasing. This is often referred to as 'the widening and deepening' debate (see Buzan and Hansen 187–211) Because it is defined more broadly, security is depicted as more valuable than strategy as an organizing framework for understanding the complex, multidimensional risks of today.

However, as Richard Betts, noted in his 1997 article 'Should strategic studies survive?', those who champion new definitions of security run two risks. First, Betts noted that even though it is appropriate to distinguish between 'strategy' and 'security' studies, security policy requires careful attention to war and strategy. In other words, military power remains a crucial part of security and those who ignore war to concentrate on non-military threats to security do so at their peril. Second, he argued that 'expansive definitions of security quickly become synonymous with 'interest' and 'wellbeing', do not exclude anything in international relations or foreign policy, and this becomes indistinguishable from those fields or other subfields'. In other words, by including potentially everything that might negatively affect human affairs, security studies creates the risk of being too broad to be of any practical value.

The contributors to this book recognize the importance of security studies while at the same time they share these concerns about the coherence of the field. Strategy remains a distinctive and valuable area of academic study. Strategy is part of security studies, just as security studies is part of international relations, which itself is part of political science. This relationship is expressed in Figure 1 (See Chapter 17).

Despite all of the changes that have occurred in world politics since the late 1980s there is in many respects an underlying continuity with earlier eras. The euphoria produced by the hope that a fundamental transformation of international relations was under way has proved

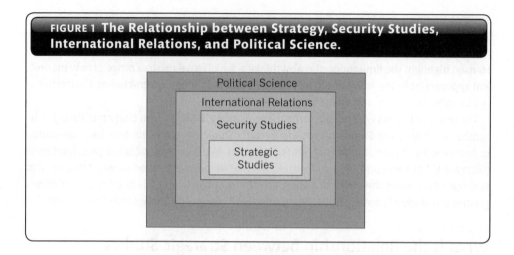

FIGURE 1 The Relationship between Strategy, Security Studies, International Relations, and Political Science.

Political Science

International Relations

Security Studies

Strategic Studies

to be ill-founded. As we have seen from the Gulf Wars I and II, the Iraqi insurgency, Bosnia, Kosovo, Chechnya, Libya, Syria, and the terrorist attacks launched by al-Qaeda and various fellow travellers, force and military power continue to be an important currency in the international system at the beginning of the twenty-first century. Certainly important changes are taking place in world politics, associated with the twin forces of globalization and fragmentation, and wars between the great powers have slipped into the background, although there are a few disturbing hints of a potential 'great power' competition between the United States and China. The sad fact remains, however, that the utilization of military power as an instrument of political purpose and therefore, strategic studies, remains just as relevant today as it has been in the past.

Our exploration of strategy in the contemporary world is divided into four sections. In Part I, our contributors describe the enduring issues that animate the study of strategy and provide a historical and theoretical overview of the topic for our readers. Our study opens with an essay on the causes of war, a complex issue that ultimately shapes approaches to mitigating inter-state violence. It then offers two essays of grand historical and theoretical sweep: one on the evolution of warfare since the Napoleonic age; the other a *tour d'horizon* of strategic thinkers and thinking. The issues of culture, morality, and war are also addressed in this section, reflecting some of the changes in methodology that have taken place in strategic studies. Despite popular imagery, cultural, legal, and moral considerations play a role in shaping both the recourse to and the conduct of war. These chapters are important because they illustrate the normative basis for strategy: to help to mitigate both the occurrence, and death and destruction produced by war.

Three further chapters focus on perennial factors that shape warfare. Geography—land, sea, air, and space, and now even cyberspace—has shaped the conduct of war and technology itself: the so-called 'revolution in military affairs' or 'transformation' continues to shape the evolution of warfare and strategies in each of these geographic settings. This is followed by a chapter on the critical issue of Intelligence in modern conflicts. A new chapter has been added to this edition dealing with cyber warfare, which has increasingly emerged as a feature of the contemporary world.

In Part II, our contributors explore issues that appear in today's headlines and that animate strategic debate today. Peacekeeping and humanitarian intervention pose unique problems for military forces, especially when treated by policymakers as an afterthought in the global war on terrorism or to encourage the movement towards greater democracy in areas like the Middle East. Fears about North Korean and Iranian nuclear programmes, and the possibility that terrorists might acquire and use weapons of mass destruction, suggest that it is time for a reappraisal of the threat posed by nuclear, radiological, chemical, and biological weapons. This section also explores emerging issues that are likely to animate debate not only about weapons of mass destruction but also about conventional military power in the decade ahead. Part II also explores emerging issues related to Homeland Defense and the link between domestic counterterror operations and strategy.

Part III offers a conclusion to our overview of contemporary strategy not by summarizing the findings of each of our contributors, but by considering new approaches to the study of security that have emerged in recent years and by charting a new way forward for strategic studies. There is also a chapter in this section on 'Strategic studies and its critics', which surveys and assesses the literature on the subject.

 Further Reading

For useful accounts of the nature and development of strategic studies:

J. C. Garnett, 'Strategic Studies and its Assumptions'. In John Baylis, Ken Booth, John Garnett, and Phil Williams, *Contemporary Strategy: Theories and Policies* (London: Croom Helm, 1975).
This is a very good analysis of the philosophy behind classical realism and the early strategic studies texts.

Andre Beaufre, *An Introduction to Strategy* (London: Faber & Faber, 1965).

Andre Beaufre, *Deterrence and Strategy* (London: Faber & Faber 1965).
Both of these studies provide an alternative and distinctly French approach to strategic studies during the cold war.

B. Brodie, *War and Politics* (London: Cassell, 1973).
A key text by one of the leading American strategic thinkers during the 'golden age' of strategic studies.

Michael Howard, *War In European History* (Oxford: Oxford University Press, 1976).
This provides an important historical analysis of war in modern European history by a leading British historian and strategic analyst.

H. Kahn, *On Thermonuclear War* (Princeton, NJ: Princeton University Press, 1960).
This book, written by one of the most important and controversial American strategic theorists of his day, provides a cold and unemotional view of how a nuclear war might be fought.

P. J. Katzenstein, (ed.) *The Culture of National Security: Norms and Identity in World Politics* (New York: Columbia University Press, 1996).
This study challenges realist and neo-realist approaches to strategic studies and argues for an alternative 'social constructivist' approach.

H. A. Kissinger, *Nuclear Weapons and Foreign Policy* (New York: Harper & Row, 1957).
This study focuses on the diplomatic role of nuclear weapons during a key part of the cold war era.

Williamson Murray, Macgregor Knox, and Alvin Bernstein (eds), *The Making of Strategy: Rulers, States, and War* (Cambridge: Cambridge University Press, 1994).
This is a very good analysis of the strategic and operational side of nuclear strategy.

R. Niebuhr, *Moral Man and Immoral Society* (London: Charles Scribner's Sons, 1932).
This book deals with the ethical issues of strategic studies written from a sophisticated realist thinker's viewpoint.

A. Rapoport, 'The Sources of Anguish', *Bulletin of Atomic Scientists* 21/10, December 1965.
This article provides a critical view of cold war strategic studies.

Part 1

······································

Enduring Issues of Strategy

······································

1 **The Causes of War and the Conditions of Peace**   19
   John Garnett

2 **The Evolution of Modern Warfare**   39
   Michael Sheehan

3 **Strategic Theory**   60
   Thomas G. Mahnken

4 **Strategic Culture**   76
   Jeffrey S. Lantis and Darryl Howlett

5 **Law, Politics, and the Use of Force**   96
   Justin Morris

6 **Geography and Strategy**   115
   Daniel Moran

7 **Technology and Warfare**   132
   Eliot Cohen

8 **Intelligence and Strategy**   151
   Roger George

The Causes of War and the Conditions of Peace

JOHN GARNETT

 Chapter Contents

Introduction	20
The Study of War	21
Human Nature Explanations of War	28
Wars 'Within' and 'Beyond' States	34
Conclusion	37

 Reader's Guide

Scholarship dealing with the causes of war is voluminous and multidisciplinary. This chapter describes and explains theories that have been advanced by biologists, philosophers, political scientists, and sociologists about why wars occur. It groups their ideas into categories and shows how different explanations of war give rise to different requirements or conditions for peace. Distinctions are drawn between immediate and underlying causes of war; between permissive and efficient causes; between learned and instinctive causes; and between necessary and sufficient causes. The chapter pays particular attention to explanations of war based on human nature and instinct, but it also considers those psychological theories that emphasize misperception and frustration as causes of aggression. The ideas of those who find the causes of war in human collectives—states, tribes, and ethnic groups, and those who favour 'systemic' rather than 'unit' explanations—are also described.

Introduction

Though 'strategy' these days is as much concerned with the promotion of peace as with the conduct of war, the phenomenon of war remains a central concern. Previous generations might have seen virtues in war, for example, as an instrument of change or as a vehicle for encouraging heroic virtues, but these ideas have been rendered obsolete by the destructiveness of modern warfare. In the twentieth century abolishing war became a top priority. The first step in ending war, however, is to identify its causes.

Historians sometimes argue that since wars are unique events, the causes of war are as numerous as the number of wars and nothing in general can be said about them. This chapter takes a different view. It identifies similarities and patterns between the causes of wars so that we can group causes under such headings as human nature, misperception, the nature of states, and the structure of the international system. Its aim is twofold. First, to relate contemporary scholarship across a range of disciplines—biology, political science, philosophy, and history—to the problem of war causation, and second, to elaborate a number of distinctions which help us to identify different kinds of 'cause' (e.g. underlying and immediate causes). Throughout the chapter these distinctions are used to identify the various causes of war and to discriminate between them.

Since there is little scholarly agreement on what causes war, this chapter is directed towards explaining the debate rather than to answering the question in a decisive way. The arguments are more than academic because, if the cure for war is related to its causes, then different causes will lead to different policy recommendations. If, on the one hand, wars are caused by arms races, then policies of disarmament and arms control are appropriate solutions to the problem of war (see Chapter 11). On the other hand, if wars are instigated by despotic or authoritarian states, then the way to peace lies in the spread of democracy. If the basic cause of war is deemed to be the 'international anarchy' which characterizes the current system of states, then attempts to rid the world of war will be geared towards promoting system change—perhaps in the direction of strengthened international law or a system of collective security or world government (see Box 1.1).

Some explanations for war offer less hope for finding a way to end armed conflict than others. For example, those that locate war in a fundamentally flawed human nature suggest a bleaker future for the human race than those that locate the causes of war in learned behaviour. If war is learned rather than instinctive, then there is a possibility that it can be eliminated through social engineering.

BOX 1.1 Five Distinctions which may help clarify our thoughts about the Causes of War

1. Instinctive vs learned behaviour.
2. Immediate vs underlying causes.
3. Efficient vs permissive causes.
4. Conscious vs unconscious motives for war.
5. Necessary vs sufficient causes.

Three conclusions emerge from this analysis. First, the search for a single cause appropriate to all wars is futile. Second, because war comes in a variety of forms and has a multiplicity of causes, its elimination will almost certainly require simultaneous domestic and international political action. Third, a worldwide 'just' peace is unattainable.

The Study of War

In the field of international relations, no question has attracted more attention than 'Why war?' The reason for this interest is that war is almost universally regarded as a human disaster, a source of misery on a catastrophic scale, and, in the nuclear age, a threat to the entire human race. But war has not always been viewed so negatively. In the nineteenth century, for example, numerous writers identified virtues in war (see the Introduction). The philosopher G. W. F. Hegel believed that war preserved the ethical health of nations, and in a similar vein H. von Treitschke regarded war as 'the only remedy for ailing nations' (Gowans 1914: 23). For Treitschke, war was one of the conditions for progress, the cut of the whip that prevents a country from going to sleep, forcing satisfied mediocrity to leave its apathy. This kind of thinking alerts us to the idea that war can be thought of as a purposive, functional thing. E. H. Carr regarded it as 'the midwife of change' (1942: 3): 'Wars . . . break up and sweep away the half-rotted structures of an old social and political order.' These authors suggested that wars herald rapid technological progress, territorial change, strengthened group consciousness, and economic development. The idea of war as a purposive, functional thing, however, sits uneasily in an age that typically interprets war as an abnormal, pathological condition that threatens us all.

Idle curiosity or an aimless spirit of enquiry has not motivated most investigations into the causes of war. Theorists have studied war to abolish it. They have believed that the first step towards eliminating war is to identify its causes because, in much the same way that the cures for disease are related to the causes of disease, so the cures for war are to be found in its causes. As long as students of war do not allow their enthusiasm for prescription to affect their diagnostic skills, no harm is done. However, there is a danger that researchers may be tempted to gloss over the more intractable causes of war in favour of those which suggest the possibility that solutions to human conflict can be readily found.

Many social scientists recoil from the idea that though particular wars may be avoided, war is endemic in the human condition. The idea that war is inevitable is pretty difficult to swallow, psychologically speaking, and that may explain why pessimistic interpretations of the causes of war meet with resistance. Take, for example, the view that the root cause of war is to be found in human nature, i.e. that aggression and violence are genetically built into humans and that we do what we do because of what we are. Despite some scientific evidence in support of this idea, there is enormous resistance to it. Why? Because, if human nature is fixed in our genes, we are helpless in the face of ourselves. For many observers, the conclusion that war is built into us is an intolerable counsel of despair, even though it is a useful reminder that just because the elimination of war is desirable does not mean that it is therefore possible.

A gloomy interpretation of human nature and an admission of its intractability, however, do not automatically lead to despair of ever being able to rid the world of war. Some would argue that wars are not caused by human *nature*; they are caused by human *behaviour*, and while it may not be possible to change human nature, it is certainly possible to modify human behaviour—by offering rewards, by making threats, by education programmes, or by propaganda. Richard Dawkins has pointed out that

> our genes may instruct us to be selfish, but we are not necessarily compelled to obey them all our lives. It may . . . be more difficult to learn altruism than it would be if we were genetically programmed to be altruistic [but we should try] to teach generosity and altruism, because we are born selfish.
> **Dawkins (1976: 3)**

Civilized societies spend a great deal of energy on making people behave themselves despite their natures. The law, the police, schools, and churches all play a part in modifying human behaviour in the domestic environment. The possibility of modifying state behaviour is also widely recognized. Diplomacy, force, trade, aid, and propaganda are all instruments used by leaders to affect the behaviour of the states they are dealing with. Deterrent strategists, for example, argue that even if human nature is fatally flawed (and most of them think it is), states can still be deterred from aggression by the threat of unacceptable punishment in much the same way that many potential criminals can be deterred from robbing banks by the threat of imprisonment (see Chapter 10).

Unlike those who believe that peace can best be promoted by removing the causes of war, nuclear deterrent strategists hardly care at all about why wars occur. Their policy is simply to make the *consequences* of war so bad that nobody will dare fight even if they want to. In other words, the strategy of nuclear deterrence is unique in that its effectiveness does not depend either on particular interpretations of why wars occur or on treating the underlying pathologies that cause people or states to fight. The only assumption that deterrent theorists make about human beings is the fairly uncontroversial one that on the whole people prefer to be alive rather than dead and hence are likely to be deterred from aggression by the threat of annihilation.

Difficulties in Studying War

No clear authoritative answer has emerged, and perhaps one never will, to the question 'Why war?' One of the reasons for this is that the word 'war' is a blanket term used to describe diverse activities. There are total wars and limited wars, regional wars and world wars, conventional wars and nuclear wars, high-technology wars and low-technology wars, inter-state wars and civil wars, insurgency wars and ethnic wars. In recent years, wars have also been fought by coalitions on behalf of the international community. It would be very surprising if these widely different activities—linked only by the fact that they involve organized military violence—could be explained in the same way.

Another reason for the absence of an authoritative answer is that the question 'What are the causes of war?' is a complicated, 'cluster' question. Under its umbrella, as Hidemi Suganami has pointed out, we may be asking a number of different questions. We may, for example, be asking 'What are the conditions that must be present for wars to occur?'; or we may be asking 'Under what circumstances have wars occurred most frequently?'; or we may be asking about how a particular war came about (1996: 4). Lumping these questions together inevitably leads to complicated and unsatisfactory answers.

An additional reason for complex answers to the question of war causation is that the concept of causation itself is fraught with philosophical difficulties. One may note that X is often a prelude to Y, but that is not at all the same as proving that X caused Y. Various writers, for example, noting that wars are often preceded by arms races between the belligerents, have claimed that arms races *cause* wars. Arms races sometimes cause war, but an *automatic* connection has not been conclusively demonstrated. Arguably, human beings do not fight because they have weapons; they acquire weapons because they already wish to fight. Further, it is worth pointing out that not all arms races have led to war. Anglo-French naval competition in the nineteenth century led to the *entente cordiale*, while the cold war arms race between the United States and the Soviet Union led to a deterrent stalemate and one of the most prolonged periods of peace in European history.

Given the difficulties inherent in the problem of causation, some writers (particularly historians) have preferred to talk about the 'origins' of wars rather than 'causes'. They believe that the best way of explaining why wars occur is to describe how they come about in terms of the social context and events from which they spring. Thus, if we are investigating the causes of the Second World War, we need to look at the Treaty of Versailles, the world depression, the rise of Hitler, German rearmament, the foreign policies of Britain and France, etc. When we have done this we are well on the way to understanding the circumstances that led to the Second World War. Those who emphasize the origins of wars hold the view that telling the story of how they come about is as close as we can get to understanding why they come about.

Historians who favour this very specific 'case-study' approach to the identification of the causes of war tend to believe that since every war is a unique event with unique causes, the causes of war are as numerous as the number of wars. Hence, providing an authoritative answer to the question 'What are the causes of war?' would involve a detailed examination of every war that has ever occurred: the uniqueness of every war means that there is nothing in general to be said about them. For investigations concerned with the causes of individual wars this is a fair point. Nevertheless, while acknowledging the uniqueness of individual wars, most political scientists see merit in shifting the level of analysis from the particular to the general so that we can see patterns and similarities between the causes of one war and another. At this more general level of analysis we may identify some causes which are common to many, if not all, wars.

Immediate and Underlying Causes

One of the most useful distinctions to be drawn between the various causes of war is between 'immediate', proximate causes and 'underlying', more fundamental causes. Immediate causes, the events that trigger wars, may be trivial, even accidental. For example, the spark that ignited the First World War was the assassination of the Austrian Archduke Franz Ferdinand who was visiting Sarajevo and being driven in an open car. The death of the Archduke was a tragedy, but it was essentially a trivial event, and no one seriously believes that its occurrence provides an adequate explanation for the momentous events that followed. What is more, it was an accident that might easily not have happened. If the duke's chauffeur had not deviated from the planned route and then stopped the car to rectify his error, the assassin would not have had an opportunity to shoot the Archduke and his wife. The assassination was undoubtedly the immediate cause of the First World War, and it is true to say that if it had not happened the war which broke out in 1914 would not have happened, but there is plenty of evidence to suggest that a war would have occurred sooner or later. In 1914 war was in the air: Europe was divided by hostile alliance systems; tensions were rising; mobilization timetables were pressuring decision-makers; and an arms race was under way. In short, the background circumstances were highly inflammable, and if the assassination of Franz Ferdinand had not set the powder keg alight, sooner or later something else would probably have provided the spark. Most commentators believe that a useful examination of the causes of the First World War should pay more attention to those underlying causes than to the immediate triggering events.

Emphasis on underlying causes is a structural interpretation in the sense that it emphasizes the importance of international circumstances rather than deliberate state policies in causing wars. It suggests that statesmen are not always in control of events; they sometimes find themselves caught up in a process that, despite their best intentions, pushes them to war. Suganami has pointed out that there are occasions when

> the background conditions appear already so war prone that the particular path through which the actual war broke out seems only to have been one of a number of alternatives through which a war like that could have been brought about.
> **Suganami (1996: 195)**

Of course, background conditions are not always a reliable barometer of the danger that war will break out. In some situations the setting seems relatively benign and responsibility for war is more easily allocated to the particular policies followed by the governments involved. Wars often come about as a result of aggressive, reckless, thoughtless, and deliberate acts by statesmen. It would be impossible to discuss the causes of the Second World War, for instance, without drawing attention to the persistently aggressive behaviour of Hitler and the weak, appeasing policies of Chamberlain. Similarly, the actions of Nasser in seizing the Suez Canal, and Eden in responding to that with military action were critically important causes of the Suez War. The same point can be made about both the Falklands War and the Gulf War. In the case of the Falklands, the Argentinian decision to invade South Georgia and Margaret Thatcher's decision to resist seem at least as important as any 'structural' causes that might be identified. In the case of the Gulf War, Saddam Hussein's decision to seize territory in Kuwait and the decision of Western governments not to allow him to get away with it were more obvious causes of the Gulf War than any background circumstances.

Efficient and Permissive Causes

Another useful distinction lies between efficient and permissive causes of war. 'Efficient' causes are connected to the particular circumstances surrounding individual wars. War may result because state A has something state B wants. In this situation the 'efficient' cause of the war is the desire of state B. Examples of these causes abound. The efficient cause of the Gulf War between Iraq and Iran was the desire of Saddam Hussein to regain from Iran the Shatt-al-Arab waterway; the efficient cause of the 1990 war between Iraq and the Western coalition was Saddam's desire to acquire Kuwaiti territory and resources. The efficient cause of the 2003 war with Iraq was the decision of the United States and the United Kingdom first to topple Saddam and second, to bring democracy to Iraq. If President Bush and Prime Minister Blair had not taken that decision to intervene militarily in Iraq there would have been no war.

Since the rise of the state system there has been a general presumption *against* this kind of intervention in the internal affairs of sovereign states. The traditional view is that states have no business meddling in the internal affairs of other states. Although the idea of non-intervention has become a basic principle of international order, in recent years there has developed a consensus that, in exceptional circumstances and as a last resort, even military intervention may be justified, both legally and morally. When, for example, genocide is being practised, when there are gross violations of human rights, when states are collapsing into chaos, and when there is a serious threat to peace and security—in these extreme situations intervention is deemed permissible, particularly if it enjoys United Nations approval. Western intervention in Libya in 2011 is a good example of this. Few would quarrel with the prevailing consensus on this point, but we have to acknowledge that in an obvious sense it is a cause of war.

In terms of success and failure, the record of military intervention is mixed. The 2003 Iraq War and its messy aftermath provides the most recent example of the difficulty of bringing military intervention to a satisfactory conclusion. As this message sinks in, the current enthusiasm for intervention may fade, and as it does, this particular cause of war may become less common.

'Permissive' causes of war are those features of the international system which, while not actively promoting war, nevertheless allow it to happen. In this context, the fact that we live in a world of independent sovereign states with no authority above them, and no institutions sufficiently powerful to regulate their relations, is a permissive cause of war. Kenneth Waltz is renowned for the emphasis he puts on 'permissive' rather than 'efficient' causes of war (1959). Although the causes of war are bewildering in their variety, notes Waltz, the most persuasive explanation for it is to be found in international anarchy—the fact that in an ungoverned international system there is nothing to prevent conflict from occurring. Because there is nothing to prevent war there is, in international relations, a permanent expectation of violence and a permanent sense of insecurity that pushes states to behave aggressively despite whatever peaceful intentions they may have. Waltz uses Rousseau's famous 'stag hunt' analogy (see Box 1.2) to show that warlike behaviour arises not primarily from any defect in human nature or some inherent flaw in states, but from the predicament in which leaders find themselves (1959: 167–8). In the face of systemic or structural inadequacy, war cannot be avoided forever and is always just around the corner.

Kenneth Thompson has made the same point in a slightly different way (1960: 261–76). He imagines a situation where, during the rush hour, someone waiting for a train on the platform of an underground railway station finds himself being pushed by a surging crowd of fellow travellers towards the electrified line. Our passenger is a good man who means

BOX 1.2 Jean Rousseau's 'Stag Hunt' Analogy

Rousseau imagines a situation in which several solitary and hungry hunters existing in 'a state of nature' where there is no law, morality, or government, happen to come together. Each of them recognizes that his hunger could be satisfied by a share of a stag, and so they 'agree' to cooperate to catch one. In Rousseau's words:

> If a deer was to be taken, everyone saw that in order to succeed, he must abide faithfully by his post; but if a hare happened to come within reach of any of them, it is not to be doubted that he pursued it without scruple, and, having seized his prey, cared very little if by so doing he caused his companions to miss theirs.

J. J. Rousseau, *A Discourse on the Origin of Inequality*

The point of the story is that in conditions of anarchy, the hunter who grabbed the hare could not feel confident that one of his fellow hunters would not do likewise if presented with the same opportunity, in which case he would go hungry. Given this predicament the sensible thing to do is to behave selfishly and seize the hare.

no harm. What should he do? The Christian ethic tells him to turn the other cheek, but if he does he will end up dead on the rail tracks: so our good man kicks and struggles and fights to stay alive. He behaves in this aggressive way not because he is wicked or violent, but because he finds himself in an environment where he cannot afford to be good. The Sermon on the Mount is not much use if you live in the jungle. And so it is with states: because they exist in a system where others behave badly, doing likewise is the only way to survive.

If the main cause of war is to be found in the anarchic international system in which sovereign states pursue their interests without the constraint of world government, then an essential condition of peace is the transformation of that system from one of competing states to a unified world ruled by a single authority sufficiently powerful to compel peaceful behaviour. The trouble with this recommendation is that there is no practical way of implementing it. We did not *choose* to live in the world of independent states that emerged from the Peace of Westphalia in 1648 and we cannot now choose not to live in it. Though the international system is constantly changing, for all practical purposes it is a *given*, something we have to accept as a fact of life. We are where we are, and whatever conditions of peace we may recommend we must take that into account. Another reason for scepticism that 'world government' will solve the problem of war is that even if we achieved it we might not like it. World government might turn out to be world dictatorship and inter-state wars might simply become civil wars.

Those who regard the ungoverned international system as the root cause of war often compare it with Hobbesian anarchy; but in reality the society of states bears little resemblance to Hobbes's 'state of nature'. Although it is not an integrated society comparable to domestic society, it is neither chaotic, nor wholly unpredictable. States do not live in conditions of permanent terror. International society is a regulated, rule-governed environment in which states can build upon their common interests, and in which international organizations, customs, habits, mores, and laws built up over hundreds of years moderate and order their behaviour. Of course, no one would claim that the world of sovereign states is the best of all worlds; it may not even be the best of all possible worlds, but it is better than some imaginable alternatives—even better, perhaps, than world government—and we ought not to try to jettison it without being very sure that what succeeds it will be an improvement.

Necessary and Sufficient Causes of War

Various writers have found it useful to distinguish between necessary and sufficient causes of war. A 'necessary' condition for war is one that *must be present* if war is to occur. In other words, if war cannot break out without that condition existing, then it is a necessary condition. The existence of armaments is a necessary condition of war because without them no war could be fought. For wars to occur it is also necessary for human beings to be organized in discrete collectives—states, tribes, ethnic groups, nations, or factions. Additionally, it is a necessary condition of war that there be no effective mechanism for preventing it. An effective *world* government, for example, would make it impossible for inter-state wars to occur, and an all-powerful *state* government would make it impossible for civil wars to occur. Thus, the absence of these mechanisms is a necessary condition of war.

There is an element of tautology in the above analysis in the sense that if we define war as organized violence between groups, then it is obvious that wars cannot occur if human beings are not organized in groups that have the capacity for organized violence. It is equally obvious that wars cannot occur if there is a mechanism that prevents them. More controversially, it has been suggested that one of the necessary conditions of war is that at least one of the parties to it must have a non-democratic government.

A 'sufficient' cause of war is one that, if present, *guarantees* the occurrence of war. A is a sufficient cause of B if B always occurs whenever A exists. If two states hate each other so much that neither can tolerate the independent existence of the other, then that is a sufficient cause of war which makes war between them inevitable. However, it is not a *necessary* condition of war: many wars occur between states which do not share that degree of hatred and are perfectly content with each other's continued existence as independent states in international society. Clearly, a cause of war can be sufficient without being necessary, and the converse of this is also true—a cause can be necessary without being sufficient. For example, the existence of weapons is a necessary condition of war, but it is not a sufficient cause of war since even the existence of high levels of armaments does not always lead to war.

The categories 'necessary' and 'sufficient' do not cover all the possible causes of war. We must not fall into the trap of thinking that the causes of war must be *either* necessary *or* sufficient because there are many causes that are *neither* necessary *nor* sufficient. For example, the desire of statesmen to annex territory belonging to neighbouring states is a common cause of war but it is neither a necessary nor a sufficient cause. It is not a necessary cause because many wars are fought for reasons that have nothing to do with territory, and it is not a sufficient cause because the desire to annex territory may not be acted upon—perhaps because of deterrence.

Key points

● The idea that war is endemic in the human condition is psychologically unpalatable, but it may nevertheless be true. Even if human nature cannot be changed, it may be possible to modify human behaviour so that wars are less frequent.

● Since there are many different kinds of war, it is not surprising that no single cause of war can be identified.

● It is often useful to distinguish between underlying causes of war and the events that trigger them.

● Efficient causes of war relate to the particular circumstances surrounding individual wars.

● Permissive causes of war are those features of the international system that, while not actively promoting war, allow it to happen.

● A 'necessary' condition of war is one that must be present if war is to occur. A 'sufficient' cause of war is one that, if present, guarantees the occurrence of war.

Human Nature Explanations of War

There is widespread agreement that one of the things that distinguishes human beings from animals is that most of their behaviour is learned rather than instinctive. No one knows what the relative percentages are and there is an ongoing debate about the relative importance of 'nature' versus 'nurture' (heredity versus environment) as a determinant of human behaviour. Inevitably this debate has raised the question of whether war is an example of innate or learned behaviour. If it is *innate* then we must accept it, since in any reasonable timescale biological evolution is too slow to modify it. If it is *learned*, however, then it can be unlearned and there is hope for us all. Liberal thinkers prefer to emphasize the importance of nurture and are naturally attracted to the idea that aggression and war can be tamed. Conservative thinkers tend to throw their weight behind nature and are therefore sceptical about the possibilities of ridding the world of war.

Though they are disposed to minimize its significance, even committed liberals admit that there is a genetic, instinctive element in human behaviour. We do not start with clean slates on which life's experiences are written to make us what we are. We come with genetic baggage, biologically programmed, with built-in drives and instincts, one of which, it is argued, is a predilection for aggression and violence. In a celebrated exchange of letters in 1932 both Albert Einstein and Sigmund Freud agreed that the roots of war were to be found in an elemental instinct for aggression and destruction. Einstein thought that 'man has in him an active instinct for hatred and destruction', and Freud believed he had identified a 'death instinct' which manifested itself in homicide and suicide (Freud 1932). In the 1960s, ethological and socio-biological research brought new life to 'instinct' theories of aggression. Konrad Lorenz argued, largely on the basis of his observations of the behaviour of birds and fish, that an aggressive instinct is embedded in the genetic make-up of all animals (including man), and that this instinct has been a prerequisite for survival (1976). Robert Ardrey, in *The Territorial Imperative*, reached a similar conclusion and suggested a 'territorial' instinct to run alongside Lorenz's four instincts—hunger, fear, sex, and aggression (1966). Edward Wilson in *On Human Nature* noted that human beings are disposed to react with unreasoning hatred to perceived threats to their safety and possessions, and he argued that 'we tend to fear deeply the actions of strangers and to solve conflict by aggression' (1978: 119).

Although Richard Dawkins in his book *The Selfish Gene* has shifted the level of analysis from the individual to the genes that help make him what he is, he too is under no illusions about human nature. His argument is that

> a predominant quality to be expected in a successful gene is ruthless selfishness. This gene selfishness will usually give rise to selfishness in individual behaviour . . . Much as we might wish to believe otherwise, universal love and welfare of the species as a whole are concepts which simply do not make evolutionary sense.
> **Dawkins (1976: 2–3)**

This analysis leads Dawkins to the bleak conclusion that 'if you wish . . . to build a society in which individuals cooperate generously and unselfishly towards a common good, you can expect little help from biological nature' (1976: 3) (see Box 1.3).

The human nature explanation of war is a persuasive one, but at least two qualifications need to be made about it. First, we need to ask whether the evidence produced by the study of animals is really relevant to the behaviour of human beings. The animal behaviourists say it is, because man is simply a higher animal, connected to the rest of the animal kingdom by evolution. To deny that human beings have instincts in the same way that animals do is to deny the almost universally accepted principle of evolution, which links all life on the planet.

BOX 1.3 The Causes of War

One may seek in political philosophy answers to the question: Where are the major causes of war to be found? The answers are bewildering in their variety and in their contradictory qualities. To make this variety manageable, the answers can be ordered under the following three headings: within man, within the structure of separate states, within the state system.

There is deceit and cunning and from these wars arise.

Kenneth Waltz, Man, the State, and War

Whatever can be said in favour of a balance of power can be said only because we are wicked.

Confucius

A steadfast concert for peace can never be maintained except by a partnership of democratic nations. No autocratic government could be trusted to keep faith within it or observe its covenants . . . Only free peoples can hold their purpose and their honor steady to a common end and prefer the interests of mankind to any narrow interests of their own.

Jonathan Dymond

It is quite true that it would be much better for all men to remain always at peace. But so long as there is no security for this, everyone having no guarantee that he can avoid war, is anxious to begin it at the moment which suits his own interest and so forestall a neighbour, who would not fail to forestall the attack in his turn at any moment favourable to himself.

Woodrow Wilson

Force is a means of achieving the external ends of states because there exists no consistent, reliable process of reconciling the conflicts of interest that inevitably arise among similar units in a condition of anarchy.

Rousseau

Even so, we cannot help wondering whether the kind of cross-species generalization engaged in by biologists is valid. After all, human beings are very different from animals. They are more intelligent. They have a moral sense. They reflect about what they do; they plan ahead. Some would claim that these differences are so important that for all intents and purposes they lift man out of the animal world and reduce his instincts to no more than vestigial significance. Waltz notes in his book *Man, the State, and War*, that arguing that human nature causes war is not very helpful since if human nature causes war then, logically, it also causes everything else that human beings do. In his words, 'human nature may in some sense have been the cause of war in 1914, but by the same token it was the cause of peace in 1910' (1959: 28). In other words, human nature is a constant and cannot explain the wide variety of activities that humans exhibit.

Frustration Explanations of War

Social psychologists, while still locating war in 'man', offer explanations for its occurrence that rely less on instinct and more on socially programmed human behaviour. Typically, they argue that aggression is a result of frustration. When individuals find themselves thwarted in the achievement of their desires, goals, and objectives, they experience frustration which causes pent-up resentment that needs to find an outlet—and this frequently takes the form of aggressive behaviour which, in turn, has a cathartic effect of releasing tension and making those who engage in it feel better. Usually aggression is levelled at those who cause the frustration, but sometimes it is vented against innocents who become scapegoats. This psychological process of transferring aggression to a secondary group is called 'displacement'. Sometimes individuals project their frustrated desires and ambitions onto the group or collective, be it tribe or state, to which they belong. In the words of Reinhold Niebuhr, 'the man in the street, with his lust for power and prestige thwarted by his own limitations and the necessities of social life, projects his ego upon his nation and indulges his anarchic lusts vicariously' (1932: 93).

There is a sense in which the 'frustration/aggression' hypothesis, which emphasizes the connection between violence and the failure of human beings to achieve their objectives, is somewhat more optimistic than instinct theories of aggression. Although frustration in life is unavoidable, it may be possible either to channel aggression into harmless activities like sport (psychologists call this sublimation), or to organize society in ways that minimize frustrations (sociologists call this social engineering).

Misperception Explanations of War

Accepting that wars cannot occur unless statesmen decide to wage them, many believe that decisions to go to war are often the result of misperception, misunderstanding, miscalculation, and errors of judgement. Essentially, those who think in this way regard wars as *mistakes*, the tragic consequences of failing to appreciate things as they are. This being the case, they are caused more by human frailty or fallibility than malice. Robert Jervis (1976), building on the ideas of Kenneth Boulding (1956), has contributed enormously to our understanding of these psychological causes of war. He makes the point that in order to make sense of the world around us, all of us develop images of reality through which we filter the welter of information that bombards our senses. These 'images' of reality are more important than reality itself when it comes to determining our behaviour; they act as a distorting lens which inhibits our ability to see reality as it is and predisposes us to judge the world in ways that confirm our pre-existing concepts.

Critically important misperceptions likely to lead to war include mistaken estimates of both enemy intentions and capabilities, inaccurate assessments of the military balance between adversaries, and failures to judge the risks and consequences of war properly. Quite frequently these kinds of misperceptions are made by both sides involved in a conflict. For example, Greg Cashman has argued that in the Gulf War, Saddam Hussein may have perceived a threat from Kuwait's reluctance to allow Iraq to cancel its debts and its unwillingness to pump less oil. He may even have perceived a joint American–Israeli–British conspiracy to deny Iraq sophisticated weaponry. On the other hand, leaders in virtually all of the Middle East capitals underestimated the degree of threat posed by Iraq and were taken by surprise when Kuwait was invaded. Thus, while Iraqi leaders overestimated the degree of threat to their interests, their opponents underestimated the hostility of Iraq (Cashman 1993: 63). But perhaps the most critical misperception of all was Saddam Hussein's failure to anticipate Western resolve and the creation of a powerful military coalition against him. There were at least as many misperceptions surrounding the 2003 Iraq War. Despite the unambiguous warnings he had received Saddam was convinced that the United States and Britain would not invade. For their part the Americans and the British believed that Saddam possessed weapons of mass destruction and was well on the way to acquiring nuclear capability. They also believed that invasion would be universally welcomed, that Iraq was a haven for terrorists, and that democracy could be created with relative ease. None of these beliefs were true, but for the participants they formed the psychological reality against which they made their decisions.

Before the Second World War, Hitler mistakenly believed that Britain would not fight and Chamberlain mistakenly believed that Germany could be appeased by concessions. Other delusions and misconceptions that contributed to the outbreak of war in 1939 have been identified by A. J. P. Taylor. Mussolini was deluded about the strength of Italy; the French believed that France was impregnable. Churchill believed that Britain could remain a great power despite the war, and Hitler 'supposed that Germany would contend with Soviet Russia and the United States for mastery of the world' (Nelson and Olin 1979: 153–4). In Britain hardly anyone expected that German blitzkrieg tactics would bring France down in a matter of weeks, and throughout Europe people grossly overestimated the power of strategic bombing. Given this plethora of misunderstandings, misjudgements, and misperceptions, it is easy to argue that statesman stumbled into the Second World War because they were out of touch with reality.

Much the same point can be made about the Falklands War. Misperceptions abounded. Britain seriously misinterpreted Argentine intentions with respect to invasion, and Argentina badly misjudged Britain's determination to resist. For years the two governments had been involved in intermittent negotiations about a possible transfer of sovereignty, and, though little progress had been made, the Conservative government could not believe that the Argentine junta would seize South Georgia before the possibilities of negotiation had been exhausted. What the British government failed to appreciate was the significance of the Malvinas in the Argentine psyche and the domestic pressures to act that this put on

President Galtieri and Dr Costa Mendez. For its part, the government of Argentina could not believe that at the end of the twentieth century a Eurocentric, post-colonial Britain was prepared to spill blood for the sake of a barren relic of empire 10,000 miles away.

There is a sense in which the misconceptions prevalent both in Germany before the Second World War and in Argentina before the Falklands War are understandable. The signals transmitted by the policy of appeasement may have suggested to Hitler that since he had got away with swallowing the Rhineland in 1936, and Austria and the Sudetenland in 1938, he could probably get away with aggression against Poland in 1939. In the case of the Falklands, the casual pace of British diplomacy and the absence of any serious military capability in the area may have suggested to the Argentines that Britain was not much interested in the fate of the Falkland Islands and was unlikely to defend them. Perhaps, in both of these cases, it was not so much that signals were *misread* but that *the wrong signals were sent*. Either way Britain's enemies made serious miscalculations of her intentions and war resulted.

If wars are caused by misperceptions and misunderstandings created by cognitive biases, then conditions of peace include more clear thinking, better communications between countries, and education. This thought lies behind the United Nations Educational, Scientific, and Cultural Organization (UNESCO) motto 'Peace Through Understanding', various 'education for peace' proposals, and the attempts that are frequently made to get potential adversaries around the conference table so that they can better understand each other. The basic idea is that if enemies can be brought to appreciate each other's perspectives, then the disputes that divide them will dissolve because they will be seen to be either illusory or not sufficiently serious to justify war. Perhaps we can detect in this approach relics of the idea of a natural 'harmony of interests', which would prevail if only misunderstandings were cleared up.

Before we are persuaded by this idea that wars can be prevented by removing misperceptions and misunderstandings, a word of warning is appropriate. It may not be possible to eradicate misperception from human affairs given the inherent cognitive weaknesses of the human mind. The need to simplify, the inability to empathize, the tendency to ethnocentrism, the reluctance to relinquish or recognize prejudices—all familiar human weaknesses—may make some degree of misperception inevitable. Herbert Butterfield recognized this point when he identified an 'irreducible dilemma' lying in the very geometry of human conflict. Butterfield imagined a situation in which two potential enemies, both armed, face each other. Neither harbours any hostile intent but neither can be sure of the intentions of the other.

> You cannot enter into the other man's counterfear [and] it is never possible for you to realize or remember properly that since he cannot see the inside of your mind, he can never have the same assurance of your intentions that you have.
> **Butterfield (1952: 21).**

Butterfield makes the point that the greatest war in history could be caused by statesmen who desperately want peace but whose cognitive limitations lead them to misinterpret each other's intentions (1952: 19). (Discerning students will realize that Butterfield's 'ultimate predicament' has, in recent years, surfaced in the literature of strategic studies as 'the security dilemma'.)

Additionally, not all wars are caused by misperceptions and misunderstandings, even though they may be surrounded by them. Some wars—perhaps most—are rooted in genuine disagreement and conflicting interests, and in these cases discussions between enemies simply promote a better understanding of the disputes that divide them. Indeed, in some situations improved understanding may actually exacerbate the divisions between adversaries. When it was suggested to him that international hatred and suspicion could be reduced by getting nations to understand one another better, Sir Evelyn Baring, British governor in Egypt between 1883 and 1907, replied that 'the more they understand one another the more they will hate one another' (Waltz 1959: 50). Perhaps it can be argued that for most of the 1930s Britain was at peace with Germany precisely because the British did not understand Hitler. When, in September 1939, the penny finally dropped, Britain declared war on Germany.

Group Explanations of War

Though embarked upon by individual human beings, war, by definition, is a group activity. It is waged by human collectives—factions, tribes, nations, states, and even perhaps by 'civilizations'. This has led some to shift the responsibility for war from human beings to the group within which they live and to which they owe varying degrees of allegiance. Those who argue in this way believe that there is nothing much wrong with human beings per se, but they are corrupted by the social structures in which they live. In the words of Friedrich Nietzsche, 'Madness is the exception in individuals but the rule in groups' (Nietzsche 1966: 15). Essentially, the argument is that there is something about human collectives that encourages violence.

Perhaps the trouble starts with the sense of difference that we all feel between 'us' and 'them'. Whenever people can make a distinction between those who belong to their own collective grouping—be it tribe, state, or nation—and other groups with which they cannot identify easily, they have laid the foundation for conflict. It is all too easy for a group to slide from recognizing that it is different from other groups to believing that it is superior to them. Hence, this sense of differentiation—what Suganami calls 'discriminatory sociability' (1996: 55)—readily leads to group selfishness, inter-group conflict, and ultimately war. As Niebuhr once observed, 'altruistic passion is sluiced into the reservoirs of nationalism with great ease, and made to flow beyond them with great difficulty' (1932: 91).

G. Le Bon was one of the earliest social psychologists to notice that the behaviour of social groups is different from—and usually worse than—the behaviour of the individuals comprising them. He developed the idea of crowd psychology, that in a crowd a new entity or collective mind comes into being. He believed that while in groups, individuals lose their normal restraints, become more suggestible, more emotional, and less rational. What is more, groups have reduced feelings of responsibility, because the more responsibility is diffused in crowds, the less heavily it weighs on each individual. Since responsibility is everywhere (and therefore nowhere), blame cannot be allocated specifically, and this frees human collectives from normal moral restraints (1897: 41). This thought was neatly captured in the title of Niebuhr's classic *Moral Man and Immoral Society*. Eric Hoffer, in discussing the appeal of mass movements, makes the same point very graphically, 'When we lose our individual independence in the corporateness of a mass movement, we find a new freedom—freedom to hate, bully, lie, torture, murder and betray without shame or remorse' (1952: 118).

Human beings have always lived in differentiated groups and it is unlikely that this will change in the foreseeable future. The interesting question is whether some groups are more war prone than others. In the context of inter-state wars, for example, are capitalist states more warlike than socialist states or vice versa? There is no clear answer to that question. Can we argue that democratic states are more peace-loving than authoritarian states? Again there is no clear answer. Although some evidence suggests that democracies do not fight *each other* very often, other historical evidence suggests that democracies fight as often as do other types of states. In the late 1990s, as wars in the Gulf and the former Yugoslavia have shown, democratic states have also demonstrated some enthusiasm for wars of intervention in support of human rights. This current fashion for waging wars in support of liberal values does not augur well for a peaceful world.

Various observers have noted, however, that democracies seldom, if ever, *fight each other*. Michael Doyle, for example, has argued that liberal states are more peacefully inclined towards each other because their governments are more constrained by democratic institutions, and because they share the same democratic values. Commercial interdependence between liberal states also gives them a vested interest in peace (Doyle 1983, 1986). If Doyle and those who share his views are right, one of the conditions of peace is the spread of democracy—a trend that has gathered pace particularly since the end of the cold war. For the first time ever, almost half of the world's governments are now democratic. The thesis that the spread of democracy will promote peace is no more than plausible, however, and it would be unwise to accept it uncritically.

Key points

- Some believe that human beings are genetically programmed towards violence, but there is an ongoing debate about whether war is an example of innate or learned behaviour.
- Social psychologists have argued that aggression is the result of frustration. Some believe feelings of aggression can be channelled into harmless activities like sport.
- Wars that result from misperceptions, misunderstandings, and miscalculations by statesmen might be prevented by better communications and more accurate information.
- Some believe that there is something about human collectives that encourages violence.
- There is some evidence, however, that though democratic states fight as frequently as other states, they do not fight each other.

Wars 'Within' and 'Beyond' States

Perhaps because of the spread of democracy, it is often argued that *inter-state* violence is now less of a problem than it was just a few years ago. Indeed, it has been calculated that since 1970 fewer than 10 per cent of armed conflicts have been inter-state wars fought for traditional objectives. Sometimes, of course, wars straddle both the 'internal' and 'inter-state' categories. The Indo-China war, for example is a case in point. What started as a colonial war developed into a civil war and became an inter-state war with the intervention of the United States and its allies in Vietnam. In Libya in 2011 resistance to Colonel Gaddafi, triggered by 'the Arab Spring' also led to Western intervention in support of the rebels. The subsequent overthrow of Gaddafi meant that the distinction between civil conflict and inter-state conflict was blurred.

One reason why it is argued that inter-state wars may be going out of fashion is that in a globalized world the expected value of conquest has diminished and its costs, both economic and political, have escalated. States bent on improving their standards of living are better advised to spend their money on education, research, and technology than on conquering other countries and trying to hold down hostile populations. The contemporary moral climate makes aggressive wars difficult to justify, and the media revolution makes it difficult to avoid the opprobrium attached to waging them.

General Sir Rupert Smith is one of the most recent in a long line of commentators who echo this fashionable perception that old fashioned wars are old hat. Violence exists, he says, but 'wars in the future will not be waged between states. Instead we will fight among the people' (Smith 2006: 1). The general may be right, but a little reflection suggests that both he and those who think like him may be premature in their judgement. The conflicts between Israel and Hezbollah in Lebanon in 2006, Russia and Georgia in 2008, and Israel and Hamas in Gaza in 2008, all took place across neighbouring borders. Levy and Thompson have argued that interstate wars are normally much more significant in their consequences than intra-state conflicts (Levy and Thompson 2010). It is also possible to envisage a scenario, perhaps not far into the future, when there is a desperate scramble for scarce resources by capitalist countries that find it increasingly difficult to sustain their profligate lifestyles as vital minerals, particularly fossil fuels, start to run out. The global economic crisis of 2008 might make this more likely.

If that should happen, advanced industrial countries might face the stark choice between going under or waging inter-state war to secure supplies of essential materials. Take oil for example. To deny a modern industrial state oil is to deny it the means of survival. Since no state has ever committed suicide, who can doubt that, faced with the destruction of their way of life, states will do whatever is necessary to secure adequate supplies of oil—including waging inter-state war. In short, inter-state war is not yet off the agenda, even for civilized states that pride themselves on their peaceful intentions.

Even if it is accepted that there has been a decline in inter-state wars, this does not explain the rising incidence of internal war. There are a number of reasons why civil wars have become common, but perhaps the most basic is that in many parts of the world sovereign states—which are usually defined in terms of the monopoly of military power that they wield within their territory—have lost that monopoly to a variety of bodies, be they tribes, ethnic groups, terrorists, warlords, splinter groups, or armed gangs. As Syria in 2012 demonstrates when governments lose their monopoly of military force they can no longer control their territory or their people. The domestic environment begins to resemble the ungoverned international system which, as we saw earlier in this chapter, is a structural, 'permissive' cause of war. In Hobbesian anarchy, ancient tensions and hatreds that were previously contained burst to the surface. We have also seen the consequences of this in Bosnia, Kosovo, Chechnya, Afghanistan, Sierra Leone, Somalia, East Timor, and Haiti.

What is particularly horrifying about ethnic wars is that people are brutalized and killed not because of anything they have done, not even because of their politics, but simply because of who they are. That is what is so terrible about the persecution of the Tutsis in Rwanda, the Tamils in Sri Lanka, the Kurds in Iraq, the Muslims in Bosnia, and the Albanians in Kosovo. Ethnic wars are quite different from Clausewitzian politically motivated conflicts where the belligerents disagree about something and seek to resolve their disagreement by inter-state war—an activity conducted according to moral and legal rules. It may be going too far to describe run-of-the-mill inter-state wars as rational and civilized, but there is a grain of sense in the thought. Ethnic wars are quite different. They are not about the pursuit of inter-ests as normally understood. They are about malevolence and they are unrestrained by any legal or moral rules. 'Ethnic cleansing', like 'the final solution', is surely one of the most sinister phrases to enter the political vocabulary of the twentieth century.

It is ironic that authoritarian governments, so frequently blamed for inter-state wars, were instrumental in preventing civil wars in countries like Yugoslavia and the Soviet Union. Hobbes's *Leviathan* may have its attractions if the alternative is genocidal violence. If the thousands of ethnic groups that exist in the world can no longer be contained within nation states, then we face the break-up of international society into a myriad of micro-groups. The consequences of 'Balkanization' on this scale are unlikely to lead to a more peaceful world.

Wars between states and wars between nations and tribes within states are depressingly familiar, but the idea that future conflicts in global politics will occur between civilizations is a new one. In a provocative and influential article in *Foreign Affairs*, Huntington predicted that the fundamental source of future conflict will be cultural. 'The fault lines between civilizations would be the battle lines of the future' (1993a: 22). In Europe, for example, as the ideological divisions of the cold war disappeared, the age-old cultural divisions between Western Christendom on the one hand and Orthodox Christianity and Islam on the other reappeared. As W. Wallace has suggested, 'the most significant dividing line in Europe may well be the eastern boundary of Western Christianity in the year 1500' (quoted in Huntington, 1993a: 30). This cultural fault weaves its way from the Baltic to the Mediterranean and conflict along it is to be expected.

Huntington argues that a civilization is 'the highest cultural grouping of people and the broadest level of cultural identity people have' (1993a: 24). He has distinguished eight civilizations—Western, Japanese, African, Latin American, Confucian, Hindu, Islamic, and Slavic Orthodox—that differ from each other in terms of their attitudes towards democracy, free markets, liberalism, church–state relations, and international intervention. The differ-ences between civilizations on these issues are deeper than those between states or ideolo-gies. As a result, international consensus and agreement will become increasingly difficult to achieve. Among the reasons for thinking inter-civilizational conflict is likely is that in many parts of the world 'Western' values are being challenged. There is a resurgence of religion and fundamentalism that has widened the gulf between peoples and the communications revo-lution has also served to make people more aware of the differences that divide them.

Key points

- As inter-state war has waned, intra-state conflict has become more frequent.
- Ethnic conflicts do not easily fit the Clausewitzian model. They are particularly violent and people are often killed because of who they are rather than because of their behaviour and politics.
- In the future, some writers suggest, wars may be between civilizations rather than between states or ethnic groups.

Conclusion

There is no shortage of 'cures' for the 'disease' of war. Some are bizarre. For example, Linus Pauling once suggested that wars are caused by a vitamin deficiency and that we could eat our way out of aggression by swallowing the appropriate tablets. Others—like calls to change human nature, to reconstruct the state system, to redistribute equitably the world's wealth, to abolish armaments, or to 're-educate' mankind—follow with faultless logic from the various causes of war which scholars have identified. But since there is no prospect of implementing them in the foreseeable future, in a sense they are not solutions at all. Henry IV's reputed comment on an equally impractical proposal for peace is still appropriate, 'It is perfect', the king said, 'Perfect. I see no single flaw in it save one, namely, that no earthly prince would ever agree to it'. Hedley Bull has rightly condemned such solutions as 'a corruption of thinking about international relations and a distraction from its proper concerns' (1961: 26–7).

We have to begin by recognizing the limits of what is possible. Maybe we can then edge our way forward by improving our techniques of diplomacy, communication, crisis avoidance, and crisis management; by developing a concept of enlightened self-interest which is sensitive to the interests of others; by extending the scope of international law and building on existing moral constraints; by learning how to manage military power through responsible civil-military relations and sophisticated measures of arms control; and by strengthening cooperation through international organizations and world trade. These are not spectacular, radical, or foolproof solutions to the problem of war. That is why practical foreign policymaking is more akin to weeding than landscape gardening. However, they are practical steps that offer the possibility at least of reducing its frequency, and perhaps also of limiting its destructiveness. Even if war could be abolished, we need to remember that peace is not a panacea in which all human antagonisms are resolved. Peace is simply the absence of war, not the absence of conflict. As the cold war demonstrated, it is just as possible to wage peace as it is to wage war. Though 'peace' and 'war' are usually regarded as opposites, there is a sense in which both are aspects of the conflict that is endemic in all social life. War is simply a special kind of conflict that differs from peace only by its violent nature. The fact that peace is not a panacea explains why, when confronted with the stark choice of peace or war, leaders sometimes choose war. Some kinds of peace—under dictatorships, for example—may be worse than some kinds of war. In other words, although almost everyone wants peace, almost no one (apart from strict pacifists) wants only peace or peace at any price. If it were otherwise, the problem of war would disappear since as a last resort states can always avoid war by surrendering. Capitulation might bring peace, but it would almost certainly entail the loss of some of those other things that states want—like independence, justice, prosperity, and freedom. When it comes to the crunch, leaders may think that some fundamental values or goals are worth fighting for.

Ideally, of course, what people want is a worldwide just peace. Unfortunately, this is an unattainable dream. It would require agreement on whose justice is to prevail. It would require a redistribution of the world's wealth from the haves to the have-nots. Just peace would require religious and political movements—Muslims, Christians, Jews, Hindus, communists, capitalists—to tolerate each other. It would also require an end to cultural imperialism and an agreement that differing cultural values are equally valid. It would probably require the disappearance of borders and differentiated societies with their 'them' and 'us' mentalities. In short, it would require human beings to behave in ways in which they have never behaved. Since justice and peace do not go together, statesmen will have to continue choosing between them. The pursuit of justice may require them to wage war, and the pursuit of peace may require them to put up with injustice. During the cold war years, Western politicians, by abandoning Eastern Europe to its fate under Communism, thought, probably rightly, that peace was more important than justice. Since the end of the cold war, they have tended to put justice before peace—witness the upsurge of violence caused by wars of intervention in support of human rights and democratic values. The critical question now is whether, in juggling the priorities of peace and justice, we have got the balance right, or whether our current enthusiasm for Western values and human rights implies an ever so slightly casual attitude to the problem of war. Perhaps, in the interests of peace, there is something to be said for the realist policy of fighting necessary rather than just wars.

 ## Questions

1. Which of the distinctions in Box 1.1 do you think is most useful for analysing the causes of war?
2. Do you think the spread of democracy will solve the problem of war?
3. To which would you allocate priority: the pursuit of peace or the pursuit of justice?
4. Is aggressive behaviour instinctive or learned?
5. How convincing is the argument that wars are a result of misjudgement and misperceptions?
6. Is war inevitable?
7. Is war an instrument of policy or an outburst of irrationality?
8. Are inter-state wars going out of fashion?
9. If international order rests on the principle of 'non-intervention', using Libya as an example, how can military intervention in the internal affairs of sovereign states be justified?
10. Can the problem of war be solved through education?

 ## Further Reading

J. S. Levy and W. R. Thompson, *The Causes of War* (Chichester: Wiley-Blackwell, 2010) provides a comprehensive analysis of the leading theories on both inter-state and civil wars.

R. Niebuhr, *Moral Man and Immoral Society: A Study in Ethics and Politics* (New York and London: Charles Scribner's Sons, 1932) is one of the best studies of ethics and conflict.

S. P. Rosen, *War and Human Nature* (Princeton, NJ: Princeton University Press, 2005) for an analysis of the contribution that neuroscientific and biological research can make to the study of war.

S. Van Evera, *The Causes of War* (Cornell: Cornell University press, 2009) provides an up-to-date analysis of the causes of war.

K. Waltz, *Man, the State, and War* (New York: Columbia University Press, 1959).
One of the best studies of the causes of war.

 ## Web Links

Russ Long, *Introductory Sociology Theoretical Perspectives* **http://www.delmar.edu/socsci/rlong/intro/perspect.htm** This source provides an interesting sociological analysis of the causes of war.

R.J. Rummel, *Understanding Conflict and War:* **http://www.hawaii.edu/powerkills/NOTE12.HTM** Rummel focuses on the psychological causes of conflict and war. This source also considers the technological, social, and intellectual roots of conflict and violence.

Robert A. Hinde, *The Psychological Basis of War* **http://www.unc.edu/depts/diplomat/AD_Issues/amdipl_7/hinde.html** Another useful source on the psychological causes of war.

Stanford Encyclopaedia of Philosophy, *Thomas Hobbes* **http://plato.stanford.edu/entries/hobbes-moral/** This source provides a useful background to the ideas of Hobbes on the anarchical nature of international relations and the causes of conflict that result.

2

The Evolution of Modern Warfare

MICHAEL SHEEHAN

 Chapter Contents

Introduction	40
The Napoleonic Legacy	40
The Industrialization of War	44
Naval Warfare	47
Total War	49
Nuclear Weapons and Revolutionary Warfare	55
Conclusion: Postmodern War	56

 Reader's Guide

This chapter looks at the way that the theory and practice of war has changed over the past two hundred years. It examines the ways in which the development of modern states have changed the way that wars are fought and looks at the impact of the Industrial Revolution on the planning for, and conduct of, war. It also looks at the influence of some of the key thinkers on war in the past two centuries. War is a social practice, and the conduct of war is influenced by changes in military theory, in the development of new technologies, and crucially, by the evolution of society itself.

Introduction

War has been a perennial feature of human history. It is condemned as a base activity in which human beings show the darker side of their nature by using violence and killing to achieve their ends. Yet at the same time war is a peculiarly *social* activity, demanding high levels of organization, and depending upon bonds of loyalty, obedience, and solidarity for its effective prosecution.

In the modern period, war between developed states assumed a particular form, characterized by a symbiotic relationship with increasingly well-organized states, the industrialization of warfare, and a growing totality in the manner in which it was conducted. In many ways this 'modern' era of warfare was historically unusual. By the end of the twentieth century however, there was some evidence that this era of 'modern' industrial warfare might be ending and a new one beginning.

What do we mean by 'modern' warfare? It is the forms of warfare shaped by and reflecting the 'modern' era of human history, but modernity and modern war mean much more than simply technological progress and wars fought with increasingly sophisticated and mass-produced weaponry. The nineteenth century military theorist Carl von Clausewitz said that the prevailing form of war always reflects the era in which it occurs, and this is certainly the case with modern warfare. It should be noted however, that in any era there is more than just one characteristic *form* of war. The nature of the combatants and the social and geographical context mean that war shows many faces, apart from that typical of conflicts between the great powers of the day.

Modern warfare developed in terms of a number of broad themes that were increasingly characteristic of society as a whole, particularly Western society, such as the growing power of the state through processes of centralization, bureaucratization, and, to some extent, democratization. It was influenced by the rise of powerful ideologies, such as nationalism. Other important developments were the rapid development of technological progress and industrialization driven by the scientific method, an associated rapid rise in national populations, and a growing insistence that in return for the benefits brought by living in an advanced state, the citizen owed a duty to defend the state.

These forces took form during the course of the nineteenth and early-twentieth centuries in terms of a military revolution focused on mass conscript armies, of ideologically motivated citizens, armed with mass-produced, long-range weapons of incredible killing power, and logistically sustained by industrialized economies that could maintain armies on distant fronts almost indefinitely. This produced a form of war where the absolute defeat of the enemy was the objective, and the entire population of the opposing state became potential targets. It was an evolution towards 'total war', which saw its apotheosis in the Second World War (1939–1945).

The Napoleonic Legacy

The second half of the eighteenth century in Europe had been characterized by comparatively 'limited' warfare. The spread of the rationalist values of the Enlightenment, and the lingering memory of the horrors of the religious wars of the seventeenth century were influential.

Socio-economic factors were also important. The dynastic states of the period had limited tax and recruiting bases. In some states, such as Britain and the Dutch Republic, there were constitutional limitations on the size of the army and the ways in which it could be used.

All states faced major difficulties both in recruiting and retaining soldiers. Military service was not popular and most armies relied upon a combination of long-service professionals and foreign mercenaries. Such professionals were expensive to recruit and train, and governments encouraged their generals not to risk such expensive assets in pitched battles.

Military factors also tended towards limitation. The linear warfare of the age required the soldiers to have great training and discipline, and such trained troops were too valuable to be lightly thrown away. Fighting in line or square meant that infantry could only move very slowly, making it difficult to take opposing armies by surprise or to pursue them to the point of destruction, no matter how keen the generals were to do so. The ferocious discipline of armies encouraged desertion, making generals reluctant to release their troops for the unrelenting pursuit that might bring absolute victory.

The horrors of the wars of the previous century also meant that commanders were reluctant to allow their soldiers to pillage. This meant that armies had to carry all their supplies with them, or else amass huge stockpiles of supplies at depots in advance, to which they were subsequently tied. Supply limitations and poorly developed road networks also restricted the size of the armies that states could put into the field.

Many of the transformative ideas that characterized the military results of the French Revolution had in fact appeared in earlier decades. French thinkers such as Montesquieu and Rousseau had promoted the idea that in a democracy, a citizen should have an obligation to defend his country and that the army should essentially be the people in arms. Nor was such thinking confined to the *philosophes*, military thinkers such as Guibert also advocated the recruiting of a citizen army. Guibert also called for the abandonment of the depot system, and a return to pillage and 'living off the land'.

The basis for change occurred in 1792, with the flight, arrest and subsequent execution of King Louis XVI, and the creation of the French Republic. To defend itself against its many enemies, the revolutionary regime embraced a radical new approach to the conduct of war, including the creation of a citizen army raised by conscription, the beginnings of economic regimentation and large-scale war production, as well as ideological warfare and indoctrination. These were features typical of modern warfare.

The introduction of conscription in 1793 led to a vast increase in the size of the French armies. The scale of warfare was also affected by other developments which changed the nature of war. These included the idea of the nation in arms, the impact of ideology and nationalist fervour, and the meritocratic promotions that altered the class basis of the officer corps.

Unlike the limited war of the eighteenth century, the purpose of ideological war became the complete overthrow of the enemy. Rather than minor territorial gains, the objective of war became massive gains or even outright annexation. In the Revolutionary and Napoleonic period the French army deliberately sought out battle, and the army's ability to manoeuvre quickly compelled the enemy to fight or retreat.

The French Revolution allowed France to raise mass armies, and these proved decisive in the early years of Napoleon's empire. Only the difficulties of supplying such huge numbers in the age before railways and mass production held back the growth in the size of armies. One of France's greatest generals from the Age of Reason, Maurice de Saxe, had argued that 50,000 men was the maximum practical size for an army, but by 1812, Napoleon invaded Russia with an army of nearly 600,000.

The huge armies raised new issues for generals and strategists. They were too large to be easily moved along a single road, but to spread them along several parallel roads left them vulnerable to being defeated in detail. The creation of the corps system overcame this danger, since each corps was essentially a small army of up to 50,000 men, with its own infantry, cavalry and artillery, powerful enough to defend against the enemy army until the rest of the French army could be concentrated, yet small enough to advance rapidly. Prior to the French Revolution, the largest unit in an army was the brigade, composed of several battalions of infantry, or regiments of cavalry. The revolution introduced the division, a grouping of several brigades into a larger formation. Napoleon then combined several divisions into *army corps*. Powerful artillery bombardment would now become a feature of battle, and casualties would reflect this. This development had been advocated before the revolution by Du Teil, who emphasized the advantage of concentrating artillery at the point of attack, rather than spreading it along the line of battle.

The new massive armies posed another problem: they were difficult to feed and supply. The traditional supply depots used by eighteenth-century armies were soon left behind by the rapidly moving corps, yet the supplies required were so great that they would dramatically slow the army if it had to transport them with it. The solution was a reversion to pre-eighteenth century practice, a practice condemned as barbaric during the Age of Reason. This was for the army to 'live off the land', to forage ruthlessly in the territories through which it marched.

This in turn meant that war necessarily had to be offensive war. Such foraging could not be practised in one's own country without producing economic and political disaster, so it must be carried abroad where the war could be made to pay for itself. However, in doing so, it encouraged an attitude of callous indifference towards the sufferings of those in the lands so pillaged, and triggered a resort to guerrilla war against the French from the peasants who had suffered at their hands.

With huge numbers of soldiers at their disposal, generals such as Napoleon Bonaparte felt able to squander the lives of their soldiers on a lavish scale in pursuit of military and political ambition. As revolutionary fervour faded, and casualty lists grew, the huge French armies had increasingly to be maintained through the use of the totalitarian powers that the new modern state possessed, which were far greater than the old monarchical regime had at its disposal. Napoleon's empire ultimately conscripted more than three million men and he boasted that he had an 'income' of 200,000 men a year. The French successes in the Napoleonic period eventually encouraged the equally erroneous assumption that *only* numbers were decisive (see Box 2.1).

The most striking feature of Napoleon's campaigns is the frequency of battle. Unlike his eighteenth-century predecessors, Napoleon commanded armies that could move rapidly enough to *force* their opponents to give battle. He exploited this capacity to the full, deliberately seeking battle in order to defeat the enemy's army, and then to destroy them with an unrelenting pursuit. Destroying a country's army in this way would then allow him to occupy and control the enemy's resources and leave them helpless to resist any political demands that France chose to make (Jones 1987: 350). A classic example of such warfare was the

---

BOX 2.1 Napoleonic Warfare

At its apogee, the Napoleonic way of war threw armies of unprecedented size on country-smashing campaigns of conquest through decisive manoeuvre and, usually, battle. The forces employed to accomplish such heroic tasks were an assemblage of professional soldiers, fairly patriotic French conscripts, and sundry (but increasingly reluctant foreign) mercenaries. The soldiery was articulated into an autonomous *corps d'armée* and led with a variable operational artistry by the Zeus of modern war, the Corsican mastermind himself, variously aided and frequently abetted by his Imperial Headquarters (*very* approximate general staff) and, after 1804, his Marshalate. In its prime, which is to say in 1805–07, the Napoleonic style at least appeared to restore the power of swift decision as an instrument of foreign policy.

Gray (2003: 140)

1806 campaign against Prussia. The Prussian army was shattered at the twin battles of Jena-Auerstädt, and then destroyed by a vigorous and continuous pursuit.

Clausewitz

Carl von Clausewitz (1780–1831) was a Prussian career soldier, with extensive experience of the conduct of war at all levels. His thought was influenced by the German nationalism of Schiller and Goethe and by numerous military writers, such as Berenhorst, who had argued that 'war is a natural social phenomenon, susceptible to analysis' (Nofi 1982: 16). Much of his later career was spent as the Director of the Prussian Military Academy, where he developed the ideas expounded in his classic book, *On War*.

Clausewitz's ideas on war marked a break from the social and political optimism of the eighteenth century. Though he saw war as a political instrument, guided by rational decision-making, he emphasized that it depended on the willingness to inflict violence and to suffer casualties. The purpose of war was to seek battle and to impose one's will on the opponent through violence.

Clausewitz emphasized that victory would come when the opponent's centre of gravity, the focal point of his power, was captured or destroyed. The destruction of the adversary's armed forces was the key to political victory, but this destruction was moral, not *necessarily* physical. It was the destruction of his capacity to resist, though for Clausewitz, decisive battle was the surest way to achieve this outcome, and the heart of the enemy army was normally the decisive centre of gravity. Though tactics and strategies could be pursued that were designed to create a decisive advantage on the battlefield, for Clausewitz, numbers were ultimately decisive, all other things being equal. For many, this logic would be decisively demonstrated in the Prussian victories over Austria in 1866 and France in 1870.

Clausewitz's view that war represented a continuation of politics, rather than its break-down, also marked a change from Enlightenment thinking. In time his ideas would become decisively influential, though many of his disciples failed to note the caveats in some of his arguments, and underplayed his emphasis on the power of the defensive in war. Although reflecting the lessons of Napoleonic warfare, Clausewitz's thinking was subtle and imaginative enough to remain of relevance throughout the period of industrialized mass warfare, and into the age of nuclear weapons and limited war (see Box 2.2).

BOX 2.2 Clausewitz's Key Ideas

- War is a normal part of politics, differing only in its means.
- War is an act of violence designed to achieve otherwise unattainable goals.
- Each age creates its own form of war.
- War is something in which the entire nation must take part.
- Since war involves people, it is inherently unpredictable.
- Victory is of no value unless it is a means to achieve a political objective.
- Other things being equal, numbers are ultimately decisive.

Key points

- The Napoleonic period saw the emergence of mass armies produced by conscription.
- Napoleonic warfare focused on seeking decisive battle in order to destroy the opponent's army and his capacity to resist.
- Ideology and nationalism helped to produce a more ruthless form of warfare and generated resistance by guerrilla war in many countries.

The Industrialization of War

During the nineteenth century, warfare became industrialized in two important senses. Modern technology was applied to the production of more sophisticated weaponry, but in addition a wide variety of developments in essentially civilian technologies proved immensely important for the future conduct of war. Weaponry, ammunition, and all the other material of war could now be mass produced. Armies of much greater size could now be sustained on campaign. Small developments such as the ability to store tinned food made it easier to provide food supplies for campaigning, even in harsher winter months. Supplies could be moved quickly to the front in great quantities using the new railways. The first rail journey was made in 1825, and by 1846 Prussia was able to move an army corps, with all its equipment, 250 miles in two days, rather than the two weeks a march would have required (Preston and Wise 1970: 244).

The use of railways meant not only that soldiers could be moved quickly, but that they remained relatively fit and unexhausted at the end of their journey, an important consideration with armies largely composed of reservists. The railway could be used to move wounded troops to rear-area hospitals, improving their chances of survival. Railways could also bring replacements and reinforcements on a more regular basis which meant that states could produce and maintain the mass armies required by Napoleonic warfare. In 1870, Prussia invaded France with an army twice the size of the one Napoleon had led into Russia 60 years earlier. The much smaller French army, which had not been able to mobilize quickly enough, was simply overwhelmed. By 1914 the forces employed had doubled again and Germany attacked France with nearly three and a half million men, and her enemies were deploying armies of comparable sizes.

The strategic value of railways was quickly realized. France moved 120,000 men to Italy during its 1859 war with Austria, but failed to move their associated supplies, limiting the army's effectiveness. Two years later however, the utility of railways for strategic advantage was clearly demonstrated in the opening campaign of the American Civil War. In July 1861, the movement of Johnson's Valley Army to Manassas enabled the Confederacy to achieve numerical parity and to win the Battle of First Manassas, when a defeat might have led to an almost immediate end to the Civil War. The United States subsequently organized a Military Railway Department which played an important role in the ultimate Federal victory in the war, but not before the Confederacy had used the railway system to achieve important strategic advantages in the Kentucky campaign of 1862 and Chickamauga campaign of 1863, while the United States countered the Chickamauga setback with a massive rail movement of reinforcements to relieve besieged Chattanooga. During the Franco–Prussian War of 1870, the superior Prussian use of railways enabled it to heavily outnumber the opposing French armies and overwhelm them.

Another civilian technology of immediate military importance was the telegraph, which allowed political leaderships and theatre commanders to maintain communications with army leaders over distances that would previously have meant delays of days or weeks in communicating orders.

During the course of the nineteenth century, however, a series of crucial developments in weapons technology transformed both strategy and tactics. Infantry weapons were revolutionized by the introduction of rifled gun barrels, smokeless cartridges, breech-loading, and eventually magazine weapons. Rifled weapons were far more accurate, and infantry could now hit their targets at ranges of several hundred yards, without necessarily exposing themselves to counterfire. Rifled weapons rapidly proved their superiority in the early stages of the American Civil War and breech-loaders became standard in European armies after the Prussian success with using them in the 1866 Austro–Prussian War. In 1884 Prussia introduced the eight-shot magazine rifle. US cavalry armed with repeating carbines achieved a decisive superiority over their Confederate opponents in the closing stages of the American Civil War. However, the machine gun, which the French army possessed in 1870, was so poorly understood and unintelligently deployed, that it initially had no impact whatsoever. By 1884, however, the development of the Maxim machine gun produced an effective weapon which would revolutionize tactics.

During the 1860s rifled artillery also became the norm, and even muzzle loading examples had ranges of two miles. By 1870 Prussia had produced efficient breech-loading rifled artillery, which outranged those of their French opponents, giving them a huge tactical advantage. In the 1890s quick-firing technology increased the effectiveness of artillery still further.

The experience of the American Civil War (1861–1865) and Franco–Prussian War (1870–1871) demonstrated that the new weapons made it extremely difficult for infantry to close successfully with their enemy and that they suffered very heavy casualties if circumstances forced them to carry such attacks through. Battles such as Malvern Hill, Fredericksburg and Gettysburg in the American Civil War, and Gravelotte in the Franco-Prussian War, were characterized by infantry suffering very heavy casualties against prepared defenders. When manoeuvrability was lost and the enemy entrenched, the difficulties for the attacker became even greater, as the final months of the Civil War in the east demonstrated (see Box 2.3).

BOX 2.3 Colonial Warfare

Although histories of war tend to focus on the collisions between the major powers in the nineteenth century, for many states, notably Britain, France, and Spain, colonial and imperial campaigns against non-European enemies absorbed much of their military energies and attention. Such conflicts were often characterized by extreme brutality. Decisive victories for the European powers were rare and were invariably followed by years of indecisive guerrilla warfare. Colonial commanders frequently resorted to massacres and the deliberate destruction of the local population's homes and food supplies in order to undermine their opponents' guerrilla campaigns. The contemporary military writer C. E. Callwell argued that 'in small wars, one is sometimes forced into committing havoc that the laws of regular warfare do not sanction' (Porch, 2001). It was a form of war from which European generals derived few lessons for European war, yet it was a precursor of the total war of the first half of the twentieth century, and a style of war that in some ways would be echoed in the so-called 'New Wars' that followed the end of the cold war.

However, European strategists largely missed the significance of this lesson between 1871 and 1914, preferring to believe, on the evidence of the Prussian wars of 1866 and 1870, that mass armies, rapidly transported to the military theatre by train, and manoeuvring swiftly thereafter, would guarantee quick victory to the side prepared to take the offensive. Over-looked was the danger posed if the defender also mobilized rapidly and used railways as efficiently to mass defenders in the attacking army's path (Quester 1977: 80). The wars of the mid-nineteenth century had provided mixed lessons. The Crimean War and Franco-Austrian War had seen the early use of rifled weapons and railways, but in many ways had been characteristically Napoleonic conflicts. The Austro-Prussian War of 1866 had seen the use of mass armies and the importance of technological superiority, but had otherwise demonstrated none of the elements of total war. This was not the case with the Franco-Prussian War, which saw not only the effective use of staff work, railways and the telegraph, but also heavy casualties produced by the new long-range rifled weaponry. Ominously the French defeat had also triggered political revolution and regime change in France, guerrilla warfare against the Prussians by the Francs-Tireurs, and often savage reprisals by the occupying German forces.

European observers in addition failed to take regard of the warnings from outside Europe. Colonial warfare was often notably savage but indecisive, and in addition, a number of the large-scale wars fought outside Europe in the second half of the nineteenth century were all too modern in many respects and demonstrated many of the features of twentieth century total war. The American Civil War was at the same time the last of the old wars and the first of the new. It was an ideological struggle to the death between two incompatible nationalisms, which saw the use of mass conscription, a wide range of novel technologies, including rifled weapons, steamships, landmines, barbed wire, and observation balloons. Over 20 per cent of the Southern population fought in the war and the Confederacy enlisted nearly 90 per cent of its available military manpower. Casualties were extremely heavy on both sides and Union forces deliberately targeted the southern civilian population in the Atlanta and Shenandoah campaigns of 1864, General Sherman declaring that 'we are not only fighting hostile armies, but a hostile people and must make old and young, rich and poor, feel the hard hand of war' (Janda 1995:15). However, for the most part it was property rather than the lives of civilians that was targeted (O'Connell 1989: 201). Even more savage was the Great Paraguayan War between Brazil, Argentina, and Paraguay which saw the death of over half of Paraguay's male population. Similarly, the Second Boer War of 1899–1902 saw heavy military casualties in the face of the new weaponry, the incarceration of Boer civilians in British 'concentration' camps, guerrilla warfare by the Boers, and repressive countermeasures by the British that soured relations between the two communities for the next century. All these lessons were repeated in the Russo-Japanese War, characterized by massive armies, horrendous casualties, battlefronts of enormous length, and battles that went on day and night, for weeks on end.

Key points

- The nineteenth century saw the Industrial Revolution dramatically alter the conduct of war.
- Civilian technologies such as railways, steamships, the telegraph, and mass production made it possible to raise, equip, and control huge armies.
- New weapons such as rifled and breech-loading weapons, machine guns, armoured warships, mines, and submarines made their appearance.
- Governments sought to mobilize their populations to support the war effort.
- Because tactics were slow to change, heavy casualties were typical.

Naval Warfare

Naval warfare went through an equally dramatic revolution during the nineteenth century. During the Napoleonic Wars warships were made of wood and powered by the wind, as they had been for centuries. As the century progressed they were increasingly armoured in metal, equipped with long-range rifled weapons, and, most importantly, given engines that enabled them to operate independently of the wind. In 1822 General Paixans published *Nouvelle force maritime*, in which he argued that ships armed with explosive shells and protected with armour plate would be able to annihilate the existing wooden, cannon-armed warships (McNeil 1982: 226). The European navies began adopting such naval artillery in the 1830s and steam engines were introduced in the 1840s. The application of armour plate soon followed.

It was France that led the way in naval design in the mid-nineteenth century, with Britain being reluctant to encourage developments that might challenge her supremacy at sea. For decades warships combined sail and steam propulsion, but as guns became more powerful, they needed to be based in revolving turrets, for which masts and sails were an obstacle. Britain launched the first battleship without any sails in 1873. So rapid was the pace of technological development in warships in the last quarter of the century that ships were sometimes obsolete before they could be launched (Howarth 1974: 331).

Although warship design was undergoing rapid evolution, strategic thinking about naval warfare was slow to evolve. Only towards the end of the century did significant developments take place. In 1890 Alfred Mahan published *The Influence of Seapower on History, 1660–1783*. The book became enormously widely read, partly because the previous decades had seen such rapid change that naval officers were struggling to keep pace with its implications. Mahan argued that naval power had always been crucial in history, that the purpose of a great power's navy was to attain command of the sea, and that the way to achieve this was to concentrate naval capabilities in a powerful battle fleet and to seek out and destroy the major battle fleet or fleets of the enemy. These ideas echo those of Jomini and Clausewitz, though Mahan himself did not encounter Clausewitz's work until much later and was more influenced by Jomini, whom he had read extensively.[1]

New schools of naval thought were emerging, which were unsettling to traditional naval commanders. For example the *Jeune École* in France argued that new systems such as torpedo boats would make commerce raiding the primary form of naval warfare in the future. Proponents of the new technologies argued that the massive battle fleets of countries like Britain would be made obsolete by submarines and torpedo boats.

These ideas alarmed proponents of traditional naval power in Britain, Germany, and Japan. Navalists, such as Colomb in Britain, Von Maltzen in Germany, and Saneyuki in Japan, argued that sea power would continue to dominate the world, because of its inherent advantages of mobility and flexibility. Admiral Columb's *Naval Warfare: Its Ruling Principles and Practices Historically Treated*, appeared at the same time as Mahan's book. Mahan himself dismissed the idea that attacks on commerce should be a navy's primary role in wartime, insisting that battle fleets would dominate the sea, and thereby dominate the world.

Mahan's ideas were in contrast to those contained in the *geopolitics* of Sir Halford Mackinder, who argued that world domination would go to the *land power* that controlled the Eurasian land mass in the era of railways. The theory downplayed the importance of naval power in the contemporary world. Navalist writers argued that national power, security, and prosperity depended on seaborne trade, and that therefore the countries with large merchant fleets and powerful navies would continue to dominate the world, as they always had.

The proponents of naval power envisaged war at sea in terms strongly reminiscent of key features of Napoleonic land warfare. Once the main enemy battle fleet had been located and destroyed, command of the sea could then be exploited by the protection of trade, and the destruction of the enemy's trade, and by the projection of military power ashore.

A somewhat more balanced view was offered by the British naval theorist, Sir Julian Corbett. Corbett stressed a different aspect of Clausewitz's thought, arguing that sea power was no more than a means to a political end. It was therefore important for a state to have a maritime strategy that was in tune with its political aspirations. However, Corbett was well aware that sea power on its own could not overwhelm a strong and resolute land power. Sea power had its limits, and a major naval power like Britain had historically always needed continental allies with land power at their disposal. He also argued that there was far more to maritime strategy than simply the pursuit of decisive battles, with trade protection, commerce raiding, amphibious warfare, and transport of armies by sea being crucial.

In practice, the armoured fleet action did not prove historically decisive. Only in the 1905 Japanese victory over Russia at Tsushima did such a victory occur. During the First World War, although small-scale battles like Coronel and the Falkland islands in 1914 showed how more up-to-date warship technology would decisively prevail, most of the new technologies failed to be decisive and simply made the fleet commanders more cautious. Britain imposed a naval blockade on Germany, which ultimately made a major contribution to the Allied victory. Britain also sought to bring the main German fleet to battle, but the encounters at Dogger Bank in 1915 and Jutland in 1916 were not immediately decisive. Jutland was a tactical victory for the German fleet, but ultimately a strategic victory for the British, since the German fleet never again challenged the

British and was therefore unable to counter the Allied blockade. Nevertheless, British commanders remained frustrated by their inability to force a decisive 'Mahanian' battle of annihilation. In fact Jutland would turn out to be the last fleet action between battleships in history.

Germany turned instead to submarine warfare, and the submarine campaigns would be vital in both world wars. By late 1917 British merchant shipping losses were becoming almost unsustainable, but as would happen in the Second World War, the introduction of the convoy system, along with better tactics and equipment, allowed the allies to defeat the German submarine challenge. In the end neither the *navalists* nor the *Jeune École* were vindicated by the outcome of the war at sea, which saw the battle fleets prove largely impotent. The torpedo proved a crucial, but not a war-winning weapon.

Nevertheless, sea power was important to the outcome of the First World War. Allied naval superiority allowed them to seize Germany's overseas colonies, and to impose the ultimately devastating blockade. It also allowed the allies to transport enormous quantities of men and material from outside Europe to the war zone, including one million French soldiers and two million American troops.

Key points

- The British navy emerged dominant from the Napoleonic Wars, which saw numerous fleet actions, culminating in the Battle of Trafalgar in 1805.
- Naval technology was revolutionized during the nineteenth century.
- Steam power gave navies even greater flexibility and manoeuvrability.
- Heavy guns in revolving turrets, plus armoured warships produced a new generation of all-gun ironclad battleships.
- Mahan argued that fleets of such warships would dominate the seas, while the *Jeune École* insisted that submarines and torpedo boats would be decisive.

Total War

By the beginning of the twentieth century, the major powers had come to accept the Clausewitzian idea that the threat and use of war were appropriate instruments of political purpose in the industrial era. The experience of the European wars of 1864, 1866, and 1870 encouraged the great powers to believe that any future war between the major powers would be both short and decisive.

By 1914 the political, economic, social, technological, and doctrinal trends of the nineteenth century had coalesced into a recipe for catastrophe. Doctrinally, armies were convinced of the virtues of Napoleonic warfare—mass armies, seeking out the army of the adversary, enveloping it, destroying it, and then pursuing the remnants of the enemy forces until his ability to resist any political demands had been crushed. Conscription and nationalism would provide the mass armies, which would be transported and supplied using the railway networks and the industrialized economies of mass production. Rapid movement, combined with the killing power of advanced weaponry, would deliver swift victory to the army that could mobilize and manoeuvre most efficiently.

The harsh reality was that by 1914 the battlefield had grown in size enormously in comparison to the Napoleonic era, and so had the armies that occupied it. By the winter of 1914, the trench line on the western front stretched from Switzerland to the English Channel. There were no flanks to go round, and no way of 'enveloping' the enemy army, which by this period consisted of over three million men on each side. Nor could the armies move as rapidly as the era of railways and aeroplanes might suggest. In 1914 warfare was still not fully mechanized. The German army advanced into Belgium and France in 1914 with fewer than 7,000 motor vehicles, but with 726,000 horses and 150,000 wagons (Addington 1994: 104).

Armed with powerful defensive weapons such as machine guns and long-range artillery, protected by trenches and barbed wire, and supplied with all the resources that the railways could deliver from a mobilized industrial economy, defending armies could not be swiftly shattered and dispersed in the Napoleonic fashion. The defending forces enjoyed an unprecedented ratio of force to space, making the stalemate which followed virtually inevitable. Once this stalemate had been created, it became a war not of rapid military offensives, but of 'economic and human endurance' (Quester 1977: 114).

Instead the enemy had to be worn down by brutal frontal assaults that produced enormous casualty figures, while technological advances were sought which might break the battlefield stalemate. Germany attacked with poison gas at Ypres in 1915, while the British used the first tanks in the closing stage of the Battle of the Somme in 1916.

The conflict also saw war moving into a new dimension as air power became increasingly important. Aircraft were used for reconnaissance from the beginning of the war, and fighters evolved to destroy the reconnaissance aircraft. As the war continued, aircraft were increasingly used for tactical fire and bombing support to ground forces, and eventually for long-range strategic bombing. In their reconnaissance and raiding roles, the aircraft of the First World War essentially took on the role played by light cavalry in the Napoleonic period, just as tanks took on the role previously played by heavy cavalry.

Increasingly too, warfare became more total in its scope and application. Because it was so difficult to break through in the main theatre of war, the geographical scope of war expanded, as the combatants sought to place additional pressure on the opponent by opening new theatres of operations, such as Italy, the Balkans, and the Middle East.

The expansion of the geographical scope of war was accompanied by a greater willingness to deliberately target non-combatants. In the First World War this was seen in the use of unrestricted submarine warfare, with merchant ships being sunk without the crews being given a chance to take to the lifeboats, as Germany attempted to prevent France and Britain from being supplied by sea. It was seen also in the blockade of Germany, which, though it made a critical contribution to Germany's military collapse in the autumn of 1918, also caused enormous civilian suffering and death in Germany. Both Germany and Britain inaugurated the long-range bombing of cities by aircraft.

Major war increasingly came to involve much of the manpower, and material, and moral resources of the state. Any objective whose destruction promised to weaken the war effort of the enemy came to be seen as a legitimate target. Warfare was increasingly directed as much against the civilians and industries that produced the weapons of war, as against the soldiers who actually used them. The idea of illegitimate objectives or targets, of criteria of justness and proportionality, increasingly came to be seen as irrelevant to the conduct of modern war.

Totality in warfare can be assessed in terms of a number of elements, including the type of weaponry employed, the strategy and tactics used, the proportion of a state's resources that are committed, the degree to which every human and material resource of the opponent comes to be seen as a legitimate target, and the extent to which social and cultural pressures towards unrestricted warfare are operating.

The elements of totality in warfare that had become prominent in the First World War came into full flower in the Second. Once again the combatants mobilized their military, economic, and human resources to the maximum extent possible. Conscription was now extended beyond the men called up in the First World War, to embrace also the female population. Women took the place of men in agriculture and industry, but also served in huge numbers in the armed forces in non-combatant roles. In some cases, such as the Soviet Air Force, they also served as combatants. Industry and the merchant navies were taken under government control and subordinated to the war effort. Rationing was introduced to conserve supplies of vital commodities such as food and oil. Germany not only drew on its own population but, by the use of conscript and slave labour, on that of its enemies as well. The social totality of war increased still further with the systematic use of censorship and propaganda, the promotion of nationalism and demonization of the enemy, and the restriction or imprisonment of groups deemed to have suspect loyalties, such as conscientious objectors or citizens of foreign descent (see Box 2.4).

At the strategic and tactical level, the Second World War saw the implementation of military doctrines designed to restore the manoeuvre and offensive capacity that had been so conspicuously absent for most of the First. Germany scored dramatic successes with its blitzkrieg tactics from 1939–41, in which combined arms tactics involving tanks, infantry, and dive-bombers sought to bypass and disrupt enemy resistance, rather than to destroy it through frontal battles of attrition (see Box 2.5) .

The effectiveness of blitzkrieg owed much to the inferior doctrine of the opposing British and French armies. The allies outnumbered the Germans in tanks in the campaign of 1940 and their tanks were superior in quality. However, the French viewed the tank as an infantry support weapon, as they had in 1918, while the Germans concentrated them in armoured divisions, with a view to rapid mechanized offensives. Germany also integrated its air power to support its ground offensives. The Luftwaffe was designed for tactical support of the army, a feature that would disadvantage it in the strategic bombing campaign against Britain in 1940–41, but which made it highly effective in the blitzkrieg land campaigns of 1939–41.

Nevertheless, despite the initial success of blitzkrieg, the technique did not produce ultimate German victory, and by subsequently declaring war on both the Soviet Union and the United States, Hitler condemned Germany to a war against overwhelming odds in which attrition and economic power would be ultimately decisive, particularly on the critical eastern front.

As with the First World War, technological advances prior to and during the war were crucial in a way that had not been typical in earlier wars. Radar helped the RAF win the Battle of Britain in 1940, while the Anti-Submarine Detection Investigation Committee ASDIC (sonar) and aircraft carriers were crucial in the antisubmarine war in the Battle of the Atlantic. Nuclear weapons played a key role in bringing about the unconditional surrender of Japan. German technological breakthroughs, such as the ME262 jet fighter, V-1 cruise missile, and

BOX 2.4 Total War

The phrase 'total war', predates the nuclear age. In the long history of warfare, it is natural that some wars will be less limited than others. The causes, the objectives of the belligerents, their cultures and the history of their previous interactions, the beliefs and values of the era, the prospects for victory, the possibility of outside intervention—these and many other factors influence the manner and means of waging war.

Totality in war is a relative rather than an absolute concept. Total war in the absolute sense would mean fighting without any restrictions. After the experience of Germany's defeat in the First World War, Erich Ludendorf, who had been Chief of Staff of the German armies on the western front, remained unconvinced by those in the interwar period who argued that a particular technology such as tanks, aircraft, or poison gas would bring swift victory in a future war. Nor did he believe that a tactical or strategic doctrine such as blitzkrieg would be able to do so.

For Ludendorf, the key to victory in war between industrialized nations was to follow to its brutally logical conclusion, the social, economic, and technological trends that had characterized warfare over the previous century. War should therefore be characterized by total mobilization of all the military, economic, and human resources of the state. The enemy's civilian population would be deliberately targeted, and one's own civilians would suffer similar assault. Mobilization of the population should therefore embrace ideological features to sustain the war effort, and a political dictatorship to focus all the state's energy on winning the war.

In total war, governments are as demanding of their own citizens as they are ruthless towards their enemies. States draw on every natural resource that they can successfully mobilize, and treat virtually every element of the adversaries' society as a legitimate target, using all the weapons that are available to them. The citizens of the state are obliged to serve in the armed forces or participate in the production of war material, civil and political rights are constrained, the economy is subordinated to the war effort, every weapon, no matter how indiscriminate or terrible, is utilized, and the armed forces, industrial capacity, and the unarmed citizens of the opponent are deemed legitimate targets, because they all contribute to the enemy war effort in either tangible or psychological ways. This logic reached its height with the systematic area bombing of civilians in the Second World War, and in the cold war plans to inflict genocidal 'assured destruction' in a retaliatory nuclear strike.

In practice, wars invariably fall short of totality in one or more dimensions, such as geographical scope, weaponry employed, mobilization of national resources and population, attitude towards neutrals, targeting strategies, and so on.

V-2 ballistic missile, became operational too late in the war to affect its outcome. In the European war it was once again mass and industrial power that proved ultimately decisive, along with Germany's strategic problem of fighting a two-front war against the American and Soviet superpowers.

Whereas in the First World War the bombing of civilians had been a secondary tactic in support of the conventional ground war, in the Second, it became one of the primary war-fighting strategies. The opponent's cities and populations were deliberately targeted in an attempt to break the will of the enemy to resist by laying waste to his economy and slaughtering his population. By destroying the enemy's productive capacity, such attacks would undermine the ability of his armed forces to operate effectively. This logic reached its peak with the nuclear attacks on Japan in August 1945, when civilian targets were deliberately annihilated in order to compel the Japanese government to bring to an end further resistance in the Pacific theatre.

BOX 2.5 Blitzkreig

Blitzkreig, or 'lightning war', was the term used to describe the successful German tactics for armoured offensives in the opening phase of the Second World War. It was an attempt to overcome the defensive dominance and static warfare characteristic of most of the First World War. Like Napoleonic warfare, it was a triumph based on superior doctrine rather than technological advantage. The theory was propounded by Basil Liddell Hart, Charles de Gaulle, and Heinz Guderian during the interwar years.

Available tanks were concentrated in a limited number of Panzer (armour) divisions, along with plenty of antitank and anti-aircraft guns, armoured cars for reconnaissance, and infantry support. The emphasis was on rapid advances designed to dislocate the enemy by breaking into the rear and throwing them off-balance. The objective was deep penetration on a narrow front. Certain supporting technologies were important, for example radios in tanks for communication and co-ordination. Because the speed of the advance made it difficult for heavy artillery support to keep up, tactical airpower was used as a form of artillery to help the breakthrough. The Ju-87 Stuka dive-bomber attacked defenders' positions and also attacked rear-area command and supply positions, reinforcements, and even refugee columns in order to create confusion and panic ahead of the advancing Panzer divisions.

The combined arms blitzkrieg doctrine was also employed to great effect by Israel during its 1956 and 1967 wars against Egypt, and was a central feature of the concept of operational manoeuvre groups designed to exploit breakthroughs in late cold war Soviet armoured offensive doctrine. A crucial requirement for successful blitzkrieg is that the attacker must achieve air superiority over the battlefield.

For much of the war, strategic bombing failed to produce the dramatic results that pre-war advocates such as Douhet had predicted. Losses among the attacking aircrew were extremely heavy, forcing both the Germans and British to carry out their attacks at night, making precision bombing virtually impossible. In the closing months of the European war, as German air defences became increasingly suppressed, the allies shifted their attacks to key production 'bottlenecks', such as oil refineries. Such attacks proved far more effective in undermining Germany's war-fighting capacity than the earlier assaults on its overall economic capability had been.

The Second World War was global in scope, and naval power was more crucial to the outcome than it had been in the First World War. As island nations, both Britain and Japan depended on resources imported by sea. In the Battle of the Atlantic, Germany sought to strangle the Anglo-American war effort by destroying the merchant shipping bringing supplies, weapons, and soldiers across the Atlantic to Britain and into the Mediterranean. Although ultimately unsuccessful, the German U-boat campaign came close to success. In the Pacific, a similar American submarine campaign had brought the Japanese war effort to its knees by the summer of 1945.

Germany succeeded in the early part of the war because land-based air power compensated for its naval weakness. British naval losses to German air attack in the Crete campaign were equivalent to a major fleet action. However, once Allied fleets had acquired effective anti-aircraft weapons and carrier-based fighter protection, navies were able to resume their offensive role once more. The early phases of the Second World War demonstrated that both on land and at sea, obtaining air superiority, or at the very least, denying it to the enemy, had become an essential prerequisite to successful military operations. Air power on its own could not guarantee victory, but its absence guaranteed defeat. By the end of the war, all major states had come to recognize that 'combined arms' or 'joint' warfare was the key to success in modern industrial war.

Amphibious operations were a minor feature of the First World War, and the largest such operation, the landings at Gallipolli in 1915, were a tactical and strategic failure. In the Second World War in contrast, amphibious operations were crucial to the final outcome in both the European and Pacific theatres. The invasions of North Africa, Sicily, Italy, and France saw major amphibious landings allow the Allies to seize the strategic initiative, while the American 'island-hopping' campaign in the Pacific outflanked and overcame Japanese power in the region while ultimately moving American forces close enough to Japan to launch devastating conventional and nuclear attacks on the Japanese home islands.

In both the antisubmarine and amphibious offensive campaigns, the role of the aircraft carrier was of decisive importance. The aircraft carrier had replaced the battleship as the primary naval weapons platform, and the Second World War saw five major aircraft carrier battles in the Pacific war, as well as 22 other major naval engagements. The Atlantic and Mediterranean campaigns also saw major naval surface actions. In the European war, sea power was a crucial, but not a sufficient cause of the Allied victory, the Soviet land-offensives being decisive. In the Pacific, however, sea power was decisive in the ultimate Allied victory.

The Second World War also saw large-scale parachute offensives. These operations were crucial in the German capture of Crete in 1941 and the Allied invasion of Normandy in 1944, as well as the Rhine crossings in 1945. The failure of the Arnhem operation in 1944, however, was a demonstration of the limitations of such forces. Unless reached by substantial heavy reinforcements quickly, parachute forces were too lightly armed to hold out against armoured forces, and large-scale parachute operations did not become a feature of the post-1945 environment, though they were employed in the 1956 Anglo-French Suez war against Egypt.

Key points

- The First World War was a conflict between mass armies, which technology made difficult to defeat decisively.

- New technologies such as chemical weapons and tanks were used in an attempt to regain manoeuvre and decision.

- Air power emerged, but was not yet a decisive weapon.

- Societies were fully mobilized for the war effort.

- All of a state's economic and human resources increasingly came to be seen as legitimate targets.

- By the Second World War, airpower had become crucial in support of forces on the battlefield and as the means to launch strategic attacks against the opposing homeland. Aircraft carriers emerged as the decisive naval weapon.

- Technology, amphibious landings, and parachute operations sought to avoid the deadlock characteristic of the First World War.

Nuclear Weapons and Revolutionary Warfare

Total war reached a peak with the Second World War. The ultimate example was the destruction of the Japanese cities of Hiroshima and Nagasaki in 1945. Yet paradoxically, the unleashing of the nuclear weapon ushered in an era of limited warfare. During the 1950s as the United States and Soviet Union acquired larger and larger stockpiles of increasingly accurate and destructive nuclear weapons, it became clear that a full-scale war between the two countries would be mutually suicidal.

As a result, both states saw it as essential to avoid a full-scale war at all costs. They there-fore sought to exercise restraint in their relations with each other and to avoid taking military actions that risked escalating to a full-scale conflict which might go nuclear. For the same reason, they sought to restrain the policies and war strategies of their allies and other states over which they had influence, in order to avoid being dragged into conflicts originating elsewhere.

The so-called 'cold war' was therefore characterized not by the total war seen between 1914 and 1945, but by limited war; wars limited in terms of objectives sought, means employed, and geographical area affected. A full-scale nuclear war would involve mutual assured destruction; a simultaneous genocide that bore no relation to the idea of war as a political act in the terms in which Clausewitz and his successors understood it.

However, while it was understood that strategic nuclear weapons could not perform a meaningful war-fighting role, their possession in large numbers was seen as necessary in order to deny a unilateral military and political advantage to the other side. They became central to the strategic doctrine of deterrence, while remaining outside the scope of practical war-fighting.

Tactical, and to some extent theatre nuclear weapons, however, were seen as retaining a function in war. With more limited nuclear yields, and assuming they were not employed in overwhelming numbers, it was believed that they could play a role in great power war, as long as a final escalation to a full-scale strategic nuclear exchange could be avoided. The dangers involved in such an ambiguous strategy were obvious, and the evidence from war games manoeuvres conducted throughout the cold war suggested that once the nuclear threshold was crossed, escalation to full-scale strategic conflict would be virtually impossible to prevent.

Conflicts during the cold war were therefore characterized by restraint shown by the nuclear superpowers in terms of the kinds of wars they fought. In Korea and Vietnam for example, the United States limited its war effort in terms of the weaponry used, the geo-graphical scope of the war, and the objectives pursued; all restraints characteristic of limited, rather than total war. Similar restraint was encouraged in others. During the 1973 Arab-Israeli War, the United States and Soviet Union pressured their allies to end the fighting, because they were concerned that it might escalate and draw them into the conflict on opposing sides.

The reluctance of the most powerful states to employ the techniques of total war created an opportunity for their opponents to employ asymmetric tactics and strategies against them successfully. In the Korean War, comparative American restraint meant that the vastly less well-equipped Chinese forces were able to achieve a military stalemate and preserve the independence of communist North Korea. In the Vietnam War, despite an even more dramatic disparity in military resources between North Vietnam and the United States, the North was able to deny the USA victory and once it had forced the US to withdraw from South Vietnam, it achieved its objective of the unification of Vietnam under a communist government. The Soviet Union encountered similar problems in its war in Afghanistan. The success of North Vietnam showed that war itself had not become an unusable instrument of policy, as some critics contended.

The cold war period was therefore characterized by smaller-scale conventional wars and by campaigns of insurgency and counterinsurgency. Conventional wars tended to be limited in their outcomes and duration, and profoundly influenced by the geopolitical context of the cold war environment. The wars between Israel and its neighbours, as well as those between India and Pakistan, and Ethiopia and Somalia were typical of this pattern. These wars were unusual in one respect however, in that they were inter-state conflicts. More typical was the prevalence of civil, rather than international war. Most wars in the second half of the twentieth century were civil wars and insurgencies, most notably in Africa and South East Asia. Many of these conflicts were anti-colonial conflicts, or conflicts generated by the arbitrary boundaries that colonialism left in its wake. While a 'Third World War' was successfully avoided, a 'Third World' war was not.

Key points

- Nuclear weapons ended the era of total war.
- Major powers subsequently engaged only in limited war.
- Superpower pressure deterred the escalation of other conventional conflicts.
- Insurgency and counterinsurgency were more typical forms of war.
- The Third World became the arena for such conflicts.

Conclusion: Postmodern War

The end of the cold war also ended the classic period of nuclear deterrence and was followed by a number of wars in Eastern Europe and Africa characterized by the employment of relatively low-tech weaponry, but with very heavy death tolls. Some of these conflicts were also characterized by great savagery, leading some commentators to suggest that these conflicts were a novel form of war and that such wars would be characteristic of the post-cold war, postmodern world: that the era of industrialized great power war had passed.

The reality is more complex than this. Some of the features identified with postmodern conflict have been present for half a century or longer and their novelty should not be exaggerated. At the same time, there are many features of the previous era that are either still recognizably present, or are evolving along trajectories that place them at odds with other aspects of postmodernity.

It can be argued that global society is in the midst of a transition from modernity to postmodernity. The architecture of world order is changing as part of a long-term process and with it will change the associated institution of war, as happened in the earlier transition to modernity in the seventeenth century. The distinctively 'modern' state is evolving in the face of globalization, and shedding many of its responsibilities, including military responsibilities, to private actors.

This transition to postmodernity can be expected to influence war as a politico-cultural institution. Certain superficial aspects of conflict in the current century seem to suggest this. 'Modern' war was conducted by the state. The postmodern era has seen a dispersal of control over organized violence to many forms of non-state actors. Modern wars were fought by formally organized, hierarchically structured, specialized armed forces of the state. Postmodern wars are fought by a disparate array of fighting forces, many of which are informal or private (i.e. non-state). These include guerrilla armies, criminal gangs, foreign mercenaries, kin/clan-based irregular forces, paramilitary groups raised by local warlords, international peacekeepers, national armies, and de-territorialized terrorist networks. Such groups do not seek decisive battle in the Clausewitzian sense; they avoid it at all costs in favour of protracted asymmetric conflict. The war objectives of such groups are usually as political as are those of states themselves, so that war has not lost its 'Clausewitzian' character. Indeed, where no such political rationale exists, it is arguable whether we can even speak of such conflicts as 'war' (see Box 2.6).

However, such conflicts were also characteristic of the cold war era, most of whose conflicts were internal, subconventional, and occurred in the Third World. The civil wars in Nigeria, Angola, and Afghanistan were typical in this respect. In many ways they also resemble earlier colonial warfare such as the conflicts between France and indigenous North African forces in the late-nineteenth and early-twentieth centuries.

At the same time as the shift downwards towards more low-tech wars, the so-called 'revolution in military affairs' has seen the United States at the leading edge of a technology-based enhancement of conventional military capability.

The purposes and objectives of armed conflict are also changing. Modern wars originated in the pursuit of perceived national interests. Wars tended to be driven by geopolitical assumptions, such as those fought in defence of the balance of power. Postmodern wars are often focused on 'identity politics'. Power is pursued on the basis of a particular identity. These wars may break out in an effort to pursue ethnic cleansing, or religiously inspired holy war. Such conflicts are often particularly ferocious, and may not have clearly defined beginnings and endings, but they are, however, no less political. They are conducted with strategic objectives, such as the acquisition of control over valuable resources or of the determination of state policy.

The political economy of war-making is also being transformed. During the modern era, military forces were maintained by state-based production and financing systems, preferably organized on a national basis. Postmodern non-state institutions of violence tend to draw material sustenance not from such formal and centralized national economies and defence industries, but from private

BOX 2.6 Revolution in Military Affairs

The nature and frequency of such revolutions is a matter of dispute. Andrew Marshall defines them in relation to technology, doctrine, and force structure, declaring that a Revolution in Military Affairs (RMA), is a major change in the nature of warfare brought about by the innovative application of new technologies which, combined with dramatic changes in military doctrine and operational and organizational concepts, fundamentally alters the character and conduct of military operations

Robertson (2000: 64)

Kapil Dek sees the second and third elements as the key, arguing that the 'historical record appears to suggest that technological change represents a relatively small part of the equation, the crucial element in most RMAs being conceptual in nature'.

Broader in concept than an RMA is the idea of a *military revolution*. Whereas many RMAs can be identified in history, true military revolutions are rare. Military revolutions are dynamically interactive social processes which, according to Williamson Murray, 'recast the nature of society and the state as well as of military organizations'.

Murray (1997: 71)

production and finance networks organized either locally or on a global scale. Such sources may include plunder and theft, hostage-taking for ransom, extortion, drug trafficking, arms trafficking, money laundering, remittances and material support from relevant diaspora communities, foreign assistance, and the diversion of humanitarian aid. For many of the combatants, such wars are an end in themselves, they are 'military entrepreneurs' exploiting a new form of 'war economy'.

Postmodernity is perhaps continuing to loosen the grip that 'modern' war has had for the past two centuries. The emergence of nuclear weapons had already initiated this process by neutralizing the most powerful weapons possessed by the leading military powers, and encouraging a particular security policy restraint. Postmodernity may be reinforcing this process. Just as feudalism and modernity each produced their own distinctive forms of war, so the transition to postmodernity is producing its own unique politico-cultural form of organized violence, even while the *nature* of war remains constant.

War remains a purposeful instrument of political violence in many parts of the world, although decisive victory has become more elusive. In all ages, older forms of war and violence do not entirely disappear even as new forms gradually supplant them.

 ## Questions

1. How valid is it to argue that the French Revolution unleashed an era of unlimited warfare?

2. Evaluate the thesis that Clausewitz still has something worthwhile to teach students of war in the contemporary world.

3. In what ways was warfare in the nineteenth century significantly affected by advances in technology?

4. Is war a catalyst for significant social and political change, or a reflection of it?

5. What do you understand by the phrase 'total war'? Does modern history provide examples of such a conflict?

6. How would you define 'limited war'? Is limited nuclear war a contradiction in terms?

7. What do you understand by the concept of *either* 'sea power' or 'air power'?

8. Is industrialized war between major powers becoming obsolete in the post-cold war world?

9. How useful is the distinction between 'revolutions in military affairs' and 'military revolutions' in understanding the evolution of modern war?

10. In what ways do the so-called 'new wars' of the post-cold war period differ from earlier forms of war?

 ## Further Reading

G. Best, *War and Society in Revolutionary Europe, 1770–1870* **(London: Fontana, 1982).**
Effectively captures the inter-relationships between politics, technology, and warfare during this turbulent and formative period in European history.

Jeremy Black, *War* **(London: Continuum, 2001).**
An interesting, and like most of Black's writings, provocative, exploration of the nature of war in the contemporary age and its likely evolution in the next few decades. Black is sceptical of the wilder claims made by the proponents of the Revolution in Military Affairs thesis.

A. Gat, *Clausewitz and the Enlightenment: The Origins of Modern Military Thought* **(Oxford: Oxford University Press, 1993).**
A good book for exploring the intellectual origins of the revolutionary military thinking of the nineteenth century. It helps bring out not only the legacy that the eighteenth century provided for

Napoleon, but also the distinctive contribution made by his synthesis of effective practice, and the equally impressive intellectual synthesis of Clausewitz.

A. Jones, *The Art of War in the Western World* (Chicago, IL: University of Illinois Press, 1987).
An impressive and very readable single volume treatment of the development and evolution of the military art over the centuries. The decisive changes in weaponry, strategy, tactics, and social environments are brought out with skill and style, and the influence of leadership is illuminated in each age. One can disagree with some of the interpretations, but this is a lively *tour d'horizon* of the history of the practice of war.

C. Messenger, *The Art of Blitzkreig* (London: Ian Allen Ltd, 1976).
A lively analysis of the effectiveness of superior doctrine over numbers and technology, and a useful case study of the impact of military evolution (or possibly revolution).

Herfield Munkler, *The New Wars* (Cambridge: Polity Press, 2005).
An insightful and thought-provoking analysis of postmodern warfare, with a historical depth lacking in most studies of this subject.

D. Porch, *Wars of Empire* (London: Cassell, 2001).
A very accessible and readable study of the 'little wars' of the nineteenth century, written by an acknowledged expert on colonial warfare and the French military experience in particular. Brings out both the fact that many European armies spent much of their energies engaged in this form of warfare and not just industrial war with other great powers, and the fact that the 'new wars' of post-1990 are in many ways not so new after all.

M. Waltzer, *Just and Unjust Wars* (London: Allen Lane, 1978).
Waltzer's book is a study in ethics, but is extremely useful in understanding traditional and contemporary approaches to the question of morality and warfare, and provides a useful basis for analysing the scale of the evolution towards total war between 1800 and 1950.

G. Wright, *The Ordeal of Total War 1939–1945* (New York: Harper & Row, 1968).
A book that brings out the scope and totality of the Second World War and the impact that it had on civilians as well as the military.

 ## Web Links

An excellent resource for the American Civil War **http://sunsite.utk.edu/civil-war/warweb.html**

A comprehensive site for Clausewitz studies **http://www.clausewitz.com/index.htm**

A useful site for the Napoleonic wars **http://www.fortunecity.com/victorian/riley/787/Napoleon/**

A good site for the First World War **http://members.fortunecity.com/mikaelxii/**

The US Army Centre for Military History. Very good on American military history **http://www.history.army.mil/**

For naval warfare, a site with excellent links to a wide range of naval warfare sources is **http://navalwarfare.blogspot.co.uk/**

Strategic Theory

THOMAS G. MAHNKEN

 Chapter Contents

Introduction   61
The Logic of Strategy   61
Clausewitz's *On War*   65
Sun Tzu, Mao, and the Jihadists   70
The Enduring Relevance of Strategy   72
Conclusion   74

 Reader's Guide

This chapter discusses strategic theory, which provides a conceptual understanding of the nature of war. It argues that the logic of war is universal. Although strategy is an art, it is one that can be studied systematically. The chapter begins by exploring the logic of strategy. It then discusses some of the most valuable concepts in strategic theory as contained in Carl von Clausewitz's *On War*. It briefly compares and contrasts these with the concepts contained in Sun Tzu's *Art of War* and the military writings of Mao Tse-Tung before considering and rebutting the main arguments about the obsolescence of classical strategic theory.

Introduction

The logic of war and strategy is universal; it is valid at all times and in all places. This is primarily because war is a human activity, and human nature has remained unchanged in the face of material progress. The same passions that motivated those who lived millennia ago continue to drive us today. Although such strategic theorists as the nineteenth-century Prussian officer and philosopher Carl von Clausewitz and the ancient Chinese author Sun Tzu wrote from very different historical and cultural experiences and thus viewed strategy from unique perspectives, the phenomenon they described—war—is the same. It is the character and conduct of war—how it is waged, by whom, and for what ends—that has changed over time.

Strategic theory provides the conceptual foundation of an understanding of war. It offers a toolkit that can be used to analyse problems of war and peace. An understanding of theory equips the student with a set of concepts and questions to guide further study. As Clausewitz wrote, the purpose of theory is not to uncover fixed laws or principles, but rather to educate the mind:

> [Theory] is an analytical investigation leading to a close *acquaintance* with the subject; applied to experience—in our case, to military history—it leads to a thorough *familiarity* with it . . . Theory will have fulfilled its main task when it is used to analyse the constituent elements of war, to distinguish precisely what at first sight seems fused, to explain in full the properties of the means employed and to show their probable effects, to define clearly the nature of the ends in view, and to illuminate all phases of warfare in a thorough critical inquiry. Theory then becomes a guide to anyone who wants to learn about war from books; it will light his way, ease his progress, train his judgment, and help him to avoid pitfalls . . . It is meant to educate the mind of the future commander, or, more accurately, to guide him in his self-education, not to accompany him to the battlefield; just as a wise teacher guides and stimulates a young man's intellectual development, but is careful not to lead him by the hand for the rest of his life.
> **Clausewitz (1989: 141)**

In other words, Clausewitz suggests, we study strategic theory in order to learn how to think strategically.

Because the stakes in war are so high, strategy is a supremely practical endeavour. The most elegant theory is useless if it is inapplicable to real problems. Strategic theory succeeds or fails in direct proportion to its ability to help decision-makers understand problems of war and peace and formulate sound strategy. As the twentieth-century American strategist Bernard Brodie put it, 'Strategy is a field where truth is sought in the pursuit of viable solutions' (1973: 452–3).

The Logic of Strategy

Strategy is ultimately about how to win wars. Any discussion of strategy must therefore begin with an understanding of war. As Clausewitz famously defined it, 'War is thus an act of force to compel our enemy to do our will' (1989: 75). Two aspects of this definition are notable.

BOX 3.1 War as a Political Instrument

War is a matter of vital importance to the State.

Sun Tzu (1963: 63)

It is clear, consequently, that war is not a mere act of policy, but a true political instrument, a continuation of political activity by other means.

Clausewitz (1989: 87)

War is only a branch of political activity; it is in no sense autonomous.

Clausewitz (1989: 606)

No major proposal required for war can be worked out of ignorance of political factors; and when people talk, as they often do, about harmful political influence on the management of war, they are not really saying what they mean. Their quarrel should be with policy itself not with its influence.

Clausewitz (1989: 608)

The object of war is a better state of peace.

Liddell Hart (1967: 351)

[Irregular warfare is] a violent struggle among state and non-state actors for legitimacy and influence over the relevant population(s).

Department of Defense Directive 3000.07 (2008: 1)

First, the fact that war involves force separates it from other types of political, economic, and military competition. Second, the fact that war is not senseless slaughter, but rather an instrument that is used to achieve a political purpose, differentiates it from other types of violence. Distinguishing war from non-war is important because it determines whether strategic theory can provide insight into the problem at hand.

It is the political context of war, and not the identity of those who wage it, that is its key characteristic (see Box 3.1). Empires, city-states, subnational groups, and transnational movements have all used force to preserve or aggrandize themselves. The fact that United Nations forces in Somalia in 1993 fought Mohammed Farah Aideed's Habr Gidr clan rather than a recognized state matters less than the fact that both sides were strategic actors possessing political objectives and that each sought to use force to compel the other. Similarly, the struggle against violent Islamic extremist groups such as al-Qaeda and its associated movements fits the classical definition of a war, in that both sides have political aims and are using military means to achieve them. It is, to be sure, a strange war, one waged by irregular forces with unconventional means. However, the fact that it is a violent clash of wills means that it is amenable to strategic analysis. Conversely, the use of force to curb criminal behaviour such as piracy is not war, because pirates seek material gains rather than political aims.

Strategy is about making war useable for political purposes. If tactics is about employing troops in battle and operational art is concerned with conducting campaigns, then strategy deals with using military means to fulfil the ends of policy. It is the essential link between political objectives and military force, between ends and means. As Germany demonstrated in two world wars, mastery of tactics and operations counts for little without a coherent or feasible strategy.

In recent decades, the definition of strategy has expanded to include peacetime activity. Edward Mead Earle, writing during the Second World War, argued that strategy was 'an inherent element of statecraft at all times' (Earle 1943: viii). With the advent of nuclear weapons, strategic theory expanded to include peacetime military competition, such as the four-decade cold war between the United States and the Soviet Union. The expanding definition of strategy has at times devalued the concept and led to confusion about the relationship between policy and strategy (Strachan 2005: 34).

Strategy is, or rather should be, a rational process. As Clausewitz wrote, 'No one starts a war—or rather, no one in his senses ought to do so—without first being clear in his mind what he intends to achieve by that war and how he intends to conduct it' (1989: 579). In other words, successful strategy is based upon clearly identifying political goals, assessing one's comparative advantage relative to the enemy, calculating costs and benefits carefully, and examining the risks and rewards of alternative strategies.

Clausewitz's formulation acknowledges, however, that states sometimes go to war without clear or achievable aims or a strategy to achieve them. Statesmen have embarked on war for ill-defined aims. At other times, statesmen and soldiers have failed to develop a strategy that will readily translate into achieving political aims. In the absence of a coherent policy, strategy becomes meaningless because it lacks direction.

Sound strategy is formulated by individuals, but all strategies are implemented by bureaucracies. As a result, even a rational strategy can fail in execution. It is often difficult to determine, even in retrospect, whether failure was the result of the poor execution of a sound strategy or a strategy that was fundamentally unsound. Historians will, for example, long debate whether the decision to disband the Iraqi army and ban the Ba'ath Party after the 2003 invasion of Iraq were mistakes in implementing a good strategy, or whether the insurgency that followed the overthrow of Saddam Hussein was inevitable.

Strategy is more an art than a science. The range of strategic choice is inevitably constrained by material and political reality. The reciprocal action of the belligerents introduces further complications. In addition, war is rife with passion, inaccurate information, misperception, and chance:

> Efforts were . . . made to equip the conduct of war with principles, rules, or even systems. This did present a positive goal, but people failed to take adequate account of the endless complexities involved. As we have seen, the conduct of war branches out in almost all directions and has no definite limits; while any system, any model, has the finite nature of a synthesis. An irreconcilable conflict exists between this type of theory and actual practice.
> **Clausewitz (1989: 134)**

Or, as Sun Tzu put it more succinctly, 'In the art of war there are no fixed rules' (Sun Tzu 1963: 93). As a result, a military problem may have many—or no—potentially correct solutions rather than one optimal one.

The fact that strategy is more an art than a science doesn't mean that it cannot be studied systematically. Rather, the theory of strategy consists of concepts and considerations instead of fixed laws.

Military success by itself is insufficient to achieve victory. History contains numerous examples of armies that won all the battles and yet lost the war due to a flawed strategy. In the Vietnam War, for example, the US military defeated the Vietcong and North Vietnamese Army in every major engagement they fought. The United States nonetheless lost the war because civilian and military leaders never understood the complex nature of the war they were waging. Conversely, the United States achieved its independence from Britain despite the fact that the Continental Army won only a handful of battles.

It is axiomatic that policy drives strategy. Policymakers and senior officers nonetheless frequently misunderstand the relationship. During the 1999 Kosovo War, for example, Secretary of State Madeline Albright was wrong in arguing that 'Up until the start of the conflict, the military served to back up our diplomacy. Now, our diplomacy serves to back up our military' (Isaacson 1999: 27) Similarly, Lieutenant General Charles A. Horner, at the time the commander of US Air Force units in Saudi Arabia, was wrong when he said that war 'should not be dragged out in an effort to achieve some political objective' (Gordon 1990: 1).

It is worth emphasizing that the primacy of politics applies not only to states, but also to other strategic actors. As Ayman al-Zawahiri, al-Qaeda's leader and chief theoretician, wrote in his book *Knights Under the Prophet's Banner*:

> If the successful operations against Islam's enemies and the severe damage inflicted on them do not serve the ultimate goal of establishing the Muslim nation in the heart of the Islamic world, they will be nothing more than disturbing acts, regardless of their magnitude, that could be absorbed and endured, even if after some time and with some losses.

Clausewitz would doubtless approve of Zawahiri's understanding of strategy, if not his goals.

The political context of warfare can in some cases extend to tactical actions, particularly when they hold the potential to change the character of a war. During the North Atlantic Treaty Organization (NATO) war over Kosovo in 1999, for example, a US B-2 bomber accidentally dropped three precision-guided munitions on the Chinese embassy in Belgrade, killing four. The incident was a tactical error with strategic consequences, triggering a diplomatic crisis between Washington and Beijing, disrupting moves to negotiate an end to the war, and prompting a halt to the bombing of targets in Belgrade for the next two weeks. More recently, the abuse of Iraqi prisoners by a group of poorly trained and led guards at the Abu Ghraib prison in Iraq represented a strategic setback to American efforts to build legitimacy among the Iraqi population.

Although policy drives strategy, the capabilities and limitations of the military instrument also shape policy. As Clausewitz wrote, the political aim 'must adapt itself to its chosen means, a process which can radically change it' (1989: 87). To choose a ridiculous example to illustrate the point, it was one thing for Russia to invade Georgia in 2008; it would have been quite another for Georgia's tiny army to try to occupy Russia.

Just as it would be wrong to view war as nothing more than slaughter, it would be misleading to believe that force can be used in highly calibrated increments to achieve finely tuned effects. War has its own dynamics that makes it an unwieldy instrument, more a bludgeon than a rapier. The pages of history are full of wars in which soldiers and statesmen sought quick, decisive victories over their foes; militaries have actually achieved such results only rarely, however.

Interaction with the adversary can make it difficult to achieve even the simplest objective. As Clausewitz reminds us, 'War is not the act of a living force upon a lifeless mass but always the collision of two living forces' (1989: 4). In other words, just as we seek to use force to compel our adversary to do our will, so too will he attempt to use force to coerce us. Effectiveness in war thus depends not only on what we do, but also on what an opponent does. This interaction limits significantly the ability to control the use of military force.

Key points

- War is an act of force to compel your enemy to do your will.
- Strategy is about how to win wars. It is the essential link between political objectives and military force, between ends and means.
- Strategy is—or should be—a rational process.
- Strategy is more an art than a science.
- Interaction with the adversary makes it difficult to achieve even the simplest objective.

Clausewitz's *On War*

Carl von Clausewitz's unfinished masterpiece, *On War*, forms the cornerstone of any understanding of strategic theory. Unfortunately, the book is all too often misunderstood. *On War* was left incomplete by the author's death from cholera in 1831. Book 1, Chapter 1 was the only part of the volume that Clausewitz considered complete. Like the Bible, *On War* is more frequently quoted than read, and more frequently perused than comprehended. It is not a book that can be understood fully after a single reading, but rather demands careful study and reflection, raising as many questions as it answers and forcing serious readers to grapple with the author's concepts.

Clausewitz's methodology, which distinguishes between 'war in theory' or 'absolute war' and war in reality, has led many mistakenly to identify him as an apostle of total war. In fact, he uses the approach of defining war in its ideal or pure form as a way of identifying the many considerations that shape war in reality. It is akin to a physicist examining mechanics in a frictionless environment or an economist describing an ideal market. In each case the observer is portraying the theoretical, not the real. In fact, Clausewitz argues that war can be fought for limited or unlimited aims with partial or total means.

As Hugh Smith has written, Clausewitz views war in four different contexts (Smith 2005: Chapters 7–10). First and foremost, in his view war is ultimately about killing and dying. He is dismissive of the notion that war can be waged without bloodshed:

> Kind-hearted people might of course think that there was some ingenious way to disarm or defeat an enemy without too much bloodshed, and might imagine that this is the true goal of the art of war. Pleasant as it sounds, it is a fallacy that must be exposed: war is such a dangerous business that the mistakes which come from kindness are the very worst.
> **Clausewitz (1989: 75)**

Second, war is a contest between armies, generals, and states. Clausewitz invokes the metaphor of wrestling to describe war as a physical and mental competition, with each side trying to pin the other while simultaneously trying to avoid being pinned.

Third, war is an instrument of policy. It is not to be pursued for its own sake, but rather to serve the ends of the state.

Finally, he argues that war is a social activity. As someone who had lived through the French Revolution and fought in the Napoleonic Wars, he was acutely aware of the fact that social conditions mould the character and conduct of war.

A number of the concepts that Clausewitz introduces in *On War* are central to the study of strategy. These include the trinity, the need to understand the nature of a war, the difference between limited and unlimited wars, the rational calculus of war, and friction.

The Trinity

Clausewitz's description of war is one of his most enduring legacies. He views war as a 'paradoxical trinity—composed of violence, hatred, and enmity . . . the play of chance and probability . . . and of its element of subordination'. He wrote that each of these three tendencies generally (but not always) corresponds to one of three groups in society: the people, the military, and the government (1989: 89). Passion is most often associated with the people, whose animosities move states to fight. Probability and chance are the realm of the military. Indeed, soldiers most constantly deal with uncertainty and friction. Reason is generally a characteristic of the government, which determines the aims of war and the means for waging it.

Clausewitz argued that the relative intensity of and relationships among these tendencies change according to the circumstances of the war:

> Three different codes of law, deep-rooted in their subject and yet variable in their relationship to one another. A theory that ignores any one of them or seeks to fix an arbitrary relationship between them would conflict with reality to such an extent that for this reason alone it would be totally useless. Our task therefore is to develop a theory that maintains a balance between these three tendencies, like an object suspended between three magnets.
> **Clausewitz (1989: 89)**

The interaction of these three tendencies thus determines the character of a war.

Understanding the Nature of a War

Clausewitz argues that understanding the nature of a war is a necessary precondition to developing an effective strategy:

> The first, the supreme, the most far-reaching act of judgment that the statesman and commander have to make is to establish by that test the kind of war on which they are embarking, neither mistaking it for, nor trying to turn it into, something that is alien to its nature. This is the first of all strategic questions and the most comprehensive.
> **Clausewitz (1989: 88-89)**

In Clausewitz's view, the nature of a war is the result of the interaction of the objectives of the two sides; the people, government, and militaries of the belligerents; and the attitudes of allies and neutrals. He goes on to write:

> To assess these things in all their ramifications and diversity is plainly a colossal task. Rapid and correct appraisal of them clearly calls for the intuition of a genius; to master all this complex mass by sheer methodological examination is obviously impossible.
> **Clausewitz (1989: 585-6)**

This is yet another example of the fact that strategy is more an art than a science.

Because the nature of a war is the product of the interaction of the belligerents, every war is unique. The nature of a war is dynamic because a change in any of its elements can change the nature of the conflict. A change in the aims of one or more of the participants, for example, can change the nature of a war. So too can the entry of new participants. China's entry into the Korean War, for example, markedly changed its complexion.

Understanding the nature of a war is both necessary and difficult. Both participants at the time and historians subsequently debated whether the Vietnam War was an international communist war against South Vietnam, a civil war between North and South Vietnam, an insurgency in the south supported by the north, or all of these. Similarly, American statesmen and soldiers largely failed to comprehend that the swift defeat of Saddam Hussein's regime would lead to a sustained insurgency. Even as the insurgency began to grow, it proved difficult for leaders at all levels to recognize it. As Linda Robinson notes:

> One of the enduring mysteries of the war, and a testament to its shape-shifting complexity, was that so many intelligent officers of all ranks made superhuman efforts to grapple with the task of analysis and prescription to relatively little effect. The long hours and press of battle and the proximity to the daily minutiae made it hard for many to see the forest for the trees.
> **Robinson (2008: 13)**

Inherent in understanding the nature of a war is gaining an appreciation of one's comparative advantage. This, in turn, forms the basis of sound strategy. The key to doing so, in Clausewitz's view, is understanding the enemy's centre of gravity:

> One must keep the dominant characteristics of both belligerents in mind. Out of these characteristics a certain center of gravity develops, the hub of all power and movement, on which everything depends. That is the point against which all our energies should be directed.
> **Clausewitz (1989: 595–6)**

In Clausewitz's view, a state achieves victory by seeking out and attacking the enemy's centre of gravity. He wrote that the centre of gravity was most likely the enemy's army, capital city, principal ally, leader, and public opinion, in descending order. In practice, however, it can often be difficult to determine the adversary's centre of gravity. In the 1991 Gulf War, for example, US decision-makers viewed Iraq's military—particularly its Republican Guard—as the centre of gravity, when in fact the 'hub of all power' was Saddam Hussein's government.

Limited versus Unlimited Wars

Wars can be fought for a wide range of objectives, from a quest for land and resources to the utter destruction of the enemy. In a note for the revision of *On War*, however, Clausewitz drew a distinction between wars fought for limited aims and those fought for unlimited aims:

> War can be of two kinds, in the sense that either the objective is to *overthrow the enemy*—to render him politically helpless or militarily impotent, thus forcing him to sign whatever peace we please; or *merely to occupy some of his frontier districts* so that we can annex them

or use them for bargaining at the peace negotiations. Transitions from one type to the other will of course recur in my treatment; but the fact that the aims of the two types are quite different must be clear at all times, and their points of irreconcilability brought out.
Clausewitz (1989: 69)

This distinction affects the way that wars are fought and how they end. In wars for limited aims, soldiers and statesmen must translate battlefield success into political leverage over the adversary. As a result, they must continually reassess how far to go militarily and what to demand politically. Such wars end through formal or tacit negotiation and agreement between the warring parties. Wars for unlimited aims are fought to overthrow the adversary's regime or achieve unconditional surrender. They end in a peace settlement that is imposed rather than negotiated.

The 1991 Gulf War and 2003 Iraq War illustrate the difference between the two types of wars. In 1991, the US-led coalition fought to liberate Kuwait from Iraqi occupation, restore Kuwait's government to power, ensure the safety of US citizens in the region, and ensure the security and stability of the gulf region. In 2003, the United States and its allies fought to overthrow Saddam Hussein's Ba'athist regime.

The end of limited wars can lead to dissatisfaction on the part of one or more of the parties as well as a prolonged military commitment. A strong case can be made, for example, that the US-led coalition ended the 1991 Gulf War prematurely, before Saddam Hussein had been forced to admit defeat. As a result, the United States acquired a prolonged commitment to the gulf region, one that led to the stationing of US forces in Saudi Arabia and fostered resentment among Muslims in the region and across the globe. The aftermath of a war for unlimited aims leads to a protracted commitment of another sort, as the victors must install or support a new government. In the wake of the overthrow of Saddam Hussein's regime in 2003, the United States and its partners faced the daunting task of nation-building under fire: creating new political, economic, and military institutions in order to build political legitimacy and provide security for the Iraqi people while combating a widespread insurgency.

The Rational Calculus of War

Another concept that flows from Clausewitz's work is the notion that there should be a correlation between the value a state attaches to its ends and the means it uses to achieve them:

> Since war is not an act of senseless passion but is controlled by its political object, the value of this object must determine the sacrifices to be made for it in *magnitude* and also in *duration*. Once the expenditure of effort exceeds the value of the political object, the object must be renounced and peace must follow.
> Clausewitz (1989: 92)

States should thus be willing to fight longer and harder to secure or defend vital interests than peripheral ones. It helps explain, for example, why the US government chose to withdraw from Somalia after the death of 18 soldiers but remained in Korea despite suffering 33,000 deaths.

The notion of a rational calculus of war would appear to be one area in which strategy most resembles a science. However, although the notion makes sense in theory, it is far more problematic to apply in practice. It is often difficult, for example, for decision-makers to determine the costs and benefits of military action beforehand. Furthermore, estimates of the political, social, and economic costs change as war unfolds. As Clausewitz notes, 'The original political objects can change greatly later during the course of the war and many finally change entirely since they are influenced by events and their probable consequence' (1989: 92). States may continue fighting beyond the 'rational' point of surrender when their leaders' prestige becomes invested in the war or the passions of the people become aroused. Alternatively, heavy losses may lead to escalation of a conflict, changing its character. During the 1990s, for example, al-Qaeda's attacks on Western targets led to a series of limited responses, such as the 1998 cruise missile strikes on Sudan and Afghanistan in retaliation against the bombings of the US embassies in Nairobi and Dar es Salaam. However, its attack on the United States on 11 September 2001, which killed nearly three thousand innocents, raised the stakes of the conflict considerably, triggering the invasion of Afghanistan, the overthrow of al-Qaeda's Taliban hosts, and a protracted series of campaigns to counter the terrorist movement worldwide.

Friction

Another concept with enduring value is that of friction, which Clausewitz defined as 'the only concept that more or less corresponds to the factors that distinguish real war from war on paper' (1989: 119). Clausewitz derived the name and the concept from physics. As he wrote in *The Principles of War*, 'The conduct of war resembles the workings of an intricate machine with enormous friction, so that combinations which are easily planned on paper can be executed only with great effort' (quoted in Smith 2005: 77). The sources of friction include the danger posed by the enemy, the effort required of one's own forces, the difficulties presented by the physical environment, and the problem of knowing what is occurring.

Examples of friction abound in recent wars. For example, the largest Iraqi counterattack of the 2003 Iraq War, which occurred early on 3 April near a key bridge over the Euphrates southwest of Baghdad, surprised US forces. US sensors failed to detect the approach of three Iraqi brigades composed of 8,000 soldiers backed by 70 tanks and armoured personnel carriers.

Key points

- Clausewitz viewed war as a paradoxical trinity composed of passion, probability, and reason. These tendencies generally correspond to the people, the military, and the government.
- Understanding the nature of a war is a necessary but difficult precondition to developing an effective strategy.
- In war it is important to identify and attack the enemy's centre of gravity. In Clausewitz's view, this was most likely the enemy's army, capital, ally, leader, or public opinion.
- Clausewitz distinguished between wars fought for limited and unlimited aims. The former are fought over territory; the latter are fought to overthrow the enemy's regime or achieve unconditional surrender.
- Clausewitz argued that there should be a correlation between the value a state attaches to its ends and the means it uses to achieve them. In practice, however, this is often difficult to determine.

Sun Tzu, Mao, and the Jihadists

There is a seemingly wide gulf between Clausewitz and Sun Tzu. The former wrote from the perspective of early nineteenth-century Europe, the latter from the perspective of ancient China. The books they wrote are also strikingly different. Whereas *On War* is often a thicket of prose, much of *The Art of War* is made up of deceptively simple aphorisms. *On War* is close to 600 pages, *The Art of War* totals fewer than 40 pages in English and 6,600 characters in Chinese. Yet as the British strategist Basil Liddell Hart observed, Clausewitz's *On War* does not differ as much from Sun Tzu's *Art of War* as it would appear to do on the surface (Handel 2001: 20).

Sun Tzu does, however, provide contrasting perspectives on several aspects of strategy. For example, the two authors exhibit different strategic preferences and offer contrasting views of intelligence and deception. Moreover, Sun Tzu's approach has inspired subsequent generations of strategic theorists as diverse as Mao Tse-Tung and a number of contemporary Islamist theoreticians.

Strategic Preferences

Sun Tzu's strategic preferences are significantly different from those of Clausewitz. Sun Tzu extols victory without bloodshed as the ideal, writing that 'to subdue the enemy without fighting is the acme of skill' (Sun Tzu 1963: 77). Clausewitz, by contrast, is sceptical of such an approach to combat, arguing that a reluctance to shed blood may play into an opponent's hands.

Sun Tzu sees war as a search for comparative advantage. He believes that success in war is less a matter of destroying the adversary's army than shattering his will to fight. In his view, the most successful strategies are those that emphasize psychology and deception.

To Sun Tzu, information represents a key to success in war. As he puts it, 'Know the enemy and know yourself; in a hundred battles you will never be in peril' (Sun Tzu 1963: 84). Typically, however, such pithy injunctions conceal the many challenges that make it difficult to understand oneself and one's adversary, including imperfect information, ethnocentrism, and mirror-imaging.

Whereas Clausewitz writes that destroying the enemy's army is most often the key to victory in war, Sun Tzu recommends that the best alternative is to attack the enemy's strategy. The next best alternative is to attack the opponent's alliances. Destroying the enemy's army ranks third on his list of preferred strategies.

Intelligence

Another contrast involves the two authors' views of intelligence. Sun Tzu is an intelligence optimist, claiming that the outcome of a war can be known in advance if the leader makes a complete estimate of the situation:

> To gauge the outcome of war we must compare the two sides by assessing their relative strengths. This is to ask the following questions: Which ruler has the way? Which commander has the greater ability? Which side has the advantage of climate and terrain? Which army follows

regulations and obeys orders more strictly? Which army has superior strength? Which officers and men are better trained? Which side is more strict and impartial in meting out rewards and punishments? On the basis of this comparison I know who will win and who will lose.
Sun Tzu (1993: 103–4)

Two aspects of this passage are noteworthy. First, he emphasizes 'relative strengths', not absolute capabilities. In other words, one's capabilities only matter when considered in relation to those of the adversary. Second, most of the factors that he identifies as being important are qualitative, not quantitative.

Clausewitz, by contrast, is an intelligence sceptic:

Many intelligence reports in war are contradictory; even more are false, and most are uncertain . . . One report tallies with another, confirms it, magnifies it, lends it color, till he has to make a quick decision—which is soon recognized to be mistaken, just as the reports turn out to be lies, exaggerations, and so on. In short, most intelligence is false, and the effect of fear is to multiply lies and inaccuracies.
Clausewitz (1989: 117)

The failure of the US intelligence community—indeed, of all major intelligence services—to determine that Iraq did not possess nuclear, biological, or chemical weapons prior to the 2003 Iraq War is evidence of the fact that despite the development of highly sophisticated means of collecting information, intelligence continues to be an uncertain business.

Sun Tzu is also a proponent of deception. He repeatedly discusses how the successful general can surprise and deceive an opponent and how he should gather good intelligence and weaken the morale of the enemy. Yet he seldom alludes to the fact that an enemy may be able to do the same.

Sun Tzu's imprint can be seen in the writings of Mao Tse-Tung. Mao never summarized his theory of warfare in a single work. Rather, his theoretical contributions are scattered throughout several different writings. Taken as a whole, they offer a blueprint for the defeat of a stronger power by a much weaker force through a sophisticated politico–military strategy involving the incremental establishment of political control over the countryside, near total mobilization of the peasantry, and deliberate protraction of a conflict. He emphasizes that social, political, and economic developments have a decisive impact on the outcome of such a conflict. The concrete manifestation of his philosophy is a three-phase approach to war that begins with the revolutionary movement on the strategic defensive, builds to a strategic stalemate characterized by

Key points

- Sun Tzu argues that success in war comes from shattering the adversary's will to fight rather than destroying his army.
- He recommends that the best alternative is to attack the enemy's strategy.
- He claims that the outcome of a war can be known in advance if the leader makes a complete estimate of the situation.
- Mao Tse-Tung offers a blueprint for insurgents to defeat a strong power through a protracted revolutionary war.

intensified guerrilla warfare, and culminates in a strategic counteroffensive that witnesses the defeat of the adversary in a decisive conventional battle (Mao Tse-Tung 1967).

Although Chinese in origin, Mao's writings have served as the template for revolutionary movements throughout the developing world. They have, in turn, influenced jihadist strategic thinkers who see in Mao's writings a model for how to overthrow a local government through a protracted insurgency.

The Enduring Relevance of Strategy

In recent years, both scholars and practitioners have questioned the utility of the classical strategic theory. Some have argued that the advent of the information age has invalidated traditional theories of warfare. They claim that technology either has or will soon overcome much of the friction that has historically characterized combat. As Admiral William A. Owens wrote several years ago:

> Military theorists from Sun Tzu to Clausewitz have pointed out the value of understanding one's enemies and the geographical-political-social-context in which they operate. What is different, however, is that some technologies—available either now or soon—will give the United States an edge that approaches omniscience, at least relative to any potential opponent.
> **Owens (1995: 133)**

Those who take this view argue that the advent of the information age demands a new body of strategic theory, one drawing its inspiration from business theory, economics, or the so-called new physical sciences. Vice Admiral Arthur K. Cebrowski and John J. Garstka, for example, wrote that 'there is *as yet* no equivalent to Carl von Clausewitz's *On War* for the information age' (emphasis added). The implicit assumption, of course, is that such a work is needed (Cebrowski and Garstka 1998: 29).

A second group agrees that the classical approach to strategy is anachronistic, but for a very different reason. These critics allege that the utility of classical strategic theory is limited to wars between armies and states, whereas war today more often involves trans- or subnational groups. In John Keegan's characterization, Clausewitzian thought makes 'no allowances for . . . war without beginning or end, the endemic warfare of non-state, even pre-state peoples' (Keegan 1993: 5). Implicit in this critique is the assumption that such conflicts obey logic distinct from those involving states. As Philip Meilinger has claimed:

> The warriors of al-Qaida, Hezbollah, Hamas, Taliban and other sects that fight us do not view war as an instrument of policy. Other cultural, biological and religious factors motivate them. They are not following the script of '*On War*'. They are not Clausewitzians. We need to understand what motivates them and not rely upon an outdated dictum for policymaking that belongs to another place and another time.
> **Meilinger (2008: 10)**

Finally, some have argued that strategy itself is an illusion. In this view, strategic concepts are misleading, even harmful. The military historian Russell Weigley wrote that

> War . . . is no longer the extension of politics by other means. It is doubtful whether the aphorism affirming that war is such an extension of politics was ever true enough to warrant the frequency with which it has been repeated.
> **Weigley (1988: 341)**

Although each of these arguments has its adherents, each is flawed. Those who criticize Clausewitz have at best a limited understanding of his strategic thought. First, although the growth and spread of stealth, precision, and information technology has had a dramatic influence on recent conflicts and portends even greater changes, there is as yet no evidence that it has altered the fundamental nature of war. The wars in Kosovo, Afghanistan, and Iraq have demonstrated the enduring value of such concepts as friction. If anything, the increasing complexity of modern war may actually multiply sources of friction.

In fact, strategic theory offers a lens through which we can assess the prospective effectiveness of new ways of war such as cyber warfare. Applying such concepts as war for limited and unlimited aims and the rational calculus of war to cyber warfare, one would expect the cyber instrument of war to be most effective in wars pitting the strong against the weak, fought for limited aims, and to gain something that the target of a cyber attack does not hold dear. It is unlikely to be decisive in other circumstances (Mahnken 2011).

Proponents of new 'theories of war' drawn from business, literature, and science frequently confuse novelty with utility. As Richard K. Betts has correctly noted:

> Critics would have to demonstrate that more recent and numerous theories in other fields are *better* theories—more useful to understanding the world—than the fewer and older ones of strategy. Theories may endure because each new one proves wanting. One Clausewitz is still worth a busload of most other theorists.
> **Betts (1997: 29)**

Second, it is unclear that war involving non-state actors is any different from that between states. The strategic questions most relevant to the struggle against Islamic terrorist networks differ little from those in previous wars. Although al-Qaeda looks and operates very differently than a conventional state adversary, it is nonetheless a strategic actor. Islamist authors such as Hasan al-Bana, Abu Bakr Naji, Abu' Ubayd al-Quarashi, and Abu Musab al-Suri have all penned works on strategy, including some that invoke the ideas of Clausewitz, Sun Tzu, and Mao (Stout et al. 2008: 123–32)

Third, those who argue that strategy is an illusion confuse the difficulty of executing strategy with the existence of an underlying strategic logic. Some strategic concepts may indeed be of limited utility in practice. For example, leaders may be unable to estimate the value of an objective before the fact, but ignoring these concepts and guidelines will only diminish the prospects of success.

That critiques of the classical approach are unconvincing is not to say that existing theories of war hold all the answers. Clausewitz has little to say about the impact of technology on war, for example. Yet those who reject the classical approach to strategy have nothing to offer in its place. Indeed, by rejecting strategic thought one must also discard the notion of the use of force as an instrument of policy.

Key points

- Some argue that classical strategic theory is obsolete because technology either has or will soon overcome much of the friction that has historically characterized combat. The evidence that this is occurring is, however, weak.

- Others argue that classical strategic theory does not explain conflict involving trans- or subnational groups. In fact, however, both states and terrorist groups may be strategic actors.

- Still others argue that strategy itself is an illusion. They confuse the difficulty of executing strategy with the existence of strategic logic.

 ## Conclusion

Strategic theory reminds us that despite significant changes to the character and conduct of war brought on by the development of new technology, the nature of war is constant. War remains the use of force to achieve political aims, regardless of whether the group seeking those aims is a state or terrorist network. Similarly, interaction with the adversary remains one of the key dynamics that prevents strategy from becoming a science.

Concepts found in Clausewitz's *On War* and Sun Tzu's *The Art of War* have similarly enduring value. Clausewitz's discussion of the remarkable trinity, the need to understand the nature of a war, the differences between limited and unlimited wars, the rational calculus of war, and friction are all useful. Sun Tzu, for his part, reminds us that victory does not always require the physical destruction of an adversary. He also highlights the importance of intelligence. Together, these concepts can help us better understand contemporary conflicts.

 ## Questions

1. Why is it important to study strategic theory?
2. In what ways is strategy an art? A science?
3. What are the main differences between Clausewitz and Sun Tzu's views of strategy?
4. What considerations should decision-makers keep in mind as they contemplate using force?
5. What limits the utility of strategic theory as a guide to action?
6. What differentiates war from other forms of violence?
7. What are the main contributions of Clausewitz to strategic theory?
8. What are the main contributions of Sun Tzu to strategic theory?
9. Does Clausewitz or Sun Tzu have a more realistic view of intelligence?
10. Which elements of strategic theory are most relevant to the world of the early twenty-first century? Which are least relevant?

 ## Further Reading

J. F. C. Fuller, *Armament and History* (New York: Scribner's, 1945) offers the most articulate consideration of the role of technology in warfare.

C. S. Gray, *Modern Strategy* (Oxford: Oxford University Press, 1999) similarly argues for the unity of all strategic experience because nothing vital to the nature of warfare changes.

He also makes a persuasive case that Clausewitz stands head and shoulders above other strategic theorists.

M. I. Handel, *Masters of War*, 3rd edn (London: Frank Cass, 2001) makes a convincing case that Clausewitz, Sun Tzu, Mao Tse-Tung, and other theorists employ a common strategic logic. What at first glance appear to be divergences and contradictions are often upon closer examination differences of methodology, definition, or perspective.

B. H. Liddell Hart, *Strategy* (New York: Praeger, 1967) argues that decisive victories usually involve prior psychological dislocation of an adversary. Rather than concentrating one's troops, the commander should force his enemy to disperse his forces. Despite the author's overly narrow interpretation of Clausewitz and selective use of history, this is nonetheless an important work.

E. Luttwak, *Strategy: The Logic of War and Peace*, revised and enlarged edition (Cambridge, MA: Belknap Press, 2001) explores the paradoxical nature of strategy. Classic treatment of paradox in strategy.

T. G. Mahnken and J. A. Maiolo, *Strategic Studies: A Reader* (Abingdon: Routledge, 2008) provides a useful compilation of many of the most valuable readings in strategic studies.

S. Tzu, *The Art of War*. The serious student should read several translations. The best are the translations by Samuel B. Griffith **(Oxford: Oxford University Press, 1963)** and Roger Ames **(New York: Ballentine Books, 1993).**

P. Paret (ed.), *Makers of Modern Strategy: From Machiavelli to the Nuclear Age* (Princeton, NJ: Princeton University Press, 1986) offers an intellectual history of strategic thought from Machiavelli to modern times. It includes chapters on Machiavelli, Clausewitz, Jomini, and Mahan, and essays on the practice of strategy.

C. von Clausewitz, *On War*, edited and translated by Michael Howard and Peter Paret (Princeton, NJ: Princeton University Press, 1989) deserves to be read in its entirety.

J. C. Wylie, *Military Strategy: A General Theory of Power Control* (Annapolis, MD: Naval Institute Press, 1989) is also a valuable work on strategy.

Web Links

The Clausewitz homepage at **http://www.clausewitz.com/index.htm** contains a variety of useful research resources, including indices and bibliographies.

The Sun Tzu Art of War site **http://www.sonshi.com/** contains a translation of *The Art of War*, reviews of the other major translations, and other works of strategy online.

The web page of the US Military Academy's Combating Terrorism Center **http://www.ctc.usma.edu/** contains the center's reports, which include some insightful analyses of jihadist strategic theory and practice.

Military history online **http://www.militaryhistoryonline.com/18thcentury/articles/thesuccessofnapoleon.aspx** This site contains many useful issues relevant to strategic theory along with a large number of case examples.

The Journal of Strategic Studies **http://www.tandfonline.com/loi/fjss20** is the premier journal of strategic studies and frequently publishes articles on strategic theory.

Strategic Culture

JEFFREY S. LANTIS AND DARRYL HOWLETT

 Chapter Contents

Introduction	77
Thinking about Culture and Strategy	77
Sources of Strategic Culture	80
Constructivism and Strategic Culture	83
Continuing Issues	84
Delineating Non-state, State, and Multi-state Strategic Cultures	88
Strategic Culture and Weapons of Mass Destruction	90
Conclusion	93

 Reader's Guide

This chapter considers the ways that strategic culture can aid academic understanding as well as analysis of security policies of many actors in the international realm. This approach is salient because of the number of conflicts that seem to exhibit cultural dimensions. To facilitate this analysis the chapter is divided into three sections. First, the chapter presents an overview of approaches exploring the relationship between culture and nuclear strategy during the cold war. This section also includes a synopsis of the various sources of strategic culture identified in the literature. Second, the chapter discusses certain theoretical issues related to strategic culture, including: the contribution of constructivist approaches to security studies; the question of 'ownership' of strategic culture; and whether non-state, state, and multi-state actors can possess distinctive strategic cultures. The final section of the chapter provides an overview of recent work that explores the relationship between strategic culture and the acquisition and threat of use of weapons of mass destruction.

Introduction

This chapter provides an overview of the scholarly and policymaking relevance of strategic culture in the contemporary world. It also presents background on certain issues that have influenced conceptual and empirical debates related to strategic culture in the past.

Many consider that culture has a profound impact on strategic decision-making, and in recent years there has been renewed academic and policy interest in exploring its role in international security (Johnson, Kartchner and Larsen 2009; FIU-SOUTHCOM 2010). Scholars and practitioners have begun to study issues like the United States' relations with countries such as China, Russia, and Iran, European security cooperation, counterterrorism policies, and weapons of mass destruction (WMD) proliferation through the lens of strategic culture. The challenges of insurgencies and instability in Iraq and Afghanistan also under-score the importance of cultural considerations at political and strategic levels.

Recognizing the impact of diverse strategic cultures seems especially pertinent in the twenty-first century security arena. The first step may be to accept, and attempt to over-come, a measure of ethnocentrism in the enterprise (Booth 1981). Jeannie Johnson, Kerry Kartchner, and Jeffrey Larsen write:

> All cultures condition their members to think certain ways, while at the same time providing pre-set responses to given situations. Thus culture bounds our perceptions and the range of options we have for responding to events. However, when a society experiences a severe shock or major disaster, it forces that culture to become more open-minded, as it becomes momentarily susceptible to new explanations, new paradigms, new ways of thinking, all in search of understanding and mitigating the shock that has befallen them. The events of 9/11 did that to America.
> **Johnson, Kartchner, and Larsen (2009: 5–6)**

Thus, it may be important to try and step outside one's own cultural perspective in order to embrace the possibility that non-Western cultures may exhibit different ways of thinking and acting. Engagement in this enterprise could help reduce the criticism that strategic studies has traditionally been too Western-centric, and also aid the contextual understanding of the study of postcolonial societies and the issues associated with nation-building, for example. This deviates from interpretations of security policy behaviour purely as a function of material opportunities and constraints in the external environment, and offers instead a route to recognize ways that 'cultural, ideational, and normative influences' impact the motivations of states and leaders (Glenn 2009: 523).

Thinking about Culture and Strategy

There are three main approaches to the study of culture and strategy. The first views culture as a value-added explanation of strategic behaviour. Culture is used to fill in the gaps of explanation by supplementing theories centred on national interest and the distribution of power. Culture is considered a variable that may influence behaviour but is characterized as epiphenomenal, or secondary to international systemic pressures. The second approach views culture as a conceptual vehicle that can explain some, if not all, strategic behaviour. This approach draws on other areas of knowledge such as political psychology in order to create a theory of strategic culture that is falsifiable and also contributes to a cumulative research programme. Strategic culture in this sense is an independent variable that explains decision-making on international security as well or better than neorealism or neo-liberal institutionalism. The third scholarly approach argues that aspects of human conduct can be understood only by becoming immersed within a given strategic culture. Consequently, the search for falsifiable theories is unachievable. Some anthropologists and sociologists consider that the relationship between culture and strategy is inordinately complex because it consists of a combination of discursive (what is said) and non-discursive (what is unsaid) expressions. Hence, they argue, it is impossible to measure the influence of culture on strategy (see Box 4.1).

Political Culture

The idea that culture could influence strategic outcomes was first captured in classic works, including the writings of Thucydides and Sun Tzu. In the nineteenth century, Prussian military strategist Carl von Clausewitz identified war and war-fighting strategy as 'a test of moral and physical forces' (Howard 1991: A23). The goal of strategy, he argued, was more than defeat of the enemy on the battlefield—it was the elimination of the enemy's morale.

The Second World War prompted a new wave of research on the distinctive 'national character' of countries, which were rooted in language, religion, customs, and the interpretation of common memories. Scholars became curious about how a country's national character could lead them to fight wars differently. Some sought to understand how Japanese culture, for example, fomented a spirit of self-sacrifice, such as in the kamikaze attacks against US warships and battles to the death over remote South Pacific islands (Benedict 1946). While this work was criticized for reifying the culture and promoting stereotypes, anthropologists including Margaret Mead and Claude Lévi-Strauss continued to refine these studies. In the 1980s,

---

BOX 4.1 Differing Perspectives on Culture

Culture is comprised of 'interpretive codes' including language, values, and even substantive beliefs like support for democracy or the futility of war.

Parsons (1951)

Culture is 'an historically transmitted pattern of meanings embodied in symbols, a system of inherited conceptions expressed in symbolic form by means of which men communicate, perpetuate, and develop their knowledge about and attitudes towards life'.

Geertz (1973)

Culture is 'the dynamic vessel that holds and revitalizes the collective memories of a people by giving emotional life to traditions'.

Pye (1985)

Political culture is 'that subset of beliefs and values of a society that relate to the political system'.

Almond and Verba (1965)

sociologist Ann Swidler defined culture quite broadly as consisting of 'symbolic vehicles of meaning, including beliefs, ritual practices, art forms, and ceremonies, as well as informal cultural practices such as language, gossip, stories, and rituals of daily life' (1986: 273). Building on the arguments of Max Weber and Talcott Parsons, she contended that interest-driven, cultural 'strategies of action' were important mediating conditions on state behaviour.

Meanwhile, political scientists Gabriel Almond and Sidney Verba had generated interest in political culture, which they defined as the 'subset of beliefs and values of a society that relate to the political system' (1965: 11). Political culture included a commitment to values like democratic principles and institutions, ideas about morality and the use of force, the rights of individuals or collectives, and predispositions toward the role of a country in the world. This political culture, Almond and Verba argued, was manifest on at least three levels: 'the cognitive, which includes empirical and causal beliefs; the evaluative, consisting of values, norms, and moral judgements; and the expressive or affective, which encompasses emotional attachments, patterns of identity and loyalty, and feelings of affinity, aversion, or indifference' (quoted in Duffield 1999: 23).

However, even though sociological models of culture became increasingly complex, subsequent studies of political culture were considered to have yielded little theoretical refinement. Critics argued that the approach was subjective and that the explanatory power of political culture was more limited than its proponents claimed. This was also a period when the behavioural revolution was making an impact in the social sciences, contributing to a loss of interest in cultural interpretive analyses in mainstream international relations scholarship.

Strategic Culture and Nuclear Deterrence

In 1977, Jack Snyder introduced culture into modern security studies by developing a theory of strategic culture to interpret Soviet nuclear doctrine. The predominant approach to nuclear strategy up to this juncture had been shaped by econometric treatments of rational utility. The United States and the Soviet Union were thus posited as rational actors responding to each others' moves in a calculated way in the strategic nuclear realm.

Snyder's alternative approach to analysing US–Soviet nuclear interaction focused on what he viewed as the distinctive strategic cultural differences between the two states. He suggested that elites articulate a unique strategic culture related to security–military affairs that is a wider manifestation of public opinion, socialized into a distinctive mode of strategic thinking. He contended, 'a set of general beliefs, attitudes, and behavior patterns with regard to nuclear strategy has achieved a state of semi-permanence that places them on the level of "cultural" rather than mere policy' (Snyder 1977: 8). Snyder concluded that the Soviet military exhibited a preference for the pre-emptive, offensive use of force and that the origins for this could be found in a Russian history of insecurity and authoritarian control (see Box 4.2).

Subsequent studies of strategic culture continued to explore the ideational foundations of nuclear strategy and US–Soviet relations. Colin Gray suggested that distinctive national styles, with 'deep roots within a particular stream of historical experience', characterized strategic development in countries like the United States and the Soviet Union. Strategic culture thus 'provides the milieu within which strategy is debated' and serves as an independent determinant of strategic policy patterns. Like Snyder, Gray considered that strategic culture would be a semi-permanent influence on security policy (1981: 35–7). At the same time, Ken Booth

> ### BOX 4.2 Definitions of Strategic Culture
>
> Strategic culture is 'a set of general beliefs, attitudes, and behavior patterns with regard to nuclear strategy that has achieved a state of semi-permanence that places them on the level of "cultural" rather than mere policy'.
>
> Snyder (1977)
>
> Strategic culture is the 'ideational milieu that limits behavioral choices', from which 'one could derive specific predictions about strategic choice'.
>
> Johnston (1995)
>
> Strategic culture is comprised of 'beliefs and assumptions that frame . . . choices about international military behavior, particularly those concerning decisions to go to war, preferences for offensive, expansionist or defensive modes of warfare, and levels of wartime casualties that would be acceptable'.
>
> Rosen (1995)

was concerned about the impact that ethnocentrism could have as a source of errors in both the theory and practice of strategy. For Booth, ethnocentrism meant that strategists might be culture-bound, unable to escape 'one's own cultural attitudes and imaginatively recreate the world from the perspective of those belonging to a different group' (1981: 15).

While these path-breaking works represented a call for new attention to ideational factors, few strategic cultural theorists viewed this as an 'either-or' debate with rationalism. Nevertheless, sceptics perceived the growth of cultural theory as a challenge to traditional strategic thought and argued that the theory was too subjective, reliant on narrow contextual historiography. Based on questions about difficulty of operationalizing culture in any meaningful sense, critics claimed that early proponents had overstated the analytic and policymaking relevance of strategic culture.

> ### Key points
>
> - Early studies linking culture and strategic action focused on 'national character' as a product of language, religion, customs, socialization, and the interpretation of common historical experiences.
> - Almond and Verba later integrated cultural approaches into political science by identifying the features of what they called 'political culture'. This involved a commitment to values like democratic principles and institutions, ideas about morality and the use of force, the rights of individuals or collectives, and predispositions towards the role of a country in the world.
> - Jack Snyder coined the phrase 'strategic culture' to focus on the relationship between culture and nuclear strategy. This led to significant applications of strategic culture to the study of deterrence.

Sources of Strategic Culture

Several sources of strategic culture, encompassing both material and ideational factors, are identified in the literature. First, geography, climate, and resources have been key elements in strategic thinking throughout the millennia and remain important sources of strategic culture today. Geographical circumstance may be one key to understanding why some countries adopt particular strategic policies rather than others. For example, proximity to great powers has been viewed as an important factor, as the cases of Norway and Finland exemplified during the cold war (Graeger and Leira 2005; Heikka 2005), while relative isolation for countries like Australia enabled a focus on continental defence in the past. Additionally, while most territorial borders are settled by negotiation, others have been forged through conflict and remain contested. Some states have multiple borders and may be confronted by multiple security dilemmas. Such factors appear to have shaped the strategic orientations of countries like Israel and could explain its motivation for acquiring a nuclear capability. Ensuring access to vital resources is also deemed critical to strategy, and this and other factors seem especially significant in changing global territorial and resource landscapes today.

History and experience are important considerations in the evolution of strategic culture. International relations theory has identified several ways to categorize states ranging from weak to strong, colonial to postcolonial, and pre-modern, modern, and postmodern. This raises the prospect that different kinds of states may confront different strategic problems and with varying material and ideational resources, apply unique responses. For newly formed states the difficulties of nation-building can compound insecurities and thereby help shape strategic cultural identities. Conversely, for those states of ancient standing, the longevity of their existence may prompt consideration of factors that contribute to the rise and fall of great powers or civilizations and shape their policies to suit.

Scholars argue that generational change and technology, particularly information and communications technology, can have important ramifications for issues of empowerment and strategic reach. While information technology has transformed societies it has also allowed individuals or groups to communicate in novel ways and cause disruption at a distance. The arrival of the Internet is a relatively recent phenomenon, yet there are now generations who have grown up with this medium of information and communication. This and other technologies may empower individual and group identities in ways unlike ever before in history.

Another source of strategic culture is the nature of a country's political structure and defence organizations. Some countries adopt a broadly Western liberal democratic style of government, while others do not. Some are considered mature democracies while others are undergoing democratic transformations. Where the latter are concerned there may be cultural variables such as tribal, religious, or ethnic allegiances that operate within and across territorial boundaries, which determine the pace and depth of consolidation. Similarly, many regard defence organizations as being critical to strategic cultures but differ over the precise impact these have. Studies of the Nordic region suggest that issues such as whether the forces are professional or conscript and their experiences in conflict are significant. Military doctrines, civil–military relations, and procurement practices may also affect strategic culture (Adamsky 2010).

Myths and symbols are considered to be part of all cultural groupings and both can act as a stabilizing or destabilizing factor in the evolution of strategic cultural identities. The notion of myth can have meaning different from the traditional understanding 'as something unfounded or false'. John Calvert writes that this can refer to a body of beliefs that express the fundamental, largely unconscious or assumed political values of a society—in short, as a dramatic expression of ideology. The details narrated in a political myth may be true or false; most often they meld truth and fiction in ways that are difficult to distinguish . . . To be effective, political myth must engage not reason, but belief and faith.

Calvert (2004: 31)

At the same time, historical narratives also impact conceptions of state roles. According to Breuning, roles are an extension of cultural 'axiomatic beliefs' regarding the state's relation to the international environment (actor versus subject orientation); the nature of the international environment (universalistic versus particularistic worldview); and understandings of rules of behaviour (intent-based versus results-oriented) (1997: 113). These roles then manifest themselves in different foreign and security policy behaviours.

Related studies of symbols also suggests that these act as 'socially recognized objects of more or less common understanding' and which provide a cultural community with stable points of reference for strategic thought and action' (Elder and Cobb, quoted in Poore 2004: 63). Political unrest and cyber-attacks in Estonia in the late 2000s show just how powerful symbols may be. This turmoil was sparked by Estonia's decision to move a Soviet war memorial from the centre of the capital, Tallinn, to a military cemetery. For Russia and the ethnic Russian population in Estonia, the statue had symbolic value related to historic sacrifice in the Second World War; for Estonia, in contrast, it represented a symbol of past occupation. The resulting protests on the streets and cyber-attacks on websites for Estonian institutions launched from Russia drove a deep wedge between the populations of the country.

Traditional analyses of peace and conflict have long pointed to the influence of key texts as formative throughout history and in different cultural settings. These may follow an historical trajectory—from Sun Tzu's *Art of War*, considered to have been written during the time of the warring states in ancient China, through the writings of Kautilya in ancient India—and into Western understanding of peace and conflict as a result of Thucydides' commentary on the Peloponnesian War and Clausewitz's writings on the nature of war stemming from his observations of the Napoleonic period. At the same time, there may be competition between texts for influence on society. In a study of Greek strategic culture, for example, the oscillating influence of two distinct strategic traditions was identified. On the one hand, 'traditionalists' derive their intellectual sustenance from the exploits of Achilles, hero of the *Iliad*, and tend to view the world as an anarchic arena where power is the ultimate guarantee of security. On the other hand, there are the 'modernists', followers of Odysseus, the hero of the *Odyssey*, who although viewing the world as an anarchic environment consider that Greece's best strategy is to adopt a multilateral cooperative approach to peace and security (Ladis 2003). This dualism in strategic culture reflects the influence of long-held myths and legends, which continue to find resonance in narratives of the modern era.

Finally, transnational norms, generational change, and technology are also regarded as important sources of strategic culture. Norms are understood as 'intersubjective beliefs about the social and natural world that define actors, their situations, and the possibilities of action' (Wendt 1995: 73). Theo Farrell and Terry Terriff consider that norms can define 'the purpose and possibilities of military change' and 'provide guidance concerning the use of force' (2001: 7). Farrell has studied how transnational norms of military professionalism have

BOX 4.3 Potential Sources of Strategic Culture

Physical	Political	Social/Cultural
Geography	Historical Experience	Myths and Symbols
Climate	Political System	Defining Texts
Natural Resources	Elite Beliefs	
Generational Change	Military Organizations	
Technology		

←————————(Transnational Forces/Normative Pressures)————————→

influenced national policies and the process by which this occurs. He considers that transnational norms can be transplanted into a country's cultural context either through a process involving pressure on a target community to accept the new norms (termed 'political mobilization'), or by a process of voluntary adoption (termed 'social learning') (2001) (see Box 4.3).

Key points

- Snyder brought the political cultural argument into the realm of modern security studies by developing a theory of strategic culture to interpret Soviet nuclear doctrine.
- Scholars have argued that national styles, with 'deep roots within a particular stream of historical experience', characterized nuclear strategy-making in countries like the United States and the Soviet Union during the cold war.
- The sources of strategic culture are considered to be: geography, climate and resources, history and experience, political structure, the nature of organizations involved in defence, myths and symbols, key texts that inform actors of appropriate strategic action, transnational norms, generational change, and the role of technology.
- Strategic cultures may be influenced by international norms.

Constructivism and Strategic Culture

In the 1990s, the influence of constructivism prompted renewed interest in strategic culture. While constructivism encompasses many theoretical positions, some scholars became interested in how ideas, norms, and cultural factors might be as influential as material factors in international security. One of the early writers in this tradition, Alexander Wendt, consequently argued that state identities and interests were 'socially constructed by knowledgeable practice' (1992: 392). For Valerie Hudson, constructivism embraced the study of culture 'as an evolving system of shared meaning that governs perceptions, communications, and actions' (1997: 28–9).

Notable studies bridging constructivism and strategic culture soon emerged. Alastair Iain Johnston's *Cultural Realism: Strategic Culture and Grand Strategy in Chinese History* (1995) is regarded as a quintessential work on strategic culture influenced by constructivism. The study set out to investigate the existence and character of Chinese strategic culture, and whether this has causal links to the use of military force against external threats. Johnston characterized strategic culture as an 'ideational milieu that limits behavioral choices', from which 'one could derive specific predictions about strategic choice'. Focusing on the Ming dynasty in China (1368–1644) for his theoretical test, he concluded China 'has exhibited a tendency for the controlled, politically driven defensive and minimalist use of force that is deeply rooted in the statecraft of ancient strategists and a worldview of relatively complacent superiority' which had a 'nontrivial effect on strategy' (Johnston 1995: 1). Other studies in the 1990s also pointed to the importance of strategic culture. Work on states like Germany and Japan directed attention to the significance of their 'antimilitarist political-military cultures' in shaping foreign policy behaviour (Berger 1998; Banchoff 1999) (see Box 4.4).

Another strand of this scholarship focuses on military and/or organizational cultures. Elizabeth Kier described the significance of organizational culture in the development of French military doctrine (1995). Steven Rosen provided an account of the ways that the military and organizational cultures in India have shaped strategy over time. Jeffrey Legro's work on military restraint during the Second World War, and Roland Ebel, Raymond Taras, and James Cochrane's (1991) work on the cultures of Latin America all concluded that culture makes a difference. More recently, a comparative strategic cultures project jointly sponsored by Florida International University and the US Southern Command found a significant role for military organizational cultures in shaping security policy behaviour in South America (FIU-SOUTHCOM 2010). Together, these studies suggest that organizational culture can be a powerful factor influencing strategic choice.

Key points

- The rise of constructivism in international relations theory helped fuel a revival of interest in strategic culture.
- Strategic cultural studies have proliferated in recent years, including works that compare strategic cultures of countries in key regions such as Europe, Latin America, and Southeast Asia.
- Another strand of this scholarship focuses on how military/organizational cultures can shape security policies.

Continuing Issues

Continuity or Change?

The focus of most studies of strategic culture is on continuity or at least semi-permanence in state behaviour. Harry Eckstein (1998) suggested that the socialization of values and beliefs occurs over time. In this view, past learning coalesces in the collective consciousness and is relatively resilient to change. Lessons of the past serve as a filter for any future learning that might occur. The process of transformation consequently is often slow and involves generational change. If historical memory, political institutions, and multilateral commitments

BOX 4.4 Case Studies of Strategic Culture

People's Republic of China

Culture plays a strong role in shaping strategic behaviour in China. Scholars have identified two dominant strands of Chinese strategic culture today—the *parabellum* focused on realpolitik and the *Confucian–Mencian* strand, a philosophical orientation used mainly for idealized discourse. Scobell contends that these two strands are sometimes intertwined to shape a 'Chinese cult of defense'. Chinese civilian and military leaders repeatedly stress China's commitment to the Confucian saying 'peace is precious' (*he wei gui*), and they assert that China has never been an aggressive or expansionist state. A recent study by Huiyun Feng also suggests that China displays a more defensive posture in relation to the use of force and that the Confucian elements of its strategic culture have been 'underrepresented' (2009: 172). But not all are agreed on this, as Scobell concludes that Chinese leaders assume that any war they fight is just and any military action defensive, 'even when it is offensive in nature' (2002: 11).

United States of America

Scholars argue that several core principles have defined US strategic culture over time. Thomas Mahnken suggests: 'American strategic culture was shaped by free security and imbued with exceptionalism . . . American military culture, the so-called American way of war, emphasizes direct strategies, an industrial approach to war, and firepower—and technologically intensive approaches to combat' (Mahnken 2009: 69–70). Many writers also point to the impact on US strategic culture of the 9/11 terrorist attacks. This resulted in the George W. Bush administration's declaration of a war on terror and the initiation of new strategic cultural orientations. These included a positive reaffirmation of US dominance in international security affairs, with priority to homeland security, a new doctrine of pre-emption that includes a willingness to use military force to achieve security objectives, and a preference for unilateral actions internationally. At the same time, the new strategic cultural orientations were packaged rhetorically as a demonstration of continuity in US support for democracy and freedom (Lantis 2005).

Japan

Throughout the cold war, Japan fostered an 'antimilitarist political–military culture' that was characterized by pacifism and dependence on security alliance with the United States. The Yoshida Doctrine stressed that Japan focus on its own economic and technological development while establishing military security through alliance with the United States. For Thomas Berger, Japan's antimilitarist sentiments became deeply institutionalized through a long historical process that included legitimated compromises. However, in wake of the 9/11 attacks and the announcement by North Korea in 2006 of a nuclear weapon test, Japan has undertaken a re-assessment of its security. The government has provided logistical support to US and multinational coalition forces fighting in Afghanistan and Iraq, and it has pursued significant defence modernization. Japan has also bolstered its contribution to United Nations peacekeeping operations around the world (Berger 1998; Hughes 2004).

The Nordic Region: Denmark, Finland, Sweden, and Norway

The strategic cultures of Denmark, Finland, Norway, and Sweden have been shaped by their proximity to great powers during the cold war (and in previous eras). Analyses of Sweden and Denmark have also revealed two forms of strategic culture. In the case of Sweden the first form

BOX 4.4 *(continued)*

emphasizes professional and technologically advanced military forces, while the second revolves around notions of a people's army based on conscription and the democratic involvement of citizens of the state. Where Denmark is concerned, the two forms have been labelled cosmopolitanism and defencism. Cosmopolitanism stresses neutrality, alternative non-military means of conflict resolution, and the importance of international institutions such as the former League of Nations and the United Nations. In contrast, defencism emphasizes the importance of military preparedness encapsulated in the dictum 'if you want peace, you must prepare for war' and the importance of regional military organizations, such as the North Atlantic Treaty Organization (NATO), in defence and deterrence (Graeger and Leira 2005; Heikka 2005).

Russia

Writers on Russia have highlighted the importance of geography, history, and ideology in the context of its strategic culture (Glenn 2004). Factors such as political stabilization within Russia's vast landmass, which stretches across much of Eurasia, concerns about future military encirclement and fears of attack on its territory stemming from past historical experience are deemed instrumental in the development of a distinct Russian strategic culture. Fritz Ermarth (2009) considers that Russian strategic culture has also traditionally been one of the most militarized of any state but that the conditions for demilitarizing its strategic culture have been increasing since the 1970s. While not ruling out the possibility of a return to the traditional military basis of Russia's strategic culture, Ermarth suggests that there has been a new assertiveness within this strategic culture centring on nationalism as the ideological foundation and 'fueled by the dramatic economic recovery of recent years that oil and gas revenues have stimulated' (2009: 93). This 'new assertiveness', he argues, 'is accompanied by assertions of a supra-national Russian mission, to advance a multi-polar world that contains US power, to establish a Eurasian geopolitical identity distinct from the West, and to combat perceived threats from Western culture' (ibid.).

shape strategic culture, then it would seem plausible to accept that strategic cultures around the world are undergoing 'enduring transformations'. Conversely, other scholars argue that strategic cultures can change more dramatically. When North Korea conducted a missile test over Japan in 1998 and detonated its first atomic bomb in 2006, for example, Japanese and other Asian strategic cultures were triggered to adapt.

Early research on strategic cultural change contends that at least two conditions can cause strategic cultural dilemmas and produce changes in security policy. First, external shocks may fundamentally challenge existing beliefs and undermine past historical narratives. This appears to be illustrated in the Japanese case over the past decade, as elites revisit questions of security in a changing threat environment. For German leaders in the 1990s, the scale of the humanitarian tragedies in the Balkans served as a catalyst for consideration of policy options outside the traditional bounds of German strategic culture. The recognition that groups were being systematically targeted for genocide and ethnic cleansing created an imperative for German action. The intensity of external shocks eroded the moral legitimacy of pacifism on the German political left and prompted a re-examination on all sides of the question of the use of military force (Lantis 2002).

Any process of change would not be easy. Potential catalysts for change, Duffield argued, might be 'dramatic events or traumatic experiences [such as revolutions, wars, and economic catastrophes]' that would 'discredit thoroughly core beliefs and values' (Duffield 1999b: 23). Yet the shock of events and the subsequent reflection on implications for core beliefs would not be likely to occur overnight. Such change would be accompanied by extreme psychological stress and require a resocialization process, involving participation by various groups in the crafting of a compromise on a new political cultural orientation.

Second, foreign policy behaviour may break the traditional bounds of strategic cultural orientations when primary tenets of strategic thought come into direct conflict with one another. Swidler recognizes the potential for dynamism 'in unsettled cultural periods . . . when explicit ideologies govern action [and] structural opportunities for action determine which among competing ideologies survive in the long run' (1986: 274). For example, a country with interpretive codes of support for democracy and an aversion to the use of military force faces a strategic cultural dilemma when confronted by a challenge to democracy that necessitates a military response. Japan's government wrestled with this dilemma in relation to the struggle for self-determination in East Timor, for example. Thompson, Ellis, and Wildavsky argue that cultures remain vital only if their core principles continue to generate solutions that satisfy human needs and make sense of the world (1990: 69–70). Products of this strategic cultural *dissonance* include occasional state defections from multilateral arrangements, the development of alternative diplomatic initiatives, or stipulations for policy cooperation.

Thus, strategic cultural dilemmas define new directions for foreign policy and demand the reconstruction of historical narratives. Changes, including abrupt and fairly dramatic reorientations of security policy, are possible. Strategic cultural analysis must be more reflective of the conditions that draw out such changes.

Who are the Keepers of Strategic Culture?

One theme of contemporary strategic cultural studies has been the effort to identify the 'keepers' of strategic culture. These studies also allude to the subtleties associated with determining whether individuals or elite and non-elite groupings have the most influence in strategic cultural outcomes.

Past work tended to describe political and strategic cultures as properties of states only, reflecting the ideas of 'collectives rather than simply of the individuals that constitute them' (Wilson 2000: 12). However, actors other than states may be important stewards of strategic cultures—ranging from elites within a country to non-state actors, transnational groups, or multi-state actors. Strategic culture may still be a function of the socialization of values and beliefs over time, yet the actual agents involved in this process may vary. Thus, strategic culture may provide useful intellectual and policymaking tools to analyse how and why non-state, state and multi-states actors take strategic decisions.

Elites (high level policymakers) may represent the primary keepers of strategic culture or purveyors of the common historical narrative. While strategic culture can have deep roots in society, newer works on policy discourse suggests that strategic culture is best characterized as a 'negotiated reality' among elites (Swidler 1986). Writers have shown how leaders play a special role in strategic cultural continuity and change. For example, Jacques Hymans contends that identity is as much *subjective* as intersubjective and that leaders often adopt their own specific conceptions of national identity from among a competitive marketplace of ideas (2006). Both the constructivist and culturalist literature agree on the possibility for norm entrepreneurs to approach events, frame the discourse, and begin constructing a new discursive path towards objectives. Sociologist Consuelo Cruz contends that elites have more latitude than scholars generally allow. They may 'recast a particular agenda as most appropriate to a given collective reality' or 'redefine the limits of the possible, both descriptively and prescriptively' (2000: 278). Post-structural constructivists also look at how elites may be both keepers and strategic users of culture, manipulating cultural frames as a way to take exception to intersubjective structural limits. This approach acknowledges a dialectical relationship between how actors make choices within specific contexts that prioritize particular responses (Milliken 1999; Miskimmon 2004; Mattern 2005).

The organizational culture literature suggests that state behaviour is a function of specific institutional orientations or prevailing cultures. Studies of Japan's and Germany's foreign policy decisions in the 1990s, for example, identified enduring institutional manifestations of strategic culture, but the keepers of the culture are not necessarily *military* bureaucracies. In Germany, the Foreign Ministry has control over foreign and security policy. In Japan, political institutions from the Diet to the Liberal Democratic Party to the Japan Self-Defense Forces share commitments to a foreign policy of restraint. Lynn Eden argued that 'organizational frames' are developed by institutions to identify problems and find solutions. These frames include 'what counts as a problem, how problems are represented, the strategies used to solve those problems, and the constraints and requirements placed on possible solutions' (Eden 2004: 51). Finally, there may be an important public dimension to strategic culture. Charles Kupchan has argued that the foundations of strategic culture are *societal*. 'Based on images and symbols', he says, strategic culture 'refers to images that shape how the nation as a collective entity defines its well-being and conceives of its security' (Kupchan 1994: 21). Broad support for a prevailing historical narrative may condition security policy responses as well as the potential for strategic cultural change.

Key points

- The focus of many studies of strategic culture has been on continuity, but new scholarship suggests potential scope conditions of change including external shocks and internal cognitive dissonance.
- Strategic cultural dilemmas may define new directions for foreign policy and foster the reconstruction of historical narratives.
- While traditional studies suggest that strategic culture is the property of collectives, new work explores the potential for agency in cultural framing.
- 'Keepers' of strategic culture may include elites, bureaucratic organizations, and society at large.

Delineating Non-state, State, and Multi-state Strategic Cultures

An exciting new area of research focuses on the degree to which non-state and multi-state actors may be said to possess strategic cultures. This approach has special implications for study of the European Union (EU). In December 2003, the EU formalized a common European Security Strategy (ESS) for the first time in its history. That document called for the development of a 'strategic culture, which fosters early, rapid, and when necessary, robust intervention' (European Union 2003: 11). This new initiative suggests that European countries may be able to foster common European responses to regional and global challenges such as terrorism, humanitarian crises, and proliferation of weapons of mass destruction (Schmitt, Howlett, Müller, Simpson, and Tertrais 2005; Vasconcelos 2009). The 2009 Lisbon Treaty promised even greater cooperation on multilateral responses through a Common Defence and Security Policy architecture.

However, scholars continue to debate whether we are witnessing the emergence of a truly new EU strategic culture. Optimists such as Paul Cornish and Geoffrey Edwards believe 'there are signs that a European strategic culture is already developing through a socialization process'. They define EU strategic culture as 'the institutional confidence and processes to manage and deploy military force as part of the accepted range of legitimate and effective policy instruments' (Cornish and Edwards 2001: 587). For Christoph Meyer, establishment of the ESS in 2003 provided a necessary 'strategic concept' around which to focus attention and resources (Meyer 2004). Conversely, Julian Lindley-French considered that Europe lacks

---

BOX 4.5 Culture and Counterinsurgency?

Can knowledge of cultural dynamics in countries like Iraq and Afghanistan bolster counterinsurgency and stability operations? This question has generated significant debate in the last decade. Some strategists have embraced the idea that cultural understanding matters for counterinsurgency operations in complicated theatres of operation. At the same time, social scientists have debated whether it is ever ethical to provide assistance for military operations.

In 2005, the US Army established an experimental counterinsurgency program called the Human Terrain System (HTS). Human terrain was defined as the 'social, ethnographic, cultural, economic, and political elements among whom a force is operating . . . characterized by sociocultural, anthropologic, and ethnographic data' (Kipp et al. 2006: 9). Five-person human terrain teams made up of regional studies experts, linguists, and social scientists, would be assigned to brigades or combat headquarters to provide 'cultural knowledge' for more effective military planning. These groups were deployed in Iraq and Afghanistan in daily civil operations, including engagement with populations in areas of insurgency, to promote more effective cooperation. By focusing on civil society as the 'centre of gravity' in counterinsurgency operations, the military hoped to make stronger links between occupation forces and local civilians.

The system was self-consciously 'designed to address cultural awareness shortcomings at the operational and tactical levels' (Kipp et al. 2006: 8). However, since the establishment of HTS, the military has provided few public statements regarding effectiveness, the program has been plagued by recruitment and operational problems, and other sectors of the government have raised questions about its value. Acting on these concerns, in 2010 the House Armed Services Committee limited funding for the program until an independent assessment was completed.

The question of assistance for military operations also fostered a bitter debate within the social sciences. While optimists saw this as a modified version of ethnographic research—and a tacit endorsement of the importance of learning about foreign languages and cultures—critics charged that these teams were collecting intelligence on local tribes for more effective targeting by the military. In other words, the work of the teams was more directed to *controlling* populations, to 'combat support', rather than civil reconstruction. In 2007, the Executive Board of the American Anthropological Association issued a statement expressing its disapproval of the program and opposing secrecy in operations that might have the effect of harming societies more than helping them (Weinberger 2008).

both the capabilities and will to establish a common foreign and security policy in the fore-seeable future. He characterized the Europe of today as 'not so much an architecture as a decaying arcade of stately structures of varying designs reflective of a bygone era' (2002: 789). Given the disagreements over threat perception and inconsistent policies in response to challenges such as the war on terrorism and the 'Arab Spring' in the Middle East and North Africa, the EU may be unlikely 'to develop a coherent and strong strategic culture' any time soon (Rynning 2003: 479). With limited consensus on values, even the institutionalization of the Lisbon arrangement may not guarantee legitimacy for any new European strategic cul-ture (see Box 4.5).

Another issue concerns whether the strategic culture frame applies to terrorist groups or groups operating across territorial boundaries where identities may be formed in the realms of both physical and cyberspace. Mark Long contends that al-Qaeda and other transnational terrorist organizations can have identifiable strategic cultures. He suggests that the study of strategic culture of some non-state actors, especially organized terrorist groups or liberation movements, may actually be *easier* than the study of state strategic cultures (Long 2009). The cyber revolution also deepens the complexity of the non-state actor threat assessment (Rat-tray 2002; Goldman 2003; Schwartzstein 1996). Victor Cha argues '[T]he most far-reaching security effect of globalization is its complication of the basic concept of "threat" in interna-tional relations' (2000: 392).

Additionally, while acknowledging that the technologies associated with globalization have enabled terrorist groups to conduct operations that 'are deadlier, more distributed, and more difficult to combat than those of their predecessors', James Kiras argues that these same technologies 'can be harnessed to defeat terrorism by those governments with the will and resources to combat it' (2005: 479). Cha concludes that technology enhances 'the salience of substate extremist groups or fundamentalist groups because their ability to orga-nize transnationally, meet virtually, and utilize terrorist tactics has been substantially enhanced by the globalization of technology and information' (2000: 392).

Key points

- One of the more complex questions that carries over through generations relates to what types of actors are most likely to have defined strategic cultures: states, regional organizations, civilizations, and even non-state groups such as terrorist networks?

- The HTS program represents a recent foray into bridging the gap between academic study and policymaking, but this counterterrorism initiative has generated significant controversy.

- Globalization and revolutions in information technology suggest that future threats will be more diffuse, more dispersed, and more multidimensional.

Strategic Culture and Weapons of Mass Destruction

What can strategic culture tell us about WMD proliferation and emerging deterrent situations? Recent studies have highlighted the role that strategic culture plays in decisions to acquire and potentially threaten to use WMD (Johnson, Kartchner, and Larsen 2009). In some ways, this work harkens back to the foundations of strategic cultural studies, but it also reflects a globalizing world characterized by more actors and rapid technological innovation. There is also renewed attention to cultural factors to explain the seeming limits of deterrence in preventing unintended consequences, including Russian nuclear modernization and the concerted drive to develop nuclear weapons in Iran and North Korea.

Among the questions being revisited are: Whether deterrence is an accepted universal norm that predetermines behaviour, or are attitudes toward nuclear strategy largely indigenous constructs that emerge from within the cultural context of particular actors? Early scholarship on this question is mixed. For example, Keith Payne considers that past 'deterrence concepts, buzzwords, and terms of art have essentially lost their meaning because the conditions of current power and political relationships have become so different from cold war conditions' (2007: 2). Jeffrey Knopf identifies a new fourth wave of deterrence literature as distinct given its asymmetric focus on deterrence relationships between the United States and rogue states or violent non-state actors (VNSAs), and the relaxation of traditional standards of deterrence (Knopf 2010).

In related work, Ian Kenyon and John Simpson contend there is significance in the 'ongoing debate between universal rationality and particular strategic cultures in relation to the mechanisms and effectiveness of deterrence, and the implications for this of threats of mass destructive actions by non-state actors and perceived "rogue states"' (Kenyon and Simpson 2006: 202). Contemporary scholarship also tends to recognize the importance of contextualizing relationships when it comes to specific settings, or scope conditions within which cultural factors may play a larger role in strategic decisions. For example, Sten Rynning posits that 'a strong strategic culture' may make a state more willing to use military force and enables it to triumph in zero-sum conflicts, while states with a 'weak strategic culture' might seek more diplomatic means of conflict resolution (Rynning 2003: 484). Further, Adrian Hyde-Price asserts that the strength of a strategic culture must be seen as a function of multiple measures, including power, history, geography, and society (2004). The democratic peace literature suggests links between political–military culture and security policy as well.

Kartchner has hypothesized that specific conditions can enable strategic culture to play a more dominant role in WMD policy. These include: when there is a strong sense of threat to a group's existence, identity, or resources, or when the group believes that it is at a critical disadvantage to other groups; when there is a pre-existing strong cultural basis for group identity; when the leadership frequently resorts to cultural symbols in support of its national group security aspirations and programmes; when there is a high degree of homogeneity within the group's strategic culture; and when historical experiences strongly predispose the group to perceive threats (2009).

New studies of 'tailored deterrence' stand squarely at the intersection of traditional and cultural approaches. Traditional deterrence theory is rife with discussions of *persuasion* of the adversary. For instance, Thomas Schelling defines deterrence as 'influencing the choices that another party will make, and doing it by influencing his expectations of how we will behave' (1963: 13). In other words, theorists of deterrence also implicitly recognize the significance of the target of their policies. Any thoughtful attempt to reflect on coercion dynamics and persuasion generates consideration of value hierarchies and vested national interests, which, in turn, can be the product of elite strategic calculations embedded within a larger cultural context. Lawrence Freedman even takes this a step further, arguing deterrence can be viewed as a 'norms-based as much as an interests-based approach' (2004: 4). Meanwhile, cultural models have offered more sophisticated and nuanced understandings of the power of cultural narratives and keepers of strategic culture to shape policy.

One of the first official references to the concept of tailored deterrence came in a US Strategic Command (STRATCOM) doctrine in early 2004, which stated that deterrence policies should be 'tailored in character and emphasis to address . . . fundamental differences in the perceptions and resulting decision calculus of specific adversaries in specific circumstances' (2004). Subsequent Joint Operating Concepts have reinforced the goal of establishing a 'customizable approach to deterrence assessment'. In 2006, the Pentagon's Quadrennial Defense Review (QDR) declared its intention to practise tailored deterrence, defined as 'context specific and culturally sensitive' conception of deterrence strategy. For Elaine Bunn, a policy-maker and strategist, tailoring deterrence represents, 'a shift from a one-size-fits-all notion of deterrence toward more adaptable approaches suitable for advanced military competitors, regional weapons of mass destruction states, as well as non-state terrorist networks' (2007: 4).

These developments may be better understood through the lens of emerging scholarship on identity and strategic choice. Alexander George has emphasized that 'the effectiveness of deterrence and coercive diplomacy is highly context dependent' (2003: 272). Much of the existing literature on strategic culture tends to focus on its role in authoritarian states, implying that there are more measurable strains of strategic culture manifest in certain types of political ideology, doctrine, and discourse. Studies of North Korea emphasize the core ideology of self-reliance (*Juche*), which prioritizes national security over all other policy concerns (even meeting basic human needs). The cult of personality of Kim Jong-Il allows some measure of continuity in expression of military priorities and other security orientations. Studies of Iran suggest that a definable strategic culture can be identified. It may be rooted in a nearly 3,000-year history of Persian civilization that lends itself to a combination of feelings of 'cultural superiority', 'manifest destiny', coupled with a 'deep sense of insecurity' (Giles 2003: 146). Gregory Giles argues that 'specific attributes of Shi'ism, which was adopted by Persia in the sixteenth century, both reinforce and expand certain traits in Iranian strategic culture' (2003: 147). In sum, cultural theories appear promising to lend greater cohesion to studies of tailored deterrence, provided we recognize some limits on conditions in which they may be most relevant (Lantis 2009).

Key points

- Strategic culture has implications for state policies regarding weapons of mass destruction.
- Though not emphasized in early theoretical work on deterrence, cultural dynamics can impact perception of threats and opportunities and help mediate attempts at persuasion. They may augment understandings of bounded rationality, for example.
- Strategic cultural understanding is directly related to the concept of tailored deterrence, from the 'fourth generation' of deterrence scholarship, which recognizes the importance of targeting and contextualizing deterrence messages carefully to potential adversaries.
- Identity and strategic choice may sometimes be a function of culture.

Conclusion

Recent events have renewed scholarly and policymaking interest in strategic culture. As NATO leaders adapt their strategic concept for a changing world and as future US presidents review the government's nuclear posture, research on strategic culture can offer important insights to improve knowledge as well as enrich policy recommendations. Today, scholars and practitioners are also reckoning with many other challenges that can be interpreted through a cultural lens, ranging from Chinese nuclear modernization and space technology advancements to Western responses to the problems of global economic recession and countering terrorism. In the last decade, scholarly work has pointed to the significance of exploring conventional and non-conventional assumptions about WMD proliferation, norms and taboos, security dilemma dynamics, and the structural determinants of power in the contemporary world. Thus, culturally interpretive models are gaining increased attention in academia and policymaking circles, and all signs point to further development of this worthwhile endeavour.

Comparative analysis represents one of the more fertile areas for advancement of cultural understandings in policymaking and academic research. Studies of strategic culture often apply the theory to a single case or make general comparisons with other like-minded countries. This tradition has produced rich and compelling works, to be sure, such as Adefuye's fascinating study of the culture and foreign policy of Nigeria (1992) or Marcin Zaborowski's study of the evolution of Polish strategic culture (2004). Yet more rigorous cross-national comparison can promote cumulative knowledge in the field. Academics, strategists, and defence planners should more openly recognize variation in instruments and incentive structures associated with deterrence of specific threats, while at the same time searching for identifiable patterns among nations. As one senior State Department official, Kerry Kartchner, argued, '[s]trategic culture offers the promise of providing insight into motivations and intentions that are not readily explained by other frameworks, and that may help make sense of forces we might otherwise overlook, misunderstand, or misinterpret' (2009: 56). In this context, there appears to be an important convergence of interest in deterrence and strategic cultural studies around the theme of contextualizing strategic choice and identifying scope conditions for more reflective models of deterrence and dissuasion for the twenty-first century.

Finally, culturalists remind us of important caveats in these pursuits, including that, in seeking to identify causal relations, there is a risk of oversimplifying the social world and, consequently, categories from one case may be applied inappropriately to others. An inadequate knowledge of a given strategic culture may lead to misinterpretation of attributes such as pride, honour, duty, and also security and stability. Even long-time proponents of cultural interpretations warn of the potential pitfalls that accompany an over-reliance by policymakers on the insights that this area of knowledge can give.

 ## Questions

1. What are the different definitions of culture and what implications do these differences have for the study of security policy?

2. What are some specific examples of strategic cultures (or historical narratives) in countries around the world?

3. What are the sources of these strategic cultures? In your opinion, which are the most important and why?

4. What should be the historical starting point for research on strategic culture?

5. What conditions might cause strategic cultural change?

6. Identify the primary themes that define a country's strategic culture. Can you imagine scenarios in which these themes might come into conflict with one another?

7. Can a strategic cultural framework be applied to a non-state or multi-state actor?

8. What are the implications of globalization for our understanding of strategic culture?

9. Why is it important to study the linkages between strategic culture and WMD proliferation?

10. What are the pitfalls of an over-reliance on strategic culture from a policymaking perspective?

 ## Further Reading

John Glenn, Darryl A. Howlett, Stuart Poore (eds), *Neorealism Versus Strategic Culture* **(Aldershot, UK: Ashgate, 2004).**
A recent classic, this book addresses head-on the theoretical debate over the explanatory power of cultural and ideational models versus the more parsimonious neorealism.

A. Hyde-Price, 'European Security, Strategic Culture, and the Use of Force', *European Security,* **13/1 (2004), 323–43.**
This article summarizes the important debate in Europe about the development of a common security and defence identity.

J. L. Johnson, K. M. Kartchner, and J. A. Larsen (eds), *Strategic Culture and Weapons of Mass Destruction: Culturally Based Insights into Comparative National Security Policymaking* **(London: Palgrave Macmillan, 2009).**
This excellent volume presents theoretical foundations for the study of strategic culture and a number of rich comparative case studies.

Edward Lock, 'Refining Strategic Culture: Return of the Second Generation', *Review of International Studies,* **36/1 (2010), 685–708.**
An interesting survey of the evolution of strategic culture scholarship, with particular emphasis on insights that were 'missed' from second-generation works.

Christoph O. Meyer, *The Quest for a European Strategic Culture: Changing Norms on Security and Defence in the European Union* **(London: Palgrave-Macmillan, 2006).**
This book provides a rich and engaging exploration of debates about strategic culture and security norms in Europe.

R. W. Wilson, 'The Many Voices of Political Culture: Assessing Different Approaches', *World Politics,* **52/2 (January 2000), 246–73.**
This is an engaging thoughtful piece that encourages reflection on the role of culture in politics.

 ## Web Links

The Florida International University-US Southern Command Comparative Strategic Cultures Project **http://strategicculture.fiu.edu/Studies.aspx** was produced in 2010. It yielded fascinating details regarding similarities and differences in Latin American strategic cultures. The study adopts a framework to examine fascinating historical traditions, keepers of culture, and the importance of military and organizational cultures across the region.

Strategic Insights **http://www.ccc.nps.navy.mil/si/2005/Oct/khan2Oct05.asp** The October 2005 special issue of the online journal, *Strategic Insights,* examines the theme of comparative strategic culture. The journal is sponsored by the Center for Contemporary Conflict at the Naval Postgraduate School in Monterey, California.

Japanese Ministry of Foreign Affairs **http://www.mofa.go.jp/** Here you can learn more about Japan's foreign and security policy posture as a reflection of its historical experiences.

The Stockholm International Peace Research Institute (SIPRI) **http://www.sipri.org/** monitors trends in military expenditures and policies throughout the world.

European Union **http://europa.eu/pol/cfsp/index_en.htm** is the main website of the EU, which
   includes valuable archival materials as well as descriptions of contemporary EU foreign and
   security policy institutions and initiatives.

Washington Institute for Near East Policy **http://www.washingtoninstitute.org/templateC04.php?**
   CID=280 This website features a compelling work linking strategic culture and contemporary
   deterrence challenges, entitled *Deterring the Ayatollahs: Complications in Applying Cold War*
   Strategies to Iran (edited by Patrick Clawson and Michael Eisenstadt, July 2007).

5

Law, Politics, and the Use of Force

JUSTIN MORRIS

 Chapter Contents

Introduction: The Efficacy of International Law	97
Why States Obey the Law	98
International Law and the Use of Force	102
Jus ad Bellum	105
Jus in Bello	109
Conclusion	112

 Reader's Guide

This chapter discusses the role of international law in international politics, focusing specifically upon the efficacy of legal constraint of the use of force by states. It is not intended that the chapter will provide a detailed examination of the substantive legal provisions relating to the use of force, though the basic proscriptions will be outlined and commented upon. Rather, the intention is to focus upon the manner in which legal regulation influences the behaviour of states and in particular the political and strategic decisions that they take. It will be argued that international law exerts a significant, though by no means always decisive, influence on the behaviour of states, and that this is the case even when states are dealing with issues which are perceived to be of great national interest and where the use of force is at issue.

Introduction: The Efficacy of International Law

There is a commonly held view that international law has little effect upon the behaviour of states. According to this view international law is simply a tool in the diplomatic kitbag that can be utilized by states to justify their politically motivated actions. Ken Matthews captures this sentiment:

> The common view seems to be that international law is honoured more in its breach than in its observance and that since it seems to be broken so much it can hardly be said to exist at all. Moreover . . . there is little evidence that international law restrains states from pursuing their interests in the international system.
> **Matthews (1996: 26)**

This assessment of international law is reflected in the dominant approach to international politics known as Realism. Realists portray the world as being dominated by states that act only in pursuit of their national interests. These states interact in a world that is anarchic, in the sense that sovereign states recognize no higher authority. In such a world, interaction is regulated through the exercise of power (and ultimately through the utilization of military power). For realists there is little scope for effective international legal regulation.

This view of the world and international law's role within it is challenged by scholars such as Louis Henkin. Henkin observed that 'it is probably the case that almost all nations observe almost all principles of international law and almost all of their obligations almost all of the time' (1968: 47). So why does the common perception of international law not reflect this? The answer lies in what one might call a 'perception–reality gap' (see Box 5.1).

The Perception–Reality Gap

The perception–reality gap operates at a number of levels. The low regard in which international law is commonly held is partially a consequence of inappropriate parallels drawn between domestic and international law, often leading to the unwarranted conclusion that international law lacks the status of true 'law'. Even among those immersed in international law such doubts sometimes appear: as Sir Hersch Lauterpacht famously commented 'international law is the vanishing point of law' (1952: 381). The common

---

BOX 5.1 Symptoms of the Perception–Reality Gap

Perception	Reality
International law is regularly flouted	International law is usually obeyed
Military conflict is the norm	Military conflict is the exception
International law regulates the use of force	International law regulates almost all aspects of inter-state activity
Law is prohibitive	Law is facilitative

assumption is that at the international level the norm in response to legal edicts is breach, whereas domestically the norm is compliance. In reality the norm in both cases is compliance, though this may be less so at the international level than at the domestic.

The common failure to recognize this is the consequence of another misleading idea, namely that to operate effectively it is essential that a system of law possesses the 'legal trinity' of a legislature, an effective and centralized police force, and a judiciary. Despite the existence of institutions such as the United Nations (UN) Security Council and General Assembly, the International Court of Justice and the International Criminal Court, at the international level, this trinity is all but absent and the conclusion commonly drawn from this is that international law is unable to influence the behaviour of states effectively. The argument is misleading because it is predicated on the notion that domestic law is synonymous with criminal law, resulting in a misguided preoccupation with issues of apprehension and enforcement, and hence the legal trinity. As the late Hilaire McCoubrey noted, 'Enforcement—specifically processes of criminal enforcement—tends to be emphasised in external observation of the operation of law and legal systems . . . but it can be argued that this is a seriously misplaced emphasis' (1998: 271).

It is, of course, true that domestic criminal law is obligatory, policed by the state, and enforced through the imposition of judicially passed sanctions—it possesses the legal trinity. And yet it is also true that this does not result in the effective control of *all* members of society and, conversely, other forms of legal regulation function effectively without such characteristics. Contract law, for example, impinges only upon the lives of those who choose to enter into contracts, its enforcement is dependent upon the parties resorting to self-help, and in many systems it does not provide a punitive response to breaches. Despite these 'deficiencies' contract law effectively regulates an important aspect of domestic behaviour and in a similar vein the fact that international law does not conform to the familiar model of criminal law does not necessarily deprive it of its efficacy.

Another reason for the perception–reality gap is the manner in which international politics is portrayed, be it in academic writings or journalistic comment. Academic writing on international relations tends to concentrate on conflict rather than cooperation. This focus has two main implications: first, that international law is often broken, and second, that its main function is to regulate the use of force. Neither are true; inter-state military conflict is the exception, and—the focus of this chapter notwithstanding—for the most part international law provides for orderly and predictable intercourse between states at a mundane, 'everyday' level that has nothing to do with military conflict. The media's coverage of world events shares academia's preoccupation with conflict, and while in the commercial world of journalism the need to generate attention-grabbing headlines and stories is readily understandable, the size of the audience makes its impact all the more deleterious.

Why States Obey the Law

The observation that states generally obey the law should come as no great surprise. International law, and indeed law more generally, is designed not to prohibit those actions which states (or individuals in the domestic setting) would normally choose to undertake, but rather to codify accepted modes of behaviour; good law is facilitative, not prohibitive.

Law reflects and strengthens social order and values, it does not seek to impose them. Were this not the case it would be both ineffective and short-lived. The law should not be viewed as an end in itself, but rather as a means to an end. It is a mechanism through which societies seek to achieve political objectives, though once these objectives have become enshrined in law, the law in turn serves to define modes of acceptable political activity (Reus-Smit 2004).

This observation raises a further difficult question: *which* social values and objectives are to be legally codified? For realists, it will always be those that secure and perpetuate the privileged position of the satisfied powers, but this is an oversimplification of the complexities involved in the development of normative frameworks (Morris 2005). Not even the most powerful are free to dictate an order purely on their terms, but rather must establish one premised upon the codification of behavioural norms in which a sufficiently large proportion of states believe themselves to have an interest. As Henkin observes, 'even the rich and the mighty . . . cannot commonly obtain what they want by force and dictation and must be prepared to pay the price of reciprocal or compensating obligation' (1968: 31). The exact nature of what such a compromise requires is likely to be a source of perpetual debate, but the basic point remains; for the international order to be stable, a sufficiently high proportion of states must perceive it to be just and conducive to their own interests (see Box 5.2).

Coercion, Self-Interest, and Legitimacy

The suggestion that states are more likely to obey the law because they deem it to be in their interests is not to reaffirm the realist position that law is simply a diplomatic tool to be employed to justify politically motivated actions. Ian Hurd's work provides a particularly lucid explanation of this point. Hurd (1999) explains how states are induced to accept rules through coercion, calculations of self-interest, and/or legitimization. Coercion involves an asymmetric power relationship in which one actor is, through the exercise of power, forced to comply with a rule. Where compliance results from calculations of self-interest, it is self-restraint motivated by the likelihood of a beneficial outcome that induces compliance. In both cases, compliance results from prudential calculation. In neither are the content of the rule or its associated institution(s) valued or relevant. What distinguishes the two scenarios is that in cases of coercion, states obey the law to avoid punishment but find themselves, in contrast to cases of self-interest, ultimately disadvantaged by doing so.

Systems that depend on coercion in order to ensure compliance are difficult to sustain because forcibly policing them is so resource-intensive. Systems that depend on self-interest

---

BOX 5.2 Why do States Obey International Law?

- Coercion: involves an asymmetric power relationship in which one actor is, through exercise of power, forced to comply with a rule.

- Self-interest: involves an ad hoc calculation of whether compliance with a rule will result in a beneficial or detrimental outcome.

- Legitimacy: compliance results from the belief that a rule is of value. Rule compliance is an integral part of an actor's identity.

to ensure observance are less costly, but they tend to be unpredictable and unstable because of their reliance on ad hoc cost–benefit calculations. For these reasons it can be concluded that legal systems that depend primarily on coercion and/or self-interest for their observance are likely to be ineffective and relatively short-lived. Sustainable and effective legal regulation depends, therefore, on a widespread shared perception of legitimacy. In such cases, compliance is motivated neither by fear of punitive sanction nor by self-interest (as we have defined) but rather by the belief that the law is, in some sense, of intrinsic value. In such circumstances its observance and general standing form a constituent element of states' interests and identities. Interest is defined in relation to the law itself rather than by consideration of the beneficial or detrimental consequences of compliance. While states are 'interested' in the sense that they pursue goals, they do so within behavioural parameters that are internally driven and hence non-compliance is the exception to the rule.

Whether in any particular case it is fear of coercion, calculations of self-interest, or perceptions of legitimacy that leads to observance of the law is likely to be unclear and any claims on the matter non-falsifiable. In keeping with the generally low esteem in which international law is held there tends to be an assumption that prudential calculations are the primary motivating factor. However, as Hurd notes:

> [It] is unreasonable to use the difficulty of proving any one motivation to justify the retreat to the default position that privileges another, without requiring similar proof . . . We have no better reason to assume coercion [or self-interest] than to assume legitimacy.
> **Hurd (1999: 392)**

In fact, given its nature, in the case of international law coercion is unlikely to be the most significant motivation. Considerations of self-interest and legitimacy provide more plausible explanations, though determining the relative importance of these motivational factors is a complex process. Consider, for example, the reputational benefits that states derive from observance of legal obligations. States seek to avoid the stigma of being branded a 'law-breaker'—or in current parlance a 'rogue state'. They expect that having a trustworthy reputation will be advantageous because others will reciprocate in future dealings with them, not simply with regard to the specific rule or agreement in question, but with regard to legal commitments more generally. This could, therefore, be said to be a prudential calculation, i.e. observation is motivated by self-interest. Against this, however, there is ample evidence that policy leaders, and particularly those who operate within systems long immersed in liberal–democratic traditions, do not want to be branded law-breakers because they attach significant value to the notion of the rule of law. They consider rule observance to be of value in itself.

A second reason for abiding by the law is the perception that it is of substantive value, in other words the modes of behaviour enshrined within particular rules warrant respect. Legal rules are a means by which societies pursue collective goals. The greater the extent to which states share these aspirations, and that a specific rule assists in their attainment, the more likely it is that the rule will be accepted and obeyed by states (Franck 1990). A third reason why state officials observe international legal obligations is that they perceive international law to be of functional value. While the importance of a particular law may be questioned, leaders recognize the contribution that legal regulation as a whole makes to international society. Since the authority of the law will be undermined if states pick and choose the rules by which they abide, all rules must be followed. In both these cases prudential and legitimacy concerns again come into play. Consider, for example, rules pertaining to non-use of force, territorial integrity, and the inviolability of borders. These clearly serve to protect states at an individual level and so it can be argued that states obey them out of self-interest. However, states have good reason to value order as a social good in and of itself and since the collapse of colonialism there is a general and growing acceptance that states have the right to political independence and to determine their own futures free from external interference.

A final factor that gives rise to the general acceptance of legal regulation and conformity to the law is inertia: states become habituated into formulating and adopting policies that accord with legal rules. This may be because under monist constitutional arrangements international legal obligations become incorporated into the body of domestic law (Brownlie 1990: 32). Where this occurs, government policies that violate international legal obligations may give rise to action in the domestic courts. There is, however, a less tangible way in which states become habituated into following the law: individuals who comprise governing elites and bureaucracies become socialized into behaving in certain prescribed ways. Moreover, where democratically elected policymakers are subject to public, media, and legislative scrutiny, policies that violate legal obligations may be perceived as electorally non-viable.

Understanding Breaches of the Law

Although states generally act in accordance with the law, they do not of course *always* obey it. What do breaches of international law tell us about its role and status in international politics? While perhaps counterintuitive, law-breaking often serves to demonstrate the strength of the law, at least insofar as it remains the exception (see Box 5.3). Because states normally obey the law, any breach is likely to occur against a background of general conformity to both the body of international law in general and to the specific rule in question. Where the breaking of a rule attracts widespread international censure, this demonstrates the efficacy, rather than inefficacy, of the rule. Iraq's 1990 invasion of Kuwait was such a clear breach of international law and was so overwhelmingly criticized that its effect was to bolster, rather than undermine, the legal prohibition of the use of force in international relations. In less clear-cut cases where there exists legal ambiguity, 'breach' may

---

BOX 5.3 Understanding Breaches of the Law

- The fact that a state breaches a rule of international law does not in itself demonstrate the inefficacy of the rule or of international law more generally.
- Breaches of the law invariably occur against a background of general conformity to both the specific rule and the law in general.
- Widespread censure following a breach reinforces the rule.
- Breach is invariably accompanied by an explanation based on recourse to legal argument.

> **Key points**
>
> - States are motivated to obey the law by a complex combination of factors (fear of coercion, self-interest, and perceptions of legitimacy).
> - Breaches of the law often serve to demonstrate its strength and not its weakness.
> - Where states break the law they very rarely seek to repudiate the validity of international law completely and invariably attempt to justify their actions in terms of the law.

result from a genuine disagreement over the legality of an act and may, therefore, in fact embody some element of conformity. The general prohibition of the use of force, for instance, is subject to numerous alternative interpretations regarding the extent of the prohibition and the permissibility of exceptions to it (e.g. pre-emptive strike and humanitarian intervention). Finally in this regard it should be noted that violations of the law are invariably accompanied by an assertion that, while the rule in question is perceived by the offending state to be ordinarily valid and applicable, exceptional circumstances or the existence of a competing principle necessitate breach. Particularly in the latter case, a degree of caution is necessary; history is replete with claims of this sort which are clearly disingenuous, but it is clear that, from invulnerable superpowers to the most delinquent of rogues, when states opt to break the law they seek to justify their actions in terms of the law. Hollow, cynical, and hypocritical these invocations of the law may be, but the very fact that they are made is instructive.

International Law and the Use of Force

The two broad functions of the laws of armed conflict are performed respectively by the *jus ad bellum* and the *jus in bello*. The *jus ad bellum* (literally the law towards war) governs and seeks to avert or limit resort to armed force in the conduct of international relations. The *jus in bello* (literally the law in war) governs and seeks to moderate the actual conduct of hostilities. It should be made clear from the outset that these sectors are distinct in both purpose and implication. The applicability of the *jus in bello* is not affected by the legitimacy or otherwise of the initial resort to armed force by either of the belligerents; if it were otherwise, the door would be opened to a return to the worst excesses not of pre-modern 'just war' concepts as such, but to its systematic historic abuses. If, despite the legal restraints of the *jus ad bellum*, armed conflict breaks out, the *jus in bello* becomes operative and equally applicable irrespective of which party initially transgressed the law. These are pragmatic objectives rooted in the practical experience of warfare. Yet the idea of legal constraint upon the waging of war, though ancient in origin, seems profoundly paradoxical. Two distinct lines of argument underpin this apparent paradox, each corresponding to the two areas into which the laws of armed conflict are divided.

The *jus ad bellum* seeks to control the circumstances in which states use force in their inter-national relations. When the logic of 'power politics' appears at its most intense, however, factors mitigating in favour of legal observance are likely to be most compromised. To quote more fully Sir Hersch Lauterpacht: 'If international law is . . . the vanishing point of law, the law of war is even more conspicuously the vanishing point of international law' (1952: 381).

BOX 5.4 The Laws of Armed Conflict

Jus ad bellum (the law towards war)

Governs and seeks to limit resort to armed force in the conduct of international relations.

Major source: Articles 2(4) and Chapter VII of the UN Charter

Jus in bello (the law in war)

Governs and seeks to moderate the actual conduct of hostilities.

Major source: the four Geneva Conventions of 1949 and the Hague Conventions of 1899 and 1907

That states do not consider the use of force as a viable or acceptable part of day-to-day international relations is clear. Yet it is equally apparent that it is considered as a policy of last resort. In such circumstances the normal rules of international intercourse are most strained. As the German Chancellor Theobald von Bethmann-Hollweg stated in his infamous Reichstag speech at the outset of the First World War:

> We are now in a state of necessity, and necessity knows no law . . . He who is menaced as we are, and is fighting for his highest possession, can only consider how he is to hack his way through.
> **Wilson (1928: 305)**

The German Chancellor's statement is of interest, however, not only because of the relationship which it suggests between necessity and law, but also because it indicates that the decision to which the Chancellor was referring (namely to invade two neutral states) was taken not in *disregard* of the law, but rather in *conscious* breach of it. The lawfulness of the action being contemplated was clearly a pertinent issue in the decision-making process.

This is not to suggest that legal questions are always at the forefront of policy-makers' minds when they contemplate the use of force. The uppermost questions will be ones relating to whether policy objectives can be achieved through the use of force at a reasonable cost and this, in turn, will depend on the perceived importance of the objective in question. In a fight for ultimate survival almost any cost may appear reasonable, whereas in one fought for political aggrandizement or to secure the welfare of non-nationals, the threshold of acceptability may be much lower. We may conceive of the notion of 'cost' in several ways. There are the direct costs of conflict, of lives and assets, both military and civilian, lost in the fray. Given the destructive power of modern weaponry these may be almost without limit; in such situations legal niceties may seem at best a tangential consideration. There are political costs: what will be the response, both domestically and internationally, to a policy involving the use of force? Much may here depend upon the outcome of the conflict, but even victory cannot guarantee acclaim. If the action is perceived to be in violation of the accepted norms of international behaviour enshrined within international law, even political allies may disapprove. Despite the improbability of effective direct sanction, legal considerations are paramount here, for international law provides the medium of political exchange on the basis of which states will formulate, articulate, and justify their responses.

Normative costs also must be considered. What will be the likely long-term impact of a breach of the cardinal rule prohibiting the use of force upon international order? Repeated violations can only undermine an order in which both the powerful and the weak have a vested interest. For the former, the incentive in preserving the existing order and its rules is readily apparent, though the rules themselves may militate against great powers adopting policies that are blatantly self-interested. For the weaker members of international society the legal framework's prohibition of the use of force is also beneficial. Many states are militarily incapable of defending themselves, and their survival is therefore dependent upon the general observance of these rules. As Robert Jackson observes: 'Ramshackle states today are not open invitations for unsolicited external intervention . . . They cannot be deprived of sovereignty as a result of war, conquest, partition, or colonialism such as frequently happened in the past' (1993: 23–4). This may have as much to do with the utility of territorial possession in contemporary international politics as with more enlightened post-1945 political outlooks, but nevertheless, for a significant number of the world's states, sovereign independence is primarily legally enshrined rather than militarily ensured.

According to this argument international law plays a crucial role in preserving international order. Conflicts do, however, still occur. What role can international law play *once hostilities have commenced*? War, as an ultimate collapse of 'normal' international relations, appears to be a situation in which the most ruthless use of force must prevail and in which the acceptance of legal constraint can serve only as a potentially fatal self-inflicted impediment to effective action. If it was indeed the purpose of legal norms to obstruct and diminish the combat efficacy of fighting forces, such strictures would be fully justified and norms so conceived could not long endure. That, however, is neither their purpose nor their effect. The real foundation of legal constraint upon warfare can be found clearly stated in a much misrepresented passage in Carl von Clausewitz's classic work *On War*. The great Prussian strategist wrote:

> He who uses force unsparingly, without reference to the bloodshed involved, must obtain a superiority if his adversary uses less vigour in its application . . . From the social condition both of States in themselves and in their relations to each other . . . War arises, and by it War is . . . controlled and modified. But these things do not belong to War itself, they are only given conditions; and to introduce into the philosophy of War itself a principle of moderation would be an absurdity.
> **Clausewitz (1982: 102)**

If war is analysed as a phenomenon in isolation, a logic of illimitable force might indeed seem to be suggested. However, as Clausewitz indicates, wars and armed conflicts do not arise in isolation, but occur in the real context of international relations, which imports expectations that not only condition reactions to armed conflict but themselves have real political and military effect.

In the first place, needless barbarity renders both the conduct and the ultimate resolution of conflict more difficult than it otherwise might be. As Colonel Klaus Kuhn commented, 'the quickest way of achieving and maintaining a lasting peace is to conduct hostilities humanely . . . It is evident that humanitarian considerations cannot be dissociated from the strategic concept of military leaders' (1987: 1).

The proscription of unnecessary barbarity is counselled not only by ethical and humanitarian considerations but also by reference to the response of other states to a belligerent power and the likelihood that conflict will be prolonged when fear of probable mistreatment renders a cornered enemy desperate. The idea is not new: it was asserted in the fifth century BC by the Chinese philosopher Sun Tzu in advising, 'Do not press a desperate foe too hard'. There is ample historical evidence to support the contention. In 1945 the forces of the Third Reich sought to resist the advancing Soviet army, whose fury was at least in part occasioned by prior German conduct, long after it was clear that all hope of success was gone and even as vast numbers hastened to surrender to the Allies in the west. All wars must eventually end, if only through the economic exhaustion of the belligerents. Peaceful relations must be resumed. This process is, *ex hypothesi*, never easy and the more brutal the conflict the more difficult post-war reconstruction will be.

A second criticism levelled at the *jus in bello* is that, to the extent that it humanizes war, it also encourages it. This argument, however, has a major flaw: the inherent cruelty of war does not prevent its occurrence. If the argument were correct, it is difficult to imagine how war could have been contemplated after the carnage of Verdun, the Somme, and Passchendaele. That war continues to occur is a reflection of the fact that its instigators rarely have to fight or otherwise become its victims. To deny humanitarian mitigation to those who do find themselves engaged in combat would be the cruellest of logics.

There are powerful ethical and practical arguments for norms of constraint in armed conflict. However, norms governing the conduct of war, in distinction from those governing resort to armed force, are by their nature no more than mitigatory in effect. If it were to be pretended that either ethics or law could render war humane, the 'absurdity' to which Clausewitz referred would rapidly become all too evident.

Key points

- Even in the most extreme of circumstances, such as those involving contemplation of the use of force, legal factors continue to influence decision-makers.
- War is a social phenomenon and hence the notion of legal regulation of warfare remains pertinent.
- Norms governing the conduct of war are no more than mitigatory in effect.

Jus ad Bellum

The *jus ad bellum* is now founded primarily upon Article 2(3)(4) and Chapter VII (Articles 39–51) of the UN Charter. Article 2(3)(4) of the UN Charter provides that:

3. All Members shall settle their international disputes by peaceful means in such a manner that international peace and security, and justice, are not endangered.

4. All Members shall refrain in their international relations from the threat or use of force against the territorial integrity or political independence of any State, or in any other manner inconsistent with the Purposes of the UN.

The basic proscription set out by Article 2(4) is recognized as having the character of *jus cogens* and as such is, under Article 53 of the Vienna Convention on the Law of Treaties 1969: 'a peremptory norm of general international law . . . accepted and recognised by the international community of States as a whole as a norm from which no derogation is permitted'.

The Article 2(4) prohibition is qualified by two essential exceptions: (1) the inherent right of individual and collective self-defence in the face of armed attack, preserved by Article 51; and (2) action for the maintenance or restoration of international peace and security authorized by the UN Security Council under Article 42.

Article 51 of the UN Charter states:

> Nothing in the present Charter shall impair the inherent right of individual or collective self-defence if an armed attack occurs against a Member of the United Nations, until the Security Council has taken the measures necessary to maintain international peace and security.
> **United Nations (1945)**

Taken in conjunction with the wording of Article 2(4), Article 51 raises a number of issues. In the case of Article 2(4) what, for example, constitutes 'the threat or use of force' and is such a threat or use which is not 'against the territorial integrity or political independence' of a state permissible? What, under the terms of Article 51, constitutes the 'inherent right of individual or collective self-defence' and at what point can the Security Council be deemed to have 'taken the measures necessary to maintain international peace and security'?

Such questions are central to debates regarding the legality of practices such as anticipatory self-defence, military intervention to protect nationals abroad, and humanitarian intervention. The terrorist attacks of 11 September 2001 and the subsequent pursuit of the so-called 'war on terror' brought such matters into even sharper focus (Gray 2008). Those who argued in favour of a relaxation of the rules prohibiting the use of force maintained that the presence of global terrorist networks, which reject all aspects of international regulation, combined with their potential use of nuclear, chemical, and biological weapons, necessitated a reinterpretation of the law so that states can legally undertake preventive military action against such networks and the states which harbour or otherwise assist them. This argument goes well beyond that traditionally put by states such as Israel that Articles 2(4) and 51 of the UN Charter must be understood to allow for acts of anticipatory self-defence. This latter argument is premised upon the idea that the 'inherent right' of self-defence includes the pre-Charter right to carry out a pre-emptive strike provided it is proportionate and undertaken only against a threat that is imminent and not preventable by peaceful means (Arend and Beck 1993: 71–9). Reformulated on account of the 'war on terror', some argued for the right to make preventive strikes, discarding the requirement that the threat of attack posed must be imminent. Security strategies issued by both the United States (United States White House 2002: 15) and the European Union (2003: 7) alluded to such a right and it was a key issue in the debates over the legality of the 2003 Iraq War. The fact that member states of the EU were, despite their 2003 declaration, bitterly divided over the conflict is evidence of how controversial the issue of self-defence had become.

Whatever the legal, moral, political, and strategic merits of the forgoing argument, its broader implications for the basic prohibition of the use of force should not be lost sight of

(Morris and Wheeler 2007). In an international environment consisting of sovereign states that recognize no higher authority, order is already vulnerable and the destructive capacity of modern warfare only heightens the need to limit the use of force. That states will, when they see no other means by which to achieve vital national goals, resort to force is an inevitable condition of international politics, but to loosen the bonds of legal control when such strictures clearly serve to limit conflict would run counter to the ultimate goals of international society. State practice, in its general renunciation of those that do resort to force, provides support for this position; exceptions to the prohibition of the use of force, it may be concluded, should be interpreted in an extremely restrictive manner.

One more issue regarding the *jus ad bellum* requires consideration, namely the relationship between the prohibition of the use of force enshrined in Article 2(4) and the collective security provisions of the United Nations (UN) Charter. The drafters of the UN Charter envisaged not only the establishment of a legal structure that would prohibit the use of force (other than in the case of self-defence) but also the creation of a collective security mechanism that would operate to ensure the security of states. In accordance with Article 39 of the Charter:

> The Security Council shall determine the existence of any threat to the peace, breach of the peace, or act of aggression and shall make recommendations, or decide what measures shall be taken in accordance with Articles 41 and 42, to maintain or restore international peace and security.
> **United Nations (1945)**

Where necessary, the Security Council may impose non-military (primarily economic) sanctions under Article 41 or military measures under Article 42. These articles are not mandatorily sequential. It is entirely lawful in appropriate cases to proceed straight from Article 39 to Article 42, as is made clear by the provision of Article 42 that it may be applied if the Council considers that non-military sanctions 'would prove inadequate'. Moreover, the usual rationale for arguing that non-military sanctions must be exhausted prior to the employment of military ones, namely the assumption that economic measures are more humane, is increasingly questionable given that economic sanctions fall disproportionately on innocent populations rather than culpable leaderships. As technology allows ever more precise military targeting, economic sanctions may come to be seen as the indiscriminate option, especially when leaders of target states are less interested in the welfare of their citizens than in the political capital which can be generated by images of suffering appearing in the world's media. The prospect of increasingly 'clean' military conflicts with minimal 'collateral damage' that modern technology appears to offer is to be welcomed, but to the extent that 'acceptable'—and ultimately legal—war comes to be equated with 'clean' war, it has very significant political implications. 'Smart' weaponry is currently the preserve of the powerful few and is likely to remain so for many years. If the use of force becomes the exclusive legal preserve of these states then the implications for the *jus ad bellum* are considerable.

The Chapter VII mechanism gives rise to a number of grey areas, not least of which is what constitutes a 'threat to the peace, breach of the peace, or act of aggression'? The Charter provides no guidance as to what constitutes such situations and it is clear from the *travaux préparatoires* that those responsible for the Charter intended that the Security Council should have a wide discretion in reaching such a determination (Goodrich and Hambro 1949: 262–72). At the time of its drafting, proposals to include a definition of aggression were rejected because states were reluctant to shackle the Council's activities. The Council was intended to act as a political rather than a judicial body and legalistic definitions were, therefore, deemed inappropriate. The Council was limited to dealing with matters that were *international*, i.e. inter-state, but this relatively restrictive interpretation has, through practice, been eroded over time. As the twentieth century drew to a close UN practice increasingly suggested that some internal use of force might fall within the Council's legitimate remit, at least to the extent that it threatens regional stability (White 1997: 45).

In addition to the—now much-depleted—restriction that the Security Council can only act with regard to international uses of force, a further crucial restriction was imposed upon the Chapter VII mechanism; the activities of the Security Council's five permanent members (the 'P5'—China, France, UK, USA, and USSR) would, as a result of the veto power granted to them under Article 27(3), be exempt from UN sanction. The veto was intend to assist in the maintenance of P5 unanimity, but it also insured the P5 states against the prospect of the UN being used as a mechanism through which their actions could be sanctioned (Russell 1958). This was a price to be paid for ensuring crucial great power participation in the UN, but it was also widely welcomed by the organization's broader membership; on balance the prospect of veto-induced stalemate seemed preferable to that of being dragged into an intra-P5 dispute which might ultimately end in large-scale conflict (Claude 1962: 161).

The vulnerability of the UN's security mechanisms to veto-induced paralysis—a condition to which the organization effectively succumbed for the first 45 years of its existence—raises one final question; should Article 2(4) be viewed as being *contingent* upon the effective operation of Chapter VII? The logic of such a proposition is not without merit, but neither the provisions of the Charter nor state practice lend it much support. Despite the absence of an effective collective security mechanism, for almost 60 years no state directly refuted the validity of Article 2(4) or, indeed, its standing as a norm with the status of *jus cogens*. But as the twentieth century closed and the twenty-first began this central facet of the UN system was subjected to two challenges. The first of these was grounded in the earlier discussed arguments in favour of a most expansive right of self-defence. The second came in the assertion that where the Security Council fails to authorize, through the passing of a resolution, action to maintain or restore international peace and security, states may themselves act in order to do so. In claiming that they were acting to enforce legally binding obligations previously imposed by the Security Council in 1991, the US and its allies made this argument the central legal point of their justification for action against Iraq in 2003 (Kritsiotis 2004). This represented a fundamental departure from previous state practice, but the largely critical international response to the initiation of the war suggests that few states were willing to endorse this challenge to the prohibitory norm.

With post-Iraq changes of government in the US and UK, the appetite for taking military action without a UN mandate appears to have dissipated. The US and UK, along with France, members of the Arab League, and other allies were careful to secure Security Council authority before military action aimed at protecting civilians through the establishment of a no-fly zone was undertaken in Libya in March 2011 (Morris and Wheeler 2012). Conversely, failure to gain Security Council backing for enforcement measures against the Syrian government as a consequence of Russian and Chinese vetoes in October 2011 and February 2012 was a major impediment to international action. Within the context of the debate about the legal use of force the import of the Syrian case should not be overstated; neither of the resolutions vetoed involved proposals for military action, with such reticence stemming primarily from prudential geo-strategic calculations rather than legal ones. Nevertheless, in its tone and content, the widespread condemnation of the Sino-Russian position served to reinforce the proposition that the Security Council is the primary source of international legitimacy, a stance all the more noteworthy for the prominence of the US and UK in asserting it.

Key points

- The *jus ad bellum* governs and seeks to limit resort to armed force in the conduct of international relations.
- Recourse to force is prohibited other than in cases of individual or collective self-defence or where action is taken to restore international peace and security as mandated by the UN Security Council.
- Exceptions to the prohibition of the use of force should be interpreted restrictively.
- The prohibition of the use of force is not viewed by most states as being contingent upon the successful operation of the UN collective security mechanism. The 2003 Iraq conflict challenged this, but elicited little support.
- No state has openly repudiated the general prohibition of the use of force.

Jus in Bello

The *jus in bello* has two principle subdivisions, which have conventionally been categorized as 'Geneva' and 'Hague' law in recognition of the principal treaty series upon which each is founded. Modern 'Geneva' law is specifically concerned with the protection of the victims of armed conflict. 'Hague' law is concerned with methods and means of warfare, including controls on weapons type and usage, and on tactics and the general conduct of hostilities. It should be noted that the Geneva–Hague distinction is today artificial; both are premised upon a humanitarian concern for the moderation and mitigation of warfare and for this reason there is a considerable degree of overlap between them. In modern usage the term 'international humanitarian law' (IHL)—historically used to refer specifically to Geneva law—is taken to comprise the whole *jus in bello* in both its Geneva and Hague dimensions.

Both sets of norms rest ultimately upon a fundamental principle of proscription concerning the infliction of militarily 'unnecessary suffering'. This principle was stated expressly in the 1868 Declaration of St Petersburg:

> The only legitimate objective which States should endeavour to accomplish during war is to weaken the military forces of the enemy . . . this objective would be exceeded by the employment of arms which uselessly aggravate the suffering of disabled men . . . [and] the employment of such arms would therefore be contrary to the laws of humanity.
> **McCoubrey (1998: 212)**

The modern foundations of the 'Hague' sector are primarily to be found in the Hague Conventions of 1899 and 1907 and the 1977 Additional Protocol I to the Geneva Conventions, which makes provision for methods and means of warfare and discrimination in

---

BOX 5.5 *Jus in bello*

'Geneva' Law

- Concerned with protection of victims of warfare.
- Based primarily on the four 1949 Geneva Conventions.

'Hague' Law

- Concerned with methods and means of armed conflict.
- Based primarily on the 1899 and 1907 Hague Conventions.

---

bombardment. Modern Geneva law is based on the four 1949 Geneva Conventions, dealing respectively with: (I) wounded and sick on land; (II) wounded, sick and shipwrecked at sea; (III) prisoners of war; and (IV) civilians. On the basis of this treaty and customary provision the basic rules of IHL are well settled, but it must be conceded that all too often its application remains inconsistent and problematic (see Box 5.5).

The causes of this inconsistency are to be found in significant part in our apparently innate ability to inflict horrendous suffering on our fellow human beings, especially those deemed to be enemies or threats, and most particularly during times of great stress and conflict. History is, alas, replete with examples of such behaviour. However, to some—no doubt more limited—extent the failure to observe IHL stems from disputes about its applicability, and in particular the degree to which it is based upon reciprocal obligation. As a starting point it is worth noting that IHL is closely related to the general law of human rights, and this creates a powerful argument that the obligations created by it are essentially unilateral and non-reciprocal in nature (McCoubrey 1998: 187). Such a view is certainly taken by the International Committee of the Red Cross (ICRC), which has commented that a state should not observe IHL simply in the hope that this will be reflected in the treatment by others of its own nationals; it should do so 'out of respect for the human person as such' (Meron 2006: 11). The Nuremberg Tribunals took a decisive stance in favour of this position when they established that, despite their containing specific statements to the contrary, Hague regulations were non-reciprocal in nature. This was so, the Tribunal determined, because though they were new and innovative at the time of their writing, 'by 1939 these rules laid down in the Conventions were recognised by all civilized nations, and were regarded as being declaratory of the laws and customs of war' (ibid.: 10). This principle was further strengthened by the Geneva Conventions, Common Article 1 which provides that 'The High Contracting Parties undertake to respect and ensure respect for the present Convention *in all circumstances*' [emphasis added] (ICRC, 1949).

Given the above, it can be seen that, at least with regard to armed conflicts between states, the applicability of IHL on a non-reciprocal basis has become increasingly embedded. There has also been significant progress toward regulating internal conflict which had, despite its tendency to involve the cruellest acts of violence, traditionally lain outside the ambit of IHL (Moir 2002). Despite these legal developments, intra-state/inter-ethnic conflicts such as those in the former Yugoslavia, Rwanda, Democratic Republic of the Congo, Uganda, and Sudan testify to the horrific barbarity that so often accompanies fighting between irregular combatants who routinely fail to conform to the—perhaps idealized—traditional expectations of regular military forces. The trend in conflict patterns toward a greater incidence of intra-, rather than inter-state conflict does not bode well in this regard, but it must also be acknowledged that regular military forces, including those of the most developed states, are not beyond reproach as accusations regarding US and British armed forces in Iraq testify.

In addition to allegations levelled at US personnel for their behaviour on the battlefield, concerns were also raised over those detained at the infamous US base at Guantanamo Bay. The accusations related, in part, to the conditions in which the detainees were held and the interrogation techniques to which they were subjected, but despite the genuine debate regarding the applicability of IHL to terrorist activity (Sassòli 2004; Barnes 2005), it was America's apparent ambivalence to its international legal obligations more generally that underpinned the furore (Forsythe 2008; Carvin 2008). The Bush Administration's claims that Guantanamo detainees enjoyed neither protection under IHL nor the right of recourse to the US domestic courts suggested that it sought to act outside the law. Both of these arguments were ultimately rejected by the US Supreme Court, but this rectification of the legal position came too late to repair the self-inflicted diplomatic and reputational damage. Such matters were clearly appreciated by the incoming President Obama who, in the first days of his presidency acted to confirm the applicability of IHL to the Guantanamo detainees and to signal the closure of the detention camp. This latter measure proved far more difficult to achieve than was envisaged however, and three years after Obama's assumption of office the camp remained open (Yin 2011). Nevertheless, the declaration and associated attitudinal shift did much to rehabilitate the US in the eyes of many; an indication of the power of perception and the role that legal compliance can play in this.

It will be apparent from the preceding discussion that IHL's applicability in theory and its application in practice are far from being the same, and to the extent that variation exists the victims of conflict suffer all the more. The 'theoretical' position does, however, remain highly significant, since the behaviour of those who violate IHL is increasingly viewed in the light of its legal demands and the ethical principles that underpin them. As such, the political implications of perceived violation are considerable, manifesting themselves in highly practical and strategically important ways. The willingness of others to become or remain allies and so to share the costs arising from conflict is among the most important of these consequences, since even the most powerful benefit from being able to socialize the costs of their actions (Reus-Smit 2007). Nor is this a purely international phenomenon. A growing public awareness resulting from 24-hour real-time TV coverage, advances in global communications, and the campaigning work of non-governmental organizations (NGOs) such as Amnesty International and Human Rights Watch are also important. The high-profile now enjoyed by humanitarian issues can place considerable domestic political pressure on governments and can have profound electoral implications. Indeed, non-state actors, be they NGOs or less formalized grass-roots movements, can play a significant role in shaping the very legal framework against which the behaviour of states comes to be judged, as, for example, the adoption of the Convention on the Prohibition of Anti-Personnel Landmines shows.

Another major advance in IHL that may yet see a closing of the gap between theory and practice was the establishment in 2002 of the International Criminal Court (ICC). The court is competent to prosecute cases of genocide, crimes against humanity, war crimes, and potentially at some future date the crime of aggression. Its jurisdiction extends over nationals of states parties and crimes committed on their territory where such states are either unable or unwilling to prosecute themselves (Schabas 2004). The court is not without its detractors, most notably the United States (Ralph 2007) and it is yet to prove its mettle, but its very existence is a development that few can realistically have even dreamt of only 20 years ago. It is early days and already there are fears that some conflicts may have been prolonged by the prospect that the parties to them, especially the vanquished, may face prosecution once hostilities cease. This has long been the nub of the argument in favour of granting immunity to belligerents and though the establishment of the ICC does not provide a definitive resolution to the debate over whether we should prioritize 'peace' or 'justice' in such situations, it does appear to be a significant step in favour of the latter.

Of course the extent to which IHL (including the ICC) is able to realize the objectives which it enshrines is contingent upon the degree to which belligerents actually eschew proscribed modes of behaviour in practice. As noted earlier, excessive concern with punishment, in this case of war crimes, misses the point that the primary function of IHL is not to punish those who violate its edicts but rather to protect the victims of armed conflict by preventing war crimes in the first place. Indeed, before any question of punishing war crimes or other enforcement action can arise, failure in this primary endeavour must be presupposed. In this sense, issues of enforcement must be viewed as secondary to the imperatives of effective dissemination and training. That in many states the latter is now a foundational element of military training bodes well, though such practice is far from ubiquitous and deficiencies in this regard are often exacerbated through shortcomings in discipline and command and control (Robinson, de Lee, and Carrick 2008).

Key points

- The *jus in bello*, often split into the subdivisions of Geneva and Hague law, and commonly known now as IHL, governs and seeks to moderate the actual conduct of hostilities.
- 'Geneva' law is concerned with the protection of victims of armed conflict. 'Hague' law is concerned with methods and means of warfare.
- Much of Geneva and Hague law has the status of *jus cogens*.
- The primary function of IHL is to protect the victims of armed conflict through preventing war crimes. Such objectives are best pursued primarily through education and training rather than through post-violation prosecution.

 ## Conclusion

The low regard in which international law is customarily held is the consequence of several factors. It is a result of our perception of the world of international politics and the extent to which we tend to see this as an environment characterized by conflict. In such a world, the notion of states forming a society appears inappropriate and it follows that law seems equally out of place. This perception is profoundly misleading. Rather than wringing our hands over the frequency of military conflict in the world we might, without forgetting the devastation and suffering inherent in conflicts when they do arise, marvel at the degree to which an increasing number of states manage to coexist in a cooperative and often mutually beneficial manner. It would be folly to suggest that this is the consequence of some great legalistic enterprise, but equally it would be foolhardy to suggest that international law has no role to play in influencing the manner in which states behave. To borrow a phrase from Robert Keohane, international law 'prescribes behavioural roles, constrains activity, and shapes expectations' (1989: 3).

At times, of course, international law, like all law, is broken. This, however, is the exception rather than the rule. Moreover, in cases where international law is broken one would be hard pressed to find a transgressor who does not at least attempt to provide a legally couched justification for their behaviour, and the more prominent and significant the breach, the greater the efforts become. Nowhere are breaches of international law more significant or prominent than with regard to the laws of armed conflict. Nowhere are the stakes higher or the pressures greater. It is, therefore, all the more noteworthy that even here, for the most part, the law prevails.

 ## Questions

1. Why is international law held in such low regard? Is this a deserved reputation?

2. Does international law really influence the behaviour of states? If so, how, and why?

3. How does the relative power of states affect the ability of international law to influence their behaviour?

4. Can you cite examples involving the use of force in which states have breached international law and not attempted to justify their actions in terms of the law?

5. Are exceptions to the prohibition of the use of force—such as anticipatory self-defence, action to protect nationals abroad, action to punish state-sponsored terrorism, and humanitarian intervention—justifiable?

6. Should the prohibition of the use of force be contingent upon the existence of an effective mechanism by means of which the security of states can be assured?

7. Are limitations upon the means by which war is waged practicable?

8. Should international humanitarian law only be applied on a reciprocal basis?

9. Is the establishment of the International Criminal Court more likely to lead to more just post-conflict settlements or to prolong conflicts?

10. What effect did the 'war on terror' have on international humanitarian law?

 ## Further Reading

In addition to the texts referred to throughout the chapter, the following texts are recommended.

H. Bull, *The Anarchical Society: A Study of Order in World Politics* **(London: Macmillan, 1977).**
This book provides the seminal discussion of the idea that states form an international society.

I. Brownlie, *International Law and the Use of Force by States* **(Oxford: Clarendon Press, 1963).**
This book provides a detailed discussion of key issues in the development of the *jus ad bellum*.

M. Byers (ed.), *The Role of Law in International Politics: Essays in International Relations and International Law* **(Oxford: Oxford University Press, 2000).**
This book comprises a collection of essays that consider the role which international law plays in international politics.

H. Duffy, *The 'War on Terror' and the Framework of International Law* **(Cambridge: Cambridge University Press, 2005).**
This book provides an analysis of international humanitarian law in the context of the 'War on Terror'.

D. Fleck (ed.), *The Handbook of International Humanitarian Law 2nd edn* (Oxford: Oxford University Press, 2008).
This book provides a comprehensive discussion of the *jus in bello*.

W. A. Schabas, *An Introduction to the International Criminal Court* (Cambridge: Cambridge University Press, 2007).
This book provides discussions on the history and operation of the International Criminal Court.

M. Weller, *Iraq and the Use of Force in International Law* (Oxford: Oxford University Press, 2010).
This book analyses legal key questions raised by the 2003 Iraq Conflict.

 ## Web Links

United Nations **http://www.un.org** This site provides a huge array of UN-related resources, including UN resolutions and minutes of meetings.

International Court of Justice **http://www.icj-cij.org/** This site provides details of how the Court is structured, how it works, and details and materials relating to past and present cases.

International Criminal Court **http://www2.icc-cpi.int/Menus/ICC/Home** This site provides details of how the Court is structured, how it works, and details and materials relating to past and present cases.

International Committee of the Red Cross **http://www.icrc.org/eng/index.jsp** This site explains what the ICRC is and provides details of the work it does. It has a particularly good section on 'War and Law'.

Human Rights Watch **http://www.hrw.org/** This site provides details of the work of Human Rights Watch, highlighting specific human rights concerns around the world.

International Campaign to Ban Landmines **http://www.icbl.org/index.php** This site looks at the specific issue of landmines, their use, the movement to have them banned, and the work that continues in addressing matters arising from their use.

Geography and Strategy

DANIEL MORAN

 Chapter Contents

Introduction: The Lay of the Land   116

Land Warfare: The Quest for Victory   117

Maritime Strategy   121

Airpower   124

The Final Frontier: Space War   128

War by Other Means: Cyberspace   129

Conclusion   130

 Reader's Guide

This chapter explores the diverging strategic possibilities that are presented by warfare in different physical environments. It identifies the particular strengths and weaknesses of forces that fight on land and sea and in the air. It also considers the strategic potential of warfare in space, and of new information technologies that may be employed as weapons. In practice modern war is almost always conducted in ways designed to seek synergies between the diverse realms in which force is deployed. To that extent what follows is not a realistic presentation of how modern war is actually conceived and conducted. Nevertheless, for purposes of analysis, and in order to understand what can and cannot be accomplished by the various forms of violence at the disposal of today's belligerents, it can be instructive to consider those forms separately.

Introduction: The Lay of the Land

Strategic theory is concerned with the use of force by political communities in relation to each other. The psychological effects that violence causes do not vary in any predictable way with respect to the means employed: a blow delivered from the sea feels much the same as one from the land, and will inspire the same desire to defend oneself, to strike back, or to give in. Carl von Clausewitz, the Prussian theorist whose work *On War* (1832) is foundational to modern strategic studies, wrote exclusively about war on land. But the distinctive characteristics of war as he conceived it—the overwhelming effects of fear, chance, and uncertainty; the escalatory dynamic that drives adversaries to extreme measures; the superior strength of the defensive; the difficulty of sustaining military action over long periods; the need for constant adaptation to the unexpected—are equally familiar to those who have fought on the land, the sea, or in the air. The contest of wills that is central to every strategic encounter will play itself out in roughly the same fashion, irrespective of the physical environment in which it occurs.

Nevertheless, in practice the conduct of war is overwhelmingly shaped by its geographical setting. It is on this basis that armed forces are characterized. All armies resemble each other more than they do the navies and air forces that fight under the same flags. A modern army also resembles an ancient one more than it does a modern navy, since its most basic problems have not changed from one millennium to the next. The same is true for the other military branches. Before any armed force can come to grips with its opponent, it must first master the immediate challenges of its physical environment. Ships must float. Aircraft must remain suspended in the air. Armies must propel themselves across a landscape rich with obstacles. War*fare*, the *making* of war, is first of all about making the most of one's chances within the constraints imposed by nature. Only after that has been accomplished can the enemy be given the attention he deserves.

Physical geography defines the tactical identities of armed forces. It also shapes their strategic effects. An explosive shell delivered from a warship, an aircraft, or an artillery piece will feel much the same to those on the receiving end. But that does not alter the fact that armies, navies, and air forces possess distinctive strengths and weaknesses when it comes to translating military effort into political results. A country that fights chiefly with an army will be confronted with strategic possibilities different from those available to one that fights mainly on the sea or in the air. The aim of this chapter is to highlight those possibilities: to consider the conduct of war in different physical environments, and to identify the strategic risks and opportunities that each presents.

It must be emphasized that the discussion that follows is a somewhat artificial exercise, a thought experiment rather than a description of reality. This is owed mainly to the invention of the airplane, and secondarily to the mastery of wireless communications. Good armies and navies today never operate without seeking to control the skies over their heads. The major weapons systems of a modern navy are aerial weapons (airplanes, missiles, etc.), tactically indistinguishable from those of an air force. An air force in turn depends on a ground-based infrastructure whose establishment and defence will generally be the work of an army. In addition, forces operating on land, sea, and in the air all communicate constantly with each other, tailoring their operations accordingly. Such synergies are at the heart of 'joint' military operations, in which land, sea, and air forces seek to cooperate to their collective advantage. The superiority of joint operations is now so apparent that it is taken for granted by military planners. Left to their own devices, armies, navies, and air forces each present a limited and one-dimensional set of strategic capabilities. Their individual strengths are offset by equally distinctive weaknesses. Joint warfare is now the norm, or rather the ideal, because it allows military organizations to exploit the strengths and mask the weaknesses of their component parts.

Yet the strengths and weaknesses remain, and they are worth contemplating as a way of understanding the choices that political leaders face when using force as an instrument of policy. The focus in what follows is thus on the distinctive strategic considerations that surround the conduct of war in different physical environments: on land and sea, in the air, in space, and finally in 'cyberspace' a metaphorical realm whose strategic possibilities have attracted sufficient attention to merit independent discussion.

Land Warfare: The Quest for Victory

Land armies are the pre-eminent form of military power everywhere. This is owed to their role in the creation of political communities, whose independent existence depends on their ability to defend themselves against others. Only land armies can secure territorial frontiers, and it is by virtue of their ability to exercise continuous control over territory that sovereign states are most readily distinguished from other political forms. Political entities that are not states can make war. But unless they can field an army they cannot control territory, and in the absence of such control they will never take their place among the sovereign nations of the world. Historically, armies and states have created each other.

The distinctive strategic advantage of armies is their defensive strength. They are the only forces intended to seize and hold, and not merely to destroy, their objectives. That armies seek to destroy each other is also true, as it is for navies and air forces. But death and destruction in war are always a means to an end, and if the end is to gain control of a human population, then only an army will do. Once an army has established such control, the difficulty of dislodging it can be considerable. 'Regime change' is accordingly, and inherently, an army mission, and cannot be contemplated by any state that is not prepared to commit its land forces to the fight on a sufficient scale to dislodge and replace the forces of the enemy.

Such a commitment is now perceived to be an especially weighty one. For a country like the United States, which is able to inflict massive damage and suffering by means of naval and air forces, the decision to employ its army is often more politically perilous than the decision to fight in the first place. Any military operation involving ground forces will have a heightened significance for public opinion in a democratic society, if only because of the additional risk of friendly casualties. Such a step is normally considered only after some form of strategic bombardment has been tried and found wanting. The major American interventions in Korea, Vietnam, and Iraq (in 1990–1991) all began with an initial decision to employ air and naval forces, followed by a separate, independently considered decision to send in the army. No such step-wise approach occurred in the invasion of Iraq in 2003 because in that instance the overthrow and occupation of the enemy state was the objective from the start.

Additional political scrutiny attaches to land warfare because the use of land forces has a kind of finality about it that does not apply to naval and air operations. If the outstanding advantage of armies is their defensive strength, their outstanding disadvantage is that they are cumbrous and difficult to move. Employing them requires enormous determination. One reason to do so is to communicate such determination to the opponent. Once the commitment has been made, however, it is difficult to undo. Land forces engaged with an undefeated adversary cannot disengage without incurring tactical risk, while also presenting a spectacle of failure for the world to see. Ships and airplanes come and go. An army comes and stays. That is its nature and purpose, both tactically and strategically.

The defensive resilience of armies necessarily renders the delivery of a successful attack extremely difficult. War on land is almost always a grinding, wearisome business. The 'art of war' is devoted to figuring out how to make it less so. The goal of all warfare, as the sixteenth-century Austrian field marshal Raimondo de Montecucolli said, is 'victory', an observation that stood out when it was made because it cast aside a variety of other objectives—honour, glory, plunder, prestige—that the aristocratic elites of earlier times rated as highly as the political interests of the state. In strategic terms victory is a political and not merely a military concept. This is why Montecucolli's modern successors tend to add the word 'decisive', meaning victory that goes beyond the accomplishment of tactical goals, and achieves results that alter the political conditions that brought the war about. For an army, victory of this kind cannot usually be gained by pushing the enemy around, or even by pushing him away. It requires that his powers of resistance be broken and disorganized, so that he confronts the possibility that, at some point in the future, he may become defenceless.

In modern times military theorists have identified three general paths to this kind of success. The first, which emerges in the strategic literature of the eighteenth century, is to manoeuvre against the flanks and rear of the opposing army. The fighting elements of land armies represent only a fraction of their manpower. The rest are devoted to maintaining the complex logistical system required to keep the army moving, eating, and fighting. Attacks directed against that system were recognized as having disproportionate disruptive effects, and they remain the most desirable form of offensive military operation. Precisely because the vulnerability of an army's logistics is so widely recognized, however, it usually proves difficult to exploit. Armies take good care to protect their communications if they can. Nor is it easy to engage in bold manoeuvre against the enemy's rear while protecting one's own against similar assault. Modern armies have worked hard to outmanoeuvre each other, and when they have succeeded, as in the German offensives against France in 1870 and 1940, the results have been impressive. But such outcomes are historically rare, because armies of similar size, fighting with similar methods, have little chance of wrong-footing each other so grievously as to win all at once. When such efforts fail, as in the German offensive against France in 1914, the grim realities of attrition swiftly reassert themselves (see Box 6.1).

An obvious solution is to have an army that is not of similar size to your opponent's, but is instead much larger. Modern states possess extensive means of mobilizing their populations for war, either by persuading them to fight or by coercing them to do so. Until the turn of the nineteenth century, governments were reluctant to call upon the mass of their subjects to bear arms, because they could not afford to equip the huge armies that would have resulted,

BOX 6.1 Manoeuvre versus Attrition

Writers on land warfare routinely distinguish between 'manoeuvre warfare' and 'attrition'. The distinction is not hard and fast. All armies try to put themselves in an advantageous position from which to engage their opponents. Conversely, opportunities for manoeuvre may only arise as a result of preparatory, systematic destruction of enemy forces, which is what one normally means by attrition. Nevertheless, the difference between the two approaches bears thinking about.

Attrition emphasizes cumulative destructiveness through the systematic application of firepower. It has often seemed the natural choice for the side with greater material resources, which does not need to do anything fancy to win. Tactical decisions focus on choices among different targets or objectives, which are prioritized according to some doctrinally codified scheme. Because attritional warfare tends to be generic and repetitive, it is also a natural choice for a country that is uncertain who its future adversaries may be, so that it must adopt methods that are thought to work well in general.

The idea of manoeuvre only has meaning in relation to a particular opponent. It seeks to capitalize on specific vulnerabilities—the fact that enemy forces move slowly, for instance, or are poorly supplied with bridging equipment, or have bad morale—in order to achieve disproportionate effects. Most people associate manoeuvre with rapid movement, but it is really a more general concept, which tries to gain exceptional advantage from the control of small amounts of space and time. The provision of local security to isolated villages by small detachments of American forces during the Vietnam War is an example of manoeuvre warfare, because the aim was not to destroy enemy forces, but to thwart the enemy's intentions by controlling small but critical bits of territory—the bits where Vietnamese people actually lived.

Manoeuvre warfare is always intended to achieve a disproportionate effect: to accomplish a great deal with limited means, by exploiting an ostensibly critical vulnerability of which the enemy is not aware, or for which he cannot compensate. Bold and aggressive manoeuvre is often the recourse of the weaker side in war, because it is the weaker side that must make up for its deficiencies by using some highly leveraged method of fighting. Yet because the aim of manoeuvre warfare is not systematic destruction, but the *systemic disruption* of the enemy's capacity to resist, it also has great appeal to a strong country like the United States, whose political goals have lately caused it to try to limit the general destructiveness of its military actions.

and because doing so entailed political risks: people mobilized for war might expect political concessions in return. The fact that a country's inhabitants had just been trained and equipped for fighting also seemed to increase the possibility that they would seize those concessions for themselves. It is not surprising that universal conscription was first attempted by a revolutionary government, that of France in 1793. The resulting army dwarfed those of France's adversaries, and could only be defeated once Europe's other Great Powers began adopting similar methods.

During the nineteenth century major land armies grew dramatically in size. The consequences of this development were amplified by modern weaponry, whose range and lethality exceeded all previous experience. As soldiers pondered this new reality, they recognized that it cut against the possibility that they might somehow outfox their opponents. Forces numbering in the millions could scarcely be manoeuvred in any meaningful sense, and once they got within range of each other no outcome seemed possible except massacre on an epic scale.

If there was a way out, the best observers concluded, it could only be found at the outset of hostilities, when it might be possible to catch the enemy unprepared, with his forces not yet ready for action. The best chance for decisive victory seemed to lie with the side that could strike hardest right at the start. Here was a third path to victory, one whose temptations have survived a considerable record of historical disappointment. A large share of the major wars of the twentieth century have begun with massive attacks designed to achieve such swift and stunning success as to render pre-war calculations of relative strength irrelevant. Examples include the Japanese offensive against Russia in 1904, and against America and Great Britain in 1941; the German offensive of 1914, and the so-called *blitzkrieg* campaigns of 1939–41; the North Korean invasion of South Korea in 1950; the Iraqi offensives against Iran in 1980, and Kuwait in 1990; Israel's attacks against Egypt and Syria in 1967, and those by Egypt and Syria against Israel in 1973. This list could be expanded without difficulty, but the basic impression would not change, which is that on the whole the advantages of attacking first have not proven sufficiently decisive to outweigh more fundamental sources of military strength. Land armies are voracious consumers of men and materiel. In general victory on land has gone to belligerents with sufficient political determination, social resilience, and economic productivity to sustain military effort over the long haul.

Many thoughtful soldiers nevertheless remain convinced that it is their duty to win quickly if they can. Not all, however. Revolutionary insurgency is a form of land warfare that embraces protraction as a source of strategic leverage, by which an opponent may be worn down. Insurgents take advantage of a terrain feature that conventional forces prefer to avoid: the civil population, within which the insurgent conceals himself, and which he holds hostage. Such methods are as timeless as war. Whenever the weak have fought the strong they have relied on ambushes, traps, terrorism, hit-and-run attacks, and so on, in the hope that, just by staying alive and engaged, victory may come to them.

If such unconventional warfare has loomed large in recent years, it is partly because of the decline of conventional land warfare as a feature of the international system. Since the end of the Second World War advanced societies, particularly those possessing nuclear weapons, have avoided fighting each other, so that major wars have only been waged by or against second-rate powers. It is also true that the insurgent's chances have improved owing to better technology, above all in the area of communications. A few radios connecting isolated rebel bands or terrorist cells can make an enormous difference at the tactical level, while the ability to communicate with the civil population via the public media has gone some distance towards evening the odds in a contest whose basic terms are always defined ideologically.

Particularly when considered in isolation from the long-range aerial strike systems that are now required to lubricate the tactical movement of large ground forces, counterinsurgency can be considered the principal and most distinctive mission of contemporary armies. This is a reality that only a minority of today's soldiers are prepared to embrace, however, if for no other reason than because doing so threatens to relegate ground forces to the role of 'exploiting' victory, rather than achieving it. The swift overthrow of an enemy army remains the acme of professional military achievement at the turn of the twenty-first century. Setting this traditional standard aside will require a re-examination of the basic assumptions on which land warfare has been conducted for three hundred years.

Key points

- Armies are distinguished from other military branches by their ability to seize and hold, rather than simply to destroy, their objectives.
- Land warfare in the industrial era has shown a strong tendency toward stalemate and attrition.
- The aim of manoeuvre warfare is to strike the enemy at times and places that achieve disproportionate destructive or disruptive effects.
- Modern wars often begin with massive initial offensives designed to win before the other side is fully mobilized.
- Revolutionary insurgency does not seek to win quickly, but rather by slowly eroding the moral and political resolve of the enemy.

Maritime Strategy

Human populations have always been concentrated near the world's oceans and the navigable rivers that lead to them. This pattern means that most of mankind lives within range of the aircraft and missiles that comprise the bulk of modern naval weapons. Nevertheless, bombarding the shore has historically been the least significant of naval missions. The distinctive strategic contribution of navies depends on their activity on the sea, always keeping in mind that nothing that happens there can matter unless it impacts the thinking and actions of those living on the land.

From ancient times until the sixteenth century the main role of navies was to transport soldiers to an enemy shore. The ability to do this conferred important advantages, above all the freedom to choose the time and place of an attack. Such navies were tactical adjuncts to armies, with no distinctive strategic role. Naval warfare existed, in the sense that when warships met on the sea they tried to fight each other. But such episodes were rare and inconsequential. What mattered were the soldiers that the ships carried. It was their combat that decided the war.

The development of sailing warships capable of traversing the world's oceans altered this ancient picture in ways whose consequences can scarcely be exaggerated. Sailing navies were the instruments by which European overseas empires were created, from which has arisen the highly integrated world system that we know today. The role of navies in this process was two-fold: to transport soldiers, merchants, missionaries, and settlers to the far corners of the world; and to protect or prey upon the expanding network of seaborne trade that resulted.

Maritime strategy as traditionally understood sought leverage from the financial advantages these trading networks afforded. The inelastic agrarian economies of continental states could offer nothing like the wealth generated by long-distance trade, which sailing navies made possible. Sailing navies were instruments of economic warfare, and achieved strategic effects mainly through their impact on international trade. When the American navalist Alfred Thayer Mahan coined the term 'sea power' at the end of the nineteenth century, it was the synergy between naval strength, commerce, and colonial expansion that he had in mind.

From Mahan's perspective, states whose navies could 'command' the sea—that is, employ it for their own purposes while denying its use to others—were destined to dominate those who could not.

By the time Mahan wrote, however, the organic relationship between naval power and maritime trade was beginning to break down. This was owed partly to the industrial revolution, which allowed continental states to match the economic productivity of overseas commerce; and also to the increasingly intricate economic dependencies that trade created. At first glance, the strategic significance of sea power seemed destined to increase in proportion to the value of the goods that moved across the world's oceans. This is what Mahan and his contemporaries thought would happen. In practice, however, the world economy gradually became too large and complex to be coerced by direct military means.

One can see this by considering the operations of the Royal Navy against Napoleonic France at the start of the nineteenth century, and against Germany at the start of the twentieth. Naval warfare in the first of these contests centred on a close blockade of the enemy's coast. British warships, too powerful and numerous to be driven off by their French counterparts, lurked in the maritime approaches to French ports, cutting them off from seaborne trade. British ships on the high seas could also stop and search any commercial vessel, on suspicion that it was trading with the enemy. Neutral powers had no choice but to accept this interference, since their own navies were no match for the British either. In time, businessmen in Europe and the Americas preferred to transport their goods in British ships, or under British license, because such vessels were immune to interference by the Royal Navy. Naval superiority also allowed Britain to seize France's overseas colonies, whose trade shifted to the British side of the ledger. None of this could prevent Napoleon's armies from running roughshod over opposing armies in the short run. But over the longer term the financial leverage that accrued to Britain and her allies proved so overwhelming that it could not be matched even by the most remarkable military conquests. The final campaigns that brought Napoleon down were not conducted by British armies, but they were paid for by the British treasury, grown rich from the exercise of maritime strategy in its classic form.

Nothing remotely similar was possible a century later. Close blockade had been rendered impracticable by the new weaponry of the industrial age—long-range coastal guns, mines, torpedoes, etc.—which made it dangerous for warships to patrol directly off an enemy's coast. Britain instead attempted a 'distant' blockade of the entire European continent, which gravely affronted the rights of neutral states, who were no longer willing to sit still for this sort of thing. Britain's own ability to wage war was critically dependent on access to world markets, and the prospect that Britain's neutral trading partners might refuse to do business with it, or even enter the war on the other side, set strict limits on how British sea power could be exercised.

Against Napoleon, the British had grown rich by cornering the market on overseas trade. Against Germany they grew poor, borrowing money from the United States in order to finance their own war effort, and to compensate neutral trading states for being cut off from their traditional customers. The task of depriving a great industrial nation of the means to carry on war proved far beyond the power of the Royal Navy; to which was added the defensive burdens of Germany's retaliatory submarine campaign, by which Britain's own overseas trade was seriously threatened for the first time. Britain's centrality to the global economy that it helped to create had ceased to be an unambiguous source of strategic leverage, and was shown to be a strategic vulnerability as well, one that is now shared to some degree by every advanced society.

Economic warfare is no longer an important naval mission, less because it is infeasible in tactical terms than because the political and economic consequences of employing it have grown unmanageable. In its absence, the strategic advantages afforded by sea power in wartime have become less distinctive; though it goes without saying that any nation separated from potential adversaries by the world's oceans will require a navy if it wishes to get across. Overall the high seas have become a vast zone of peace and tranquillity, a safe haven across which an enormous share of world trade can pass unmolested—a fact that should not be obscured by incidental concerns about piracy or speculation about the supposed vulnerability of maritime straits to closure by terrorists. Systemically, the sea today is part of the ballast that keeps the world economy, and global order generally, on an even keel. If that should cease to be true, the world would very rapidly become a very different, and much more dangerous, place.

At present there is only one nation—the United States—that possesses a navy of global strategic significance. That significance rests upon the leading role that it plays in maintaining good order at sea, and also on its ability to project power from sea to shore. In this latter role it functions like a specialized sort of air force, which compensates for the short range of its weapons by the ability to move its bases around. The advantages of being able to do this should not be underestimated. Land-based air forces require a massive fixed infrastructure, whose location may limit how those forces can be used. Aircraft operating from bases sufficiently remote to be safe from enemy attack may have to fly through neutral air space to reach their targets, for which permission may be denied in moments of crisis. Forward bases constructed to avert this requirement need time and resources to build, and are no more defensible than any other fixed asset within range of enemy weapons. If such bases are built on enemy territory, then the territory must first be seized. If they are built on neutral or allied territory, then operations again become subject to political requirements that may be difficult to control. Warships do not suffer from these liabilities, but can approach their targets directly from international waters. Once on the scene, they can sustain operations almost indefinitely, being continuously replenished and resupplied at sea (see Box 6.2).

BOX 6.2 Gunboat Diplomacy

'Gunboat diplomacy' is a derisive phrase from the hey-day of European imperialism. It referred to the fact that colonial powers might convey their wishes to those less powerful than themselves by dispatching a warship in lieu of an ambassador, with a few rounds of gunfire substituting for the customary diplomatic note. Such practices have gone out of fashion, and the phrase with it; but the underlying reality to which it refers remains important to understanding the strategic leverage that navies afford.

A powerful navy generally has a significant proportion of its ships at sea even in peacetime. Armies and air forces are garrison troops. They are only deployed for combat when danger looms. Naval forces on the high seas, on the other hand, have much the same capabilities in peacetime as they would in time of war. They are armed and ready, and can appear wherever they can find water under their keels.

A nation that maintains significant naval forces at sea acquires significant strategic options. Warships can convey a threat to an opponent, or reassurance to a friend, without engaging in any warlike act whatever. Because they are already 'out there' they are almost always the first to respond in a crisis. The speed with which warships on station can respond to trouble also helps to deter certain kinds of bad behaviour in the first place. While long-range land-based aircraft can go anywhere, the military options they offer when they arrive are limited to blowing something up, or not. Naval forces provide a more diverse array of choices, ranging from prolonged observation through the delivery of an implied threat, to the conduct of air strikes and the mounting of an amphibious assault.

The ability to do such things has never been the primary reason to have a navy, but it is an important extra benefit if you have one anyway. Like any military action the practice of 'gunboat diplomacy' entails risk, including that of providing adversaries with isolated targets of opportunity—a peril illustrated by the surprise attack on the *USS Cole* during a port visit to Yemen in October, 2000. Nevertheless, warships continuously at sea are well suited to a security environment characterized by diffuse threats and rapidly emerging crises, including natural catastrophes like the Indian Ocean tsunami of 2004, in which the first effective humanitarian relief was delivered by warships on station in the area.

There can be no guarantee that such advantages will last forever. The strategic utility of a powerful navy is ultimately subject to the continuing evolution of long-range strike systems and other weapons of 'access denial' that are designed to hold warships so far off shore that they cannot fight effectively against an enemy on land. Such weapons are easy to envision, but they are far from being realized in practice. In the meantime, naval forces offer a combination of striking power, speed, and flexibility that is well suited to a security environment in which threats cannot be anticipated long in advance. The ability of naval forces to perform the kind of constabulary function required in a world of brushfire conflicts and rapidly emerging crises is one of their most distinctive contributions to the contemporary world picture.

Key points

- Sailing navies achieved strategic influence mainly by their impact on international trade.
- The strategic leverage of navies in war has declined in the industrial era, as continental economies have become more robust, and as the complexity of the global economy has increased.
- The ability of warships to operate freely in international water can afford direct strategic access to an opponent, which may otherwise be unavailable.
- Nowadays the traditional goal of naval warfare—to 'command the sea'—has largely been displaced by the challenges of projecting military power from sea to shore.

Airpower

Few human inventions have been as eagerly anticipated as the 'flying machine', images of which can be found in art and literature since the Renaissance. What such a machine might look like was anyone's guess, but few doubted that it would find many remarkable applications in war. The history of air warfare has been shaped to an unusual degree by exaggerated theoretical expectations of one kind or another, compared to which the real capabilities of air forces have often fallen short.

The tens of thousands of military aircraft that fought over the Western Front in World War I did so mainly to perform reconnaissance, in the hope of getting the vast armies beneath them moving again. They possessed nothing like the striking power envisioned by H.G. Wells a few years before in his novel *Wings* (1908), in which a vast air armada, launched from Germany, devastates New York City. Technological advances over the next 20 years increased the ability of aircraft to lift explosives off the ground, however, and by the end of the Second World War British and American air forces were wreaking havoc on a scale resembling the apocalyptic fantasies of airpower enthusiasts like Giulio Douhet, whose book *Command of the Air* (1923) claimed that aerial bombardment would be so terrible that it would bring any war to a swift conclusion.

This prediction failed to come true between 1939 and 1945, however, and afterwards many wondered whether the aerial devastation of German and Japanese cities had not merely amplified the horrors of modern war, spreading them haphazardly among civil populations that might have been spared. The grim prophecy of British Prime Minister Stanley Baldwin, looking at the other side of the coin, had proven equally faulty. He had told an alarmed House of Commons in 1932 that 'the bomber will always get through.' They had not. By 1945 the Royal Air Force had suffered more casualties than the Royal Navy, testimony to something real airmen always understood: war in the air is difficult, dangerous, and disappointing, just like war everywhere else.

The integration of aerial weapons into the conduct of war was the central military problem of the twentieth century. Looking backwards from the twenty-first it is apparent that a great deal was accomplished, so that a surprisingly clear and convincing picture has emerged. The frustrations of the world wars were owed partly to immature technologies, partly to the tendency of institutional interests to compromise objective analysis. The strongest advocates of airpower were convinced that only independent air services, co-equal with armies and navies, could master this new method of fighting. Their desire for institutional independence led to exaggerated claims that the long-range bombardment of economic and civil infrastructure could decide the outcome of war. Such claims inspired equally exaggerated scepticism that airpower was all that important. The resolution of these bureaucratic quarrels (always in favour of independent air forces), combined with the progress of technology, have given rise to a more stable picture, in which airpower is featured not so much as the universal solvent of modern war, but as the all-purpose glue that makes modern combined arms operations possible (see Box 6.3).

If airpower retains an independent strategic role, it is at the extreme ends of the conflict spectrum. Nuclear weapons, if they are ever employed by an organized government, will almost certainly be delivered by aircraft or missiles, and it is easy to believe that their detonations, if sufficiently numerous, will render the activities of armies and navies inconsequential. More interesting, and more unexpected from the point of view of traditional airpower theory, is the role of air weapons in conflicts where only limited force is required. Airpower has become the main tool by which strong countries seek to coerce weak ones, for two general reasons. The first is that Stanley Baldwin's prophecy has now come true. Bombers almost always do get through, owing to doctrinal and technological developments that allow the best air forces to suppress all but the very best air defence systems. Although any pilot flying

BOX 6.3 Command of the Air

Guilio Douhet was an Italian artillery officer in the First World War, whose experience of the grinding carnage of trench warfare made him, and many others of his generation, eager for any tactical alternative that promised a swift and decisive military result. After the war he became an important proponent of airpower. He thought that the air, like the sea, could be 'commanded' by a superior force in a way that would deny its use to the enemy. The passages below illustrate his efforts to work out the strategic implications of this vision.

To have command of the air means to be in a position to prevent the enemy from flying while retaining the ability to fly oneself. . . . An aerial fleet capable of dumping hundreds of tons of bombs can easily be organized; therefore, the striking force and magnitude of aerial offensives, considered from the standpoint of either material or moral significance, is far more effective than those of any other offensive yet known. A nation which had command of the air is in a position to protect its own territory from enemy aerial attack and even to put a halt to the enemy's auxiliary actions in support of his land and sea operations, leaving him powerless to do much of anything. Such offensive actions can not only cut off an opponent's army and navy from their bases of operations, but can also bomb the interior of the enemy's country so devastatingly that the physical and moral resistance of the people would also collapse. . . .

In order to assure an adequate national defense, it is necessary—and sufficient—to be in a position in case of war to conquer the command of the air. And from that we arrive at this second corollary: All that a nation does to assure her own defense should have as its aim procuring for herself those means which, in case of war, are most effective for the conquest of the command of the air. . . .

Any diversion from this primary purpose is an error. In order to conquer the air, it is necessary to deprive the enemy of all means of flying, by striking at him in the air, at his bases of operation, or at his production centers—in short, wherever those means are to be found. This kind of destruction can be accomplished only by aerial means, to the exclusion of army and navy weapons. . . .

Victory smiles upon those who anticipate the changes in the character of war, not upon those who wait to adapt themselves after the changes occur. In this period of rapid transition from one form to another, those who daringly take to the new road first will enjoy the incalculable advantages of the new means of war over the old. This new character of war, emphasizing the advantages of the offensive, will surely make for swift, crushing decisions on the battlefield. . . . Those who are ready first not only will win quickly, but will win with the fewest sacrifices and the minimum expenditure of means.

Giulio Douhet, *The Command of the Air*, translated by Dino Ferrari
(New York, 1942; reprinted Washington, 1983) 24–30.

a combat mission is undoubtedly risking his or her life, the risk is small compared to any other comparably destructive act of war. It disappears entirely if the blow is delivered by ballistic or cruise missiles, or by unmanned aircraft, whose numbers and versatility have increased markedly in recent years. Once through, moreover, bombers and missiles now strike their targets with a consistency that was scarcely imaginable in earlier times. In the world wars aerial weapons were synonymous with indiscriminate destruction. Today they are synonymous with stealth and precision, which have gone a long way towards reducing the risks traditionally associated with their use.

Whether this is a good thing depends on how one views the gap between peace and war, which has narrowed by virtue of the ease with which aerial strike operations can be mounted. The use of bombardment to punctuate a diplomatic demand or enforce a sanctions regime may pose little risk to the personnel involved, but the possibility that such attacks will inspire an escalatory response from the other side cannot be dismissed. The aim of violence in war is always to break the enemy's will. Yet it may equally well harden his heart, stiffen his spine, and stimulate his imagination.

Which of these will happen is never easy to anticipate. Strategic theory is a branch of social theory. It concerns itself with the way social groups use and experience force against each other. The effective use of force is accordingly dependent on how accurately belligerents envision and understand each other. Theories of war in the air illustrate this clearly. Strategic bombing as originally conceived envisioned the enemy society as a single entity mobilized for war. Enemy governments were seen as authentic expressions of those societies, all of whose members were complicit in the conduct of the regime. This view provided a moral justification and a tactical rationale for the far-reaching destruction that aerial bombardment entailed, in which damage inflicted anywhere was supposed to be felt everywhere. An army could be disabled without the ugly necessity of confronting its weapons, by demolishing the factories that made those weapons, along with the homes and bodies of the people who worked in the factories. Civilian deaths were not just tolerated, but sought, because they might demoralize or delegitimize the government.

Liberal democracies, at least, are inclined to think of their adversaries differently now. They no longer take the psychological unity of armed forces, state, and society for granted. On the contrary, these are now seen as being artificially stitched together by political convenience, brute force, or some other fragile thread. The resulting seams have become the principal targets of strategic bombardment in its current form. The aim of an air campaign conducted with precision weapons is to inflict suffering against the government, the armed forces, and the critical infrastructure that supports them, while sparing as much of the surrounding society as possible. Apart from its greater humanity, this approach has the additional advantage of making the reconstruction and rehabilitation of a defeated enemy easier. But whether these psychological assumptions are more reliable than those that prevailed in the past is an open question. Today's understanding of how airpower works has been refined in campaigns against isolated, despotic regimes. Such experiences may have made democratic countries too quick to doubt the moral resilience of their opponents. Totalitarian and criminal regimes, particularly those arising from revolution, may be quite firmly rooted in their surrounding societies, and correspondingly difficult to coerce without inspiring the kind of escalatory reactions that lead to general war.

Key points

- The integration of aerial weapons into warfare was the dominant problem confronting the armed forces of advanced societies in the twentieth century.

- Expectations about what air forces can achieve have often run ahead of what has been possible in practice.

- Modern air campaigns are no longer oriented towards the infliction of mass destruction, but are intended to disable an enemy government and its armed forces, while inflicting the least damage possible on the surrounding society.

- Precision weaponry has made aerial bombardment the weapon of choice in the conduct of war to coerce a concession from a weaker enemy.

The Final Frontier: Space War

Compared to the land or the sea, the air has proven to be a remarkably permissive arena of war, at least for those who can operate there unopposed. Yet its characteristics can still be improved upon. Beyond the earth's atmosphere lies, well, nothing. That is what space is: a perfectly transparent, friction-free environment, which has never yet been employed for any warlike purpose other than to observe and support activity on the planet's surface below. In this regard it has acquired immense importance. Space is nothing, but it is not empty. Thousands of military and commercial satellites are already there, performing all manner of communication and reconnaissance functions, and providing the terminal guidance that has made the accuracy of major weapons systems increasingly independent of their range. Whenever we speak of 'precision' weapons, we are almost always talking about systems that depend, in some degree, on assets deployed in space. If the land, sea, and air forces of the United States were deprived of their ability to communicate with the space-based systems orbiting overhead, the effect would be comparable to a major battlefield defeat. To that extent, space war already exists.

Whether space holds strategic possibilities independent of the contribution that space-based systems already make to the conduct of war is a matter of speculation. The military use of space is governed by two international legal norms. The first holds that claims of national sovereignty do not apply beyond the earth's atmosphere; the second that actual weapons cannot be deployed there. Like most such agreements, these provisions are not so much barriers to action as reflections of a prevailing consensus. The first has contributed to the exploitation of space for reconnaissance and communications. Any country capable of launching a satellite is free to peer down on its neighbours. This arrangement contributed to the stability of strategic deterrence during the later years of the cold war, by affording both the United States and the Soviet Union a high degree of confidence that each knew what the other was up to.

The ban on putting weapons in space is less a matter of perceived mutual advantage than of apparent futility. The transparency that makes space such an ideal environment for reconnaissance and communications makes it a poor place for weapons. They would be highly vulnerable to detection and destruction, without offering tactical capabilities significantly different from those available on the planet's surface. War in space would also rapidly create conditions that could make itself impossible. Once satellites take to destroying each other, the low-orbital space in which most of them operate will rapidly fill up with junk, even small bits of which pose a lethal risk to whatever working systems remained in orbit. Even though space war is absent, this problem already exists, to the point where scientists have become concerned about the cascading effect that will result if existing bits of junk start smashing into each other. The immensity of space per se should not conceal the fact that only small slices of it are of practical use to humanity. Those slices are already becoming seriously contaminated by human use.

It is fairly easy to imagine military actions designed to render space militarily useless. If one sets that atavistic possibility aside, however, the strategic application of space appears likely to remain confined to the collection and distribution of information, for purposes of precision targeting, and also for the collection of general intelligence. Challenges in the latter area lie less in collecting data than in employing it effectively. It is easier to launch satellites capable of recording every cell phone conversation in Afghanistan, or of photographing every flatbed truck in Shanghai, than it is to field the army of Pashtun speakers and photo-analysts required to interpret the results. Those who have gone to war have always hungered for more information. Technically speaking, that hunger is now on the verge of satiation. Yet the results may prove less digestible than our ancestors imagined.

Key points

- Space systems are vital to the conduct of war on land, sea, and in the air. Advanced military information systems often depend on space-based components, whose destruction would severely degrade their performance.
- So far as is publicly known there are no weapons currently based in space, because the tactical advantage of placing them there is unclear.

War by Other Means: Cyberspace

Up to now modern war has been all about people hurling pieces of metal at each other. Its historical development has been marked by a steady increase in the size, velocity, range, and variety of the pieces, and by the introduction of more powerful explosives to propel them along and amplify their lethal effects once they reach their destinations. Nuclear weapons represent a modest departure from this pattern, since their destructiveness is achieved by different means. Yet they too are products of a massive industrial-age infrastructure, and impose huge economic, logistical, and organizational burdens on those who employ them.

What if it were otherwise? What if war could be fought without the need to store up and discharge massive amounts of kinetic energy? What would that be like? No one has the faintest idea. But the flourishing of information technology has at least removed the question from the realm of fantasy. Whether 'cyberspace' really deserves to be treated as an independent realm of war may be disputed. It is a wholly imaginary place, originally conceived in a work of science fiction, and now conjured up by physical systems that are no less subject to direct attack than any other military or civilian object. The centrality of those systems to the conduct of war today has already been alluded to. To that extent 'cyberwar,' like 'space war,' already exists.

One reason information warfare has come in for so much scrutiny is the uneasy realization that complex information systems, on which the conduct of even mundane military operations now depends, are unusually vulnerable to attack compared to other military assets. This is a grave problem, but it remains a tactical one, and should not be confused with the direct use of information as a strategic weapon. The latter is also readily distinguishable from propaganda (also known as 'the war of ideas'). Strategy is not about persuasion, at least not primarily. It is about the *forcible* imposition of one's will upon an adversary.

Whether such imposition can be accomplished by the manipulation or disruption of information alone is difficult to say. A computer virus that disabled a national stock exchange might have consequences comparable to those of a military attack. If such a blow were delivered during a 'shooting' war it would require no explanation, and would merely be another means by which one side sought to injure the other. On its own, however, a cyber-attack of this kind would be difficult to exploit for strategic purposes, if only because, once its source and purpose were revealed, it might invite a conventional military response by way of rejoinder.

The risk of indiscriminate collateral damage is also immense, and can only be controlled with difficulty. This is illustrated by the cyber-attack mounted in 2010 against the Iranian nuclear programme, by parties as yet unknown, employing a computer 'worm' known as Stuxnet. The Stuxnet attack is the most successful example of 'precision' cyber-warfare that has yet been seen. That success, like those in other fields of strategic endeavour, required the investment of a great deal of money and time, plus painstaking intelligence. If you take those things away, a cyber-device set loose on the world might end up anywhere. In this respect information war suffers from some of the same limitations as biological warfare, which has loomed ominously on the strategic horizon for over a century without ever having been realized in practice, because its fratricidal risks have outweighed its prospective benefits.

Whether this will remain true in the cyber realm is impossible to say. For now the strategic geography of cyberspace remains *terra incognita*. It is a place where it is cheap to operate, and perhaps to fight undetected, provided you are willing to settle for indiscriminate mayhem as your desired result. For the time being its greatest appeal may be to terrorists and others who lack the means to fight openly elsewhere; who do not mind if they are not given credit for their deeds; and who are not especially dependent on information technology themselves. As a consequence, information warfare appears to be mainly a defensive problem for advanced societies.

Key points

- As modern weapons have come to rely on precision sensors and advanced communications systems, the question whether information itself may become a weapon has gained increasing attention.
- The information technologies on which modern societies now rely pose an attractive target to potential adversaries, above all those that are not especially dependent upon similar technologies.

 ## Conclusion

It would be naïve to suppose that the expansion of war into the new and nebulous realm of cyberspace, should it occur, will have a moderating effect on its destructiveness. However and wherever war is waged, it will remain the brutal business it has always been, in which victory will go to those with the material and emotional resources required to stand the strain.

 ## Questions

1. The commitment of ground forces in war appears to require a higher level of political commitment than the commitment of air and naval forces. Does this have the effect of eroding, or strengthening, the psychological barrier that separates peace and war?

2. If having a large and powerful navy is a good idea, why is the United States the only country that has one? Are there any circumstances under which we can expect this to change?

3. In peacetime, strategic decision-making often translates into decisions about how to spend money on defence. Where, between its army, navy, and air force, should an advanced society be investing its marginal defence dollars today?

4. Would your answer to the previous question be different for a developing nation? Or for a country like Iran or North Korea, which feels threatened by the United States?

5. Given that advances in the precision weaponry are now entering an era of diminishing returns (after several decades of rapid advance), where should air, sea, and land forces be looking to improve their combat effectiveness?

6. If you could invent a new weapon, what would it do?

7. If you could invent a new defensive technology or system, what would it do?

8. Do you expect the current international consensus against placing weapons in space to continue? What kinds of developments would you expect to undermine it?

9. Revolutionary insurgency has proven more successful in modern times than in the more remote past. Why is this? Do you expect this pattern to continue? Or would you expect that regular armed forces will eventually reassert their historical mastery of the battlefield.

10. Is it more helpful to think of information as a weapon in its own right, or as a means of making other weapons more effective?

 ## Further Reading

David Gates, *Sky Wars: A History of Military Aerospace Power* (London: Reaktion Books, 2003).
From the Wright Brothers to the problems of missile defence.

Peter L. Hays et al. (eds), *Spacepower for a New Millennium: Space and US National Security* (New York: McGraw-Hill, 2000).
On the strategic exploitation of space.

Daniel Moran, *Wars of National Liberation* (Washington, DC: Smithsonian Books, 2006).
An account of the revolutionary wars that accompanied the retreat of European empires after 1945.

Gregory J. Rattray, *Strategic Warfare in Cyberspace* (Cambridge, Massachusetts: MIT Press, 2001).
Looks beyond tactical issues to consider the strategic implications of information warfare.

Hew Strachan, *European Armies and the Conduct of War* (London: Routledge, 1988).
A compact survey of the history of war on the continent where it first achieved modern form.

Geoffrey Till, *Seapower: A Guide for the Twenty-first Century* (London: Frank Cass, 2004).
An up-to-date analysis including a good introduction to naval theory.

 ## Web links

http://www.fas.org/index.html The Federation of American Scientists. A comprehensive site dealing with defence planning and technology.

http://www.gwu.edu/~nsarchiv/ The National Security Archive of George Washington University. An online repository of documents and commentary pertaining to strategic issues.

http://www.globalsecurity.org/ Exceptionally strong on weapons and other military systems.

http://www.clausewitz.com/ The Clausewitz Home Page. An extensive site devoted to the greatest of all military theorists.

http://www.au.af.mil/au/aul/bib97.htm Air University Bibliographies. Hundreds of specialized bibliographies, tailored to the needs of students, on topics relevant to the study of war, strategy, and international politics.

Technology and Warfare

ELIOT COHEN

 Chapter Contents

Introduction: Technophiles and Technophobes	133
Some Ways of Thinking about Military Technology	133
Mapping Military Technology	136
The Revolution in Military Affairs Debate	138
Challenges of the New Technology	146
Conclusion: The Future of Military Technology	147

 Reader's Guide

Although the development and integration of technology into military forces and strategy is often depicted as a simple matter, the role of technology in war is controversial. Debate exists about the relative importance of technology when compared to other factors, such as training or morale, in achieving victory in battle. Scholars also offer competing explanations about how and why certain technologies are integrated into military organizations while others are ignored. The pace of technological change is also not uniform: some technology and procedures become fixtures in militaries while others become obsolete quickly and are discarded. To complicate matters further, some observers today believe that the world is witnessing a revolution in military affairs, a relatively rare event when technologies are combined to produce a fundamental transformation in the way war is fought. This chapter explores these issues and describes some changes that the revolution in military affairs is producing in military organizations. It also offers some observations about the emerging technological trends that are likely to transform future warfare.

Introduction: Technophiles and Technophobes

Military historians—and sometimes soldiers themselves—cannot make up their minds about how to view military technology. Some technical experts and enthusiasts are fascinated by the nuances of the various models of the German Panzerkampfwagen Model IV; much contemporary policy debate centres on technical decisions—how many aircraft to buy, what type, over what period of time, and so on. The general public tends to ascribe remarkable—sometimes even magical—properties to modern military technology.

By contrast, many military historians and soldiers deprecate the importance of technology. They believe that the skill and organizational effectiveness, not pieces of hardware, determine the outcome of battle. Although technical enthusiasts and sceptics sometimes clash in their assessment of a particular contest, rarely does the debate occur at a conceptual level. Only one major figure in the last century—Major General J. F. C. Fuller, a British war planner, pioneer of armoured warfare, and prolific military historian—attempted to write theoretically about the role of technology in strategic studies (1926, 1932, 1942, 1945). This chapter therefore introduces some concepts about military technology, and then discusses the key technological issues and trends of our time.

Some Ways of Thinking about Military Technology

Consider as a point of departure the question: 'Where does military technology come from?' We often think of technology as something predetermined. In this common view, scientists develop technology in war much like people walking down a corridor lined with closed rooms containing treasure chests. Progress consists of walking along the hallway, unlocking the doors, and picking up the chests. The fruits of technology, in other words, are available to those who have the keys to the doors and the strength to carry away the treasure chests.

In fact, however, historians of technology and engineering usually reject this view. A variety of forces shapes technology, whose final form is far from being predetermined (MacKenzie 1990). The most common view along these lines is that 'form follows function': military technology evolves to meet particular military needs. There are, however, other possibilities. One author, Henry Petroski, talks about 'form following failure', a concept first applied to his study of the history of bridge building, but applicable to military technology as well (1982). In this view, new technology emerges as a response to some perceived failure or fault in existing technology. Other theories of technological invention include the suggestion that technologies emerge from aesthetic or other non-rational considerations, such as custom or organizational convenience (Creveld 1989). These different theories offer varying explanations of how innovation occurs or fails to occur. Why, for example, did it take more than 30 years for the United States, which successfully deployed unmanned aerial vehicles (UAVs) in Vietnam, to introduce them into the armed forces? The technology may have been immature (the corridor-and-doors theory); there may have been no mission crying out for UAVs (form follows function); there may have been no visible failure in the existing technology (form follows failure); or, finally, the technology may have been thwarted by pilots hostile to the notion of aircraft without pilots (non-rational explanations).

No one of these theories is completely satisfying. Their very range, however, should prompt us to look more closely at how and why military technologies come into existence. There are distinctive national styles, for example, in military technology: the Israeli Merkava tank differs subtly from American M1 Abrams. These changes reflect differences in design philosophy stemming from where the two countries believe they will fight (the slow Israeli tank is designed for the rocky Golan Heights; the much faster Abrams tank can best exploit its high speed in desert warfare). The Israelis have given exceptionally high value to crew safety. They accepted mechanical inefficiency by placing the engine in front of the crew space rather than (as is normal) behind it. In armoured warfare, most hits occur on the frontal armour of the tank, and the engine can thus absorb the impact of a hit. The Americans, by purchasing a fuel-hungry high-powered turbine engine, assumed that they could readily resupply their tanks with fuel in vast quantities on the battlefield (see Box 7.1).

National styles in technology may reflect political assumptions about war at the time that a design was frozen. By 2012, for example, the United States was poised to buy large numbers of the F-35 Joint Strike Fighter (JSF), a short-ranged fighter bomber. This decision reflected a political assumption, namely, that the United States would fight its wars within a few hundred miles of its opponents, and, presumably, with extensive access to secure fixed bases.[1] This assumption may well prove incorrect.

BOX 7.1 The M1A2 vs the Merkava

	M1A2	Merkava (Mk3)
Weight (fully armed) (tons)	69.54	62.9
Length (gun forward) (metres)	9.8	8.8
Height (metres)	2.9	2.8
Width	3.7	3.7
Range (miles)	265	311
Crew	4	4
Road speed (km/hour)	90	55
Main armament	120mm	120mm
Engine	Gas turbine	Diesel

Although similar in some respects, the Merkava is very different from the M1 in others. It is much slower (perhaps half as fast): the Israelis value absolute speed much less than the ability to manoeuvre under fire, particularly over the lava-strewn Golan Heights. They also lack the super-fast infantry fighting vehicles to keep up with the tanks. There is a rear hatch on the Merkava that allows the evacuation of wounded or resupply of ammunition without exposing the crew—again, requirements derived from the peculiar problems of keeping a firing line on the Golan Heights. Finally, the Israeli engine is at the front of the tank, where it can absorb an incoming round—a sacrifice of mechanical efficiency for crew protection. The M1 gets a similar effect by unusually good (and expensive) armour.

Sources: http://www.army-technology.com/projects/merkava/
          http://www.army-technology.com/projects/abrams/

Note: the stated speed for the M1A2 is considerably too slow.

One way to penetrate the essence of national design style is to ask what kind of trade-offs designers accepted. All engineers make choices among desired features of hardware; all pieces of military technology reflect those choices. A tank has three fundamental characteristics: protection, firepower, and mobility. Increase the amount of armour and one sacrifices the tank's ability to move quickly; put a small-bore, low-recoil cannon on it and one gains a great deal of mobility for a penalty in firepower; increase horsepower and pay a penalty in terms of the size of the tank (and hence protection) or how far it can go (and hence mobility).

Military technology also reflects processes of interaction. Tanks did not grow to be today's 60-ton monsters because of the growth of their power plants or guns. Developments in armour were to blame. Tank armour once consisted of rolled homogeneous steel. Today, it may consist of a variety of substances—exotic metals such as depleted uranium, composites that include alternating layers of metal and ceramics, and sandwiches of metal and high explosive. These changes reflect the development of ever more powerful antitank weapons—depleted uranium rods and so-called shaped charges (explosives configured to create a jet of hot metal that burns its way through armour). Even in peacetime, measure and countermeasure rule the choices designers make. These interactions create a kind of evolutionary process, by which a weapon system settles into its own 'ecological' niche. Birds and lizards evolve an amazing variety of counters to their predators, who in turn come up with a range of adaptations that enable them to find and devour their prey. So too with weapon systems. As in nature, interaction may yield odd outcomes, where one kind of highly sophisticated adaptation to a particular environment makes a platform utterly unsuited to a different battlefield. The first two generations of stealth aircraft, for example, evolved to avoid detection through the use of adroitly shaped surfaces that would disperse or absorb radar energy: they were difficult (not impossible) to detect using the radar technology of the time. Their odd shaping, however, made them slower and less manoeuvrable than other aircraft; they therefore became night-time-only systems that were vulnerable to optical detection during the day.

In assessing military technology one should look at invisible technology as well. What gave the German tanks an edge over their French counterparts in the Second World War, for example, was not superior armour, guns, or engines, so much as a piece of technology barely noticed by outside observers—the radio (Stolfi 1970). Often, the most important elements of a military system are not the ones most evident to the casual observer, yet mastery of such technologies may weigh most in battle. American forces in the south-west Pacific in the Second World War struggled not only with the Japanese, but also with disease. The insecticide DDT, as much as any bomber or battleship, won the fight for New Guinea.

One should consider the role of systems technology and not just its parts. A novelist described a Second World War warship this way:

> One way of thinking of the ship was as of some huge marine animal. Here on the bridge was the animal's brain, and radiating from it ran the nerves—the telephones and voice tubes—which carried the brain's decisions to the parts which were to execute them. The engine-room formed the muscles which actuated the tail—the propellers; and the guns were the teeth and claws of the animal. Up in the crow's nest above, and all round the bridge where the lookouts sat raking sea and sky with their binoculars, were the animal's eyes, seeking everywhere for enemies or prey, while the signal flags and wireless transmitter were the animal's voice, with which it could cry a warning to its fellows or scream for help.
> **Forester (1943: 22–3)**

As the war progressed, the brain of the ship vanished into its bowels, so to speak—becoming the combat information centre of modern vessels. But Forester's point was that the effectiveness of the ship rested not simply on the working of all the different technologies individually, but rather on their effectiveness as a whole. The very use of the term weapon *system* implies that the art of putting technologies together is more important than their individual excellence. In war, more than in most other activities, the whole can be far greater than the sum of its parts.

Our last concept is that of the technological edge. It is not always decisive, but it is almost always important. J. F. C. Fuller (1945: 18) once suggested that Napoleon himself would have succumbed to the semi-competent British general in the Crimea, Lord Raglan, simply because the latter's army had rifles, while the former had smoothbore muskets. It is only recently that the advanced powers have assumed that they would go to war with a decided technological edge over their opponents, and that this advantage would prove decisive. Technological superiority does not necessarily extend across the board. In the Persian Gulf War of 1991, for example, some Iraqi artillery pieces (their South African made G-5 howitzers) outranged Western counterparts such as the American Paladin system, by 6 kilometres or more (30 vs 24km, to be precise)—much as Russian-made 130mm guns outranged their American 155mm counterparts in Vietnam.[2] The poorer, smaller, or weaker side may have some niche competencies that will surprise a richer and more powerful opponent. The technological edge may be dramatic (the quintessential case being the Dervish armies of the Khalifa crumpling under the fire of Lord Kitchener's Anglo–Egyptian infantry using the Henry–Martini rifle), or quite subtle—a matter of a few seconds' difference in the flight time of an air-to-air missile, or a few hundred yards in the effective range of a tank gun. The technological edge may have a psychological dimension that vanishes over time, as with Second World War-era German dive bombers with their unearthly wailing sirens, or American heliborne infantry in Vietnam appearing from the skies in remote jungles; or it may reflect fleeting disparities in commercial technology (e.g. commercial global positioning system navigation receivers purchased by Americans, but not Iraqis, in the Gulf War).

Key points

- There are a range of divergent and contradictory theories about how military technology develops.
- Military technologies often reflect different national styles.
- Different national styles are determined by a variety of considerations, such as political assumptions, trade-offs between various features of hardware, processes of interaction, invisible technologies, systems technology, and the search for technological edge.

Mapping Military Technology

It can be difficult enough to understand military technology when it remains static: the authors of novels about the Napoleonic era war at sea, such as Patrick O'Brian or C. S. Forester, have a considerable challenge (which those two meet wonderfully well) in describing the complex technology of early nineteenth-century naval warfare. The problem of understanding modern military technology is more difficult because it changes continuously. Indeed, since the middle of the nineteenth century, change in military technology has become a constant, through what Martin van Creveld has called 'the invention of invention'. The traditional picture of soldiers suspiciously rejecting new technology in favour of old standbys was always overdone: before the First World War, for example, the armies of Europe embraced the machine gun and the aeroplane. Their difficulty lay, and lies today, in recognizing what broader changes new technology may entail. For powerful institutional reasons, military organizations tend to fit new technologies into old intellectual and operational frameworks.

One question to ask in assessing technological change is whether what one is witnessing is a change in *quantity* or a change in *quality*. It is a more complicated question than it might appear. Marginal increases in speed, protection, mobility, or payload, to take just a few design parameters, are quantitative: they may have cumulative effects, but in and of themselves should not bring about radical changes in war. Sometimes, however, a seemingly incremental improvement augurs, in fact, qualitative change. Early firearms, for example, delivered rather less effective lethality than a good longbow; oil-fired ship engines offered moderate increases in speed over their coal-powered counterparts; and the first generation air-to-air missiles provided only marginal improvements over a well-aimed burst of cannon fire. All of these changes, however, foreshadowed tremendous upheavals in the conduct of war. Mastery of the longbow could take a lifetime. Mastery of the musket took a few months of drill, and its incidental qualities—the noise, smoke, and flash, none of which had direct effects on the enemy—made it a more fearful, that is, psychologically effective, weapon. Oil propulsion reduced the size of crews, increased the speed of ships, and, perhaps most importantly, made the world's oilfields prime strategic real estate. Air-to-air missiles improved far beyond the capability of mature aircraft cannon, to the point of engaging targets well beyond visual range.

Contemporary observers will often get it wrong. Military organizations (the US navy in particular) had experimented with satellite-based navigation systems since the early 1960s (Friedman 2000). It took the experience of the Gulf War in 1991, however, to make average sailors, pilots, and soldiers realize that the global positioning system could transform all aspects of navigation from art to science, or rather mere technique. By contrast, the advent of nuclear weapons in the late 1940s and 1950s convinced some professionals that all military organizations would have to be radically restructured to accommodate the new weapons. As it turned out, however, only selected military organizations needed to adapt their tactics and structures to the new devices (Bacevich 1986). Military organizations and platforms do not change at a uniform rate. Some aspects of military technology change very little over the decades. Visit an aircraft carrier's deck, and one is struck by how little many procedures have changed in well over half a century. Steam catapults—themselves solid pieces of mid-twentieth-century engineering—loft jet aircraft off angled decks devised shortly after the Second World War. The crews, in multicoloured jerseys, each of which identifies their function, work pretty much as their fathers did during the Korean War. Inside, the Air Boss and his (or her) staff track the movement of aircraft using model aeroplanes on a large flat table; below decks illuminated glass grids show the status of all aircraft. There are important changes—more accurate and powerful bombs, far better intelligence flowing in, better aircraft—but the structure is remarkably durable. The same might be said of a battalion of paratroopers ready to drop on an airfield and seize it. Their aircraft, C-130s designed in the early 1950s and first fielded in 1956, are crammed with men carrying parachutes whose fundamental design goes back to the Second World War.[3] The process of training, loading, and deploying those men remains, in its essentials, the same.

Some military processes change to a considerably greater extent. A large desert armoured battle, for example, bears some resemblance to the clashes of the Second World War: masses of ponderous armoured beasts manoeuvring over open ground, generating vast clouds of smoke and dust, swirling in a mêlée where the advantage goes to the quicker shot and calmer head. But much has changed, too. Today's armoured battle might take place at night, using thermal imaging devices that are in many ways better than optical sights even on a clear day. This is a far cry even from the night battles of the 1973 Yom Kippur War, in which Syrian tanks using crude infrared projectors attacked after daylight; for the modern armoured force, there is no important difference in visibility between day and night. The armour, gun power, and speed of the tanks today are much greater than during the Second World War, as is tank size. Those are important quantitative changes, but the biggest shift is in the accuracy of their weapons. A well-calibrated gun, with even a moderately competent crew (aided by laser range finders and ballistic computers) can score a first-round hit at a distance of several kilometres—a significant change in the way tank battles are fought.

Sometimes there are changes that fundamentally alter war-fighting. The first night of an air operation, for example, is now completely different from what occurred during the Second World War, Korea, and Vietnam. In one or two nights a competent air force can shut down an enemy's air defence system, rather than wearing it out by a process of attritional struggle with defending fighter aircraft. Precision weapons—now ubiquitous in the arsenals of developed countries—mean that an initial attack can, in theory at least, prove paralysing. It is not the case that air power can do more efficiently that which it did in the past—it can do things that it never could have done before. Thus, for example, with adequate intelligence and planning, a well-conducted air strike can cripple a nation's telecommunications system, in part by attacking targets (relay towers or switching centres) that previously were not susceptible to mass attack. And precision munitions, delivered by remotely piloted vehicles on the basis of meticulously gathered imagery intelligence have been used extensively by the United States to assassinate suspected terrorists in South Asia and the Middle East.

Key points

- One of the problems of understanding the role of military technologies is the constant process of change that takes place.
- One difficult issue concerns the relationship between qualitative and quantitative change.
- Another difficulty is that some technology is slow to have an effect, while some is much more immediate and radical in its impact.

The Revolution in Military Affairs Debate

When a set of changes comes together, the result (some soldiers and historians would argue) is a revolution. Normally, military technology merely evolves, at greater or lesser speeds, and unevenly. Occasionally, however, several developments will come together and yield a broader transformation. Thus, in the middle of the nineteenth century the combination of the telegraph (which allowed real-time links between civilian authority and military commanders, and between commanders in large military organizations), the railway (which permitted mass movements of troops and their sustenance during winter or while conducting sieges), and the rifle (which made infantry engagements lethal at greater ranges than ever before) transformed war. The mass conflicts of the wars of German unification and the American Civil War involved industrialized masses, and spelt the end of battles conducted in compressed periods of time and narrowly defined locations. They foreshadowed the slaughter of the First World War, as a few prescient observers noted.

Since the late 1970s, a number of observers have suggested that a revolution in military affairs is under way. Soviet writers—senior military officers, including the then Chief of the Soviet General Staff, Nikolai Ogarkov—suggested that modern conventional weapons would soon have the effectiveness of tactical nuclear weapons. Long-range sensors, including powerful radars mounted on aircraft, combined with precision weapons, would allow the detection and destruction of armoured units long before they ever approached the battlefield. Soviet military leaders believed that the United States, with its superior technological base, would drive these developments, and that their consequence would fall very much to the disadvantage of the Soviet Union, reliant as it was on waves of armoured forces that could move into Europe from their mobilization areas in the western USSR.

In the West, a number of technologists had similar, if less well-articulated, aspirations for weapons systems that would combine accuracy, range, and above all 'intelligence'—the ability to home in on, or even select, their own targets. It took the 1991 Gulf War to convince a broad spectrum of officers that very large changes in the conduct of war had occurred. The lopsidedness of that war, the undeniable effectiveness of precision weapons, and the emergence of a host of supporting military technologies (stealth, for example, which is actually a cluster of technologies) convinced many observers that warfare had changed fundamentally. The developments first noted in the Gulf War continued in a decade of smaller-scale military engagements thereafter, including repeated American and British strikes against Iraqi targets, and North Atlantic Treaty Organization (NATO) operations against Yugoslavia as a result of the wars in Bosnia in 1995 (Operation Deliberate Force) and in Kosovo in 1999 (Operation Allied Force). Attacking both by night and by day, and using primarily guided weapons, the United States and (to a lesser extent) its allies conducted operations with extraordinary accuracy and negligible combat losses. Similarly, the combination of special operations forces, UAVs, and aircraft delivering precision weapons (and unguided ones for that matter) had a devastating effect on admittedly ragtag Taliban troops in Afghanistan in 2001. These and American regular ground and air forces occupied Iraq, and crushed the regime of Saddam Hussein, and its admittedly fragile and obsolescent military, in less than three weeks in 2003.

An adequate conceptual description of these changes, however, remained elusive. The Vice-Chairman of the American Joint Chiefs of Staff, Admiral William Owens, described what he termed 'the system of systems' as the ultimate potential of the new technologies, if not their actual achievement (Owens and Offley 2000). By integrating long-range, precision weapons with extensive intelligence, surveillance, and reconnaissance, and vastly improved capabilities for processing information and distributing it, he believed the United States could hope to detect and destroy any enemy target over swathes of the earth's surface as large as 200 by 200 miles. Some in the military scoffed at this as a technologist's fantasy, pointing to the persistence of what Carl von Clausewitz termed 'the fog of war' even in seemingly immaculate military operations against feeble opponents—the limited success of NATO aircraft in knocking out Serb tanks in 1999 being a case in point. Owens himself declared that enormous bureaucratic impediments—the persistence of individual service cultures, in particular—stood in the way of his dream being achieved.

In truth, the revolution in military affairs debate remains unsatisfying. Clearly, large changes are at work, but a mere recitation of new technologies does not describe the kinds of changes emerging in warfare. The military tests that have occurred thus far involved the wildly disproportionate forces of the United States and its allies against far smaller opponents. In 1999, for example, Yugoslavia's gross national product was barely a fifteenth the size of the American defence budget. The outcome of such ill-matched encounters could serve as indicators, perhaps, but not proof of a large change. It is possible that a revolution in military affairs has occurred, but it will require evidence gathered in a much larger conflict to become manifest. It is more likely that it would require the pressure of major great power competition in the arena of conventional armament to press modern armed forces to realize such changes to their fullest. At the moment, such competition does not exist, although in theory the rise of China in opposition to American dominance in the Pacific could provide the occasion for a real revolution to make itself known. One can, however, discern at least three broad features of the new technological era in warfare: the rise of quality over quantity, the speciation of military hardware, and the centrality of commercial military technology.

The Rise of Quality Over Quantity

Historians will describe the period extending from the French Revolution to at least the middle of the twentieth century as the era of mass warfare (e.g. Howard 1975: 75ff). During this time, the dominant form of military power was the mass army, recruited (in wartime, at least) by conscription, and uniformly equipped with the products of heavy industry. Those countries that could mobilize men and military production most effectively could generate the most military power—and this was true of the largest powers (like the Soviet Union) and the smallest (like Israel). Broadly speaking, the bigger the force the better—a far cry from the days of the eighteenth century when military authorities believed that armies could not operate beyond a certain optimal size, and when the way of war and contemporary economics dictated the protection of civil society from widespread compulsory military service.

The age of the mass army is over (see Moskos et al. 2000). The near annihilation in 1991 of the Iraqi army, the world's fourth largest, marked the emergence of a world in which modestly obsolescent technology had become merely targets for more sophisticated weapons. Around the world, states abandoned compulsory military service and shrank the size of their armed forces, even in those countries (China and Turkey, for example) where they actually increased their defence expenditures substantially. Several converging developments produced these changes: the growing incompatibility between civil and military culture, the increased expense of military training and technology, and the vulnerabilities created by large forces. But nothing mattered more than the emerging importance of the technological edge in combat.

A simple *gedanken* experiment confirms this. Ask any group of field grade army officers which side they would prefer to command: an American armoured battalion task force of 54 M1 tanks plus small numbers of infantry and other supporting arms, or an Iraqi Republican Guards division of over 300 moderate-quality T-72 tanks, with the full panoply of divisional artillery and support. They will choose, unanimously, the American armoured task force. The combination of superior technology and better-trained and -led soldiers means that, in certain kinds of combat, force ratios hitherto thought utterly unacceptable—1 to 3, or even worse—could nonetheless yield victory to the seemingly hopelessly outnumbered side. To be sure, this observation may not apply equally to all forms of combat, or might not hold true in particular situations, but the broad truth remains: to a degree far greater than, say, during the Second World War, quality now trumps quantity. That quality, moreover, lies in the combination of manpower and technology. Superbly trained troops in mediocre tanks and aircraft might do well against mediocre troops in correspondingly magnificent weapon systems, but in the real world such match-ups rarely occur. The old systems of estimating military power no longer apply, be they the crude tabular comparisons of forces that appear in the newspapers or weekly news magazines, or the seemingly scientific calculations of attrition-driven Pentagon models. The emergence of quality as the dominant feature in military power has rendered obsolete, if not absurd, today's systems of calculating relative military power.

The Speciation of Weapons

In the nineteenth century, and for most of the twentieth, the armed forces of the world shared similar weaponry. There have always been minor differences: even an early twentieth-century Mauser differed from a Lee Enfield or Lebel rifle. More important differences began to emerge in the First World War when, for example, the Allied states invested heavily in tanks, where the Germans did not; and certainly by the Second World War, when the United States and Great Britain developed heavy bombers that were imitated by neither their enemies nor their chief ally, the Soviet Union. The British, moreover, concentrated on aircraft optimized for night bombing, with heavy payloads and sophisticated night navigation, but little defensive ability, where the Americans concentrated on daylight bombing of industrial targets. Still, during the Second World War, and even during much of the Cold War, basic weapons systems were similar. By the end of the twentieth century, however, weapons had evolved much like a sophisticated ecological system. This development had three parts: the evolution of the actual implements of destruction, the emergence of unique platforms, and the creation of larger systems of military technology.

An example of the first development is the 1980's British runway-attack munition JP233. This system discharged 30 penetrating rockets and over 200 scattered mines from a low-flying Tornado fighter bomber. The RAF developed tactics and practised skills suited to its capabilities; when put to the test in the Gulf War, however, it proved nearly useless and indeed dangerous for pilots who had to fly low and straight over Iraqi runways. JP233, an extremely expensive munition was, in truth, designed for a single scenario, that is, conventional conflict in Europe. Its purpose was to slow down a surge of Soviet fighter planes early in an East–West war by temporarily disabling Warsaw Pact airbases, allowing outnumbered NATO forces to gain air superiority over time. In Iraq, however, the numerical (not to mention the qualitative) balance was on the other side; Iraqi airbases were far larger than their Warsaw Pact counterparts, meaning that RAF pilots had to make longer (and hence more dangerous) runs over defended perimeters. Iraqi bases also had numerous runways and taxiways (unlike their Warsaw Pact counterparts) and could still service fighter aircraft—which, however, being outnumbered and outclassed, had very little inclination to take off! (See Box 7.2.)

The day of the simple high-explosive bomb is, if not over, close to it. Antitank missiles may carry not one but several warheads specifically designed to detonate layers of reactive armour and then to penetrate the sophisticated composite armour of tanks. A guided bomb may have a sophisticated nose that will not merely penetrate several layers of concrete and dirt, but actually count the number of floors it has penetrated before detonating (presumably) at the right one.

Military technology has diversified in another way. Whereas in the past all powers of the first rank had similar kinds of weapons systems, that is no longer the case. Only one country, the United States, can afford a large, stealthy, long-range bomber like the B2. Relatively few countries can afford large sophisticated surface warships. Most countries, by contrast, can afford highly accurate surface-to-surface ballistic and cruise missiles, UAVs, and the latest (and most lethal) antitank missiles. This does not guarantee success to one side or the other, but it means that to the extent they still occur, arms races are more likely to be asymmetric.

BOX 7.2 Second World War Fighter Aircraft

	Spitfire	P-51	Bf-109	Zero
Date entered service	July 1938	April 1942	September 1939	July 1940
Weight (fully loaded, lb)	5,800	8,800	5,523	5,313
Range (miles)	395	950	412	1,160
Speed (mph)	364	387	354	331
Armament	8 3 303in. machine guns	4 3 20mm cannon	2 3 7.92mm machine guns 2 3 20mm cannon	2 3 7.7mm machine guns 2 3 20mm cannon
Engine horsepower	1,030	1,150/1,590	1,100	940

Many aspects go into the performance of an aircraft: the statistics here are but a few of the key indicators of effectiveness—others include climb and turn rates, for example. But some anomalies here are suggestive. The Japanese extracted tremendous range out of the Zero, which they needed for operations in the Pacific region. They got that by good design—and by stripping out armour. The result was a highly manoeuvrable but vulnerable aircraft that when hit was often destroyed. The P-51 was a hulking brute of an airplane; once the powerful Merlin engine was installed—a power plant with 50 per cent more capacity than its competitors—the Allies had a long-range fighter that could escort bombers to the heart of Germany or deliver bombs as well as cannon fire. More subtle differences (for example, the American and British preference for standardized weapons, as opposed to the mix of armaments on the Bf-109 and Zero) speak to national styles of weapons design, to include a strong priority on aerial firepower.

Thus Syria, which once hoped to achieve conventional parity with Israel in the late 1970s and early 1980s, has stopped trying to match the Israeli Air Force in the air. It relies, instead, on sophisticated Russian-made air defences and thousands of surface-to-surface missiles and rockets of varying types and quality. So too, for that matter, does a non-state militia— Lebanon's Hezbollah.

A third form of military evolution has to do with the development not of weapons systems per se, but of meta-systems of extraordinary complexity. Networked sensors and command and control, such as the air operations centres that managed Allied air forces in the Gulf and Yugoslav Wars, are one example, but others will surely emerge. The US Navy's Cooperative Engagement Capability, which allows all the ships in a task force to share a common picture based on the sum of all data in the system, is a prototypical example. So too are the space command and control systems that allow military staffs to track most objects in close orbit, and to coordinate the movements of spacecraft. Increasingly, these systems reflect less a traditional system of military command and control—in which information flows up and decisions down—than a far less hierarchical sharing of information and with it a certain dilution of authority as traditionally understood.

Engineers use the term 'systems integration' to describe the art of putting together a complex of technologies to achieve a purpose. Not all countries excel at it: the United States and several European states have, as the triumph of their aerospace industries indicates. Japan has found it more difficult, while China and Russia have mixed records (Hughes 1998). Conventional military power rests, increasingly, on the ability of states to put together combinations of sensors and weapons and to make them function together in a fluid environment. Other forms of military power (terror or low-intensity warfare at one level, weapons of mass destruction at the other) do not demand these qualities.

The Rise of Commercial Technology

Some percentage of military technology has always derived from the civilian sector. The famous Higgins boat of the Second World War, for example, which landed hundreds of thousands of Allied soldiers on beaches around the world, was a modification of a small craft originally designed for work in the Everglades swamps of Florida. More broadly, civilian technologies have, from time to time, had an enormous effect on the conduct of war. The telegraph and the railway were, of course, both civilian technologies. Following the Second World War, however, to an unprecedented degree the armed forces of the developed world created vast research establishments operating on the cutting-edge of technology; military inventions tended to spill over into the civilian realm more than the other way around. The transistor and modern jet engines, to take two radically different-sized technologies, emerged from military research and development. This held true at the Department of Defense's ARPANET—a system developed by the Advanced Research Projects Agency to enable the transmission of messages in the event of nuclear war. Similarly, space-based sensing emerged out of Western and Soviet efforts to exploit space for military purposes.

The information age is fundamentally different in this respect. Civilian technology, particularly in the area of software, leads military applications. Civilian encryption systems, and the fibre optic cables that carry secret information, have put secure communications within the reach even of non-state actors. Even when civilian technology does not yet lead military technology (in space-based sensing, for example) it is not very far behind: civilian satellites today can achieve resolutions (one metre or less) barely imaginable for their military counterparts only a decade or two ago. Tourists looking for maps, satellite imagery, and GPS coordinates, as well as automated directions, can obtain them all—for free—with a tap on the keyboard of any computer connected to the Internet. These trends will continue as vast sums of money for research and development—and with it talented scientists—turn to the civilian and away from the military sector. Information has no value without military technology to act on it, to be sure, but information, and the ability to process it, is the heart of modern conventional warfare.

These three trends—the rise of quality, the speciation of weapons, and the increased role of commercial technology—generally work to the benefit of developed open societies. They require a sophisticated industrial base for their manufacture, a skilled workforce for their maintenance, and, above all, flexible organizations for their intelligent use. These are qualities most likely to be found in democracies. As recently as a few decades ago, many thoughtful observers believed that democratic states stood at a near-ineradicable disadvantage vis-à-vis authoritarian or totalitarian counterparts, and indeed many of those weaknesses persist: the potential for indecision and volatility, indiscipline, and more recently, a pervasive sensitivity to casualties. Outweighing these and other weaknesses, however, are liberal democracies' strengths: their wealth (which makes military hardware affordable), their citizens' relative comfort with technological change, and fluid, egalitarian social relationships that breed a willingness to share rather than hoard information. For the moment, at any rate, the rise of the information technologies seems to ensure the conventional dominance of liberal democracies.

Key points

- There are three main features of the new era in warfare; the importance of quality over quantity; the speciation of military hardware; and the increased role of the commercial technologies.

- On occasions in history several developments have come together to create a revolution in military affairs (RMA).

- Following the Gulf War in 1991, changes in accuracy, range, and intelligence led many to believe a new RMA was taking place.

- Recent conflicts between unequal adversaries make it difficult to discern if a real RMA has occurred.

Asymmetric Challenges

There is an apparent strategic paradox in the increasing technological edge of advanced, conventional powers who find themselves baffled or even defeated by irregular opponents. Israel's unsuccessful decade-long war (from 1991 to 2000, although preceded by skirmishes beforehand) with Hezbollah guerrillas in southern Lebanon, is a dismaying example of how a vastly superior force, armed with high-tech weapons, can find itself defeated by an adroit opponent who knows how to play on the sensitivity of a democracy to its own casualties, and on world concern for civilians caught in a crossfire. American forces in Iraq following the overthrow of the Saddam Hussein regime in 2003 were bedevilled by a robust insurgency that, through the use of improvised explosive devices (IEDs), suffered far heavier casualties than it did during the swift, violent, and overwhelming march to Baghdad. These experiences, like those of Russia in Chechnya in the preceding decade, have caused some to suggest that guerrilla or irregular warfare can reduce or eliminate the importance of technological advantage on the modern battlefield.

This is not quite true. Modern guerrillas and terrorists make use of cell phones, electronic triggering devices, and extremely sophisticated explosives for their bombs; those countering them use even more sophisticated forms of electronic sweeping and neutralization, UAVs looking for those who plant IEDs, and precision-guided missiles to destroy specific vehicles or rooms in a building. In the hard urban fight for Falluja in November 2004, US Army and Marine forces took casualties in the scores, not the hundreds that would have been characteristic of city fighting even during Vietnam. The Israelis experienced similarly low losses in their operations in the urban environment of the West Bank and Gaza in the years preceding. Technology remains critical even in low-intensity conflict, and technological competitions—between bomb-maker and bomb-seeker, between guerrilla in ambush and convoy ready to fight its way through, between those protecting voting places and those seeking to prevent elections—persist.

The same might be said of another asymmetric strategy for technologically inferior powers—the resort to missile forces equipped with weapons of mass destruction, which offer non-democratic states the possibility of counterbalancing some, if not all, of the conventional predominance of their richer and more sophisticated opponents. Even the best missile defences (and these have been deployed, and are being developed further) cannot guarantee a state's safety against such threats. Yet on the other hand, in the competition between advanced and less developed states, a real nuclear edge, if such a thing exists, will go to the more developed state. In the ensuing stand-off, low-intensity conflict will flourish.

It is true, no doubt, that irregular warfare evens the playing field somewhat, but more in terms of strategy than operations. Guerrilla or terrorist strategies work when public opinion and political resolve are vulnerable to attrition of will. It is not clear that prosperous liberal democracies can always cope well with these threats. Democracy can wage conventional warfare and remain true to itself; it is far more difficult for it to battle terror and insurgency without resorting to strategies—to include extensive surveillance of its own citizens, population control, and even assassination—that are, in the long run, corrosive to its values. No society of this type, moreover, has yet had to absorb sudden, massive levels of casualties comparable to those suffered by the inhabitants of Tokyo, Dresden, or Hiroshima at the end of the Second World War. How resilient rich, free countries will be in the face of such suffering remains to be seen.

On the other hand, thus far it turns out that advanced liberal states can use modern technology—from biometrics to robotics—to fight irregular opponents, and succeed. Israel's success in containing the second Palestinian intifada, reducing its own casualties, and inflicting crippling losses on the middle and senior levels of leadership of extremist organizations, speaks to the effectiveness of high technology, and the kind of will that can be evoked in the face of what society agrees is a serious threat. Similarly, the United States public has displayed remarkable persistence in a counterinsurgency operation in Iraq that has inflicted substantial casualties (some 4,500 deaths as of 2012, and nearly seven times as many wounded), and that was, arguably, badly mismanaged in its early phases, but won in its final period. In both cases, high technology played a role in limiting losses and achieving some successes.

Challenges of the New Technology

The asymmetric threat to the dominance of the new military technologies may take some time to make itself fully felt. Meanwhile, it is difficult enough for modern militaries to cope with the challenges posed by the information revolution. One difficulty has to do with personnel issues. Industrial age militaries could compete fairly easily with private enterprise because, at some level, they resembled it. A caste system resting on soldiers, non-commissioned officers, and officers mirrored a civilian stratification of workers, foremen, and managers. Compensation and deference structures were similar, although room could be made in the military, as in the civilian world, for more highly paid technical experts.

In the information age, the similarities between military and civilian organizations have broken down. Military organizations remain more hierarchical than many of their civilian counterparts, but more importantly, they find it increasingly difficult to obtain the human resources they need. A software engineer in the civilian sector is a highly paid, fairly autonomous employee, working with relatively little supervision. It has become acutely difficult for armed forces to recruit (and more importantly, retain) skilled men and women in these fields. Similarly, talented and aggressive young officers are far more aware than ever before of the possibilities open to them outside the military. Retaining their services in an age of economic opportunity is difficult not merely because of compensation inequities—those have always existed—but because the civilian sector can often offer far more opportunity for change, autonomy, and unfettered responsibility.

The information technologies have other, perhaps more subtle effects on the conduct of war. As a general rule, the greater the flow of information, the more possibility for centralized control. During the Second World War, for example, the Royal Navy and then the United States centralized antisubmarine warfare in shore-based organizations that exploited reliable long-range radio communications and critically important advances in intelligence gathering. Such a development was very much the exception, however. Today, videoconferencing and the electronic transmission of data mean that generals in national capitals can exercise close supervision over their subordinates. This effect exists throughout the military hierarchy: the challenge for mid-level and senior leaders has become one of controlling the instinctive desire to take charge of a junior officer's problems. That impulse has become all the greater the more politically visible military action has become: when the result of a botched operation shows up immediately on CNN and a hundred websites, the inclination of higher authority to exercise the control that technology makes possible becomes all the greater.

Warfare often now occurs under the watchful eyes of the video camera and satellite uplink. In the Somalia intervention of the early 1990s, for example, American naval commandos (SEALs) slipped ashore (on 8 December 1992) in advance of a larger force, only to find a reception party of journalists awaiting them, brilliant lights blinding the wary sailors. Today insurgents put pictures of attacks on NATO forces in Afghanistan within hours, and sometimes minutes, of their taking place. There are exceptions: the Russians excluded the press from much of the second Chechen war, and the Rwanda massacres occurred before journalists could cover them adequately. The Arab–Israeli conflict, however, which resumed in 2000 with a Palestinian insurrection, may prove to be more the norm: rock throwing and shooting watched by (indeed, often staged for) journalists. Propaganda, always an adjunct of war, became a central element in the Arab–Israeli struggle, and both sides found themselves structuring military action with reference not only to the traditional considerations of geography and tactics, but also to the consideration of publicity. Adults manoeuvred Palestinian stone-throwing children into positions for optimal camera shots of 14-year-olds with rocks up against 19-year-olds with rifles. Meanwhile, after some abysmal failures (helicopter gunships blowing up empty houses), the Israelis reverted to sniper work and night-time kidnappings and assassinations precisely to avoid teams of journalists. Both sides created their own, and wrecked their opponents', websites as the conflict extended into cyberspace. The real and the virtual battlefields had become a complex and inextricable whole. This development persisted in the Iraq War, which took a much grislier turn. Insurgent strategy included kidnappings and gruesome beheadings, which were the stuff not only of broadcasts on Arab-language television, but of film clips on jihadi websites, seeking to intimidate opponents, discourage foreign development aid, and enlist new supporters. To some extent, moreover, it worked.

Key points

- The civilian sector poses a major challenge to maintaining military expertise.
- Information technology may lead to greater centralization of military control.
- Media coverage of conflicts pose challenges for military and political leaders.

 ## Conclusion: The Future of Military Technology

Military technology has contributed to a far more complicated environment for war than that of previous centuries. To the extent one can generalize about its effects, one would have to say that where the dominant forms of war in the past were few, today they are many. The challenges for armed forces are correspondingly immense.

Nor have the changes wrought by the new technologies come to an end. The increasingly easy access by countries to space, and their reliance on space for routine communications, navigation, and information gathering, seems almost certain to propel war into the heavens. For the moment, no country seems to have placed, or at least used, weapons in space that can disable or destroy either other satellites or targets on earth. Similarly, countries have experimented with, but not yet used, technologies on earth capable of affecting space-based systems. Technology, however, clearly permits this, in the form of lasers that can blind satellites, or mere lumps of metal that can hurtle from space to earth delivering enormous amounts of kinetic energy against their targets hundreds of miles below. The opening of space to full-fledged warfare would be as large a change as the opening of the air was during the First World War. New organizations, new operational conditions, new incentives to strike first, new ways of war, will blossom overnight.

Warfare also appears to be moving to cyberspace. Thus far, despite persistent stories about mischievous teenagers, clever criminals, or nefarious agents creating havoc with computer systems, there is little evidence of large-scale, lethal damage done by cyber-attack. It remains a theoretical possibility, however, and the unleashing of a potent virus (STUXNET) on the Iranian nuclear program in 2009 is reported to have had considerable success in retarding, though not stopping, that enterprise. As with the opening up of space, the realization of the potential for war in cyberspace would elicit an efflorescence of organizations, concepts, and patterns of conflict parallel to, but very different from, those of conventional warfare. (See Chapter 16, particularly 'A coming change in the character of war?' for a strong case that cyberpower may transform conflict.)

A third sort of change already under way consists of advances in manufacturing, particularly in what are known as the nanotechnologies, robotics, and artificial intelligence. While it is highly unlikely that human beings will ever leave the battlefield (if only because the battlefield will surely come to them), more of the dangerous work may devolve upon small autonomous, intelligent machines that creep or fly, or merely sit and wait, classifying and attacking opponents. Animated, superintelligent minefields transposed on land might make movement or manoeuvre by conventional forces extremely difficult. More importantly, the creation of such machines will mean that humans have gradually begun to cede much of their ability to make decisions to silicon chips. It is a process already well under way in some areas—modern aircraft, for example, are so intrinsically unstable that an automatic system, rather than a human being, must adjust their trim.

In all these cases, the most interesting and important consequences of technological change will probably flow from its effect on how human beings think about and conduct war: how they conceive of military action, how they assign responsibility, how they calculate military effects, how they attempt to harmonize means and ends. But a fourth set of changes, perhaps the most profound of all, looms larger still. The biological sciences increasingly make it possible to change the nature of human beings themselves (Fukuyama 1999). The intriguing theoretical possibility of Greek philosophers has become, in our age, the challenge of scientific researchers. One can scarcely doubt that an Adolf Hitler, or for that matter a Saddam Hussein, would have availed himself of the resources of bio-technology to breed new kinds of human beings—super-soldiers, for one thing, insensitive to fear and truly loyal to the death—who could serve his purposes. Our common understanding of war rests on some of its deeply human features, which have not changed since the days of Homer or Thucydides. This is so, however, only because the same species, *homo sapiens*, has continued to wage it. If—when?—humans are replaced by a variety of creatures, some subhuman, and others, in some respects, superhuman, war itself will have become an activity as different from traditional human conflict as are the murderous struggles between competing anthills or the stalking of herds of deer by packs of wolves.

 ## Questions

1. Take a representative military technology such as the tank. Using several examples, how would you characterize the national style embedded in the design of these armoured vehicles?

2. What is stealth technology? Does the concept of interaction apply to it?

3. In what cases does military technology require high levels of technical expertise and education, and in what cases does it actually reduce or even eliminate such a requirement?

4. What are some of the military technologies that only the United States has available to it? Other great powers? Smaller states? Non-state actors?

5. What are some examples of 'the technological edge'? How fragile are such leads by one state or another?

6. Is cyberwarfare really 'warfare'? Are there other metaphors that might explain it better?

7. What implications are there if warfare extends to space—will it impact more on commercial or military technology?

8. What are some of the technologies most useful to the conduct of irregular warfare, to include guerrilla and terror operations?

9. Are democracies better placed than authoritarian/totalitarian regimes to adapt to the changing nature and problems of technological warfare?

10. What would be the strategic and moral implications of advances in biological science that would allow governments to enhance soldier performance far beyond current norms?

 ## Further Reading

J.D. Bergen, *Military Communications: A Test for Technology* (Washington, DC: Center of Military History, 1986), chapters 16–17, 367–408.
Describes an interesting competition in communication technology and electronic warfare between an extremely sophisticated state (the USA) and a considerably more backward one (North Vietnam) in which the more developed society did not necessarily do well.

A. Beyerchen, 'From Radio to Radar: Interwar Military Adaptation to Technological Change in Germany, the United Kingdom, and the United States', in Williamson Murray and Allan R. Millett (eds), *Military Innovation in the Interwar Period* (Cambridge: Cambridge University Press, 1996).
A good example of how national style appears even in the electronic realm.

W. Churchill, *The World Crisis, 1911–1914* (New York: Charles Scribner's Sons, 1926), chapter 6, 'The Romance of Design', 125–49.
Brilliantly describes some of these challenges from the point of view of a decision-maker.

A. C. Clarke, 'Superiority', in *Expedition to Earth* (New York: Harcourt, Brace and World, 1970), 92–104.
A science fiction story with a whimsical but wise warning on the dangers of becoming too sophisticated.

M. van Creveld, *Technology and War from 2000 BC to the Present* (New York: Free Press, 1989).
Considerably more up to date than Fuller 1945.

J. F. C. Fuller, *Armament and History; A Study of the Influence of Armament on History from the Dawn of Classical Warfare to the Second World War* (New York: Charles Scribner's Sons, 1945).
Remains an excellent short treatment of the relationship between technology, tactics, organization, and strategy.

W. Hughes, *Fleet Tactics: Theory and Practice* (Annapolis, MD: Naval Institute Press, 1986).
A thoughtful treatment of the role of technology in warfare.

H. Petroski, *To Engineer is Human: The Role of Failure in Successful Design* (New York: Random House, 1982).

According to the author, 'form follows failure', that is, engineering advances occur only as a result of the failure of current materials or designs—and in turn, advances set up further failures as technologies are stressed to their limits.

G. Raudzens, 'War-Winning Weapons: The Measurement of Technological Determinism in Military History', *Journal of Military History*, 54 (October 1990), 403–33.

A sceptical view of technology's importance. A sceptical view of the impact of technology on war.

P. W. Singer, *Wired for War: The Robotics Revolution and Conflict in the 21st Century* (New York: Penguin, 2009).

The first comprehensive look at the impact of unmanned technologies on the conduct of war—surely an augur of things to come.

 ## Web Links

Janes: **http://www.janes.com/** This website has many reputable articles on the links between technology and warfare.

Aviation Week: **http://www.aviationweek.com/aw/** The same applies to this reputable website.

Global Security: **http://www.globalsecurity.org/military/systems/index.html** This website also hosts articles on a range of technology issues, including valuable primers on the subject.

Military Technology: **http://www.monch.com/** This website has regular updates on recent developments in military technology.

Wired Danger Room **http://www.wired.com/dangerroom/** This website has excellent reporting, particularly on cyber-related issues.

http://www.army-technology.com/projects/merkava/; **http://www.army-technology.com/projects/abrams/**. Note: the stated speed for the M1A2 is considerably too slow.

8

Intelligence and Strategy

ROGER GEORGE

 Chapter Contents

Introduction	152
What is Intelligence?	153
Intelligence as Enabler of US Strategy	157
Strategic Surprise: Causes and Correctives	160
The Post-9/11 World of Intelligence	164
Conclusion	168

 Reader's Guide

This chapter examines how intelligence enables but does not guarantee successful strategy. It opens by discussing what intelligence is and how strategists have talked about its utility. It then traces the development of US intelligence in its efforts to support cold war strategies of containment and deterrence. The chapter examines the challenges and causes of 'strategic surprise', bringing to bear key historical cases of Pearl Harbor, the 1962 Cuban Missile Crisis, the 1973 Yom Kippur War, and the 11 September 2001 attacks. While suggesting some possible correctives, it concludes that there are no complete solutions to inevitable intelligence failures. It also identifies some of the new challenges intelligence faces in a world of globalization, transnational threats, information overload, and strategies of counterterrorism and counterinsurgency.

Introduction

Good strategy is dependent on understanding the nature of war, key aspects of the international system and an adversary's intentions and capabilities.[1] Inherently, then, strategy must be based on good intelligence. Yet, while strategic theorists have acknowledged the importance of intelligence, many also express their discomfort with its quality and reliability. Theorists can be categorized as either optimists or pessimists regarding the role of intelligence. Sun Tzu, the optimist, advised the warrior to 'know the enemy and know yourself and in a hundred battles you will never be in peril'. Carl von Clausewitz (1982), the pessimist, barely acknowledges the value of intelligence in his writing, concluding that 'many intelligence reports are contradictory, even more are false, and most are uncertain'. Nevertheless, both recognize that no strategy can be formulated or implemented without assessing the challenges and opportunities that it might encounter. Today, decision-makers are no different. As one senior American US official described policymakers from several past administrations: 'The ones that were skeptical when they came in [to government] became increasingly dependent or, at least reliant on it. The ones that loved it at the beginning began to say, "Is that all you can do for me?"' (Center for the Study of Intelligence 2004).

Throughout history, intelligence has played a role in the development and execution of national strategies. Moses sent his spies into Canaan. In Napoleon's time, diplomats often assumed the roles of spies while serving as representatives of their monarchs and prime ministers. Some would say Paul Revere provided the first 'warning' of war to the colonists that the British were coming. General George Washington was, in effect, the first head of American intelligence, as he doled out funds for agents who worked against the British. In 1941, decoding of Japanese military communications provided American negotiators with a tip-off that Tokyo was breaking off negotiations and contemplating war. Although this warning was not understood well enough to avert the Pearl Harbor attack, this code-breaking ultimately helped to destroy the Japanese fleet at the 1942 Battle of Midway. In 1944, General Dwight Eisenhower constructed one of the most daring strategic deception campaigns to mislead Hitler's Germany regarding the Normandy invasion; a deception campaign that was based on an accurate reading of Nazi preconceptions of Allied intentions. Indeed, Eisenhower and British Prime Minister Winston Churchill stand out as decision-makers with a keen sense of how to use Allied intelligence for wartime purposes.

Intelligence was a major element of strategies aimed at supporting America's containment and deterrence policies during the cold war. Today, it is central to the challenge of defeating terrorism and the spread of weapons of mass destruction (WMD). As intelligence activities have grown and become more complicated, there is increasing concern that they need to be effectively guided to support national security strategies. Far from becoming irrelevant in the post-cold war world as some thought in the 1990s, the 2009 US *National Security Strategy* highlights its principal missions to be combating violent extremism, proliferation, and cyber threats in addition to providing strategic warning and supporting ongoing military operations (National Security Strategy 2009).

What is Intelligence?

The term intelligence is commonly used to describe only that information provided to policy officials by government organizations, in order to distinguish it from a much broader body of information available to those inside and outside the US Government. Intelligence is often secret information, which is collected through clandestine means or technical systems (e.g. satellites in earth-orbit, monitoring communications or electronic signatures). The sources and methods used to collect this information are risky, expensive, and often fragile, so their unauthorized exposure to adversaries would weaken US national security. Part of the intelligence mission, then, is to protect this information (called counterintelligence) as well as to penetrate the intelligence services of adversaries (counterespionage). Intelligence information also is 'tailored' to respond specifically to the requirements and needs of government officials. Generally speaking, intelligence is focused on the policies, intentions, and capabilities of foreign governments and increasingly on the plans and activities of non-state actors that threaten the United States and its allies. Intelligence can also be understood as the programmes and processes used by the 16 separate agencies currently comprising the US intelligence community to collect, analyse, and disseminate secret information throughout the US Government. The production of finished intelligence reflects this 'intelligence cycle': decision-makers' needs are translated into information requirements for collection, which lead to analysis and the writing of finished intelligence reports, which are then disseminated back to the original requestors of that information (see Box 8.1).

These intelligence programmes and processes require the coordination of hundreds of separate programmes and thousands of individuals across the US Government. In 2010, such

BOX 8.1 Definitions of Intelligence

The term 'foreign intelligence' means information relating to the capabilities, intentions, or activities of foreign governments or elements thereof, foreign organizations, or foreign persons.

National Security Act (1947)

Intelligence, as I am writing it, is the knowledge, which our highly placed civilians and military men must have to safeguard the national welfare.

Sherman Kent (1949)

Intelligence is information not publicly available, or analysis based at least in part on such information, that has been prepared for policymakers or other actors inside the government.

Council on Foreign Relations (1996)

Reduced to its simplest terms, intelligence is knowledge and foreknowledge of the world around us—the prelude to decision and action by US policymakers.

CIA Consumer's Guide to Intelligence (1999)

The product resulting from the collection, processing, integration, analysis and interpretation of available information concerning foreign nationals, hostile or potentially hostile forces or elements or areas of actual or potential operations.

JCS Joint Publication 1-02, November (2010)

Warner (2002)

activities constituted as many as 100,000 people and as much as US$53 billion dollars per year (Director of National Intelligence, 2010). On a daily basis, individuals and organizations must collect huge volumes of raw (unevaluated) information, sift through it to separate fact from rumour, propaganda and fiction, search for the most valuable insights, interpret facts to form important analytic judgements about their meaning and significance to US policy interests, and communicate it to senior civilian and military policymakers in the United States or to allied and friendly governments.

Intelligence Collection

The collection of raw intelligence information takes the lion's share of American intelligence resources (roughly 80 per cent). Most collection efforts are located inside in the Department of Defense. Its National Security Agency operates major signals intelligence (SIGINT) programmes while the National Reconnaissance Office builds and operates major satellite reconnaissance programmes and the National Geo-spatial Intelligence Agency exploits and analyses the imagery produced by the satellite collection systems. These agencies are considered so vital to the conduct of US military operations that they are designated 'combat support' elements of the US intelligence community, and the Secretary of Defense takes special care to ensure that they are properly funded, manned, and managed. The Central Intelligence Agency (CIA) runs the other major intelligence programme focused on collecting clandestine HUMINT or human intelligence. The classic job of recruiting secret agents who can penetrate the internal workings of foreign adversaries and terrorist groups falls to the CIA's National Clandestine Service. Its case officers are deployed all over the world to identify important intelligence targets and learn the plans and intentions of America's enemies, which cannot be so easily gleaned from overhead satellites or intercepted electronic messages.

Although not new, global collection of the so-called 'open source' information has taken on greater prominence. There has always been an interest in reading foreign publications or listening to and watching radio and TV broadcasts. The advent of the Internet, however, has caused a dramatic explosion in the volume and scope of foreign open source information, leading to the development of the intelligence community's Open Source Center. The Center monitors millions of publications, broadcasts, and websites, and media reports are produced for intelligence analysts and decision-makers alike. Moreover, in the battle against violent extremism, information warfare now involves monitoring and disrupting jihadist websites often used for recruitment and communications (see Box 8.2).

Intelligence Analysis

The least expensive part of the intelligence enterprise is analysis. Country and functional analysts must make sense out of the millions of clandestine reports, electronic intercepts, or digital imagery that are gathered by their collection partners. These analysts are to be found in the Central Intelligence Agency, the Defense Intelligence Agency, the Department of State's Bureau of Intelligence and Research, as well as in smaller units in the FBI, the

---

BOX 8.2 Intelligence Collection: Sources and Methods

Finished all-source intelligence rests on the collection and careful weighing and evaluation of multiple pieces of clandestinely or openly gathered information. This information comes from a variety of sources.

- *Human intelligence (HUMINT)* is gained overtly by diplomats and military attachés or secretly from foreign agents who have access to the plans, intentions, and capabilities of foreign adversaries.

- *Signals intelligence (SIGINT)* is the technical interception and exploitation of an adversary's communication and other electronic systems.

- *Imagery intelligence (IMINT)* is collected from ground, overhead, and space-based imaging systems (often satellites) using visual photography, electro-optics, radar, or infra-red sensors.

- *Open source (OPINT)* intelligence is the collection, translation, and analysis of foreign broadcasts, news media, and increasingly Internet websites.

Department of Homeland Security, and other national security agencies. They have the responsibility of giving US policymakers the knowledge needed to fashion and implement effective national security strategies. They provide this analysis to a wide array of government officials throughout the Executive Branch and the Congress in written, oral, and electronic formats. From the most sensitive and limited production of the President's Daily Brief (PDB) to the posting of numerous intelligence assessments on the Intelligence Community's classified website (called INTELINK), these assessments are tailored to suit a variety of decision-makers, from the President down to diplomats and field commanders. The purpose of these reports is both to inform as well as to enable decision-makers to construct and implement policies that advance US strategies, identify threats, and evaluate the actions and intentions of foreign adversaries. Seldom, however, do intelligence analysts provide sufficient factual details or highly confident forecasts that completely satisfy policymakers.

The task for intelligence analysts, then, is to distinguish carefully between what they know and do not know and then to present what they believe might happen and explain why it is significant. It is up to the decision-maker to decide how to fashion strategies and policies that take note of these intelligence judgements. Intelligence analysis, however, faces increasing competition from other sources of information. Decision-makers often consider themselves analysts, who are also utilizing the Internet, have their own networks of experts and have more direct contact with foreign government officials than analysts working at the CIA or other intelligence agencies. Hence, analysts must work hard to develop special insight and expertise based on their access to a wider range of sources of intelligence. In some cases, analysts' credibility can rest as much on their academic credentials, foreign area travels, and language skills as on their access to highly classified information. Such experts also have the advantage of focusing their entire workday on a single issue or country and the ability to task intelligence collectors to provide new information of use to decision-makers. By quickly preparing new assessments directed at the specific interests or needs of a decision-maker, they can provide actionable (useful in taking decisions) information.

Special Intelligence Missions

While collection and analysis form the core of the intelligence mission, these missions rest on effective counterintelligence and counterespionage. Information provided to key decision-makers must be protected from falling into the hands of enemies. Strategic deception can occur—a situation when an adversary understands how an opponent perceives a threat and succeeds in undermining or distorting accurate threat perceptions. The ongoing Wikileaks controversy—that is, the unauthorized disclosure of hundreds of thousands of classified US diplomatic and military reports—continues to complicate US foreign relations and demand greater government controls over how the nearly 2 million government and contractor employees handle sensitive information.

To ensure that intelligence agencies are not penetrated, it is necessary to conduct counter-espionage operations; these activities are aimed at recruiting agents inside hostile intelligence services, in order to determine if they have recruited agents inside one's own government or intelligence services. This competition often prompts Hollywood to develop fantastic versions of what is often called the 'spy-versus-spy' game. In real life, counterespionage is far less romantic but no less vital to protecting information which intelligence provides to the most senior decision-makers in a government.

Another distinct mission for intelligence is conducting covert action. While most intelligence merely enables the use of military, economic, informational, and diplomatic power, covert action is in fact the *covert* use of these instruments. Sometimes known as 'special activities', covert action is run in the United States by the CIA at the specific request of the President. These actions are kept secret in order to achieve important strategic objectives, without directly associating them with the US Government. First established by the National Security Council in the late 1940s, special activities have become a tool of US foreign policy, used by virtually every President in some fashion. In a post-9/11 environment, such special activities are vital to disrupting terrorist plans and proliferation networks. However, any strategist will need to weigh the risks and benefits of covert actions as they often create controversy when they become known to an adversary, the US public, or the international community.

The intelligence community's role in covert activities has steadily grown since 9/11, as US strategists have increasingly relied upon non-conventional approaches to combating terrorism and overcoming internal conflicts in Iraq and Afghanistan. Major Presidential Findings have been issued for CIA to conduct extensive covert activities to disrupt, defeat, and destroy terrorist cells around the world. The most significant aspect of these special operations was the location and elimination of Usama Bin Laden in Pakistan in 2011. This event highlighted both the utility but also the controversiality of using combined intelligence and military assets to eliminate a major terrorist figure operating in a safe haven. In addition, the US military and intelligence agencies have operated unmanned airborne vehicles (UAVs or 'drones') to identify and kill key al-Qaeda leaders. The extent to which the US will be able to rely on such methods remains to be seen, as they are not only highly effective, but also fiercely criticized by countries, against which the US has used them without their explicit approval. (Gorman 2011)

Key points

● Strategy rests on accurate perceptions of an adversary's plans, intentions, and capabilities, and intelligence enables decision-makers to develop and implement good strategy.

● Intelligence is more than just information. It is focused on the special needs of decision-makers and usually requires secret collection methods to uncover the true plans and intentions of a foreign actor.

● Producing actionable (useful in decision-making) intelligence requires careful collection, exploitation, analysis, and dissemination of intelligence. This is called the 'intelligence cycle'.

● Good intelligence requires good counterintelligence aimed at understanding an adversary's efforts to penetrate one's own intelligence apparatus.

● US intelligence also has the responsibility for carrying out special activities designed to hide the US role in using military, political, or economic measures against an adversary. This is commonly known as covert action.

● Covert activities have grown significantly as the US counterterrorism and counterinsurgency strategies have demanded more sensitive, small-scale paramilitary operations to complement and reinforce major military operations.

Intelligence as Enabler of US Strategy

When the cold war began, the United States was in search of both a national security strategy as well as a concept of intelligence. Neither was well defined until important seminal thinking had occurred within the US Government and in the major research centres of the time. George Kennan coined the containment strategy in 1946–1947 and further developed the concept while at the State Department's Policy Planning Staff. A deterrence strategy was also emerging from the strategic thought of Bernard Brodie and Herman Kahn among others, working at the Rand Corporation in the early 1950s. In the meantime, Sherman Kent—a Yale historian and colleague of both Kennan and Brodie at the National War College—developed the concept of strategic intelligence. In his groundbreaking 1949 book, *Strategic Intelligence for an American World Policy*, Kent laid out the basic principles that should drive intelligence. In it simplest sense, intelligence should 'raise the level of discussion' around the policymaking tables. In Kent's view, intelligence should not advocate a specific policy position; instead it should inform policy. Intelligence analysts should be cognizant of, but detached from, any specific policy agenda. Kent knew that lively debates among strong-willed policymakers would make intelligence prone to manipulation and that intelligence analysts had to maintain their objectivity and integrity in presenting unbiased intelligence. Stating this objective, however, was not to say it would be easy to achieve in practice. Nor were intelligence assessments uncontroversial when matters of war or peace were to be based partly on their findings. Throughout the cold war, time and again US intelligence was faulted for being wrong, biased, or both. It also became embroiled in debates over strategy and was sometimes accused, rightly or wrongly, of becoming 'politicized' (distorted by political agendas).

The Soviet Target

As the cold war developed, the principal function of American intelligence was to penetrate the veil of secrecy that surrounded the Soviet Union. The highest collection priorities were aimed at understanding Moscow's communist ideology and internal policy process as well as its strategic objectives and military–industrial complex that presented the key military threat to US and allied security interests. Early intelligence failures drove changes in the operation of US intelligence. The invasion of South Korea in 1950 led to widespread reforms in the CIA and the national estimates process, bringing Sherman Kent to the CIA and creating the Board of National Estimates. This estimates process became a centrepiece of intelligence support to Presidents and the National Security Council in shaping national security policies vis-à-vis the Soviet Union, the Warsaw Pact, and its communist allies in Asia and the Third World. An elaborate schedule of national estimates was designed to monitor and forecast the growth of Soviet strategic and conventional forces, so that Washington's defence planners could build and size US forces appropriately. Other estimates were aimed at comprehending Moscow's global political strategy to spread its influence beyond its East European sphere of influence and into the developing world: still others were produced to assess how resilient were parts of the free world and the so-called non-aligned countries, where the East–West contest was fought through proxies and wars of liberation.

US intelligence assessments were far from perfect but better than most critics care to believe. While US intelligence underestimated the pace of Soviet and Chinese programmes to build their first atomic weapons, it tracked the development of Soviet and Chinese military forces reasonably accurately. Accurate forecasts of Soviet decisions to deploy or use military forces, however, proved the most elusive. Analysts were unprepared for the Soviet placement of nuclear-armed missiles in Cuba in 1962, the invasion of Czechoslovakia in 1968, and the occupation of Afghanistan in 1979 (see Box 8.3).

Periodic intelligence failures, however, were small compared to the steady focus that intelligence agencies placed on the development of Soviet military capabilities, the state of the Soviet economy, and the machinations of the Soviet leadership whose political system was

---

BOX 8.3 The National Intelligence Estimate and the President's Daily Brief

National Intelligence Estimates (NIEs) are prepared for the President, his Cabinet, the National Security Council and other senior civilian and military decision-makers. NIEs focus on strategic issues of mid- or long-term importance to US national security policies. They represent the combined views of all 16 intelligence agencies that comprise the US intelligence community. The NIE process has evolved over time, since first being established in the 1950s by the Board of National Estimates. As practised today, they are produced by the National Intelligence Council, reviewed by all heads of the US intelligence community, and signed off by the Director of National Intelligence.

More importantly, the PDB has become the most well known and highly prized daily intelligence report. Written explicitly for the President and his principal White House and Cabinet-level advisors, it constitutes what the IC believes are the most important intelligence developments and most sensitive information. Delivered by senior intelligence briefers, these reports can often lead to new policy decisions and actions. The PDBs are largely prepared by CIA, however, analysts in the Defense Intelligence Agency and State Department's Bureau of Intelligence and Research (INR) also submit items for inclusion on occasion.

becoming increasingly unstable through the 1970s and 1980s. By the end of the 1980s, the CIA warned that the system was becoming increasingly untenable and that Mikhail Gorbachev's reforms risked either destroying the system or forcing his more conservative critics to replace him. While US intelligence was slow to forecast the end of the Soviet Union—a conclusion that few outside experts or Soviet leaders themselves had reached—American presidents had been largely well served by the CIA and the rest of the US intelligence community in their sober assessments of Soviet military capabilities and political actions. The development of impressive technical intelligence collection systems in the 1970s and 1980s also enabled intelligence analysts to track Soviet strategic systems. This, in turn, enabled US policymakers to develop effective defence and arms control policies that preserved a stable US–Soviet strategic balance and fostered effective deterrence and containment strategies.

Evolution of the Intelligence Community

Over the past half century, the profession of intelligence has continued to evolve. With each decade, there were problems to be addressed, organizational changes to be made, and new substantive issues to be followed. By the end of the cold war, the intelligence community amounted to over a dozen large and small agencies, most of which were contained within the departments of defense, state, justice and now homeland security. This growing 'intelligence community' drove the need for better organization of intelligence activities, highlighting the need for a far stronger role than the Director of Central Intelligence (DCI) could provide. The DCI, who had to lead the CIA, could not effectively coordinate the far-flung activities of a dozen or more intelligence agencies.

As intelligence became a more acknowledged function of government, there was more appreciation and criticism for its role in shaping strategy and policy. Since its very beginning, the CIA and other intelligence agencies inspired controversy. The very role of intelligence in a democratic society caused law-makers to be anxious about having sufficient controls over its methods and its uses. Most recently, the revelations regarding counterterrorist intercept programmes and the interrogation methods employed by the US intelligence community has sparked congressional outrage and enquiries. Not only have American leaders worried about 'spying' on Americans and the breaking of US laws, but they also periodically charge that intelligence is being used or manipulated to serve narrow political purposes. Whenever debates over US strategies began to arise, there was a good possibility that US intelligence would be dragged into these disputes as well. The Vietnam War occasioned major intelligence arguments. Senior US military and civilian leaders challenged and sometimes overruled pessimistic CIA estimates, so they did not undermine the conduct of the war itself. The 1970s American détente and arms control policies designed by President Nixon and Henry Kissinger were also bedevilled by intelligence debates over the nature of the Soviet military threat, Moscow's willingness to fight a nuclear war, and the adequacy of the US–Soviet strategic balance. At the heart of those debates were the strategic intelligence assessments made by the CIA and the Defense Intelligence Agency.

During the 1980–1988 tenure of President Ronald Reagan, US intelligence was sometimes viewed as having taken too benign a view of the Soviet military threat and having allowed itself to become 'politicized' by adopting the 'détentist' tendencies that would support Henry Kissinger's arms control agenda. Most recently, intelligence assessments on Saddam Hussein's nuclear, chemical, and biological weapons capabilities became the focus of multiple investigations to determine how such important judgements could be so incorrect. The Robb-Silbermann WMD Commission cleared the CIA and other agencies of wilful 'politicization' of intelligence but sternly criticized their poor collection and analysis regarding such a central issue to America's national security. Likewise, CIA analysis on Iran and North Korea's nuclear programmes continues to generate criticism for its quality and possible politicization.

The post-9/11 era silenced the calls for eliminating the CIA that were often heard after the end of the cold war, but they were soon replaced by demands for major improvements in the way the United States runs the intelligence community. Major organizational changes were instituted to enable better information sharing and coordination of 16 major foreign and domestic intelligence agencies (including the creation of a Department of Homeland Security). Reforms included the establishment of a new position of Director of National Intelligence, separate from the Director of the CIA, as head of the US intelligence community. The philosophy reigning at the moment is that the Director of National Intelligence would become the leading presidential advisor on and organizer of all intelligence activities, while the CIA was to concentrate on collecting HUMINT, producing all-source intelligence analysis, and conducting covert action at the direction of the President. This new organizational division of labour remains untested and will no doubt be open to further adjustments as needs and conditions change.

Key points

- US intelligence was created with the start of the cold war and focused primarily on the Soviet Union and related threats.
- The intelligence community provides both estimative analysis (NIEs) and current intelligence products (PDBs).
- The intelligence record on the Soviet Union is better than often portrayed, as significant intelligence failures were few compared to massive amount of accurate intelligence on the USSR's military and economic performance.
- The CIA was joined by more than a dozen other intelligence agencies during the cold war to form what is now commonly called the 'intelligence community'.
- Intelligence has been embroiled in controversies, regardless of president or party, as it became a focus for disputes over how to deal with the Soviet Union or other adversaries.

Strategic Surprise: Causes and Correctives

The US intelligence community was created after the 1941 Pearl Harbor attack in an effort to prevent another strategic surprise. The notion of strategic surprise, highlighted in Roberta Wohlstetter's seminal work on Pearl Harbor, continues to drive the development of US intelligence capabilities and the standard by which the CIA and other intelligence agencies are often judged. A working definition of strategic surprise has at least three key elements:

1. It is a development having significant negative impact on national interests;
2. Alternative strategies might have been chosen to avert the consequences; but
3. Accurate and timely intelligence information was lacking, not transmitted or not correctly understood by senior officials.

This definition makes a distinction between a strategic surprise and an intelligence failure; the former is often the result of ineffective interaction between strategists and intelligence professionals in identifying and responding to major threats. An intelligence 'failure' generally places the blame for some disaster on the intelligence community and constitutes only one element of the broader notion of strategic surprise. In fact, some intelligence failures may not jeopardize overall US strategy because their consequences are not so grave or the strategy itself is not so dependent on specific intelligence judgements.

Causes of Surprise

There are many causes of strategic surprise and intelligence failures. A strategic surprise can occur when decision-makers fail to absorb and use information and analysis provided by intelligence professionals. Cases of this include not only Pearl Harbor, where information was available, but also the Soviet placement of nuclear-armed missiles into Cuba in 1962, the 1973 Yom Kippur War, and most recently the 9/11 attacks on New York City and the Pentagon. In each case, there was some warning of a possible threat, but the information was scanty or not properly interpreted. Moreover, policymakers as well as most intelligence analysts dismissed the possibility of such bold actions being plausible and therefore took no steps to avert those actions or mitigate their effects. In virtually all these cases, both decision-makers and intelligence professionals share the blame. In the Pearl Harbor case, there was information indicating Japan planned attacks against US interests in the Pacific; however, it was not disseminated quickly to senior commanders, nor did commanders imagine the attack might be as far forward as Pearl Harbor so they took minimal and mostly ineffective preventive or defensive actions. In the Cuban Missile Crisis, US intelligence was observing Soviet military transfers to Cuba, but analysts as well as President Kennedy's advisors dismissed the possibility that Moscow would place nuclear weapons on an island 90 miles from American shores. In the 1973 Yom Kippur War, both US and Israeli intelligence had good information that Arab states were planning an attack, but they misinterpreted available information as evidence of military exercises rather than preparation for war. Ironically, US and Israeli decision-makers discounted such moves believing that Egypt and Syria would not contemplate attacking Israel after their decisive defeat in the 1967 Middle East War (often called the Six-Day War because of the rapidity with which Israel dispatched both combatants).

The September 2001 attack by al-Qaeda is a classic case of an intelligence failure that led to decision-makers' inattention to a strategic warning that then contributed to a major strategic surprise. The 9/11 Commission Report documents the fact that terrorism analysts at the CIA's Counterterrorism Center were well aware of the growing danger that al-Qaeda posed to American interests. Counterterrorism analysts believed an attack was likely to occur in the autumn of 2001 but they could not provide details of how, when, or where such an attack might occur. As summer 2001 ended, senior intelligence officials provided 'strategic warning' by telling the George W. Bush administration that something big was planned and that counterterrorism analysts were monitoring a huge increase in activity ('chatter'). On 6 August 2001, the President was briefed on a possible terrorist attack on the American homeland, but American intelligence had no specific, tactical intelligence on when or where this might occur. Sadly, as the Commission recounts, there was information held by the FBI and other agencies, which was not effectively combined with what the CIA knew about al-Qaeda in time to realize that the plotters were already in the United States and making their final preparations for the attack. Moreover, the 6 August briefing did not lead decision-makers in other parts of the government to highlight the threat or take any actions that might have tightened airport or airline security. Unheeded strategic warning and the lack of more specific tactical intelligence reporting, according to some intelligence practitioners, encouraged policy inaction, setting up the conditions necessary for a major strategic surprise (Pillar 2011).

Key Factors: Seven Deadly Sins

No single factor is the cause of a major surprise or intelligence failure. Indeed, seven factors are often present in some combination. First, there is usually a collection failure. As Clausewitz warned, information is often lacking or contradictory, or both. Second, analysts can often misinterpret the available information because of an outmoded or inadequate understanding of an adversary's objectives, plans, or capabilities; this is often termed the 'mindset' problem. Even the best experts can develop a benign or 'stylized' view of the adversary that clouds their ability to see how an enemy might take great risks or attempt an unconventional attack. Third, deception employed by an adversary can often feed analysts' inaccurate mindsets and cause them to misread tell-tale signs of danger. Fourth, an adversary can deny—through excellent operational security—to intelligence analysts sufficient information to form an accurate picture of the threat. Fifth, information available to intelligence collectors or analysts might not be rapidly or effectively shared among themselves. Compartmentation (security rules limiting the sharing of information through a 'need to know' principle) can inhibit intelligence organizations from passing what they know to other agencies that can compare it with their own information. Sixth, there can be a failure to communicate threat information effectively to decision-makers, so leaders do not appreciate the dangers in time to take appropriate action. And finally, decision-makers may suffer from their own outmoded mindsets regarding the adversary's intentions and capabilities, and therefore dismiss intelligence warnings or take no countermeasures.

At the core of the problem of strategic surprise and intelligence failures is the presumption that decision-makers and intelligence analysts correctly and completely understand the intentions and capabilities of an adversary. In fact, most strategic surprises result from an inaccurate assessment of how an enemy sees his own situation and how that opponent assesses the benefits and risks of war. Stalin dismissed intelligence that Germany would launch an eastern offensive in the spring of 1941. Hitler suffered the same fate of believing he correctly understood how an Allied invasion would begin in 1944, which Eisenhower reinforced with the Allied deception plans. Israelis underestimated the risk-taking of Arabs in 1973 after their drubbing in 1967, which Egyptian President Anwar Sadat exploited by launching a surprise attack under the cover of military exercises. US analysts and decision-makers likewise underestimated the risk-taking calculations of Soviet leaders in the 1962 Cuba case and again in the

1979 Soviet invasion of Afghanistan. All of these examples highlight the role of human perceptual frailties, to which all analysts as well as strategists are prone. Such cognitive biases, as many psychologists would recognize, are hard to identify and even harder to eliminate.

Correctives, not Cures

Correctives to future strategic surprises or intelligence failures are difficult if not impossible to guarantee. As intelligence scholar Richard Betts has put it, 'intelligence failures are almost inevitable', because there is almost no way to guarantee sufficient information and correct analysis of all threats in order for policymakers to pre-empt them (Betts 2007). Nonetheless, there are three correctives that can be employed to reduce the chances of strategic surprise and intelligence failures. First, improved collection, of course, is always to be hoped for; however, few analysts can depend on perfect intelligence information to guide their analysis. Analysts can assess the gaps in their information and accordingly qualify their judgements to alert decision-makers to the 'unknowns' present in any decisions they make. Second, analysts can assess an adversary's motives and capabilities for conducting major deception and denial campaigns. Typically, the weaker the adversary, the more it might rely on surprise—using deception and denial—to compensate for an opponent's stronger military forces. Third, analysts can develop a greater awareness of their own mindset and other cognitive biases, which can distort their interpretation of available information. There is a growing social science literature on structured analytic techniques, which analysts can use to make their work more rigorous. These techniques—such as devil's advocacy, team A/team B, analysis of competing hypotheses, or scenario analysis—can help analysts to challenge analytical assumptions, make analytic arguments more transparent to peers as well as decision-makers, guide intelligence collectors to filling significant information gaps, and ultimately caution users of intelligence on the limitations of available information to their decision-making processes (see Box 8.4).[2]

Strategists must appreciate that all intelligence is imperfect and not likely to be sufficient to make all decisions with high confidence. Whether it is the case of the 1962 Cuban Missile Crisis or the more recent example of the 2002 Iraq WMD National Intelligence Estimate, intelligence is not entirely right or wrong but rather has both strengths and weaknesses. In 1962, Sherman Kent's estimators misread Soviet intentions and its risk calculations when they judged that the Russians were unlikely to place nuclear-armed missiles in Cuba. Despite

---

BOX 8.4 Warning Problems: The Inevitability of Intelligence Failures

Major insights into intelligence failure have emerged from strategic surprises, such as Pearl Harbor, the German invasion of the USSR, the North Korean attack and Chinese intervention of 1950, the Middle East wars of 1967 and 1973, the Tet offensive and the Soviet invasion of Czechoslovakia in 1968, the 1979 Soviet invasion of Afghanistan, the Argentinean invasion of the Falkland/Malvinas islands in 1982, the 1990 Iraqi attack on Kuwait and other cases. All involve two common problems. First, evidence of impending attack was available but did not flow efficiently up the chain of command. Second, fragmentary alarms that did reach decision-makers were dismissed because they contradicted strategic estimates or assumptions.

Richard Betts (2007: 22)

this flawed estimate, it was intelligence—via U-2 flights over Cuba—along with SIGINT and some HUMINT that gave the Kennedy administration sufficient insight into subsequent Soviet moves to then face down Moscow and eventually negotiate the missiles' removal. For those 12 days in October, the Kennedy administration had good enough intelligence supporting the secret EXCOM meetings (Kennedy's high-level policy team), where options were debated and actions were planned and executed.

In like fashion, the 2002–2003 Iraq intelligence story is not entirely negative. To be sure, the October 2002 National Intelligence Estimate on Iraq's WMD capabilities was deeply flawed. The intelligence community misinterpreted outdated, limited, and in some cases fabricated information, thereby basing its judgements too heavily on outmoded mindsets and on Saddam Hussein's earlier success at deception and denial (Iraqi WMD Commission 2005). However, while these estimates of Saddam's WMD capabilities were wildly off the mark, two other important estimates were largely correct regarding how Saddam would conduct the war and what conditions the United States would face in a post-conflict Iraq (Kerr 2005). As is often the case, some intelligence judgements are always closer to the truth, while others are not. In the Iraq case, what is most remarkable is how little attention was actually paid to intelligence, regardless of whether it was right or wrong (Pillar 2006).

Key points

- Strategic surprise can result when decision-makers fail to act upon intelligence warnings, or when those warnings are ineffectual or not provided at all.

- Intelligence failures result from inadequate collection, effective deception and denial operations, flawed analysis, poor information sharing, and poor communication of warning.

- Analysts can suffer from cognitive biases that create inaccurate perceptions of an adversary's intentions and capabilities, often termed a 'mindset'.

- Decision-makers also run the risk of dismissing intelligence warnings if they harbour strong mindsets of an adversary's intentions and capabilities that do not conform to reality.

- An adversary can employ deception and denial to reinforce flawed mindsets to mislead decision-makers as to a possible attack.

- Averting surprise requires better collection and greater attention to possible deception efforts as well as analysts' cognitive biases and mindsets.

- Strategic surprises and intelligence failures are impossible to eliminate, but taking steps to improve collection and analysis can reduce the odds of them occurring.

The Post-9/11 World of Intelligence

The 9/11 attacks dramatically altered how US strategists think about the role of intelligence. Not only has the threat changed but also the strategic paradigm—both the ends and means of strategy—has shifted. The George W. Bush administration developed explicit strategies for counterterrorism and counterproliferation. Part of this review of US strategy necessarily involved rethinking intelligence priorities and programmes. The 2004 Intelligence Reform and

Terrorism Prevention Act (IRTPA) is the most dramatic reorganization and revitalization of the US intelligence community in nearly six decades. It expanded the scope and missions of the intelligence community to make it a far more powerful set of institutions and agencies. First, the legislation created a new national chief of intelligence in the form of a Director of National Intelligence, aimed at giving this official more authority than previous Directors of Central Intelligence possessed. Next, it created new institutions like the National Counterterrorism Center and the National Non-proliferation Center aimed at better integrating the different activities and skills or the 16 agencies. Finally, it took note of the creation of a new Department of Homeland Security, one element of which had intelligence functions and would, in conjunction with the FBI, constitute a more prominent domestic intelligence arm of the US Government. Large increases in funding and personnel followed, which have also been employed in providing intelligence to support the ongoing conflicts in Iraq and Afghanistan.

Reliance on Strategies of Counterterrorism and Counterinsurgency

Part of the rationale for the intelligence reforms and resource increases undertaken since the turn of the century was to support the evolving US national security strategies. Where the US once relied on deterrence or containment of strategic threats emanating principally from states like Russia and China, now the focus is on preventing the emergence of strategic threats emanating as much from non-state actors. The Bush Administration's initial reliance on preventive and pre-emptive strategies generated controversy not only for their justification but also over their feasibility given the significant intelligence requirements they required. To be sure, the United States has long relied on elements of prevention and pre-emption. Efforts to interdict and disrupt terrorist plans or the transfer of WMD-related technologies—using either covert action or overt paramilitary operations—predated the George W. Bush administration and has always depended on good intelligence. Most recently, the US has become engaged in ambitious counterinsurgency strategies in both Iraq and Afghanistan. They too require unique forms of intelligence information, often not easily acquired through technical or traditional means. Indeed, senior US military officials have lamented that the intelligence community is ill-suited and not well positioned to provide the kinds of societal and tribal information needed by commanders and diplomats to understand the nature of the insurgencies they are facing in Afghanistan (Flynn 2010)

The Information Glut

The twenty-first century intelligence world is not solely the result of the 11 September attacks. Indeed, many new challenges would have existed regardless of the emergence of al-Qaeda or the global war on terror. Among the most pressing are the information technology revolution and a more global and multifaceted definition of national security threats. Along with rising terrorism and proliferation threats, these global developments require different strategies for coping with the world. As in the past, different national security strategies will often redefine national intelligence strategies and policies.

Information technology is changing the world and the workplace. As it does, it puts more information in the hands of decision-makers and makes it available at increasingly faster rates. Nanotechnology and miniaturization of communications and computing systems makes information flow around the world virtually instantaneously. Not only is time for analysis and action reduced, but also the amount of information that must be absorbed to reach judgements and decisions is far greater. In 2006, then Director of National Intelligence John Negroponte noted that 'the National Security Agency estimates that by next year [2007] the Internet will carry 647 petabytes of data each day . . . By way of comparison, the holdings of the Library of Congress represent only 0.02 petabytes' (Negroponte 2006). The advent of the computer era has also magnified the targets of intelligence value, for example, capture and analysis of the so-called 'Sinjar', The take-down of Usama Bin Laden also resulted in the capture of valuable computer disks and other media that yielded invaluable information on the al-Qaeda organization's future plans and organization. (Oppel, New York Times 2007) But this data often requires detailed scrutiny, translation, and interpretation. Technology can partly solve the problem it has created, but the point has been reached where no single analyst or policymaker can possibly be an expert on all aspects of an international problem. As a senior intelligence official noted recently, intelligence will be more team-based to take advantage of the special knowledge that political, economic, military, and science and technology (S&T) analysts collectively bring to a problem (Medina 2008). In her view, such multidisciplinary analysis will increasingly become routine, as most global problems are not easily dissected into an exclusively political, or military, or economic issue.

Providing intelligence assessments has already become a 24/7 operation and different users will pull their products off as fast as the electrons allow. The danger lies in making intelligence operate faster than the analyst can think or even verify the quality and reliability of the information being passed on to policymakers. Processing raw information is one thing, but making sense of information is still a human factor that cannot be accomplished without time to weigh evidence, identify key strategic dangers, and map their likely consequences. Information technology can assist the analyst in processing large volumes of information by providing analytic tools to help filter and find patterns in the data, but the human mind is still required to see the significance of such patterns to the policymaker. Both the producers and the users will have to work harder to preserve the quality of intelligence as it becomes more ubiquitous and timely.

Global Coverage

The 2008 American housing and financial crisis illustrated how globally interconnected the world had become. European, Middle Eastern, and Asian countries initially thought themselves to be insulated from such turmoil but soon found their financial institutions equally threatened because of the interdependence of national financial transactions and the global market. Likewise, the 2011 'Arab spring' revolutions were swiftly 'globalized' by CNN and other international news services and rose to a top-tier intelligence priority. What had been thought of as an intelligence backwater—e.g. the Libyan opposition—suddenly became a critical intelligence priority as the Obama administration struggled to understand the nature of this opposition, its intentions, and capabilities. Given the inherent unpredictability of world events, the intelligence community must often surge from one part of the world to another, never knowing where the next hotspot will be, but knowing it will be called on to have ready expertise and knowledge to support new policies.

Providing what the US intelligence community would describe as 'global coverage' has been a major issue, especially since the end of the cold war. Gone is the monolithic Soviet threat, to be replaced by fast-breaking crises around the world. Current hotspots—be they in the Middle East or Asia or elsewhere—demand that agencies rapidly commit more collection and analytic resources (so-called 'surging') to meet policymakers' demands. More than a decade ago, the House Permanent Select Committee on Intelligence warned that 'the IC's ability to maintain an intelligence 'base' cannot be sacrificed in order to focus entirely on other, more immediate concerns' (HPSCI 1996). Some of this global coverage will have to be increasingly drawn from open source analysis. The Director of National Intelligence (DNI) issued an Intelligence Community Directive that also underlined the importance of developing global expertise by engaging in more outreach to academic and non-government experts and centres of excellence. Former DNI Dennis Blair also noted in 2009 that the intelligence community is now leveraging its vast array of information by integrating the people and knowledge through better use of technology; to illustrate this, he cited a networked system of computers available to aid workers, diplomats, and military officers in Afghanistan, where one could access information on the latest military attacks, the current crop yields, or the village leaders' photos. (Blair 2009)

The globalization phenomenon now draws our attention to less traditional topics of national security interest. In the past decade, climate change, environment and energy, scarce resources, pandemics, demographics, religious radicalization, and non-state actors have been added to the list of national security concerns. Collecting information as well as developing expertise on such diverse topics will call for new intelligence strategies. Many intelligence professionals have recognized the changing nature of the global challenges we face. Gregory Treverton, former Vice Chairman of the National Intelligence Council, noted in 2003 that the intelligence community is going to have to deal with more mysteries than 'secrets', as policy increasingly turns to questions like global finances, climate change, and pandemics (Treverton 2003a). In its latest *Global Trends 2025* document, the National Intelligence Council is pointing the way towards a world in which 'there will be a global multi-polar international system' and where 'strategic rivalries are most likely to revolve around trade, demographics, access to natural resources, investments and technological innovation' (McConnell 2008). In this world, there will be an unprecedented transfer of global wealth and economic power from West to East. While this report forecasts changes in America's world prominence, it reaffirms the important role the United States will continue to play. Hence, as this role changes, one would expect to see new strategies and continued interest in intelligence on both traditional as well as new international topics.

Key points

- The September terrorist attacks have put new emphasis on strategies of prevention and pre-emption, which will demand even better intelligence than the strategies of containment and deterrence.

- Relying on preventive and pre-emptive strategies requires solid information to justify taking military action even before an enemy has acted.

- Globalization has been accompanied by a global information revolution, speeding up the rate and volume of information flow which the intelligence community must monitor and understand.

- Globalization has changed the definition of national security, so that new intelligence topics now include climate change, energy and resource scarcities, global health problems, and broad demographic and religious trends.

Conclusion

Intelligence remains a vital ingredient to the development of effective national security strategies. It will have to adapt constantly to keep pace with changing conceptions of national security interests and the associated strategies that emerge. As in earlier times, no intelligence system will ever produce entirely perfect insight or prescient forecasts. The world is simply too complex and the decision-making styles of foreign adversaries too unpredictable to know how they will choose to challenge the interests of the United States and its friends and allies. What we can say, however, is that decision-makers will require intelligence to reduce the uncertainty surrounding the future actions of strategic rivals as much as possible.

As in the past, strategic surprises and intelligence failures cannot be ruled out. Steps have been taken, however, to improve collection, analysis, and the intelligence–policy relationship to reduce the likelihood, severity, and consequences of surprise and intelligence failure. Moreover, the need for decision-makers and intelligence professionals to work together makes it clearer than ever that strategy depends on a good understanding of what intelligence can and cannot do. Although centuries old, Sun Tzu's advice to 'know oneself' as well as the enemy is as relevant today as it was then.

 Questions

1. Is intelligence a necessary ingredient to good strategy?

2. How does a strategist use intelligence to improve on strategy?

3. What roles can intelligence play in improving strategy?

4. What are the key limitations of intelligence that a strategist should be aware of?

5. What lessons can be learned from past intelligence failures? What is a working definition of failure?

6. How successful have efforts been to reform intelligence activities to help inform decision-makers? What have been the problems?

7. What is the role of covert action in assisting the strategist?

8. How useful do you think the role of analytic bias or 'mindsets' are in explaining intelligence failures?

9. What can be done to improve intelligence analysis? Is failure inevitable as some writers suggest?

10. How does intelligence need to adjust to the new post-11 September realities?

 Further Reading

R. Betts, *Enemies of Intelligence: Knowledge and Power in American National Security* (New York: Columbia University Press, 2007).
A recapitulation of the author's many excellent articles on intelligence that takes a balanced view between many critics and the few apologists for US intelligence.

R. George and J. Bruce (eds), *Analyzing Intelligence: Origins, Obstacles, and Innovations* (Washington, DC: Georgetown University Press, 2008).
A collection of articles focused on improving the profession of intelligence analysis written by leading practitioners and scholars.

Robert Jervis, *Why Intelligence Fails: Lessons from the Iranian Revolution and the Iraq War* (Ithaca New York: Cornell University Press, 2010).
An excellent post-mortem by a recognized intelligence scholar on the sources of cognitive and bureaucratic bias in intelligence analysis.

L. Johnson and J. Wirtz, *Intelligence and National Security: The Secret World of Spies: An Anthology* (Los Angeles, CA: Roxbury Publishing Company, 2008).
An excellent collection of articles that surveys key intelligence issues, including the challenges of analysis and collection, politicization, covert action, and the ethics of intelligence.

M. Lowenthal, *Intelligence: From Secrets to Policy,* 5th edn (Washington, DC: CQ Press, 2011).
The best and most well-known introduction to the role of US intelligence.

Paul R. Pillar, **Intelligence and US Foreign Policy: Iraq, 9/11, and Misguided Reform** (New York: Columbia University Press, 2011).
The best well-argued, if provocative defence of the intelligence community's performance and scathing critique of recent intelligence reforms by a senior retired intelligence official.

J. Sims and B. Gerber (eds), *Transforming US Intelligence* (Washington, DC: Georgetown University Press, 2005).
A volume of insightful articles on how intelligence organizations and processes need to change.

G. Treverton, *Reshaping National Intelligence for an Age of Information* (Cambridge: Cambridge University Press, 2001).
A scholar and practitioner's view of how the intelligence enterprise needs to be reformed, which takes a critical look at intelligence agencies' preoccupation with secrecy and reliance on secret sources.

 ## Web Links

Federation of American Scientists **http://www.fas.org** This website contains a treasure trove of intelligence assessments and studies useful to students interested in seeing actual products.

CIA **http://www.cia.gov** CIA's website includes the Center for the Study of Intelligence, where CIA's official 'Studies' journal is available, along with many other descriptions of the intelligence process and products.

The Office of the Director of National Intelligence **http://www.odni.gov** The ODNI's website houses official press releases, statements, and directives; it also contains unclassified national intelligence estimates and other community products like the Global Trends series.

Defense Intelligence Agency **http://www.dia.mil** DIA's website explains the roles and missions of defence intelligence organizations and offers an unclassified history of the agency.

National Security Agency **http://www.nsa.gov** NSA's website provides some glimpses into the US Government's most secret agency and its new responsibilities regarding cyber defense.

Central Intelligence Agency factbook **https://www.cia.gov/library/publications/the-world-factbook/** This website houses the voluminous CIA factbook that catalogues the key facts regarding nearly 300 countries including their demographics, economy, history, political structure, and other pertinent characteristics.

Part II

Contemporary Problems

9 Irregular Warfare: Terrorism and Insurgency   173
   James D. Kiras

10 The Second Nuclear Age: Nuclear Weapons
   in the Twenty-first Century   195
   C. Dale Walton

11 The Control of Weapons of Mass Destruction   213
   John Baylis

12 Conventional Power and Contemporary Warfare   230
   John Ferris

13 Iraq, Afghanistan, and American Military Transformation   247
   Stephen Biddle

14 Homeland Security: A New Strategic Paradigm?   267
   Jacob N. Shapiro and Rudolph P. Darken

15 Humanitarian Intervention and Peace Operations   286
   Sheena Chestnut Greitens and Theo Farrell

16 The Rise of Cyberpower   303
   John B. Sheldon

Irregular Warfare:
Terrorism and Insurgency

JAMES D. KIRAS

 Chapter Contents

Introduction	174
Subverting the System: The Theory and Practice of Irregular Warfare	176
Protecting the System: Counterinsurgency and Counterterrorism in Theory and Practice	184
Irregular Warfare Now and in the Future	189
Conclusion	192

 Reader's Guide

Western democracies have had some difficulty adjusting to the 'new reality' of global violent extremist terrorism and revolutionary violence. These difficulties are reflected in two themes that run through the long history of irregular warfare. The first is that all types of irregular warfare, including terrorism and insurgency, are appealing to those who are seeking to change the status quo. But what role can politics possibly play for those who are willing to kill themselves and others for rewards in the afterlife? For reasons that will become clear in this chapter, global violent extremists and modern revolutionaries, including anarchists, share much in common with their historical antecedents. The second theme is that conducting irregular warfare successfully to achieve change is a very challenging undertaking. Historically the balance sheet favours those who fight against terrorist and insurgent groups. For dissatisfied groups and individuals, however, irregular warfare will continue to be used as it offers the promise of change to right perceived injustices and wrongs. Irregular warfare is often the only practical method of violence that weaker elements can wear down, coerce, or destroy their opponents to gain political power.

Introduction

At the height of the period in irregular warfare known as the 'wars of national liberation' (1962–1965), journalist Robert Taber, who had spent time in Cuba during the revolution there, stated that

> the guerrilla fighter's war is political and social, his means are at least as political as they are military, his purpose almost entirely so. Thus we may paraphrase Clausewitz: *Guerrilla war is the extension of politics by means of armed conflict.*
> **Emphasis in original; Taber (1970: 26)**

More recent critiques suggest identity or culture explain substate violence; conflict today is, as General Rupert Smith suggests, 'war amongst the people' instead. In addition, the technologies associated with globalization, including the Internet, are reshaping politics and violence.

The aim of this chapter is to demonstrate that the spirit of Clausewitz is still very much relevant to current and future irregular campaigns. Historical experience cannot be summarily dismissed. Religious, social, cultural, and economic factors provide the context that shapes the conduct of irregular conflicts. Terrorists and insurgents, however, ultimately seek to achieve a *political* result from their use of force. These political results in turn serve goals defined by states fighting insurgencies or those aspiring to change the system through armed conflict.

Such motives are discernable even in the case of al-Qaeda and the resurgence of the Taliban in Afghanistan. The very nature of the extremist interpretation of Islam impedes Western understanding of the violence. As Johannes Jansen points out 'Islamic fundamentalism is both fully politics and fully religion.' (Jansen 1997: 1). For Westerners, the affairs of the church and those of the state are separable while within the militant Salafist strain of Islam they are not. Indeed adherence to religious tenets becomes a form of governance. While religion justifies killing and suggests spiritual rewards, leaders such as Ayman al-Zawahiri stress political power and control:

> Victory of Islam will never take place until a Muslim state is established in the manner of the Prophet in the heart of the Islamic world, specifically in the Levant, Egypt, and the neighboring states of the Peninsula and Iraq.
> **al-Zawahiri (2005: 2)**

From this established political base, the revolution can continue to spread.

Definitions

The first problem associated with the study of terrorism and irregular warfare relates to the relative and subjective lenses that one applies to the subject. One cannot simply compare accidental death figures, such as those from traffic fatalities, with purposeful violence intended to spread fear among the populous. Critics suggest that the Department of Homeland Security's 2012 budget of $57 billion dollars far exceeds the nature and scope of the threat. Much of the confusion associated with terrorism and irregular warfare stems from the use of either value-laden or emotive language. The term 'freedom fighter' suggests heroism while 'terrorist' conveys cowardice. The term 'guerrilla' still evokes the romance and adventure of rebellion embodied by the iconic Ernesto 'Che' Guevara. There is also little agreement on what to call these types of violence: political violence, terrorism, irregular warfare, military operations other than war (MOOTW), low intensity conflict (LIC), people's war, revolutionary warfare, guerrilla warfare, hybrid warfare, among others. Terrorism and insurgency are still viewed at best as a nuisance by many military professionals, or a form of 'dirty war' at worst. The line between combatants and non-combatants is unclear, objectives unclear, and timeline for victory unknown. In addition, military forces conduct policing functions in this environment, with all of the dangers but little glory.

Irregular warfare, which is different in form but warfare nonetheless, describes types of violence conducted by substate actors including terrorism and insurgency (see Box 9.1).

Terrorism is easily the most contentious and elusive type of violence to define. For the purposes of this chapter, terrorism is defined as *the sustained use of violence against symbolic or civilian targets by small groups for political purposes, such as inspiring fear, drawing widespread attention to a political grievance, and/or provoking a draconian or unsustainable response.*

Terrorism cannot result in change on its own. By provoking a response, terrorists hope that their opponent will overreact and reveal their true nature. Some debate exists over whether terrorism is a tactic within a broader strategy of insurgency or whether groups can conduct a strategy of terrorism (O'Neill 1990: 24). What separates terrorism from other forms of violence is that the acts committed are legitimized to a degree by their political nature. Hijacking, remote bombing, and assassination are criminal acts but the legal status of those who conduct them can change if the violence is carried out for a recognized political cause. Two examples illustrate the point. The bombings conducted by Anarchists against monarchs in the late 19th and early 20th century are considered acts of terrorism given their stated objective of changing the political environment. Any one of the number of hijackings of ships off the coast of Somalia and in the Indian Ocean, in contrast, are criminal acts as the motivation behind them is financial gain. Problems exist in determining *who* recognizes the cause, beyond the terrorists themselves, as well as shifts in motive over time. Terrorists seek attention to generate domestic and international empathy and support for the cause that 'drove' them to arms.

Defining insurgency is equally problematic. Insurgency is perhaps best understood by first considering what it is not. Insurgency is not conventional war or terrorism, for example, but it shares with them the use of force to achieve a political end. The crucial difference is the scope and scale of the violence. Terrorism rarely results in political change on its own while

---

BOX 9.1 T.E. Lawrence on Irregular Warfare

Thomas Edward Lawrence, better known as 'Lawrence of Arabia', explained the essence of irregular warfare

In fifty words: Granted mobility, security (in the form of denying targets to the enemy), time, and doctrine (the idea to convert every subject to friendliness), victory will rest with the insurgents, for the algebraical factors are in the end decisive, and in them perfections of means and spirit struggle quite in vain.

Lawrence, T.E. (1920), *'The Evolution of a Revolt,' The Army Quarterly*, 1(1), 69

insurgency attempts to bring about change through force of arms. The principle difference between irregular and conventional war is relatively simple: the latter involves adversaries more or less symmetric in equipment, training, and doctrine. In an insurgency, the adversaries are asymmetric and the weaker, and almost always a substate group attempts to bring about political change by administering and fighting more effectively than its state-based foe through the use of guerrilla tactics. These tactics are characterized by hit-and-run raids and ambushes against local security forces. Confusion often results from insurgent movements using terrorist tactics to achieve local results. Insurgency, unlike terrorism, is characterized by the support and mobilization of a significant proportion of the population. Individual insurgencies differ widely in terms of character (social, cultural, and economic aspects) and type (revolutionary, partisan, guerrilla, liberation, or civil war) but obtaining power and political control is the desired outcome. Finally, external physical and moral support for an insurgent cause is a prerequisite for success.

Definitions are not the final word on a subject but merely act as gateways. Capricious categorizations can lead to a misleading and seemingly irreconcilable divide between forms of irregular conflict. Terrorism and other forms of irregular warfare are plainly not the same activity. But how does one then classify the so-called 'urban guerrilla' phenomenon and its ideological impact on terrorist groups during the 1960s? In addition, some terrorist groups adopt parallel efforts that are more commonly associated with insurgencies—have they now become insurgents, do they remain terrorists, or have they become something else? The Lebanese organization known as Hezbollah has used terrorist tactics (kidnappings and suicide bombings), it fought both long and short guerrilla campaigns against Israeli forces (1983–2001 and 2006), but it has also provided social welfare to local communities, even if funded by Syria, Iran, and illicit commercial operations. Ultimately, some arbitrary distinctions must be made in order to grasp the business at hand, without losing perspective on the numerous 'grey areas' endemic to this and other areas of strategic studies.

Key points

- Terrorism is a tactic of violence, can form a strategy of violence as well, and it differs from criminal acts in that it is conducted for a political purpose.

- Insurgencies differ from terrorism in the degree of popular support for the cause behind the violence, as well as the scope and scale of the means employed using guerrilla tactics.

- Trying to separate types of political violence too exclusively is problematic given how groups and campaigns change over time.

Subverting the System: The Theory and Practice of Irregular Warfare

Those undertaking insurgency and terrorism are trying to find a way to use their strengths such as mobility, organization, and relative anonymity or stealth, against the weaknesses of their more powerful adversary. Bernard Fall reduced this equation even further when he suggested that 'When a country is being subverted, it is being out-administered, not out-fought' (Fall 1998: 55). But subversion is a time-consuming and resource-intensive activity that does not guarantee success. In almost every case, the length of terrorist and irregular warfare campaigns is measured in *decades* not years. They achieve success by gaining an advantage over their adversaries in terms of time, space, legitimacy, and/or support.

These dimensions of conflict are not mutually exclusive and excellence in one dimension will not compensate for drastic shortcomings in the others. Regardless of the space and time available, for example, a terrorist or insurgent campaign will almost always fail if it cannot attract substantial internal or international support. As in all forms of strategy, insurgencies or terrorist campaigns are dialectical struggles between competing adversaries; outcomes are determined by the interaction between opponents (Gray 1999: 23–5). The goal for the irregular leader is to pit the organization's strengths against enemy weaknesses. The value ascribed by different writers to and perceived relationships between time, space, legitimacy, and support create substantial variations in the theories of irregular warfare. These theories often reflect the circumstances that are unique to specific conflicts, a fact that has contributed to failed government efforts to stop insurgents or terrorists. The unconsidered application of a theory based on a specific context to another conflict can lead to disaster.

Time

Time is the most important element required for the successful conclusion of an insurgent and terrorist campaign as it is a commodity that can be exchanged to make up for other weakness. With sufficient time, an insurgent group can organize, sap the resolve of its adversary, and build a conventional force capable of seizing control of the state. Mao organized time in his writings into three interrelated phases: the strategic defensive, the stalemate, and the strategic offensive (see Box 9.2).

Each phase, carefully conducted, would lead one step closer to victory no matter how long it eventually takes. Mao once stated, for example (in 1963), that his forces had 'retreated in space but advanced in time.' He understood that the sequence of phases leading to victory was not necessarily linear; unforeseen circumstances could lead to setbacks and perhaps regression to a previous phase of the insurgency. Endless struggle without an obvious victory would eventually lead to the exhaustion, collapse, or withdrawal of the enemy. The dimension of space works with time, providing insurgents with the leeway to manoeuvre and demonstrates their superior legitimacy to the population. Perceived legitimacy in turn will generate internal and external support for the insurgents. With popular support, insurgents will be able to raise a superior army, launch bolder attacks, and achieve victory.

Many irregular campaigns result in deadlock after a period of time with neither side able to conclude the conflict decisively. The Liberation Tamil Tigers of Eelam (LTTE) waged insurgency within Sri Lanka for more than four decades; the *Fuerzas Armadas Revolucionarias de Colombia–Ejército del Pueblo* (FARC) has conducted insurgent and terrorist campaigns within Columbia for almost a half-century. Only very rarely does guerrilla struggle end quickly. The most famous quick insurgent success is the Cuban revolution (1957–1959). Led by Fidel Castro, this irregular war was concluded in just three years. A number of factors contributed to the rapid collapse of the government forces; in the vast majority of cases, however, few states are as corrupt, inept, and fragile as the Batista regime in the late 1960s.

BOX 9.2 Mao's Three Stages of Insurgency

Stage I, Strategic Defensive

This phase is characterized by avoidance at all costs of pitched, set-piece battles. Tactical offensives, with local numerical superiority, are carried out to further stretch enemy resources. The moral superiority of the guerrillas is established with the local population, political indoctrination is carried out, and new recruits are trained to fight as irregulars in remote, safe bases.

Stage II, Stalemate

This phase begins the prolonged battle to attrit the enemy's physical and moral strength. Government control, in the form of local officials, is targeted and its representatives killed or forced to leave. With government presence in rural areas neutralized, the population can be drawn upon for moral and physical support. That support must be channelled into building capable, conventional 'main' forces.

Stage III, Strategic Offensive

The end game of the conflict, in which popular and main forces conduct the battle of manoeuvre and use overwhelming force to destroy decimated enemy forces in their defensive positions.

Tse-Tung, Mao (1966), *Selected Military Writings of Mao Tse-Tung* (Peking: Foreign Languages Press), 210–19

Such brittle adversaries are rare but local circumstances can convince insurgents or terrorists that time works against them. Carlos Marighella believed that circumstances in Brazil in the 1960s demanded a response other than organizing and waiting for the right revolutionary conditions. Marighella favoured immediate action as he believed the state grew stronger every month while the Brazilian Communist Party did little but talk. By taking action, Marighella believed that the 'urban guerrillas' would build a critical mass for the guerrilla organization, catch the Brazilian state authorities off-guard, and provoke an extreme response. In other words, he believed that the state of affairs within Brazil called for reversing the typical relationship between the guerrilla and time.

Space

Space allows irregulars to decide where and when to fight. If their adversary appears in overwhelming numbers, irregulars can make use of space to withdraw and fight when the odds are in their favour. Defenders against sedition cannot be everywhere at once without spreading their forces too thinly and inviting attack from locally superior guerrilla forces. This becomes particularly problematic for those fighting irregulars when they cross state borders or operate across different geographic domains such as air, land, and sea.

The exploitation of formidable terrain that limits the manoeuvre of government forces is a potent way in which lightly armed and mobile terrorists or insurgents offset their relative weaknesses in technology, organization, and numbers. Insurgents have often used difficult terrain for tactical advantage, often against foes ill equipped to deal with the challenges presented by mountains, jungle, swamps, and even deserts. For example, Afghan Mujahidin guerrillas used mountainous terrain to ambush predominantly road-bound Soviet forces, just as their forefathers did against the British. Triple-canopy jungle limited US and South Vietnamese attempts to apply overwhelming manoeuvre and firepower against the Viet Cong and North Vietnamese forces. Urban terrain can also be an arduous obstacle as the Russians found in 1994. Chechen guerrillas used buildings and narrow roads to offset their weakness and isolate and destroy Soviet formations during the battle for Grozny and Iraqi insurgents tried to do the same in Fallujah a decade later. Terrain difficult for government forces provides insurgent forces with the opportunity to establish safe areas or bases from which to expand the struggle.

Force-to-space ratios also influence the course and duration of insurgencies. If much territory needs to be defended by a government, terrorists or insurgents can compensate for their operational or strategic inferiority by massing forces locally to achieve tactical superiority. Government forces often attempt to defend territory or resources that have political, economic, social, and/or military value. For example, governments under siege often abandon the countryside in favour of more defensible cities and military bases. More often than not, states have the resources to protect many, but not every local target as their resources are stretched. Col. T. E. Lawrence, for instance, used the Arab force-to-space ratio advantage against the Turks to good effect during the Arab Revolt (1916–18). Given the amount of terrain to be covered, Lawrence calculated that the Turks would need 600,000 troops to prevent 'sedition putting up her head' across the entirety of the Transjordan, a figure six times larger than the forces available to the Turks (Lawrence 1920: 60). One of the most persistent criticisms against US and coalition leaders in defeating insurgency in Afghanistan and Iraq is the lack of enough forces, including competent Iraqi and Afghan ones, for the space of each country.

Force-to-space ratio superiority does not require irregulars to operate over huge geographic area in order to be successful. In the case of the guerrilla campaign conducted against the British in Cyprus, the nationalist group EOKA was limited to a space little more than 3 per cent of that roamed by Lawrence's forces. EOKA's leader, George Grivas-Dighenis, based his strategy on the assumption that substantial numbers of British troops would attempt to put down the insurgency. EOKA members operated in small groups and conducted ambushes, bombings, and assassinations. These actions convinced the British that the benefits of remaining in Cyprus were not worth the political and military price to be paid.

Support

Few insurgencies or terrorist campaigns succeed without some form of support. In addition to munitions, insurgents must also look after casualties and continually replenish their supplies, including food and water. In addition, they must constantly update their intelligence on the whereabouts and activities of government forces as well as train new recruits. Support, however, is interlinked with and inseparable from the legitimacy of the organization. Violence conducted without a comprehensible political purpose will generate little popular support. Without support, insurgents and terrorists will eventually succumb to the efforts of the state or a hostile population. Clausewitz suggested that support, in the form of public opinion, was one of the centres of gravity in a popular uprising (Clausewitz 1993: 720).

Insurgents and terrorists can look for support from both domestic (internal) and international (external) sympathizers. Almost all theorists agree that substantial popular support is required to compensate for the resources available to the state. Even Carlos Marighella, who believed initially that urban guerrillas could find and seize the necessary resources in major towns and cities to sustain the struggle, eventually relented and recognized the need to cultivate rural popular support. Domestic support can be forced from the population, using terror and intimidation, but long revolutionary struggles should not rely exclusively on such measures.

Although it is now a cliché, Mao's analogy describing the relationship between the guerrilla and the people is still evocative. The guerrillas were likened to 'fish' that swim in a 'sea' of popular support. Without the sea, the fish will die. A dramatic example of the consequences of failing to have domestic support is the fate of Che Guevara. Guevara believed that conditions in Bolivia in 1967 were ripe for a guerrilla insurrection led by his 'foco' (see Box 9.3).

He overestimated, however, the amount of support he could receive from local Communists and farmers in Bolivia. The Bolivian Communists were hostile to advice from outsiders on how to run their revolution. More importantly, the local peasants were indifferent to the message preached by Guevara given government sponsored land reform initiatives that addressed some of their grievances. Guevara and his 'foco' lacked popular support; the insurgents were either killed or captured within seven months of the first shots being fired.

Support is also contingent on the circumstances within a specific country. A danger exists in trying to reproduce success elsewhere using a previously effective revolutionary formula without first identifying the specific base of potential popular support. The uprising of the urban proletariat was considered a necessity in Marxist-Leninist revolutionary theory but failed dismally when attempted in China (1930) and Vietnam (1968). The agrarian character of China and Vietnam doomed urban revolts to failure; in both states most of the rural population were peasants. As a result, Mao Tse-Tung and Vietnamese General Vo Nguyen Giap respectively modified their strategies and eventually succeeded.

External support for irregulars largely depends on both the geography of the country and the political relations maintained by the insurgents or terrorists. Such support can be material, in the form of resources or cross-border sanctuaries, or moral, in the case of political recognition and lobbying. Many Marxist terrorist groups during the 1970s, such as the German *Rote Armee Faktion*, received physical support from Soviet Union or its client states. Tangible support included money, advanced weapons, and training. Insurgent and terrorist leaders in countries ranging from the Dutch East Indies (1950, later becoming Indonesia) and British Palestine (1948, later becoming Israel) received external support, as part of a backlash against colonialism, that tipped the balance in their favour. States harbour or support terrorist or

---

BOX 9.3 Ernesto 'Che' Guevara and the Theory of the 'Foco'

Ernesto 'Che' Guevara de la Serna Rosario (1928–1967) developed (and Regis Debray expanded on) the idea of *foco* or the centre of gravity of the guerrilla movement. Practically, the *foco* refers to the initial critical mass of the guerrillas, the vanguard of the revolution, from which all else is derived. Philosophically, the *foco* represents the political and military 'heart' of the insurgency and from it Guevara and Debray believe that *the guerrilla movement itself* can generate the conditions for a revolutionary victory (the title of a book by Debray reflects this shift: *The Revolution In The Revolution*). They believe that guerrilla success will eventually 'inspire' local peasants to come to support them, allowing the organization to grow in strength.

insurgent groups for reasons of political expediency and to suit their own policy objectives rather than genuine sympathy for the cause such groups espouse. The ruling authorities in Jordan and Afghanistan made decisions regarding the relative political cost of providing sanctuary for their respective 'guests': the Palestinians in Jordan (1970) and Osama bin Laden and al-Qaeda under Taliban protection in Afghanistan (2001). In addition, irregulars can serve to fight proxy wars against their patron's rivals. For example, Iran and Iraq sponsored rival terrorist groups designed to conduct attacks against one another below the threshold of conventional war. With the regime of Saddam Hussein deposed, Iran continues to provide support and sanctuary for terrorist groups operating against coalition and Iraqi forces until their specific policy goals, namely a regime amenable to Iranian influence, are met. More recently, the inability or unwillingness of Pakistani leaders to deal with Taliban and al-Qaeda support structures in its Western tribal areas has been a source of tension for both its immediate neighbour, Afghanistan, as well as its ostensible partners and allies fighting against violent extremism.

Legitimacy

Insurgents and terrorists fighting irregular wars require internal or external support to sustain their struggle. Terrorists and insurgent leaders need to convey the reason for their actions or lose sympathy for its cause. They often seek to legitimize their use of violence and translate this into meaningful support for their cause by demonstrating moral superiority over those who represent the state; supplanting the functions of the state at the local level; and, spreading a persuasive message.

The moral superiority of the guerrillas is a cornerstone of all irregular and terrorist theory especially those fuelled by religious zeal. Insurgents derive support from the people and they often cultivate their relationship with them. Mao went so far as to outline a 'code of conduct' for the guerrillas, known as 'The Three Rules and Eight Remarks', as a way to demonstrate their moral superiority (see Box 9.4).

The most important job of the guerrilla is to demonstrate this moral superiority in routine contact so that people differentiate the guerrillas from bandits or 'counter-revolutionaries'. Che Guevara insisted that the peasants understand that the guerrillas were as much social reformers as they were protectors of the people.

Peasants who cooperate with the insurgents often face harsh retaliation from the government but frequently this only further legitimizes the revolutionary cause. Abdul Haris Nasution, who fought against the Dutch in Indonesia from 1945–1949, suggested that government responses to subversion only served to drive the people further into the arms of the insurgents. Government brutality also allows insurgents to act as the avengers of the people, helping to cement the ties between them. Carlos Marighella, for example, hoped that the actions of the Brazilian authorities would demonstrate conclusively that

[the] government is unjust, incapable of solving problems, and that it resorts simply to the physical liquidation of its opponents. The political situation in the country is transformed into a military situation in which the 'gorillas' appear more and more to be the ones responsible for violence, while the lives of the people grow worse.
Marighella, 1969

BOX 9.4 Mao's 'Three Rules and Eight Remarks'

Rules

1. All actions are subject to command.
2. Do not steal from the people.
3. Be neither selfish nor unjust.

Remarks

1. Replace the door when you leave the house.*
2. Roll up the bedding on which you have slept.
3. Be courteous.
4. Be honest in your transactions.
5. Return what you borrow.
6. Replace what you break.
7. Do not bathe in the presence of women.
8. Do not without authority search the pocketbooks of those you arrest.

*The translator to this edition, retired US Marine Corp Brigadier General Samuel B Griffiths, notes that 'In summer, doors were frequently lifted off and used as beds.'

Tse-Tung, M. (1961), *Mao Tse-Tung on Guerrilla Warfare* (New York: Praeger), 92

Of course, the admonitions to behave better than government troops are often applied only to those who actively assist insurgents in their struggle. In a number of irregular conflicts, guerrillas and government forces alike regarded an unwillingness to help with aiding and abetting the enemy. Absolute popular support can never be guaranteed. Populations invariably split into willing assistants, staunch foes, and the undecided majority. To help make up the minds of those undecided, insurgents can demonstrate legitimacy by becoming the de facto government in areas under their control. This can include taking 'positive measures' such as the establishment of schools and clinics or 'negative measures' such as tax collection. In Afghanistan, for example, the Taliban have used a system of mobile judges as a positive measure to provide swift and impartial justice, as well as negative measures including the imposition of taxes, public beheadings, and threats of violence through 'night letters' to cement their control over the population. The use of terror as a negative measure to intimidate the population is a matter of debate by irregular warfare practitioners to this day. For Che Guevara, terror tactics were unjustified because they invariably delegitimize the guerrilla's message. Both Mao and Marighella disagree, noting that acts of terror may be necessary to convince the population of the occupational hazards of working for the government, or to provoke a repressive response. Negative measures backed by proselytizing can be an effective way of legitimizing the insurgent cause by showing conclusively that the government can no longer protect them. Intercepted communications between al-Qaeda leaders suggest that negative

BOX 9.5 Popular Support and Negative Measures in the Jihad in Iraq

The following correspondence between Ayman al-Zawahiri and Abu Musab al-Zarqawi which was intercepted and translated in October 2005, suggests senior al-Qaeda leadership are keenly aware of the importance of popular support:

> And it's very important that you allow me to elaborate a little here on this issue of popular support . . . If we are in agreement that the victory of Islam and the establishment of a caliphate in the manner of the Prophet will not be achieved except through jihad against the apostate rulers and their removal, then this goal will not be accomplished by the mujahed movement while it is cut off from public support, even if the Jihadist movement pursues the method of sudden overthrow . . . In the absence of this popular support, the Islamic mujahed movement would be crushed in the shadows, far from the masses who are distracted or fearful . . . Therefore, the mujahed movement must avoid any action that the masses do not understand or approve . . . meaning we must not throw the masses–scant in knowledge–into the sea before we teach them to swim.

al-Zawahiri, A. (2005) 'Letter from al-Zawahiri to Zarqawi,'
translated by the Foreign Broadcast Information Service

measures remain a concern for contemporary insurgents and terrorists in that short-term gains may upset long-term goals (see Box 9.5).

The most powerful method of legitimizing a struggle is to link military operations with a justifiable political end. Causes vary, but self-determination has been the most pervasive and successful rallying cry. Given the fundamental rights outlined in the Atlantic Charter (1941) and the United Nations Charter (1945), it was difficult for nations such as Great Britain, France, the Netherlands, and Portugal to maintain possession of overseas colonies in the face of native insurgencies claiming the right of self-governance. Likewise the legitimacy of the East Timorese claim of independence led to internal and external pressure on the Indonesian government to end a 25-year insurgency. Other successful causes blend social, cultural, and economic issues into a powerful political message that the government or an international audience finds difficult to counter or resist.

Key points

- Terrorism and insurgencies can be examined in terms of time, space, legitimacy, or support, reflecting specific local contexts rather than predetermined goals attributed to a general theory.

- Time is an important element in the success of insurgencies, involving a non-linear progression that includes: the space to manoeuvre and to gain legitimacy and/or support, all of which are necessary for eventual victory.

- Terrain is important to offset weaknesses and gain tactical advantages, including gaining 'force-to-space' superiority at the time and place of your choosing.

- Support is dependent on legitimacy; it is derived internally from the quality of the interaction with the local populace and externally via resources from allies and sympathizers.

- Moral justification provides the cornerstone to sustain the struggle, usually blending cultural and social causes with political ends.

Protecting the System: Counterinsurgency and Counterterrorism in Theory and Practice

The difficulties facing governments besieged by insurgents or terrorists may seem insurmountable at first glance, but numerous works have been written to explain how to quell them. This literature ranges from general theories and practical suggestions, based on hard-won experience, to complicated empirical models purporting to predict outcomes or test practical advice. Commentators have reduced complicated political-military struggles against forceful usurpers to a number of principles or formulas for success (see Box 9.6). Brigadier General Samuel B. Griffith suggested in 1961 that anti-guerrilla operations could be summed up in three words: location, isolation, and eradication (Mao Tse-Tung 1961: 32). Griffith's summary is a useful reference point for exploring how to apply the strengths of a state (or group of states) against an irregular threat.

Location

The most important phase of any counterinsurgency or counterterrorism campaign is recognizing that the threat exists. Counterinsurgency expert Robert Thompson believed it necessary to tackle an insurgency during its subversion and organization phase or at the first signs of a sustained campaign of violence (Thompson 1966: 50). In other words, he believed it necessary to defeat insurgents in both physical space *and* time. The problem for counterinsurgents and counterterrorists is distinguishing between lawful or unlawful forms of discontent. Restricting guaranteed rights and freedoms every time a bomb is detonated will undermine the credibility and intentions of the government. Waiting too long to uphold the rule of law, however, will give the insurgents or terrorists the necessary time to build a robust organizational infrastructure that only the most dedicated efforts might hope to defeat.

Terrorism and insurgency can be staved off with enough early warning, but this implies that an effective intelligence-gathering and assessment organization is operating. Few states possess such resources or foresight. Those willing and able to destroy the system need to be identified and tracked: this requires the assistance of a supportive populace. The question in pluralist systems is whether or not *potentially* seditious individuals can be monitored or arrested without violating civil liberties and undermining the rule of law, as recent debates in Sweden, the United States, and Great Britain suggest.

Upholding the rule of law is crucial if states are to preserve the legitimacy of their cause and maintain the moral high ground over insurgents or terrorists. Methods to counter ter-rorism, for example, must be effective yet stay within the boundary of the rule of law. This applies to both domestic and international measures. Citizens of democratic states are loath to give up rights and freedoms to combat threats especially if they intrude upon per-sonal privacy. Managing how and when (and in what measure) to begin counterinsurgency and antiterrorism efforts, such as imposing curfews and controlling media access while upholding the rule of law, is the primary challenge to any government under siege. In most democratic societies, however, steps to counter terrorists are rarely preventive and are almost always taken *after* horrific acts of violence have been committed, as the Indian reac-tion to the Mumbai attacks of November 2008 suggest. Democracies run into greater

BOX 9.6 Principles, Prerequisites, and Laws of Counterinsurgency and Counterterrorism

Material quoted from specific texts in chronological order.

Charles W Gwynn: Principles from *Imperial Policing* (1934)

- Policy remains vested in civil government
- Minimum use of force
- Firm and timely action
- Cooperation between civil and military authorities

David Galula: Laws of counterinsurgency from *Counterinsurgency Warfare* (1964)

- Support of the population necessary
- Support gained through an active minority
- Support from population is conditional
- Intensity of efforts and vastness of means are essential

Robert Thompson: Principles of counterinsurgency from *Defeating Communist Insurgency* (1966)

- Clear political aim
- The government must function in accordance with the law
- The government must have an overall plan
- The government must give priority to defeating the political subversion, not the guerrillas
- The government must secure its base areas first (in the guerrilla phase)

Frank Kitson: Framework for an effective counterinsurgency campaign from *Bunch of Five* (1977)

- Good coordinating machinery (between civil and military agencies)
- Establishing the sort of political atmosphere within which the government measures can be introduced with the maximum likelihood of success
- Intelligence (right information = sensible policy)
- Law (upholding the rule of)

US Government: The long-term approach, building democracy and representative institutions, as well as the four priorities of action, from the *National Strategy for Combating Terrorism* (2006)

- Advance effective democracies as the long-term antidote to the ideology of terrorism;
- Prevent attacks by terrorist networks;
- Deny weapons of mass destruction to rogue states and terrorist allies who seek to use them;
- Deny terrorists the support and sanctuary of rogue states;
- Deny terrorists control of any nation they would use as a base and launching pad for terror; and
- Lay the foundations and build the institutions and structures we need to carry the fight forward against terror and help ensure our ultimate success.

US Army/Marine Corps: Principles of counterinsurgency from FM 3-24, *Counterinsurgency Field Manual* (2007)

BOX 9.6 *(continued)*

- Legitimacy is the main objective
- Unity of effort is essential
- Political factors are primary
- Counterinsurgents must understand the environment
- Intelligence drives operations
- Insurgents must be isolated from their cause and support
- Security under the rule of law is essential
- Counterinsurgents should prepare for a long-term commitment

British Army: Principles of counterinsurgency from British Army Field Manual Volume 1, Part 10: *Countering Insurgency*

- Primacy of political purpose
- Unity of effort
- Understand the human terrain
- Secure the population
- Neutralize the insurgent
- Gain and maintain popular support
- Operate in accordance with the law
- Integrate intelligence
- Prepare for the long term
- Learn and adapt

---

trouble when their international actions appear to contravene their domestic laws and international norms. The vexing issues of al-Qaeda detainees and so-called 'aggressive interrogation methods' will not be resolved with a stroke of a presidential pen but will continue to influence US counterterrorism measures adversely until its credibility is restored internationally.

Once an irregular threat has been identified, various civil and military agencies must localize the threat while coordinating their response. They must identify safe houses, group members, and sources of supply. Gathering such information about the terrorists can be daunting, given the desire of most subversives to keep the organization small, stealthy, and secret. For a state providing direct counterinsurgency or counterterrorism support into a geographically and culturally unfamiliar country, as the United States did in South Vietnam, obtaining even basic information on subversives takes time. This problem is compounded when a state either does not have an effective and efficient security apparatus (Afghanistan) or the existing one evaporates and must be painstakingly reconstructed (Iraq). The time gained is used by insurgents to retain the initiative and develop their organizational base further.

Isolation

Isolating insurgents and terrorists from their bases of support is probably the most important element of successful campaigns against them. Isolation can take the form of physical separation or political alienation. Physical separation can be achieved by moving villagers into more easily defended compounds, known in Malaya and Vietnam as 'strategic hamlets'. Preventive measures such as curfews, prohibited ('no-go') areas, food rationing, aggressive patrolling, and overt presence can also physically isolate insurgents. As with any form of deterrence, the threat posed by patrolling and presence must be a credible one and not consist simply of half-hearted 'cordon and search' operations. Isolation also means limiting the mobility and range of the insurgents or terrorists, in effect taking away their space and their time. Insurgents and terrorists can also be cut off from their external sources of support by a combination of diplomatic pressure and military measures. The French managed to block external support from reaching the *Armée Liberation Nationale* during the Algerian insurgency (1954–1962): the border between Algeria and its neighbours Morocco and Tunisia was shut down by a combination of wire barriers, guardhouses, and patrols. Experts suggest that the insurgencies in Iraq and Afghanistan cannot be dealt with effectively until supply routes from neighbouring countries are cut off.

Segregating insurgents and terrorists from the population involves more than just physically separating them. To impose meaningful isolation, the state must defuse the irregular's most powerful asset: its political message. Widely held grievances that foster a potent source of recruitment and support must be mitigated by the government. Obviously, some messages are more influential than others: self-determination is difficult to counter by an external or occupying power, whereas demands for land reform or increased political representation can be more easily satisfied. The words of the government must be accompanied by effective deeds to show that the state can and will respond to what amounts to political extortion. The terrorist's or insurgent's 'propaganda of the deed' must be diffused by government displays of a firm, yet lawful response. The displays can range from enforcing a 'no negotiations with terrorists' policy to simple measures like providing basic necessities and local security. The onus is on the representatives of the state to prove that they are *morally superior* to the guerrillas and terrorists and will provide for the needs of their citizens, including responding to the sources of disgruntlement that led to armed insurrection in the first place. Likewise, the terrorist or insurgent cause must be discredited. Leniency should also be extended to those insurgents and terrorists who give up the armed struggle. Above all, citizens must be convinced that the state's fight is their fight. One of the keys to success in Iraq has been the so-called 'awakening' of the Sunni tribal leaders in Anbar province where a degree of local autonomy has been traded for turning against the local al-Qaeda-affiliated group. Popular support for the terrorists or insurgents must be denied through credible and efficient actions to win what Sir Gerald Templar called 'the hearts and minds' of the population. With little internal or external sustenance flowing to the rebels and a population willing to support the government, it is only a matter of time before the state's forces destroy the irregular threat.

Eradication

Eradication involves the physical destruction of the insurgents or terrorists, although few would go so far as to follow Robert Taber's rhetorical advice: 'There is only one means of defeating an insurgent people who will not surrender, and that is extermination. There is only one way to control a territory that harbour's resistance, and that is to turn it into a desert' (Taber 1972: 11). The state has numerous advantages over its opponents given its control over social, fiscal, and military resources. The most important question in democratic states is whether or not the leaders of the state can apply their resources effectively to extinguish the insurgent flame without alienating popular support for their own authority. Cultural context matters when determining a response. For example, the leaders of some European countries were hesitant to cast actions against al-Qaeda after September 2001 as a 'war' for cultural and political reasons based on their historical experience. Indeed many continued to see the phenomenon of violent extremist terrorism exclusively as a domestic law enforcement issue within their sovereign borders, requiring civilian police or paramilitary forces, and not as a *global* problem that might require the use of military forces.

Regardless of the forces used, theory and doctrine is rife with plans that discuss the destruction of guerrillas. These plans range from French Marshal Lyautey's innocuous-sounding 'oil patch' method applied in Morocco in the first quarter of the twentieth century to the more sinister-sounding Nazi German 'spider's web' and 'partridge drive' tactics. All theorists agree that eliminating the insurgents' safe havens must be a priority. Numbers also make a difference. US counterinsurgency doctrine suggests that 20–25 personnel are required for every 1,000 inhabitants (Department of the Army FM 3-24: 23). Most theorists also assert that 'special forces' are also needed to defeat the irregulars at their own game. Some advocate the use of technologies not available to the insurgents, such as helicopters and remote sensors, to enhance the force-to-space balance between government and irregular forces and to achieve superior mobility. Others suggest that a 'kill/capture' strategy, using a mixture of special forces and airpower in a relentless campaign to remove key leaders, managers, and facilitators, will eventually erode terrorist groups into irrelevance.

There also are passive ways in which that state can subvert an insurgency and thereby diminish the number of guerrillas or terrorists. One such method combines psychological warfare techniques, promises of amnesty (e.g. the *Chieu Hoi*, or 'Open Arms' programme used in South Vietnam), cash incentives, or land to convince insurgents and terrorists that their struggle is in vain. Other methods, such as those tried with mixed success in Yemen (the so-called 'Koranic Courts'), attempt to rehabilitate terrorists and reintegrate them into society. Political and economic pressure can be placed on states or groups providing safe havens for terrorists and insurgents. Other passive measures include engaging in political dialogue with, and offering support for, moderates within an irregular organization, convincing them of the need to start talking and stop fighting and causing groups to fracture, splinter, and perhaps turn on themselves.

Political will must underlie efforts to counter terrorism and insurgency. The eradication of an irregular movement is a gradual process of attrition that requires a significant and consistent investment in time and resources. Rarely have national leaders been able to sustain the political will necessary to defeat insurgents or terrorists, particularly when those leaders are intervening in irregular conflicts in other states. Equally daunting is the fact that the underlying causes of discontent often resurface and the embers of insurgency are rekindled in a different form. For example, the government of the Philippines conducted a textbook campaign to 'defeat' a communist insurgency during the 1950s with inspired leadership and US assistance. Barely a decade later, another Marxist-inspired insurgency flared up. Today Philippine leaders continue to struggle against Marxist and Muslim separatist groups. Some commentators have suggested that terrorism and irregular warfare are analogous to the mythical hydra: cut off one head and several more appear in its place.

The effects of terrorism can be limited through a combination of offensive and defensive measures, but ultimately bringing terrorists to justice, especially for crimes beyond state borders, can be accomplished by a combination of the political will to sustain the struggle, maintaining core societal valves and upholding norms, and making the best use of its capabilities. Bringing individuals to trial for actions below the threshold of 'an act of war' takes even greater reserves of time, patience, resolve, negotiation, and treasure. It took the United States 12 years and considerable third-party support, for example, to bring those allegedly responsible for the Lockerbie bombing to trial. In the end, the side that will prevail will be the one most willing to continue the struggle and make the least damaging choices throughout its course.

Key points

- Methods used by the state in response to local threats are aimed crucially at maintaining a lawful, hence political/moral, legitimacy.
- The strategy of state success is based on isolating the insurgents both physically and politically.
- The eradication of insurgents is often a slow process and will take different forms in different political and cultural contexts.

Irregular Warfare Now and in the Future

The supposition that terrorism and irregular warfare involve the use of force strictly for political ends has recently been challenged. As stated in the introduction, some suggest that the irregular conflict is no longer about politics. In other words, wars of national liberation, ideological terrorism, and revolution have joined colonial small wars in the museum of 'conflict past.' Instead, some suggest that contemporary and future irregular threats are driven by a mixture of culture, religious fanaticism, and technology.

Culture

Samuel Huntington famously argued in 1996 that future conflict on the macro level will result from differences in culture between incompatible civilizations. Others believe that on a micro level, substate warrior cultures will become the predominant irregular threat. Westerners fight wars according to established norms and modalities. States, which retain the monopoly on the use of force, go to war with one another to achieve political aims. Examples from Chechnya, Somalia, and the Democratic Republic of Congo, as well as in Afghanistan and Iraq, suggest a new form of irregular warfare is emerging. In this 'fourth generation warfare (4GW),' networks of warriors will utilize their social and culture advantages to offset the technological advantages of Western soldiers (Hammes 2004). According to this argument, soldiers are no match for warriors. Proponents of this view suggest that the availability of modern small arms and disdain for Western rules of warfare give cultural warriors their military superiority. Political aims matter not to Somali clansmen, high on *khat*, driving around Mogadishu in heavily armed civilian vehicles. Warrior culture dictates goals—honour, plunder, or manhood—instead of politics.

Other observers argue that in the future violence will be ethnic or identity based. The political basis for war, Clausewitz's trinity of the people, the state, and the armed forces, is irrelevant. Where states cannot effectively govern, they cannot represent the will of the people. Without a state to sustain the armed forces, the only surviving element of Clausewitz's trinity is the people, which splinter in competing cultural and ethnic communities. The moral resolve of such cultural and social networks is superior precisely because they exist to fight. The conventional armed forces of developed nations will be increasingly irrelevant in the face of such superior will and approaches to warfare that offset technological advantages. The net effect is chaos and mayhem among substate groups with 'state' borders as the new norm for war.

Religious Fanaticism

Religious beliefs often shape terrorists' and insurgents' causes and are used to obtain support among a community of the faithful. Throughout history, religion has been a powerful stimulus for political violence by Muslims, Christians, Jews, Sikhs, and other faiths as well. In exchange for personal sacrifice, earthly representatives of some faiths promise terrorist martyrs a glorious afterlife for conducting attacks, suicide or otherwise, that kill non-believers. Religion does, however, provide insurgent and terrorist leaders with a number of advantages for their cause. First, leaders such as Osama bin Laden use religion to provide a competing value structure and ideology to rally the deprived and disillusioned behind their cause. What bin Laden and his followers offer is an alternative to the Western, materialist culture and an attempt to recapture previous glories of mythic past. What has surprised Western analysts is the resonance that this vision has across cultural and ethnic lines—in other words, the degree of popular support for his message. Second, religion offers a rationale for action. Much like Che Guevara, Osama bin Laden and his followers see themselves as social reformers. Terrorist attacks serve to raise the consciousness of the global Islamic community (the *ummah*) to the existing struggle as well as to demonstrate to others that there is an alternative to their current situation. Religion can also blind the faithful to certain realities as well. Religious-inspired terrorist movements often overestimate the appeal of their message. As with political ideologues, including Mao Tse-Tung, religious ideologues convince themselves that the future is predetermined based on the righteousness of their cause. Particularly heinous or indiscriminate actions over time may lead even the staunchest supporters, much less allies of convenience, to question the legitimacy and viability of religiously sanctioned terrorism. For example, some affiliated insurgent groups and external supporters of al-Qaeda in Iraq are distancing themselves from attacks that target or have killed large numbers of fellow Muslims as opposed to occupying coalition forces. The inability of Western democracies to influence a fundamentalist segment of Islamic population raises the spectre of an interminable war of annihilation of the type mentioned earlier by Robert Taber.

Technology

Weapons of Mass Destruction (WMD)

The congruence of religion and WMD—including biological, chemical, radiological, and even nuclear weapons—portends a frightful and very real 'apocalypse now.' Modern religious fanatics, do not have the political restraint of their terrorist predecessors and may be interested in just killing as many non-believers as possible. Experts point to the ease with which chemical and biological agents, or 'poor man's atom bombs,' can be manufactured or acquired; the decreasing frequency but increasing lethality of terrorist acts; and the breaking of a so-called WMD taboo by Aum Shinrikyo in Tokyo in 1995 and the mailing of anthrax spores to the US Congress in October 2001. Those who track terrorist attempts to acquire WMD suggest that the question is not 'if' such attacks will occur but rather 'when'—and whether Western democracies will be able to manage the consequences.

Information Technology

The Internet transcends borders, and therefore some observers believe that future irregular wars will be fought in cyberspace. Given the vulnerability of websites and servers to hackers, terrorists inevitably will become cyberterrorists through the World Wide Web. Serbian and Indonesian hacking of opponents' websites, as well as the 'defacing' of al-Qaeda affiliated websites by groups such as TeAmZ USA, are examples interpreted by some as evidence that cyberwar is a reality. Hacking and defacing provide glimpses into what ambitious cyberterrorists and activists can accomplish. Policymakers fear that cyberterrorists and infosurgents will conduct electronic raids on vital national systems controlled by computers (e.g. financial services, transportation networks, and power grids). Particularly daunting is the prospect that terrorists or other insurgents will harness the Stuxnet code, and in particular its unique payload delivery system, to sabotage critical infrastructure, such as banking networks, power plants, or other key control systems. Fear is no longer based on the prospect of violence: information and the ability to control it has become the new form of power.

Whether or not terrorist and insurgent campaigns will be entirely 'virtual' is a matter of speculation. A technological reality is that access to the Web, satellite communications, and portable computers greatly enhances the capability of aspiring terrorists and insurgents. According to media reports, the group which rampaged through and besieged part of Mumbai in November 2008 made use of readily available cellular and satellite phones, as well as publically available satellite maps and Global Positioning Satellite data, to coordinate their attack. Such technology and information was once the exclusive purview of major powers. Websites, portals, and weblogs allow the quick dissemination of propaganda, training materials, and 'best practices,' while basic equipment such as a laptop, software, and a CD burner allows materials to be produced professionally and disseminated clandestinely. With a computer and connection to the Internet, an individual can do more damage than armed terrorist cells or small insurgent movements, as the example of American-born Anwar al-Awlaki suggests. His various electronically produced and distributed products, including the online *Inspire* magazine, have encouraged individuals around the globe to take up arms. More importantly, some senior al-Qaeda leaders view the future of the movement as a 'leaderless resistance' of compartmented, geographically dispersed cells. The net effect, observed in the Philippines, Iraq, and elsewhere, is that individuals or small insurgent cells can obtain training and mission planning materials, share information, and coordinate their activities with little fear of being caught by security forces.

Key points

- Religion is useful as a rallying point and enabler for terrorism but cannot provide a strategy to achieve the desired objectives.
- Culturally inspired insurgents might change the nature of uprisings from traditional 'trinitarian' wars to chaotic ethnic conflict.
- The replacement by religious fanatics of the political with 'apocalyptic millenarianism' possibly portends the lethal combination of martyrs with weapons of mass destruction.
- Information technologies and the World Wide Web have provided terrorists with new capabilities to reach across time and space, creating vulnerability in a state-based system where control of information equals power.

 ## Conclusion

States will be plagued by terrorism and irregular warfare as long as individuals are willing to use violence for political purposes. The shocking cultural details of irregular conflicts, such as the Taliban and al-Qaeda's recorded beheadings of captives and the use of starvation as a weapon in Sudan and Somalia, can obscure the political purpose behind the fighting. Terrorism and irregular warfare have long been used to change political systems and acquire power; more recently, cultural schisms have led to a rise in terrorism carried out for religious and personal reasons.

Current re-evaluations of irregular warfare and terrorism often lack context. Religion, culture, ethnicity, and technology remain important elements of irregular warfare. They define how and why individuals take up arms against perceived injustices. But the *ultima ratio* for the use of irregular methods of war is to achieve *political* results. US militia and patriot groups, for instance, hope to provoke a response to redress the *political* imbalance between what they perceive as illegitimate federal authorities and individuals' rights and freedoms established in the Constitution. Terrorist use of WMD is a frightening prospect. Yet Shoko Asahara, the spiritual leader of the Aum Shinrikyo cult, only attempted to use chemical and biological agents *after* his political ambitions were thwarted in 1990. Revenge for his humiliation at the polls was perhaps the most significant reason for launching chemical and biological attacks. Likewise the stream of veiled threats of WMD use by al-Qaeda leaders, including Osama bin Laden, should draw attention to the fact that the movement had failed since 2001 to achieve its stated objective of creating a theocracy to undertake social reform.

Warrior cultures may appear to espouse violence for its own sake but at the root of their struggle is the quest for political autonomy, control, or power. The protracted guerrilla war fought by the Chechens against the Russians is little different from the one conducted in 1856: the Chechens' desire is to gain political autonomy from Moscow. Somali warlords seek to gain political power and influence for their clans. Native Americans fought against the US Army in the nineteenth century to maintain autonomy and protect their traditional hunting grounds. Even ancient irregulars, classified as *barbarii* by the Romans, were resisting attempts to have *Pax Romana* imposed upon them.

So is the trinity of Clausewitz no longer relevant? To suggest so misrepresents its foundation and misconstrues the reasons why irregulars fight in the first place. After all, primordial violence (the people) serves no purpose unless it is subordinated ultimately to policy (the government). Violence undertaken for personal gain, be it financial or to enhance one's reputation, is nothing more than a criminal act in civil society and should be treated as such.

 ## Questions

1. What is the difference between terrorism and insurgency and why is it important to distinguish between them?

2. Can terrorists and insurgents sacrifice the element of time to achieve political change and if so, under what conditions?

3. Why is the element of space easy to discuss in theory but difficult to incorporate in practice?

4. Why are irregular warfare theorists divided on the use of terror as a method of compelling support?

5. Is irregular warfare governed by the principles of war or does it have its own principles?

6. What did Bernard Fall mean when he said that subversives are out-administering their opponents? Why does he place such emphasis on organization rather than fighting?

7. Why is locating terrorists and insurgents so difficult?

8. How is the balance struck between force and the rule of law on both sides of an irregular campaign?

9. How can those countering insurgents and terrorists prevail?

10. Have religion, culture, and technology changed the nature of terrorism?

 ## Further Reading

Department of the Army. *FM 3-24, Counterinsurgency Field Manual* **(Chicago: University of Chicago Press, 2007).**
Never has a work of doctrine been so often quoted and publicized which is due in part to its oversight by General (now retired) David Petraeus. Explains in generic terms much about how to conduct a counterinsurgency campaign and some of the differences between 'classic' and contemporary counterinsurgency.

D. Galula, *Pacification in Algeria, 1956-1958* **(Washington, DC: RAND, 2006).**
Galula's lesser-known, but more informative work describes both his theory of counterinsurgency, developed by reading, travelling, and interviewing, as well as the considerable difficulties of translating counterinsurgency operations from theory into practice.

B. Ganor, *The Counter-Terrorism Puzzle: A Guide for Decision Makers* **(New Brunswick, NJ: Transaction, 2005).**
Emphasizes the dilemmas and practical difficulties associated with various counterterrorism policy options.

B. Hoffman, *Inside Terrorism***, revised and expanded edition (New York: Columbia University Press, 2006).**
The best single-volume work on the development of terrorism, its evolution over time, and current and future prospects for defeating it.

B. Jenkins, *Will Terrorists Go Nuclear?* (New York: Prometheus, 2008).
A level-headed analysis by one of the most well-respected terrorism analysts that put into perspective the likelihood of terrorists using nuclear weapons.

S. Kalyvas, *The Logic of Violence in Civil War* (Cambridge: Cambridge University Press, 2006).
Although written on the subject of civil war, Kalyvas' work explores how and why irregular wars are conducted from both organizational and individual perspectives.

D. Kilcullen, *The Accidental Guerrilla: Fighting Small Wars in the Midst of a Big One* (Oxford: Oxford University Press, 2009).
Part theory and part travelogue, this book attempts to link together a cautionary tale of Western military interventions that only fuel local terrorist and insurgent campaigns into a wider 'global insurgency'.

A. Kurth Cronin, *How Terrorism Ends: Understanding the Decline and Demise of Terrorist Campaigns* (Princeton, NJ: Princeton University Press, 2011).
A straightforward, accessible, yet deeply analytic survey of the seven ways in which terrorist campaigns terminate, leading to a discussion of how al-Qaeda might end.

R. Thompson, *Defeating Communist Insurgency: Experiences from Malaya and Vietnam* (London: Chatto & Windus, 1966) was the most influential work of its day as it provided counterinsurgency advice derived from the author's role in the successful Malayan campaign. The quintessential example of 'classic' counterinsurgency principles and practices.

Mao Tse Tung, *Selected Military Writings of Mao Tse-Tung* (Peking: Foreign Languages Press, 1966), is a collection of Mao's most important tracts, including the seminal 'On Protracted War,' which lays out a theory of guerrilla warfare yet unmatched in logic and linking means to ends.

 ## Web Links

RAND Corporation **http://www.rand.org/hot_topics/counterinsurgency/** Although RAND offers numerous downloadable reports on all aspects of irregular warfare, its counterinsurgency section features contemporary analysis as well as a wealth of historical reports useful to the researcher.

This is Baader-Meinhof **http://www.baader-meinhof.com** This site contains excellent information on the Baader-Meinhof group. It has a section for students and researchers as well as links to or the complete text of seminal works such as Carlos Marighella's 'Minimanual of the Urban Guerrilla' **http://www.baader-meinhof.com/book-minimanual-urban-guerrilla/**

Combating Terrorism Center **http://www.ctc.usma.edu/** Founded in 2001, the CTC website provides access to a range of outstanding reports and products, based on declassified documents and other primary source research, that are available for download. The Center also produces a free monthly electronic journal entitled *CTC Sentinel*.

The Small Wars Journal **http://smallwarsjournal.com/** This portal offers access to the blog, journal, and professional reading lists posted by a range of practitioners, academicians, and subject matter experts.

Marx to Mao Website **http://www.marx2mao.com/** Provides the full text of most of Mao's writings on guerrilla warfare as well as those of V.I. Lenin.

The Counterterrorism Blog **http://counterterrorismblog.org/** Expanded from a blog to a portal, this website features expert commentary and cutting-edge coverage of recent terrorism trends and incidents. This site features a treasure trove of news items and documents but requires a level of familiarity with the subject.

Abu Muquwama blog site **http://www.cnas.org/blogs/abumuqawama** This blog, posted by Andrew Exum and hosted by the Center for a New American Security, is informative on Middle Eastern issues including terrorism and insurgency, contains many valuable links, shys away from no topic, and is often humorous as well.

10

The Second Nuclear Age: Nuclear Weapons in the Twenty-first Century

C. DALE WALTON

 Chapter Contents

Introduction	196
The First Nuclear Age	197
Risks in the Second Nuclear Age	200
Adapting to the Second Nuclear Age	205
Conclusion: Looking Towards the Third Nuclear Age	209

 Reader's Guide

This chapter sets out to consider the role that nuclear weapons have played in international politics, both during the cold war and in the post-cold war era. In particular, a distinction is drawn between the spread of nuclear weapons to more states, which is creating an increasing threat to international security, and the decline in the absolute number of nuclear weapons due to the reductions in the nuclear arsenals of the United States and Russia. Some attention is also given to other contemporary issues such as ballistic missile defences, the cultural dimensions of nuclear weapons acquisition, and the possibility of terrorists using nuclear weapons in the future.[1]

Introduction

Since their invention, nuclear weapons have played an important role in the international system, even though they have not been used in wartime since 1945. During the cold war, both the United States and the Soviet Union built large and diverse nuclear arsenals, which included a mix of many different types of weapons and delivery vehicles. During this era, academics and policymakers struggled with many difficult issues related to these weapons, but in the United States and other North Atlantic Treaty Organization (NATO) countries special attention was paid to deterrence, particularly the use of nuclear weapons to deter the Soviet Union from launching an invasion of western and central European NATO countries. Thus, one might say that the main 'theme' of Western nuclear debate during the cold war was the use of nuclear weapons to prevent superpower war, either nuclear or conventional.

This First Nuclear Age—which lasted approximately from 1945 to the 1991 fall of the Soviet Union—was dominated by the Soviet and American superpowers, which first tested nuclear weapons in 1945 and 1949, respectively. Three other countries also became declared nuclear powers during the First Nuclear Age (Great Britain, France, and China), while at least three other polities (South Africa, Israel, and India) became undeclared nuclear states, but the arsenals of all of these countries combined were dwarfed by those of either of the two superpowers. As a result, serious thinking about nuclear issues tended to focus on the United States and Soviet Union—the cold war era was a bipolar one, and that fact was reflected in the superpower nuclear arsenals (see Table 10.1).

TABLE 10.1 Growth in the Number of Nuclear Powers

Nuclear Weapon States	Date of First Test	Still Possesses Nuclear Weapons?
United States	16 July 1945	Yes
USSR/Russia	29 August 1949	Yes
United Kingdom	3 October 1952	Yes
France	3 December 1960	Yes
China	16 October 1964	Yes
Israel	2 November 1966	Yes
India	18 May 1974	Yes
South Africa	22 September 1979	No
Belarus	N/A	No
Kazakhstan	N/A	No
Ukraine	N/A	No
Pakistan	28 May 1998	Yes
North Korea	9 October 2006	Yes

Note: Some countries possessed nuclear weapons for several years before conducting their first nuclear test. Belarus, Kazakhstan, and Ukraine inherited nuclear arsenals with the break-up of the USSR.

Today, Moscow and Washington still possess the world's largest nuclear arsenals, but international political circumstances have changed dramatically in recent years. The United States and Russia currently do not have a particularly antagonistic relationship, and the danger of a massive nuclear conflict in the foreseeable future appears small. However, in other respects, the international environment is more dangerous than it was during the cold war era. The world has transitioned into a Second Nuclear Age, in which these weapons will proliferate horizontally to more states, including very dangerous and unstable regimes. Therefore, it is quite likely that the odds of a nuclear war occurring in any given year are much greater now than was the case in the First Nuclear Age.

The objective of this chapter is to explore the strategic role that nuclear weapons play in international politics and study how it has changed over time. The transition from the First to the Second Nuclear Age receives particular attention, and the chapter demonstrates how horizontal nuclear proliferation, the spread of nuclear weapons to more states or other international actors, is creating new threats to the international security environment as an increasing number of states obtain these weapons, even as the fears associated with the bipolar cold war stand-off are decreasing. (Vertical nuclear proliferation, by contrast, is an increase in the number of nuclear weapons. Therefore, a country that has five nuclear weapons has proliferated vertically if it produces a sixth one. Today, however, the total number of nuclear weapons worldwide is decreasing because of the shrinking Russian and American nuclear arsenals.) The chapter explains briefly how ballistic missile defences (BMD) can influence the strategic utility of nuclear weapons. Moreover, it will address the possible roles that nuclear weapons may play in the future, including their possible use by terrorists.

The First Nuclear Age

The first nuclear test occurred on 16 July 1945 in New Mexico; less than one month later, on 6 and 9 August, nuclear weapons were used against two Japanese cities, Hiroshima and Nagasaki. These devices—nicknamed 'Little Boy' and 'Fat Man'—differed in their designs, but both were fission nuclear weapons. These weapons were the fruit of the Manhattan Project, a massive 'crash programme' to which the American government—worried that Nazi Germany might be the first country to obtain nuclear weapons—devoted billions of dollars and thousands of scientists, technicians, and other personnel.

For a brief time the United States was the only power capable of building nuclear devices, and thus enjoyed an atomic monopoly. This monopoly was, however, short-lived, partly because Soviet spies were providing data from the American nuclear programme to Moscow even as the (supposedly very secret) Manhattan Project was ongoing. In 1949, the Soviet Union tested its first nuclear weapon.

By the mid-1950s both Washington and Moscow had tested fission–fusion nuclear weapons (more commonly referred to as thermonuclear weapons), which were even more powerful than their fission predecessors. Thermonuclear weapons use fissile material more efficiently than fission devices do, making larger yields—in essence, bigger explosions—possible. Nuclear yields are measured in kilotons, thousands of tons of TNT (dynamite) equivalent, and megatons, millions of tons of TNT equivalent. A five kiloton weapon, for example, yields an explosion equivalent to 5,000 tons of TNT, while a two megaton warhead's explosion equals 2,000,000 tons of TNT (see Box 10.1).

Almost immediately after the bombing of Hiroshima, a great debate began over the meaning of nuclear weapons for the future of international relations and, indeed, humanity itself. The first major text examining the impact on nuclear weapons on world politics was edited by Bernard Brodie and titled *The Absolute Weapon*. The book's title is indicative of Brodie's views regarding the importance of these devices—like many other observers, he believed that nuclear devices were something other than 'normal' weapons and that their existence, in turn, would have a radical impact on the future course of international politics. Over the next several decades, a huge body of literature developed which addressed a myriad of issues related to the existence of nuclear weapons. For the purposes at hand, however, the most important writings addressed nuclear deterrence. In essence, nuclear deterrence examined how nuclear weapons could be used to prevent an opponent from undertaking an undesirable action.

In the context of the cold war perhaps the most critical deterrence issue, from the Western perspective, was preventing the Soviet Union from invading NATO's European members. Throughout the cold war, the Soviet Union enjoyed an enormous advantage over NATO in conventional military forces (all forces except for weapons of mass destruction, a category which includes nuclear, chemical, biological, and radiological weapons, are considered conventional). Strategists struggled with how to ensure that Moscow would not attempt to conquer vulnerable NATO countries, and their answers almost invariably relied on nuclear deterrence.

It was generally believed that Soviet leaders would not attack NATO countries if they were convinced that the United States would retaliate by using nuclear weapons against the Soviet Union. This is known as a countervalue threat—something that Soviet leaders valued, in this case the Soviet homeland itself, was held hostage to their good behaviour. Another sort of deterrence threat is a counterforce threat—the warning that nuclear weapons would be used against the 'sinews' of state power: military forces, leadership targets, targets relevant to military command and control, and so forth. In general, one can say that the United States relied on a mix of countervalue and counterforce threats to deter the Soviet Union (see Box 10.2).

During the First Nuclear Age, the two superpowers each built enormous arsenals of tactical nuclear weapons (TNWs) and strategic nuclear weapons. The distinction between the two types of weapons is somewhat artificial, but as a rule of thumb, TNWs are delivered by means such as tactical aircraft, artillery, or short-range ballistic or cruise missiles. TNWs are generally intended for use in battle, against troop concentrations, ships, or similar targets. (The superpowers even developed nuclear depth charges for use against enemy submarines.) Strategic

---

BOX 10.1 Fissile Material

For the building of nuclear weapons, the most important fissile materials are uranium 235 (U235) and plutonium 239 (P239). These radioactive isotopes are difficult to acquire. A given quantity of mined uranium contains very little U235; the latter must be separated from non-fissile uranium. Plutonium is not found in nature in any significant quantity—it is a by-product of nuclear processes guided by humans. The control of fissile materials is very important in preventing nuclear proliferation, but the generation of nuclear power requires fissile material. The International Atomic Energy Agency (IAEA) is tasked with ensuring that non-nuclear weapons countries which have nuclear power plants do not divert fissile material and use it to build nuclear weapons.

BOX 10.2 Credibility

Credibility is central to the success of any deterrence threat. If a threat is not credible—if, in short, the state being threatened does not believe that its foe will carry out the threat—it is likely to ignore deterrence warnings and do what it wishes. One might compare this to crime: if a would-be thief believes that it is very improbable that he will be caught when robbing a house, it is unlikely that he will be deterred. If, on the other hand, he believes that it is probable that he would be caught, it is likely that he will conclude that it is in his best interest not to rob the house. This is surety of punishment. A related concept is severity of punishment: the thief is more likely to be deterred if he believes that the punishment he would receive if caught would be heavy than if he assumes that it would be light. Generally speaking, a deterrence threat that is both credible and severe is far more likely to deter an opponent than one that falls short in either, much less both, of these dimensions.

Every deterrence relationship is unique, and a would-be deterrer must try to understand what their counterpart values and how difficult it will be to dissuade the deterree from undertaking specific actions. Some activities may be easy to deter, while it might be very difficult or even impossible to prevent other ones. If deterrence does fail, a state must then decide whether to carry out its previous threats—and if it does not do so, its credibility will suffer. Thus, there is no simple deterrence formula that applies to all potential opponents; it is always important to understand the motivations and desires of those whom one is attempting to deter.

nuclear weapons, by contrast, are usually delivered at very long ranges by intercontinental ballistic missiles (ICBMs), submarine-launched ballistic missiles (SLBMs) of intercontinental range, or long-range heavy bombers. These weapons can strike deep into enemy territory, thousands of miles from the point at which they were launched (see Table 10.2).

The United States and Soviet Union built tens of thousands of strategic and tactical warheads with an enormous variety of yields that ranged from less than one kiloton to tens of megatons. In many cases, several warheads were placed on a single delivery vehicle—the American MX ICBM, for example, was designed to carry up to ten Multiple Independently Targetable Reentry Vehicles (MIRVs). MIRVed warheads were first deployed in the 1970s. Before this time, there had been missiles with several warheads, but they were not independently targetable, which means they could not strike different targets.

Key points

- Nuclear weapons have not been used in conflict since atomic bombs were dropped on Hiroshima and Nagasaki, Japan in 1945.

- Nuclear weapons are categorized, along with chemical, biological, and radiological devices, as weapons of mass destruction.

- Competition in the building of nuclear weapons was very closely tied to the cold war between the United States and the Soviet Union and the theoretical models relating to deterrence that were built during that time reflect the bipolar competition between the two superpowers.

- Nuclear weapons are divided into a variety of categories, depending on their design, means of delivery, and other factors. Two of the most important distinctions are between fission and thermonuclear weapons and between tactical and strategic weapons.

TABLE 10.2 **Approximate Force Levels of Nuclear Weapons Worldwide, 1945–2000: Declared Nuclear Powers**		
Date (End of Year)	**Quantity**	**States Included**
1945	6	USA
1950	374	USA, USSR
1955	3,267	USA, USSR, UK
1960	22,069	USA, USSR, UK
1965	38,118	USA, USSR, UK, France, China
1970	38,153	USA, USSR, UK, France, China
1975	46,830	USA, USSR, UK, France, China
1980	54,706	USA, USSR, UK, France, China
1985	63,416	USA, USSR, UK, France, China
1990	55,863	USA, USSR, UK, France, China
1995	27,131	USA, USSR, UK, France, China
2000	21,851	USA, USSR, UK, France, China

Source: National Resources Defense Council

Risks in the Second Nuclear Age

It would be excessive to claim that nuclear deterrence is either easy or always impossible in the twenty-first century. Deterrence concepts developed during the cold war continue to be useful when discussing today's challenges, but it perhaps is naïve to assume that twenty-first century actors—particularly, but not only, 'rogue' states such as Iran and North Korea—will act in a manner consistent with the assumptions of cold war deterrence theory. The assumptions regarding behaviour that underpin the body of deterrence theory are not universally applicable; every political culture is unique (indeed, every leader is unique), and it should not be expected that states will always act in a manner consistent with deterrence theory. Deterrence is not a panacea—threats, whether presently emerging or as yet unforeseen, cannot all be addressed successfully by consulting 'the cold war Deterrence Manual'.

Far too often, observers of international politics simply assume that leaders will not undertake particular actions because it would not be in their best interest to do so—with 'best interest' being defined by the observer. Thus, it is widely assumed that North Korea or Iran would, for example, never provide nuclear devices to terrorists or pre-emptively attack South Korea or Israel with such weapons. In both of these extreme examples, this assumption is likely to be correct—certainly, Pyongyang and Tehran are aware that such actions would be extraordinarily risky. However, even a very high probability that an event will not occur is not the same as a certainty that it will not occur.

There are still a great many continuing controversies concerning the reliability of deterrence during the cold war. To claim that deterrence theory was proven to have worked well because there was no US–Soviet military conflict, much less a nuclear war, is to assume a causal relationship that may or may not exist. Certainly, the United States attempted to deter Soviet military aggression, but whether American deterrence actually prevented war between the two powers is unknown and, ultimately, unknowable. History, unlike a laboratory experiment, cannot be repeated, and we have no 'control cold war' to compare to the real cold war.

If American strategists had not developed a sophisticated body of deterrence theory, perhaps a nuclear conflict would have occurred—*or perhaps not*. Similarly, perhaps a US–Soviet nuclear conflict would have occurred despite American deterrence if not for historical happenstance. If we are unable to say with certainty that deterrence prevented the cold war from turning hot, we should be all the more cautious when attempting to predict the future behaviour of opponents whose decision-making is opaque and whose values are foreign to those prevailing in the West. To say that 'State X' will not commit a particular act because it would not be in its best interest to do so requires a judgement regarding the interests of that state. However, it is rare for all of a state's key leaders to hold essentially indistinguishable views on their country's wellbeing; for an outsider to simply assume that their own perspective will inevitably be reflected in that country's policy is perilous indeed.

Prudent leaders must factor in the risk of an unlikely event when making decisions; the mere fact that the use of nuclear weapons in a given situation may be imprudent, or even outright foolish, is no guarantee that such weapons will remain unused. This is not good news for the reliability of deterrence. It is especially troubling when one considers that the two states mentioned above are not the only unpredictable countries that now own, or may soon have, nuclear weapons (see Box 10.3).

BOX 10.3 Terminology

- *Ballistic missile.* A missile with rocket motors that flies on a ballistic trajectory. Ballistic missiles carry a payload of conventional or WMD warheads, also known as reentry vehicles. Early ballistic missiles were inaccurate and could only carry relatively small payloads for short distances, but advanced missiles can be of intercontinental range and carry independently targetable warheads.

- *Cruise missile.* A missile with an air-breathing motor; in essence, a small, pilotless aircraft. Current models travel at subsonic speeds. Bombers can be equipped to carry nuclear-tipped cruise missiles.

- *Decapitation strike.* An attack intended to destroy the leadership and command, control, and communications (C3) network of an enemy nation.

- *Disarming strike.* An attack that attempts to destroy an enemy's nuclear forces. If a disarming strike is successful, the enemy state will not be utterly destroyed, but will be militarily helpless and compelled to negotiate a peace on the disarmer's terms.

- *Fallout.* Radioactive debris resulting from a nuclear explosion. Heavier particles tend to settle in the area of the explosion, while lighter ones often travel great distances. Fallout contamination can result in serious, even fatal, health effects.

- *Triad.* The combination of SLBMs, ICBMs, and nuclear-armed long-range bombers that together comprise the strategic nuclear forces of the United States and Russia.

Adapted from Payne and Walton (2002: 162)

The simple answer to these uncertainties is to deny nuclear arsenals to rogue, or potentially rogue, states. However, there is every reason to believe that it will be impossible to do so consistently. Rather, we should expect the number of nuclear states to increase over time. This is not to say that there will be no non-proliferation victories. Some states seeking nuclear weapons will be dissuaded from acquiring them (as Libya was by the United States), and on rare occasions a nuclear state may even denuclearize (as South Africa did).

It is, however, very unlikely that this means that the spread of nuclear weapons can be reversed overall. Knowledge about any technology can be expected to be dispersed over time and nuclear weapons are an old invention—they were first built more than 60 years ago. Unsurprisingly, there are increasing numbers of individuals from (currently) non-nuclear countries who are knowledgeable about nuclear weapons technology. The growing number of states with nuclear energy programmes makes it all the more difficult to eradicate proliferation.

The A. Q. Khan network provides an example of how difficult it may be to prevent nuclear proliferation in the Second Nuclear Age. Khan is regarded as the 'father' of the Pakistani nuclear weapons programme, and has long been treated as a national hero in that country. Yet over the course of time it became increasingly clear that he was at the centre of an international network trading in nuclear technology; in 2004, he publicly admitted to such activities, stating that his operation was not undertaken with the knowledge of Pakistan's government. However, he later renounced this confession, contending that it had been made under pressure, and that he was a 'scapegoat' whose activities were actually endorsed by his government.

The degree to which Khan acted with official approval remains disputed, but it is clear that his operation was a very extensive one that provided proliferation-related information to a number of states. Notably, the Khan apparatus appears to have provided important assistance to the Iranian and North Korean nuclear programmes, but, beyond this, it demonstrated the increasing difficulty of controlling the spread of nuclear knowledge and materials, especially when informal criminal networks make it difficult to prove a state intended to help others proliferate. Events in recent years have also highlighted the difficulty of even ascertaining accurately whether a country is attempting to proliferate. In 2007, for example, the Israeli government struck an alleged Syrian reactor facility at which apparently a number of North Koreans were working—an event that shocked many observers, as Syria was not widely suspected to have a serious nuclear weapons programme, much less one closely coordinated with Pyongyang.

Although well-designed counterproliferation efforts can slow the spread of nuclear weapons, further proliferation should be regarded as being extremely likely. This, in turn, means that there will be more powers that possess the physical means to initiate nuclear war and, consequently, an increasingly complicated deterrence environment worldwide. The 'Second Nuclear Age' is distinct from the first in a number of key respects, one of the most important of which is the increasing unreliability of deterrence. As nuclear weapons proliferate horizontally, the risk of nuclear war occurring *somewhere* on earth can be expected to increase—especially as many of the proliferating states are not models of good international citizenship. While nuclear weapons have not been used militarily since 1945, we should not expect that this record will necessarily continue for another six decades. Moreover, if a truly undeterrable leader ever comes to possess nuclear weapons and is determined to use them, deterrence would be impossible. Leaders ultimately *choose* to be deterred, which is to say that they decide not to accept the consequences that would flow from taking a particular action—in essence, they are frightened away from doing something that they otherwise would do. If, however, they are willing to accept the consequences of an action, they may do as they like.

While it is often assumed, based on the experience of the cold war, that nuclear weapons make countries more cautious and therefore less likely to go to war, there is reason to doubt that this will be true in all cases. We know very little indeed about nuclear weapons decision-making in certain countries, such as North Korea. Moreover, it is impossible to know how a country such as Iran, which apparently does not yet have nuclear weapons, but likely soon will obtain them, will act once it possesses a nuclear arsenal. There also are many questions about how willing a country such as China might be to risk nuclear war during a future crisis.

In all likelihood, the countries that are most reliably predictable in regard to nuclear strategic decision-making are stable democracies, which have a relatively long track record of nuclear possession; states such as Great Britain, France, and the United States would fit into this category. It is, however, far more difficult to anticipate how a country such as North Korea, Iran, Russia, China, or Pakistan will act in the future (see Box 10.4).

In the case of most of these countries, we have little trustworthy information about their nuclear doctrine. Doctrine guides countries in their use of military power, and in the case of nuclear weapons it helps lay out a 'road map' as to the circumstances in which these devices might be used. While the cold war superpowers proved very reluctant to use nuclear weapons in combat, there is no guarantee that all states will be similarly reluctant to do so. Indeed, governments which possess relatively weak conventional forces may see nuclear weapons as offering an inexpensive trump card that they may use against better-armed enemies. Over time, we will have a clearer notion of how various nuclear states will use their arsenals in negotiations and conflict. In any case, however, it is clear that in this Second Nuclear Age deterrence must be carefully tailored to the cultural, political, military, and other characteristics of the state that one is endeavouring to

---

BOX 10.4 Unstable Nuclear States: The Pakistani Case

In the Second Nuclear Age, certain unstable states possess or are attempting to acquire nuclear weapons, and it should be remembered how quickly, and profoundly, the governments of troubled countries can be transformed. Pakistan provides one example. While Pakistan currently has an elected civilian government, it is widely feared that an internal coup, civil war, or other event could lead to massive political change; a radical, perhaps even Taliban-led, regime could take power and/or the country might splinter, much as the Soviet Union did in 1991. The security situation has worsened in recent years as the conflict in Afghanistan has increasingly spilled over into Pakistan, with Taliban forces presenting a very serious threat to the latter country's internal stability.

Today, India and Pakistan appear to have a reasonably stable deterrence relationship—one could argue that mutual deterrence is working tolerably well in South Asia, and even that a common fear of nuclear usage prevented a hot war from breaking out between the two countries in 2002. However, if a radical government comes to power in Pakistan, or if the country disintegrates, deterrence stability could vanish. This highlights one of the dangers of horizontal proliferation to unstable countries—even if the government that obtains nuclear weapons is responsible, its successors may not be.

deter. Not all leaders are similar to the individuals who led the USSR; even if deterrence truly 'worked' during the cold war, it should be assumed that deterrence theory as it developed during that period is not infallible and that deterrence failure is entirely possible.

Another difference between the two nuclear ages that likely will be critical relates to the deployment of missile defences. During the First Nuclear Age, the deployment of BMD was a matter of heated debate. BMD opponents warned that such defences would destabilize the nuclear balance between the superpowers and, therefore, encourage both countries to build more warheads so as to overwhelm the other side's BMD. This arms race and the general sense of instability might, it was feared, in turn increase the likelihood of a US–Soviet war. Regardless of whether the claims of BMD foes were accurate, the end of the First Nuclear Age has very much altered the international security environment. It was not unreasonable to believe that a superpower that already possessed thousands of nuclear weapons might build many thousands more. However, many of the small states constructing nuclear arsenals would be financially and technically incapable of building great numbers of missiles and warheads. In such a case, the fact that other states deploy BMD is unlikely to drive vertical nuclear proliferation. While some missile defence opponents worry that American construction of ballistic missile defences will convince countries with small nuclear arsenals to build many more warheads, in most cases they simply will not have the resources to do so.

In 1971, the United States and Soviet Union agreed to the Anti-Ballistic Missile (ABM) Treaty. This agreement barred both countries from constructing comprehensive national missile defences (however, it did not absolutely ban all missile defences, as it allowed each power to maintain a very strictly limited BMD capability). The Treaty was representative of a specific vision of deterrence based on mutual assured destruction (MAD), in which it was assumed that both the United States and the Soviet Union would not use nuclear weapons if they believed that, no matter how successful a first strike might be, it would be impossible to eliminate the ability of the other power to execute a devastating retaliatory strike. MAD, in short, envisioned deterrence stability as requiring that any nuclear war be utterly devastating to both sides. At present, however, only the United States and Russia have nuclear arsenals sufficient to allow them to practice MAD reliably. Moreover, MAD is largely irrelevant to the current Moscow–Washington relationship, because the contemporary international system differs radically from the cold war environment. Therefore, countries such as the United States can now look beyond MAD and ask how they can best address the potential threats offered by smaller nuclear powers, while the latter countries (as well as would-be new nuclear powers) have to take account of the possibility that the arsenal that they build may be defeated by a foe's missile defence.

The United States renounced the ABM Treaty in 2002, leaving it free to build missile defences, and that country now possesses a basic homeland missile defence. However, it is not the only state contemplating BMD defence of its territory. A wide variety of countries, including both nuclear and non-nuclear powers, have indicated interest in deployment of BMD. It is likely that as the Second Nuclear Age matures, an increasing number of countries will deploy such defences, a fact that will complicate the targeting strategy of all nuclear powers, particularly ones with modest arsenals.

Key points

- With the end of the cold war, the world has entered a Second Nuclear Age in which the number of actors possessing nuclear weapons is progressively increasing even as the absolute number of such weapons is falling.

- Deterrence may prove unreliable in the future. Deterrence theories that were developed in the context of the struggle between the United States and the Soviet Union may prove to be inapplicable to other powers such as North Korea and Iran.

- Strategic culture influences how a country uses its nuclear arsenal for deterrence and/or warfighting.

- Ballistic missile defences will be an important factor in nuclear decision-making in the future, and the existence of BMD may discourage some countries from attempting to acquire nuclear weapons.

Adapting to the Second Nuclear Age

In many respects, humanity as a whole is far safer today than it was during the cold war. A US–Soviet nuclear war could well have spelt the end of modern civilization, at least in the northern hemisphere. Today, there appears to be little immediate danger of a civilization-shattering nuclear conflict. It is far more likely that the next nuclear war will involve, at most, a few dozen warheads rather than the tens of thousands that might have been used in a US–Soviet apocalypse. It may be cold comfort when one contemplates the horrors that even a 'small' nuclear war would entail, but the reality that there appears to be little danger of the modern world being wiped out in an afternoon is important nonetheless.

In this Second Nuclear Age, several presumptions, common in the cold war era, may prove to be problematic: that nuclear-armed powers will always be 'reasonable'; BMDs undermine deterrence; and that arms control and disarmament treaties are the best means to counter-proliferation. The potential problems with the first two assumptions have already been addressed, and we shall now address the third one.

Non-proliferation and counterproliferation both relate to efforts to prevent the horizontal proliferation of nuclear weapons. While it is sometimes difficult to distinguish between the two activities, as a general rule the term 'non-proliferation' is used in reference to international legal arrangements such as the Nuclear Non-Proliferation Treaty (NPT). Counterproliferation, a term that has become popular in recent years, is more often used to refer to the *enforcement* of the NPT and other international agreements. Counterproliferation can involve a variety of measures, including military force (see Chapter 11).

The NPT, which was opened for signature in 1968 and went into force in 1970, is an international agreement that recognizes only five states—China, Great Britain, France, the Soviet Union/Russia, and the United States—as legitimate nuclear powers. All other states that signed the Treaty agreed to refrain from obtaining nuclear weapons. India, Israel, Pakistan never signed the NPT, while North Korea was formerly a signatory but withdrew from the Treaty in 2003.

The overall success of the NPT is debatable. While the number of nuclear powers has not exploded in the years since the agreement first came into effect, it should be noted that the great majority of countries signing the NPT surely would not, in any case, have obtained nuclear weapons—most states are too small and/or too poor to afford nuclear arsenals, and many of those which could afford to maintain a nuclear force are inhibited by domestic pressures from obtaining one or simply feel that they do not need such weapons to ensure their security. Most leaders in countries such as Germany, Japan, and South Korea, for example, believe that their countries are well-protected by the American 'nuclear umbrella' and therefore think that a national nuclear arsenal is unnecessary.

A major vulnerability of the NPT and similar universal disarmament agreements is that compliance is essentially voluntary; such treaties have very weak provisions regarding inspection of suspect sites and no mechanism for seriously punishing bad actors. (The reason for this, in turn, is that in order to maximize the number of signatories, such treaties basically accept the 'lowest common denominator'—the provisions must be acceptable to as many states as possible, including would-be bad actors which otherwise would refuse to accede to the agreement.) (See Box 10.5.)

The case of Iraq before its occupation by the United States illustrates some of the shortcomings of the NPT and other universal arms control agreements. As a militarily defeated state (in the 1991 Persian Gulf War), Iraq submitted to far more intrusive International Atomic Energy Agency (IAEA) inspections than are the norm. It was quickly discovered that not only did Baghdad have a nuclear weapons programme, which was generally assumed even before the war, but that it was quite close to actually building such devices. Despite this, the Iraqi government managed to avoid full disclosure of its WMD programmes and capabilities—and, of course, it is now clear that most of the world's intelligence agencies grossly overestimated the progress of the Iraqi WMD programmes in the years between 1991 and 2003. If Iraq could mislead outsiders under such conditions, one can readily imagine how easy it would be for other states to do so.

Iraq's Ba'ath Party government eventually paid an enormous price for its refusal to cooperate fully with IAEA inspections, but this was the result of Washington's initiative, not that of the IAEA or the United Nations. Moreover, as the cases of North Korea and Iran presently illustrate, apparent non-compliance with agreements such as the NPT does not necessarily carry a prohibitive price—indeed, North Korea at times has profited financially from its NPT non-compliance, thanks to the largesse of countries such as Japan, South Korea, and the United States, which have agreed to provide that country with fuel oil, food, and other goods

---

BOX 10.5 Arms Control Treaties and the International Environment

History seems to indicate that arms control treaties, by themselves, do little or nothing to reduce the danger level in the international environment. If they did, there would never have been a Second World War, because the period after the First World War was a 'golden age' of arms control, with war itself essentially being banned by the 1928 Kellogg–Briand Pact. For example, the fact that the number of warheads possessed by Russia and the United States decreased radically after the end of the cold war is instructive. One could argue that the successful negotiation of the bilateral Strategic Arms Reduction Talks (START) I, START II, Strategic Offensive Reduction Treaty (SORT), and New START agreements did not fundamentally alter the overall geostrategic environment, and that these treaties merely reflected the fact that the Russo–American relationship itself had changed radically. (See Chapter 11 for further detail on arms control.)

in exchange for ending its nuclear weapons programme. North Korea took the pay-off and built nuclear weapons nonetheless.

Counterproliferation measures, such as the Proliferation Security Initiative (PSI)—a US-led programme that allows states to cooperate in various ways to prevent the transfer of WMD materials and knowledge—attempt to plug the 'holes' in the NPT. While one cannot expect arms control and disarmament agreements to solve all proliferation problems, they *can* provide useful leverage for countries that are dedicated to stopping WMD proliferation and are willing to actively enforce counterproliferation (see Box 10.6).

Together, non-proliferation and counterproliferation efforts may succeed in slowing considerably the horizontal proliferation of nuclear weapons, although one should not expect that they can stop it altogether.

Having considered the history of nuclear weapons and their continuing horizontal proliferation, it is useful to consider briefly how the political and military roles of these devices will develop as the Second Nuclear Age matures. Will the 'nuclear taboo' grow stronger, with

---

BOX 10.6 The Difficulties of Assertive Disarmament

Assertive disarmament is the use of military force to destroy a successful proliferator's actual nuclear arsenal or a would-be proliferator's capability to build nuclear weapons. However, assertive disarmament is very difficult and controversial, and for those reasons it has rarely been undertaken. The difficulties associated with the invasion and occupation of Iraq, a military undertaking largely motivated by WMD proliferation concerns, illustrate how costly assertive disarmament can be in both financial and human terms for the would-be disarmer. The United States has expressed deep concern over the North Korean and Iranian nuclear programmes for years and in both cases has, at times, hinted that it might assertively disarm these states. However, it has never actually attempted to do so, for a variety of reasons.

Even if the United States possessed highly detailed and specific intelligence on the location and character of all the sites relevant to the North Korean and presumed Iranian nuclear programmes (and it is unlikely that it does in fact have such near-perfect intelligence), it is quite possible that Washington would not choose to strike these facilities. In regard to North Korea, the United States would surely fear that a full-scale war on the Korean Peninsula would result. Given that North Korea possesses great numbers of conventional artillery tubes and could inflict massive conventional damage on Seoul—and kill tens of thousands of civilians—just in the early hours of a conflict, the risks of escalation strongly discourage a disarming strike.

The Iranian case is not quite so dire, but it is generally assumed that Iranian facilities are widely dispersed and that destroying them would result in a large number of civilian casualties. Moreover, American policymakers greatly fear that such a move would set back reform in Iran and turn the Iranian public against the United States. It is also possible that Iran would retaliate by undertaking terrorist attacks against US targets.

Some observers expect that Israel will strike Iran's facilities, but this would require Israeli leaders to accept the difficulties and dangers that would accompany such an action. It is far from certain that they are any more willing to than their American counterparts to accept these consequences. North Korea and Iran present proliferation challenges that are unlikely to be resolved through the use of military force. Thus, responsible policymakers and military planners must work under the assumption that these powers either do possess nuclear weapons and will continue to do so (North Korea) or will have nuclear weapons in the future (Iran).

nuclear weapons eventually being banned outright worldwide? Will technological developments render these devices obsolete? Or will nuclear weapons continue to play a role in international politics?

There appears to be little likelihood that nuclear weapons will cease to be an international political tool, either being eliminated altogether or placed in the hands of an international authority such as the IAEA. Indeed, there has been no compelling evidence that progress has been made towards universal nuclear disarmament in recent years. The absolute number of nuclear weapons in the world is decreasing as the United States and Russia continue to adapt to post-cold war conditions by decreasing the overall size of their arsenals, but this is quite different from complete disarmament. Neither of these countries, nor any other declared nuclear states, have surrendered their nuclear arsenals or indicated a willingness to do so at any time in the foreseeable future, though they have all agreed publicly that universal disarmament is a laudable goal. Moreover, horizontal proliferation is still, of course, continuing (see Box 10.7).

The question of whether nuclear weapons will become outdated is a rather more complex one. While a few elegantly simple weapons have remained on the battlefield for millennia, it is usual for a weapon to have a fairly straightforward life cycle, offering great advantages to

BOX 10.7 A Nuclear Taboo?

Many observers contend that there is a taboo against the use of nuclear (as well as chemical and biological) weapons. From this perspective, the use of these devices is considered so disreputable and immoral that states are extremely reluctant to use such weapons; the use of such weapons would make the state in question an outcast, despised by its peers, including those which might otherwise be sympathetic to it. Therefore, the taboo is a strong firebreak that helps to prevent the occurrence of nuclear war. Certainly, the use of nuclear weapons is controversial, and the fact that they have not been used in combat since 1945 is strong evidence that states possessing these weapons are reluctant to use them. However, 'taboo' is a very powerful word, implying a deep-rooted and long-standing repugnance shared by almost all members of a particular society (most cultures, for example, have a taboo against cannibalism).

One must, however, consider the fact that there have been no truly hard cases in which a nuclear state chose not to use its arsenal; for example, no nuclear-armed country has chosen to allow itself to be destroyed rather than use its arsenal against an invader. Indeed, since 1945 no nuclear-armed state has even fought a war in which it lost as many as 100,000 troops, a small figure compared to the millions of fatalities suffered by various major powers in the World Wars (the Soviet Union alone suffered approximately 27 million deaths in the Second World War). Perhaps the closest that any state has come to using nuclear weapons in recent decades was Israel in the early part of the 1973 Yom Kippur War, when it was faced with possible invasion by the armies of several Arab states. Israel supposedly prepared for possible use of its arsenal, but eventually the invasion was turned back by conventional means. If the Arab armies had instead achieved a decisive breakthrough and the survival of Israel was thought to be in danger, it is quite possible that the Israeli cabinet would have permitted nuclear use.

In this light, the fact that nuclear weapons have not been used is not particularly impressive, as no nuclear-armed country has faced very intense pressure compelling it do so. Real proof of the existence of a strong nuclear taboo would be found if states proved willing to suffer truly terrible consequences rather than use these weapons.

its possessors when first introduced and then, progressively, growing more outmoded as new weapons are invented until, eventually, it disappears entirely from military use. In due course, this perhaps will be the fate of nuclear weapons, but this life cycle process may require many decades, if not centuries. It is possible that the nuclear weapon will be dethroned from its position as 'the absolute weapon' by an even more devastating new weapon of mass destruction (there has been speculation, for example, on the feasibility of an 'antimatter bomb' that would be enormously powerful), and, certainly, militaries on the technological cutting-edge will continue to deploy ever more potent conventional weapons. However, for the foreseeable future, nuclear weapons will remain the most powerful engines of destruction possessed by human beings.

Given this reality, it is clear that nuclear weapons will continue to have an international political role. While it is not possible to predict precisely how many states will come to possess these devices over the next few decades, it is very likely indeed that the number of nuclear-armed states will increase, perhaps dramatically. As more states acquire nuclear weapons—and as the nuclear club becomes more diverse ideologically and culturally—we will learn more about how robust deterrence is under a variety of conditions involving different actors. Perhaps we will find that there actually is a strong nuclear taboo which prevents leaders worldwide from 'pushing the button'. It is, however, all too plausible that we will instead see the breaking of the long nuclear truce.

Key points

- Non-proliferation and counterproliferation measures are used to control, and ideally prevent, the horizontal proliferation of nuclear weapons.

- The NPT acknowledges only five nuclear weapons states (China, France, Great Britain, the Soviet Union/Russia, and the United States) and forbids all other signatories from obtaining nuclear weapons. Most of the world's states are signatories, although some (including nuclear-armed countries such as India, Israel, and Pakistan) are not.

- Effective enforcement of universal disarmament agreements such as the NPT has proven difficult, especially as such agreements generally only have very weak inspection provisions.

- It is very unlikely that nuclear weapons will become obsolescent in the next few decades, or that the world's nuclear powers will all agree to dismantle their arsenals.

 ## Conclusion: Looking Towards the Third Nuclear Age?

Since 1945, nuclear weapons have played a central role in international relations, but over time that role has changed subtly. During the decades immediately following the invention of 'the bomb', nuclear weapons were only possessed by a small number of states, with the two superpowers amassing arsenals far larger than those of all the world's other countries combined. However, as the world has transitioned to the Second Nuclear Age, the 'nuclear club' has become far less exclusive, and even some relatively minor powers, such as Pakistan and North Korea, now possess nuclear arsenals and the means to deliver them. (North Korea tested nuclear devices in 2006 and 2009.)

While non-proliferation and counterproliferation efforts may slow the spread of nuclear weapons, it should be expected that the number of nuclear-armed countries will continue to grow. There are several reasons for this, but the military utility and consequent usefulness of these devices for deterrence and coercion, as well as the prestige associated with possessing a nuclear arsenal, are the most important. Nuclear weapons are particularly valuable to states that, in conventional terms, are militarily weak relative to their foes. For example, in a conventional conflict, most states would find the military power of the United States overwhelming, but even a small nuclear arsenal would greatly complicate US war planning and raise the possibility of horrific American and allied casualties. In some cases, it might even be possible to prevent the United States from undertaking any military action, making it possible for a country such as North Korea or Iran to prevail in a crisis. Nuclear possession is also associated with high status in the international community, since most very powerful states have nuclear arsenals. Although owning nuclear weapons alone does not make a country a great power, there certainly is a unique status associated with nuclear possession, and this surely is one of the reasons why some of the aforementioned lesser powers went to such extraordinary (and expensive) efforts to circumvent international non-proliferation regimes.

While deterrence theories developed during the cold war continue to provide useful guidance, as the group of nuclear-armed states has diversified, the continued validity of these theories has become questionable. As we have seen, every country has a unique strategic culture, and cultural factors can have a significant influence on decisions related to nuclear acquisition, deterrence, and use. We should not expect that the very diverse group of leaders who will wield nuclear weapons in this century will all act as their Soviet and American counterparts did during the cold war.

The simple 'MAD worldview', which assumes that any nuclear war would involve thousands, or even tens of thousands, of nuclear warheads, and be utterly devastating both to the participants and other countries (which would experience the environmental side-effects of the massive nuclear exchange), is obsolete. In the cold war, the greatest fear of both superpowers was that the other would be able to disarm it almost entirely in a well-planned first strike. There was relatively little concern over whether surviving nuclear weapons, especially those mounted on SLBMs and ICBMs, might hit the enemy; so long as the command and control system and a modest percentage of a superpower's arsenal remained intact, it could execute a devastating counterstrike. Certainly, some warheads would fail to strike their targets for any number of reasons—mechanical failure, simple inaccuracy, or whatnot—but the superpower nuclear arsenals were so large that such problems would not undermine the ability to deliver a fatal blow.

Most of today's nuclear powers possess rather small arsenals, and missile defences can complicate nuclear war planning exponentially. When a state with a small nuclear arsenal considers attacking a foe with a missile defence, the attacker cannot be certain how many, if any, of its warheads will break though the defence and strike their targets. It is likely that the proliferation of missile defences in this century will provide many states with a 'shield' that they can use to defend against the nuclear sword wielded by their enemies. Moreover, many states no doubt will, like the United States, seek to have both a nuclear sword and a BMD shield. Thus the argument, commonly made in the West during the cold war, that building defences against nuclear weapons is a waste of effort because many warheads (presumably) would 'leak through' any defence is irrelevant with regard to most of the countries that are, or will be, nuclear-armed in this century. When a state only has a small number of nuclear weapons, it is conceivable that they could all be intercepted by a well-designed missile defence.

In the two decades of the Second Nuclear Age, we have seen clear patterns develop, such as continuing horizontal proliferation and an ongoing decrease in the size of the Russian and American nuclear arsenals. Most recently, the latter trend was reinforced by the New START treaty, which limits the two countries to 1,550 deployed warheads each. However, other countries, such as China and India, are both increasing the size of and modernizing their nuclear arsenals. This, combined with the spread of missile defences over time, has resulted in a complicated environment with many potential nuclear deterrence relationships.

There are still many uncertainties regarding how nuclear weapons will be used politically in the current nuclear age. Thus far, fortunately, most of the 'emerging' nuclear powers have been relatively cautious in regard to issuing nuclear threats. There are, however, many potential flashpoints—for example, India and Pakistan have a perpetually uneasy relationship, and if the North Korean government suffered a succession crisis or began to collapse internally, it is impossible to be certain how it might try to leverage its nuclear arsenal. Moreover, although we have not yet seen a cascade of nuclear proliferation where many states simultaneously sought nuclear weapons, it is possible that one will occur in the future. The Middle East may be a particularly fertile environment for a nuclear cascade, given Iran's ongoing nuclear efforts and the current political instability of most Arab countries. What sort of governments that will emerge from the 'Arab Spring' and the events following it is unknowable, but it is entirely possible that some of them will prove to be less reticent concerning nuclear proliferation than were their predecessors.

The great theme of the Second Nuclear Age is unpredictability—there is a lack of surety concerning how many nuclear-armed states there will be in coming years or how those states will use their arsenals for political gain. Perhaps even more worryingly, it is possible that one or more terrorist groups or other violent non-state actors will obtain nuclear weapons. There are many good reasons to celebrate the end of the First Nuclear Age and the consequent greatly diminished probability of a massive nuclear exchange, but it is, regrettably, all too possible that, sooner or later, nuclear weapons will be used *somewhere* in the world. If that were to occur, it might well mark the beginning of a Third Nuclear Age—and that epoch might well be an era of both unbridled horizontal proliferation and repeated use of nuclear weapons.

 ## Questions

1. What were the key characteristics of the First and Second Nuclear Ages? In what key respects do the two nuclear ages differ?

2. Why might the cold war model of nuclear deterrence be less relevant in the Second Nuclear Age? In what respects might it still be relevant?

3. Does the horizontal proliferation of nuclear weapons make nuclear war more likely? If so, why?

4. If many countries acquire ballistic missile defences, how might this affect vertical and horizontal proliferation worldwide?

5. How might the history of the A. Q. Khan network demonstrate the difficulties of controlling horizontal proliferation in the Second Nuclear Age?

6. Is it possible to halt the continuing spread of nuclear weapons? If so, how?

7. If it is not possible to stop the spread of nuclear weapons, is it at least possible to significantly slow the proliferation of these devices? If so, how?

8. Is there a strong taboo against the use of nuclear weapons?

9. Is a complete global abolition of nuclear weapons a plausible goal? If so, how might it be achieved?

10. Is it ever appropriate for a state to use military force to prevent a would-be proliferator from obtaining nuclear weapons? If so, under what conditions might it be appropriate to do so?

 ## Further Reading

F. Barnaby, *How to Build a Nuclear Bomb: And Other Weapons of Mass Destruction* (New York: Nation Books, 2004).
This book explains, using accessible language, how a state or non-state actor might go about building weapons of mass destruction.

L. Freedman, *Deterrence* (Cambridge: Polity Press, 2004).
This short work introduces key deterrence concepts and explores how deterrence theory has evolved over time.

C. S. Gray, *The Second Nuclear Age* (Boulder, CO: Lynne Rienner, 1999).
This book describes the concept of the Second Nuclear Age in detail.

W. Langewiesche, *The Atomic Bazaar: The Rise of the Nuclear Poor* (New York: Farrar, Straus and Giroux, 2007).
This work explores a number of issues related to horizontal proliferation, including the A. Q. Khan network and the danger of nuclear terrorism.

P. R. Lavoy, S. D. Sagan, and J. J. Wirtz, *Planning the Unthinkable: How New Powers will Use Nuclear, Biological, and Chemical Weapons* (Ithaca, NY: Cornell University Press, 2000).
This edited volume offers perspectives on a variety of issues related to the horizontal proliferation of WMDs.

D. Miller, *The Cold War: A Military History* (New York: St. Martin's Press, 1998).
This work provides a general discussion of how the US and Soviet nuclear arsenals developed during the cold war.

P. Morgan, *Deterrence Now* (Cambridge: Cambridge University Press, 2003).
This work considers some of the arguable flaws in deterrence theory and makes recommendations regarding how they may be corrected.

K. B. Payne, *The Great American Gamble: Deterrence Theory and Practice from the Cold War to the Twenty-first Century* (Fairfax, VA: National Institute Press, 2008).
This work explores the development of deterrence theory and how it may be applied today and in the future.

 ## Web Links

Alsos Digital Library for Nuclear Issues **http://alsos.wlu.edu/** This digital library, hosted by Washington and Lee University, is an excellent resource containing annotated descriptions books, articles, and other materials. It is affiliated with the Nuclear Pathways project.

Federation of American Scientists **http://www.fas.org/nuke/** The website of this anti-nuclear group contains a substantial amount of information about the nuclear arsenals of various countries.

National Resources Defense Council **http://www.nrdc.org/nuclear/** The website of this anti-nuclear organization also includes a variety of relevant information.

Nuclear Age Peace Foundation **http://www.nuclearfiles.org/** The Nuclear Files site is maintained by another anti-nuclear group. It contains considerable material concerning nuclear weapons and deterrence.

Nuclear Pathways **http://www.nuclearpathways.org/browse.php** This project, which is part of the US National Science Digital Library, gathers together a great variety of information on historical and current nuclear weapons issues.

National Resources Defense Council **http://www.nrdc.org/nuclear/nudb/datab19.asp**

The Control of Weapons of Mass Destruction

JOHN BAYLIS

Chapter Contents

Introduction	214
Arms Control during the Cold War	214
The Residual Role of Arms Control in the Post-Cold War Era	218
From Arms Control to Counterproliferation	220
The Challenges of Counterproliferation	222
The Diplomatic Option: Strategic Responses Withheld?	223
The Return of Arms Control: Attempts to Reduce the Saliency of Nuclear Weapons	224
Conclusion	227

Reader's Guide

One of the most important questions facing humanity during the nuclear age has been how to control weapons regarded as uniquely abhorrent or particularly destructive. During the cold war, this had an added urgency because the numbers and destructive capacity of such weapons meant that they possessed the unique capability to destroy civilization as we know it. Is the best way to try to negotiate the elimination of nuclear weapons and other weapons of mass destruction completely? Is a better approach to try, through diplomatic means, to manage these weapons to create as much stability in the international system as possible? Or, should more forceful means be used to prevent the proliferation of these weapons, especially to those 'rogue states' or terrorist organizations, who might be tempted to use them to upset the status quo. These questions and the changing international approach to dealing with weapons of mass destruction are the subject of this chapter.

Introduction

Establishing controls over weapons or delivery systems is a difficult and painstaking process. Despite this, efforts to eliminate weapons through disarmament have a long history, and at least one writer has traced a lineage back to ancient times (Croft 1996). As an academic subject, however, arms control—the mutually agreed management of military relations—is a more recent arrival. A decade or so after the onset of the cold war in 1947, academic analysis and international policy began to converge, as the prospect of using arms control to stabilize the superpower relationship began to find favour. The hair-raising experience of the Cuban Missile Crisis only served to drive home that the relationship could be dangerously unstable and could not be relied upon to run itself. In a wider context, the lesson of the twentieth century seemed to be that warfare would almost always escalate upwards to the most destructive level, and increasingly it was not only the superpowers that possessed the most destructive technology. The spread of weapons of mass destruction (WMD), a term coined and defined by the United Nations in 1948, therefore became a key concern.

This chapter charts the shift that took place during the cold war from disarmament to arms control, and the shift in relative importance that has taken place in the post-cold war period from arms control to more forcible means to tackle proliferation. The chapter shows how concerns emerged in the 1980s and 1990s about the continuing utility of arms control as an effective means of dealing with weapons of mass destruction and how new ideas began to take shape, first in the Clinton administration, and then in the Bush administration, about more militarily driven approaches, associated with counterproliferation. The chapter ends with a discussion of 'the return to arms control' by the new Obama administration.

Arms Control during the Cold War

Following the arms races and the slide to war in the late 1930s, disillusionment with disarmament, as a way to achieve peace and security, characterized official attitudes in the immediate aftermath of the Second World War. The limited attempts at arms control or disarmament that were made by the two emerging superpowers in the new cold war that developed only helped to reinforce the sceptical judgement of the day. Neither side was prepared to take risks with their own security (as they perceived it), especially when it came to weapons which could be a decisive influence in a future conflict. Far from easing the growing tension between the two superpowers in the late 1940s, the modest international control negotiations that were undertaken only exacerbated mistrust and heightened hostility.

By the mid-1950s, the lack of success in disarmament negotiations and growing awareness of the dangers of nuclear war produced a change in approach to arms control. Efforts to negotiate a general and comprehensive disarmament treaty were abandoned in favour of what were known as 'partial measures', such as the 1955 'Open Skies' agreement and negotiations designed to try to ban nuclear testing. Arms control was increasingly viewed as a way to deal with specific problems created by the cold war arms race.

This move towards greater flexibility at the policy level led to what has been described as 'new thinking' within the defence community. Although the ideas that emerged were not as original as the proponents sometimes claimed, a new literature began to appear in the late

1950s developing the theory of arms control (see Box 11.1). These new arms control theorists intended to work within the prevailing system of nuclear deterrence rather than to try to abolish it. Arms control was designed to 'strengthen the operation of the balance of military power against the disruptive effects of the arms dynamic, especially arms competition, arms racing and technological developments that tend to make nuclear and non-nuclear deterrence more difficult' (Buzan and Herring 1998: 212). Its essential aim was to reduce the likelihood and costs of war and to reduce expenditures on both nuclear and conventional arsenals.

As the superpowers edged back from the nuclear abyss after the Cuban Missile Crisis in October 1962, both realized, more than ever before, that they had a mutual interest in effective crisis management. The crisis highlighted the dangers of inadvertent escalation and miscalculation during periods of military confrontation and intense political instability. In June 1963, the United States and the Soviet Union signed a 'hotline' agreement to provide a secure, official, and dependable channel of communication between Moscow and Washington. The intensity of the crisis also highlighted the issue of nuclear testing. Reflecting the less ambitious agenda of the new arms control school, the United States, Britain, and the Soviet Union agreed on a Partial Test Ban Treaty in August 1963. The treaty prohibited all nuclear tests in the atmosphere, but allowed tests to continue underground. Significantly, neither French nor Chinese officials (who tested nuclear weapons in 1960 and 1964 respectively) were prepared to accede to the Treaty because they believed it benefited more advanced nuclear states (see Box 11.2).

Limited as the Treaty was, it encouraged further arms control initiatives. Between 1963 and 1968, the superpowers focused on their mutual interest in trying to negotiate a wider agreement to prohibit further nuclear proliferation. This culminated in the Non-Proliferation Treaty (NPT), which was signed in July 1968. Once again, initially, China and France refused to sign, and a number of other states rejected the treaty on the grounds that it froze the nuclear status quo and incorporated only a limited commitment by the nuclear powers to give up their own weapons. This latter criticism became perennial and was to bedevil the NPT process in later years.

The nuclear explosion by India in 1974, ostensibly for peaceful purposes, highlighted the weaknesses of the Treaty. Despite this, the Treaty provided some limited, but not

---

BOX 11.1 Definitions of Arms Control

While the terms 'arms control' and 'disarmament' are sometimes used interchangeably, they reflect very different views about international politics. Hedley Bull, in his book *Control of the Arms Race*, defines disarmament as 'the reduction or abolition of armaments. It may be unilateral or multilateral; general or local; comprehensive or partial; controlled or uncontrolled'. Arms control, on the other hand, according to Bull, involves 'restraint internationally exercised upon armaments policy, whether in respect of the level of armaments, their character, deployment, or use'.

John Spanier and Joseph Nogee in their study of *The Politics of Disarmament* provide a similar, although more specific definition of the differences between arms control and disarmament. In their formulation 'while disarmament refers to the complete abolition or partial reduction of the human and material resources of war, arms control deals with the restraints to be imposed upon the use of nuclear weapons'.

Spanier and Nogee (1962: 15)

BOX 11.2 What Are Weapons of Mass Destruction?

In the run-up to the 2003 war in Iraq, the term 'weapons of mass destruction' (WMD) took on a public profile that it had hitherto lacked, and a term that had previously been used largely by specialists (scientists, analysts, government officials, and activists) was now part of political rhetoric. Buzan and Herring (1998: 53) define WMD as 'weapons of which small numbers can destroy life and/or inanimate objects on a vast scale very quickly', but note that this could conceivably be applied to weapons (such as fuel-air explosives) that are normally regarded as 'conventional' weapons.

The term does in fact have an internationally accepted definition, one formulated by the United Nations Commission for Conventional Armaments in 1948. This defined WMD as: 'Atomic explosive weapons, radioactive material weapons, lethal chemical and biological weapons, and any weapons developed in the future which have characteristics comparable in destructive effect to those of the atomic bomb or other weapons mentioned above'.

This definition formed the basis for subsequent international agreements on controlling WMD. Nonetheless, the term should be used with more care than is usually the case in political rhetoric, since by its nature it conflates very different forms of weapon. Today, it can be regarded as a blanket term for nuclear and radiological, chemical and biological weapons.

Nuclear weapons work by nuclear fission using plutonium or uranium (fission or atom bombs) or by nuclear fusion (thermonuclear or hydrogen bombs). There are seven known nuclear-armed states in the world (Britain, China, France, India, Pakistan, Russia, and the United States). Israel neither acknowledges nor denies it has nuclear weapons but is widely believed to have them. North Korea is believed to possess a small and rudimentary capability, and Iran may be pursuing such a programme.

Radiological weapons are sometimes referred to as 'dirty bombs', and would work by surrounding conventional explosive with radioactive material. They do not involve any nuclear explosion, but rather the large-scale dispersal of radioactive toxic materials, thereby inflicting doses of radiation on nearby victims of the explosion. These weapons are widely associated with terrorists and other non-state actors.

Biological weapons are bacteria, viruses, or biological toxins that are intentionally disseminated in order to infect or poison individuals, such as troops or civilians. Examples of biological substances used in weapons include anthrax, smallpox, and ricin. Similarly, *chemical weapons* use the toxic effects of chemical substances to cause death, permanent harm or incapacity to human beings. Examples include phosgene, mustard gas, and VX (nerve agent).

---

unimportant benefits. It became the central plank of the nascent non-proliferation regime, which helped restrain the pace of further nuclear proliferation. It also emphasized the opportunities for cooperation between the superpowers during rocky times in their relationship.

By the mid-1970s, the superpowers also recognized their mutual interest in trying to control the use of pathogens and toxins as weapons of mass destruction. The Biological Weapons Convention (BWC), which entered into force in 1975, banned the development, production, and stockpiling of biological and toxin weapons. It also required states to destroy 'the agents, toxins and weapons equipment and means of delivery in the possession of the parties' to the treaty. The main problem with the Convention, however, was that there was no provision for verification of compliance.

Between 1969 and 1972, the superpowers focused for the first time on the difficult task of limiting strategic armaments. In May 1972, the Strategic Arms Limitation Treaty (SALT) I was signed and covered a number of different areas, including limitations on ballistic missile defence. The aim of SALT I was to 'cap' missile and anti-ballistic missile (ABM) deployments at specific levels to prevent a future unrestricted arms race, which would lead to greater international instability. Despite the unprecedented nature of the agreement it quickly became the subject of criticism, both within the United States and in the arms control community itself. According to domestic critics it froze the numerical superiority of the Soviet Union while at the same time allowed the Soviet Union to compete in those qualitative areas where the United States was in the lead. This failure to address the all-important qualitative issues (including missile accuracy and the placement of multiple warheads on ballistic missiles) was particularly disappointing even for many arms control supporters, who were concerned that the arms race had simply been moved from a quantitative to a qualitative arena.

Given the shortcomings of SALT I, it was not long before new negotiations began in Geneva. Progress, however, proved to be slow. The SALT II Agreement eventually reached in 1979 followed closely guidelines reached at Vladivostok five years earlier. The ceiling for strategic delivery vehicles were set at 2,400, with sublimits on ballistic missiles armed with Multiple Independently Targetable Re-entry Vehicles (MIRVs) and strategic bombers.

Almost immediately, however, the arms control process was derailed by the Soviet invasion of Afghanistan and in January 1980 President Carter asked the Senate to delay the ratification of the Treaty. Although the SALT II remained unratified, both the United States and the Soviet Union continued to abide by the limits of the Treaty. Despite this tacit agreement, however, the following three years were characterized by frequent accusations by the Reagan administration that the Soviet Union was in breach of the Agreement.

By the end of the cold war, despite the 1987 Intermediate Nuclear Force (INF) Agreement, (banning missiles with ranges between 500 and 5,000 kilometres) there was a growing disappointment in many quarters with the overall benefits of arms control. There had been periods of détente when arms control appeared to have played a part in helping to enhance confidence between the adversaries, especially by providing a forum for discussion of strategic thinking, the purposes behind force deployments, and concerns about the opponent's force structure and operations. This happened in the aftermath of the Cuban Missile Crisis and in the early 1970s. However, these periods were short-lived and more hostile relations followed. The effects of arms control were clearly limited and temporary. The critics of arms control felt that there was very little evidence that arms control had helped to improve superpower relations during periods of intense hostility. Indeed, they felt that the evidence seemed to support the view that differences over arms control more often than not exacerbated the problems which existed.

Key points

- The late 1940s and early 1950s saw a growing disillusionment with disarmament in dealing with the problems posed by weapons of mass destruction.
- The late 1950s brought 'new thinking' and the development of the theory of arms control.
- The aim of arms control was to make the prevailing system work more effectively.
- The Cuban Missile Crisis ushered in a new 'golden age' of arms control agreements.
- By the late 1970s, however, arms control as an approach to peace and security faced increasing problems.
- There were continuing difficulties in the 1980s, which meant that despite the INF Agreement in 1987 there was a growing feeling that the disadvantages of arms control outweighed the benefits.

The Residual Role of Arms Control in the Post-Cold War Era

The ending of the cold war brought a flurry of arms control activity and some remarkably far-reaching progress which rebutted some of the criticisms that had been levied against the arms control concept. Following a number of years of detailed negotiation in 1991, a Strategic Arms Reduction Treaty (START I) was finally signed. Instead of merely imposing limits on increases in weapons, START reduced the number of strategic delivery vehicles and warheads in a verified process of drawdown.

With the disintegration of the Soviet Union, President Boris Yeltsin of Russia and President Bill Clinton continued the momentum of the early post-cold war years by signing a START II Treaty in 1993 reducing the number of warheads held by both sides even further. As a result of a Protocol to the START I Treaty signed in May 1992, it had been agreed, however, that START II would only enter into force once START I had been ratified by the United States and Russia and entered into force. This proved to be difficult because of increasing Russian concerns about the Treaty's costs and strategic effects, the need to resolve a new debate over the ABM treaty before agreeing START II limits, and growing hostility towards North Atlantic Treaty Organization (NATO) expansion plans.

These bilateral difficulties were also evident in a number of other fields. Despite the notable achievement of securing indefinite extension of the NPT in 1995, significant disagreements continued between the nuclear and non-nuclear states over the pace of nuclear disarmament (enshrined in Article 6 of the Treaty). At the same time the nuclear tests carried out by India and Pakistan in May 1998 demonstrated the fragility of the non-proliferation norm outside the Treaty in certain parts of the world. Similarly, an apparent breakthrough achieved with the Comprehensive Test Ban Treaty (CTBT) in 1996 ground to a halt in late 1999 when the US Senate refused to ratify the Treaty (see Box 11.3).

Attempts to control other weapons of mass destruction also ran into difficulties at about the same time. The Chemical Weapons Convention (CWC), signed in 1993, and which entered into force in April 1997, also suffered from a number of serious weaknesses. The Convention was designed to ban the use of chemical weapons, as well as their development, production, transfer, and stockpiling. Stockpiles and production facilities were to be destroyed. Although there was some provision for verification through the OPCW based in The Hague, the widespread industrial and commercial production of chemicals made the Convention virtually impossible to police effectively. By 2002, 145 states had ratified both the Biological and Toxins and the Chemical Conventions, but in both cases, there were concerns that a significant number of states were developing weapons covertly.

There were also increasing concerns about the proliferation of nuclear weapons as the new century dawned. Despite the Strategic Offensive Reductions Treaty (SORT) of May 2002 (the Moscow Treaty), further reducing the number of US and Russian warheads to around 2,000 each over the following decade, there appeared to be an increasing incentive for some states and terrorist groups to acquire nuclear weapons and other weapons of mass destruction. With the cold war over, and the United States now the dominant power in the world, those who feared US hegemony or intervention in their internal affairs (like North Korea and possibly Iran) had an interest in developing their own 'ultimate' weapon. After 9/11 there were also concerns that terrorist groups, like al-Qaeda,

BOX 11.3 International Regimes on WMD

The three key categories of WMD (nuclear, biological, chemical), plus the missile delivery systems usually associated with them, each have an international regime devoted to their control. They are in various stages of development (some might add disarray) and they have not advanced or progressed at an even pace.

The Treaty on the Non-Proliferation of Nuclear Weapons (NPT) entered into force on 5 March 1970 and currently has 189 member states. Only India, Israel, North Korea, and Pakistan remain outside it. The NPT's signatory states are divided into two categories: nuclear weapon states (NWS) and non-nuclear weapon states (NNWS). Under the terms of the treaty the latter agree to forgo nuclear weapons entirely, while the former (the five states, Britain, China, France, Russia, and the United States, that possessed nuclear weapons at the signing of the Treaty) are committed to 'pursue negotiations in good faith' on nuclear disarmament. This stipulation, set out in Article 6 of the Treaty, has proved recurrently controversial, since none of the five NWS has ever looked likely to move seriously towards such an end.

The other 'devil's bargain' in the NPT is drawn from Article 4, which notes the 'inalienable right' of the NNWS to develop civil nuclear power with the 'fullest possible exchange' of information with the NWS. This exchange of information is subject to various safeguards and inspections conducted by the International Atomic Energy Agency (IAEA—see http://www.iaea.org).

The *Chemical Weapons Convention* (CWC) is a multilateral treaty banning chemical weapons. It entered into force on 29 April 1997, currently has 164 states parties, and is implemented by the Organization for the Prohibition of Chemical Weapons (OPCW—see http://www.opcw.org). The Convention bans development, acquisition, or possession of chemical weapons by signatories; their use or preparation for use; the transfer of chemical weapons or any encouragement of chemical weapons in other states; and the destruction of chemical weapon stockpiles by signatories. The latter is significant: unlike the NPT, the CWC *compels* states parties possessing the banned weapons to dismantle their stocks, and sets out clear timetables and deadlines for this work. In cases of non-compliance, the OPCW can recommend that the states parties take punitive action, and in extreme cases can refer the case to the UN Security Council.

The *Biological Weapons Convention* (BWC) entered into force on 26 March 1975 and currently has 150 states parties. It bans development, stockpiling, acquisition, retention, and production of biological agents and toxins, and all weapons designed to use them. Unlike the CWC, it does not ban the use of such weapons, which is affirmed in the 1925 Geneva Protocol.

with nothing to lose, have an interest in acquiring such weapons to further their regional and in some cases global ambitions. As such, the new geostrategic realities of the post-cold war era meant that attempts to control weapons of mass destruction faced new challenges.

By the close of the twentieth century, the picture was therefore a mixed one. Nuclear non-proliferation appeared to have successfully prevented the Kennedy-era fears that the number of nuclear-armed states might exceed 20 by the year 2000, the destruction of chemical weapons was proceeding globally if haltingly, and biological weapons remained, for the great majority of states, beyond the pale of normal military arsenals. Nonetheless, the new century's advent was haunted by a growing feeling that as weapons of mass destruction proliferated to weak states and non-state actors, it would be increasingly difficult to bring traditional arms control techniques and principles to bear to address the new emerging threats.

From Arms Control to Counterproliferation

The United Nations and International Atomic Energy Agency inspectors of Iraqi WMD, after the 1991 Gulf War, found that Iraq had made considerably more progress on developing a nuclear capability than intelligence assessments had supposed. This suggested that proliferation might be moving more quickly than was apparent. The implications of this were far-reaching. Prior to 1990, US intelligence estimated that 20 states in the world possessed chemical weapons and ten were working on biological ones; it now appeared that either this number might be an underestimate, or that those states might be considerably more advanced than anyone suspected. Concerns about hidden horizontal and vertical pro-liferation were therefore strengthened by the experience with Iraq, which in turn led to louder calls for more tools to tackle this problem.

Thus it appeared that the end of the cold war had spawned a new set of threats that might be smaller in scale, but more numerous and potentially more acute. In such conflicts, nuclear weapons were regarded as being likely to be deployed to deter, but chemical and biological weapons were potentially more likely to be deployed in order to be *used* (Lavoy et al. 2000). The CIA Director James Woolsey put this succinctly when he said that 'it was as if we were struggling with a large dragon for 45 years, killed it, and then found ourselves in a jungle full of poisonous snakes' (Woolsey 1998).

The seriousness with which the threat was taken was due to an uncomfortable awareness that WMD might erode the ability of the United States to project military power around the world. Richard Betts alluded to this when he argued that WMD, particularly nuclear weapons, were now 'weapons of the weak—states or groups that are at best second class' (Betts 1998: 27). General Sundarji of the Indian Army similarly argued that 'One principal lesson of the Gulf War is that, if a state intends to fight the United States, it should avoid doing so until and unless it possesses nuclear weapons'.[1]

Betts and Sundarji were both suggesting that, if Iraq had possessed a nuclear capability in 1991, Operation Desert Storm might never have been possible: the United States and its allies might have been deterred from intervening in Kuwait. Washington's confidence in its ability to resist the deterrent strategies of small hostile states might therefore be significantly eroded once these small states possess nuclear weapons. This may also be true for other NATO members who participated in the coalition, such as Britain, or for important regional allies such as Turkey.

Moreover, this problem was exacerbated by a perception (not one universally shared) that some states, or at least their leaders, are simply not deterrable. This is often raised in the context of the so-called 'rogue states'. Officials and analysts in the United States frequently claim that these states are not susceptible to deterrent-based strategies because their leaders are fanatical (i.e. too wedded to ideological or religious fervour), morally bankrupt (i.e. unlikely to recoil from mass casualties on their own soil), or simply crazy or irrational.

These concerns, centring around the possibility that WMD proliferation might either make it difficult for the United States to win a Gulf War-type conflict at acceptable cost, or deter it from acting at all, were at the heart of the Clinton administration's decision, announced in the Bottom Up Review of 1993, that WMD represented the most direct threat to US security. In December of the same year, US Secretary of Defense Les Aspin unveiled the Defense Counterproliferation Initiative (CPI) in a speech to the National Academy of Sciences.[2]

Aspin noted that the United States and NATO had used nuclear weapons as 'the equalizer' to compensate for Soviet conventional superiority. 'Today,' he continued, 'it is the United States that has unmatched conventional military power, and it is our potential adversaries who may attain nuclear weapons. We're the ones who could wind up being the equalizee.' In Aspin's view, potential US opponents were all at least capable of producing biological and chemical agents so that US commanders now had to assume that US forces were threatened by potential battlefield use of WMD.

The goals of the CPI were subsequently defined as:

1. to deter the acquisition of WMD;

2. to 'reverse WMD programmes diplomatically where proliferation has occurred';

3. to ensure that the US had 'the equipment, intelligence capability, and strategy to deter the threat or use of WMD'; and

4. to defeat an enemy armed with WMD (Davis 1994: 9).

The goals of 'counterproliferation', however, were considerably better defined than the concept itself, and indeed the term ought to be used carefully, since it is used to mean different things by different people. Harald Müller and Mitchell Reiss noted in 1995 that there were at least four different definitions of exactly what constituted counterproliferation (Müller and Reiss 1995). See Box 11.4 for an explanation of the term and its usage.

Key points

- Strategic responses against WMD proliferation are those involving military means. This is sometimes referred to as 'counterproliferation'.

- Post-cold war interest in such responses is driven by a combination of the emergence of smaller but potentially more immediate threats, and a sense that arms control may be of limited use.

- Concern about proliferation of WMD, particularly nuclear weapons, is significantly driven by a concern that they may be used to deter US-led intervention.

- The 1993 Counterproliferation Initiative was an attempt to develop a coherent strategy to allay those concerns.

- The most far-reaching Counterproliferation came in 2003 with the war against Saddam Hussein.

BOX 11.4 What's in a Name? The Emergence of Counterproliferation

Counterproliferation is defined by Butcher as 'the military component of non-proliferation, in the same way that military strategy is a component of foreign policy' (Butcher 2003: 17). This sounds relatively straightforward, but the term is in fact rather slippery and caution should be exercised when using it.

The term was popularized by Les Aspin's Counterproliferation Initiative (CPI). A couple of months after his 1993 speech, a National Security Council memo set out a possible definition of counterproliferation:

> the activities of the Department of Defense across the full range of US efforts to combat proliferation, including diplomacy, arms control, export controls, and intelligence collection and analysis, with particular responsibility for assuring US forces and interests can be protected should they confront an adversary armed with WMD or missiles.
>
> Davis (1994: 8)

The Bush administration set out its WMD strategy in a companion document published in December 2002 (White House 2002). The term counterproliferation was given a rather clearer definition than it had hitherto possessed, and for the first time it appeared to be privileged over non-proliferation, of which it had hitherto been viewed as a subset. Counterproliferation was defined as having three key elements: interdiction of WMD transfers to 'hostile states and terrorist organizations'; deterrence of use; and defence. Significantly, the document explicitly states that 'US military forces and appropriate civilian agencies must have the capacity to defend against WMD-armed adversaries, including in appropriate cases through pre-emptive measures.'

The Bush administration's National Security Strategy 2002 appeared to herald a genuine change in this policy. As the administration was attempting to make a case for a pre-emptive/preventive attack on Iraq, its National Security Strategy appeared to generalize from this to make such attacks a part of a wider strategy against proliferation. Within a very short time after publication of the National Security Strategy, the United States had embarked upon the most far-reaching anti-WMD operation ever undertaken. This came with the war against Saddam Hussein's Iraq, undertaken in the face of widespread global suspicion and opposition.

The following year, the US Joint Chiefs of Staff published a statement of its doctrine on countering WMD (Joint Chiefs of Staff 2004). This defined non-proliferation as actions to 'prevent the proliferation of WMD by dissuading or impeding access to, or distribution of, sensitive technologies' (2004: II.1), and specifically cited arms control and international treaties (especially the regimes and treaties on WMD) in the range of relevant activities. Counterproliferation was defined as military activities taken to defeat the threat or use of WMD, with its objective being to deter, interdict, attack, and defend against the range of WMD acquisition, development and employment situations. The inclusion of acquisition and development as counterproliferation (that is, military) targets is significant.

The Challenges of Counterproliferation

There are several problems and dilemmas associated with military responses to proliferation. The foremost difficulty, as we have seen in Box 11.4, is one of definition: the term 'counterproliferation' can refer to everything from protective clothing for troops to air strikes on nuclear facilities or even regime change. In the latter cases, it requires the surrounding 'political logic' to be more fully developed than is currently the case. Recent documents issued from Washington may suggest an increasing clarity of definitions.

One possible place to develop this logic is the international regimes on WMD and the UN. The great unanswered question of these global WMD regimes has always been: what happens in cases of non-compliance? Counterproliferation can be seen as a response to this question that grew from the initial response of 'defend yourself from WMD attack' to more robust ways to use military force. In specific cases (e.g. the Israeli attack on Osirak in 1981) it has proven controversial, and has yet to make the transition in 'political logic' from its origins in national military strategy to an accepted international context. In general cases, such as the Proliferation Security Initiative (PSI), it is undeveloped but potentially more consensual.

Another, more difficult problem is the issue of operations in the face of an 'imminent threat'. This would perhaps get around the difficulties of generating institutional agreement in the UN for military operations, but still faces the prospect of assessing exactly what constitutes an 'imminent' threat (officials on both sides of the Atlantic have, since the invasion of Iraq, gone to extraordinary lengths to deny that they ever presented Iraq as an imminent threat).[3] As the authors of a recent report noted, the United States (and any state, for that matter) has 'the inherent right and a moral obligation' to take pre-emptive military action in the face of imminent threats, but needs clarification of the standards for 'imminence' (Perkovich et al. 2005: 38).

Key points

- Finding a 'political' logic into which preventive or pre-emptive action can be fitted has not always been easy.

- Pre-emptive operations tend to find their rationale and legitimacy in the context of an ongoing war, such as the 1991 Gulf War operations.

- Preventive operations find their justifying logic in the international norms surrounding WMD, such as the Proliferation Security Initiative, or in an existing strategic doctrine such as Israel's attack on Osirak in 1981.

The Diplomatic Option: Strategic Responses Withheld?

North Korea and Iran currently represent the foremost nuclear proliferation issues. North Korea was an NPT member state that withdrew membership, suspended withdrawal, and subsequently followed through with formal withdrawal. It is commonly believed to possess a small number (6–8 is the largest estimate) of atomic weapons, and, in 2009, was engaged in a number of missile tests. Iran remains an NPT member, but the ongoing crisis over its plans for its nuclear power programme shows little sign of resolution. Despite cyber attacks on Iran's facilities in 2010, Iran has continued to enrich uranium (see Chapter 16). Intelligence estimates in 2011 varied over how long it would take to produce nuclear weapons but a consensus existed that this was the intention of the Iranian government.

In the case of North Korea, an operation against the Yongbyon facility was, apparently, seriously considered by the Clinton administration (Sokolski 2001: 96). The plans were not taken up, although one member of the Clinton administration wrote in 2003 that 'Washington still has the option' of attacking Yongbyon, and that 'even if US forces struck after the plant goes hot, radioactive contamination would likely remain local' (Samore 2003: 18). No such plans were reported in the Iranian case, although the Bush administration's mantra was always that this option is emphatically 'not ruled out'. The Obama administration pledged a policy of engagement and 'tough but direct diplomacy', indicating a growing international sense that time was running short to head off a serious Iranian breakout capability.

In these cases, the 'red line', noted by Müller, against attacking facilities that contain nuclear fuel, combined with the political consequences of preventive operations, appears to have kept military action off the agenda. Samore goes on to point out that although the United States could launch a unilateral attack on North Korean nuclear facilities in theory, 'the reaction in Seoul and Tokyo could splinter the alliance' (Samore 2003: 19).

Presumably, similar reasoning can be applied to the Iranian case, and it is noticeable that Washington maintained its commitment to the six-party talks in North East Asia, and the EU3 dialogue with Iran, as the preferred way to deal with these proliferation threats. Multilateral-ism and institutions (the IAEA and the UN) are [at the time of writing] the tools of choice for tackling the Iranian issue, although Washington has repeatedly suggested that this will not continue indefinitely. For example, the American envoy to Iran declared in September 2003 that diplomatic solutions were always possible but would require Tehran to 'change its course and cooperate fully with the IAEA'. The most likely consequence of a breakdown in diplomatic efforts, however, would be to refer the issue to the UN Security Council, rather than a unilateral decision to launch a preventive attack. The Obama administration departed from the line of its predecessor by promising direct nuclear talks with Iran; however, Gary Samore of the Council for Foreign Relations and subsequently a government official stated bluntly in January 2009 that 'the key to all of this is not the inducement that the US offers but the threats it can mobilize if Iran turns down the offer' (BBC 2009). Significantly, during recent years Iran's nuclear facilities were subjected to cyber attacks and sabotage which killed key nuclear military and scientific personnel, and many strategists believed that a preventive or pre-emptive strike by Israel on Iranian facilities cannot be ruled out.

Key points

- Preventive strategies are directed at the process of proliferation, and aim to snuff out development or acquisition of WMD.
- Pre-emptive strategies are directed at the deployed weapons and/or facilities, and aim to prevent their use in war.
- The dilemma over North Korea and Iran has been whether to continue with diplomatic initiatives or whether to pursue a preventive or pre-emptive strategy.

The Return of Arms Control: Attempts to Reduce the Saliency of Nuclear Weapons

Cold war lessons suggest that arms control agreements have had some role to play in contributing to international security. The cold war experience also suggests that arms control is rarely of decisive importance and it is not wise to see them as a way of fundamentally resolving the world's problems. There are 'good' and 'bad' arms control agreements. Arms control, however, has rarely been seen as decisively important or a solution in its own right. On the contrary, it has traditionally been a fundamentally conservative policy, aimed solely at introducing some measure of predictability into an adversarial relationship. It cannot *by itself* create stability, much less peace, and to hope otherwise is to saddle it with unreasonable expectations that are bound to go unfulfilled.

Viewed in that more sober and cautious light, arms control as a means to control weapons of mass destruction should be viewed as a means to an end, never as an end in itself, and relies on the assumption that two or more states that are hostile to one another can also see a mutual interest in avoiding outright conflict. The decline in interest in arms control after the cold war was a function of the fact that the confrontation was over, and the role of arms control was now no longer needed to inject some stability or predictability into the conflict itself, but to assist in eliminating what was now surplus military capability. By 2001, it was believed that consolidation of ageing cold war arsenals no longer required formal, verified treaties.

Elsewhere, in the context of the global regimes, the Biological and Toxin Weapons Convention (BTWC) appeared to be in stasis, the OPCW in good shape, and the NPT, following the 2010 review, in slightly better shape than in previous years, but still suffering from some important weaknesses (in terms of verification issues, withdrawal sanctions, and threshold capabilities).This does not imply that the NPT is necessarily in terminal decline. The two outstanding nuclear proliferation issues, the weapons programmes in Iran and North Korea, are both being dealt with inside a negotiated framework grounded in the non-proliferation regime. The NPT regime, however, remains under great pressure. Should Iran develop a nuclear weapons capability others may well follow in the Middle East. And a strike by Israel against Iran would bring forceful counterproliferation back into focus (see Box 11.5).

Although forceful counterproliferation seems likely to remain part of the strategy of the way some states deal with the proliferation of weapons of mass destruction, criticisms following the war in Iraq led to a renewed interest in the United States and elsewhere in the continuation and updating of arms control arrangements. What is emerging is a broader

---

BOX 11.5 Israel's Attack on Syria 2007

In September 2007 Israeli intelligence feared that Syria was seeking to purchase a nuclear device from North Korea. Syria had already acquired North Korean-made Scud-C missiles and were believed to have chemical warheads which could be fitted to these missiles. In early September a North Korean ship carrying what Israel believed to be nuclear materials arrived in Syria. This raised the possibility that Syria might soon acquire a nuclear capability which could be delivered by its Scud-C missiles.

In the light of this, the Israeli air force carried out an attack on a facility in northern Syria near the Turkish border on 6 September, apparently successfully destroying a target believed to contain the nuclear materials. Subsequent to the attack, virtually no information was released in either Syria or Israel.

Precisely what the mysterious target was and how close Syria was to developing a nuclear capability remains unclear. Given the limited time that elapsed from the arrival of the North Korean ship and the attack, it seems that Israel was taking early preventive action to signal its continuing determination not to allow any of its neighbours to acquire an effective nuclear capability.

strategy than in the past for controlling weapons of mass destruction. This framework or architecture consists of attempts to shore up the non-proliferation regime, renewed interest in traditional bilateral and multilateral arms control measures, counterproliferation arrangements, together with what has been described as a 'network of partnership' activities designed to act as 'a web of denial' or a 'toolkit' that can be used against those states and non-state actors intent on proliferating weapons of mass destruction (Bernstein 2008). These latter activities include the Proliferation Security Initiative (PSI), UN Resolutions 1540 and 1887, the Global Initiative to Combat Nuclear Terrorism, the Global Nuclear Energy Partnership, the Cooperative Threat Reduction Programme, and the April 2010 Nuclear Security Summit.

In recent years there has also been the rise of what some have called 'the New Abolitionists'. In the *Wall Street Journal* in January 2008 George Shultz, William Perry, Henry Kissinger, and Sam Nunn called for new urgent action to reverse the continuing reliance on nuclear weapons globally in order to prevent their further proliferation 'into potentially dangerous hands'. The world they said was on 'the precipice of a new and dangerous nuclear era'. In particular, Shultz and his colleagues urged action on bringing into force the Comprehensive Test Ban Treaty, a Fissile Material Cut-off Treaty, as well as further cuts in the offensive strategic capabilities of both the United States and Russia. These measures were needed, they argued, to shore up the Non-Proliferation Treaty which was in 'a precarious position'. These views were supported by four former British foreign and defence secretaries (Rifkind, Owen, Robertson, and Hurd) in an article in *The Times* on 30 June 2008 (Hurd et al. 2008). They argued for a new initiative to achieve progress on multilateral arms control and disarmament. In their view 'the ultimate aspiration should be to have a world free of nuclear weapons'. Even though this would take time, they argued that, with the necessary 'political will and improvements in monitoring the goal is achievable'. For such hard-headed individuals on both sides of the Atlantic to be supporting a new phase of arms reductions, leading possibly to complete nuclear disarmament, is of some significance. Even more significant, in a speech in Prague in April 2009, President Obama also indicated his support for a 'zero option' (see Box 11.6). The achievement of a nuclear-free world, as President Obama indicated, would be likely to take a long time, and remains very problematical. It would certainly require much more far-reaching arms control efforts but also more effective measures to achieve conflict resolution than presently exist.

BOX 11.6

Today, the cold war has disappeared but thousands of those weapons have not. In a strange turn of history, the threat of global nuclear war has gone down, but the risk of a nuclear attack has gone up. More nations have acquired these weapons. Testing has continued. Some argue that the spread of these weapons cannot be checked—that we are destined to live in a world where more nations and more people possess the ultimate tools of destruction. This fatalism is a deadly adversary. For if we believe that the spread of nuclear weapons is inevitable, then we are admitting to ourselves that the use of nuclear weapons is inevitable. So today, I state clearly and with conviction America's commitment to seek the peace and security of the world without nuclear weapons. This goal will not be reached quickly—perhaps not in my lifetime. It will take patience and persistence. But now we, too, must ignore the voices who tell us that the world cannot change.

President Obama (Prague Castle, 5 April 2009)

Whether traditional arms control can re-emerge as a significant and sustained approach to international security and play an important role in the control of weapons of mass destruction in the future remains unclear at the time of writing. There are currently some reasons for optimism but also some important challenges ahead. The NEW START Treaty in April 2010 between the US and Russia agreed to a limit of 1,550 strategic warheads on either side, a 30% reduction from the levels agreed in the 2002 Moscow Treaty. Both sides also agreed to continue negotiations to deal with stored and non-strategic weapons. The 2010 US Nuclear Posture Review also argued for the reduction in the role of nuclear weapons in US security policy. This attempt to reduce the saliency of nuclear weapons and to breathe new life into the arms control process, however, still faces major challenges. The CTBT Treaty remains some way from ratification and little progress has been made in negotiating the Fissile Materials Cut-off Treaty (FMCT). Also, quite apart from some continuing great power suspicions, Russian concerns about US plans for a missile defence system and its own conventional inferiority indicated that there were still important problems to be resolved. There were also criticisms from opponents in the US that such drastic cuts were premature at a time when Iran seemed to be continuing on the road to developing nuclear weapons and North Korea was still developing its nuclear capability. At the same time, there were also concerns about the need to bring India, Pakistan, and Israel into the Non-Proliferation regime in some way (even though they are not members of the NPT) as well as the need to secure regional arms control arrangements in areas like the Middle East. Dual use and new technologies, especially nanotechnologies, also pose particularly hard problems for non-proliferation arrangements.

Key points

- Arms control should be seen as a means to an end, not an end in itself, and depends upon mutual interests.
- Criticisms of counterproliferation following the Iraq war led to renewed interest in arms control, more broadly defined.
- Recent years have seen a rise of what have been called the 'New Abolitionists', who argue for new arms control initiatives as a result of new proliferation dangers and terrorist threats.
- The new Obama administration has attempted to reduce the importance of nuclear weapons through supporting a 'return to arms control', leading to new nuclear arms control agreements. This initiative, however, still has some way to go.

 Conclusion

Overall therefore, there would appear to be no single approach, whether it be disarmament, arms control or counterproliferation, which provides an easy and sustainable solution to the problem of controlling weapons of mass destruction. The vision of a world free of such weapons should not be dismissed and nor should forceful counterproliferation be discounted in certain extreme situations. Both, however, raise serious problems. Equally arms control, both traditional treaties and new partnership arrangements, is not a panacea. However, the new initiatives introduced by the Obama administration aimed to re-invigorate the arms control process were welcomed by many observers as an important contribution to global security. Once again there was a growing consensus that, despite their imperfections, arms control arrangements, more widely and consistently applied and more dependably verified and policed, can help provide preventive barriers, greater assurance, and trust between states, which is essential in dealing with the critical political issues that cause states to arm themselves, as well as the contemporary dangers of terrorist groups using weapons of mass destruction.

Questions

1. What are the differences between disarmament and arms control?
2. What role did arms control play in the cold war in preserving strategic stability?
3. What were the key criticisms of arms control by the end of the cold war?
4. How useful has arms control been in helping to preserve peace and security in the post-cold war period?
5. Is arms control compatible with counterproliferation?
6. Account for the growing interest in strategic military responses to proliferation.
7. Is traditional arms control coming back?
8. Is it possible to talk about a 'New Arms Control' and, if so, what does this mean?
9. What are the contemporary difficulties facing arms control?
10. What issues arise for strategists with low numbers of nuclear weapons?

Further Reading

I. Anthony and A. D. Rotfeld (eds), *A Future Arms Control Agenda* (Oxford: Oxford University Press, 2001).
This provides an analysis of post-cold war thinking on arms control.

H. Bull's classical study *The Control of the Arms Race* (London: Weidenfeld and Nicolson, 1961).
This study developed the first modern concept of arms control.

I. Daalder and T. Terry (eds), *Rethinking the Unthinkable: New Directions in Nuclear Arms Control* (London: Frank Cass, 1993).
This is a useful source on thinking about arms control shortly after the cold war ended.

S. Feldman, 'The Bombing of Osiraq–Revisited', *International Security* 7/2 (Autumn 1982).
This is a useful source on the Israeli attack on Osiraq in 1981.

C. S. Gray, *House of Cards: Why Arms Control Must Fail* (Ithaca, NJ: Cornell University Press, 1992).
This study provides an interesting and controversial critique of the utility of arms control.

E. Herring (ed.), *Preventing the Use of Weapons of Mass Destruction* (London: Frank Cass, 2000).
This study explores the options for preventing use, rather than simply spread, of WMD.

Jeffrey A. Larsen and James J. Wirtz (ed.), *Arms Control and Cooperative Security* (London: Lynne Rienner, 2009).
This study contains some interesting articles on the relationship between arms control and its contribution to cooperative security.

H. Müller, D. Fisher, and W. Kötter, *Nuclear Non-Proliferation and Global Order* (New York: Oxford University Press, 1994).

This study examines the relationship between non-proliferation and issues relating to international order.

T. Schelling and M. Halperin, *Strategy and Arms Control* (Washington, DC: Pergamon-Brassey's, 1985).

This is a classical study that helped to develop the concept of arms control.

William Walker, *A Perpetual Menace: Nuclear Weapons and International Order* (London: Routledge, 2011).

This study provides an excellent analysis of the history of nuclear weapons and how they have affected international order.

 ## Web Links

The Acronym Institute for Disarmament Diplomacy **http://www.acronym.org.uk** provides a useful, and often critical, view of Western arms control policies.

International Atomic Energy Agency **http://www.iaea.org** provides information about IAEA activities in helping to stem proliferation of weapons of mass destruction.

The Defense Threat Reduction Agency **http://www.dtra.mil** covers the various approaches adopted by the US to reduce the threats to its national security.

Organization for the Prohibition of Chemical Weapons **http://www.opcw.org** provides information on the progress to control chemical weapons.

Arms Control Association **http://www.armscontrol.org** gives information on a wide range of issues relating to arms control.

Center for Nonproliferation Studies, Monterey **http://cns.miis.edu/** provides information on the activities and research undertaken by the Center.

Joint Chiefs of Staff, *Joint Doctrine for Combating Weapons of Mass Destruction* (2004) Washington, DC: Department of Defense. Available at **http://www.dtic.mil/doctrine/new_pubs/jp3_40.pdf** provides detailed information about US Counterproliferation planning.

Conventional Power and Contemporary Warfare

JOHN FERRIS

 Chapter Contents

Introduction: Power and War—A History	231
New World Orders: 1945, 1989, 2001	232
Power and Hyperpower	234
Military Affairs: Revolution and Counter-Revolution	235
Arts of War	237
Military Balances	239
World on the Scales	241
War, What is It Good For?	242
Conclusion	245

 Reader's Guide

This chapter assesses conventional power today. It analyses how, and how far, conventional forces shape the contemporary world, whether by fighting wars or backing policy in peace. This chapter examines how they function in areas ranging from distant strike to urban warfare, and compares their role to that of other forms of force, like WMDs and terrorism. It ends by discussing the conventional strength of states in the world, and trends in its development and distribution.

Introduction: Power and War—A History

In romance, this is war. States fight, therefore armies enter *decisive battle*. One wins, the other loses, the victor gains, immediately, and both return to their seats. Sometimes war is like a waltz, but mostly not. Often, it is long and destructive, costing both sides more than they gain. Even victors suffer unintended damage. Battles are inconclusive, or victories have no value. Enemies refuse to surrender, or recover from defeat and force you to fight again. They reject your rules, evade your strength, attack your weaknesses, and impose their will on you. In this competition, intentions and effects become confused, and paradox rules. Politicians imagine armies are military scalpels for political surgery, but in war, one operates with a battleaxe and without a medical licence on a patient who is trying to amputate your arm; in the dark.

This chapter examines the present and emerging state of conventional military power, including its distribution, what it can and cannot do, what is changing and what is not. One may understand these trends only by considering the record of conventional war. Nor can one look just at the states that most often fight them, or have the biggest toys. Third-rate powers shape conventional war as much as advanced ones, and they all do so by their weaknesses as well as their strengths.

Refined power yields armed forces, which are usually small in size and hard to maintain. Sometimes, states regularly field hundreds of thousands of soldiers (in China between 453 and 221 BCE or Europe between 1660 and 1870 ACE)—millions in the twentieth century. Yet these periods are unusual, because armies erode the wealth of nations and the power of states. In classical Greece, armies were usually fewer than 15,000 men, rarely 50,000; so too European empires of the nineteenth century. Since 1989, armies have again slipped in size. The greatest power on earth can barely send 100,000 soldiers on one expedition beyond its borders. Navies have been even smaller, because they are a rich man's weapon, dependent on industry and wealth. Expensive to build and maintain, fleets vanish without a regular programme of shipbuilding. Navies usually die in the dockyard, not battle. Few states maintain large navies for long; and these command the seas as armies rarely do the land. Sea power is the child of wealth and resolve; so too, air power. Military power has social roots, many forms, and a competitive nature—your system compared to the enemy's in specific circumstances. The edge of the razor is comparative advantage, your strengths, and ability to force them on the enemy. Numbers and technology matter, but not enough to win every time. A belligerent able to take heavy losses without surrendering beats one with high technology and low willpower. Able armies with no material edge whip larger enemies. Politics and willpower defeat firepower and technology, or vice versa. Small elite forces crush half-trained hosts, or not. It depends on the circumstances (see Box 12.1).

Until 1945, the greatest form of military power was conventional force. It was the weapon of choice for the strong, particularly useful against the weak, common between neighbours. It could inflict more precise and powerful damage than irregular forces and keep battle from your home, yet it had limits. Sometimes conventional war is unavoidable or an effective way to achieve ends. Merely to avoid defeat is good. More is possible if one is strong and smart, or the enemy weak and foolish—preferably both at once. Yet, as in any competition, the use of conventional force has unpredictable outcomes. Decisive battles are like strikes of lightning—they happen, rarely. The greatest of world powers emerged through long runs of

> ### BOX 12.1 The Intricacies of Power
>
> Power is an alloy, formed from the interaction of material factors (geography, demography, and economy) and the administrative capacity and political structure of a state—its ability to command a people and tap their resources. The first group defines the potential power of a state, the second how much can be tapped. Their relationship converts material power from crude to finished form—from resources to forces. Overwhelming strength in one element may not a great power make, nor weakness in one destroy it. A poor country may remain a great power because its forces are large, its geopolitical position favourable, its institutions stable, and its statesmen able; thus, Prussia, 1740–1866. A rich country may not convert its wealth to power, and so matters less in world affairs than possible, viz., Japan and most European states since 1960. Rich states rarely tap their resources systematically for strategic purpose. That bolsters the position of anyone willing to do so, rich or not. In power, resolve outweighs wealth. Power is a concrete quality; the resources a state taps for strategic purposes, as against those it might, but does not. It takes different forms in diplomacy, a short campaign between two countries, or a prolonged and total war of attrition involving most members of a state system. Usually, institutions are the main factor in power, because they turn raw into refined strength—a hard task, dominated by marginal superiority. For most of history, a state able to jump from tapping 1 per cent of its potential power to 2 per cent might so double its military capacity. The edge provided by institutions dulled from 1870 because, ironically, they became more effective, numerous, and common. Advanced states adopted many systems (conscript armies, General Staffs, central banks, military-industrial complexes) which were better at turning wealth into power. Brute demographic and industrial strength was the key predictor of power in the First and Second World Wars. The value of institutional superiority rose again after 1945, at least for developing states. Israel's battlefield success stems from the fact that it possesses techniques like conscription and a quickly mobilized reserve while its neighbours do not.

decisive victories over many enemies—Romans, Arabs, Mongols, British. These circumstances are significant, but not common. The classic example of a decisive battle is Cannae in 216 BCE—yet its victor lost that war. The average outcome of war is attrition, slow and costly to both sides. Conventional war is like gambling. All that is sure is an entry cost, and some combination of risk and gain. Some people love the risk, forget the odds, and think the pay-off certain; others fear to play; skill matters, and the strength of your hand; so does chance.

New World Orders: 1945, 1989, 2001

Between 1815 and 1945, Western military systems beat all others at once. Europeans conquered the earth, and then destroyed each other. From the wreck emerged a new *world order*, defined by decolonization, the cold war, and nuclear weapons. The industrialized states were divided between two alliances, unequal in economics but balanced in destructive capability. They waged the greatest arms races ever known, with conventional and nuclear, chemical, and bacteriological weapons of mass destruction (WMDs). A war between them carried the risk of suicide. This made conventional strength just one part of power, imposed an upper limit on *the rationality of force*, and reshaped world politics. The industrialized states possessed more power than in 1939, but their influence declined. Decolonization was the primary political force; the cold war was a local phenomenon of the industrialized world.

The European empires shattered, breaking the world into bits. Power had to be gained in each region. Success in one did not determine events in another. The USSR and the United States dominated the industrialized world, but neither picked up the pieces of imperialism. They simply established ties with regional successor states, some of which became stronger than most advanced countries.

Since 1945, the major industrialized states have not fought each other nor, excepting the guerrilla wars which accompanied decolonization, many countries at all. War has rarely been fought by the strong nor practised at the state of the art. The core of world power was not the centre of world war. That was Asia and Africa, where most states lacked the economic or administrative abilities to fight total wars or to win quick and cheap victories. Most of these conflicts stemmed from the end of imperialism, whether wars of national liberation to overthrow it or of succession between new states, striving to determine strength, status, and frontiers. They ended by 1975. Wars in Africa were prolonged, indecisive, and destructive, because neither side could tap its resources well for military purposes. In Asia, some conventional wars were long and costly, but usually both sides halted long before their resources were exhausted. Asian regimes pursued limited aims with limited means. Conventional war was an important, but uncommon, aspect of international affairs. In these Third World wars, many states had modern weapons but few used them well. There was no dominant style of war because no one set of military conditions ruled. The relationship between victory on the battlefield and at the peace table was complex. Rarely did force achieve great aims, or precise ones.

In 1989, with the collapse of the Soviet bloc, the distribution of power in the world altered again, as did its nature. Western states, overwhelmingly superior in military technology, cut their forces and spending by 25 per cent, and assumed they could master the new world order. They were misinformed. The end of the cold war prompted the collapse of several states and another wave of wars of succession. In most of Asia, strong non-Western states became more powerful, continuing to dominate their regions and acquire WMDs. Arab powers slipped in status, because they no could longer gain free weapons from superpowers. In the Middle East, the United States used force for realpolitik, crippling Iraq and checking Iran. Otherwise, power became decoupled from policy. When Western states used their power, they did so in an odd way. Their peoples, reluctant to fight except for vital interests sometimes wished one foreign party would cease to bully another and deployed token forces to achieve that end. They pursued international acts of charity through multilateral military means, driven not by reasons of state but public opinion, aiming not to defeat a foe but to do good and no bad. Such ends were hard to achieve or to pursue. Outrage did not make bullies mend their ways. The West found it hard to help the weak, or to prevent ethnic cleansing and mass murder in Rwanda or Bosnia.

Then, on 11 September 2001, al-Qaeda launched an act of 'propaganda by the deed', to rally Muslims against the United States. This attack tied together every level of force, from terrorism to WMDs, and plugged power back into politics. Rich states, fearing for their security, took firmest actions. The United States ceased to swing between isolationism and internationalism. It bolstered its conventional power, declared policies of unilateralism and pre-emptive attack against anything it deemed a threat, and occupied Afghanistan and Iraq. The lonely hyperpower, pillar of the world order, was wounded. It pursued absolute security, which many states saw as a threat to themselves. It used all types of power to reshape all forms of politics everywhere in the world, at once. This affected the distribution of power, and its use.

Key points

- Several forms of a unified world political system have existed since 1800. Conventional force played a different role in each one.

- Conventional power was used frequently between 1815 and 1945. Military superiority underwrote European imperialism.

- After 1945, major states rarely used conventional force against each other, but did so more often against weaker states, which fought each other frequently.

- Since 1945, the power of conventional force has been limited by WMDs, and guerrilla warfare.

Power and Hyperpower

If riches made strength, Europe would be the greatest power on earth, the United States second, and Japan and China third, all close together; but the issue is the marriage of will and wealth. One may divide conventional military powers in four groups: *the United States, advanced states* (industrialized, capitalist, mostly liberal-democratic, ranging in size from Singapore to Germany), *developing powers* (with small-to-large industrial bases, and mostly authoritarian governments, like China, India, Russia, and Turkey) and *weak states* (most of those in Africa, and some in Asia). Weak states have little offensive power; their strength is the difficulty of occupation. Any rich country can speedily increase its conventional forces, and so change the distribution of strength in the world or its regions, but their will to power varies. Most European states have little power to project, and less will. Characteristically, between 2001 and 2012, those with forces in Afghanistan usually forbade them to fight. They are unlikely to be attacked by conventional force or to fight each other. With out-of-area capabilities small, they are most likely to use force against the weakest of weak states, in humanitarian interventions. Britain and France can launch sizeable expeditionary forces, barely. Australia and Canada retain smaller expeditionary capabilities. Advanced states in Asia, like Singapore, South Korea, and Japan, maintain powerful defensive capabilities. Conventional power matters more to Israel than any other nation on earth, except North Korea. Many developing states tap far more of their resources for forces, and are far stronger in their own regions, than any rich country except Israel, South Korea, and the United States. Russia and China remain the world's second-strongest conventional powers, while others have large forces and some offensive capability. All these states stand well behind the state of the art, and are cautious about using such forces. Russia's experiences against Georgia in 2009, and those of Britain and France against Libya during 2011, show that even major powers cannot easily defeat fourth-rate foes.

Americans have a taste for, and the infrastructure to exercise, power across the world. Their post-9/11 expansion in military spending has stalled, but at far higher levels than in 2000. No other state has had the absolute and relative conventional power it possessed in 2012.

Overwhelming strength at sea and in air strikes, and space, dissuades any head-on challenges in these key areas. The United States has more aircraft carriers than the rest of the world combined, able to launch ten times as many aircraft. Its air force, the only one with the most advanced equipment, like stealth technology, matches every other one on earth together. This capacity underwrites Pax Americana just as sea power did Pax Britannica. It augments nuclear power as a means to deter attack and sustains the United States' loose leadership over all advanced countries, the structure through which Washington exerts political influence. This creates a key phenomenon in contemporary politics, that rich states will not fight each other and often will cooperate. Yet these edges are of limited value in land combat—indeed, the cost needed to develop them weakens American power in that sphere. Its relative advantage lies in distant strike, compellence, deterrence, and dissuasion, and its weakness in close-quarter combat and occupation. The United States could smash the air and naval power of almost any developing country, but can occupy few of them. Threats of force serve Washington more than its use. These are just some of the paradoxes of conventional power in the contemporary world.

Key points

- Overwhelming conventional power, along with nuclear weapons, make the United States the world leader. This strength supports dissuasion better than war.
- Many rich states have powerful conventional forces at home. Some have expeditionary capabilities.
- Some developing powers have powerful conventional forces at home. None can project it far from their borders.
- Most states have weak conventional forces.

Military Affairs: Revolution and Counter-Revolution

Between 1989 and 2006, American military policy was driven by efforts to ride a Revolution in Military Affairs (RMA). Armed forces would act without friction on near-perfect knowledge, through the fusion of precision weapons, information technology, and command, control, communications, computers, intelligence, surveillance, and reconnaissance (C4ISR). They would jettison hierarchies, adopt flat structures based on the Internet, and conduct net-centric warfare (NCW). Conventional force would have more power as a tool of state and the leading powers greater superiority in it, than ever since Omdurman, the heyday of European imperialism.

These ideas were tested in three recent conflicts. They failed in Kosovo during 1999, where forces suffering from over-centralization and confusion between levels of command, engaged an enemy with good strategy, camouflage, and air defence. Air power did little damage nor did the allies achieve clear victory. In Afghanistan and Iraq during 2001–2003, the conversion of military to political success also proved hard. Still, larger forces, better used, unleashed on worse foes, coordinated command and intelligence with unprecedented skill. This multiplied the strength of all forms of centralized firepower and rapid, precise, and long-distance weapons. These leaps in quality, and in the quantity of aircraft and precision-guided munitions (PGMs), let strike forces matter far more than ever before, equalling armies in land warfare.

Yet victory did not flow straight, or simply, from the RMA. Its keys were air supremacy, the incompetence of Iraqi command and the power of coalition artillery and tanks. Classic problems of information overload, friction between headquarters and inexperienced personnel, swamped commands. Command and intelligence were no better than in 1944–1945, but the enemy was worse. Distant strike succeeded only when the machine performed without friction. Any friction yielded failure; no system is always perfect. Close-quarter battle shaped land war as much as distant strike, and mattered far more against guerrillas. The main lesson from these campaigns is that Western powers cannot easily defeat any enemy with competent leadership, a decent army, and fair public consent. Nor are Americans the only people who can learn lessons.

These tests show the limits to ideas about *transformed forces*. They posit a world without strategy, a one-dimensional and one-sided struggle. The United States can always play to its strengths, and need never defend its weaknesses. High-technology conventional forces assault against weak enemies, without initiative. They play to your strengths. A fine-tuned, high-performance machine works perfectly, without any effort being made to hamper its effect. It is convenient when an enemy chooses to be foolish and weak, but that is its choice, not yours. A smart but weak foe may refuse any game where you can apply your strengths, and make you play another. A tough and able foe might turn the characteristics of your game into a strength of its own, by attacking any precondition for your machine to work and imposing its rules on you. By doing what suits them, they change their strengths and weaknesses—and yours.

The idea of an RMA was oversold, but has some value., In assessing power for air and sea, C4ISR matters as much as hardware (command, control, communications, computers, intelligence, surveillance, and reconnaissance; a schematic model of how military institutions gather, interpret, and act on information). C4ISR and NCW would function in a system as a person sees the world, turns data to knowledge, and acts on it, through intution rather than analysis. An air force with better C4ISR matches one with far more aircraft. The RMA did many things, but not everything. It has *multiplied American strengths, but not reduced its weaknesses.* The RMA increased the value of high technology and firepower in conventional war, but for little else; where these things matter, they do more than ever; where they do not, nothing has changed. Its advocates assume that conventional power has grown steadily more powerful, and everything else weaker, that the RMA has universal force across all arms, instead of strength in some and weakness in others. Their arguments look at only one development, instead of the reciprocal relationship between several of them. The revolution is advancing; so is the counter-revolution.

Thus, strike weapons enable a new version of gunboat diplomacy, letting one destroy targets from a distance, so as to make a political point. They enable conventional forces to hit harder, further and more accurately than ever before; they reshape operations at sea and in the air, and what one can do with them; but that is not all of war, nor is it new. Since 1933, air forces have applied NCW to some aspects of combat—Fighter Command was the world's first net-centric force, before the Internet existed!—and navies since 1955. These command and intelligence systems were sophisticated. They could do far more than was done with them—weapons systems were restrained by limits to weapons, not systems. So too, the RMA stems less from changes in C4ISR than weapons. Technology enables transformation; that in 2003 it transformed the power of aircraft far more than that of armies is suggestive. In land warfare, command and intelligence have never worked as they do at sea or air.

Perhaps conventional forces are midway through a decade-long transition from one set of forms—armies, navies, and air forces—to another: close quarters land forces, navies, strike weapons, and space power. If so, some services may not survive as they are. If no combat aircraft have pilots, air forces and artillery might merge, and dominate blue water, where no large surface warships can survive the hostility of the United States. However, this transition is far from over and it will affect armies least of all—perhaps not much. No recent piece of technology except the atom bomb or nerve gas has changed land warfare so greatly as did bayonets, quick-firing artillery, machine guns, tanks, antitank guns, or aircraft. In the foreseeable future, land warfare will involve an equal and overlapping combination of close quarters and distant firepower, as it has done since 1940—or 1916.

At one and the same time, the strike capacity of advanced states has risen as has the power of terrorists against them, while nothing has changed in close-quarter combat or guerrilla warfare. Nor can any one master all these domains at once.

Key points

- Conventional forces take many forms. Their strength is hard to compare.
- High-technology forces can strike blows of unprecedented precision and weight, which has transformed sea power, air power, and all forms of distant strike.
- The power of armies has not been transformed for close-quarter combat, or against guerrillas.

Arts of War

Armies cannot evade economics. To buy one thing is not to buy another. One maintains large standing forces only by reducing the procurement of new equipment, and vice versa. The entry cost for the RMA is high; to pay it incurs opportunity costs. This situation forces choices on all states, each with a mixture of costs and benefits. The United States will take an unassailable lead in transformed forces, albeit at cost in other areas, because it cares about them while no one else can keep up. Even a military budget equal to almost every other state on earth has limits. So to make anyone else think twice about competition, the United States will keep the entry cost to the RMA high. This will hamper its friends as well as its enemies. Nor is the new American way of war a model for everyone. In transformed power, the United States is a giant and everyone else a dwarf. Transformation gives no one else quite the same bang for a buck. It will be less cost-efficient for weak than for strong states. Its pressure on defence budgets reinforces the tendencies toward demilitarization in Europe, while complicating life for all other advanced powers. The RMA will give them the edge over enemies which cannot adopt such innovations, but not revolutionary ones. Israel does not need transformation to master Arab armies. It will not silence North Korean artillery in range of Seoul.

Comparative advantage takes many forms. The United States will own sea power, air power, and strike, with everything that that promises. Even forcing enemies to asymmetry has advantages, as unconventional means often solve problems worse than conventional ones. Between 1914 and 1945, surface fleets let one use the sea, while submarines merely limited one's power to do so. Of course asymmetry can be more successful. Air defence systems cheaply cripple the power of aircraft. Asymmetric means are unlikely to wreck (as against degrade) American strengths in the air or blue water, but the story is different on land. American choices for transformation will leave its enemies strong cards to play. Between 1870 and 1989, the standard form of armies was large conscript forces, able to deliver and absorb heavy punishment. Given their costs in money and skilled personnel, transformed armies will be smaller professional services, with unprecedented reliance on firepower and technology. Like eggshells armed with hammers, they can inflict damage, but not take it; closer to the model of artillery than infantry. When they are good they will be very good. They will be better than ever at anything dominated by firepower, but worse at anything else. They cannot take losses; they cannot easily deploy their strengths or shield their weaknesses in close-quarters combat. Once, an army able to defeat an enemy was big enough to occupy it—now, one can easily be powerful enough to crush a foe but too small to hold its territory. Western regular forces in Iraq and Afghanistan have had to rely heavily on their reserves and mercenaries to function. Nor do Special Forces change this equation. These units are useful, but not new, essentially equalling the light infantry or cavalry maintained by states over past centuries, their mobility multiplied by air power.

Again, until 1945, nothing limited the upper edge of force except one's ability to get there. If one could annihilate an enemy, one did. No longer is that true, because of the mixture of images, ethics, and opinion aroused by modern media. A desire to minimize the deaths of enemy civilians, even of soldiers, confuses the use of power by Western states, as one tries to avoid overstepping the upper level of permissible force. Indicatively, legal advisors serve on military staffs, to ensure that international law shapes the selection of targets for strike weapons. Because they are the safest means to navigate near the tolerated limits on force, precision and control are the fundamental gains from transformation, while the most obvious use of PGMs is to assassinate individuals in irregular warfare. These gloves would come off, however, if any people thought its vital interests were at stake—then conventional weapons could wreak mass destruction, to the surprise of the unwary instigator. States like Russia and China might do so from the start. Meanwhile, terrorists drive their devastation into levels once occupied by conventional forces, because images of ruthlessness and power play to their home demographic.

Developing states will maintain large and good forces for close-quarter combat. One lesson from Iraq and Kosovo is the difference a decent army and second-rate kit makes. This is not a new lesson. Over the past century, developing states like Turkey, Vietnam, and Japan created armies able to inflict heavy punishment while absorbing even more, making willpower a decisive theatre and often beating richer but less resolute enemies. In ground war, defenders will be most strong and attackers least so, home field advantage will matter, and Western armies must handle cities. Urban combat sucks up time and resources. It divides the value of training, technology, and firepower and multiplies that of morale and the ability to take losses; it creates unpredictable consequences which turn victory to defeat. Civilian casualties, refugees, and relief efforts shape victory or defeat as much as tactics. Western forces will not enter urban warfare unless every other option is exhausted, and the choice is assault or defeat. These are dicey options. Urban warfare and the price of occupation are the functional equivalents of WMDs for weak states. They will deter attack.

Developing countries will also aim to negate high-technology forces through asymmetric strategies. The first step for an able enemy in a war with the United States would be to jam any communications on the electromagnetic spectrum. This would damage American power far more than their own, and perhaps stall its entire war machinery, given its reliance on thick and fast communications. That would have happened in 2003 had Iraq been able to jam geographical positioning systems, a central node in C4ISR and an easy target. Cyberwar, psychological warfare, black propaganda, and deception, will also shape postmodern conflicts.

Above all, the final *asymmetric* response of enemies to American conventional power will simply be to pick up its pieces and go home—to WMDs or terrorism.

Key points

- The RMA will help the United States more than any other country.
- Transformed fighting services have weaknesses and strengths.
- When they can play to their strengths, they will succeed.
- Rational foes play to their strengths and your weaknesses. Developing countries may trump the RMA through asymmetric strategies, WMDs, urban warfare, guerrilla warfare, terrorism, or good forces with low technology.

Military Balances

Sometimes, conventional power is easy to calculate. Each side fights the same way and has so many archers or armoured fighting vehicles (AFVs); you multiply the quantity by some coefficient representing quality, and Bob's your uncle. Today, simply to gauge conventional power is problematic, because its forms vary and are changing. Perhaps one can measure power in PGMs for all states, simply by multiplying their quality and quantity by some coefficient representing C4ISR. So too with blue water navies, as they are rare and commentators agree on what makes power for them (that story ends at the green water mark). Such measurements are harder with armies. Those of developing powers have a strong but short punch, great on their borders but not beyond; perhaps best measured by the number of combat soldiers they could deploy on their frontier. North Korea or China could throw millions of soldiers to their frontiers, India, Pakistan, or Turkey 400,000. Rich states have armies with longer range but less weight. Their strength is best measured by the combat troops ready for expeditionary service: Germany, Canada, and Australia might deploy 2,000 each, France and Britain, 10,000, and the United States, 140,000. World conventional power rests on a combination of a blue water fleet and an expeditionary capability, in which the United States stands alone in its class; Britain and France punch above their weight, while Australia, Canada, and India are the only bantams. To compare these different forms of force is like gauging apples and oranges; the point is where the struggle occurs. In Fukien, the Chinese army would reign supreme; 50 miles off shore, it would drown.

The balance of military power is changing most in Asia. India's competition with Pakistan is unlikely to end, but is one-sided. Pakistan strains its resources to remain in the game. India has 165 per cent more infantry, 175 per cent more tanks, 240 per cent more guns, and 160 per cent more aircraft, at par. Pakistan can exploit India's greatest weakness, the political fractures of a multinational state, but it could endanger its rival only with help from China or the United States. Indian cooperation with Washington trumps that ace. Indian leaders distort the danger of Pakistan, because a weak enemy suits them. India, however, does not seek to conquer its neighbours, however much it wishes them subordinate—few things could be more disastrous for India than conquering Pakistan and having to rule its people. Meanwhile, India can already project force far from its shores. It aims to be one of two dominant powers in the Indian Ocean, alongside the United States. Its naval bases are good, as is its locale for land-based aviation. Its old carrier and 25 decent destroyers and frigates form the equivalent of a weak carrier battle group. This power will rise notably after 2015, as it junks old kit and acquires new, above all purchasing an ex-Soviet carrier, building an Indian one at home, and deploying the Indo-Russian BraMos cruise missile. As long as it acts on its declared policies, India has and will keep the world's fourth-greatest fleet, if qualitatively below the top three. It cannot sail against American opposition, but then neither can Britain or France. As long as India continues its drift towards alignment with the West, and the moderate but sustained investment in new forces of the past generation, it will be a major but regional sea power. That will strengthen its influence throughout the Indian Ocean littoral, but to what effect remains uncertain. Since 1949, India has found power and strategy hard to handle. It uses power merely as one means to demonstrate status, rather than as a tool to pursue interests. India, the least of the great powers, punches below its weight. It has more power than it can use.

China has less than it needs. It has great ambitions, and moderate strength. It aims to absorb Taiwan and remove the American containment of its coasts; easier said than done. Until 2000, Taiwan had the maritime and air ability to block Chinese invasion. Chinese power outweighs Taiwan's defences. The true competition is the United States, on terrain where it is strong and China weak—sea and air power. Since 1949, China has pursued the anti-access and area-denial maritime strategy of a continental power—to keep rivals far away through land-based force and a brown water navy. China hopes to push that perimeter toward Japan and Taiwan, but is painfully slow in gathering the means, such as cruise missiles, better aircraft, and bigger ships. Its fleet has shrunk over a generation, as much old kit is junked and little acquired, though it has built some modern ships , and shows signs of striking for blue water. Nor can an Indian-sized investment in sea power achieve Chinese aims. Its efforts are unlikely to bear much fruit before 2020. For decades afterward, the sea and air power of an American-Taiwanese alignment can easily pin China on its coast, if they wish. Only if and when Taiwan joins China will it break that barrier and reach blue water and so become a world power.

These calculations are confused by a further issue. Sino-Japanese relations are unstable. Their interests clash and their leaders evince mutual suspicion. No major power is more affected by the rise of China than Japan. None could do more to counter it. If Japan wished, it could easily and immediately become the world's second sea and air power. Certainly it intends to acquire more advanced fighters than China has (see Box 12.2).

Key points

- Conventional power is hard to calculate. It depends on circumstances.
- Conventional forces take many forms, to handle different problems.
- They succeed by exploiting comparative advantages over competitors.
- Only years of sustained effort enables any state to challenge an established air or sea power.

BOX 12.2 Arms and Power

Over the past century, many developing countries built good armament industries, resting on effective links between businesses and bureaucrats, and decent kit. They entered the state of the art, learning to copy and then innovate, by forming liaisons with arms producers in many states, buying much material and acquiring more via espionage, making weapons under licence and reverse engineering, training labour to build munitions and designers to make them. While a score of states entered such arrangements, two cases particularly changed world power. In 1921 all Japanese warships and naval aircraft were versions of British equipment, gained through purchase or joint ventures. Over the next 20 years, it developed good naval and aeronautical industries through hard work and copies of all the kit it could buy. So too, Soviet tanks of 1941 stemmed from refinement of Western technology purchased a decade earlier. Its aircraft industry of 1951 relied heavily on Western designs acquired by aid, accident, and espionage.

Since 2000, arms sales have been driven by the hunger of firms for profits in harsh markets, and the desire of their political masters to strengthen those industries while acquiring political influence through their product. The United States makes massive arms sales to its allies, especially in the Persian Gulf, needing means to keep Iran in check. So too have France and Britain. Since 1992, Russia has led in the transfer of advanced military technology, so to salvage its military-industrial base, the only area where its firms can compete on world terms. This provided its only success in industrial exports, but enabled China to strip Russian technology, and become a strategic and industrial competitor. India has licenses to build or has entered into joint ventures with Russia on much modern equipment, like the Sukhoi-30 MKI aircraft and the T-90 tank. China purchased leading Russian aircraft, missiles, destroyers and submarines, and also stole the technology for radar and data link systems, and fighters.

World on the Scales

In 2012, the world confronts the biggest changes in power since 1989. China's rise alarms its neighbours, though it is decades away from being a global power. Europe, rich and weak, slides to strategic irrelevance as actor, though not object. The United States, a chastened superpower, must slash capabilities, especially in land forces. Just because a power declines while others rise, however, need not mean that it will fall, immediately. Its position may hold steady for decades, or tip suddenly at any time. In power, tipping points matter as much as trends. Unfortunately, they are harder to foresee.

The United States has reconsidered its strategies of 1989 and 2001. Indications are that it will maintain far and away the largest military expenditure on earth, but still cut it well below the level of inflation, forcing bitter budgetary battles, and killing some programmes. The United States will remain an unmatched military power for decades to come, but its power is declining, and hyperpolarity vanishing, for reasons beyond its control. Other states, especially India, China, and Russia, are exercising their weight. Meanwhile, the first general rise since 1989 in the size and quality of armed forces is occurring, as all major states pursue great programmes of rearmament to counter the rust-out of kit. Only some will succeed. Talk is cheap, weapons are not. Major weapons constantly rise in price as they become more sophisticated, driving down numbers of orders, which immediately increases unit costs. In order to maintain national arms industries, states rarely buy equipment off the shelf from others, but instead prefer indigenous firms, usually more costly and less good than the best on earth. Without constant orders, every arms firm withers. These factors drive supply and demand for the arms trade.

After 2000, military budgets jumped, but then stalled and now are falling. Western states almost doubled their military spending between 2000 and 2008, while that of China trebled, but most of that increase was lost to inflation. Governments are shocked to find how so much can buy so little. All navies and air forces are in crisis, as numbers of personnel and kit plummet to allow recapitalization. Western ones must explain why they need new equipment, when they already have the world's best, and threats are so weak and far away. The US Navy, a vaunted 600-ship navy in 1989, has 300 in 2012. Since 2001, the US Air Force has slashed personnel to produce tiny numbers of its next two generation of fighters, the F-22 and F-35—183 F-22s eliminated 20,000 airmen, almost 10 per cent of its personnel. These pressures drove Western states to develop aircraft by international consortia, including the Eurofighter and the F-35. Washington's refusal to do so with the F-22, and so to maintain the secrecy of stealth technology, shaped its astronomical unit cost, of US$339,000,000 per aircraft. In order to buy new kit, between 1990–2009, Russia cut its army by 70 per cent, to 500,000 men, as China did its army by 20 per cent and its air force by 50 per cent. Moscow and Beijing have linked their status as powers to massive new arms programmes, like the Indo-Russian project for the fifth-generation Sukhoi/HAL fighter aircraft, intended to compete where American power is strongest. If these aims fail, so will their policies.

In the decade after 2012, the countries least affected by the recession may meet their declared policies. South Korea, China, India, and Japan are almost bound to become militarily more powerful, though the effect may be largely just to check each other. Most countries, however, will not match words with deeds, however much they try to hide decline through bluster, as squid flee behind ink. The choices are hard. In 2011, Britain scrapped its naval aviation capacity for a decade, and gutted its surface fleet and air force, in order to build two super-carriers, one of which it plans to sell upon completion! Unless Russia makes military investments at the scale which bankrupted the USSR, it will slip from the second to the third division of power. Only an Anglo-French marriage in procurement and deployment can let the couple matter militarily, as both did recently on the singles market. Cost barriers and the recession cripple the ability of states to keep their place, and also to develop dominant weapons systems. These factors will disrupt the production of modern fighters, and aircraft carriers.

A struggle will occur between the economic power and political will of major states, embodied in military procurement; the outcome will be measured in the quantity and quality of conventional forces. The only safe bets are that the United States will remain the greatest of great powers, that any country which fails in rearmament will fall in power, and many will do so. Their efforts to achieve these ends, and their success compared to their rivals, will add uncertainty to the base of a new world order. Nothing drives a state towards desperation more than the fear that it is declining while a rival is rising (see Box 12.3).

War, What is It Good For?

Wars occur from combinations of intention and error. They are unusually likely when the nature and distribution of power change rapidly, as states misconstrue their strength while declining ones strive to hold what they have and growing ones to take more. Those circumstances

BOX 12.3 The Future for Power Relations

Power, in Asia and elsewhere, turns on the military application of industry. China and India have large sectors in those areas, government-run, and burdened with the deadweight of failed socialism, and widespread corruption. Their defence industries and governments have tangled relations. Firms in Chinese provinces, caught in local political fiefdoms, rarely cooperate with those elsewhere, preventing economies of scale, or rationalization. In India, attempts to let private arms firms compete with state ones face paralysing resistance from industrial, labour, and political lobbies. Indigenous production of aircraft and the acquisition of foreign ones are delayed for decades as firms and state tinker with contracts, especially over arrangements for technology transfer, though this happens in rich nations too. The developing states with the most advanced military industrial bases are Russia, through the wasting legacy of its superpower past, and Brazil, which produces large numbers of good indigenously designed aircraft and AFVs and aggressively pursues technology transfer agreements with advanced powers—on a continent where conventional power has little positive influence. This capacity, however, will matter in coming years if Brazil seeks to acquire power to match its wealth.

China and India depend on access to foreign technology; but each works with many partners, through which it builds advanced AFVs, aircraft and cruise missiles, and tries to leapfrog time-consuming stages of technology. Their civil economies have able elements in high technology, but weaknesses in innovation. China seeks to establish defence industries of the top rank by 2025, an ambitious, but achievable, aim. Since 1995, China has performed consistently at the top level of expectations; no other power has risen so fast and far. During those years, its air force leapt from 1970 to 1995, just below the best secondary powers. Its rise exploited every relationship and technique, combining joint licences, reverse engineering and espionage, to strip Western technology in the 1980s, and Russian since then, so to build an air industry of decent quality. Chinese capabilities are hard to calculate, because it tries to make foreigners overestimate its development of leading assets like aircraft carriers and fighters. Nonetheless, its firms produce fighters which are comparatively decent compared with any others deployed in 2012, except the F-22. India, while rising, depends more on its suppliers and performs worse in programmes, though aided by the greater willingness of foreigners to exchange technology with Delhi, than Beijing. In 20 years, China and India will probably have established good military industries, and closed the gap with leading economies, even in defence electronics and information technology. Though the edge will remain with the rich, they may then be the world's second and third strongest economies and conventional powers, and growing fast.

Key points

- The distribution of conventional power is changing.
- Western countries are in decline.
- New world powers are emerging, especially China and India.
- The impact of these changes will vary with the desire of states to tap economic power for strategic purposes, and the skill of their policies.

exist today. The American drawdown from Iraq and Afghanistan opens uncertainty across Asia. Classic confrontations loom between rising and declining powers. Mexican stand-offs rule Asia: between India and Pakistan; North Korea vs South Korea, Japan and the United States; and Beijing vs most of its neighbours, and Washington. Chinese power waxes steadily, but is not yet significant in WMDs or maritime power. Since 1949 China has aimed to maximize its power, and has often provoked high-risk incidents, in the belief that teaching lessons to neighbours is a good thing, while it can control the worst cases—characteristics shared, to lesser degrees, by the United States. Both countries believe they are on the defensive over Taiwan, and respond to aggression in a tough and self-righteous manner. Meanwhile, as the Soviet collapse reshaped power in Asia, so would any resurgence of Russia—or Japan.

The Middle East is governed not by stalemate but vacuum. Several Arab states, particularly Syria and Egypt, match Israel numerically in the main categories of land and air force, while Saudi Arabia and the Gulf States make large purchases of advanced weaponry. Outside Jordan and Hezbollah, these forces are poor in quality, while Israeli ones are excellent. The failure of its 2006 war with Lebanon shocked Israel into improving its army, which performed better next time, in Gaza during 2008–2009. Israel, the military master of the Arab world, can overawe its neighbours and wreck any threat, yet cannot directly translate that strength into political power, as demonstrated by its irrelevance during the greatest political change in the Middle East for generations, the Arab Spring of 2011. Turkey, militarily weaker but diplomatically stronger, has risen in regional import. Israel and America cannot use conventional force to block big dangers, such as the rise of jihadist regimes in Egypt or Saudi Arabia; though that could aid them in containment, as it did with Iraq and Iran between 1991 and 2003. Nor, short of occupying Lebanon or Gaza, can Israel destroy the ability of Hamas and Hezbollah to bombard its territory with thousands of missiles. Meanwhile, the military weakness of Arab states and the turmoil within them make that region even less stable than usual.

In these cases, conventional force is part of power, but not the whole. It does not primarily define the balance between Israel, the United States, and Iran. A tough neighbourhood may drive Japan to increase its conventional power, but Tokyo has more to gain from nuclear weapons. China can strengthen its hand against the United States through conventional force to match American strengths, asymmetric force to degrade them, politics, or WMDs. The latter options are its best chances for success. For most developing states, WMDs offer the simplest military solution to strategic problems. For China in Taiwan, and Iran in Iraq and Afghanistan, political influence is a better instrument than armies, just as terrorism is a tool of policy by other means.

Bigger questions loom behind these matters, like the use of WMDs in conventional war. When only one side has chemical weapons, it routinely uses them, but not nuclear weapons. How far can states equipped with WMDs use conventional force against each other? They have often done so, but the rules for these games remain obscure. All major belligerents in Europe during 1939–1945 were equipped for gas warfare, but did not use it; so too in the Gulf War of 1991. Nuclear powers have fought each other, most notably India and Pakistan in the isolated region of Kargil during 2000; but Soviet pilots shot down many American air intruders over their territory in the 1950s and attacked allied airmen in the Korean War, and Israeli ones during 1970. Again, the single greatest factor in world politics since 1989 has been the relationship between overwhelming American power, and its erratic use. Its search for absolute security made all its rivals insecure, looking for ways to defend themselves or escape the firing line. Its power and threats frightened many hostile states into changing their ways, but also convinced any serious rival that it must neutralize that threat, by being able to endanger America. The dominant concept in the public rhetoric of Chinese strategy, opposition to hegemony, was once a code word for resistance to the USSR; today it is the United States. American success in conventional power will drive any rational enemy to abandon head-on competition, and pursue asymmetry or WMDs, and the latter are easier to build and have a more certain deterrent effect.

Key points

- Wars occur from accident and intention.
- Conventional power is part of the balance in every zone of conflict.
- Its limits matter no less than its strengths.

 ## Conclusion

Conventional power is a great but limited tool of state. Once it was a spear for the strong against the strong; now, it is most valuable as a weapon against the weak. It remains the main shield for most states, but the sword of choice for few. It is more useful as a negative than a positive tool: to stop others from moving, as against doing so oneself. It is a fundamental means to demonstrate resolve, or support any strategies of dissuasion and compellence, though no more so than nuclear power or diplomatic influence. Any state threatened by conventional force must match it or die. Such forces can save oneself, aid one's friends, destroy one's enemies, and, occasionally, strike like lightning. Still, their utility has slipped steadily over the past century, as has the willingness of states to use them. Conventional force has failed to achieve specific results predictably or cheaply. The outcome of its use has been more uncertain than ever before. Often, it has caused complex collateral damage, or trapped its users in the mire of world war, or guerrilla conflict. Conventional force will be more discussed than used. When deployed, it will face characteristic problems, or victory traps. If one uses cruise missiles for diplomacy, a few civilian deaths will mess your message. No matter the cause—*raison d'état*, or humanitarian intervention, whether single-handed, or under UN control—Western states will use conventional power primarily where the entry cost seems low and chances for success high: against weak or failing ones. This raises immediate questions. Can outsiders end a civil war? Does occupation cause resistance? Will Western publics tolerate the violence necessary for victory except for defence of vital interests? Nor can armies be used on any great issue without raising the issue of WMDs.

Conventional force affects the policies of single actors, and the system as a whole. Many consequences of conventional power lie outside that plane, in what it drives states to do elsewhere. Its impact is most critical in deterring people from using an obvious tool, and in driving them to develop others. In theory, levels of force are divided; in reality, they are intertwined. For example, an American air strike on Iranian nuclear power stations might spark terrorism across the Middle East. The pure game of conventional power is played in a narrow field between two limits: WMDs, and terrorism and guerrilla warfare. To be too good in this game is not a simple blessing. Too much success drives one's rival off this field to play on others. A rational enemy plays to its strengths, not yours. Conventional power remains a strong card, perhaps the king of trumps in a game where the ace is unplayable, but it cannot take every hand. Perhaps it can take only one out of 13. The trick will be learning how to play that card only when it can take the game; and to know when that game is worth the gamble.

 ## Questions

1. Did the United States win, or did Iraq lose, the Gulf War of 2003?

2. How does sea power matter today, why, and to whom?

3. What use are air power and precision weapons to the United States, compared to nuclear power?

4. What is a decisive battle? How many of them have happened since 1945?

5. How will the economic decline of the United States, and the rise of China, affect their military power by 2025?

6. Compare and contrast the conventional military power of Israel, Iran, and India. What good does it do them? What are the limits to its value?

7. How far can states equipped with WMDs engage in conventional war?

8. Is attrition the normal state of conventional war? Is indecisiveness its normal outcome?

9. How, and how easily, can conventional forces defeat terrorists or guerrillas?

10. How will Russia and Japan respond to the rise of China?

 ## Further Reading

C. Archer, J. Ferris, H. Herwig, and T. Travers, *A World History of Warfare* (Lincoln, NE: University of Nebraska Press, 2002) offers a good modern account of the history of conventional war.

V. D. Hanson, *Carnage and Culture: Landmark Battles in the Rise of Western Power* (New York: Anchor Books, 2001) also offers a good modern account of the history of conventional war.

J. Lynn, *Battle, A History of Combat and Culture* (Boulder, CO: Westview Press, 2003) also offers a good modern account of the history of conventional war.

R. Weigley, *The Age of Battles, The Quest for Decisive Warfare* (Bloomington, IN: Indiana University Press, 1991).

International Institute of Strategic Studies, *The Military Balance* (London: IISS and Routledge). An authoritative, comprehensive, and annual assessment of conventional forces and weapons.

Janes (various publications) also provides a credible source for information on conventional forces and weapons.

 ## Web Links

Useful websites on modern military matters, which include copies of many semi-official and official publications, and links to other websites, are:

The Air War College Portal to the Internet **http://www.au.af.mil/au/awc/awcgate/awcgate.htm** An excellent source for official, semi-official, and unclassified studies of current military topics, with links to official, semi-official and unclassified websites.

The Center for Strategic and International Studies **http://www.csis.org** An excellent source for analyses of international strategic issues and conflicts, particularly useful for instant and informed studies of conflicts as they occur.

Global Security **http://www.globalsecurity.org** An excellent source for statistical breakdowns and analyses of international military issues, with links to many other sources, and extensive archives. Now on a subscription basis only.

The RAND Corporation **http://www.rand.org** An excellent and wide-ranging source for studies of contemporary strategic policy and military forces, often surprisingly detailed.

Carnegie Endowment for International Peace **http://www.carnegieendowment.org/** An excellent source for analyses of international strategic issues and conflicts, from a liberal perspective.

International Crisis Group **http://www.crisisgroup.org/** An excellent source for analyses of international strategic issues and conflicts, particularly useful on internal political dimensions, and the application of area expertise.

Iraq, Afghanistan, and American Military Transformation

STEPHEN BIDDLE

 ## Chapter Contents

Introduction	248
Afghanistan and the Transformation Thesis	249
Iraq 2003 and the Transformation Thesis	255
An Alternative View	259
Conclusion	263

 ## Reader's Guide

This chapter considers two recent examples of major combat operations (MCO), in Afghanistan in 2001–2, and Iraq from March to April of 2003. Both proved highly influential for subsequent US defence policy debates, and particularly so for arguments over the need to 'transform' the American military to meet the needs of twenty-first century warfare. Does the actual experience of combat in these two campaigns support the view that warfare has changed dramatically and now requires a very different kind of military for success? The chapter argues that, in fact, the conduct of both campaigns was more traditional, and less transformational, than widely supposed. In particular, both campaigns involved extensive close combat on the ground against unbroken defenders who survived precision air strikes and fought back when struck by US and allied ground forces. Although there were many new tactics and technologies in both campaigns, there was also a great deal of continuity with prior military experience: to focus only on the change and ignore the continuity is to misunderstand the nature of warfare in the early twenty-first century.

Introduction

The wars in Iraq and Afghanistan began as inter-state conventional conflicts. Each subsequently morphed into insurgency and irregular warfare, and ultimate success in either theatre will be shaped chiefly by the outcomes of these low-intensity follow-ons to the initial, conventional campaigns. However, some outcomes are already clear: the Taliban regime in Afghanistan was toppled in 2001; the Ba'athist regime in Iraq fell in 2003; the military campaigns of 2001–2 and 2003 that did this proved highly influential in the American defence planning debate.

In particular, these campaigns gave powerful impetus to a collection of proposals for radical change—or 'transformation'—in the US military. Even before 2001, it was widely believed that a transnational revolution in information processing was transforming the nature of war. The increasing power of networked information, many claimed, was erasing the need for massed conventional ground forces, substituting stand-off precision strike for the close combat of the past and replacing the breakthrough battle with the struggle for information supremacy as the decisive issue for success. The campaigns in Afghanistan and Iraq powerfully reinforced these perceptions: the speed and radically low casualties of the Coalition offensives in Afghanistan and Iraq seemed to offer trenchant empirical evidence to show that the hypothesized changes were in fact real.

This in turn reinforced a series of interconnected proposals for transforming the US military from what has often been described as a heavy, slow-moving, cold war relic into a leaner, faster, higher technology force that exploits the connectivity of networked information to outmanoeuvre, outrange, and demoralize enemy forces without requiring their piecemeal destruction in close combat. Some transformation advocates would even bypass the enemy military in the field altogether, using deep strikes from possibly intercontinental distances to destroy key nodes in a hostile economy or political control system in 'effects-based' operations (EBO) that prevail by coercive bombing rather than brute force on the battlefield.

These proposals have not gone unchallenged. In particular, critics have long argued that this transformation agenda overlooks the demands of inherently labour-intensive, low-technology missions such as counterinsurgency (COIN), or stability and support operations (SASO). Critics argue that the kind of streamlined, technology-dependent military that transformation advocates want would leave the United States unable to wage sustained counterinsurgencies of the type now ongoing in Afghanistan: and the future, they often claim, lies in exactly such low-intensity conflicts (LIC), rather than the high-intensity major combat operations (MCO) around which most high-tech transformation proposals turn.

Yet this critique skirts a more fundamental issue: is the transformation thesis valid even for major combat itself? In particular, is it a valid interpretation of the reasons for the quick success and low cost of MCO in Afghanistan or Iraq in 2001–2 and 2003? Was the actual conduct of either of these campaigns consistent with the claims of the transformation thesis?

In fact the answer is no—the transformation thesis is not consistent with the actual conduct of either campaign. This suggests that, whatever one thinks of the need for future COIN or SASO, the network-centric, EBO version of American military transformation is ill-advised. What the evidence from MCO in Afghanistan and Iraq actually shows is that speed and stand-off precision will work as claimed only against enemies who lack the skills necessary to evade their effects. Against unskilled enemies such as the Iraqi military or the indigenous Afghan Taliban, a transformed US military would be highly successful—in fact, it is probably the ideal force for such a job. However, against enemies with at least the combat skills shown by the Taliban's foreign allies in Afghanistan—and especially al-Qaeda— traditional close combat capability is needed for success. A transformed military in which close combat capability is traded for increased emphasis on stand-off precision strike could be radically less effective than a traditional military against such enemies. This suggests that a transformation agenda that trades mass for speed, and close combat for stand-off precision, could be a very risky undertaking in a world where it is uncertain where or against whom the US military may be called to fight.

The chapter presents this case in four steps. First, it discusses the conduct of the 2001–2 campaign in Afghanistan and its consistency with the transformation thesis. Next, it does the same for the 2003 major combat phase of the war in Iraq. It then presents an alternative explanation for the low cost and rapid conclusion of these campaigns, and concludes with some implications of the findings for US defence policy.

Afghanistan and the Transformation Thesis

The heart of the transformation school's interpretation of MCO in Afghanistan is that American airpower is held to have used targeting information provided largely by a handful of US special operations forces (SOF) on the ground to destroy the Taliban's military at stand-off ranges, before the Taliban could overrun US commandos or the indigenous allies working with them. In this account, it is the precision munitions that did the real military work; everything else is there to support stand-off firepower delivery and the precision fires are held to have been sufficient in themselves to destroy the enemy and enable a collection of ostensibly ragtag local militias to advance. This ability to destroy the enemy by stand-off precision is in turn central to this view's implications for the transformation debate: if Afghanistan shows that stand-off precision has made close combat largely unnecessary, then restructuring the military away from close combat and towards stand-off precision makes sense.

In fact, in its early stages the war did indeed go mostly the way transformation proponents assume. US precision took the Taliban by surprise, and their initial dispositions were poorly chosen for protection against such firepower. Taliban defenders typically deployed on exposed ridgelines with little effort at camouflage or concealment. Entrenchments were haphazard, lacking overhead cover for infantry positions or proper emplacements for combat vehicles. As a result, Taliban positions could be identified from often extraordinary distances; once located, their poor entrenchment and exposed movement made them easy prey for precision weapons.

The result was slaughter. At Bishqab on 21 October 2001, for example, US SOF pinpointed Taliban targets at ranges of over 8 kilometres. Sceptical Northern Alliance commanders peered through their binoculars at Taliban positions that had stymied them for years and were astounded to see the defences suddenly vaporized by direct hits from 2,000-pound bombs. At Cobaki on 22 October Taliban observation posts were easily spotted at 1,500–2,000 metres and annihilated by precision bombing. At Zard Kammar on 28 October, Taliban defences were wiped out from a mile away. At Ac'capruk on 4 November, exposed Taliban combat vehicles and crew-served weapons on hillsides west of the Balkh river were spotted from SOF observation posts on the Koh-i-Almortak ridge line some 4–5 kilometres distant and obliterated by US air strikes.

The Taliban were not the only ones surprised by this: some allied Afghans initially thought the lasers US SOF used to designate bombing targets were actually death rays, since they apparently caused defences to vanish whenever caught in their cross hairs. Both sides, however, learnt fast.

Within days of the first SOF-directed air strikes, US commandos were already reporting that Taliban vehicles in their sectors had been smeared with mud to camouflage them. By 5 November, the Taliban's al-Qaeda allies were already making aggressive use of overhead cover and concealment. In the fighting north of Kandahar and along Highway 4 in December, al-Qaeda defences were well-camouflaged, dispersed, and making use of natural terrain for expedient cover. This pattern continued into Operation Anaconda in March, by which time al-Qaeda forces were practising systematic communications security, dispersal, camouflage discipline, use of cover and concealment, and exploitation of dummy fighting positions to draw fire and attention from their real dispositions. Indigenous *Afghan* Taliban in the war's early battles were radically exposed, but as the war unfolded the opposition came increasingly to comprise better trained, more adaptive foreign—and especially al-Qaeda—forces. As these foreign forces adapted their methods they reduced their vulnerability significantly: and as they did, the war changed character.

Finding Hidden Targets

Among the more important changes was increasing difficulty in finding targets for precision attack. At Bai Beche on 2–5 November, for example, a mostly al-Qaeda defensive force occupied an old, formerly Soviet system of deliberate entrenchments. With proper cover and concealment, the defenders were able to prevent US commandos from locating the entirety of their individual fighting positions, many of which could not be singled out for precision attack.

By the time of the December fighting along Highway 4 south of Kandahar, even less information was available. In fact, concealed al-Qaeda defences among a series of culverts and in burnt-out vehicle hulks along the roadside remained wholly undetected until their fire drove back an allied advance. An al-Qaeda counterattack in the same sector using a system of wadis for cover approached undetected to within 100–200 metres of allied and US SOF positions along the highway before opening fire on friendly forces.

At the village of Sayed Slim Kalay north of Kandahar between 2 and 4 December, concealed al-Qaeda defenders likewise remained undetected until they fired upon unsuspecting US and allied forces. An al-Qaeda counterattack using local terrain for cover manoeuvred into small-arms range of friendly defenders before being driven back.

At Operation Anaconda in March 2002, an intensive pre-battle reconnaissance effort focused every available surveillance and target acquisition system on a tiny, 10-by-10-kilometre battlefield. Yet fewer than 50 per cent of all the al-Qaeda positions ultimately identified on this battlefield were discovered prior to ground contact. In fact, most fire received by US forces in Anaconda came from initially unseen, unanticipated defenders.

How could such things happen in an era of persistent reconnaissance drones, airborne radars, satellite surveillance, thermal imaging, and hypersensitive electronic eavesdropping equipment? The answer is that the earth's surface remains an extremely complex environment with an abundance of natural and man-made cover available for those militaries capable of exploiting it.

Militarily exploitable cover is commonplace in almost any likely theatre of war. For targets who observe radio listening silence, as al-Qaeda now does, foliage degrades all current remote sensor technologies; urban areas provide overhead cover, create background clutter, and pose difficult problems of distinguishing military targets from innocent civilians. Each is widely available. More than 26 per cent of Somalia's land area is wooded or urban, as is more than 20 per cent of the Sudan's, 34 per cent of Georgia's, or 46 per cent of the Philippines'. In most countries, the central geostrategic objectives are urban areas; even where the bulk of the national land area is open desert (as in Iraq), the cities are both the key terrain and an ample source of cover (Baghdad alone covers more than 300 square kilometres). The natural complexity of such surfaces offers any adaptive opponent with the necessary training and skills a multitude of opportunities to thwart even modern remote surveillance systems. Against such opponents, remote surveillance will still detect some targets, and remote sensors remain crucial assets, but the only sure means of target acquisition is direct ground contact: a ground force whose advance threatens objectives that the enemy cannot sacrifice and thus must defend compels them to give away their locations by firing on their attackers. Skilled attackers can eventually locate any defensive position by observing the source of the fire directed at them—and this, in fact, is how the majority of the al-Qaeda positions at Anaconda were found.

Close Combat in Afghanistan

As the enemy adapted, their decreasing vulnerability to stand-off attack meant an increasing burden of close combat. Little of this was guerrilla warfare. At least until Anaconda in March 2002, the Taliban sought to take and hold ground in very orthodox ways—they tried to defend key geographic objectives, not harass their enemies with hit-and-run tactics. These defences, however, were sufficiently covered and concealed to allow important fractions of them to survive American air attack. The resulting ground combat was neither trivial nor wholly one-sided: many battles were close calls, with either initial reverses, serious casualties, or both.

At Bai Beche on 5 November, for example, dug-in al-Qaeda defenders refused to withdraw after more than two days of heavy US bombing. To dislodge them, Northern Alliance cavalry was ordered to charge the position. The first attempt was driven back. The attached American SOF observed this reverse and began calling renewed air strikes in anticipation of a second assault. In the process, however, a SOF warning order to the cavalry to prepare for another push was mistaken by the cavalry as a command to launch the assault, with the result that the cavalry began its attack much sooner than intended. The surprised Americans watched the Afghan cavalry break cover and begin their advance just as a series of laser-guided bombs had been released from American aircraft in response to the SOF calls for air support. The SOF commander reported that he was convinced they had just caused a friendly fire incident: the bomb release and the cavalry advance were way too close together for official doctrinal limits, and the air strike would never have been ordered if the SOF had known that the cavalry was then jumping off for the second assault. As it happened, the bombs landed just seconds before the cavalry arrived. In fact, the cavalry galloped through the enormous cloud of smoke and dust that was still hanging in the air after the explosions, emerging behind the enemy defences before their garrison knew what was happening. The defenders, seeing Northern Alliance cavalry to their rear, abandoned their positions in an attempt to avoid encirclement (see Box 13.1).

The result was an important victory—in fact, the victory that turned the tide in the north—but the battle involved serious close combat (cavalry overrunning prepared, actively resisting defences), and the outcome was a very close call. The assault profited from an extremely tight integration of movement with suppressive fire—far tighter, in fact, than either the cavalry or their supporting SOF would ever have dared arrange deliberately. Luck thus played an important role in the outcome. The Northern Alliance might well have carried the position eventually

BOX 13.1 Key Events in the Afghanistan Campaign's Major Combat Phase, 2001–2002

The Afghan campaign began the night of 7 October 2001, with a programme of air strikes aimed initially at destroying the Taliban's limited air defences and communications infrastructure. Early air attacks produced few results, however, because the country had little fixed infrastructure to destroy. By 15 October, SOF teams designated to make contact with the major Northern Alliance warlords had been inserted. A three-part campaign followed, divided roughly into a northern phase revolving around control of the city of Mazar-i-Sharif, a southern phase centred on the city of Kandahar, and subsequent battles against Taliban and al-Qaeda forces at Tora Bora and during Operation Anaconda in the Shah-i-Kot Valley.

The fight for Mazar-i-Sharif began when General Abdul Rashid Dostum, supported by US SOF, took the village of Bishqab on the banks of the Dar-ye Suf south of Mazar on 21 October. This was followed by engagements at Cobaki, Chapchall, and Oimetan over the next few days as Dostum fought his way up the river valley. The key battle came when Dostum's troops overran hostile forces occupying old Soviet-built defensive positions at the hamlet of Bai Beche on 5 November. Shortly thereafter, General Muhammed Atta's forces and their accompanying SOF captured Ac'capruk on the Balkh River, and the door swung open for a rapid advance to Mazar, which fell to Atta and Dostum's troops on 10 November. The fall of Mazar unhinged the Taliban position in northern Afghanistan. Kabul fell without a fight on 13 November, and after a 12-day siege, a force of some 5,000 Taliban and al-Qaeda survivors encircled in the city of Kunduz surrendered on 26 November.

With the fall of Kabul and Kunduz, attention shifted to the Taliban's stronghold of Kandahar in the south. SOF teams and Hamid Karzai's allied Afghan forces advanced on the city from the north; Gul Agha Shirzai's allied Afghans and supporting SOF advanced from the south. After a series of battles, on the night of 6 December Mullah Muhammad Omar and the rest of the senior Taliban leadership fled the city and went into hiding, ending Taliban rule in Afghanistan.

Allied forces, meanwhile, tracked a group of al-Qaeda survivors thought to include Osama bin Laden to a series of redoubts in the White Mountains near Tora Bora. These redoubts were taken in a 16-day battle ending on 17 December, but many al-Qaeda defenders escaped death or capture and fled across the border into Pakistan.

In March 2002, a second concentration of al-Qaeda holdouts was identified in the Shah-i-Kot Valley east of Gardez. In Operation Anaconda, Western and allied Afghan forces descended on these al-Qaeda defenders, killing many and dispersing the rest. Anaconda would be the last action of the war's major combat phase; after this, the Taliban shifted increasingly to insurgent methods and the war changed character.

even without the good fortune of an extraordinary integration of fire and movement; this was clearly a crucial battle, and they would presumably have redoubled their efforts if the second attempt had failed. However, as fought, the outcome involved an important element of serendipity.

Nor was Bai Beche unique in demanding hard fighting at close quarters. As already noted, al-Qaeda counterattackers reached small-arms range of US and allied forces before being driven back at Sayed Slim Kalay and at Highway 4. At Konduz in late November, al-Qaeda counterattackers penetrated allied positions deeply enough to compel supporting American SOF teams to withdraw at least three times to avoid being overrun. In Anaconda, allied forces associated with General Mohammed Zia and supported by US SOF were assigned to drive al-Qaeda defenders from the 'Tri-cities' area (the villages of Shirkankeyl, Babakuhl, and Marzak) in the Shah-i-Kot Valley floor; they were instead pinned down under hostile fire from prepared defences in the surrounding mountainsides and eventually withdrew after they proved unable to advance. Only after the al-Qaeda defenders pulled back under joint, multinational attack by allied airpower, Western infantry, and multinational SOF, were Zia's troops able to enter the Tri-cities and adjoining ridgelines. At Tora Bora, massive American bombing proved insufficient to compensate for allied Afghan unwillingness to close with dug-in al-Qaeda defenders in the cave complexes of the White Mountains; this ground force hesitancy probably allowed Osama bin Laden and his lieutenants to escape into neighbouring Pakistan.

Among these examples, the fighting along Highway 4 in December is particularly instructive. The US-allied Afghans here were divided among two factions. The first, commanded by Haji Gul Alai, were very capable troops by Afghan standards. They used terrain for cover and concealment, maintained good intervals between elements in the advance, moved by alternate bounds, exploited suppressive fire to cover moving elements' exposure, and were able to exploit the effects of US air strikes by coordinating their movement with the bombing (which many Afghan factions could not). The second faction, by contrast, was much less skilled: the attached SOF commander characterized them as 'an armed mob—just villagers given weapons' (US Army Military History Institute 2003). Their tactics consisted of exposed, bunched-up movement in the open, with no attempt to use terrain to reduce their exposure, and little ability to employ supporting or suppressive fires. At the Arghestan Bridge on 5 December, this second faction launched an assault on a dug-in al-Qaeda position south of the Kandahar airport. Driven back repeatedly, they proved unable to take the position, in spite of US air support. Only after these troops were withdrawn and Haji Gul Alai's forces took over the assault the following day could the al-Qaeda positions be taken.

Of course, the alliance ultimately ousted the Taliban, and precision US airpower was a necessary precondition for this—together with its SOF spotters it was what turned a stalemated civil war into a rapid toppling of the Taliban regime. However, while precision bombing was *necessary* for this, it was not *sufficient*. It could annihilate poorly prepared fighting positions, and it could inflict heavy losses on even well-disposed defences, but it could not destroy the entirety of properly prepared positions by itself, and unless such positions are all but annihilated, even a handful of surviving, actively resisting defenders with modern automatic weapons can make great slaughter of unsophisticated indigenous allies whose idea of tactics is to walk forward bunched up in the open. To overcome skilled, resolute defenders who have adopted the standard countermeasures to high-firepower air strikes still requires close combat by friendly ground forces whose own skills are sufficient to enable

BOX 13.2 The Combatants in Afghanistan's Major Combat Phase

Neither the Taliban nor the Northern Alliance forces allied with the United States comprised homogeneous or uniformly trained armies in 2001–2. The Taliban consisted of at least three militarily very different subcomponents: indigenous Afghan Taliban, mostly with very little training or tactical sophistication; better-trained and better-motivated foreigners fighting on behalf of the Taliban; and the subset of foreign fighters who had been through Osama bin Laden's al-Qaeda training camps, and who provided the most capable of the Taliban's troops. The Northern Alliance comprised a similarly diverse collection of warlords with forces whose military proficiency varied widely as a function of their past military experience in Afghanistan's civil war. Some had skills comparable to the al-Qaeda fighters, others were much less adept. Strength estimates for these armies are necessarily inexact. Most accounts, however, credit the Taliban overall with some 40,000–50,000 troops in autumn 2001, of whom perhaps 8,000–12,000 were foreign. The Northern Alliance is sometimes credited with 20,000–30,000 troops in autumn 2001, though after the campaign began, additional forces were organized from Taliban opponents in the central and southern provinces of Afghanistan in what is sometimes termed the 'Southern Alliance'. Western forces in Afghanistan consisted, initially, of American and multinational SOF, which were later augmented by US regular army infantry (chiefly from the 10th Mountain and 101st Airborne divisions), US Marines from Task Force Rhino, and multinational regular infantry (prominently including a battalion from the Canadian Princess Patricia's Light Infantry Regiment, which played an important role in Operation Anaconda in March 2002). Afghanistan was unique as the first major campaign in which US Special Operations Forces were the 'supported' rather than a 'supporting' command—meaning that their mission was the main effort in the theatre of war.

them to use local cover and their own suppressive fire to advance against hostile survivors with modern weapons.

By and large, America's main Afghan allies in this war either enjoyed such fundamental skills or profited from accidentally tight coordination of their movement and American fires (as at Bai Beche) or both. The Northern, and later the Southern, Alliances were not uniformly the motley assortment of militiamen they are sometimes said to have been. Enough of them were capable of implementing complex tactics to allow them to exploit the tremendous potential that precision airpower can bring to armies capable of integrating their movement with its firepower (see Box 13.2).

Not all of America's allies in this war were up to this job. Though the typical combat units on each side were about equally matched (as the stalled pre-intervention battle lines imply), both sides in Afghanistan were actually diverse mixtures of better and worse trained, more and less motivated troops—and this diversity offers a couple of valuable opportunities to observe instances of unequally skilled forces in combat. In such unequal fights as the first day at Arghestan Bridge and the assault on the Tri-cities in Anaconda, the results suggest that, where the indigenous allies are overmatched tactically, US airpower and SOF support alone may not be enough to turn the tide.

In 2001–2, America's Afghan allies, eventually combined with the US and Canadian infantry that fought at Anaconda, together provided significant ground forces that ultimately shouldered an essential load of old-fashioned close combat against surviving, actively resisting opponents. Even with twenty-first-century firepower, without this essential close combat capability the outcome of major combat in Afghanistan could easily have been very different.

Key points

- Early in the 2001–2 campaign, indigenous Afghan Taliban targets were ill-prepared and exposed. US SOF were able to locate them from great distances and destroy them with stand-off precision air strikes.

- Later, as the indigenous Afghan Taliban were replaced with better-trained foreign and al-Qaeda fighters, exposed targets became less common, stand-off precision became less effective, and close combat became more frequent.

- Against motivated defenders in properly prepared positions, success required a combination of stand-off precision with ground manoeuvre by infantry with the skills needed to reduce their exposure to defensive fire.

Iraq 2003 and the Transformation Thesis

The transformation school's interpretation of the major combat phase in Operation Iraqi Freedom (OIF) focuses on American speed, precision, and situation awareness. These are held to account for the campaign's quick conclusion and low casualties by leaving the Iraqis unable to inflict significant losses: in this view, much of Iraq's military refused to fight against such overwhelming technology, and those who did were destroyed by stand-off precision strike before they could pose a real threat to Coalition ground forces. Iraqi threats of scorched earth, moreover, are held to have been pre-empted by the speed of the Coalition advance: it was widely feared that Saddam would destroy Iraq's economic infrastructure rather than allow it to fall into Coalition hands, yet Iraqi oilfields, ports, and bridges were overrun before Saddam's forces could destroy them. Much of the emphasis on speed, especially in the post-2003 defence planning debate, stems from this interpretation of its role in Saddam's fall. Also, the apparent role of stand-off precision in limiting Coalition losses gave further impetus to the transformation argument that had already been strengthened by the conventional interpretation of the 2001–2 campaign in Afghanistan.

However, while speed, precision, and situation awareness were surely helpful, they were far from sufficient to explain the low cost of Saddam's ouster. To see why, I will consider in turn the role of close combat, and the absence of scorched earth, in the major combat phase of the war in Iraq.

Close Combat in Iraq

The logic of the transformation account of the Coalition's low MCO casualty rate implies that Coalition losses were averted by avoiding close combat—by reducing the scale of close-quarters fighting against willing combatants on favourable ground to the point where the Iraqis could not inflict heavy casualties. Yet there was actually substantial close combat in Iraq against Iraqi fighters on urban terrain who proved willing to take extraordinary risks to kill Americans and Britons—certainly there was far too much close combat to accept explanations that turn on its ostensible infrequency.

The key here is urban warfare. Urban terrain is ordinarily thought highly defence favour-able; defenders in cities should be able to fight at a considerable tactical advantage. The basis for most pre-war fears of heavy Coalition casualties in conventional combat was concern with urban warfare, and in fact there was substantial close combat in Iraqi cities in Operation Iraqi Freedom (OIF).

In Baghdad, for example, the US 3rd Infantry Division's 2nd Brigade conducted two successive penetrations (or 'Thunder Runs') into the heart of the city on 5 and 7 April 2003. On both occasions it was met with a fusillade of Iraqi rocket-propelled grenade (RPG) and small arms fire, at point blank range, along nearly its entire route. In fact, on 5 April, every single vehicle in the brigade column was hit at least once by Iraqi RPGs, and many took multiple hits. Opposition was especially intense at highway overpasses and key intersections; Iraqi positions there were destroyed but subsequently reoccupied by fighters who infiltrated back behind the moving American columns. The 5 April penetration was a raid, and returned to its origin at the Baghdad International Airport after reaching the city centre, but the 7 April assault established a brigade perimeter at the Tigris River bend to hold the ground. This required a resupply column to be sent forward after nightfall to replenish depleted fuel and ammunition stocks. This resupply convoy, too, had to fight its way through defences that had been reoccupied after having been destroyed in the earlier advance; it lost one ammunition and two fuel trucks in a wild ride through a series of desperate fire fights, suffering two soldiers killed and thirty wounded en route. The next morning, the brigade was counterattacked by waves of paramilitaries hanging over the sides of some 50–100 civilian vehicles and firing small arms and RPGs as they poured over the Tigris River bridges towards the brigade perimeter.

When the division's 3rd Brigade entered Baghdad from the north it, too, fought its way through volleys of massed RPGs fired from practically point-blank range. Every armoured vehicle in 3rd Brigade suffered either a hit or a near miss from RPGs while fighting their way into the city.

Similarly, in Nasiriyah Iraqi paramilitaries and elements of the Iraqi 11th Regular Army division waged a week-long urban battle against the US Marine Corps' Task Force Tarawa, a reinforced three-battalion regimental-scale formation. In Samawah, Iraqi paramilitaries fought for a week against the US Army's 3–7 Cavalry, the 3rd Brigade of the 3rd Infantry Division, and the 2nd Brigade of the 82nd Airborne Division in turn. In Najaf, urban warfare in and around the city centre continued for more than a week, tying down in series multiple brigades of US infantry.

The exact strength of the willing, surviving Iraqi opposition in these and other urban battles cannot be known, but it was clearly enough to produce a major volume of potentially lethal fires at very close quarters. Perhaps 30,000 Iraqi paramilitaries were predeployed in Baghdad, Basra, Najaf, and Nasiriyah before the war began. Another 15,000 Special Republican Guards (SRG) were predeployed in Baghdad and its suburbs. Some 10,000 paramilitary reinforcements were moved south from Baghdad into Nasiriyah and Najaf after it became clear that major battles were under way there for control of the bridges running through these cities. SRG infantry and paramilitaries in mostly civilian clothing were poor targets for Coalition deep strikes, which were aimed chiefly at Iraqi leadership, command, air defence, and heavy weapons targets. While paramilitary losses were heavy in close combat with Coalition forces, there is little evidence to suggest that they suffered much attrition prior to contact with invaders on the ground. Combat motivation, while very weak in the Iraqi Regular Army and some Republican Guard units, was stronger elsewhere—and especially among paramilitary fighters in Iraqi cities. In fact, paramilitary combat motivation bordered on the suicidal in 2003. In Nasiriyah, Samawah, Basra, Najaf, Baghdad, and elsewhere, Iraqi para-militaries executed repeated frontal assaults against US armoured vehicles using civilian sport utility vehicles, pick-up trucks, minivans, and even bicycles. In Samawah, Iraqi SUVs rammed American armoured vehicles. Even after initial waves of such kamikaze charges were mowed down, others followed. In Baghdad, Iraqi reinforcements reoccupied devas-tated positions to resume resistance after US columns drove on. Iraqi defenders of Nasiriyah and Samawah kept fighting long after being bypassed by American spearheads. Basra's gar-rison held out through a two-week siege until defeated by a British variant on the Baghdad Thunder Runs: multiple British armoured columns drove into the urban centre and broke the resistance by direct fire. This is inconsistent with a model that Iraqi forces were too malde-ployed or too demoralized by Coalition speed or precision to offer meaningful resistance.

Of course, none of this is to suggest that Iraqi paramilitaries or SRG infantry were a serious threat to halt the Coalition advance; even at full strength, neither had much chance of hold-ing Iraq's cities against a determined assault. The Thunder Runs in Baghdad and Basra do appear to have broken the defenders' morale once it became clear to them that their best efforts were proving futile, and speed, precision, and situation awareness did leave much of the Iraqi military out of position, unwilling to fight, or destroyed by deep strikes.

What was left—what the Iraqis did manage when in close combat with Coalition ground forces on favourable, urban terrain—was in principle more than enough to have caused much heavier Coalition casualties. The Thunder Runs in Baghdad alone received a volume of fire that with historical loss rates might have been expected to have devastated at least two brigades of Coalition forces. Before the war, the US Marines estimated that even with maximum profi-ciency, their own troops could expect no better than about a 1:1 loss exchange ratio in offen-sive urban warfare. If the surviving, actively resisting components of the Iraqi paramilitary and Special Republican Guards in Iraq's cities had comprised even 10 per cent of their pre-war totals, an exchange ratio like this could easily have increased Coalition losses by a factor of ten or more. That this did not occur is thus hard to attribute to speed, precision, and situation awareness. While helpful, these capabilities did not in themselves preclude a volume of urban close combat that would normally be expected to yield much heavier casualties.

Scorched Earth in Iraq

Transformation advocates have argued that speed prevented the Iraqis from destroying the Rumaila oilfield, sabotaging the port facilities at Um Qasr, blowing the primary bridges over the Tigris and Euphrates, or flooding the Karbala Gap in 2003. Yet there is substantial evidence to suggest that Coalition speed was less important than Iraqi choices for these outcomes. Properly wired bridges, oil wells, pipelines, cranes, or levees can be blown in seconds from safe locations with the pressing of a single button. Secure landline cables connecting switchboxes with explosives would make such commands very difficult to interdict. Pre-delegated detonation authority could have afforded local commanders the ability to beat invaders to the punch even if unable to communicate with Baghdad. Had the Iraqis taken such precautions, massive damage could have been done in seconds—long before even the fastest invasion could have reached them—and the United States could not have prevented them from doing so if they had chosen to.

Of course, they did not. Far from it: in fact, the Iraqis did remarkably little to implement Saddam's threat of scorched earth. They neither prepared their infrastructure for destruction on more than a token scale, nor were they in the process of doing so, either before the war or during the fighting. On the contrary, some key facilities were left in their possession for weeks after the fighting actually began, yet were left undamaged and found unprepared for demolition when Coalition forces finally captured them. It is hard to see how the difference between a fast and a slower Coalition advance would have been decisive when even weeks of time could pass without the Iraqis implementing threats that could in principle have been realized in a fraction of that time, yet were not. At the margin, speed may have made adequate preparation harder for the Iraqis, but it could not make it impossible, and it does not appear to have been the main reason why the threat was not carried out.

Consider, for example, the issue of oilfield destruction. Of the more than 250 wells in the Rumaila oilfield, only 22 had actually been prepared for demolition when the Marines secured the field on 21 March. Of these 22, only 9 were actually detonated, causing just 7 fires. No gas–oil separation plants (GOSPs), pumping stations, or pipelines were wired for destruction. Nor was there evidence of ongoing efforts at preparing additional wells or other oilfield facilities for destruction in the days before the invasion or the early stages of the invasion itself. Twenty-two wells had been prepared for demolition in advance of the war; the Iraqis then stopped and did not significantly expand their preparations either just before or during the war's initial stages. Even after the war began, and even with a very fast-moving offensive, there were still some 48 hours available to the Iraqis between the beginning of hostilities and the time the field was actually secured—they had considerable, but unused, time for setting charges or destroying additional facilities even after they knew the war was on.

In fact, the Kirkuk oilfield in the north remained in Iraqi hands for more than three weeks after the invasion began. Yet at no point in that interval were any oil wells destroyed, or any facilities demolished, or any fires set in the Kirkuk field. No evidence of preparation for demolition was discovered when American troops finally took possession of the field after 7 April; in fact, dirt had been piled around a number of wells to protect them from accidental destruction in the fighting. Even if one were to argue that the Iraqis would have demolished Rumaila if they only had more time, at Kirkuk they had the time—by any standard. Yet they did less demolition at Kirkuk than at Rumaila.

There are many possible explanations for the Iraqis' lack of preparation, ranging from disobedience by oilfield workers to organizational incompetence in the Iraqi military to a lack of intent at the highest levels: perhaps the threat of scorched earth was merely a bluff to deter a Coalition attack. Either way, though, none of these possibilities are consistent with a claim that only a fast-moving advance prevented mass destruction of the Iraqi oil industry. None implies a process which would have yielded significantly wider destruction if the campaign had lasted weeks or even months longer than it did. If time were all the Iraqis needed, then at a minimum, Kirkuk should have been razed. Yet it was not.

Iraqi bridges, port facilities, and inundation follow a similar pattern. The Coalition advance was obviously premised on its ability to use a series of key bridges over the Euphrates River. The towns at these crossings were in fact major battlefields in the war, as the Iraqis apparently understood their importance and sought to contest the bridge sites. Yet few of these bridges were wired for demolition, and even fewer were actually destroyed. At Nasiriyah, the Iraqis fought a week-long battle for a city whose military importance turned on its bridges—yet the Iraqis made no systematic effort to destroy them. Of the five bridges surrounding Basra, only one was wired, and none were actually destroyed. At Objective Peach south of Baghdad, the key bridge was found wired for demolition, but undestroyed. The key port of Um Qasr, critical to the potential prosperity of post-war Iraq, was undamaged in the war and captured intact by Coalition forces, even though the Iraqis held the port and its facilities for two days prior to its capture and could have done extensive damage had they used this time to do so. American commanders had worried that the Iraqis would flood the Karbala Gap, a key choke point on the road to Baghdad and a potentially promising target for Iraqi weapons of mass destruction (WMD) use against stalled Coalition ground forces. Yet nothing of the kind happened—the closest the Iraqis came to deliberate flooding was some small-scale tactical inundation in the Subiyat Depression near Nasiriyah.

Key points

- There was substantial close combat against unbroken defenders in Iraq's cities in 2003, in which Coalition forces received heavy fire often at short ranges.
- Saddam Hussein had threatened a scorched earth campaign to destroy Iraq's economic infrastructure if the Coalition attacked, yet few preparations had been made to carry out this threat.
- Not speed, nor precision, nor situation awareness was sufficient to deny the Iraqis ample opportunities to inflict casualties on Coalition forces in close combat, or to destroy Iraqi oilfields, port facilities, or bridges.

An Alternative View

The transformation school's implications are thus at odds with important elements of the actual conduct of the 2001–2 and 2003 campaigns. In particular, there was too much close combat in either campaign for stand-off precision to have played the role often attributed to it, and Saddam's failure to impose higher costs via scorched earth had little to do with Coalition speed or technology. What, then, was responsible?

Part of the answer lies in idiosyncratic features of Ba'athist Iraq: the Iraqis' failure to destroy oilfields and other economic infrastructure, for example, was ultimately their choice. Either Saddam never meant to carry out this threat, or his people refused to follow his orders, or his organization proved unable to implement his plan. The failure of scorched earth was caused more by Iraqi than by Coalition actions—even a different or less capable Coalition military might still have averted scorched earth given the Iraqis' apparent unwillingness to carry out their threat, and even a very capable Coalition would have failed if the Iraqis had been able and willing to follow through.

Much of the answer, however, lies in the interaction between Coalition strengths and the enemies' particular weaknesses. Technology's performance depends heavily on its targets' behaviour: armies who present massed, exposed targets against twenty-first-century firepower suffer gravely for their error. Armies who can reduce their exposure and fight effectively from dispersed, concealed positions pose much tougher targets—and especially, targets that are very difficult to destroy through stand-off precision fires alone. The indigenous Afghan Taliban of

2001 and the Iraqi military of 2003 presented precisely the kind of massed, exposed targets against which modern technology can reach proving ground lethality levels, and when weapons' proving ground lethality is as great as today's, the results can be extremely one-sided. An exposed enemy thus enabled US firepower to destroy the Afghan Taliban at stand-off ranges, almost without close combat. While urban terrain enabled Iraqi paramilitaries and Special Republican Guards to avoid annihilation from stand-off distances, their radically exposed close-combat tactics made it possible for even a small, but well-equipped, Coalition ground force to annihilate them in close combat at very low cost to itself. By contrast, the same precision strike technology that wiped out exposed indigenous Afghan Taliban from stand-off range proved insufficient to do the same against better trained, less-exposed al-Qaeda opponents in actions such as Bai Beche, Sayed Slim Kalay, Highway 4, or Operation Anaconda. There is every reason to expect that a more skilled Iraqi opponent in 2003 would have posed much greater challenges than the exposed enemies seen in the actual event.

Iraqi Ineptitude in 2003

To see why, it is useful to review some of the more serious of the Iraqis' many military shortcomings in 2003, and how these interacted with particular Coalition strengths. Perhaps the most serious Iraqi shortcoming was their systematic failure to exploit the military potential of urban terrain. Cities offer a natural source of cover and concealment, they canalize attacks, they facilitate barrier construction, they pose difficult problems of intermingling and collateral damage avoidance, and they make effective employment of stand-off precision weapons much harder. The most plausible pre-war scenario for heavy Coalition casualties was the prospect of prolonged urban battles in the streets of Baghdad, Tikrit, Najaf, Nasiriyah, Samawah, Basra, Mosul, or Kirkuk.

Yet the Republican Guard and Iraqi Regular Army systematically avoided major cities, deploying instead in rural areas and suburban outskirts. They appear to have been deliberately denied access to major city centres by the Iraqi high command.

The great majority of the true urban combat in 2003 was waged against lightly armed irregular paramilitaries, who fought mostly on the tactical offensive, sallying out into the open to charge Coalition armoured vehicles. Not only did the paramilitaries lack the heavy weapons or armour protection of Iraq's large mechanized formations, they also forfeited the tactical potential of urban terrain by taking the offensive in exposed, unprepared frontal assaults.

More conventional SRG units deployed some heavy weapons, especially in Baghdad, but these were a tiny fraction of the total available to the Iraqi military and even the SRG failed systematically to make effective use of urban terrain for their employment. The SRG's prepared positions were almost entirely outdoors, typically in shallow foxholes dug along the roadside or in simple sandbag emplacements on building roofs or at intersections. SRG tanks were often just parked in the open at major intersections, with no effort at cover or concealment. Practically no buildings received the interior preparations that would be normal for urban warfare in Western practice, such as interior barricades, wall reinforcement, loophole construction, or wire entanglements. Outdoor obstacles, barriers, or minefields were almost completely absent.

This systematic failure to exploit urban terrain may be attributable to poor training: the Republican Guard and Iraqi Regular Army had received no instruction whatsoever in urban warfare in the years leading up to the war. In fact, Guard and Army commanders found the entire concept of city fighting unthinkable in 2003. As one Iraqi colonel put it: 'Why would anyone want to fight in a city?' His troops 'couldn't defend themselves in cities' (US Army Military History Unit 2003). Only the SRG was given any systematic training in conventional urban warfare, and even this was poor quality. The paramilitaries who shouldered much of the burden of actual city fighting in 2003 received no sustained conventional military training of any kind.

Urban Warfare and the Interaction of Iraqi Shortcomings and Coalition Strengths

The Iraqis' failure to exploit urban terrain's potential in 2003 enabled the Coalition's close combat technology—together with very skilled employment—to annihilate Iraqi urban defenders at very low cost to the Coalition attackers even without stand-off precision engagement. In particular, the modern armour technology of the US M1 and British Challenger tanks offered extraordinary protection, and their fire suppression, blast localization, and crew escape systems often made it possible to survive even a large-calibre penetration of the armour envelope. The ability of US Bradley Fighting Vehicles as well as Abrams tanks to shoot on the move with both accuracy and tremendous volumes of fire made them extremely lethal even to hostile armoured vehicles, much less paramilitary foot soldiers. For the latter to launch themselves in frontal assaults at such well-protected, highly lethal targets with nothing more than civilian pick-up trucks and RPGs was clearly suicidal. Even where the paramilitaries fought on the tactical defence, as in their resistance to 2nd Brigade's Thunder Runs in Baghdad, the combination of the paramilitaries' shortcomings and the Americans' lethality meant that tremendous numbers of Iraqis would be mowed down: without adequate cover or concealment once firing had given them away, Iraqi paramilitaries were dangerously exposed. Whereas the Iraqis' fire often missed, Coalition return fire was both voluminous and deadly accurate—exposed paramilitaries thus rarely survived to fire again (see Box 13.3).

Yet there is every reason to believe that better trained Iraqis could have produced a very different outcome even with exactly the same equipment on both sides. The light weapons wielded by Iraqi irregulars *can* penetrate M1 and Challenger tanks—in fact, at least nine M1s were disabled by RPG fire during the MCO phase of the war in Iraq. If the hundreds of RPGs fired at 2nd Brigade in the two Thunder Runs alone had been fired accurately, the penetration rate could have been dramatically higher. If the shooters had been firing from covered, concealed positions, they could reasonably have expected to survive their first shot at a much higher rate, enabling them to shoot again and thus increasing the hit rate even further.

Most important, though, a skilled urban defender could not have been broken by an all-mounted assault of the sort waged in Baghdad and Basra. The Iraqis of 2003 were exposed and could thus often be slaughtered in the open even within the city centre without the attacker dismounting from its armoured vehicles. By contrast, a defender who exploited the natural potential of urban terrain by remaining in cover to fire from within buildings, who prepared those buildings for maximum cover and concealment, who used barriers and obstacles to canalize attacks into prepared ambushes, and who used covered retreat routes

BOX 13.3 Key Events in the Major Combat Phase of the War in Iraq, 2003

The campaign in Iraq began on the night of 19-20 March with an attempt to decapitate the Iraqi regime by bombing locations where Saddam Hussein was believed to be meeting with senior lieutenants. These air strikes failed to eliminate the Iraqi leadership or induce concession, however, and a joint air–ground invasion of Iraq was launched on the night of 20–21 March.

This invasion was conducted on several fronts. In the north, US SOF teamed with air strikes and Kurdish allies on the ground in an economy of force action designed to hold Iraqi forces in place on the 'Green Line' dividing the Kurdish autonomous zone from Iraq proper. In the west, SOF and supporting US conventional forces secured potential Scud missile launching sites and searched for Iraqi WMD.

The main effort was in the south, however, where US and British conventional forces invaded Iraq from bases in Kuwait along three primary axes. On the far right, the British 1st Armoured division cleared the Faw peninsula and advanced on Basra. To their left, the US 1st Marine Expeditionary Force (I MEF) secured the Rumaila oilfields, then moved north toward Baghdad. On the far left was the US Army V Corps, led by the 3rd Infantry Division (3ID). As these forces advanced, Coalition air forces struck Iraqi air defences, command facilities, WMD-capable fire support, and combat manoeuvre units in depth.

Iraqi forces were disposed with a combination of regular army and paramilitary forces defending the major approach routes in the south. Behind them, a ring of higher-quality Republican Guard divisions defended a 'Red Line' of positions around Baghdad. Within the city itself, a combination of paramilitaries and Special Republican Guards defended prepared positions along key roads and intersections. To the north, a mix of regular army and reinforcing Republican Guard divisions defended the Green Line opposite the Kurds.

The initial advance from Kuwait moved quickly. In the process, many Iraqi units simply melted away, abandoning their arms and disappearing into Iraqi society in civilian clothes. Iraqi defenders of the southern cities of Nasiriyah, Najaf, and Samawah, however, mounted unexpectedly heavy resistance. Sharp battles at these critical river crossing sites cost the Iraqis heavy casualties while delaying the Coalition advance only slightly.

When the ground advance finally struck the Republican Guard, beginning on 31 March, it overran the remaining resistance in battles at Objectives Peach, Murray, and Montgomery, completing the encirclement of Baghdad on 7 April. In the meantime, an initial probe into the Baghdad metropolitan area proper was conducted by the 2nd Brigade Combat Team (2 BCT) of the 3rd Infantry Division; this Thunder Run consisted of a mounted raid into the city along Highway 8, then back out to a destination at the International Airport. Two days later, a second Thunder Run drove straight into the city centre, reaching and then holding positions on the Tigris River bend. Subsequent advances into Baghdad from the north and east led to the rapid collapse of the city's defences. By 9 April when the statue of Saddam in the city centre was pulled down, Ba'athist rule had effectively ended; though President Bush did not announce the end of 'major combat operations' until 1 May, for all intents and purposes the initial goal of toppling the Ba'athist regime had been accomplished by 9 April, after just 21 days of combat operations.

to slip away for subsequent engagements a couple of blocks away, would have been a much tougher target. Historically, it has been impossible to destroy such urban defenders without coupling armoured advances with dismounted infantry who can enter building interiors to clear rooms, kill concealed defenders, and hold the building interiors to prevent their re-occupation by defenders. Mounted vehicle crews simply cannot find properly concealed defenders in building interiors, and unless such defenders are cleared before the armoured vehicles advance, the vehicles' weaker roof, rear, and flank armour surfaces risk easy penetration from bypassed but unseen defenders. Working together, skilled dismounted infantry and supporting armour can clear urban terrain, but they cannot do so cheaply if the defender makes the most of that terrain: even with skilled attackers, and even with armoured support, dismounted building clearance against skilled defenders has typically been very costly. Urban warfare on the scale of Iraq's in 2003 could easily have produced thousands of Coalition casualties and a fundamentally different outcome for OIF if the Iraqi defenders had been better skilled, even given the technological advantages of the Abrams, the Bradley, and the Challenger, and even given the Coalition's speed, precision, and situation awareness.

Key points

- Iraqi defenders in 2003 systematically failed to exploit the defensive potential of urban terrain, fighting mostly outdoors and often on the tactical offensive in frontal assaults against heavily armoured Coalition forces.

- Exposure to twenty-first century firepower can be very costly; the 2003 campaign's combination of Iraqi exposure and Coalition firepower enabled Coalition forces to destroy ill-prepared urban defences with limited casualties and little need for risky dismounted building clearance.

- If the Iraqis had had the skills needed to exploit urban terrain to reduce their exposure, they could well have inflicted much heavier casualties in spite of the Coalition's technological advantages.

 ## Conclusion

The radically low cost of toppling the Taliban and Saddam cannot thus be explained by reference to Coalition strengths alone. Speed, stand-off precision, and situation awareness all surely contributed to these outcomes, and some combination of these may be sufficient to account for Saddam's or the Taliban's ouster per se. Still it is not their ouster as such that made these campaigns influential for the subsequent debate—it was the MCO campaigns' radically low cost and apparent ease that has fuelled the case for transformation. Not the Coalition's speed, its precision, nor its situation awareness were sufficient to prevent Iraq, for example, from waging enough close combat, at point-blank range under nominally favourable conditions, to have caused much higher Coalition casualties if Iraq's fighters had been tactically proficient. These Coalition strengths did not prevent Iraq from carrying out Saddam's threat of scorched earth, which was more a result of Iraqi choices than Coalition capabilities. To explain this outcome thus requires an interaction effect between friendly strengths and enemy weaknesses—and in particular, a synergy between advanced Coalition technology and a major skill imbalance in both Iraq and especially the early stages of the Afghan campaign.

This is not to say that speed is a bad idea, or that either precision or situation awareness is undesirable. Moreover, to say that with hindsight it seems unlikely that the Iraqis would have torched their oilfields or destroyed their ports with more time is not to say this could have been known at the time. A rapid advance made sense given the credible possibility that Saddam might carry out such threats, and both precision and situation awareness were important contributors to the aggregate technological sophistication needed to exploit the enemy's mistakes in both campaigns.

However, not all contributors to these campaigns' outcomes were equally important, and the difference matters, especially in post-war hindsight. Views of past wars always shape future policies, and views on the relative importance of contributing causes can have serious post-war policy implications. It makes a difference which contributors mattered most.

In particular, it would be a serious mistake to overestimate technology or speed's contribution, and to underestimate the skill differential's importance, as many accounts of these campaigns now do. Getting the relative importance of these factors wrong can lead to at least two serious dangers.

First, it could lead to a mistaken assumption that precision and situation awareness can produce similar results against other opponents with better skills than the Iraqis' or the indigenous Afghan Taliban's. Even with skilled US forces, this is a risky proposition. In 2001–2 and 2003, US technology could operate at near-proving-ground effectiveness against exposed, ill-prepared opponents. Enemies who do a better job of exploiting the natural complexity of the earth's surface for cover and concealment pose much tougher targets—as al-Qaeda (as opposed to the indigenous Afghan Taliban) showed in Afghanistan. Precision-strike technology's performance is strongly affected by the nature of its targets, and the Afghan Taliban and Iraqi military's targets were extremely permissive in 2001–2 and 2003. To overlook this is to risk exaggerating technology's potential against better skilled enemies.

Second, misunderstanding cause and effect in Afghanistan and Iraq could lead to a mistaken assumption that speed can substitute for mass, and that stand-off precision can substitute for close combat capability. If speed were sufficient to explain these campaigns' outcomes (either alone or in conjunction with precision), and if speed and mass are antithetical, then reducing mass to enable greater speed would make sense. However, if speed was *not* sufficient, and if unskilled enemies were necessary to produce the apparent successes of stand-off precision in 2001–2 and 2003, then to trade speed for mass in US force structure would be a dangerous bargain. Against enemies like Iraq or the indigenous Afghan Taliban, small, fast-moving ground forces with massive stand-off firepower and excellent situation awareness may well succeed again—in fact, against such foes this could well be the optimum solution—but if future warfare involves better skilled opponents, then a small but agile US ground force could find itself unable to cope with concealed, covered enemies in numbers too great to overcome without mass of its own.

This in turn suggests that the common use of Iraq and Afghanistan as evidence to fuel transformation proposals is often mistaken. The ineptitude of Saddam's and the Taliban's militaries played an important role in the low cost of major combat operations. If one cannot guarantee such inept enemies in the future, then one must be cautious in drawing implications from these conflicts for force planning and defence policy.

 Questions

1. How did transformation advocates in 2001–3 believe the US military must change to meet the challenges of modern warfare?

2. In what ways does the experience of major combat in Afghanistan and Iraq support the transformation argument?

3. Are there inconsistencies between the transformation thesis' expectations and the actual conduct of MCO in Afghanistan and Iraq?

4. In what ways were the Afghan and Iraq campaigns similar? What were the most important differences?

5. How did the nature of the fighting in Afghanistan change over the course of the 2001–2 campaign?

6. Why was the Coalition loss rate so low in the 2003 invasion of Iraq?

7. If the Iraqi military had used US or British tactics and methods, what effect would this have had on the performance of Coalition technology?

8. Before 2003, some had argued that a war in Iraq should be fought using the 'Afghan Model', that is, replacing large, conventional US ground forces with small numbers of SOF commandos, PGMs, and indigenous allies. Would this have been wise or unwise in light of what we now know of the conduct of the Afghan and Iraqi campaigns?

9. The US Army has been evaluating a variety of proposals for lighter, faster, more transportable armoured vehicles that would rely on networked information for survivability rather than on

weight of armour protection. How might such vehicles have fared in the invasion of Iraq, and what does the 2003 Iraq experience imply for the viability of such proposals?

10. To what degree are the Afghan and Iraq campaigns useful guides to future warfare?

Further Reading

Systematic histories of major combat in Afghanistan and Iraq are only beginning to appear. Probably the best one-volume treatments to date in what is still a very limited literature are:

G. Berntsen and R. Pezzullo, *Jawbreaker: The Attack on Bin Laden and Al-Qaeda: A Personal Account by the CIA's Key Field Commander* (New York, NY: Crown Publishers, 2006).
A detailed account of critical events in the early phase of the Afghan campaign.

G. Fontenot, E. J. Degen, and D. Tohn, *On Point: The United States Army in Operation Iraqi Freedom* (Fort Leavenworth, KS: US Army Training and Doctrine Command, 2004).
The US Army's official history of the invasion of Iraq; very detailed on unit movements and battles.

M. Gordon and B. Trainor, *Cobra II: The Inside Story of the Invasion and Occupation of Iraq* (New York: Random House, 2006).
Especially strong on the pre-war campaign planning for the invasion of Iraq.

T. Ricks, *Fiasco: The American Military Adventure in Iraq* (New York: Penguin, 2006).
The best critique of the US invasion of Iraq.

K. Sepp, R. Kiper, J. Schroder, C. Briscoe, *Weapon of Choice: US Army Special Operations in Afghanistan* (Fort Leavenworth, KS: US Army Command and General Staff College Press, 2004).
The US Army's official history of the early stages of the war in Afghanistan; extensive details on planning and logistics for special forces' employment.

By contrast, the literature on military transformation is both voluminous and growing. Good starting points include:

S. Biddle, *Military Power: Explaining Victory and Defeat in Modern Battle* (Princeton, NJ: Princeton University Press, 2004).
Provides more extensive theoretical and historical perspectives on the argument in the chapter text above.

A. Cebrowski and J. Garstka, 'Network-Centric Warfare', *U.S. Naval Institute Proceedings* (January 1998).
An influential argument on networked information's future role, by two prominent transformation advocates.

E. Cohen, 'A Revolution in Warfare', *Foreign Affairs* 75/2 (March/April 1996), 37–54.
A classic account from an early and influential transformation advocate.

US Joint Forces Command, *A Concept for Rapid Decisive Operations* (Norfolk, VA: Joint Forces Command J9 Joint Futures Lab, 2001).
An official blueprint for operations in the transformed future.

Web Links

Federation of American Scientists: **http://www.fas.org/programs/ssp/man/miltutorials/general_ intro.html** Tutorials on the aircraft, ground and naval assets, missiles, and munitions at the centre of the Transformation debate.

US Department of Defense Annual Report on Afghanistan: **http://www.defense.gov/news/ 1230_1231Report.pdf** The US Department of Defense's annual report on progress in the Afghan counterinsurgency campaign following the 2001–2 invasion.

US Department of Defense Iraq reports: **http://www.defense.gov/home/features/iraq_reports/** The US Department of Defense's quarterly reports on progress in stabilizing Iraq.

Brookings Institution's Afghanistan and Iraq indexes: **http://www.brookings.edu/~/media/Files/ Programs/FP/afghanistan%20index/index.pdf** and **http://www.brookings.edu/saban/ iraq-index.aspx** These indexes provide a combination of historical and current statistics on progress in each theatre of war since the respective invasions.

Iraq Coalition Casualty Count: **http://icasualties.org/** An independent source of data on casualties in Afghanistan and Iraq since the US interventions, covering US and allied military and civilian deaths and injuries.

Council on Foreign Relations: **http://www.cfr.org/region/iraq/ri405** and **http://www.cfr.org/region/ afghanistan/ri280** Analyses of Iraq and Afghanistan by Council on Foreign Relations analysts and affiliates.

Homeland Security:
A New Strategic Paradigm?

JACOB N. SHAPIRO AND RUDOLPH P. DARKEN

 ## Chapter Contents

Introduction	268
A New Threat?	268
What Should Preparations Look Like?: Dealing with the Small-N Problem	273
What is the United States Preparing For?	274
Conclusion	282

 ## Reader's Guide

How has the threat of catastrophic terrorism reshaped the strategic environment? We argue that in fact the threat is not dramatically new: what is new is the salience of this threat to the public in some states, particularly the United States. However, the secretive nature of counterterrorism actions necessarily means that the public is ill-informed about the potential efficacy of government's activities and so cannot assess if their rhetoric matches their actions. Thus public statements can easily be tailored to what decision-makers think the public wants to hear, rather than to what decision-makers genuinely believe. We consequently rely on an examination of how the United States budgets and exercises for the war on terrorism to illuminate what American decision-makers believe are the links between domestic counterterror operations and strategy. Along the way we look at the tools states have to prepare for counterterrorism, and the challenges of doing so. We find strong evidence that the United States remains strategically focused on relationships between states, and argue that this is probably an appropriate focus.[1]

Introduction

On September the 11th, 2001, America and the world witnessed a new kind of war. We saw the great harm that a stateless network could inflict upon our country, killers armed with box cutters, mace, and 19 airline tickets. Those attacks also raised the prospect of even worse dangers—of other weapons in the hands of other men. The greatest threat before humanity today is the possibility of secret and sudden attack with chemical or biological or radiological or nuclear weapons.[2]
President George W. Bush, 11 February 2004

It has become something of a truism to say that 'the world changed on the morning of September 11th'. Indeed, the introduction to this volume makes that very argument. This chapter is sceptical of that claim, at least with respect to strategy. We believe that in fact the threat of transnational terrorism is not a new phenomenon, nor is the scale of destruction threatened by transnational Islamist terrorist groups discontinuous with past terrorist campaigns, nor are the goals of the current threat out of line with past experience. In sum, it is not a phenomenon demanding a radically new strategic response. That said, there can be no doubt that the salience of terrorism as a political issue has increased out of proportion to the impact of terrorism on Western societies: but if the salience of terrorism has increased to domestic publics, does that necessarily mean those concerned with the exercise of military power for political objectives need a new paradigm?

This chapter examines the challenges involved in preparing the domestic response to the terrorist threat and compares the actions these suggest to the preparations actually being made by the United States. We find a puzzling disconnect between what must theoretically be done to adequately combat this adversary, and what is being done on a daily basis. One explanation is that the government simply does not know what to do. Rejecting this perspective, we suggest that the United States is behaving as though terrorism after 9/11 does not require a new response, or at least not more than a rebalancing of the current response. Instead, the United States maintains an artificial distinction between what has been termed Homeland Security, Homeland Defense, and counterterrorism actions overseas. This artificial distinction is a key indicator that American leaders remain focused on traditional concerns about the use of force between nation states. Our analysis suggests that given the challenges of properly preparing to meet the terrorist threat in contrast to the low expected costs of not doing so optimally, this is an appropriate choice. We begin our analysis by examining claims about how new, or different this threat might be.

A New Threat?

Four claims are generally made to support the argument that after 9/11, the world faced a dramatically different strategic environment. The first is that transnational terrorism, groups operating without geographically defined objectives, requires a strategic response that is different from that required by nationalist groups. The second is that modern communications technology and the ready availability of technical know-how have rendered transnational organizations newly capable of achieving strategic impact. The third is that the frequency of attacks around the world has increased to the point where terrorism should be a matter of central strategic concern. The fourth is that the ideology behind the Islamist groups of current concern drives them to seek a fundamentally new scale of destruction. In other words, their goals are sufficiently different to require a different strategic response. We argue that none of these claims can stand up to scrutiny (see Box 14.1).

A New Strategic Response?

To evaluate what may be different about today's transnational groups requires a careful parsing of the strategic objectives of transnational terrorist organizations. Al-Qaeda's strategic plan, as espoused by Ayman Al-Zawahiri, entails several steps. Step one is to compel Western powers to stop supporting apostate Arab regimes. Step two is to replace these regimes with an Islamic caliphate, something only possible once they no longer have Western support. Step three is to expand the caliphate to spread Islamic rule to the world. This type of plan is nothing new. Left-wing terrorist organizations in Europe have held similar goals since the 1890s. The Italian Red Brigades, for example, also had a three-stage plan. Stage one was to conduct terrorist attacks to both mobilize industrial workers to communist causes, and to weaken the state. Stage two was to lead a revolution within Italy. Stage three was to spread the revolution to other states in Western Europe. The similarities in the ideological plans are striking.

While transnational goals are not new, what may be new is that the proximate targets for the first stage of al-Qaeda's plan are located in many different states. Yet this too is not fundamentally different. The Palestine cause was moved to the front burner of Israeli–Arab relations by a series of attacks outside Israel. The most important of these were a series of eight attacks by the Popular Front for the Liberation of Palestine (PFLP) against commercial airliners between July 1968 and September 1970, and the 1972 Black September attacks at the Munich Olympics (Abrahms 2004). In the case of the PFLP attacks, three were against Israeli

---

BOX 14.1 Key Terms

- *Counterterrorism*. Refers to the practices, strategies, and policies that governments employ to fight terrorism.

- *Terrorism*. Over 120 definitions have been offered. The authors prefer the following: the use of force by non-state actors that: (1) is intended to influence an audience beyond its immediate victims; and (2) violates the standards of discretion and proportionality for the use of force under the customary Law of Armed Conflict.

- *Transnational terrorism*. Following Enders and Sandler (2004), we define an incident as transnational when an incident in one country involves victims, targets, or institutions of at least one other country. Thus, an attack by Iraqis, on Iraqis, intended to influence Americans is transnational terrorism, as is an attack in Spain, by North African immigrants, intended to influence Spain.

- *Homeland Security*. The American catch-all term that refers to all non-military actions taken to protect people on American territory from terrorism, industrial disasters, and natural disasters. Homeland Security does not include Homeland Defense, the term for all military actions taken within the United States Northern Command area of responsibility (AOR) to protect the United States from threats by external actors, both state and non-state.

airlines operating in Europe, five were against American or European airlines. Notice that the targets were neither geographically concentrated, nor were they all of one nationality. Instead, the idea was to sow terror broadly to compel a change in state policy, a similar mode of action to that taken by current Islamist groups.

What was the strategic response to these attacks, what ended this wave of transnational terrorism? Two elements were critical. The first was the installation of additional security precautions in airports, including metal detectors. This forced terrorists to move out of hijacking into less efficient methods of sowing terror, such as individual kidnappings (Enders and Sandler 2004). The second critical element was recognition by the Palestinian leadership that while terrorism brought political attention, it was not bringing the desired changes. In the case of the PFLP, the goal was to serve as a Marxist revolutionary vanguard, not simply to bring attention to the Palestinian cause (Abrahms 2004: 536–7). The transnational goals of the PFLP in the late 1960s had more in common with al-Qaeda's goals than with those of its nationalist contemporaries. In the case of the PLO, the negative public reaction to the Munich attacks led the group to disavow links to Black September, to essentially retire that organization. Notice that neither critical element involved the use of military power by states to achieve the political goal of ending transnational terrorist attacks. Historically, dealing successfully with transnational terrorism has not required a strategic response. Rather, it has required some combination of political change and effective law enforcement and counterterrorism activities.

A New Level of Impact?

Now consider the claim that changes in technology have rendered groups newly capable of achieving strategic impact. The concern here is with Thomas Friedman's 'super empowered individuals' (Friedman 2002). Friedman and others rest their arguments on an analysis of the immediate destructiveness of attacks. They suggest that the ready availability of information on how to make bombs, or the potential use of contagious biological agents facilitated by advances in bio-technology, make individual attacker's orders of magnitude more dangerous than before.[3] This cannot be a satisfactory perspective for strategists who see violence as but a means to an end. From a strategic perspective, the well-placed bullet, or well-timed grenade, can have impact commensurate with the largest of bombs. In June 1914 Gavrillo Princip, a member of the left-wing militant group Narodna Odbrana, triggered a chain of events leading to the First World War by killing Archduke Franz Ferdinand of Austria. That war killed millions and set the stage for the Second World War 21 years later. Certainly Princip had strategic impact far beyond that of the 9/11 plotters, even though the immediate destructiveness of his attack paled in comparison.

Note also that questions about destructiveness cannot be considered in isolation from the overall level of activity in a society. Here there is little good empirical evidence. Abadie and Gardeazabal (2004) provide evidence that in a rich country (Spain), terrorist activities (by the Basque separatists) have significant negative macroeconomic consequences. Blomberg, Hess, and Orphanides (2004) show an inverse relationship between terrorism and investment in poor countries, especially in Africa. However, neither study shows that these negative consequences are increasing over time.

By the United States government's own estimates, the potential economic costs of most major terrorist attack scenarios are small compared to those of natural disasters and even of labour disruptions. According to the April 2005 draft National Planning Scenarios, the estimated costs of a biological attack using the plague bacterium is millions of dollars, while that of a chemical attack with a blister agent is US$500 million. By comparison, cost estimates for the 11-day closure of 29 west coast ports due to a 2002 dock-workers' strike range between US$140 million and US$2 billion per day for a minimum cost of US$1.5 billion. Even the 9/11 attacks do not exceed the scale of the worst natural disasters. Insurance payouts related to the 9/11 attacks totalled approximately US$20 billion, less than the US$20.8 billion paid out for Hurricane Andrew and far less than the estimated US$125 billion cost of Hurricane Katrina.[4]

The most recent example of the use of technology as a force multiplier was not anticipated by Friedman and others. The impact of social media on the recent 'Arab Spring' events was profound. While it did not directly bring to bear a new threat or potential to destroy life or property, it did show how technology can vastly shorten the links of a social network and thus accelerate a desired outcome. In this case, the desired outcome was not terrorism but rather political reform. It could be that social media is in some ways reducing the terrorist threat by offering an alternative (and a proven successful alternative at that) to terrorism as a means to political change. In the context of this discussion, even this instance does not make the case for a new strategy based on increased destructiveness.

None of this is meant to argue that terrorism is not a serious problem. We simply seek to point out that, when considered within the context of the massive increases in economic activity over the last 50 years, the relative destructiveness of terrorism has not increased in a way that demands fundamental rethinking of strategy.

Communications and the Frequency of Terror

Perhaps communications technology and new modes of organization have led to a sufficiently large increase in the rate of attacks worldwide that strategists should be more concerned with terrorism than before. The statistical evidence for a secular increase in the rate of terrorism since 1990 is quite ambiguous, with total attacks dropping from 1990–2001 and then increasing until 2006 when the numbers began to decline again.[5] The deadliness of incidents has gone up over that period, but has been rising much more slowly than the total number of incidents. What has increased substantially since 1990 is the use of the most spectacular terrorist tactic, suicide terrorism. However, if the communications revolution were the cause of this increase, then we should see a steady increase in the use of suicide terrorism by all groups that employ it as communications technology spreads more deeply. This has not been the case, leading us to believe the increase is driven by the strategic dynamics of particular conflicts, and not by a secular change in technology.

Note also that these findings come from data that does not count incidents that are of a terrorist nature but are not labelled terrorist (e.g. massacres of civilians in rural Africa). Consequently, the data cannot distinguish between an increasing reliance on terrorism as a tactic, or a general secular increase in the number and activity level of rebellions and violent social movements. Nor can the data tell us whether an increase in terrorism reflects an increase in the frequency of terrorist acts, or an increasing tendency for governments to label acts as terrorist because of the new political salience of terrorism.

Furthermore, there is scant evidence to confirm that any increase in terrorist activity is due to increased electronic communication capabilities or that the Internet and other advances broaden the population of terrorists more than was previously possible. In fact, the most widespread terrorist movement of the last 200 years, the anarchist movement of the 1890s and 1900s which killed thousands, spread its ideology and inspired attackers throughout the world without the benefit of electronic communications.

New Destructiveness Demands a New Strategy?

The evidence is equally ambiguous as to the last claim, that Islamist groups have fundamentally more destructive goals than past groups. Certainly an examination of the strategic writings of jihadi groups reveals the same fundamental task that preoccupies leaders of other terrorist organizations: the controlled use of violence for well-specified political ends (Al-Zawahiri 2001; Lia and Hegghammer 2004). The organizational manuals and lessons-learned pamphlets of these groups suggest they struggle with the same organizational dilemma that has plagued covert extremist organizations since the 1890s: how to achieve the appropriate use of violence in an environment in which identification by the government equals operational failure. Islamist groups struggle with these dilemmas because excessive violence hurts their cause. Foreign terrorist organizations in Iraq dealt themselves a fatal political blow by engaging in too much wanton violence. Al-Qaeda's then second in command Ayman al-Zawahiri warned about this problem in July 2005 and by late 2006, Iraqi militias had turned against the foreign fighters and began driving them out of many areas.

Even if we accept the proposition that Islamist terrorist groups simply seek to maximize violence, this is nothing new. In the 1970s the Bader Meinhoff Gang attempted to acquire tactical nuclear weapons from the United States' arsenal in Europe, while members of Aum Shinrikyo successfully acquired and used sarin, a nerve agent (Sagan 2005).

A more problematic point is that those who argue that the new destructiveness of terrorist attacks demands more offensive strategies do not show that such strategies will reduce the risk of catastrophic terrorist attack. There are a number of reasons why taking the offensive may not mitigate the risks of attacks. Chief among these is that offensive actions may create more terrorists than they destroy. Former United States Secretary of Defense Donald Rumsfeld addressed the uncertainty behind an offensive strategy when he famously asked:, 'Are we capturing, killing or deterring and dissuading more terrorists every day than the madrassas and the radical clerics are recruiting, training, and deploying against us . . . Is our current situation such that the harder we work, the behinder we get?' (Rumsfeld 2003). He is right to be concerned. An interesting finding from the Israeli–Palestinian conflict is that targeted killings can be counterproductive, increasing the stock of terrorists because they serve as a recruiting call (Kaplan et al. 2005). Conventional arrests do not have this counterproductive effect. So if the probability of a catastrophic attack is increasing the number of active terrorists, an offensive strategy may actually increase the net risk of catastrophic terrorism.

Does the Current Threat Demand a New Strategy?

We found little support for the claims that the terrorist threat today is dramatically worse than it has been in the past. We thus argue that a new strategic response is not needed. However, while the mechanics of the threat are not new, the political salience of the threat is, particularly in the United States. As the threat does not merit a new strategic response, but does merit a new political response, we should not be surprised to see a great divergence between what government claims to be doing to prepare for terrorism, and what government actually does. In the next section we will explore what preparations for this threat should look like, in order to better answer the question of what the United States is preparing for.

Key points

- The transnational goals of the current Islamist terrorist organizations are not a new phenomenon: many terrorist groups have had transnational goals in the past.

- Historically, successful responses to transnational terrorism have not involved a new strategic perspective, but rather a combination of political change and law enforcement.

- Evidence does not support the claim that technology has given terrorists the capability to achieve a fundamentally greater level of destruction.

- Evidence does not support the claim that modern communications have increased the frequency of terrorist actions or that modern communications have increased the number of terrorists.

- Evidence does not support the claim that modern terrorists have more destructive goals than previous terrorist threats.

What Should Preparations Look Like?: Dealing with the Small-N Problem

During the cold war, the threat against which Western countries had to prepare was a well-defined adversary: the Soviet bloc. Strategy was made simple by the fact that it could be designed with only one enemy in mind. In dealing with terrorism, the 'adversary' isn't one alliance system with a unified command and control organization, but many smaller, highly varied organizations. Jemaah Islamiyah is organized in a fairly hierarchical fashion, mimicking traditional military structures. The cells involved in the 2004 Madrid bombings were organized around a small core of charismatic leaders who used their connections to draw on a wide variety of individuals for particular resources and expertise. Hamas is somewhere in between. Consequently, any 'model' of the adversary is likely to be misleading. Thus, crafting a serious strategic response to terrorist operations requires taking into account the great variety of terrorist organizations. This poses tremendous problems for government.

Essentially, building models that can handle the variety of terrorist organizations, and help government craft strategies against them, depends on having a large amount of data. Unfortunately, such data does not exist because the number and frequency of attacks by terrorist organizations is inherently low. This 'small-N' problem means that it is quite difficult, if not impossible, for government to track trends and tendencies in the behaviour of a terrorist adversary. Because the adversary's activities do not follow a strong central tendency, policy adaptation is quite difficult.[6] Changes made in response to one threat may open up a series of new vulnerabilities. To deal with these data problems would require a robust exercise programme with a substantial simulation and experimentation component. As we will show, such elements are noticeably lacking, at least in the United States.

There is another, more problematic, 'small-N' issue related to what government must prepare for. In designing programmes to deal with large-scale warfare against the Soviet bloc, American military planners could safely prepare the best response to the other side's average operating patterns. Against a terrorist threat, government must get it right for each cell. It is no longer enough to figure out what is the right strategy on average. Thus, while government is getting less data than before on how the enemy will behave, government's responses must be more discriminating and carefully calibrated. Simply put, there isn't enough data to model any of the terrorist organizations well, and modelling the 'average' adversary doesn't model any of them at all.

Given the analytical challenges presented by the very nature of the terrorist threat, it is unlikely that a single strategy can be articulated. However, a number of areas for increased attention can be identified. First, the lack of a central tendency to the threat places a significant weight on collecting operational intelligence as a primary prevention mechanism. Second, because an offensive military strategy can be counterproductive—by increasing the total number of terrorists—and because it is impossible to kill all terrorists overseas, local law enforcement must play the major role in prevention. Getting good at filling this role requires that local police officers should be able to respond to information generated within the intelligence community. This in turn requires systems to share information and exercises to practise using them. Third, border security takes on an added importance because of the essentially infinite target set found within the United States. Fourth, a greater focus should be placed on securing the most dangerous weapons and materials. Fifth, the small-N problem we've already discussed means that preparing for a highly variable threat is critical. Given the problematic data on terrorism, the best way to prepare is through simulation and exercises that incorporate the variety of adversaries we actually face, rather than using a standardized threat.

If the terrorist threat is truly grave, then preparedness efforts should place significant attention on these five focus areas. As we show in the next section, only border security, and to a lesser extent the use of intelligence in prevention, are receiving that attention.

Key points

- The number of terrorist events useful for analysis is still so small that it is difficult to statistically determine patterns of behaviour or to predict future trends.

- Current models of the terrorist adversary are generalized across the data. This means they do not match any specific adversary.

- If the threat does merit a new strategy, that strategy should include placing increased attention on five areas: Intelligence as a prevention mechanism, the use of intelligence by local law enforcement, border security, securing WMD, and preparing for a highly variable threat.

What is the United States Preparing For?

Given that no major international attacks have occurred in the United States since 9/11, and given that many strategic actions are largely invisible to analysts, there are two places to look to understand how the United States is preparing for this adversary: budgets and exercises.

By investigating both budgeting choices and the US exercise programme we can develop a holistic view of the nation's strategic perspective on counterterrorism and Homeland Security; we can develop insight into what the American decision-makers feel is most important. In this section we will examine the five focus areas implied by the nature of the terrorist threat:

1. Collecting operational intelligence for prevention;
2. Creating an effective link between operational intelligence and law enforcement;
3. Border security;
4. Securing the most dangerous weapons and materials; and
5. Preparing to respond to a highly variable threat.

Operational Intelligence Collection and the Link to Law Enforcement

In the previous section, collecting operational intelligence and the link to law enforcement were identified as critical focus areas given the nature of the terrorist threat. Because American intelligence budgets are classified, and because efforts to collect operational intelligence against terrorists are among the most highly classified programmes in government, we cannot directly assess how much emphasis is being placed on intelligence for counterterrorism. We do know from press accounts that significant technical and human intelligence assets were shifted from counterterrorism targets to prepare for the 2003 invasion of Iraq, but we do not know the impact of these shifts (Stone 2003).

What we can observe is how the American intelligence community participates in exercises, especially in the National Exercise Program. By observing this participation we can answer two questions: (1) does the intelligence community appear to be preparing to collect against an adversary that matches the characteristics of terrorist groups? and (2) are the intelligence and law-enforcement communities realistically practising the sharing of information to disrupt and prevent terrorist attacks?

On both counts, the answer is no. The reason is that the exercise programme for homeland security relies on models developed for traditional military engagements. In military simulations, intelligence is highly constrained and predictable, with an emphasis on the use of sensors and digital streams of data where the signal-to-noise ratio—the amount of correct information relative to bad information—is quite high. The key intelligence challenge in these simulations is for the intelligence system to distribute the raw data through systems that are designed for handling classified data to people with clearances. Combat units then act on this information according to well-defined doctrine.

Notice how different this is from the intelligence challenge in counterterrorism. In counterterrorism the analyst must first sort through false alarms and ambiguous reporting to find information that is truly about terrorists. He faces an extremely low signal-to-noise ratio, relies much more heavily on human intelligence, and must interpret this data in light of an enemy whose operating patterns are highly variable. The resulting warnings and actionable intelligence must then be scrubbed of information on sources and methods so that they can be passed to law enforcement organizations that lack the classified systems and cleared personnel to receive them in raw form. Finally, these organizations must act on the information without the benefit of standardized doctrine or rules of engagement.

The challenging tasks involved in developing operational intelligence against terrorist organizations and acting on it have only recently been incorporated into exercise play. The National Exercise Program[7] first included in intelligence play with the third Top Officials Exercise (TOPOFF-3). Here the intelligence play focused on the passing of intelligence injects to relevant homeland security officials in several nations. Two critical elements were not exercised. First, the exercise did not test the ability of intelligence analysts to pick out and integrate relevant information from the stream of reports crossing their desks. This is understandable given that the press of real-world concerns makes it hard to flood analysts with exercise intelligence, but it still indicates an unwillingness to sacrifice some intelligence in non-terror areas to better prepare intelligence analysts for counterterrorism. Second, the exercise did not stress the ability of the intelligence community to pass information received from classified channels rapidly down to local law enforcement.

In TOPOFF-4 improvements were made, but it still appears that the role of intelligence is mainly as injects for other aspects of the exercise (Department of Homeland Security 2007a). In the TOPOFF-4 After Action Quick Look Report, an objective of the exercise was 'to test the handling and flow of operational and time-critical intelligence between agencies prior to, and in response to, a linked terrorist incident'. Part of this was accomplished through an Arizona-based fusion centre that allowed for information sharing from federal to state and local levels. While this is a clear improvement, the actual end effect of information sharing in terms of prevention, response, or mitigation is not apparent—and that is the point of information sharing in the first place.

So, while there have been recent improvements in intelligence community participation in a variety of exercises, the fact remains that intelligence has historically been the 'odd man out'. Intelligence is used for injects that stimulate actions of other players in an exercise, but analysts ability to recognize the right signals, to share this information, and to determine the end effect of their actions is not being trained. Having intelligence participate in an exercise and having intelligence analysts benefit from the exercise are not the same thing. TOPOFF-4 happens to be one of the better examples of effective exercising of intelligence. The TOPOFF exercise series has since been discontinued but the National Exercise Program remains very active. As we look beyond the National Exercise Program into state and local exercises, the problem intensifies. Not only is there little to no intelligence play in state and local exercises, but the role of local law enforcement in using and developing intelligence is almost never addressed. When we read about problems of 'information sharing' and the complications associated with it, we mean intelligence sharing from the Federal level down to the local, and vice versa. This is exactly the second focus area we identified. Unfortunately, notwithstanding official statements to the contrary, we could find no evidence that either of the first two focus areas is receiving serious attention.

Border Security

In the area of border security, we do see increased spending and exercise activity since 2001. Border security has been the focus of considerable attention in both the national and state exercise programmes. At the federal level, United States Northern Command (NORTHCOM), the American military command responsible for the continental United

States, has participated in a number of exercises that involve border security. These exercises have not focused on the detection of threats crossing the border, but have still focused on important issues. For example, Ardent Sentry included a biological outbreak in Mexico and examined the repercussions to Border States. A number of exercises have included mass migration issues. More typically, a terrorist successfully crossing a border into the US is used as the backdrop to an exercise. TOPOFF-2 examined issues related to the Canadian border in the Pacific north-west. While not a focus of TOPOFF-4, the inclusion of the US Territory of Guam introduced elements of border security as related to the specific objectives of the exercise. At the state and local level, border states are actively involved in exercises that include border security. Arizona, for example, has participated in several exercises that involve the economic impact of restricting border crossings, checking visas during a mass exodus from Mexico, and shutting down a port of entry in response to a terrorist threat.

Notice though that none of these exercises has focused on what matters about border security for counterterrorism: the ability to catch terrorists trying to cross the border. To our knowledge, there has been no 'red teaming' in which government agents test the effectiveness of border security by trying to cross with false documents or under names that should trigger suspicion.

The picture appears equally mixed when we examine spending priorities. Federal spending on border security increased from US$5.5 billion in 2001, to US$8.5 billion in 2002, and reached only US$8.7 billion in 2005 (Congressional Budget Office 2005: 6). Compared to an overall 300 per cent increase in discretionary spending for homeland security during the four years after 9/11, the increase in border security spending looks paltry. Much of the increase in border security funding has gone towards technical detection equipment that makes the borders more secure against groups trying to smuggle in radiological or chemical weapons. However, as Flynn (2004) points out, the number of detection systems is still woefully inadequate to the task at hand. This suggests to us that the increased budgeting for border security is driven less by a desire to secure the United States against a strategic threat, than by border-state legislators who see spending on border security as an effective way to get more direct federal spending to their districts.

Securing the Most Dangerous Weapons and Materials

The gravest potential threat posed by terrorists is that they might acquire and detonate a nuclear weapon or other weapon of mass destruction (WMD) in a major city. Thus, securing WMD worldwide, and securing targets whose attack through conventional means can lead to WMD-scale destruction, should be a major strategic goal if we believe the threat of terrorism is so grave. Yet, funding for the Nunn-Lugar Cooperative Threat Reduction Program to help the states of the former Soviet Unions secure nuclear weapons and materials has not been dramatically increased since 9/11. United States government funding for Nunn-Lugar was higher in 2000, US$458.1 million, than it has been in any year since.[8] Moreover, efforts to secure nuclear stockpiles in the United States have not been treated with great urgency. In late 2003 a Government Accountability Office (GAO) report revealed that security at American nuclear weapons production and storage facilities did not meet the currently required standards, and that those standards were too low for the threat at hand.[9]

The situation is even starker with respect to targets that can be hit with traditional means to yield WMD-scale destruction. Chemical plants represent the greatest threat in this category, and so are illustrative of the government response. Recent DHS analysis suggests that 'about 600 facilities could potentially threaten between 100,000 and a million people.[10] About 2,000 facilities could potentially threaten between 10,000 and 100,000 people.' Based on an analysis of all terrorist attacks against chemical facilities since 1900, Kosal (2005) identifies several strategies that would best prevent mass casualties in the aftermath of an attack. These strategies include:

1. enhancing perimeter security;

2. modifying certain processes to reduce the risks of release;

3. switching to less toxic precursors and solvents;

4. minimizing the amount of stored materials by switching to more 'just in time' production; and

5. strengthening the physical structures in chemical plants.

None of these steps would enhance profitability, so they would require government mandates. Yet the current United States approach to chemical plant security has been to request voluntary increases in perimeter security. No additional security mandates have been issued. This suggests strongly that the United States government does not view securing the most dangerous materials as a strategic imperative.

This view is supported by what we know about TOPOFF-4 (Department of Homeland Security 2007b) which was based on National Planning Scenario No. 11 (NPS-11), a radiological attack, most likely some form of 'dirty bomb'. It had three coordinated attacks, the first being a dirty bomb detonation in Guam followed by similar attacks in Portland and Phoenix. From the after-action reports, it appears that rather than focusing on securing dangerous materials, TOPOFF-4 was geared more towards response and mitigation, assuming the attack was imminent.

Preparing for a Highly Varied Threat

The best insight we have on what type of threat the United States is preparing for comes from the National Planning Scenarios. The scenarios include a nuclear detonation, anthrax attacks, biological disease outbreaks, pandemic influenza, chemical or radiological weapons, and natural disasters. The scenarios are meant to be templates or starting points for exercise development, not as a literal exercise design. Even so, it is apparent that the focus of the scenarios is on post-event activities, not pre-event or prevention activities. Further, there is clearly a bias towards WMD-focused exercises: 8 of 15 scenarios involve WMD. This reveals an assumption that the current adversary specifically wants to maximize damage and/or loss of life. Only the cyber-attack scenario would deal with a scenario where the adversary seeks to trigger an economic disaster. Yet, we know from Al-Zawahiri (2001) and other sources that economic disruption is as strategically important to al-Qaeda as physical devastation. There are many ways in which an adversary can cause economic devastation without using large-scale physical devastation. In fact most of the scenarios do not closely match historical evidence on the weapons of choice for modern terrorist actions. So who is the threat behind these scenarios?

The most telling piece of the puzzle is the 'Universal Adversary' (UA). The UA is intended to be a generic adversary developed for the purpose of simulation. While many of the details of the UA are classified, we know that the UA is meant to cover a number of categories of conspirators including:

- Foreign (Islamic) terrorists;
- Domestic radical groups (e.g. antiwar, civil rights, environmentalist, and right-wing groups);
- State-sponsored adversaries (e.g. rogue states);
- Disgruntled employees.

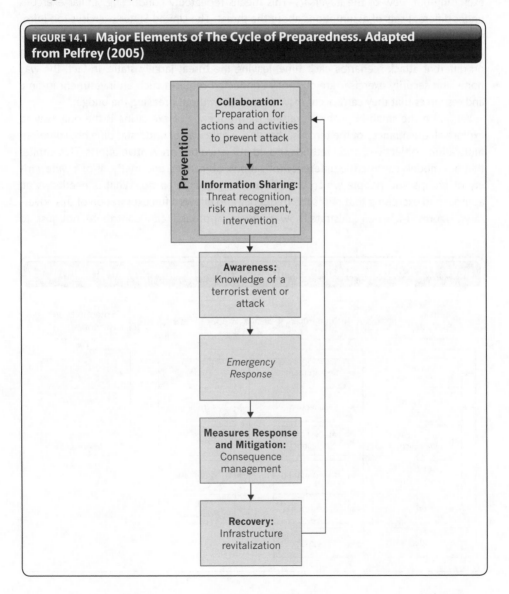

FIGURE 14.1 **Major Elements of The Cycle of Preparedness. Adapted from Pelfrey (2005)**

Within any one of these subgroups, the variability in behaviour is enormous. Taken over all of these groups, the UA becomes so general as to be meaningless. This generality has pernicious effects. By preparing for a general adversary, we don't prepare for any threat we are likely to face. The Department of Homeland Security seems to be agreeing with this view as the use of the UA has been far less evident in recent exercises than it has been in past years. However, there also does not appear to be a specific plan for what to replace the UA with that will be more representative of the actual threat. In recent years we have seen an increase in funding for human behavioural modelling that would in part address this shortfall, but results thus far have had minimal impact. We expect to see continued work in this area in the coming years.

Getting around this problem, exercising to meet a highly variable threat, would require exercising our view of the adversary. This means repeatedly conducting similar exercises under different sets of assumptions about the threat. The United States exercises too infrequently to be able to do this. When active, TOPOFF exercises happened every two years, leaving little room for variability in the adversary. Other exercises happen quarterly, but focus on different attack scenarios each time, leaving the threat largely static. In fact, the way homeland security exercises are currently conducted requires such an investment in time and resources that they can't occur more frequently without breaking the budget.

Yet, given the small-N problem, raising the frequency of exercising is the only way to explore all the nuances of the terrorist threat, the only way of understanding how different motivations, objectives, and methods should influence our preventive efforts. This implies that our models capture the different motivations, objectives, and methods of a wide variety of groups and people which we are currently unable to do. What is needed is an approach to exercising that raises the frequency and allows a full exploration of this adversary; Figures 14.1–14.3 illustrate how such an approach can contribute not just to

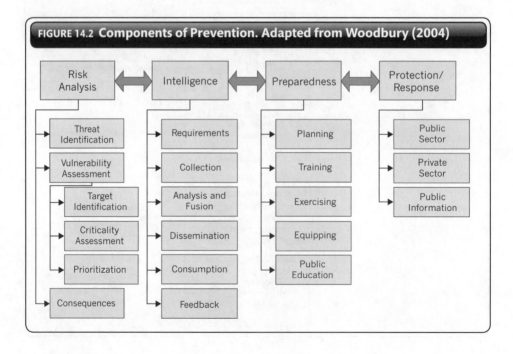

FIGURE 14.2 **Components of Prevention. Adapted from Woodbury (2004)**

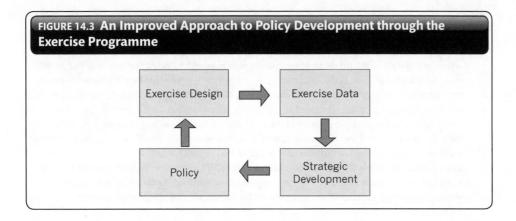

FIGURE 14.3 An Improved Approach to Policy Development through the Exercise Programme

preparedness, but to the production of effective policy. A more extensive understanding of the components of preparedness and prevention will help us to develop exercises that exploit gaps in our capabilities, thus improving our stance while addressing the dynamic nature of this adversary.

Exercise design produces exercise data (measures of performance). That data should be used to develop strategies that result in policy. That policy can then be tested within a simulation environment to determine its projected outcome over a wide variety of scenarios (and adversaries). The process then repeats with the data from those exercises refining the strategy and resulting policies that can again be tested through exercises and experimentation. This is only possible if and when exercising becomes cost-effective and a ubiquitous, routine part of preparedness.

Taking counterterrorism seriously requires exercising to determine what we need to do differently with respect to each adversary, it requires considering a much wider spectrum of adversarial behaviour than is currently done. We see no evidence that such an approach is being implemented, or even seriously considered.

Key points

- There is little evidence that government is preparing for the unique intelligence challenges involved in counterterrorism. These include: interpreting ambiguous signals with a heavy emphasis on human intelligence, and passing this information to local law enforcement for action.

- Increased budgets and a robust exercise programme suggest at first glance that border security is receiving increased attention. However, the exercises are not practising what matters for counterterrorism, nor are the budget increases as large as they should be if counterterrorism requires a new strategic response.

- Efforts to secure the most dangerous weapons and materials have not increased.

- Exercises have been directed at a general threat and have not explored how variations in the threat should relate to variations in response. Understanding this relationship is critical against a highly variable adversary.

➕ Conclusion

As the previous pages demonstrate, despite a large exercise programme for counterterrorism within the United States, there are some curious gaps in how the United States prepares. Specifically, despite rhetoric about the importance of intelligence, the National Exercise Program gives little attention to the preventive role of intelligence. No work is done to inject signals into the system and ensure they are processed so that timely action is taken. This is despite the fact that many signals that might have prevented the 9/11 attack were missed, not because they were never received, but because they were never passed to people who could/would act upon them.[11] In like manner, the role of local law enforcement in preventing terrorist attacks has not been exercised to any significant extent in the Top Officials Exercise (TOPOFF) series, the major Homeland Security exercise involving local agencies. The most important elements of border security have been similarly neglected, as have efforts to secure WMD abroad and the most dangerous materials in the United States.

However, the largest lacuna in the exercise programme has been the lack of attention paid to the war of ideas. There has been an abundance of rhetoric with regard to the 'war of ideas', or 'winning the hearts and minds of the adversary'. It is hard to argue that this is how terrorism will eventually be defeated, but are these just words, or are serious efforts being made to accomplish this? Here is where a better exercise programme can help. With a better understanding of who the adversary is (particularly the psychological and/or political profile of different groups), developed out of a more robust exercise programme because of the small-N problem, we could begin to experiment with ways to influence the adversary towards peaceful ends. The business world has models of consumer behaviour—why we buy what we buy, how much we buy, when we buy—the same can be done for terrorists. That no serious efforts to build such models are under way, suggests strongly that the 'war on ideas' is not being taken seriously.

Finally, there are a number of strategic decisions that should be made with respect to terrorism that have not been made. As Biddle (2005) points out, the United States has not made the fundamental choice between trying to contain the threat of Islamic terrorism and trying to rollback Islamic extremism worldwide. While the United States continues its withdrawal from Iraq, it has not done so to try to contain the terrorist threat there, as implied by a containment strategy, nor has it committed the full measure of national power to the stabilization of Iraq, as implied by a rollback strategy. The choice of strategies has huge implications for how government tries to protect the people. Choosing a containment strategy would imply that the choice between placing radiological scanners in every port and funding additional military forces should be decided in favour of the radiological scanners. A rollback strategy would suggest a greater focus on offensive counterterrorism operations, and hence the opposite priority. That the decision has not been made is informative as to how seriously senior American decision-makers take the terrorism issue.

Our analysis leaves us with a question: why isn't the United States exercising to deal with terrorism in a way more suited to the problem at hand? After all, politicians in the United States face strong incentives after 9/11 to be seen as proactively preparing for the terrorist threat. A tentative answer may be that the general population does not have the time, or expertise to evaluate government's efforts critically. As a result, it is enough for politicians to say 'we are exercising'. They do not need to be able to show that they are exercising well or in a way that is likely to succeed, in order to get political credit for their counterterrorism efforts. Given this disconnect, if senior leaders do not believe a new strategy is required, they will not put the necessary pressure on agencies involved in counterterrorism to overcome bureaucratic inertia. Since we have not seen a new paradigm in how the United States exercises, we can only conclude that senior leaders do not see a dramatically new strategic environment. Instead, the increased salience of terrorism has led to a domestic emphasis on preparing to deal with an attack, without the concomitant links to a strategy for the conflict.

We have seen that the nature of the terrorist threat has not changed significantly since 9/11. What has changed is that the threat has become more salient to domestic publics. This disconnect between the magnitude of the threat and the public perception has led to a poorly thought-out response in the United States; at least as revealed by the National Exercise Program. To address this threat seriously would require a wholesale revamping of the use of exercises and budget priorities to prepare for strategic threats. Such changes have not yet occurred. Indeed, since late 2006, Homeland Security as a field has all but dropped off the United States public's radar screen. The 2005 TOPOFF-3 exercise generated significant attention in the national news media while the 2007 TOPOFF-4 exercise was scarcely reported in major United States newspapers.[12] The dramatic drop in the prominence of Homeland Security from policy debates in the United States provides dramatic evidence that the terrorist threat is simply not a strategic concern for American policymakers.

The bottom line is that United States actions reveal that 'new' security threats take a back seat to traditional threats of inter-state war on the military side and natural disasters domestically. Our assessment is that this is probably an appropriate approach.

 Questions

1. Does terrorism require a new strategy? Are the authors missing important aspects of the problem?

2. If terrorism does require a new strategic approach, what would be some elements of that approach, based on your understanding of terrorist groups?

3. Given the fundamental differences in motivation, capability, and objectives of existing terrorist groups, are the elements of your approach in Question 2 compatible with each other? How would you address incompatibilities at a policy level?

4. Are there other areas of strategy where political leaders' rhetoric does not match their actions? Why can they get away with it in those areas?

5. How would you prepare for a highly variable threat? Could you use computer simulations as an integrated part of the exercise programme? What forms of analysis would it enable that are not possible now? What critical questions could be addressed?

6. How does the small-N problem relate to our understanding of the adversary? Is the Universal Adversary approach sufficient or is there more that can be done?

7. How would you use exercises, simulations, and analysis to evolve or further develop the National Strategy and the policies that we use to attain preparedness?

8. How do the key elements of preparedness identified in Figure 14.1 vary across: (1) threats; and (2) types of attack? How many of these elements can the average member of the informed public actually observe?

9. Are existing national exercise programmes sufficient to prepare for the existing terrorist threat? What would you change and why?

10. Given that no existing simulation can safely make accurate predictions of terrorist behaviour or actions, what is simulation good for and how would you utilize it in a national exercise programme?

Further Reading

M. Abrahms, 'Why Terrorism Does Not Work', *International Security* 31/2 (Fall 2006) 42–78.
Analysing the campaigns of 28 prominent terrorist organizations, this article shows that terrorist groups mostly fail to achieve their strategic objectives. Groups that focused on attacking civilians systematically failed to achieve their policy objectives.

S. D. Biddle, *American Grand Strategy After 9/11: An Assessment* (Carlisle, PA: Strategic
     Studies Institute, 2005, available at http://www.strategicstudiesinstitute.army.mil/pubs/display.
     cfm?pubID=603) on strategy for the War on Terror.
This very important monograph analyses the costs and benefits of two strategic choices for the war on terror: containment and rollback. Biddle demonstrates that the American strategy in 2004 was incoherent and ineffective because it neglected the choice between these strategies.

S. Flynn, *America the Vulnerable* (New York: Harper Collins, 2004) and *The Edge of Disaster:
     Rebuilding a Resilient Nation* (New York: Random House, 2007) on Homeland Security
     vulnerabilities.
These books identify a number of serious shortfalls in American Homeland Security efforts. The analysis is strengthened by the author's in-depth knowledge of specific vulnerabilities and how they could be remedied.

A. H. Kydd and B. F. Walter, 'The Strategies of Terrorism', *International Security* 31/1 (Summer
     2006): 49–80.
This excellent article lays out the broad strategic logic that drives terrorism and reviews the specific strategies terrorist organizations have used.

J. Record, *Bounding the Global War on Terrorism* (Carlisle, PA: University Press of the Pacific,
     2003).
Written in late 2003, this outstanding analysis of the limitations of the 'war on terror' seems prescient given the course of events in Iraq. Record identifies real limitations to American power and works through their implications.

Sageman's follow-on work, *Leaderless Jihad: Terror Networks in the Twenty-First Century*
     (Philadelphia, PA: University of Pennsylvania Press, 2007) develops a more complete
     argument about why individuals participate in decentralized terrorist organizations.

M. Sageman, *Understanding Terror Networks* (Philadelphia, PA: University of Pennsylvania Press,
     2004).
The best-researched account of why individuals join al-Qaeda and affiliated organizations. Uses biographical and network data on more then 300 former and present participants.

See also R. Pape, *Dying to Win: The Strategic Logic of Suicide Terrorism* (New York: Random
     House, 2005).

 ## Web Links

Homeland Security Institute http://www.homelandsecurity.org A federally funded research centre.
     Provides many useful links to GAO reports, government documents, and the like.

US Department of Homeland Security:

http://www.dhs.gov/files/training/gc_1179350946764.shtm

http://www.fema.gov/

http://www.dhs.gov/xfrstresp/training/

The sites above describe the National Exercise Program. They contain details on the major recurring exercises and provide contact information for further research.

Homeland Security Exercise and Evaluation Program **https://hseep.dhs.gov/** Provides a series of tools and evaluation criteria for organizations wishing to exercise their homeland security capabilities. Invaluable for gaining insight into what is really being emphasized in homeland security exercises.

15

Humanitarian Intervention and Peace Operations

SHEENA CHESTNUT GREITENS AND THEO FARRELL

 Chapter Contents

Introduction	287
The Changing Face of Peacekeeping	287
The Politics of Humanitarian Intervention	292
The Military Character of Peace Operations	295
Conclusion: Problems and Prospects	300

 Reader's Guide

Since the early 1990s, there has been a significant increase in the number of humanitarian interventions and peace operations organized by the United Nations (UN), as well as an expansion of their scope. This chapter begins by considering the transition from traditional peacekeeping to more ambitious post-cold war peace operations; it discusses some of the difficulties of practice and principle that have emerged in that transition. The next section examines the politics of intervention and the constraints imposed by both international and domestic politics. It then explores the applicability of the main principles of war to peace operations, and how these principles interact with the political imperatives involved in peace operations. Finally, the chapter concludes by examining the effects of peacekeeping and the perspectives of the individuals and communities targeted by intervention and peacekeeping efforts. This final section also outlines future challenges for peacekeeping.

Introduction

Humanitarian intervention is directed towards two purposes: protecting fundamental human rights and providing emergency assistance. It can take non-military forms, such as emergency aid (money, medicine, food, and expertise) in the aftermath of a natural disaster, or human rights promotion using diplomacy and sanctions. When reporters and policymakers speak of humanitarian intervention, however, they usually mean 'forcible military intervention in humanitarian crises'. In countries where ongoing conflict threatens aid operations, or regimes engage in massive human right abuses, intervening forces can undertake operations aimed at suppressing conflict and creating security.

During the cold war, humanitarian intervention was rare for three reasons. First, the great powers focused their military efforts on building up massive nuclear and conventional forces to deter the outbreak of World War III. They did intervene in Third World conflicts, but for the purpose of supporting their own (or undermining the other side's) client states. Such military interventions funded and armed clients engaged in human rights atrocities, and fuelled proxy wars rather than stopped them. Second, Eastern and Western publics viewed these conflicts as elements of a larger cold war battle in which national security was a higher priority than human rights, so there was insufficient public pressure on governments to induce them to respond to humanitarian crises by intervening. Third, cold war politics paralysed the United Nations Security Council (UNSC) and prevented international collaboration on intervention. To be legal under international law, intervention must be authorized by a Security Council resolution, but that resolution can be vetoed by any of the permanent five members (P5) of the Security Council. With the P5 split—Britain, France, and the United States versus the Soviet Union and later communist China—the sides traded 279 vetoes during the cold war.

The end of the cold war created demand, opportunities, and incentives for intervention, and led to an unprecedented increase in the number and scale of military interventions by United Nations forces. A series of regional peace agreements (in Afghanistan, Angola, Namibia, Central America, and Cambodia) demanded peacekeeping forces to supervise ceasefires, demobilizations, and elections. At the same time, great power cooperation in the UN became possible, a new surplus of military power could be redeployed towards humanitarian ends, and public pressure to respond to large-scale civilian suffering increased. Between 1988 and 1993, 20 new peacekeeping missions were established. The annual UN peacekeeping budget shot up from US$230 million in 1988 to between $800 million and US$1.6 billion throughout the 1990s.

As humanitarian interventions have grown in size and frequency, they have increased in importance. Strategic studies, however, has traditionally devoted relatively little attention to low-intensity conflict, focusing instead on war between major powers and the nuclear-armed superpowers. Now, like soldiers and statesmen, students and scholars must understand the dynamics of humanitarian intervention and peace operations.

The Changing Face of Peacekeeping

The UNSC authorized a few limited 'traditional peacekeeping' missions during the cold war. Commonly referred to as 'Chapter VI-and-a-half' operations, traditional peacekeeping lay somewhere between the UN's Chapter VI (on 'pacific settlement of disputes') and Chapter VII, which provides for the use of force to uphold international peace and security. Only once did the UN authorize a Chapter VII peace enforcement mission—in 1950 in Korea—and on one other occasion (1960–1964), it allowed the peacekeeping mission in the Congo to turn into peace enforcement. Thirteen traditional peacekeeping missions were established between 1948 and 1978, and none between 1978 and the end of the cold war. These missions typically occurred only after a conflict had ended and if the UN obtained the consent of belligerent parties. Their contingents were small, lightly armed, and supplied by neutral or non-aligned states. They relied on impartiality and goodwill to fulfil their mandates, which were typically to monitor ceasefires and supervise truces.

UN humanitarian interventions in the post-cold war era have become larger, more complex affairs. They involve a wider range of tasks, including protecting territory, people, and aid operations, disarming belligerents, monitoring demobilization, policing demilitarized sites, monitoring and running elections, and helping to reconstruct governments, police forces, and armies. The British Army initially called these operations 'wider peacekeeping', reflecting the broader range of tasks involved and the fact that many of them lay closer to peace enforcement (UK Army Field Manual 1995). Initially, some warned that peacekeeping and peace enforcement should be strictly separate because the two tasks were fundamentally different (see Box 15.1).

The US Army, however, grouped peacekeeping and peace enforcement together under the rubric of peace operations (Department of the Army 1994), and the British Army has since moved closer to this position. Both doctrines began to reconceptualize the relationship between consent, impartiality, and force. They recognized that peacekeepers were often intervening without full consent of local parties to a conflict, and that strict impartiality against warring parties was unlikely or impossible in cases of genocide or when spoilers sought to use violence to undermine peace (Stedman 1997: 5). To accomplish the tasks assigned under these broadened mandates, peacekeepers used more force, and used it more often, than had been expected previously.

Peacekeeping after the Cold War

Three major operations in the 1990s affected the discourse and thinking on peacekeeping: Somalia, Bosnia, and Rwanda. These interventions illustrated the difficulties of adapting to a more expansive international peacekeeping mandate. They also illustrated the debate between intervention optimists, who believe that the international community can and should intervene forcibly to rebuild failed states and reform murderous ones, and intervention pessimists, who are generally sceptical about or opposed to international intervention into

---

BOX 15.1 Peacekeepers and Peace Enforcers as Pigs and Parrots

[P]eacekeeping and peace enforcement cannot be guided by a set of common principles. The peacekeeper to peace-enforcer is as referee to football player. The objectives of each are different. One is there to win, the other to ensure fair play . . . Like pigs and parrots, the differences between peacekeepers and peace-enforcers outweigh their similarities.

Colonel Charles Dobbie (1994: 141–2)

humanitarian crises and conflicts. (Others fall somewhere between these two positions.) Optimism led the UN to launch an ambitious and ultimately failed operation in Somalia, while pessimism led it to avoid dealing with spoilers in Bosnia and to fail to stop genocide in Rwanda.

In 1991, fighting in Somalia escalated into full-blown civil war. In 1992, a deadly famine gripped the country. The breakdown of the ceasefire and inability of the approximately 500-person UN peacekeeping force (UNOSOM I) to secure humanitarian aid led to the deployment of a US-led, multinational United Task Force (UNITAF) of 37,000 in December 1992. Under UNSC Resolution 794, UNITAF was mandated to use 'all necessary means [to establish] . . . a secure environment for humanitarian relief operations.' UNITAF successfully set up and defended demilitarized zones around aid operations. In mid-1993, however, its replacement (UNOSOM II, 28,000-strong) arrived with an expanded, ambitious aim: to forcibly disarm warring factions and reconstruct the Somali state. The optimistic Clinton administration and UN leadership under Secretary-General Boutros-Ghali were soon set on a collision course with Somali warlords. Over the summer of 1993, UNOSOM II clashed repeatedly with Somali militias in Mogadishu, and a US Quick Reaction Force hunted warlord General Aideed from helicopters. In October 1993, the deaths of 18 US soldiers prompted the withdrawal of US forces supporting UNOSOM. Though the mission dragged on until 1995, it achieved little.

Despite pouring money (US$1.6 billion), material, and personnel (157 peacekeepers killed) into Somalia, the United Nations failed to restore order and rebuild the state. Compared to UNITAF, UNOSOM had fewer command capabilities and less combat power, but it tried to achieve more ambitious aims, and its failure eclipsed UNITAF's modest successes. Secretary-General Boutros-Ghali, previously a supporter of more robust peacekeeping efforts, shifted back towards an emphasis on consent, impartiality, and the non-use of force. President Clinton, who had sought to expand America's commitment to multilateral peace operations, revised his Presidential Decision Directive-25 to emphasize America's lack of support for expanded peace operations. Failure in Somalia—sometimes called the 'Vietnam' of peacekeeping—contributed to American and international reluctance to intervene in Bosnia and Rwanda.

Bosnia, on the other hand, illustrated the need to be able to neutralize peace spoilers and the consequences of failing to do so. In February 1992, after the multiethnic Bosnian state voted for independence, Bosnian Serb forces opposed to independence and supported by Serbia attacked the Bosnian military. Fighting soon broke out all across Bosnia, principally between Bosnian government forces and Bosnian Serb and Bosnian Croat entities backed by Serbia and Bosnia. The UN deployed a UN Protection Force (UNPROFOR) with the mission of protecting civilians in safe areas established by the UN and delivering humanitarian aid. Although the UN Protection Force lacked the land power to protect aid convoys and civilians in its safe areas, it refused to call in air strikes against Bosnian Serb spoilers, who engaged in widespread ethnic cleansing and attacks on civilians (see Box 15.2).

General Rupert Smith did call in air strikes by the North Atlantic Treaty Organization (NATO) after the shelling of Sarajevo in August 1995– but only after the failure to protect two safe areas (Srebrenica and Zepa) had led to the slaughter of their male civilian inhabitants. Combined with advances by Bosnian government and Bosnian Croat forces in Eastern Bosnia (the latter of whom had joined Bosnian government forces after a separate Croat–Bosniak agreement was signed in 1994), NATO's military pressure convinced the Bosnian Serbs to sue for peace.

BOX 15.2 The UN's Failure to Stop Serb Spoilers in Bosnia

With the benefit of hindsight, one can see that many of the errors the United Nations made [in Bosnia] flowed from a single and no doubt well-intentioned] effort: we tried to keep the peace and apply the rules of peacekeeping when there was no peace to keep . . . None of the conditions for the deployment of peacekeepers had been met: there was no peace agreement—not even a functioning ceasefire—there was no clear will to peace and there was no clear consent by the belligerents . . . Nor was the provision of humanitarian aid a sufficient response to 'ethnic cleansing' and to an attempted genocide . . . The Bosnian Muslim civilian population thus became the principal victim of brutally aggressive military and paramilitary Serb operations to depopulate coveted territories in order to allow them to be repopulated by Serbs . . . In the end, these Bosnian Serb war aims were ultimately repulsed on the battlefield, and not at the negotiating table. Yet the [UN] Secretariat had convinced itself early on that broader use of force by the international community was beyond our mandate and anyway undesirable.

Kofi Annan (1999)

While much of the world's attention focused on the Balkan conflict, an estimated 800,000 people were massacred in Rwanda in approximately 100 days between April and July 1994. In 1993 a three-year civil conflict between the Hutu regime and the Tutsi Rwandan Patriotic Front (RPF) had ended in a ceasefire and precarious peace and power-sharing agreement (the Arusha Accords). After the assassination of Hutu president Habyarimana in April 1994, Hutu extremists seized control and began a campaign of mass slaughter against the Tutsi and moderate Hutus. The UN peacekeeping force then present, the 2,500-strong UN Assistance Mission for Rwanda (UNAMIR), had been deployed with a limited mandate to monitor the ceasefire between the RPF and the government, and assist in relief operations. Under-staffed, under-resourced, and unauthorized to use force to prevent war crimes, UN forces were overwhelmed by the carnage. National contingents were either withdrawn entirely (including soldiers from Bangladesh and Belgium—the latter after Hutu extremists killed ten Belgian soldiers), or they evacuated Europeans while failing to protect Rwandans from the massacres unfolding around them. In late April, UNAMIR was reduced to 270 personnel and remained focused on re-establishing the ceasefire. Not until 17 May did UNSC Resolution 918 expand the mission to 5,500 and authorize it to protect the population. A month later, however, UNAMIR still had only 500 troops; member states declined to contribute forces. Eventually, the genocide ran out of steam and the Rwandan Patriotic Front offensive, sweeping down from Uganda under the leadership of Paul Kagame, pushed back Hutu extremists, who fled across the border to then-Zaire under the protection of a French 'Humanitarian Protection Zone'. Since then, fighting in eastern Congo has raged in what is sometimes called 'Africa's World War'—involving eight countries, a myriad of armed groups, and over 5 million estimated deaths. The war resulted in the largest peacekeeping mission mounted by the UN at that time (the UN Organization Stabilization Mission in the Democratic Republic of the Congo, known by its French acronym MONUSCO), though the joint UN-African Union mission in Darfur may eventually be larger.

The catastrophic consequences of inaction in Rwanda prompted debate over what could and should have been done. Sceptics claimed that the pace of genocide prevented an effective response; even the United States, the only nation capable of rapid deployment, would have required four weeks to mount a ground intervention (Juperman 2000). Others argued that the UN, which had reliable forewarning of the genocide, could have bolstered the UN Assistance Mission for Rwanda prior to the genocide and perhaps prevented it; they suggest that an estimated 5,000-strong force could have halted the killing, or that other measures short of ground intervention could at least have slowed its pace. Ultimately, an independent inquiry charged the UN with 'overriding failure', and concluded that 'the Security Council bears responsibility for its lack of political will to do more to stop the killing.'

Peacekeeping Since 2000

The notable failures of the mid-1990s led to a temporary lull in peacekeeping (Tharoor 1995-96). Despite some lower-profile successes, only one major UN mission was launched between 1993 and 1998, in Eastern Slavonia (Fortna and Howard 2008: 287-88). Eventually, a reform initiative culminated in the Brahimi Report (2000), which attempted to rejuvenate peacekeeping. The Report re-asserted a strategic perspective on peacekeeping, expanded the UN's Department of Peacekeeping Operations, and reformed the practices and processes of peace operations.

At the same time, the reform initiative was paralleled by two developments that opened space for more permissive norms of humanitarian intervention. First, new institutions like the International Criminal Court and tribunals in Rwanda, the former Yugoslavia, and elsewhere began to hold leaders accountable for breaches of humanitarian law. Second, internal conflict and mass atrocity were redefined as potential threats to 'international peace and security' (invoking Chapter VII). These developments have placed significant qualifications on the norm of state sovereignty.

Today, there are more peacekeepers deployed globally than at any point in the past: almost 122,000 personnel in 16 operations on four continents as of October 2011—a ninefold increase since 1999 (UN Peacekeeping 2011). This expansion in scope, coupled with a continued expansion in the mandates given to peacekeeping forces, has led to operations that today are 'unparalleled in their organizational complexity and the scope of their ambition' and has created serious concern about overstraining the institutions responsible for peacekeeping activity (Paddon 2011). Awareness of the limitations of UN capacity has resulted in the regionalization of peace operations in some cases, and a diversification of actors or division of labour between various organizations in others. African states, in particular, have been encouraged to develop a regional capacity for peace operations on the continent—an area with high demand for peace forces which the US and others are less keen to fill. The hybrid UN-African Union operation in Darfur, the first of its kind, is an example of this shift towards regionalization. NATO also deployed massive forces in Bosnia and Kosovo in the 1990s, and has since conducted operations in Afghanistan and Libya. Often a single state or a regional organization has led an intervention, but done so either with the authorization of a UN resolution, and/or with a less coercive UN peacekeeping force following behind (Fortna and Howard 2008: 291-2).

Regional coalitions were initially thought to enjoy several advantages over UN operations: greater force cohesion, better local knowledge, greater commitment to the mission, and more suitable force structure. But this has not always been true. The case of the Economic Community of West African States Ceasefire Monitoring Group, which attempted to restore order to the failed Liberian state in 1990-1996, highlighted several problems with regionalization. The group was divided by subregional rivalries between Francophone and Anglophone

West African contributing states; it exhibited poor understanding of Liberia's political dynamics; it only maintained mission commitment by relying on local surrogate forces who had an interest in continuing the conflict; and it lacked the equipment, training, and logistical support for counterinsurgency operations. The intervention raised serious questions about regionalization that remain unresolved today.

Thus, as the context of peacekeeping has changed and developed, the principles that have traditionally guided peacekeeping—impartiality, consent, and restraint on the use of force—have also been subject to continuous debate and renegotiation. Impartiality has been redefined as a lack of favouritism or prejudice rather than as neutrality, and UN guidelines emphasize that impartiality is not an excuse for inaction where mandates call for civilian protection. Consent, while still revered at the strategic level, is acknowledged to break down in tactical situations where forceful action is sometimes needed to execute the mandate. And the non-use of force has been abrogated when necessary for self-defence of the mission's forces or when necessary to defend the mandate—which often now includes the protection of civilians. As each new situation poses different challenges to these principles, these debates will undoubtedly continue.

Key points

- Limited traditional peacekeeping operations have given way in the post-cold war era to larger, more complex, and more ambitious peace operations.

- The debate between intervention optimists and pessimists played out in UN interventions in Bosnia, Somalia, and Rwanda. Critics charge that the UN failed to deal with spoilers in Bosnia, tried to do too much in Somalia, and did not do enough in Rwanda.

- The shift toward peace operations has prompted a rethinking of the relationship between impartiality, consent, and the use of force.

The Politics of Humanitarian Intervention

Political considerations focus international attention selectively on humanitarian crises, prompting a stronger response at some times and places than others. Serbia's repression in Kosovo triggered Western humanitarian intervention; Russia's repression in Chechnya has not. Iraqi attacks on Kurds in 1991 resulted in the creation of a Kurdish 'Safe Haven' in Iraq, guarded by thousands of troops and Allied airpower, though even deadlier Iraqi attacks on Kurds several years earlier had led to no response. Politics also shapes the speed and scale of humanitarian intervention. Political constraints and incentives define crises and shape responses at both the level of domestic politics, and the level of international geopolitics—most commonly seen in the UN Security Council.

Security Council Politics

The 15 members of the UN Security Council are responsible for authorizing humanitarian interventions. Authorization requires a majority of nine UNSC members, but real power resides with the P5, who each have the right of veto. Conflict between the P5 during the cold war made the Security Council a moribund instrument for managing international security. Although cooperation between the P5 has improved since then, four political problems still dog UNSC sponsorship of humanitarian intervention.

First, the P5 are states with great power interests and aspirations. Great power differences can produce a 'veto problem' if one P5 member simply refuses to contemplate a UN intervention that it considers threatening to its interests. This was evident in Russia's approach to Kosovo in the late 1990s: Russia refused to recognize the humanitarian dimensions of the evolving crisis and was prepared to veto UN intervention. The problem was solved by independent action on the part of NATO, which argued that force was justified on the grounds of 'overwhelming humanitarian necessity' even without a Security Council resolution.

Second, there may be a 'logrolling problem'. If a particular crisis is associated with a certain P5 member (or members), others may withhold support or threaten to veto unless, in exchange, they are promised support for their interests. In the mid-1990s, for example, Russia and later China obstructed UNSC Resolutions on peace operations in Haiti because Russia wanted UN endorsement of its own intervention in Georgia, while China wanted a public apology from Haiti for inviting Taiwan's Vice-President to Haiti's 1996 presidential inauguration.

Third, even if the P5 agree to authorize a UN peace operations force, they must still overcome a 'posturing problem', which is a tendency to 'talk the talk but not walk the walk'. The great powers sometimes pass grand-sounding Security Council resolutions that are not backed by force. The creation of 'safe areas' in Bosnia is a classic example of this type of posturing problem. These areas were not actually safe because the Security Council was not prepared to deploy additional forces to protect them (see Box 15.2). Several UNSC members and the UN Secretariat warned at the time that 'without the provision of any credible military threat' these safe areas would be meaningless, but the great powers went ahead anyway.

Fourth, even if the P5 are prepared to walk the walk, they can disagree on which direction to take. Great powers may disagree on the nature of the humanitarian crisis, or on the most effective response. This 'coordination problem' was evident in Bosnia. The United States and its European allies had different perceptions of the conflict, leading them to disagree on the appropriate response. The European powers saw an ethnic conflict to be solved by partition. The United States saw it as a war started by Serbia, and opposed partition because it would reward Serbian aggression. Only in 1995, when the United States accepted that partition was a necessary evil, was the international community able to solve the coordination problem and take effective action.

Public Opinion and Domestic Politics

Policymakers and commentators alike believe that Western public opinion can make or break humanitarian interventions. The 'CNN effect', coined after the Cable News Network's total televised coverage of the 1990–1991 Gulf War, suggests that public opinion can prompt intervention when domestic audiences respond to media images of suffering by pressurizing policymakers for action. Thus 'extensive media coverage of emaciated Somalis ensured a suitable international outcry (the Do Something response)' (von Hippel 2000: 59) and in Bosnia, 'the reason the West finally, belatedly intervened was heavily related to media coverage' (Holbrooke 1999: 20).

BOX 15.3 The CNN Effect as a Double-edged Sword

The fact that the USA pulled the plug on its Somali intervention after the loss of 18 US Rangers in a firefight in October 1993 indicates how capricious public opinion is. Televised images of starving and dying Somalis had persuaded the outgoing [George H. W.] Bush administration to launch a humanitarian rescue mission, but once the US public saw the consequences of this in terms of dead Americans being dragged through the streets of Mogadishu, the Clinton administration was forced to announce a timetable for the withdrawal of all US forces from Somalia. What this case demonstrates is that the 'CNN factor' is a double-edged sword: it can pressurize governments into humanitarian intervention, yet with equal rapidity, pictures of casualties arriving home can lead to public disillusionment and calls for withdrawal.

Wheeler and Bellamy (2005: 564–5)

Policymakers and pundits also assume that public support for humanitarian intervention depends on minimal peacekeeper casualties. The argument suggests that the public will be particularly sensitive to casualties in humanitarian interventions because these military actions are freely entered into by their government: they are 'wars of choice' as opposed to 'wars of necessity' fought to defend national security. Policymakers appear to believe that media coverage of peacekeeping deaths will collapse public support. Somalia is often cited as an example of casualty aversion producing a 'body bags effect' because US domestic support for humanitarian operations evaporated following the deaths of 18 American soldiers (see Box 15.3).

Critics suggest that both effects are misleading. The CNN effect may underestimate the extent to which governments can frame the media debate, and thereby choose the place and moment of intervention. Leaders are most likely to be able to do this when they are certain as to their desired course of action, and when those lobbying for intervention can mobilize politicians for their cause. Disunity, therefore, increases public responsiveness to media coverage and reduces the executive's ability to drive the media agenda. In Somalia, the Bush administration's uncertainty and a pro-intervention lobby in US aid agencies and Congress pushed the United States toward intervention. By contrast, the Clinton administration was able to resist calls for ground intervention in Kosovo because it was sure that it opposed that policy and because it had support among opposition politicians in Congress.

Claims of a body bags effect can be similarly misleading. Empirical evidence suggests that peacekeeper casualties do not necessarily result in public calls for immediate withdrawal. Casualties can sometimes lead to a rallying of public support. In the case of Somalia, most Americans actually favoured increased US military involvement immediately following the killing of US soldiers. Long-term American support depended more on the perceived attitude of the Somali public. In other words, if ordinary Somalis wanted US troops to go home, then ordinary Americans saw little reason for their soldiers to stick around. When doubts were subsequently raised in Congress about the course and purpose of US intervention in Somalia, this apparent confusion over policy led to a decline in public support for intervention.

Key points

- Humanitarian intervention is affected by domestic politics and politics in the Security Council; both levels operate to define crisis and shape international responses.

- UN Security Council cooperation on humanitarian intervention can be hindered by one or more of the P5 seeking to advance their own national interests, either through logrolling or vetoing behaviour.

- Even when the P5 agree to act, effective intervention can be hampered by posturing (where tough talk is not matched by action) or lack of coordination (where states disagree on the best course of action).

- The CNN effect, which suggests that televised images of humanitarian suffering can produce public demand for intervention, may underestimate the extent to which political elites can frame public debate to affect the place and timing of intervention.

- The body bags effect, which assumes that casualties lead to a collapse in public support for intervention, underestimates the public's stomach for casualties. Political rather than public sensitivity is often the decisive factor.

The Military Character of Peace Operations

To protect civilians or stop conflict, peace forces must be prepared to engage in combat. Most often, these military forces have been designed, equipped, and trained according to fundamental principles of war. These principles, however, do not always apply straight forwardly to peace operations.

Principles and Practicalities

The four main principles of war—identification of the objective, unity of effort, massing of forces, and surprise—are problematic when it comes to peace operations. First, the principle that military operations should be conducted towards clearly defined, decisive, and attainable objectives is difficult to achieve in peace operations. In peace operations, objectives are often poorly defined. In a UN intervention, for instance, objectives are established by Security Council mandate; in non-UN interventions, objectives are set by the contributing national governments. Security Council politics, however, often prevent the construction of a mandate that contains a clear mission objective. Mandates may be deliberately vague to overcome the coordination problem among the great powers. They may be imprecise, non-credible, or simply unattainable when Security Council members want to threaten or coerce but are reluctant to commit to tough action, or when for the sake of posturing they assign grand-sounding mandates to under-resourced missions. Finally, mandates may be unclear if those writing them fail to realize that peace operations in themselves are decisive only for short-term effects like securing aid routes or stopping a massacre. Long-term goals like political stability and economic security are projects that depend on a host of non-military components beyond peacekeeping.

Commanders will attempt to translate their mandates into clear and attainable mission objectives. Limited objectives are often clearer and more attainable, but this paradoxically makes them less decisive in the long term. In Somalia, UNITAF sought to create a secure environment for aid operations by keeping armed bandits at bay rather than disarming them. In Bosnia, UNPROFOR protected humanitarian aid by escorting aid convoys rather than securing aid routes because the latter would have involved using force to clear Serb and Croatian roadblocks, while the former did not. In the short term, they could and often did achieve these goals. Ultimately, however, the secure environment in Somalia did not outlive UNITAF, and whether aid continued to flow in Bosnia depended on the decisions made by belligerent parties rather than UNPROFOR's power.

The second principle, unity of effort, is achieved in war through unity of command by placing all forces under a single commander. The coalition forces that liberated France in 1944 were led by one general (Dwight Eisenhower), as were those that liberated Kuwait in 1991 (Norman Schwartzkopf). Unity of command, however, is less assured in peace operations. Forces in peace operations are often drawn from a wider variety of troop-contributing states than are forces in normal coalition warfare. Differences in military culture, lack of prior joint operational experience, and potential political rivalries between contributing states all inhibit the creation and operation of an effective command structure. Sometimes the differences are so great that they render the chain of command inoperative, as in the bitter 2000 dispute between an Indian commander and the Nigerian and Zambian contingents in the UN force in Sierra Leone. The governments of troop-contributing countries also limit what the UN can do with their troops. National governments place restrictions on the rules of engagement, or they bypass the mission command structure and issue instructions directly to their forces in the field. Further complicating lines of authority is the fact that some Western powers have supported UN missions with combat forces that were not actually placed under UN command. The Anglo-French Rapid Reaction Force in Bosnia, the US Quick Reaction Force in Somalia, and British military forces in Sierra Leone, for example, all remained under national political and military command.

Even if unity of command can be achieved, commanders of peace operations must also coordinate their actions with civilian agencies—often a multitude of UN, non-government, and local aid actors—to achieve unity of effort. Here differences in military and civilian organizational cultures are even more pronounced, and can pose high barriers to effective and timely coordination. In Somalia, civil–military cooperation under UNITAF broke down when the military way of doing things—controlling movement and information—infuriated civilian aid agencies that objected to military meddling in their operations.

Third, commanders also seek to mass force, usually by concentrating troops at places and times that have greatest impact on the enemy or by synchronizing the effects of combat power to create decisive effect. When it comes to peace operations, however, forces are more commonly dispersed than concentrated, in order to maintain high visibility and provide security on the ground. In Somalia, for example, US Marines were sometimes parcelled out to villages in small units. Force dispersal limits the ability to mass force for decisive impact, and means that fewer elements of combat power will be available for centralized and decisive action. Additionally, the problems of under-resourcing and disunity of command that are endemic in peace operations greatly reduce possibilities for massing force. Massing force may prove difficult even to provide emergency support to a unit in trouble. UNOSOM II had trouble pulling together the force of Malaysian and Pakistani tanks and armoured cars that finally rescued the US Quick Reaction Force from Aideed's ambush in the streets of Mogadishu.

The fourth principle, surprise, highlights the importance of striking the enemy when and where they least expect it. The critical ingredients for surprise are speed, secrecy, and deception. Lack of unity of command makes it difficult for peace forces to achieve speed in observing and shaping developments in their area of operations. Secrecy is often compromised by the imperative for unity of effort, which requires peace forces to share operational information with civilian agencies, many of which in turn hire and share information with local staff. In Somalia, for instance, Aideed had excellent intelligence about UNOSOM II operations partly because he used local aid workers as spies. Deception is also problematic in urban environments, because the local population can act as eyes and ears for belligerent parties.

Public Opinion and Operational Pathologies

The political imperatives that shape peace operations pull them even further away from the traditional principles of war. In addition to the difficulties mentioned above, the political sensitivity to casualties in these 'wars of choice' results in a focus on managing public opinion to maintain support for intervention. In Kosovo, for example, NATO launched an elaborate public relations campaign to counter Serbia's portrayal of itself as a victim of NATO aggression. And during NATO's 2011 intervention into Libya, the Barack Obama administration tried to focus public attention on the human rights violations taking place, though this was never the sole aim articulated (see Box 15.4)

Concerns with public opinion produce three specific pathologies in interventions and peace operations. First is the strategic compression of the battlefield. In conventional war, strategic outcomes are shaped by military action at the operational level. The British campaign to drive the Argentinean military off the Falklands, or the allied campaign in 1990–1991 to push the Iraqi Army out of Kuwait are examples of operational campaign successes.

BOX 15.4 NATO's Intervention in Libya

In March 2011, UNSC Resolution 1973 authorized a no-fly zone over Libya, demanding a ceasefire and an end to attacks on civilians. The resolution also imposed tighter sanctions on the Libyan government and forbade any 'foreign occupation force' on Libyan soil. It passed unanimously, with ten votes in support and five abstentions (by Brazil, China, Germany, India, and Russia). The stated aim of UNSC Resolution 1973 was 'to protect civilians and civilian areas targeted by Colonel Muammar Al-Qadhafi, his allied forces, and mercenaries.' Members of the Obama administration, however, advanced at least five additional reasons for intervention: promoting regime change; sending a message to other dictators; supporting Libya's rebel movement; repaying European support in Afghanistan; and the belief that it would be easy to achieve the desired end-state. These actions were intended to increase public support for the intervention, but they also made it harder to maintain a clear mission focus. As Micah Zenko noted,

> When presidents authorize military action, they must have a clear objective in mind. Without a singular, defined goal, policymakers cannot appropriately match means and ends, which increases the likelihood of failure . . . In the case of Libya, there was only one overarching rationale provided—the protection of civilians—yet the initial intervention and now the 97-day bombing campaign has been about so much more.

Sources: Zenko 2011; UNSC 2011

By contrast, in interventions or peace operations, tactical military actions can have heightened strategic consequences. For example, NATO strategy was disrupted following the bombing of the Chinese embassy in Kosovo. This means that military commanders make decisions with more awareness of the domestic political consequences of their actions, either through direct communication with those at home or through pressure from civilian authorities.

The second operational pathology is a heightened focus on full force protection to ensure that intervening or peace forces are not vulnerable to attack. Making full force protection an operational imperative can hinder effective execution of a mission. It concentrates force in situations when the dispersal of forces would more effectively promote the security of aid operations. It often requires ground personnel to wear body armour and travel at high speeds, visibly demonstrating distrust and insecurity towards the local population in situations when a more relaxed force posture would make it easier to build relations with the local communities. American forces seem particularly sensitive to this issue, although US military ranks appear divided in their approach to force protection. Senior officers closer to political pressures are more intent on force protection, while junior officers focus more on the impediments that force protection requirements can create for mission success.

The third issue is an over-reliance on airpower and unrealistic expectations of what it can accomplish (see Box 15.5). The 1990–1991 Gulf War vividly demonstrated that airpower is most effective when employed in synergy with land power: the allied air campaign destroyed Iraqi military infrastructure and softened Iraqi land defences, while the land campaign (with air support) smashed the Iraqi army in Kuwait. Given the aversion to casualties in wars of choice, however, Western powers are deeply reluctant to put 'boots on the ground'. They seek to achieve force protection by making sure that the only forces deployed are in fast jets thousands of meters above the conflict.

Western airpower can sometimes be combined with local land power to achieve mission success. NATO bombing of Bosnian Serb bases in 1995, combined with a successful Bosniak-Croat land offensive against Serb territory in Eastern Bosnia, forced Bosnian Serbs to sue for peace. NATO air operations in Libya in 2011 provided critical support to rebel forces seeking to advance and overthrow Muammar Qadhafi. At other times, however, Western leaders' rejection of ground intervention has had negative consequences for humanitarian outcomes. In Kosovo in 1999, NATO's restriction of its campaign to airpower alone gave Serb forces

---

BOX 15.5 Fatal Attraction: America and Airpower

Use of airpower can help sustain domestic support or coalition unity [by reducing the risks of own casualties and collateral damage], but it cannot eliminate underlying political constraints. In Eliot Cohen's words, 'Airpower is an unusually seductive form of military strength, in part because, like modern courtship, it appears to offer gratification without commitment.' This view poses a challenge for airpower. Because policymakers often see airpower strikes as a low-risk, low-commitment measure, airpower will be called on when US public or allied commitment is weak—a situation that will make successful coercion far harder when casualties do occur or when air strikes fail to break adversary resistance. Airpower, like other military instruments, cannot overcome a complete lack of political will.

Byman and Waxman (2000: 38)

room to terrorize the Albanian population and drive them out of the province. The Kosovo Liberation Army (unlike the Croatian Army in Bosnia) could not generate enough combat power to be an effective surrogate ground force for NATO. As a result, Serb forces held out against NATO bombing for 78 days before capitulating—which they did only under threat of a ground invasion, and after the province had essentially been 'cleansed' of Albanians.

These operational pathologies have also been visible in coalition military operations in Afghanistan and Iraq (see Chapter 13). The initial US-led invasions of Afghanistan in 2001 and Iraq in 2003 are not examples of humanitarian interventions. Both campaigns were primarily about protecting the national security of the United States and its coalition partners from the threats posed by terrorism and weapons of mass destruction. Nevertheless, US policymakers predicted that humanitarian outcomes and democracy promotion would be by-products of these operations.

The character of ongoing post-conflict stabilization operations led by the United States in Iraq and NATO in Afghanistan has been similar to that of peace operations. Coalition forces have taken considerable casualties in both operations—as of late 2011, the United States had suffered more than 4,400 military fatalities in Iraq and more than 1,800 in Afghanistan. Although these losses resulted in a marked decline in US public support for the operations and mounting political pressure for withdrawal, the mission did not collapse as support waned. The United States 'surged' 30,000 additional troops to Iraq in 2007 and similarly augmented its forces in Afghanistan in 2010 before withdrawing American troops from Iraq in December 2011. Force protection concerns also informed the US counterinsurgency strategy in both campaigns. Not until 2007 did US forces move away from conducting armoured patrols from large bases on the outskirts of Iraqi cities, towards more dispersed deployments in 'security stations' within Iraqi communities.

Although over-reliance on airpower has not been a major criticism of these campaigns, American experiences in Iraq and Afghanistan were critical to informing the Obama administration's decision to rely almost exclusively on airpower for NATO's intervention in Libya in early 2011. Precedents from the United States' global counterterrorism efforts have also shaped the 2011 'armed humanitarian intervention' in central Africa, where American special forces have been tasked to help regional militaries capture Joseph Kony and counter his Lord's Resistance Army, while engaging in combat only in self-defence. Despite the fact that they were not undertaken primarily for humanitarian purposes, the operations in Iraq and Afghanistan will exert an influence on future Western humanitarian interventions and peace operations.

Key points

- In practice, peace operations often contravene one or more of the four main principles of war—objective, unity, mass, and surprise.

- Political imperatives, such as the need to manage public support for intervention and peace operations, can create a number of operational pathologies.

- The operational pathologies imposed by political considerations include command complications caused by the strategic compression of the battlefield, prioritizing force protection at the expense of mission success, and an over-reliance on air power.

Conclusion: Problems and Prospects

This chapter has explored the issues and debates surrounding humanitarian intervention and peace operations. Peacekeeping forces must balance consent, impartiality, and the need to use force to defend their mandates. Inability to strike the correct balance has led to a variety of failures in past operations. Additionally, peace operations do not always closely follow the principles of war. Instead, they are shaped by domestic and international political pressures and incentives. Each of these issues can pose challenges for successful peacekeeping.

Today, there are also acute concerns about whether the international community's renewed will to act has been matched by the appropriate capacity and resource commitments. The UN's Department of Peacekeeping Operations 'New Horizon' agenda, promulgated in 2009, has sought to expand partnerships as a means of providing effective and timely responses to conflict and crisis. For the reasons outlined in preceding sections, however, partnerships are an unlikely panacea.

Nevertheless, peacekeeping is here to stay. Despite some debate about the most effective form and organization of peacekeeping, there is broad consensus that it works. Studies that examine peace operations in the context of inter-state war as well as in cases of civil conflict suggest that the presence of peacekeepers makes re-emergence of civil war much less likely, even after peacekeepers go home (Fortna 2003, 2008; for a partially contrasting view, see Greig and Diehl 2005). And theoretical debates aside, there are more peacekeepers deployed now than ever before: 122,000 as of late 2011.

Future debates are likely to centre on what relationship peacekeeping should have with transitional administration and attempts at state building. Under transitional administrations, the UN not only takes on the tasks of multidimensional peace operations, but assumes executive authority over the state's administration and government. The process has only been attempted a handful of times—for example, during UN efforts in Namibia, Cambodia, Croatia, Kosovo, and East Timor.

The key question is whether the United States, United Nations, or any third-party external actor can build a state, or a democracy, for others. One school of thought is optimistic. It emphasizes the possibility of success if the intervening actors have the right strategy, sufficient resources, and a strong political will. Others are more pessimistic, arguing that the success of intervention depends far more on local capacity and local political dynamics than on anything foreigners do. The international community might be very good at building a telecommunications network, the argument goes, but it is far worse at transforming local political culture to meet Western standards in areas like the rule of law (Stewart 2011). This emphasis on local actors parallels a call among scholars of peacekeeping for more attention to the 'perspectives of the peacekept' to assess how local actors respond to intervention and peacekeeping efforts—a topic that so far has received relatively little attention (Clapham 1998; Pouligny 2006).

Humanitarian intervention and peace operations remain a fixture on the landscape of global politics. Given their importance, the questions and debates that surround these operations are likely to influence international practices—and the field of strategic studies—for years to come.

 ## Questions

1. Why was humanitarian intervention rare during the cold war?

2. How did peacekeeping change in the 1990s? Why?

3. Is regionalization of peace operations a good idea?

4. Is impartiality possible during peacekeeping? Why or why not?

5. Could the UN or other powers have done more to stop genocide in Rwanda? If so, what exactly could have been done? What should have been done?

6. To what extent can public opinion 'make and break' humanitarian interventions? Why? What operational pathologies can public opinion create?

7. What four problems associated with the UN Security Council hinder effective action in response to humanitarian crises?

8. How well do the principles of war apply to peace operations?

9. Does peacekeeping work?

10. Are you an intervention optimist or pessimist? Why?

 Further Reading

A. J. Bellamy, P. Williams, and S. Griffin, *Understanding Peacekeeping,* **2nd edn. (Cambridge: Polity, 2010).**
An excellent and up-to-date introductory text.

V. P. Fortna and L. M. Howard, 'Pitfalls and Prospects in the Peacekeeping Literature,' *Annual Review of Political Science* **11 (2008: 283–301).**
A concise but thorough review of contemporary debates and questions about peacekeeping. The books written by each of these authors individually are also worth a careful read.

H. Langholtz, B. Kondoch, and A. Wells, *International Peacekeeping: The Year Book of International Peace Operations,* **ed. by (Leiden: Martinus Nijhoff Publishers, 2003).**
Essential reading for scholars and students of peace operations.

L. Minear and T. G. Weiss, *Mercy Under Fire: War and the Global Humanitarian Community* **(Boulder, CO: Westview Press, 1995).**
A classic text on the application of humanitarian principles to intervention in complex emergencies.

R. Paris, *At War's End: Building Peace After Civil Conflict* **(Cambridge: Cambridge University Press, 2004).**
Advances a critique of the democratization and marketization agenda inherent in many peace operations.

W. Shawcross, *Deliver Us From Evil: Warlords and Peacekeepers in a World of Endless Conflict* **(London: Bloomsbury, 2000).**
A highly readable (and in places damning) account of UN peace operations in Cambodia, Somalia, Rwanda, Bosnia, and Kosovo.

R. Stewart, 'What Can Afghanistan and Bosnia Teach Us About Libya?' *The Guardian,* **7 October 2011, available at http://www.guardian.co.uk/world/2011/oct/08/ libya-intervention-rory-stewart.**
A sceptical view of intervention that argues for the importance of local capacity.

United Nations Blue Book Series (New York: United Nations).
Includes volumes on Cambodia, Mozambique, Somalia, and Rwanda, each one offering a collection of key primary source materials and a lengthy commentary by the Secretary General.

J. Welsh (ed.), *Humanitarian Intervention and International Relations* **(Oxford: Oxford University Press, 2004).**
An examination of issues and cases of humanitarian intervention through the lens of international relations theory.

N. J. Wheeler, *Saving Strangers: Humanitarian Intervention in International Society* **(Oxford: Oxford University Press, 2000).**
Considers the ethical case for forcible humanitarian intervention, and analyses cases of interventions during and after the cold war.

🔲 Web Links

UN Department of Peacekeeping Operations: **http://www.un.org/en/peacekeeping/** The UN Department of Peacekeeping Operations website contains a brief history of peacekeeping, discussion of principles and processes related to peacekeeping, overviews of current operations, and reports on past ones.

United States Institute of Peace Library: **http://www.usip.org/publications/peacekeeping-web-links** A fairly comprehensive list of web links on peacekeeping.

Report of the Panel on United Nations Peace Operations (aka the Brahimi Report): **http://www. un.org/peace/reports/peace_operations/** This is the text of the 2000 report that sparked significant changes in peacekeeping practice.

Website of the International Coalition for the Responsibility to Protect: **http://www.responsibility toprotect.org/** This site allows you to access a number of helpful resources on humanitarian intervention, including the two-volume report by the International Commission on Intervention and State Sovereignty, which offers a comprehensive analysis of its ethical, political, and military implications and case study analyses of past interventions.

Stimson Center Program on the Future of Peace Operations: **http://www.stimson.org/programs/ future-of-peace-operations/program-related-news/** This program's webpage offers research and news commentary on current issues related to intervention and peace operations.

Security Council Report: **http://www.securitycouncilreport.org/** This non-profit website provides monthly and thematic reports on the role of the United Nations Security Council, including its activities related to intervention and peacekeeping.

International Peace Institute: **http://www.ipacademy.org** Formerly the International Peace Academy, IPI focuses on conflict prevention and settlement, and has provided training to UN peacekeepers. Also linked from this page is the Global Observatory, a site that provides interviews, maps, and other key resources on conflicts worldwide.

New York University Center for International Cooperation: **http://www.cic.nyu.edu/** This research centre's programmes on global peace operations, humanitarian intervention, and peacebuilding offer helpful events and publications.

16 The Rise of Cyberpower

JOHN B. SHELDON

Chapter Contents

Introduction	304
Terms and Definitions	304
Cyberspace, Cyberpower, and the Infosphere	308
A New Dimension for Conflict	311
A Twenty-first Century Revolution in Military Affairs?	315
Conclusion	317

Reader's Guide

Recent years have seen the rapid spread of information-communication technologies around the world, creating a globally connected domain called cyberspace. Every aspect of modern society, from how we communicate to how we wage war, can now be said to be cyberdependent. Nearly every function of modern society is enabled by cyberspace. This is both an advantage and a serious vulnerability. A variety of actors—ranging from individuals and small groups to non-state actors and governments—are developing cyber-attack capabilities that can disrupt, and even destroy core elements of modern society. Defence against these threats is challenging because, in cyberspace, the offence is the dominant form of warfare. Yet, despite this advantage, cyber-attack entails risks. The pervasiveness of cyberspace, and the growing importance of cyberpower, is having a tangible impact on international politics and the use of military force in the twenty-first century. What are the implications of these trends, and why should strategists care about them?

Introduction

The first electronic computer, the Electronic Numerical Integrator and Computer, had to be housed in a large building. It was developed in 1946 for the US Army to plot scores of artillery targets rapidly. Since then, computers have shrunk in size, become much more powerful, and now pervade every aspect of modern life. These developments—and the rapid and inexorable rise of the World Wide Web and the Internet—have produced startling and indelible changes in modern societies, the global economy, and in the conduct of politics and warfare. Indeed, these changes have occurred in such a relatively small space of time and with such scope that analysts and scholars have still to discern all of the implications of the rise of cyberpower.

The implications for strategy are similarly challenging to identify, though broad trends and issues are sufficiently well known that strategists are now able to analyse trends. Because cyberpower is having a broad and meaningful impact on the conduct of war, it is producing significant challenges for strategic studies. These broad and meaningful impacts, along with their attendant challenges and opportunities, may also be driving a change in the character of war. This chapter outlines these trends and issues and explains what it all means for the future of strategy and conflict.

Terms and Definitions

Strategic studies, not unlike other disciplines, place a premium on definitions even though they are contextually and culturally situated. For example, an American definition of airpower may not necessarily resonate with, say, a Ugandan definition, given the vast differences in historical and operational experiences, as well as differences in capability and how the instrument of airpower is wielded to achieve political objectives set out by the respective polities. Ultimately, however, definitional debates about airpower, as well as land and sea power, tend to revolve around a handful of competing definitions.

Not so with cyberspace, and its consequential product, cyberpower. There is a plethora of competing definitions of cyberspace (see Box 16.1) and a number of competing definitions of cyberpower (see Box 16.3). Much of this definitional fruit salad can be explained away by the fact that as strategic phenomena, both cyberspace and cyberpower are relatively new when compared to land, sea, air, and space power. Of equal plausibility, however, is that many strategists are confronted with the uncomfortable notion that cyberspace is an intangible, fluid, and counterintuitive phenomenon (or if one prefers, a domain, which is discussed later) that defies the neat categorizations of the other strategic domains. The strategic effects that can be produced from cyberspace—cyberpower—are somewhat easier to grasp.

Cyberspace

The term cyberspace was first coined in a 1982 short story titled 'Burning Chrome,' by Canadian science fiction writer William Gibson, and later popularized in his famous 1984 novel *Neuromancer*. Gibson defined cyberspace as a 'consensual hallucination,' (Gibson 1984: 51) that takes place when humans interact with networked computers. The term has morphed and evolved ever since.

BOX 16.1 Selection of Competing Definitions of Cyberspace

Cyberspace is that intangible place between computers where information momentarily exists on its route from one end of the global network to the other.

Winn Schwartau, *Information Warfare, 2nd edition* (1996: 71)

'Cyberspace' is the information space consisting of the sum total of all computer networks.

Dorothy Denning, *Information Warfare and Security* (1999: 22)

Cyberspace consists of electronically powered hardware, networks, operating systems, and transmission standards.

Gregory J. Rattray, *Strategic Warfare in Cyberspace* (2001: 65)

Cyberspace: Domain characterized by the use of electronics and the electromagnetic spectrum to store, modify, and exchange data via networked systems and associated physical infrastructures.

General James E. Cartwright, *Vice-Chairman of the Joint Chiefs of Staff, Memorandum on Joint Terminology for Cyberspace Operations* (No Date: 7)

A global domain within the information environment consisting of the interdependent network of information technology infrastructures, including the Internet, telecommunications networks, computer systems, and embedded processors and controllers.

The Hon. Gordon England, Deputy Secretary of Defense (2008; quoted from Kuehl 2009: 27)

I think that a more accurate analogy can be found in the realm of science fiction's parallel universes—mysterious, invisible realms existing in parallel to the physical world, but able to influence it in countless ways. Although that's more metaphor than reality, we need to change the habit of thinking about cyberspace as if it's the same thing as "meat" space.

Jeffrey Carr, *Inside Cyber Warfare* (2010: xiii)

For the strategist, definitions attempt to lend cyberspace a certain tangibility and uniformity similar to the definitions of land, sea, air, and space power. Given the plethora of definitions circulating today, each emphasizing one or more aspects of cyberspace over others, the task of rendering a commonly held definition that all can refer to is most unlikely in the near future. Many definitions fail to emphasize the physical manifestations of cyberspace—such as computers and networks and other parts of the infrastructure—and the code that makes the machines and networks function. Other definitions depict cyberspace as an informational and virtual place that exists within an infrastructure that is implied. Such definitions emphasize the cognitive element where the human being interacts directly with information created, stored, and transmitted within cyberspace. Very few definitions combine the physical and cognitive elements of cyberspace; though cyberpower theorist Martin C. Libicki offers a characterization of cyberspace that includes the physical infrastructure, the code that provides the logic for computers to operate, and the human-computer interface that involves cognition (see Box 16.2).

All of the definitions in circulation today vary in terms of what constitutes cyberspace. As a result, some definitions include certain features that may be found in cyberspace, and others omit the same features. Definitional wars by nature can be tedious to those not directly involved, but, in the case of cyberspace, what is and what is not included in any definition may have serious implications for its strategic application:

BOX 16.2 Libicki's Three layers of cyberspace

Libicki divides cyberspace into three layers:

Physical comprising hardware, cables, satellites, routers, and other components of the physical infrastructure.

Syntactic comprises the code (software) that formats, instructs, and controls information.

Semantic comprises the cyberspace-human interface where information is meaningful to human beings.

Control of any one layer of cyberspace does not confer control of the other two remaining layers.

Martin C. Libicki, *Conquest in Cyberspace: National Security and Information Warfare* (2007: 8–9)

The issue of defining cyberspace is not trivial. What we decide to include or exclude from cyberspace has significant implications for the operations of power, as it determines the purview of cyberspace strategies and the operations of cyberpower.

Betz and Stevens (2012: 36)

An example of this issue can be found among cyberspace definitions that include the naturally occurring electromagnetic spectrum (EMS) and those that do not. The point being that inclusion or exclusion of the EMS in definitions can determine how, and by whom, cyberspace operations are conducted.

For the purposes of this essay, cyberspace is defined as:

> . . . a global domain within the information environment whose distinctive and unique character is framed by the use of electronics and the electromagnetic spectrum to create, store, modify, exchange, and exploit information via interdependent and interconnected networks using information-communication technologies.
>
> **Emphasis in original; Kuehl (2009: 28)**

Cyberpower

If cyberspace is the domain where information can be created, stored, transmitted, and generally manipulated, then cyberpower is the process of converting information into strategic effect. This strategic effect ultimately manifests itself in the cognitive processes of human beings, but can also indirectly manifest itself in the strategic domains of land, sea, air, and space, as well as cyberspace itself.

Compared to cyberspace, there are relatively fewer definitions of cyberpower. Cyberpower definitions emphasize how cyberspace can be used to fulfil the ends of strategy. One category of definition emphasizes the instrumentality of cyberpower without discussing the dialectic process of exercising that power in the face of an adversary. The other category of definition, acknowledges that cyberpower is used against a wilful and intelligent adversary that will probably also attempt to use cyberpower for their own ends. This chapter defines cyberpower as: the ability in peace, crisis, and war to exert prompt and sustained influence in and from cyberspace.

BOX 16.3 Competing Definitions of Cyberpower

The ability to use cyberspace to create advantages and influence events in all the operational environments and across the instruments of power.

Daniel T. Kuehl, *'From Cyberspace to Cyberpower: Defining the Problem.'* (2009: 38)

Cyberpower can be defined in terms of a set of resources that relate to the creation, control, and communication of electronic and computer-based information-infrastructure, networks, software, human skills. This includes not only the Internet of networked computers, but also Intranets, cellular technologies, and space-based communications. Defined behaviorally, cyberpower is the ability to obtain preferred outcomes through use of the electronically interconnected information resources of the cyberdomain.

Joseph S. Nye, Jr., *The Future of Power* (2011)

Cyberpower is the national ability to disrupt [the] obscured bad actor somewhere in the digitized globe, whether nonstate or state, in proportion to its motivations/capabilities to attack with violent effects and yet be resilient against imposed or enhanced nasty surprises across all critical nationally sustaining systems.

Chris C. Demchak, *Wars of Disruption and Resilience: Cybered Conflict, Power, and National Security* (2011: ix)

. . . cyber-power can be understood as the variety of powers that circulate in cyberspace and which shape the experiences of those who act in and through cyberspace . . . [C]yber-power is therefore the manifestation of power in cyberspace rather than a new or different form of power.

David J. Betz and Tim Stevens, *Cyberspace and the State: Towardsa Strategy for Cyberpower* (2012: 44)

Cyber War?

In early 2010, former US Director of National Intelligence Vice-Admiral Mike McConnell, US Navy (retired), asserted that, 'The United States is fighting a cyberwar today, and we are losing. It's that simple.' (McConnell 2010). McConnell is among numerous commentators and authors who use the term cyberwar (or cyber warfare or cyber conflict) to describe the range of nefarious activities that take place in cyberspace every day. The vast majority of these activities range from young hackers showing off their skills and online political protest and dissent called hacktivism, to criminal activity and espionage; very few can actually be described as actual cyber-attacks that might cause serious harm to the national security of a state. This is not to deny that hacker pranks and hacktivism are bothersome, even serious, or that crime and espionage carried out by cyber means are not significant issues in need of coherent policy responses. There is a question, however, as to whether these activities together constitute a cyberwar and therefore merit the type of response that a war might warrant.

Some authors argue, however, that the rise of cyberspace has changed the character of war significantly, making any malign cyber incident conducted against a state or its society or economy a new form of conflict. Actors who hold some form of animus toward their target and create a cyber incident to coerce that target to acquiesce to their political objective are often seen as engaging in cyberwar. Chris Demchak describes this emerging situation as a change in the very nature of conflict:

> The nature of 'war' moves from societally threatening one-off clashes of violence between close neighbors to a global version of long-term, episodically and catastrophically dangerous, chronic insecurities that involve the whole society.
> **Demchak (2011: 4)**

There are few examples of cyberpower being used in actual combat and the veracity of accounts of these isolated examples are subject to debate. For military planners, it is this use of cyberspace that is of significant interest. Since cyberpower in this context is used to achieve definable objectives as part of an overall strategy, it is perhaps more accurate to speak of 'cyberpower in war, or war by cyber means,' (Sheldon 2011) rather than the more misleading term cyberwar.

Definitions of both cyberspace and cyberpower are at a conceptually embryonic stage, leaving strategists to sort out what is true, what is false, and what is eminently arguable in cyberspace. This state of affairs might lead some to argue that cyberspace as a strategic sphere is not only immature, but is perhaps unworthy of consideration within the mainstream of strategic studies. Both assumptions would be a mistake. As a strategic sphere, cyberspace has been active in a variety of ways for many years now; and, given the pervasiveness of cyberspace in every aspect of modern life, its workings and dynamics are of the greatest concern to strategic studies and to any practicing strategist. After all, humans had been fighting on the land and at sea for many centuries before strategic theorists came along to define those activities and render them meaningful to political discourse. Why should cyberspace be any different?

Key points

- Definitions matter, but because cyberspace is a relatively new phenomenon within strategic studies it is likely that the definitional winnowing-out process will take at least several decades to complete.
- The popular term 'cyberwar' to some is a reflection of the changed character of war, but is also contentious.
- Despite the plethora of definitions, cyberpower has been used for several decades. Practice drives theory, not the other way around.

Cyberspace, Cyberpower, and the Infosphere

One can identify known characteristics and attributes of cyberspace and cyberpower. These characteristics and attributes are based on empirical observations of how cyberspace works and how cyberpower is wielded. It is too soon to tell how many of the characteristics and attributes are permanent features of cyberspace and cyberpower, or whether they may change along with changes in cyber technologies or the motivations of actors that use cyberspace.

The Infosphere

The infosphere, also known as the information environment or domain, is a realm without which cyberspace is meaningless and cyberpower does not exist. The infosphere is best thought of as a place in space and time where information exists and flows (Lonsdale 2004: 181). The currency of cyberspace is information found in the infosphere, and the use of the information to achieve political objectives is cyberpower. Information—how it is created, stored, communicated, and manipulated—is a product of the infosphere, yet cyberspace far from composes the sum of all infosphere activities. Cyberspace is merely a subset of the infosphere, albeit an increasingly significant one. The infosphere consists of everything from direct human interactions where information is exchanged, and mediated communication through such technologies as the telephone, and printed matter. Cyberspace, however, is rapidly filling the various functions of the infosphere. It seems, for example, that young people today actually would rather 'text' than talk to each other.

Cyberspace Characteristics

With its subordination to the infosphere noted, certain characteristics of cyberspace can be deduced and identified.

Low-cost of entry: the resources and expertise required to enter, exist in, and exploit cyberspace are extremely modest compared to the resources and expertise required for exploiting the land, sea, air, and space domains. Anyone with access to networked information-communication technologies can use it.

Multiple actors: the low-cost of entry into cyberspace means that the number and types of actors able to operate in the domain and potentially generate strategic effect is virtually unlimited when compared to the land, sea, air, and space domains. Individuals, groups, organizations, corporations, non-state actors, as well as states all participate in cyberspace.

Cyberspace relies on the electromagnetic spectrum: cyberspace cannot exist without being able to exploit the naturally existing electromagnetic spectrum. Without the electromagnetic spectrum, not only would millions of information and communications technologies be unable to communicate with each other, but these technologies themselves would be unable to function.

Cyberspace requires man-made objects to exist: this makes cyberspace unique when compared to the land, sea, air, and space domains. Without integrated circuit boards, semiconductors and microchips, fibre optics, and other information and communications technologies, there would be no cyberspace.

Cyberspace can be constantly replicated: There can be as many cyberspaces at any one time as one can possibly generate. With cyberspace, there can be many in existence at any one time—some contested, some not. For the most part, nothing is final in cyberspace. With airpower, enemy aircraft can be destroyed, and there the matter ends. In cyberspace, a jihadist website can be purposefully shut down, only for the same jihadists to start a new website within hours on a different server using a different domain name. Similarly, networks can be quickly repaired and reconstituted, thanks to relatively inexpensive and readily available hardware.

Cyberspace is near instantaneous: information traverses cyberspace at what is called net-speed—the speed at which any part of the network at any one time is able to move information. In many cases net-speed is nearly the speed of light; in other cases it is not quite that fast. For a human user, however, modern networks can seem to move information almost instantaneously. While this characteristic is becoming commonplace about cyberspace, it can mask another reality that is perhaps more mundane. Information has to be sent and emerge into a comprehensible and useful form by human beings. The near-instantaneous speed of cyberspace can seemingly collapse time and space, yet the cognitive processes so crucial to cyberpower—creativity, or the response to strategic effect—still take place at a very human pace.

Cyberpower Attributes

Cyberpower is pervasive: Land, sea, air, and space power are able to generate strategic effect on each of the other domains, but nothing generates strategic effect in all domains so absolutely and simultaneously as cyberpower. Cyber dependencies are a matter of fact in the military, economy, and society of a growing number of countries, and they critically enable land, sea, air, and space power—as well as other instruments of power, such as diplomacy, media, and commerce.

Cyberpower is complementary: unlike land, sea, and airpower, but in many ways like space power, cyberpower is largely a complementary instrument. It is indirect because the coercive ability of cyberpower is limited and is likely to remain limited. Shutting down a power grid via cyberpower, for example, would undoubtedly have catastrophic consequences, but rather than coercing its victim to concede to an attacker's demands, it may, in fact, only invite an even more catastrophic response.

Cyberpower can be stealthy: One of cyberpower's attractions for many users is the ability to wield it surreptitiously on a global scale without it being attributed to the perpetrator. Malicious software can be planted in enemy networks without knowledge until the cyber weapon is activated and causes its intended damage. Databases can be raided for classified or proprietary information, and the owners of that information may not be any the wiser as terabits of data are stolen. Similarly, private citizens can go about their day-to-day lives only to discover that cyber criminals have used their credit cards or ruined their credit rating by stealing their identity. This ability to use cyberpower stealthily, aided by the inherent difficulties of attributing the identity and motivation of most attackers, makes it a very attractive instrument for those who want to undertake clandestine nefarious activities.

A global Commons or 'Globally Connected Domain'

Cyberspace is often described as, and assumed to be, a global commons—an internationally recognized legal status granted to the international high seas, Antarctica, and outer space. This is an understandable assumption to make given the near ubiquity of cyberspace and its low cost of entry. Seemingly anyone and everyone can access cyberspace for free. The reality is somewhat more prosaic. Figures vary somewhat, but it is estimated that up to 90 per cent of the infrastructure that comprises cyberspace is privately owned, with the remaining 10 per cent or so owned by governments. Private and government ownership of an entity like cyberspace immediately calls into question the assumption that it is a global commons. Furthermore, to interact with cyberspace, one has to somehow gain access to a computer and a network. Although users only have to pay marginal costs for gaining access to cyberspace, sometimes these costs can be substantial, especially if high capacity systems are required to achieve some objective.

Some authors recognize these facts but still proclaim cyberspace to be a global commons, citing the ubiquity of cyberspace and the ever-increasing tens of millions of people around the world who are interacting with it on a daily basis, perhaps giving cyberspace the *appearance* of being a global commons. Yet, such claims are problematic as more and more states—democracies and authoritarian regimes alike—are increasingly asserting sovereignty in cyberspace, leading to what some have identified as the growing territorializing of cyberspace. In response to claims that cyberspace is a global commons, others, such as the US government, recognize the unique elements of cyberspace—its global ubiquity, over a billion users, and massive international information flows—and have instead labelled it a 'globally connected domain'. (US Joint Chiefs of Staff 2011: 3) This description is far from perfect, but is perhaps a more accurate reflection of the status of cyberspace in domestic and international politics.

Key points

- Cyberspace exists within the long-established information environment, or infosphere.
- Cyberspace has numerous characteristics that make it unique compared to the strategic domains of land, sea, air, and space power.
- Cyberpower possesses several attributes that make it an increasingly important strategic instrument.
- Cyberspace is often described as a global commons, but is perhaps best described as a globally connected domain.

A New Dimension for Conflict

With over a billion users combined with the growing ubiquity of cyberspace in societies, it is not surprising that cyberspace has become a place of constant conflict, resulting in disruption, deception, and theft. While conflict is an ever-present feature of cyberspace, not all conflicts there equate to what many would regard as war in the Clausewitzian sense. Disputes involve personal vendettas, organizational rivalries, and private citizens motivated by nationalist sentiment. Attacks often involve the cyber networks of states, commercial enterprises, and individuals. States have also attacked cyber targets in other states, as is alleged to have happened in the Stuxnet malware attack against the nuclear facility at Natanz, Iran, in 2009 (see Box 16.4).

Since cyberspace is offence-dominant for now, the advantage in cyber conflict can be said to favour the attacker. As a result, it might seem that cyberspace is a target-rich environment for any would-be attacker, though it should be noted that cyber-attack is not without its problems and challenges. Some scholars believe that the ease of cyber-attack against targets

---

BOX 16.4 Stuxnet

Stuxnet is an unusual type of malicious software (malware) that targets computers and networks that meet very specific configurations. Where other types of malware harm every computer in infected networks, Stuxnet only harmed a specific set of computers in one location, namely a nuclear enrichment plant at Natanz in Iran. Discovered and made public in the summer of 2010, Stuxnet is said to have first appeared in June 2009, with follow-on variants detected in March and then April, 2010.

It is now widely believed that Stuxnet was developed by a state (most speculation suggests Israel, possibly assisted by the United States) to target centrifuges used to enrich uranium at a nuclear facility at Natanz, Iran. It is believed that of the approximately 4,700 centrifuges in operation at Natanz, about 1,000 were destroyed from late 2009 through to early 2010. It is believed that Stuxnet destroyed the centrifuges by infecting their operational control system. According to reports, operators of the control system were unaware of anything untoward happening, apparently due to a feature of Stuxnet that deceived operators into believing that centrifuge operations were normal. In reality, Stuxnet compromised control of the centrifuges and spun approximately 10 per cent of them so fast that they were destroyed.

Stuxnet is believed to have set back the Iranian nuclear programme by several months, though at one point Israeli intelligence believed that the programme had been delayed by several years. Since then, the Iranians have redoubled their efforts in their nuclear programme, and it seems that while Stuxnet successfully struck its target its effect was temporary.

Despite this, Stuxnet is now widely regarded as a major turning point in the evolution of offensive cyber capabilities and cyber warfare in general. Stuxnet proves that an offensive cyber capability can more or less precisely target a remote system, compromise it, and cause physical destruction.

---

vital to the everyday functioning of modern societies heralds an age of perpetual disruption, the worst effects of which can only be mitigated by an emphasis on resilience in the networking of critical infrastructures and the storage and transmission of sensitive information.

The Problem of Cyber Security

In cyberspace the offence enjoys an advantage over the defence, and so the challenge for those charged with cyber security is to be successful in maintaining defences all of the time; an impossible expectation to meet indefinitely. For any would-be cyber-attacker, the challenge is significantly easier in many respects: they only have to be successful once to attack a target system or network.

Effective cyber security cannot hope to prevent every cyber-attack from occurring. It can, however, mitigate the worst effects of any cyber-attack by reducing the prospects of any catastrophic consequence of an attack or by taking steps to reduce the extent or duration of any disruption caused by the initial attack. These mitigation measures involve technical solutions, inculcating a culture of cyber security, and implementing measures to ensure resilience.

Technical solutions to cyber-attack include up-to-date cyber security software, capabilities, and methods applied to information and communication technologies and networks, such as firewalls, anti-virus software, and thoroughly trained system administrators who maintain networks. Inculcating a culture of cyber security includes educating workforces who must use cyberspace in best cyber security practices and how to spot potential threats and problems, as well as enforcing laws and regulations against anyone who knowingly or negligently endangers cyber security. Resilience measures include better protection of sensitive information, perhaps by excluding it from accessible networks, as well as removing the interface between critical infrastructure and accessible networks to prevent remote, unauthorized access to services and systems that are important to societies.

Cyber security is also plagued by the problem of attribution. Cyber-attacks can be masked, routed through various countries, and even designed to give the appearance of originating from somewhere other than their true point of origin. For any victim of a cyber-attack, this makes it difficult to attribute a cyber-attack to its true perpetrator, limiting opportunities to apportion blame or formulate a response that might include a retaliatory cyber-attack or even the use of military force. Apportioning blame and formulating an appropriate response to cyber-attack is problematic because attribution can be extremely difficult.

Attribution is more than just locating the geographical origins of a cyber-attack. It is also about attributing the identity of the attacker and their motivations for the attack. Just because a cyber-attack may be attributed to have originated from a certain country, it does not necessarily mean that those who carried out the attack did so with the knowledge and authorization of the government of that country, or that the attack in question was indeed intended to be an act of war. Attribution of attacker identity and motivation is extremely hard to ascertain reliably and again stymies the attribution of responsibility for a cyber-attack, as well as the formulation of an appropriate response. For example, a cyber-attack might be attributed to have originated from a certain country, but cyber forensic tools and methods are unable to ascertain reliably whether the attack in question was carried out by a gang for criminal purposes or by agents of that country's government for the purposes of espionage.

With the significant challenges involved with cyber security, coupled with the offensive advantage enjoyed by cyber-attack, a number of scholars have promoted the idea of cyber deterrence as a means of preventing catastrophic cyber-attacks. Conceptually, there is no such thing as cyber deterrence, there is only deterrence. Yet, still the notion that cyber-attacks might be deterred has some merit, depending on the deterrence strategy employed. A large portion of the literature concerned with cyberspace and deterrence focuses on deterrence by punishment strategies, whereby a cyber-attack is punished by a retaliatory cyber-attack or some other military response. The problem with the deterrence by punishment strategy is that it presumes that not only will the victim of the cyber-attack be able to attribute the location of where the attack originated, but also the identities and motivations of the attackers. Given that attribution is still a significant challenge, a deterrence by punishment strategy in cyberspace is both unreliable and carries a high degree of risk of not only overreaction to any attack, but even complete miscalculation that results in the punishment of innocent bystanders. Furthermore, knowing that attribution is a challenge, any would-be cyber-attacker would find the deterrence by punishment strategy lacking in credibility, making it potentially worse than useless.

Deterrence by denial strategies, on the other hand, places the onus of miscalculation on the would-be cyber-attacker. Greater investment in cyber defences, creating a culture of cyber security, and resilience measures can raise the risks and reduce the benefits of mounting cyber-attacks. Handfuls of cyber-attacks might get through here and there, but the effort placed into the attack may prove to be too costly if successes are too few and far between.

The problem with deterrence by denial strategies in cyberspace is that they are costly to implement because they create operational inefficiencies and lead to a never-ending requirement for state of the art equipment and services. Creating a meaningful culture of cyber security among users of cyberspace to foster deterrence by denial forces users to comply with stringent security requirements that may not always be followed by users. Resilience measures are also very costly to implement because they require stand-alone platforms and back-up systems that are run in parallel to systems used on a day-to-day basis.

The Challenges and Unknowns of Cyber-Attack

While cyber security is beset by challenges, it might seem that cyber-attack enjoys a free reign in cyberspace. In reality, while the offence is dominant in cyberspace, cyber-attack is not only without its own challenges, but is also beset with a number of unknowns.

It is alleged that the Israelis took the lead on the Stuxnet operation but required the backing and assistance of allies. Cyber operations of this scale have many moving parts and are thus subject to the friction that will inevitably arise out of such complexity. Advanced technical expertise, meticulous intelligence preparation, sophisticated logistics and tens, if not hundreds, of millions of dollars are required to pull off cyber-attacks on the scale of Stuxnet. All of these activities have also to be undertaken under the cover of the strictest secrecy to prevent the target from taking defensive measures that would eliminate operational or technical weaknesses before they can be exploited. Cyber-attacks involve extensive planning and preparation, and may fail long before they can be implemented.

Cyber-attacks are burdensome and time-consuming because their success depends on extensive intelligence collection and surveillance of targets. Intelligence collection and surveillance of targets in cyberspace requires penetrating adversary computers and networks, running the risk of discovery. Furthermore, though cyber-attacks might be successful, they will entail unforeseen and unintended consequences, including the risk of blowback. For example, malicious software (malware) might take down an intended target in cyberspace, but may then propagate throughout the network attacking unintended targets (hence the term 'blowback'), including cyber assets belonging to the attacker. An example of unintended consequences would be a cyber-attack against the critical infrastructure of a state that results in civilian casualties because hospitals were affected in the aftermath of power and telecommunication outages.

The rapid offence-defence cycle and sustaining the offence in cyberspace are also challenges. The rapid offence-defence cycle between cyber-attack capabilities and defences means that the effectiveness of offensive cyber weapons will be short lived. Once a belligerent tips their cyber-attack hand it does not take long for a defender to come up with a defence to a new offensive capability. This means that the employment of cyber-attack weapons will ideally be for a large strategic payoff, rather than a short-term tactical advantage. It also means that after a short time, the ability of an attacker to sustain the offence in cyberspace becomes increasingly challenging as the initiative starts to shift towards the defence.

> ### Key points
>
> - Cyber security—or cyber defence—is exceptionally challenging due to the offensive advantage enjoyed by cyber-attackers.
> - Attribution of attacker identity and motivation is particularly challenging, and can stymie an effective response.
> - In cyberspace, deterrence by denial strategies is more effective than deterrence by punishment.
> - While it is easier to attack rather than defend in cyberspace, cyber-attack is not without its risks and challenges.

A Twenty-first Century Revolution in Military Affairs?

Individuals, organizations, non-state actors, and states are using cyberspace, and wielding cyberpower, every day in new and innovative ways for the purposes of achieving political objectives. Cyberspace and cyberpower enable existing human activities and types of military power, but they do not render them obsolete. Cyberpower, however, also changes the character of human activity. For instance, cyberspace has radically changed how corporations organize themselves. Cyberspace has also created the opportunity for super-empowered individuals to emerge in the realm of economic activity. In the realm of strategy, cyberpower is recasting the context in which all strategic activity takes place, namely international politics. Cyberpower also blurs the distinction between war and peace, undermines the privileged role of the state in war, and might possibly have long-term implications for how military forces are organized.

Cyberpower Recasts International Politics

The pervasiveness of cyberspace, and the ubiquity of cyberpower, has an impact on international relations and the privileged role of the state in international politics.

The rise of cyberpower has helped developing states accelerate their economic development, while enabling their military, diplomatic, and cultural instruments of national power. Cyberpower has allowed a number of developing states to enjoy significant economic growth and a commensurate increase in the potency of their instruments of national power, thus enabling them to catch up with developed states. This phenomenon, best encapsulated in the rise of Brazil, India, and China has recast the distribution of power within international politics resulting in net gains for rising powers, and relative losses for established, developed powers.

The rise of cyberpower has also empowered individuals, organizations, and non-state actors, allowing them to have a global reach, a form of global influence, that hitherto was unavailable to them because it was too expensive or beyond their technical capabilities. It also enables individuals and groups with belligerent intentions to use cyber capabilities offensively against targets across the world. This empowering of individuals and groups has led to a redistribution of power within international politics that further undermines the monopoly of power traditionally enjoyed by states. Nevertheless, this empowerment through cyberpower only goes so far. States still enjoy capabilities and capacities for the employment and projection of power that are beyond the reach of individuals and groups. Although many scholars believe that cyberpower significantly undermines state power by weakening state sovereignty, states are finding various ways of asserting their sovereignty in cyberspace.

Claims that cyberpower has recast international politics for individuals and groups at the expense of states has greater plausibility than the assertion that cyberpower renders state sovereignty irrelevant. The state will continue to be the primary actor in international politics, despite the irritation felt in capitals across the globe about certain activities undertaken by individuals and groups in cyberspace.

A Coming Change in the Character of War?

Cyberpower is a useful strategic instrument since it can be wielded globally with a certain degree of anonymity in peace, crisis, and war. Cyberpower enables global reach, creating the ability to attack critical systems such as national infrastructure remotely, dupe individuals into divulging sensitive information, and disrupting services. Such attacks, deception operations, and disruptions by cyberpower potentially blur the distinction between peace and war. Terrorism, and the use of terrorists as proxies by states, already blurs this distinction but cyberpower adds to what might potentially be a dangerous ambiguity between peace and war. States subject to countless cyber-attacks that lead to significant societal disruption, or suffer the loss of sensitive information related to national defence may perceive that they are the victims of actions that are a prelude to war or merit a military response. Misperception and miscalculation are major risks in such circumstances. If these kinds of attacks, disruptions, and deception operations become the norm in international politics, they might come to be perceived as a kind of background noise to the everyday dynamics of international relations. For some observers, these trends indicate that we are entering an age of perpetual disruption.

Cyberpower creates great efficiencies in how people organize activities. Cyberpower also magnifies the ability of individuals to control operations and transmit virtually unlimited amounts of data across the planet at virtually no cost, creating opportunities that were unimaginable only a few decades ago. Cyberpower has already demonstrated these opportunities and benefits in the economic sphere, with corporations increasing both productivity and profit margins while using fewer people and leaner, flatter, and more responsive organizational structures. Modern militaries are also subject to these greater efficiencies and magnified effects thanks to cyberpower, creating leaner force structures and more automated capabilities, which place a premium on recruiting more highly skilled personnel. Military hierarchies are likely to shrink in size, as will numbers of personnel required to staff them. There is already a growing reliance on automated capabilities and systems, such as remotely piloted vehicles, and the cost of training even the lowest-ranking servicemen and women is increasing due to the complex technical skills required in modern militaries. The implications of these cyberpower trends within militaries are debatable, and cannot be divorced from the context of how, when, and for what purpose military force will used in the twenty-first century. Nevertheless, it is plausible to suggest that as military organization and structure changes due to the pervasiveness of cyberpower, when and how military force will be used might also change. These changes might culminate in a twenty-first century revolution in military affairs (RMA) if they lead to new military doctrines, force structure, and changes in the conduct of war.

Key points

- Cyberpower has contributed to the redistribution of power taking place in international politics today.

- Cyberpower has empowered individuals, organizations, and non-state actors, allowing them greater participation and influence in international politics.

- Cyberpower has not rendered the state irrelevant. Cyberpower has made sovereignty more porous, but states are increasingly asserting sovereignty in cyberspace.

- Cyberpower is impacting not only the structure of military force, but also how it is used and in what circumstances. Cyberpower might produce a revolution in military affairs in the twenty-first century.

- Some believe that the rise of cyberpower heralds the arrival of an age of perpetual disruption.

 ## Conclusion

Cyberspace continues to pervade ever more deeply into every function of modern societies around the world. The dependencies and complex interactions that emerge in cyberspace benefit societies because of the low-cost communication it facilitates and because of the efficiencies and automation of tedious functions it creates and enables. These dependencies and complex interactions also create a host of vulnerabilities throughout modern society. These vulnerabilities can be exploited by those intent on launching cyber-attacks.

As more and more state functions, including military capabilities and command and control, become increasingly dependent on cyberspace, strategists should concern themselves with the vulnerabilities and opportunities created by cyberspace. The challenge is finding the right balance between absolute cyber security that will invariably constrain the use of cyberspace and unconstrained cyber-attack that ricochets throughout networks with unintended consequences, creating a real risk of blowback.

Nearly every facet of strategy in the contemporary world is affected, influenced, and shaped by cyberpower. The implications of this have yet to play out fully, and it is for these reasons that cyberspace and cyberpower are of vital interest and importance to the strategist and strategic studies.

 ## Questions

1. Why are there so many definitions of cyberspace and cyberpower in circulation? Are definitions important, or is it more important that various actors are using cyberspace?

2. What is the difference between cyberspace and cyberpower?

3. Is there such a thing as cyber war?

4. What is the relationship between the infosphere and cyberspace? What is the difference between the two?

5. What makes cyberspace unique compared to the other strategic domains?

6. What other attributes might cyberpower possess?

7. Why is cyber security so challenging? What is your opinion of the cyber security solutions offered in this chapter? What would you do differently?

8. What makes cyber-attack so dangerous, despite the fact that it is easier to do when compared to cyber security?

9. Is the rise of cyberpower a potential revolution in military affairs? If your answer is yes, why? If your answer is no, why not?

10. Relate cyberpower to other strategic issues covered in this book—what possible connections are you able to discern?

Further Reading

J. Arquilla and D. Ronfeldt (eds), *In Athena's Camp: Preparing for Conflict in the Information Age* (Santa Monica, CA: RAND, 1997) a groundbreaking collection of essays that helped define the field, including Arquilla and Ronfeldt's classic essay, 'Cyberwar is Coming!'

S. W. Brenner, *Cyberthreats: The Emerging Fault Lines of the Nation State* (New York: Oxford University Press, 2009) is a comprehensive analysis of cyber threats and the problem of attributing them.

J. Carr, *Inside Cyber Warfare* (Sebastopol, CA: O'Reilly Media, 2010) is an in-depth primer on the actors, capabilities, and methods of cyber warfare.

R. A. Clarke and R. K. Knake, *Cyber War: The Next Threat to National Security and What to Do About It* (New York: Ecco, 2010) provides some thought-provoking solutions to the cyber security problem, as well as other policy issues pertaining to cyberspace, from a US perspective. Regarded by many to be alarmist in its assessment of cyber threats.

C. C. Demchak, *Wars of Disruption and Resilience: Cybered Conflict, Power, and National Security* (Athens, GA: The University of Georgia Press, 2011) is an intricate and scholarly treatment of cyberpower and the future of conflict and international politics.

F. D. Kramer, S. H. Starr, and L. K. Wentz (eds), *Cyberpower and National Security* (Washington, DC: Potomac Books, 2009) is an excellent collection of essays covering all the major cyberspace policy issues of concern to any modern state.

M. C. Libicki, *Conquest in Cyberspace: National Security and Information Warfare* (Cambridge: Cambridge University Press, 2007) is one of the major theoretical works on cyberspace and cyberpower in recent years.

D. J. Lonsdale, *The Nature of War in the Information Age: Clausewitzian Future* (London: Frank Cass, 2004) a landmark work that applies Clausewitzian strategic logic to cyberpower, and demolishes the arguments of cyber true-believers.

J. S. Nye, Jr., *The Future of Power* (New York: Public Affairs, 2011) provides an interesting analysis of how cyberpower is significantly impacting international politics.

W. A. Owens, K. W. Dam, and H. S. Lin (eds), *Technology, Policy, Law, and Ethics Regarding US Acquisition and Use of Cyberattack Capabilities* (Washington, D.C., The National Academies Press, 2009) is a US National Research Council report that provides an exhaustive and detailed survey of the implications of acquiring and using cyber-attack capabilities.

Web Links

Atlantic Council's *Cyber Statecraft Initiative* **http://www.acus.org/tags/cyber-statecraft-initiative** This site provides excellent analysis of cyberpower issues and their impact on national security, statecraft, and international politics.

The Citizen Lab **http://citizenlab.org/** Hosted by the Munk School of Global Affairs at the University of Toronto, this innovative outfit stands at the intersection of digital media, global security, and human rights. The Citizen Lab has helped produce a series of reports that have, among other things, uncovered an alleged Chinese cyber espionage ring and exposed the sale of Internet filtering technologies by Western corporations to authoritarian regimes.

Cyber War News **http://www.cyberwarnews.info/** A useful news aggregation site for cyber warfare and cyberpower issues.

Cyber War Blog **http://cyberwarblog.com/** Devoted specifically to commentary on cyberwar, cyberethics, and cyber-attacks.

Cyber Conflict Studies Association **http://www.cyberconflict.org/** A not-for-profit organization that conducts rigorous and in-depth research on cyber warfare issues.

Part III

The Future of Strategy

17	**A New Agenda for Security and Strategy?**	323
	James J. Wirtz	
18	**Strategic Studies and its Critics**	341
	Columba Peoples	
19	**The Practice of Strategy**	358
	Colin S. Gray and Jeannie L. Johnson	
20	**Does Strategic Studies have a Future?**	377
	Lawrence Freedman	

A New Agenda for Security and Strategy?

JAMES J. WIRTZ

 Chapter Contents

Introduction	324
The Need for a Conceptual Framework	325
Population: The Demographics of Global Politics	327
Commons Issues	329
Direct Environmental Damage	332
Disease	334
Sensitivities and Vulnerabilities	338
Conclusion	339

 Reader's Guide

This chapter explores a series of issues that have not been included traditionally on national security agendas or considered to be within the purview of strategy. Unlike most assessments of non-traditional security issues, it does not define a specific problem as a threat to national security simply because it creates the possibility of casualties, damage to personal property, or threatens economic prosperity. Rather, it develops a utilitarian assessment of environmental, resource, and population issues to discover if strategy, military force, or existing strategic literature can address these issues and problems in a useful way. If strategy, strategists, or military force can address a specific problem, or if it can be determined that they are a cause of a particular problem, or if they can be forced to change in response to some transnational trend, then the issue should be a subject for strategy and strategists. The chapter also suggests that non-traditional security issues are beginning to influence core national security considerations in ways that were not fully anticipated by proponents of a new agenda for security and strategy.

Introduction

During the cold war, high politics dominated national security agendas. Issues of war and peace, nuclear deterrence and crisis management, summit diplomacy, arms control, and alliance politics preoccupied those people with a professional or personal interest in world politics or military strategy. By contrast, low politics—the environment, the management of scarce resources, or efforts to constrain population growth—were often perceived as a source of trouble, but rarely as a threat to national security. Occasionally, issues of low politics managed to reach national security agendas. Fallout from nuclear testing in the atmosphere prompted a growing awareness of the environmental consequences of the nuclear arms race, leading to the Partial Test Ban Treaty (1963). The oil shocks of the 1970s made Americans aware of their dependence on foreign oil and the important role conservation could play in preserving US economic prosperity and diplomatic leverage. However, for the most part, high and low politics were treated as separate issues by policymakers and scholars alike.

Starting in the late 1980s, some scholars came to believe that the hierarchy between high and low politics had been reversed. They suggested that non-traditional issues should be placed at the top of national security agendas. Several theories of international relations can explain the rise to prominence, so to speak, of low politics. Realists, for example, might suggest that, as the overarching preoccupation with the cold war evaporated, issues once considered 'lesser included threats' could be expected to appear more important. They would also note that with the collapse of the cold war divide, management of these global issues might become increasingly possible, especially if the United States, the lone superpower, used its diplomatic, economic, and military leverage to good effect. Neo-institutionalists would probably add that new forms of transnational management are increasingly important in world affairs. They might point to the prominent role played by international governmental organizations (IGOs, e.g. the United Nations), international non-governmental organizations (INGOs, e.g. the Carnegie Endowment for International Peace or Greenpeace) or even a plethora of grass-roots movements in tackling tough issues that transcend international boundaries. These local organizations and movements not only push global issues—women's rights, ozone depletion, the acquired immune deficiency syndrome (AIDS) epidemic—onto national agendas, they also help initiate and coordinate international responses to transnational problems. Scholars who focus on the way the communications revolution is changing human interaction often highlight the fact that groups of people scattered across the globe can now orchestrate political or informational campaigns using the Internet. Grass-roots organizations now monitor deforestation in the Amazon or search for unauthorized development along the California Coast. Individuals, educated and empowered by new communication technologies, are increasingly aware of the suffering of others in distant lands. There is a growing awareness, especially among people in the developed world, that international boundaries are a weak barrier to the problems that afflict the poorest parts of the planet.

At the dawn of the new century, however, perspectives about the relative importance of low and high politics again changed when the darkest side of the information revolution became apparent. Al-Qaeda and its supporters exploited modern communication and transportation systems to launch terrorist attacks against innocent civilians in New York,

London, Madrid, and Bali. The debate about the relative importance of high and low politics seemed to come full circle. The low politics of the information revolution, globalization, and demographics are now the stuff of high politics, influencing national security and homeland defence agendas around the world.

The Need for a Conceptual Framework

To say that low politics are perceived as more important in the aftermath of the cold war is beyond dispute. Major research projects had already been undertaken in the 1990s by Thomas Homer-Dixon and his colleagues at the University of Toronto and by the International Peace Research Institute, Oslo (PRIO), to demonstrate a link between resource scarcity and the outbreak of war or other forms of violence (Homer-Dixon 1991). Other researchers have noted that damage to the environment should be considered as a threat to national security because it can cause casualties or even kill. Marc Levy, for instance, has suggested that damage to the earth's ozone layer should be considered to be a security threat because it causes cancer, blindness, and even death (1995). However, to say that environmental damage or resource scarcity should now be considered as national security issues raises a host of problems, especially for those who are concerned with the development of military strategy. It is not exactly clear, for instance, how military forces can help reduce the build-up of greenhouse gases in the atmosphere to prevent global warming. Similarly, it is not clear how military action can help stop the AIDS epidemic that is sweeping Africa and other parts of the world. Non-traditional threats to national security clearly exist, but it is difficult to discern how military formations, strategy, or strategists can respond constructively to these matters. Further complicating the issue is the fact that low and high politics are interacting in complex ways; issues of low politics are not completely divorced from grand strategy. For example, the possibility that Tehran might acquire nuclear weapons does not pose an immediate threat to Middle East energy reserves, but it does have a global economic impact by causing the price of oil to rise in already tight energy markets. Low politics, while not posing direct security threats themselves, are shaping and are in turn being shaped by traditional strategic concerns.

Those who suggest that environmental or global issues are a national security threat often resort to Malthusian scenarios to justify their judgements (Orme 1997). Resource scarcity or the disorder produced by overpopulation or rapid depopulation, for instance, are identified as causes of war, but these Malthusian scenarios are not entirely plausible, and recent studies have found only an extremely modest impact of resource scarcity on the outbreak of violence (Goldstone 2002). Malthusian scenarios seem to suggest that the military should prepare to contain the symptoms of nagging transnational problems before they burst into some sort of cataclysmic fury. One might also hope that educational, technical, or social action could be taken before environmental, resource, or population pressures produce wars that literally involve battles for human survival. No one would disagree that these environmental or global issues are important, it just seems unlikely that negative trends will continue indefinitely into the future and produce raging resource wars (see Box 17.1).

Already, there are positive signs on the horizon. Population growth rates, which reached a peak of 2 per cent per year in the 1960s, are declining and will continue to do so just as long as people grow healthier, wealthier, and better educated.

BOX 17.1 Thomas Robert Malthus

Malthus was born on 13 February 1766. He graduated from Jesus College, Cambridge in 1788, worked for a time as a minister and returned to Cambridge as a fellow in 1793, the year Louis XVI was guillotined by revolutionaries. Malthus took a dim view of utopian philosophies advanced by William Godwin and M. Condorcet. In response, in 1798 he published *An Essay on the Principle of Population as It Affects the Future Improvement of Society*. Using data supplied by none other than Benjamin Franklin on the population growth rates of American villages, Malthus offered a startling observation: populations grow in a geometric fashion while food supplies only increase by merely an arithmetic ratio. In other words, if current trends continued, the human race would inevitably outpace the food supply, leading to cataclysmic social collapse. Two factors might hold off this day of reckoning: efforts to reduce birth rates, which Malthus termed 'preventive measures'; and war, disease, and starvation, developments described by the misnomer 'positive measures'. Luckily, Malthus's predictions proved incorrect. He failed to account for the fact that trends rarely continue indefinitely into the future. In fact, the amount of raw materials used per unit of economic output has actually been decreasing over the last century, while available resources have been increasing. Once adjusted for inflation, *The Economist's* index of prices of industrial raw materials has dropped 80 per cent since 1845.

Defining some transnational issues as a national security threat can create a new set of problems. Often military forces are the only units available that possess the logistical capabilities or able-bodied and disciplined workforce needed to cope with the aftermath of natural or political disasters. As the effort to provide disaster relief to victims of the 2004 tsunami demonstrated, military and naval forces drawn from 19 countries and non-governmental organizations worked together to provide food, shelter, and medical supplies, especially to people left isolated by the effects of the tidal wave. Regardless of circumstances or initial intentions, however, the introduction of military forces risks making things worse by turning a public health crisis or police problem into an armed conflict. The UN intervention in Somalia, for instance, quickly deteriorated from an effort to prevent mass starvation into a particularly nasty form of warfare; urban combat. Launching a *war* on drugs inevitably leads to casualties among innocent bystanders, disruption of peasant life, increased rural poverty, and armed resistance. Soldiers also complain that humanitarian operations, peacekeeping duties, or conducting border patrols divert resources and training away from their primary responsibility: preparing to engage in conventional combat and win the nation's wars. Although military forces will continue to play a critical role in responding to natural disasters, simply defining environmental, resource, or population problems as security issues is not without costs or risks.

Instead of becoming mired in the debate about the gravity of today's environmental problems or what constitutes an appropriate mission for military units, it would be better to assess this new security agenda to determine if and how strategy can respond to these issues. This utilitarian assessment would unfold along three dimensions. First, if military units can take some action that addresses a particular problem or issue in a useful way, then the subject is of importance to strategy and strategists, but if the threat of force, the use of force, or even the logistical or technical assistance that can be supplied by military units does little to respond to a given problem, it is probably best not to treat the specific issue as a security threat. Second, if military action somehow produces environmental, resource, or demographic consequences, then these issues are of interest to strategists. The time has arrived to measure the cost of conflict by using more than just the immediate losses of blood and treasure. A global perspective requires strategists to consider the long-term environmental consequences of war and preparations for war. Third, low politics are of strategic interest when they create effects that are likely to shape the way force is used in the future. In other words, will low politics create changes in the international security environment that will force a significant transformation of strategy, military force structure, or doctrine? This utilitarian assessment stands in contrast to typical discussions of environmental or resource issues because it defines security threats in terms of what constitutes an appropriate response (i.e. use of force), rather than the potential of an issue to threaten a nation's or an individual's wellbeing (i.e. scarcity of potable water).

Is there a new agenda for security and strategy? The answer might in fact be yes: especially if strategy, strategists, or military force can address a specific problem, can be the cause of a specific problem, or can be forced to change in response to some transnational trend. What follows is a brief survey of the relationship of strategy to several transnational issues that are said to make up a new agenda for security and strategy.

Key points

- Scholars debate whether to include non-traditional issues—pollution, threats to biodiversity, disease—on national security agendas.
- Malthusian scenarios remain popular as a justification for treating environmental issues as security problems.
- Defining social or environmental issues as a national security problem is not without costs and risks.
- A utilitarian assessment may be useful to determine if there is a new agenda for security and strategy.

Population: The Demographics of Global Politics

Nearly every problem identified in this chapter is rooted in the population explosion that occurred in the twentieth century. Since the mid-century, the number of people living on the planet has grown by 3.5 billion; over 6 billion people were alive at the start of the twenty-first century. With luck, total population should stabilize somewhere between 9 and 10 billion people by 2050. Fertility rates are decreasing not just in developed countries, but also in urban areas in the developing world as women gain more access to education, health care, and job opportunities. Estimates seem to agree that the rate of global population has been slowing for several decades; global population will actually start *declining sometime between 2050 and 2100* (United Nations 2011).

Although the news about the world's population problem is not all bad, three caveats are often raised about these positive trends that paint a somewhat darker picture of both our immediate and medium-term future. First, most of the population growth in the years ahead will occur in the poorest countries that are already strained to the limit when it comes to feeding, housing, and educating their existing populations. By contrast, in the developed world, population growth rates in many cases have dipped below 'replacement levels', creating a different sort of crisis. Too few people of working age will be available to contribute to pay-as-you-go pension systems, creating the possibility of a systemic social crisis. Second, most of the population growth is taking place in urban areas. By 2015, the world will have 26 megacities with populations exceeding 10 million and almost all of the population growth in the developing world over the next 20 years will be absorbed by urban areas. Urban planners, government officials, and military officers are concerned that megacities will tax social and basic services well beyond their limits, leaving millions of people to live in urban squalor and chaos. Megacities can also erupt into spontaneous violence following some local insult or even a sporting event. Even cities in the developed world can burst into violence: thousands of armed gang members can plunge sections of Los Angeles into chaos and looting for days before police and national guard units are able to restore order. Third, most of this additional population will be very young, leading observers to note that, in parts of the developing world, it will be some time before population growth rates peak (see Figure 17.1).

Although strategists find little to dispute in the observation that over-population creates enormous social, resource, and environmental strains, they are most interested in exploring the divergent demographic trends at the heart of the population problem. In other words, what are the strategic implications of an ageing and shrinking Western population on the one hand, and an explosion in the number of young people in the developing world on the other? For the developing world, the concern is that the inability to provide basic services to this surging population will produce poverty, chaos, and hopelessness. Some observers believe that young people, concentrated by the millions in megacities, will fall under the sway of a virulent nationalism, messianic leaders, or millenarian movements, leading to waves of local violence or international terrorism. Most major revolutions have been accompanied by a so-called 'youth bulge', while scholars have also noted that youth bulges are associated with the outbreak of small conflicts (Goldstone 2002). Young men with little prospect of a traditional home, family, or occupation might find an outlet for their ambitions in war. By contrast, the slow or even negative population growth in the West will make it

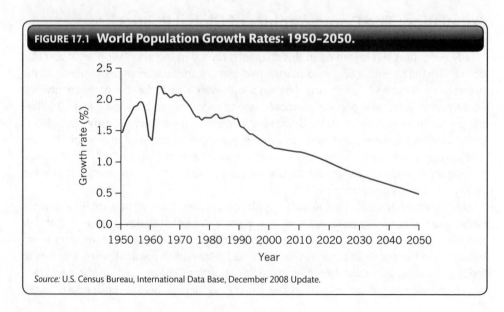

FIGURE 17.1 **World Population Growth Rates: 1950–2050.**

Source: U.S. Census Bureau, International Data Base, December 2008 Update.

increasingly difficult to fill the ranks of the armed forces, forcing militaries to rely on technology to compensate for an absence of volunteers. The demands for health care and the high pension costs created by an ageing population will also make it difficult for industrialized nations to afford large defence budgets.

These population demographics constitute a strategic issue because they will force changes in defence policies and strategy in the years ahead. Differences in population growth create fundamental trends that influence military strategy and defence policy. Exactly how will demographics transform this strategic setting? Martin van Creveld (1991) and Stephen Cimbala (1997) offer a pessimistic view of these trends. They believe that nation states are losing their monopoly on the use of force as urban mobs and transnational movements take matters into their own hands. Violence is becoming less politically organized; the world is descending into chaos and warlordism. By contrast, some observers would predict that these population demographics are already producing different attitudes towards the death and destruction of war. In the West, a rising aversion to casualties is already shaping national strategies. In the developing world, warrior cultures glorify war, swelling the ranks of millenarian, fundamentalist, or anarchist movements with thousands of untrained and lightly armed volunteers. It is probably not a coincidence that most of the terrorists who participate in al-Qaeda suicide attacks are unmarried males. It is probably wrong, however, to suggest that warrior culture offers a superior approach to the conventional battlefield than the combined arms attack that can be unleashed by military professionals. No amount of élan will save units caught in the open by a well-timed artillery barrage or an air strike using fuel-air explosives, although basic infantry tactics, such as the use of cover, can help mitigate the lethality of modern weaponry (Biddle 2003a). On a more positive note, some observers have suggested that as birth rates decline, people everywhere will be less willing to see what may be their only child sacrificed in some dubious military adventure: and if democracy continues to spread, they would have the means of making these feelings known to their elected officials.

Key points

- Although population growth rates are slowing, total world population will continue to increase for the next 30 years.
- Future population increases will be centred in the developing world, leading to a concentration of young people in megacities.
- Because they influence the context of diplomatic and military policy, divergent demographic trends will shape strategy and strategic thinking.

Commons Issues

Issues that transcend international boundaries are often referred to as commons problems. Although some countries can contribute more or less to a specific commons problem, efforts to stop the tragedy of the commons, to borrow Garrett Hardin's famous phrase, require some form of collective action on the part of most members of the international community. Most low politics problems could be classified as commons issues, but environmental and resource issues generally come to mind when policymakers and scholars think about transnational issues.

Air pollution, especially the release of carbon dioxide from motor vehicles and coal-fired electric plants, destruction of the ozone layer through the release of chlorofluorocarbons, and global warming produced by greenhouse gases are all quintessential commons problems.

In other words, it would be impossible for a single state or a group of states to slow the destruction of the ozone layer, for example, by banning the manufacture of chlorofluorocarbons if other states continued to release these substances into the atmosphere. Water pollution, depletion of underground aquifers, and the protection of migratory species (e.g. fish) are often depicted as commons problems, although their effects are generally confined to specific regions. Michael Klare, for instance, sees water scarcity as a source of conflict among countries that share major water systems. The River Nile (shared by Egypt, Ethiopia, and the Sudan); the River Jordan (shared by Israel, Jordan, Lebanon, and Syria) the Tigris and Euphrates Rivers (shared by Turkey, Syria, Iraq, and Iran); and the River Indus (shared by Afghanistan, India, and Pakistan) are identified as likely conflict points by Klare (2001). Sometimes, depletion of aquifers and fish stocks can create local economic catastrophes when farmers lose the water needed to irrigate their crops and fishers are forced to abandon traditional means of earning a living.

Threats to biodiversity, especially deforestation of tropical rainforests, occur on specific national territories, but they are slowly destroying the 'common heritage of humankind'. Deforestation destroys habitats needed by the planet's non-human inhabitants: tropical rainforests are home to half of the world's known species. Deforestation can also have regional climatic effects because trees are a key link in the evapotranspiration cycle between soil and the atmosphere. Trees also help to protect delicate topsoil by providing erosion control against landslides and flooding. Forests help to slow global warming because trees act as a major sink of carbon dioxide in the atmosphere. Global or regional environmental problems can sometimes have acute local consequences (see Box 17.2).

By contrast, local environmental damage can produce global environmental consequences. Sometimes commons problems are created when the effects of localized insults to the environment have a global impact and sometimes they are created when millions of small and relatively innocuous events have a cumulative effect that produces global consequences or local disasters. The distinguishing characteristic of all of these issues, however, is the fact that either their causes or their effects are beyond the reach of any one state.

Although commons issues pose an existential threat to all humanity, at times they do shape decisions about war and peace. Concerns about access to oil supplies (one natural resource that remains key to modern industrial economies) was a clear motivation behind the formation of a US-led international coalition to oust Iraq from Kuwait in the early 1990s. By contrast, concern about disrupting tight oil markets has slowed the international response to an apparent Iranian effort to create a nuclear weapons industry. Shots have also been exchanged in fishing disputes as boats and crews are seized for poaching in waters claimed by a specific state. Water wars are possible in the future, especially as rivers and aquifers are drained to make deserts in one state bloom at the expense of fields in neighbouring countries. Therefore, as a proximate cause of war, commons issues should be a concern to strategists; but, so far at least, with the exception of the Gulf War, shots have been exchanged only in a limited way.

BOX 17.2 The Tragedy of the Commons

Imagine you lived near the west coast of the United States and every spring you had the opportunity to go salmon fishing. The fish were plentiful and it was easy for you to catch a couple of dozen fish in a single morning. This makes you very happy because you have many friends and relatives who like salmon. In any event, there are plenty of fish in the sea, and no matter how full you loaded up your boat you could never make much of a dent in the salmon population. There would always be fish willing to take your bait. Now imagine if thousands of your neighbours up and down the coast went fishing too and proceeded to fill their boats with fish. Even though no one wanted it to happen and no one individual would be responsible, it would not be long before salmon became mighty scarce, producing a tragedy of the commons.

The tragedy of the commons is an example of the tyranny of small decisions, a situation in which unintended and negative consequences are produced by individuals following their reasonable, albeit narrow, self-interest. Each fisher, rationally acting to fulfil their self-interests, gains the extra benefit of their large catch, while the entire community bears the cost of depleting the fishery. Even if individuals refrain from filling their boats, it would only make it safe for others to 'free-ride' on their self-restraint. In other words, collective action is needed to capture the externalities involved in exploiting the fishery (i.e. getting fishers to pay the full cost of their catch) and to prevent free-riding. When a commons problem occurs within national boundaries, it is easy for the state to capture these externalities and to corral free-riders. When fisheries are open, for example, the State of California limits salmon catches to two fish per day by licensed fishers. Fish have to be longer than 24 inches and it is illegal to take protected salmon species (e.g. Coho salmon). However, when the commons crosses international borders, capturing externalities and corralling free-riders requires international collaboration.

By contrast, most commons problems are probably beyond the reach of strategy. It is difficult to imagine how military action might resolve many transnational problems. For instance, the existence of strategists, strategy, and military infrastructure did little to deplete aquifers; it is difficult to see how they can help conserve or replenish these underground water supplies. Moreover, because war is a state activity undertaken to achieve political objectives, there is little political motivation to undertake military action in response to commons issues. In other words, few would suggest that wars should be launched to stop individuals in other states from killing tigers, from practising slash and burn agriculture, or from constructing electric power plants that use coal as an energy source. Even if it were possible to use military force to solve a commons problem, it would be highly unlikely that any single state would launch this type of military endeavour. By definition, the benefits gained from using military force to resolve commons problems are outweighed by the costs of action. Everyone would benefit, but the state taking action would bear all of the costs. This is the very dilemma that lies at the heart of the tragedy of the commons. Collective action is needed to capture the externalities (the unpaid costs that are inevitably involved in all human activity) that lie at the heart of most commons problems. Strategists might contribute to the effort to devise a collective response to commons issues, but it would probably be better if this response were based on enlightened self-interest, not point of the gun environmentalism. Although commons issues might some day force military action or shape military strategies (e.g. military action to protect oil supplies), it is probably best not to treat commons issues as military problems.

Key points

- The tragedy of the commons is generally produced by an international failure to undertake collective protection of the environment or to conserve resources.
- The resolution of commons issues probably lies beyond the realm of strategy.

Direct Environmental Damage

Military action or the manufacturing of military weapons can result in significant environmental damage, although these insults to the environment probably fall short of constituting a commons problem. Sometimes the impact of military activity is limited or unknown. For example, military aircraft often jettison fuel in an emergency, but it is unclear if much environmental damage occurs in peacetime from this practice. As MP Archie Hamilton noted in 1992:

> RN (Royal Navy) and RAF (Royal Air Force) pilots are instructed to jettison fuel under carefully controlled conditions which ensure that the great majority of fuel evaporates before it reaches the ground. There is, therefore, minimal environmental impact at ground or sea level. The evaporated fuel is widely dispersed. Most of it is biodegradable and that which remains has no known effects on the atmosphere. There are no products in military aviation jet fuel known to cause greenhouse effects, damage to the ozone layer, or air pollution in the lower atmosphere.

Hamilton is probably correct that dumping jet fuel in the atmosphere does not pose much of a problem in peacetime: British flyers were only forced to jettison fuel on average about twice a month in the 1980s. However, in wartime, mission requirements might cause enormous amounts of fuel to be jettisoned. If this happened over a relatively small area, would it have an environmental impact?

An issue that often bedevils assessments of the environmental impact of military activity is the effort to use 'green' arguments to derail programmes for political purposes. A case in point is the alleged negative environmental and long-term health consequences produced by the use of depleted uranium (DU) in heavy tank armour, antitank munitions, and even as counterweights in commercial aircraft. DU is used primarily as a kinetic-kill projectile because it is very heavy and dense: no nuclear reaction occurs when a DU projectile strikes a tank, for example. Depending upon the type of impact, small amounts of DU may be released in the form of tiny, relatively insoluble particles of uranium oxide or even as larger pieces of metallic uranium. There is little scientific data on the health effects of DU, although studies exist about the health effects of uranium, a similar material. Based on studies undertaken on uranium workers, no negative health effects have been established following exposure to radiation through ingestion and inhalation of DU particles or through wounds contaminated by DU. Nevertheless, many media reports and Internet campaigns decry the environmental and health impact of the use of DU on the battlefield.

Some military weapons can potentially produce catastrophic damage to the environment and extremely significant health risks, even if they are not used in battle. The cost of dismantling and destroying these weapons is staggering and involves scientific and engineering capabilities that are far more advanced than the original efforts to make the weapons themselves. Successful programmes are possible. For example, in November 2000, after nearly 10 years of operation, the Johnston Atoll Chemical Agent Disposal System (JACADS) finally eliminated the remnants of the US chemical weapons stockpile. JCADS was the world's first full-scale facility built to destroy chemical weapons. Johnston Atoll, located 717 nautical miles south-west of Oahu, is one of the most isolated atolls in the world and had been used repeatedly as a US nuclear, biological, and chemical weapons testing and storage facility. Remaining off-limits for the indefinite future, Johnston Atoll will soon serve as a wildlife refuge.

Other facilities, especially those involved in nuclear weapons programmes, are neither as isolated nor as easily cleaned up. In the mid-1990s, the US Department of Energy estimated that it would cost at least 160 billion dollars to clean up facilities once involved in the manufacture of nuclear materials at Hanford Reservation, Savannah River, Oak Ridge, Idaho National Engineering and Environmental laboratory, and Rocky Flats. The Department of Defense also identified 26,500 other locations at existing or former military bases that have been contaminated by nuclear or industrial pollutants. Only 1,700 of these sites had been cleaned up by 1996 (see Table 17.1).

The environmental problems facing the Russians are also severe. Scores of old nuclear-powered submarines lie rusting at their berths throughout the Russian north and far east, and Russian spent fuel storage facilities are nearly full. A lack of resources makes it nearly impossible for the Russians to undertake a complicated clean-up process. The submarine

TABLE 17.1 US Stockpile Destroyed by JACADS

Agent	Item	Quantity	Pounds
HD-blister	155mm projectiles	5,670	66,339.0
HD-blister	105mm projectiles	46	136.6
HD-blister	M60 projectiles	45,108	133,970.7
HD-blister	4.2 mortars	43,600	261,600.0
HD-blister	Ton containers	68	116,294.0
GB-nerve	M55 rockets	58,353	624,377.1
GB-nerve	155mm projectiles	107,197	696,780.5
GB-nerve	105mm projectiles	49,360	80,456.8
GB-nerve	8in. projectiles	13,020	188,790.0
GB-nerve	MC-1 bombs	3,047	670,340.0
GB-nerve	MK 94 bombs	2,570	277,560.0
GB-nerve	Ton containers	66	101,158.0
VX-nerve	M55 rockets	13,889	141,769.8
VX-nerve	155mm projectiles	42,682	256,092.0
VX-nerve	8in. projectiles	14,519	210,525.5
VX-nerve	Land mines	13,302	139,671.0
VX-nerve	Ton containers	66	97,360.0

must be retired from active status; its missiles must be removed. Spent nuclear fuel must be extracted; making it safe to disconnect its reactor and reactor circuits. Spent fuel can then be transported for reprocessing and low- and high-level waste collected for storage. The reactor compartment can then be cut away from the rest of the hull so that it can be sealed for long-term storage.

Although the costs of cleaning up after the cold war are only now being assessed, clearly strategists and policymakers need to take into account the environmental impact of yesterday's and today's defence policies. Of course, at the time, these costs paled in significance when compared to the perceived military threats posed by the cold war, but the lasting legacy of nuclear, chemical, and biological weapons manufacturing and disposal must be considered by strategists and policymakers. Full disclosure of these 'hidden' costs might cause those who seek to develop a robust nuclear arsenal—here Indian, Pakistani, or Chinese leaders come to mind—to think about the potential consequences of their defence industrial policy.

Key points

- Military action can result in direct environmental damage.
- Surplus or lost munitions and industrial processes related to military activity can create serious environmental hazards.
- Military operations often entail 'hidden' costs that sometimes become apparent many years after weapons have been produced or hostilities cease.

Disease

Although disease has been a scourge throughout human existence, public health initiatives (providing people with clean water and proper sanitation), vaccination, quarantine, and the discovery of antibiotic drugs in the mid-twentieth century helped to reduce the outbreak of communicable disease, at least in the industrial world. Today public health officials in the West focus on modifying people's lifestyles to reduce the incidence of cancer (caused by smoking) and cardiovascular disease (accelerated by modern diets and a lack of exercise). The human genome project also holds out the prospect of new treatments for all types of illnesses, especially those linked to genetic disorders. Life expectancies have increased steadily over the last century. More people survived infancy because of prenatal care, public health, and vaccination against childhood diseases and treatments emerged to arrest, if not completely cure, disorders (cardiovascular disease, cancers) that killed previous generations by the time they reached their seventieth birthday. Progress was even achieved on a global scale: ask your parents (grandparents?) to show you their smallpox vaccination. (See Table 17.2.)

If one takes a global perspective, however, the news is not so encouraging. Public health officials are bracing themselves for a long-overdue outbreak of a deadly strain of influenza. They fear the outbreak of new diseases that are resistant to existing treatments and drugs. They worry that unknown bacteria or viruses that have lain dormant deep within tropical

TABLE 17.2 Pathogenic Microbes Identified since 1973 and the Diseases they Cause

Year	Microbe	Type	Disease
1973	Rotavirus	Virus	Infantile diarrhoea
1977	Ebola virus	Virus	Acute haemorrhagic fever
1977	Legionella pneumophila	Bacterium	Legionnaires' disease
1980	Human T-lymphotrophic virus	Virus	T-cell lymphoma
1981	Staphylococcus aureus	Bacterium	Toxic shock syndrome
1982	Escherichia coli 0157:H7	Bacterium	Haemorrhagic colitis
1982	Borrelia burgdorferi	Bacterium	Lyme disease
1983	Human immune deficiency virus	Virus	Acquired immune deficiency syndrome (AIDS)
1983	Helicobacter pylori	Bacterium	Peptic ulcer disease
1989	Hepatitis C	Virus	Parentally transmitted non-A, non-B liver infection
1992	Vibrio cholerae 0139	Bacterium	New strain/epidemic cholera
1993	Hantavirus	Virus	Adult respiratory distress syndrome
1994	Cryptosporidium	Protozoa	Enteric disease
1995	Ehrlichiosis	Bacterium	Severe arthritis
1996	NvCJD	Prion	New variant Creutzfeld–Jakob disease
1997	HVN1	Virus	Influenza
1999	Nipah	Virus	Severe encephalitis

rainforests will soon be disturbed by encroaching humans, producing new epidemics of dangerous diseases.

World Health Organization officials also warn that the seven infectious diseases that caused the highest number of deaths at the turn of the century will remain serious threats for decades to come.

Human Immune Deficiency Virus/Acquired Immune Deficiency Syndrome (HIV/AIDS)

At the turn of the century, about 40 million people across the globe were living with HIV/AIDS. Infection and death rates have slowed in the West in response to preventive measures and expensive multi-drug treatments. The pandemic continues to spread throughout the developing world and is making inroads in India, Russia, and China. Sub-Saharan Africa is the centre of the AIDS epidemic: already 10–20 per cent of the adults in the region are infected with the disease. The social and economic costs of the disease are staggering. African economies are experiencing a steady decline in gross domestic product (GDP) due to the AIDS epidemic and entire generations of children will become AIDS orphans.

Tuberculosis (TB)

Once thought to be controlled in the developing world by public health efforts and drug treatments, TB is increasing in Russia, India, South East Asia, sub-Saharan Africa, and parts of Latin America. About eight million new cases of TB each year were reported worldwide at the turn of the century. Particularly disturbing is the emergence of a drug-resistant form of TB. Up to 50 per cent of the people infected with drug-resistant TB will die despite treatment. Many TB infections occur in conjunction with HIV/AIDS. By 2020, TB will probably rank second behind HIV/AIDS as a cause of death by infectious disease.

Malaria

Once thought to be coming under control by public health measures and prophylaxis treatments, malaria is a tropical disease that is on the rise. In sub-Saharan Africa infection rates jumped 40 per cent over the last 30 years and new drug-resistant strains of the disease are emerging. One potential consequence of climatic change could be an increase in malaria's geographic range.

Hepatitis B and C

Worldwide, 350 million people are chronic carriers of these viruses. Up to 25 per cent of the people infected with the virus will develop cirrhosis of the liver or liver cancer. There is no vaccine against hepatitis C.

Influenza and Respiratory Infections

Airborne viruses pose an increasing threat in an age of air travel. Coronaviruses that can be spread by person-to-person contact (e.g. coughing or sneezing) are difficult to contain. In February 2003, an outbreak of severe acute respiratory syndrome (SARS) in Asia quickly spread to more than 24 countries around the world. Over 8,000 people became infected and about 700 of those infected died. Fears have also emerged about avian influenza, especially the strain H5N1. In humans, the disease has generally been contracted by individuals who have come into close contact with infected birds, but transmission from person to person has been recorded. The virus has not completely jumped the species barrier, but because viruses can change quickly, scientists fear that H5N1 could someday easily infect humans, a species with little natural immunity to this virus. H5N1 might be capable of producing a lethality rate in excess of 50 per cent in humans.

Diarrhoeal Diseases

Infection with *Escherichia coli* is the most common cause of this disease, but dysentery and rotaviral diarrhoea occur throughout the developing world and are now beginning to affect parts of the former Soviet Union. Contaminated food and water spread the disease. In 1996, for the first time in a century, there also was a major outbreak of cholera in Latin America. Most of the victims of diarrhoeal diseases are children under the age of 5 in the developing world.

Measles

Because of the relatively low vaccination rates in sub-Saharan Africa, measles kills just under 1 million people a year and infects about 4 million children every year. Measles is also the leading cause of death among refugees and displaced persons, especially during recent humanitarian operations.

Several developments are responsible for the increasing threat of infectious diseases. First, refugee movements caused by political and natural disasters subject millions of refugees to primitive living conditions that breed and spread disease. Ethnic conflict, civil wars, and famine spread disease quickly as refugees move across borders. Second, unprotected sex with multiple partners and intravenous drug use are largely responsible for the spread of AIDS. Third, modern technology and production practices are not fool-proof. Imported food produced by non-hygienic practices can spread pathogens and bacteria (*Cyclospora ssp*, *Escherichia coli*, and *Salmonella*) quickly across national borders. Modern food production practices have also created problems in the food supply. Bovine spongiform encephalopathy (mad cow disease), for example, was spread by the practice of including mammalian tissues in animal feed intended for cows and other ruminants. Fourth, land use practices, even efforts to restore natural habitats, can breed and spread disease. For example, reforestation in the United States and Europe is responsible for an increase in Lyme disease as deer ticks have more opportunities to find human hosts. Encroachment on rain forests also brings people in close contact with animals carrying malaria, yellow fever, leishmaniasis, or even heretofore unknown and potentially dangerous diseases. Fifth, international travel and commerce can spread viruses, pathogens, and bacteria faster than the incubation period of the diseases they cause. Today's cross-border movement of over 2 million people per day guarantees that disease outbreaks will be difficult to contain. Sixth, the widespread use of antibiotics in livestock production and the overuse and misuse of antibiotics by people have accelerated the evolution of a variety of strains of drug-resistant microbes. An expanding number of strains of TB, malaria, and influenza are virtually impossible to treat and HIV also displays a high rate of adaptation to drug treatments.

War and civil strife can lead to disease outbreaks by creating refugee disasters and a breakdown in public health care. Throughout history, war has often been accompanied by disease. Soldiers have spread disease in the field and have brought it back with them when they returned home. Today, for instance, the so-called 'Gulf War Syndrome'—a strange mix of debilitating symptoms—is said to occur among US soldiers who returned otherwise unhurt from the 1991 Coalition victory against Iraq. Military forces can be enlisted to help fight the spread of disease through efforts to quarantine affected populations, to move supplies into regions stricken by epidemics, or to use field medical facilities to treat local populations. From a strategic perspective, infectious diseases continue to shape military strategy because disease can create casualties just as easily as enemy fire. In fact, throughout most of history, disease killed far more soldiers than enemy action. Although military forces are at best a third- or fourth-order defence against the spread of disease (and are just as likely to help spread disease as to contain it), infectious disease shapes the security environment and should be included on the new security agenda.

Sensitivities and Vulnerabilities

Although talk of increasing globalization and interdependence is clichéd, non-traditional security issues have begun to influence strategy and defence priorities in ways that were not fully anticipated by advocates of the new agenda for security in the early 1990s. Malthusian scenarios have not materialized, but low politics are having an impact on real-world conflicts and are shaping national security strategies. Some countries are increasingly sensitive or even vulnerable to developments in the realm of low politics.

Sensitivity and vulnerability are terms drawn from Robert Keohane and Joseph Nye's work on complex interdependence (2001). Sensitivity refers to the ability of developments outside national boundaries to influence domestic events in other countries. An outbreak of H5N1 in Asia, for example, might cause officials in the United States to alert domestic public health officials to monitor hospital admissions for patients who might be exhibiting signs of H5N1 infection. Such a precautionary measure would entail some costs and be a matter of potential public concern, but it would not pose a fundamental disruption to life in the United States. By contrast, vulnerabilities can cause significant disruption to domestic economic, social, or political activity. The emergence and spread of SARS in 2003, for example, crossed the line from sensitivity to vulnerability because it significantly affected international travel and Asian economies.

Sensitivities and vulnerabilities now seem endemic across a whole range of issue areas, produced by complex global systems and relationships that are not well understood. The 2008 economic crisis rocked global credit and equity markets as policymakers and investors alike learned too late about the 'risks' that were buried deeply inside their portfolios. National economies were highly coupled in unexpected ways, producing a global economic downturn. The world economy is also dependent on a global energy market to move petroleum and natural gas from producers to consumers, but scholars worry that that market might collapse in the face of 'peak oil': a situation where oil demand outstrips production. They worry that a market mechanism might be slow to create alternative energy sources, might not build needed production capacity in slow economic times, which would lead to wild and politically destabilizing swings in price during an economic upturn. They also worry about the potential for the militarization of energy security, especially if some governments lose faith in the market mechanism to supply the energy they need. The stability of the energy market itself, not necessarily the price or location of energy resources, thus becomes an issue of national strategic interest and subject of concern to strategists.

Key points

- Although they have not risen to the top of national security agendas, issues of low politics are beginning to interact with local political and military events to produce global consequences.
- Countries are beginning to exhibit sensitivities and vulnerabilities to issues of low politics.
- Complex social, political, and economic relationships are emerging that can threaten regional and global stability, often in unanticipated ways.

 Conclusion

Those who advocate including resource, environmental, or population issues on national security agendas might suggest that this chapter ignores a critical point: many of these global developments threaten the health and welfare of both individuals and states and therefore should be considered as threats to security. They might suggest that the fact that military forces or strategists are ill-equipped to deal with emerging problems demonstrates that traditional ways of thinking about security are simply not up to the challenge of dealing with emerging twenty-first century security issues. A decision not to treat the emergence of a drug-resistant strain of TB as a threat to national security, for example, would thus be viewed as an effort to minimize the importance of the issue, but the fact that something is a threat to health and welfare does not make it a security problem in the sense that strategy or military force can minimize it. Hundreds of thousands of people every year are killed in road accidents, but no one would suggest that military force should somehow be used to improve highway safety.

By contrast, the purpose of this chapter was not to dismiss these global trends and transnational issues as threats to national or individual security or to minimize the gravity of the challenges created by environmental damage, disease, or population growth in the developing world. Instead, it offered a mixed assessment of the ability of strategy or military force to respond to global issues. On balance, there was a significant and growing interaction between strategy and many of the items on the new agenda for national security. While not a security issue per se, demographics or resource issues (tight energy markets) are interacting with other trends to shape the global security environment and influence strategy. The complexity of these energy and financial markets can also act as a wild card, making it hard for strategists to gauge the impact of events on distant shores and across disparate issue areas. The spread of infectious disease might also play a greater part in the making of strategy and defence policy in the years ahead. Environmental damage caused by the manufacture, maintenance, and disposal of weaponry is also an issue of concern to strategists. Indeed, the issues that appear to be beyond the reach of strategy are the environmental, resource, and commons problems that generated interest in a new concept of security in the first place. Those who see these issues as important should be relieved by the assessment presented in this chapter. Defining these issues as engineering, public health, or educational problems is far more constructive than somehow trying to resolve them by the threat or use of force. In an increasingly globalized and complex world, issues of low politics appear to be capable not of creating conflict, but of exacerbating the effects of political and military disputes.

 Questions

1. Why are low politics now given priority by policymakers and scholars?

2. Why would globalization help to slow population growth rates in the developing world?

3. Although other resources are vital, why is it that states have only fought recently over oil?

4. Can you think of a way to threaten or use force to resolve commons issues?

5. What would be the social or political consequences of attempting to use military units to enforce a disease quarantine?

6. Do you think it is realistic to expect that countries currently building a nuclear infrastructure would want to do so in a way that protects the environment?

7. What are the emerging points of interaction between low and high politics today?

8. Will people pay attention to environmental issues if they are not defined as threats to national security?

9. Is the process of globalization increasing the relevance of low politics on national security agendas?

10. Do you think that demographic trends will inevitably lead to decades of violence and instability?

 ## Further Reading

P. F. Diehl and N. P. Gleditsch, *Environmental Conflict: An Anthology* (Boulder, CO: Westview, 2000).
An overview of research on the relationship between the environment and security.

Nils Petter Gleditsch, 'Whither the Weather? Climate Change and Conflict' *Journal of Peace Research* 2012 49/1 pp. 3–9.
A selection from a special issue of *the Journal of Peace Research* that finds only a modest relationship between climate change and the occurrence of conflict.

R. O. Keohane and J. S. Nye, *Power and Interdependence* (Reading, MA: Addison-Wesley, 1989).
On the theoretical implications of the differences between high and low politics.

D. Moran and J. A. Russell (eds), *Energy Security and Global Politics: The Militarization of Resource Management* (New York: Routledge, 2009).
Discussion of energy markets and the prospects that the search for energy supplies could produce conflict.

S. I. Schwartz, *Atomic Audit: The Costs and Consequences of US Nuclear Weapons since 1940* (Washington, DC: Brookings Institution, 1998).
An effort to assess overall costs of the US nuclear programme.

Richard A. Matthew, Jon Barnett, Bryan McDonald, and Karen L. O'Brien (eds), *Global Environmental Change and Human Security* (Cambridge, Massachusetts: MIT Press, 2010).
Assesses the impact of environmental change on human security.

On the environmental costs of the cold war, the Woodrow Wilson Center, which runs the Environmental Change and Security Project (ECSP), publishes an annual report that contains articles, reviews, conference reports, and contact information for a host of issues and projects related to the new national security agenda. ECSP can be contacted by email at **ecspwwic@wwic.si.edu**

 ## Web Links

Over Population **http://www.overpopulation.com/** Provides data and analysis about negative consequences of demographic change.

US Center for Disease Control **http://www.cdc.gov** Provides information about disease outbreaks.

US Food and Drug Administration **http://www.fda.gov/default.htm** Provides public health information.

US Census Bureau **http://www.census.gov/main/www/popclock.html** Provides data and analysis of US and international demographics.

Center for Contemporary Conflict **http://www.nps.edu/Academics/Centers/CCC/** Provides research reports, research links, and scholarly articles on all facets of strategic studies.

18

Strategic Studies and its Critics

COLUMBA PEOPLES

 Chapter Contents

Introduction	342
Strategy and its Critics in the 'Golden Age'	342
Strategic Studies Strikes Back	345
Critical Approaches to Strategic Studies	348
A Continuing Debate?	355
Conclusion	356

 Reader's Guide

This chapter introduces readers to the criticism levelled at strategic studies from the 'Golden Age' of nuclear strategy through to contemporary critiques. It begins by reviewing prominent critiques of deterrence theory in the 1960s, a time when several fundamental criticisms of strategic studies were made. The chapter then outlines how these critiques were subsequently addressed by strategic theorists. As strategic studies has evolved and changed, however, so too have the arguments made by its critics. Numerous critical approaches to strategic studies have developed multifaceted critiques that encompass issues ranging from the use of gendered terminology to an alleged Western-centric bias. The chapter assesses the current status of the relationship between strategic studies and its critics, and the important role critics might play in the future development of strategic studies.

Introduction

For as long as the activity of theorizing conflict has existed, there have been those who have endeavoured to render its purpose irrelevant. Just as modern strategic studies can be said to have its pre-history in the broader study of how to fight and win wars, encompassing thinkers such as Sun Tzu, Machiavelli, and Clausewitz, there is an oppositional history of thinkers such as Immanuel Kant and the Abbé de Saint Pierre that have endeavoured to theorize the conditions in which war might itself become outdated and obsolete as an activity (see Dunn 1991: 59; Waltz 1962: 331). This latter tradition of attempting to identify the possibilities for 'perpetual peace' (as Kant would have it) was at odds with the basic assumption made by classical strategists: that war is an inevitable occurrence, which in turn necessitates sustained reflection on its purpose and effective conduct. These parallel traditions of 'thinking war' on the one hand and 'thinking peace' on the other remained largely independent, albeit related, intellectual activities.

Modern strategic studies has been marked by a more direct engagement between proponents of strategic theory and those who criticize its purpose and existence. The dawn of the 'nuclear age' and the exponential rise of strategic studies as a subdiscipline of international relations during the cold war gave rise to extensive criticism of strategic studies. With the advent of nuclear weapons and, by the 1960s, the condition of 'Mutual Assured Destruction', many began to criticize strategic studies as contributing to (rather than diminishing) the prospect of nuclear conflict. The study of nuclear strategy was variously decried by critics as unethical, unscholarly, and uncritical of the status quo in world politics. As Hedley Bull noted in his seminal 1968 article 'Strategic Studies and its Critics', 'civilian strategic analysts . . . have from the first been subject to criticism that has called into question the validity of their methods, their utility to society, and even their integrity of purpose' (Bull 1968: 593).

Yet the relationship between strategic studies and its critics is more complex than is presented by a picture of nuclear strategists under siege from their opponents. Proponents of strategic studies have, in response to criticism, often articulated trenchant defences of the study of strategy, and strategic studies has also been subjected to internal critiques that have fostered its development. In addition, although some of the original criticism of nuclear strategy identified by Bull persists, the nature and range of critical assessments of strategic studies have diversified beyond many of these initial concerns.

This chapter draws together key themes in critiques of the study of strategy to heighten awareness of how strategic studies has developed into its current form. Even if certain disputes between proponents and critics of strategic studies remain seemingly irresolvable, reviewing this debate provides a more holistic picture of the state of strategic studies and the prospects for its future development.

Strategy and its Critics in the 'Golden Age'

The period running from the aftermath of the Second World War through to the end of the 1960s is often referred to as the 'Golden Age' of strategic studies (Gray 1982a; Wæver and Buzan 2010: 467–70). During this period, a new breed of strategic thinker rose to prominence: the so-called 'civilian strategist' (Jervis 1979; Williams 1993: 104). Whereas previously issues of strategy had largely been the preserve of military practitioners, a 'second wave' of non-military academics such as Bernard Brodie, Herman Kahn, Thomas Schelling, and Albert Wohlstetter became the dominant voices of strategy in the new, nuclear age (Freedman 1986). The academic study of strategy also grew exponentially as did its prominence and influence on policy through academic think tanks such as the RAND corporation (Kaplan 1983).

The role of these civilian strategists was, as the title of Herman Kahn's (1962) work famously put it, *Thinking about the Unthinkable*; the world had, mercifully, only witnessed the use of nuclear weapons in conflict on two occasions, Hiroshima and Nagasaki. However, limited experience with these revolutionary weapons meant that military practitioners had only marginally greater claim to expertise on the question of nuclear warfare than non-military experts. Additionally, the vast destructive power of atomic weapons convinced many in government that strategy *really was* too important a matter to be left to the generals. Given the paucity of battlefield experience, Kahn and other civilian strategists consequently argued that 'scientific' methods such as game theory and systems analysis were necessary additions to the strategist's intellectual armoury. They looked to theoretical innovations drawn from fields such as economics and mathematics to better think through possible paths to nuclear conflict and the means by which to prevent it. Mathematical demonstrations of the vulnerability of American missile silos to a Soviet nuclear strike, for instance, were argued to provide meaningful constructions of the 'unthinkable' scenario of nuclear conflict (Barkawi 1998: 172). As Wæver and Buzan note, the US government actively fostered the growth of deterrence theory in this phase as the theories produced and promised 'ever new and ever more complex' frameworks for attempting to understand the nuclear dimension of the cold war, and 'all this seemed highly useful because the theories actually produced their own reality of abstractions, the world of "secure second strike capability", "extended deterrence", and "escalation dominance"' (2010: 468).

The magnitude of the task taken on by the civilian strategists ensured that these 'Wizards of Armageddon' (Kaplan 1983) had a high political—and public—profile. For example, well-informed viewers of Stanley Kubrick's (1964) film *Dr Strangelove: Or how I learned to stop worrying and love the Bomb* could easily recognize the parody of Herman Kahn in the figure of the film's eponymous central character, Dr Strangelove, and his blasé proposals on how a select band of elites might survive a nuclear conflict and its aftermath in facilities deep underground. Elements of Strangelove's dialogue were virtually paraphrased from Kahn's *On Thermonuclear War* (Kaplan 1983: 231). The Strangelove character—and indeed the film's central narrative plot, in which the United States accidentally begins an all-out nuclear war—though fictional, provides a window into a particular view of nuclear strategy that began to emerge in the 1960s: that the new 'science' of theorizing nuclear conflict was an incomprehensible activity that was at best morally questionable and at worst bordered on the absurd.

Strategy and Conscience: The Moral Foundation of Criticism of Strategic Studies

This critical view of nuclear strategy was most notably articulated in the work of Anatol Rapoport (1964) and Philip Green (1966). Green himself noted that his own critique of nuclear strategy was inspired by 'a feeling of strangeness induced by a lengthy study of the literature of nuclear deterrence' (Green 1966: 5), and both Rapoport and Green found it difficult to fathom the idea that otherwise well-educated scholars could countenance the idea of building theories about the possibility of nuclear war. At issue for these critics of the civilian strategists was a perceived evasion of a fundamental moral and ethical question: namely, whether it was ethical to encourage the planning and study of nuclear warfare.

The most prominent text in this line of criticism was Rapoport's *Strategy and Conscience*, which, as described in its preface by Karl Deutsch, was 'written as a protest against a glib and shallow fashion of contemporary thought [nuclear strategy] that embodies and enhances man's inhumanity to man' (Rapoport 1964: vii). Rapoport argued that scholarly proponents of nuclear deterrence had overlooked basic questions of conscience. While Kahn and others speculated about the possibilities of surviving and prevailing in nuclear conflict, Rapoport wondered how those engaged in such thinking could live with themselves in the first place.

Rapoport and Green both argued that the study of nuclear strategy, and its pretensions to scholarly and scientific rigour, essentially neglected key moral questions. For Green, euphemisms associated with deterrence theory such as 'delicate balance of terror', 'rational' responses to a nuclear strike and 'making the unthinkable thinkable' obfuscated the moral reality of nuclear war and the unavoidable fact that whole populations could be wiped out in a nuclear holocaust (Green 1966: xi). Green argued that nuclear strategy, rather than operating in a moral vacuum, actually contained 'a hidden ethical stance' (1966: 226). The civilian strategists had erroneously convinced themselves, Green believed, that questions of nuclear deterrence were scientific rather than moral issues: 'The real error in all theorising of this type', Green asserted, 'lies in the attempt to somehow separate the "analytical" components of a policy problem from the political and moral ones' (1966: 239). Green believed that strategists could never remove themselves entirely from their own values and attitudes in spite of their pretensions to 'scientific' objectivity. These calculations, construed in abstract terms, could eventually produce consequences that would make Hiroshima and Nagasaki seem like minor events.

The Dangerous Games Of Strategy

The critics of the civilian strategists did not, however, limit themselves to statements of moral outrage. The protests of anti-war and anti-nuclear protestors had long fallen on deaf ears within the strategic studies community of the post-war era. The civilian strategists perceived themselves to be involved in the business of protecting the United States and its Western allies from an obdurate, nuclear-armed opponent, and calls for nuclear disarmament were consequently dismissed as a dangerous form of idealism. Hence, Rapoport and Green both took the view that a more sustained critique of deterrence theory's claims to scientific rigour was required. Rapoport, for example, was motivated by a genuine abhorrence of what he perceived to be the callousness of strategic thought when it came to discussing nuclear conflict. Because he believed that moral critiques of strategy tended to be dismissed, Rapoport argued that the moral force of criticism needed to be supplemented by a critique of the civilian strategists' pride in the 'rationality' of nuclear deterrence. Rapoport made a plea to 'come to grips with these issues instead of playing games of strategy for enormous and unrecoverable stakes' (1964: xxiii).

Rapoport noted the tendency of the civilian strategist to portray himself as a 'master of a new science, whose principles are spelt out in abstract, often mathematical, terms' (1964: xviii). *Strategy and Conscience* thus attempted to engage strategic studies on its own terrain:

that of systems analysis and, in particular, game theory as employed in the work of Kahn, Thomas Schelling, and Glenn Snyder. Rapoport, himself eminently qualified in the fields of mathematical theories of social interaction and game theory, argued that the adoption of game theoretic models (such as prisoner's dilemma and the chicken game—see Web Links for a brief introduction) into nuclear strategy encouraged oversimplification of the realities of the cold war stand-off. Rapoport questioned the assumption of rational actors—with similar interests—that operated at the heart of game theory. In his view, this assumption lacked any relation to reality. His critique of the nuclear strategists described the actual differences between American and Soviet ideologies in practice as a means of countering the argument that 'players' in game scenarios could be regarded as holding equivalent interests. Green was likewise critical of systems analysis, ideas for civil defence, and game theory. He argued that

> All that a reference to game theory can possibly do is provide an algebraical illustration of a verbal argument that one has already made. The illustration can be no better than the verbal argument; in most of the cases . . . it is actually worse.
> **Green (1966: 125)**

Ultimately, Green argued of deterrence theorists, 'their air of authority was and is completely spurious' (Green 1966: xi).

Key points

- The 'Golden Age' of strategic studies between the mid-1950s and mid-1960s saw the rise of a new breed of 'second wave' civilian strategists that favoured the incorporation of game theory and systems analysis into the study of nuclear strategy and deterrence.

- The rise of deterrence theory generated strident moral critiques that questioned the ethical foundations of the activity of theorizing nuclear war.

- These moral critiques were accompanied by attacks on deterrence theorists' pretensions to scientific objectivity and on the application of abstract mathematical and economic models as the basis for thinking about nuclear war and formulating US nuclear policy.

Strategic Studies Strikes Back

The most prominent response to Rapoport and Green's critiques came in Hedley Bull's 1968 article 'Strategic studies and its critics', which provides not only a comprehensive overview of these critics' arguments but also a staunch rebuttal of most of their criticism. Bull was sympathetic to some elements of Rapoport and Greene's critiques, agreeing that strategic studies had become prone to abstract and technical analysis. Nevertheless, Bull largely refuted the charges levelled at strategic studies and argued that the suggestion that strategists were either immoral or amoral was misguided. Strategists did operate according to a moral calculus in his view: that of protecting the national interest (Bull 1968: 596). The purpose of deterrence, Bull also noted, was primarily to *prevent* the outbreak of nuclear war, an ultimately moral goal. Bull believed that strategic studies was a largely positive force in the post-war era.

Strategists, he argued (and this would become a common refrain of later defences of strategic studies), dealt with the realities of world politics, the threat of nuclear war included. They 'take for granted the existence of military force', he argued, as a means of establishing greater knowledge about its dynamics and how it might be controlled (Bull 1968: 600). Strategic studies was thus more realistic than proposals for the abolition of either nuclear weapons or the use of military force in its entirety, and Bull argued that proposals for disarmament were in themselves based on a particular form of strategic reasoning because they make a claim about the relationship between military force and the possible ends of policy and in this sense are 'not a statement about [strategic studies] from outside' (Bull 1968: 606).

Defenders of strategic studies attempted a series of responses to Rapoport, arguing, for example, that Rapoport overstated the influence of game theory within American strategic thought of the 1960s. Many within strategic studies, however, were also beginning to recognize the ill effects of game theory and pretensions to scientific objectivity. Bull, for example, though ultimately a defender of strategic studies, lamented the general absence of analysis of historical context and reference to concrete cases from strategic studies in the 1960s. Similarly Bernard Brodie, who had initially encouraged the incorporation of economic theories into strategic studies in the late 1940s, also came to regret the level of abstraction encouraged by the use of various types of formal analysis by nuclear strategists (see Betts 1997: 16).

As strategic studies evolved and attempted to redress these perceived failings, Rapoport's critique increasingly appeared to be tied to the Golden Age of strategic thinking. His critique of strategy as a 'mode of thought', as Rapoport himself acknowledged, centred on the issue of 'rationality' as understood and prized by second wave strategists such as Kahn, Snyder, and Schelling—those whom Rapoport referred to as 'abstractionists' (Rapoport 1964: 177). Yet, as a new generation of strategic thinkers—described as 'neo-traditionalists' by Rapoport—began to question these same issues the substantive part of Rapoport's critique became somewhat anachronistic (Rapoport 1964: 180).

By the 1980s a 'third wave' of strategists had emerged (Jervis 1979; Williams 1993: 293–324). These strategic thinkers saw themselves as engaged in a *reconstructive* critique of strategy: that is, a form of critique intended to rectify perceived flaws of the 'second wave' thinking that was so heavily criticized by Rapoport and Green. This third wave differs markedly from Rapoport and Green, however, because most of the thinkers associated with it distanced themselves from these radical moral critiques of strategic studies. Instead, critique was now seen as a means of revitalizing, rather than vilifying, strategic studies. As Colin S. Gray, one of the foremost thinkers in the third wave, argued: 'An important distinction should be drawn between friendly, as opposed to unfriendly, critics of strategic studies' (see Box 18.1) (Gray 1982b: 44).

'Friendly' critics included Bull as well as Gray himself. Building on the analysis offered by Bull, Gray dismissed the kind of radical opposition to strategic studies offered by Rapoport and Green. Gray argued that the failings of 'abstractionist' second wave strategic thinking should not be construed as a failure of strategic studies per se; it was, he argued, 'more sensible to criticize what may be termed the vulgarization of strategic thinking in the second half of the 1960s, and the near cessation of innovative strategic thinking in that period and later' (Gray 1982b: 19). The advent of game theory and systems analysis was indeed, in Gray's view, a retrograde step with regard to nuclear strategy. Nevertheless, Gray saw 'little merit in many of the criticisms voiced from the left of the political spectrum' (Gray 1982b: 5). In common with Bull, Gray argued that proponents of disarmament and alternative world orders had as

BOX 18.1 Strategists Respond to the Critics

To be blunt, deterrence theory justifies the indiscriminate killing of innocent persons under certain circumstances.

Green (1966: 225)

Pseudo-science such as that of deterrence theorists . . . constitutes a disservice not only to the scholarly community, but ultimately to the democratic political process as well.

Green (1966: 276)

Strategic thinking has produced thus far at best something like 'The Intelligent Robot's Guide to International Politics'.

Karl Deutsch (in the preface to Rapoport 1964: xiv–xv)

Strategists as a class, it seems to me, are neither any less nor any more sensitive to moral considerations than are other intelligent and educated persons in the West . . . What critics take to be the strategists' insensitivity to moral considerations is in most cases the strategists' greater sense of the moral stature of the American and Western political objectives for which war and the risk of war must be undertaken.

Bull (1968: 596–7)

Strategists are just as attracted to conditions of permanent peace as others, but they insist upon proper identification of the problems of political transition. They resent quite vehemently the charge, or intimation, that *they* themselves comprise an important part of the problem.

Gray (1982b: 8–9)

It is difficult to escape the conclusion that even though the civilian strategists have sometimes committed errors . . . they have served us well.

Bull (1968: 605)

yet failed to illustrate the validity of such options (Gray 1982b: 41–2) and that strategic studies remained a necessity of the nuclear age.

Yet Gray himself admitted to being 'far from uncritical of contemporary strategic studies' (Gray 1982b: 5). Those associated with the third wave—including, most prominently, Gray and Robert Jervis—challenged prior assumptions of deterrence theory, especially the concept of rational deterrence itself. In opposition to the abstract nature of game theory and systems analysis, the third wave of theorizing 'stressed the need for inductive methodologies and called for concrete historical evidence to counter and correct the misconceptions which, it argued, had resulted from the abstract rationalism and deductive reasoning of second wave strategy' (Williams 1993: 105).

One strand that emerged from this reassessment of strategic studies replaced prior abstract rationalism with a focus on political and strategic culture as a factor in particular 'national styles' (Gray 1986) of different states with regard to nuclear strategy. Ken Booth had previously charged strategic studies with 'ethnocentrism': that is the phenomenon by which 'societies look at the world with their own group as the centre, and they perceive and interpret other societies within their own frames of reference' (Booth 1979: 13). Booth noted that the deterrence theorists of the Golden Age failed to anticipate that there might be other ways of thinking about strategy. They assumed their own standards of rationality to be universally applicable and consequently believed that strategic thinking that deviated from it must be inferior. This assumption of a universal rationality created a serious risk of misperception, in particular misperception of Soviet strategic thinking and intentions by US strategic planners (Snyder 1977). This was a theme also picked up by Robert Jervis' (1976) *Perception and Misperception in International Relations*, in which Jervis sought to investigate the psychological dimension of deterrence, which was largely absent from second wave thinking.

The more controversial aspect to emerge from this third wave critique, however, was Gray's claim that 'American strategic studies is remarkably thin at the level of operational analysis . . . civilian scholars have almost totally neglected the question of how we fight a nuclear war and for what objectives—if deterrence fails' (Gray 1982b: 12). The advent of the Ronald Reagan era in the United States—and with it the onset of the so-called 'second cold war'—saw this question gain a new degree of prominence and notoriety. Gray and Keith Payne considered possible scenarios in which deterrence mechanisms might be inadequate or even fail (Gray and Payne 1980). They also countenanced the possibility of fighting and prevailing in a nuclear conflict with the Soviet Union should deterrence fail. Gray and Payne argued that this position was morally preferable to sole reliance on a theory in which both the US and the USSR risked mutual annihilation. The Reagan administration was seen to be sympathetic to this view, with Reagan himself commenting widely on his dissatisfaction with the condition of mutual assured destruction. Yet the idea of nuclear conflict remained to many unnerving, and theories for 'victory' in nuclear conflict represented 'a new and dangerous mythology about nuclear weapons' (Lawrence 1988: 4) that risked reversing the 'taboo' (Tannenwald 1999) on the use of nuclear weapons. As a result, the attempt to revitalize strategic studies associated with the third wave of strategic studies generated a new round of criticism from outside the strategic community.

Key points

- Proponents of strategic studies in the 1970s defended its moral virtues on the grounds that the study of nuclear strategy and the prevention of nuclear war were more realistic than the idea of nuclear disarmament.

- Though they did not accept prior moral critiques of strategic studies, theorists associated with the 'third wave' of strategic studies acknowledged the level of abstraction associated with 'second wave' deterrence theory as problematic.

- Deterrence theorists such as Colin S. Gray and Robert Jervis also questioned deterrence theory's reliance on a monolithic notion of 'rationality'.

- Thinkers associated with the third wave attempted to redirect strategic studies back towards a focus on cultural particularity, history, and 'national styles' in the making of nuclear strategy.

Critical Approaches to Strategic Studies

Since the early 1980s, a subtle but distinct shift in the criticism levelled at strategic studies has emerged. The moral dimension of the critique still remained a feature. Indeed, the literature on the ethics of nuclear war and the ethics of strategic studies became more sophisticated (Nye

1988; Lee 1996). In reaction to the conditions of the 'second cold war', however, the type of moral outrage found in earlier critiques came to be associated more with a populist rather than a scholarly critique of strategic studies. Examples of the latter could still be found (Lawrence 1988); but moral objections to strategic studies increasingly came to be enveloped within a broader opposition to nuclear weapons in general (Schell 1982, 1984). As Lawrence noted, 'Paradoxically . . . the new security of the Reagan era made individuals feel less secure and put defence issues into the centre of political debate' (1988: x). At a public level, this shift was manifest in the growth in popular anti-nuclear movements such as the Campaign for Nuclear Disarmament (CND) in Western Europe and the Nuclear Freeze movement in the United States.

With the cold war's end, strategic studies came under increasing scrutiny. As Ken Booth and Eric Herring note, the importance of the military dimension of world politics is not in question in the post-cold war era; but:

> What is in question is the appropriate intellectual status of strategic studies in relation to the study of international politics as a whole, its relationship with other subfields (such as 'security studies'), the utility of the military factor in the contemporary world, and what an appropriate strategic studies syllabus looks like now that its forty-year politico-military context has disappeared.
> **Booth and Herring 1994: 110**

As part of a broader 'critical' turn within the discipline of International Relations (see Smith, Booth, and Zalewski 1996), several scholars began to question not only the dominance of strategic studies as a mode of approaching world politics, but also the impact of its once privileged place within the discipline. What were the implications, critical scholars now wondered, of viewing the world through the lenses of strategic studies?

The attempts to address this question are grouped here under the heading of 'Critical approaches to strategic studies'. The phrase is used as shorthand to denote understandings of strategic studies that are not necessarily overtly polemical (even though they may sometimes be so), but draw on 'critical' theories (such as poststructuralism, feminism, and variants of Marxian theory) to question the place and effects of strategic studies (see Peoples 2007). The development of these types of critiques can be linked to the so-called post-positivist turn in international relations theory (Smith, Booth, and Zalewski 1996) and the emergence of 'critical security studies' (see Krause and Williams 1997; Booth 2005). The latter development, critical security studies, is predicated on a critique of 'traditional' security studies (effectively a synonym for strategic studies), so it is unsurprising that we find a range of critiques of strategic studies here.

The World According to Strategic Studies

Typical of this critical move against strategic studies is Bradley S. Klein's *Strategic Studies and World Order: The Global Politics of Deterrence*. Klein argues:

> Questions of war and peace are too important to leave to students of Strategic Studies. Or to put it another way, insights from social and political theory can help us enhance our appreciation of such social constructs as 'the balance of power', 'alliances', 'security' and 'deterrence'. Each of these is, after all, a social practice, not a primordial given.
> **Klein (1994: 3)**

Klein's argument, and its emphasis on 'social construction', identifies a fundamental difference between strategic studies and those critical approaches that seek to question it. Defenders of strategic studies such as Bull and Gray claimed that study of strategy took conflict and violence to be a given feature of world politics on a pragmatic basis. In other words, strategic theorists defended their position on the basis that they were simply attempting to theorize practices in the world 'out there', where military force is frequently and invariably used to gain political ends.

Klein, like many others who adopt a critical approach to strategic studies, attempts to unsettle this logic. 'The ability of strategic violence to reconcile itself with liberal discourse and modern civil society is possible', Klein argues, 'only because that violence draws upon a variety of discursive resources that are themselves constructed as rational, plausible, and acceptable' (Klein 1994: 5). Strategic studies does not simply acknowledge the existence of violence in world politics; it also prescribes and precludes the use of violence in certain ways and for certain purposes. Similarly Ken Booth, extending the logic of his earlier reflections on ethnocentrism, declares that:

> What gradually dawned was that what purported to be rational and objective strategic theory was often a rationalization of national prejudice, and that strategic practice was best understood as applied ethics—a continuation of (moral) philosophy with an admixture of firepower. Strategic theory helped to constitute the strategic world, and then strategic studies helped to explain it—self-reverentially and tautologically.
> **Booth (1997: 96)**

From this point of view, strategic studies is not simply an objective attempt taking place at a scholarly distance to understand the use of force. Instead, it is part of the broader legitimation of strategic violence for the purposes of maintaining a particular vision of world order, and this vision reflects the geographical–political context in which the disciplinary study of strategy evolved in the twentieth century (that is, primarily in Britain and the United States). Strategic studies has, Klein argues, provided a map of the world in which Western society has always ended up on the 'good' side (Klein 1994: 5) and has thus been a complicit and pivotal part in the making of the 'modern west' (Klein 1994: 16). In a similar vein, Barkawi and Laffey (2006: 335–338) argue that strategic studies is indelibly marked by its Anglo-American origins and, they contend, a persistent tendency towards 'Orientalism' in which non-Western states and subjects are rendered as passive objects. Western states and values are those that have most often been implicitly and explicitly defended and operative within strategic studies according to Klein: thus 'Strategic studies today . . . is an essential component in the articulation of the world order in terms that create and perpetuate a global political vision in which Western values, institutions, and political economies are valorized' (1994: 41).

This Western-centric view, Klein argues, applies not only to deterrence theory's concern with the survival and maintenance of the Western alliance during the cold war, but also to the resistance to the spread of nuclear weapons to non-Western states (see also Mutimer 2000). Additionally, Klein points to the work of pre-nuclear strategists such as Alfred Thayer Mahan as indicative of a broader but largely unacknowledged linkage between geopolitics and geoeconomics in Western strategic studies (for a related argument see O'Tuathail 1996). During the cold war deterrence did not only fend off major power conflict; it was also, Klein argues, 'a part of the ongoing making and remaking of a post-war order in which sovereign states have been integrated, at times forcefully, within a global market system' (Klein, 1994: 80). Strategic studies, for Klein, played a pivotal part in justifying institutional integration and alliances (such as the North Atlantic Treaty Organization) during the cold war, but equally obscured the economic and cultural dimensions of such integration. By concentrating attention on the military stand-off between non-communist West and communist East, strategic studies during the cold war helped draw focus away from Western economic and military intervention in the global 'South', a legacy that it has yet to shake off entirely. For Klein, 'Strategic Studies represents a reification of the politics of Western culture, enshrined in a geopolitical, statist representation of the sovereign spaces within which that culture may legitimately pursue its projects' (1994: 125).

The Ends of Strategy and The Role of Defence Intellectuals

If strategic studies as a discipline stands charged with constructing a particular vision of world order that historically privileges a Western set of values and geopolitical vision, then its proponents are, from a critical perspective, equally culpable. Cold war strategists 'found their vocation', Tarak Barkawi argues, 'in meaningful constructions of the conflict, of the nature of the Western "self" to be secured and the Communist "other" it was to be secured from' (Barkawi 1998: 161; see also Barkawi and Laffey 2006). In doing so, strategists and defence intellectuals, critics argue, contributed to a political project—the construction and maintenance of Western superiority—even when they conceived themselves simply to be contributing to an objective field of study (see Garnett 1987: 22–3).

Many strategic theorists have long been aware of this critique. Indeed, some have seen it as a virtue of the profession. Hedley Bull argued that post-war strategists were motivated by a 'greater sense of the moral stature of the American and Western political objectives for which war and the risk of war must be undertaken' (Bull 1968: 597). Likewise, Michael Howard candidly declared that:

> I myself am one of those fortunate people for whom the existing order is tolerable, and I want to maintain it . . . If the existing framework of international order is to be preserved, a deterrent capacity must be maintained against those, whatever their ideological persuasion, whose resentment at its injustices tempts them to use armed force to overthrow and remould it.
> **Cited in Klein (1994: 99)**

This debate about scholarly support to Western foreign and defence policy raises the issue of the role of the 'defence intellectual', and the relationship between strategic theory and policy. Although contemporary strategists may not have the same access to government circles enjoyed by the civilian strategists of the 1960s, proponents of strategic studies still move freely between the academic and policy worlds. Indeed, strategic studies still aspires to the status of a 'policy science' (Barkawi 1998: 160) and aims to be relevant to policymakers—even if practitioners are not always convinced that the academic world can produce ideas that are of practical relevance (see Chapter 20 of this volume by Lawrence Freedman: 'Does Strategic Studies have a Future?').

From a critical perspective, this aspiration to provide direct advice to government officials is problematic for several reasons. First, there is the unresolved issue of identifying the proper relationship between academics and practitioners. This is not an issue that is exclusive to strategic studies, nor is it an entirely novel question, although it is often depicted as ethically problematic given the perceived relationship between 'strategy and slaughter' (Wallace 1996; Gray 1982a; Shaw 2003: 269).

Second, Marxist and other critically oriented scholars have also often charged Anglo-American strategic studies as being complicit in the perpetuation of the 'military–industrial complex' (Wright 1956; Sarkesian 1972), whereby strategic studies is seen as the legitimating academic arm of the 'war industry' (Wæver and Buzan 2010: 468).

Third, critics argue that the aspiration towards the status of policy-science has encouraged strategists to concentrate on the means rather than the ends of military force (Barkawi 1998: 160; Wyn Jones 1999: 131). Since strategists tend to assume that the 'national interest' is there to be served, they consequently focus on identifying the best means available to achieve those ends. This focus on the means, not the ends of strategy, critics argue, is why proponents of strategic studies had such an overt preoccupation with missile numbers and weapons' characteristics during the cold war, and hence their continuing emphasis on the study of technological innovation and the effects of the so-called 'revolution in military affairs' today. Richard Wyn Jones, for instance, asserts that 'Strategy has tended to be the preserve of the bean counters and those whose parameters extend little further than a detailed knowledge of the latest weapons system' (Wyn Jones 1999: 131). Against the self-image of the subdiscipline, Wyn Jones charges that strategic studies is consequently much less Clausewitzian—in taking account of the *relationship* between means and ends—than its exponents often claim. This tendency towards 'means-fetishism', as Wyn Jones terms it, leads him to suggest that strategic studies is not necessarily immoral but rather amoral. Concentration on the means and techniques by which the practice of strategy is to be pursued leads to what he (drawing on the critical theory of the Frankfurt School) identifies as a form of 'instrumental rationality' within strategic studies, a form of study that is more concerned with the instruments of violence than the ends they are used to achieve (Wyn Jones 1999; Booth 2005: 267–8) and the ethical and political consequences associated with those ends.

Sex, Death and The Language of Strategic Studies

Critics of strategic studies often focus on the language and terminology employed within strategic studies, in particular the use of euphemisms, metaphors, and technical jargon to describe the instruments and activity of war. This critique has antecedents in the criticism levelled at US cold war strategic planners and deterrence theorists. The activity of 'thinking about the unthinkable', as Herman Kahn had called it, led theorists of nuclear war to imagine scenarios of nuclear conflict and develop terminology to articulate these scenarios. Hence deterrence theory came to be suffused with terms such as 'MIRVing', 'throw-weights', and 'penetration aids' as well as the copious use of acronyms (Green 1986). Critics argued that this not only rendered the study of nuclear strategy arcane and inaccessible to non-specialists, but that the tendency towards euphemism and metaphor, by introducing a level of technical abstraction into the language of strategy, helped distance strategic theorists and planners from the human consequences of nuclear conflict. Philip Green wrote in 1966 that

> More than any other aspect of the thought of deterrence theorists, perhaps this reliance on euphemism reveals the deep problem of ethical justification which is central to their writings . . . Perhaps they are unwilling to face those questions directly.
> **Green (1966: 223)**

This idea that strategists shirk from accurately describing their subject of study has more recently been restated by several critical approaches to strategy. These approaches place crucial emphasis on the role of social construction. That is, whereas most strategists have tended to assume that we can make objective claims about the world and the place of conflict in it, critical approaches to strategy assume that the ways in which we interpret and discursively construct the world through language in itself has major significance. According to Carol Cohn, strategic studies has a 'specialized language', which she terms as 'technostrategic' in order to denote the 'intertwined, inextricable nature of technological and nuclear thinking' (Cohn 1987: 690). Cohn, on attending a workshop on nuclear weapons taught by defence academics in the mid-1980s, was struck by the fact that 'there seems to be no graphic reality behind the words, as they speak of 'first strikes', 'counterforce exchanges', and 'limited nuclear war', or as they debate the comparative values of a 'minimum deterrent posture' versus a 'nuclear war-fighting capability'. She comes to the conclusion that 'language both reflects and shapes the nature of the American nuclear strategic project, that it plays a central role in allowing defence intellectuals to think and act as they do' (Cohn 1987: 690).

Beginning from a feminist perspective, Cohn was struck by the gendered and sexual connotations of much of the terminology used within the male-dominated field of strategic studies:

> Lectures were filled with discussion of vertical erector launchers, thrust-to-weight ratios, soft lay downs, deep penetration, and the comparative advantages of protracted spasm attacks . . . Sanitized sexual abstraction and sexual and patriarchal imagery, even if disturbing, seemed to fit easily into the masculinist world of nuclear war planning.
> **Cohn (1987: 692, 687; Cohn 1993)**

Yet Cohn warns that we should avoid the 'uncomfortably reductionist' temptation to conflate the motivations behind strategic planning too easily with notions of male sexual desire or underlying psychological dynamics (see Caldicott 1986). What is most conspicuous about the language of strategy, Cohn argues, is its 'domesticated' nature: that is, the extent to which modern strategic terminology denotes means and methods of destruction with familiar domestic images (the 'Christmas tree farm' cited by Cohn in Box 18.2 is a prime example). As a result, the terms used to describe nuclear conflict are

> racy, sexy, snappy. You can throw them around in rapid-fire succession. They are quick, clean, light; they trip off the tongue. You can reel off dozens of them in seconds, forgetting about how one might just interfere with the next, not to mention with the lives beneath them.
> **Cohn (1987: 704)**

Cohn argues that theorists and practitioners can think and act as they do by articulating the 'unthinkable' via familiar words and imagery. Even though Cohn's critical assessment of strategic studies derives from the cold war context, its analysis remains highly relevant,

BOX 18.2 Sex and Death in the World of Nuclear Strategy

On a Trident submarine, which carries twenty-four multiple warhead nuclear missiles, crew members call the part of the submarine where the missiles are lined up in their silos ready for launching 'the Christmas tree farm'. What could be more bucolic—farms, silos, Christmas trees? In the ever-friendly, ever-romantic world of nuclear weaponry, enemies 'exchange' warheads; one missile 'takes out' another; 'coupling' is sometimes used to refer to the wiring between mechanisms of warning and response, or to the psychopolitical links between strategic (intercontinental) and theatre (European-based) weapons. The patterns in which a MIRVed missile's nuclear warheads land is known as a 'footprint'. These nuclear explosives are not dropped; a 'bus' 'delivers' them. In addition, nuclear bombs are not referred to as bombs or even warheads; they are referred to as 'reentry vehicles', a term far more bland and benign, which is then shortened to 'RVs,' a term not only totally abstract and removed from the reality of a bomb but also resonant with the image of recreational vehicles of the ideal family vacation.

Cohn (1987: 698)

given that contemporary warfare increasingly relies on complex technology. With conflict mediated via technological means and nuclear and conventional simulations of conflict scenarios now the norm when it comes to the formulation of military strategy (for advanced Western militaries at least), the prevalence of techno-strategic language within strategic studies is even more apparent. 'Information warfare', 'network-centric warfare', 'smart bombs' are just a few examples of techno-speak common within the language of contemporary strategic studies. What Cohn, Klein, and Wyn Jones seek to alert us to is the risk that the familiar and 'snappy' nature of strategic language can create a conceptual distance between the process of theorizing strategic violence and its actual effects. The potential problem in Cohn's eyes is not that the language of strategy is inaccessible, but that, once learned, it is all *too* accessible, making it too easy to reduce human conflict to a series of sanitized euphemisms and abstractions.

Key points

- Recent critical approaches to strategic studies have focused on its role in constructing a particular West-centric vision of world order, the relationship between strategic theory and policymaking, and the language of strategic studies.

- Strategic studies has been accused of promoting a vision of world order that has legitimated and justified Western dominance, particularly during the cold war when strategic studies' concern with the superpower rivalry obscured increased Western intervention in the non-Western world.

- Critical approaches to strategic studies have questioned strategists' aspirations to the status of a 'policy science', arguing that an unquestioning focus on serving the national interest has led to an overly technical and instrumental approach.

- The role of social construction and the language of strategic studies has also come under scrutiny. Feminist scholars have argued that strategic studies has tended to employ gendered terminology, and uses words and images that lead to a sanitized, domesticated, and ultimately more permissive view of military force.

A Continuing Debate?

There has been little recent direct engagement between contemporary proponents and critics of strategic studies. In part, this is due to a growing degree of incommensurability between the two camps: that is, because proponents and critics of strategic studies tend to begin from increasingly divergent assumptions, dialogue and substantive engagement between the two has been relatively sparse. Additionally, most scholars operating from critical perspectives are not seeking to create a 'better' form of strategic studies, but alternatives to this enterprise. Rather than seeking to regenerate strategic studies, critical approaches to strategic studies have contributed to a more expansive conception of security studies that encompasses multiple non-military issues, such as economics, the environment, health, and migration. These new approaches tend to depict strategic studies as their more traditional and restricted alter ego.

This process has been accelerated by the alleged inadequacy of strategic studies for dealing with post-cold war issues. Indeed, those operating from critical approaches have been prominent in questioning the relevance of strategic studies in the contemporary world. Although some proponents of strategic studies continue to espouse its 'timeless' principles, critics argue that strategic studies is outdated and anachronistic (see Box 18.3).

One of the strongest criticisms mounted against strategic studies in the post-cold war era is that it no longer offers appropriate tools to study major issues, even conflict, in world politics. Whereas strategic studies tended in the past to focus on state and superpower rivalries, the 'new wars' of the post-cold war era have mainly tended to be intra-state civil and ethnic conflicts (Kaldor 1999). Because military threats, particularly those related to global terrorism, are non-state in character some critics have predicted the 'gradual supercession' of strategic studies (Shaw 2003).

It is this issue of relevance that has produced the greatest reaction among proponents of strategic studies. They have generally recognized the need for further evolution from the types of studies that preoccupied them during the cold war. Many have acknowledged that strategic studies may have been 'too dominant' (Baylis 2001: 1; Betts 1997: 32) within the study of world politics during the cold war and that during that period 'the political framework ha[d] been taken too much for granted and strategic studies ha[d] become infatuated

---

BOX 18.3 The Continuing Relevance of Strategic Studies?

Whether humans navigate by the stars or via the satellites of the US Global Positioning System (GPS), and whether they communicate by smoke signals or via space vehicles, matters not at all for the permanent nature of strategy.

Gray (1999b: 182)

In the historical military sense preferred by Gray, [strategy] faces not rapid redundancy but gradual supercession . . . The demand for justice in war has, of course, facilitated a limited rehabilitation of military power . . . However . . . it hardly provides sufficient scope for a general rehabilitation of strategic thinking about force.

Shaw (2003: 276–7)

with the microscopic analysis of military technology and the acquisition of equipment by the forces of both sides' (Freedman cited in Barkawi 1998: 181; see also Chapter 20 of this volume, 'Does Strategic Studies have a Future?').

 ## Conclusion

Viewed from the perspective of its critics, strategic studies is ripe for an overhaul in the twenty-first century and, as many of the contributions to this volume attest to, has already begun to address a much wider range of issues relevant to the contemporary world. Contemporary strategic studies is clearly more than simply the study of nuclear war and nuclear weapons, even as this remains a central concern. There will always be those who view strategic studies, pejoratively, as nothing more than the 'conjectural art of butchering one's neighbour' (Danchev 1999: 313), and strategy simply as an accomplice of 'slaughter' (Shaw 2003). Yet those who oppose the purpose and existence of strategic studies need to mount sustained and viable critiques of a field of study that is attempting to evolve away from its cold war incarnation. The extent to which strategic studies can do so, and its ability to address the critiques reviewed here, should be the source of critical analysis in the future. Critique, friendly or even unfriendly, can still play a major role in this regard by questioning the assumptions of contemporary strategic studies and by holding a critical mirror up to its development.

 ## Questions

1. Why did strategists seek to apply game theory to the study of nuclear deterrence, and what are the main criticisms of this application?

2. How convincing are moral critiques of strategic studies? Are strategy and ethics compatible?

3. Is it possible to achieve scientific objectivity in the study of strategy?

4. What are the main differences between 'second wave' and 'third wave' strategic thinking?

5. Why do critical approaches to strategic studies emphasize the role of social construction?

6. Does strategic studies have an inherent Western bias?

7. Why is the relationship between strategic studies and policymaking potentially problematic according to critics?

8. What are the main foundations of feminist critiques of strategic studies?

9. Do critical approaches to the study of strategy have anything to contribute to the development of strategic studies?

10. Is strategic studies still relevant to the study of contemporary conflict?

 ## Further Reading

R. K. Betts, 'Should Strategic Studies Survive?', *World Politics* 50/1 (October 1997).
A qualified but robust defence of the relevance of strategic studies in the post-Cold War era.

H. Bull, 'Strategic Studies and its Critics', *World Politics* 20/4 (July 1968).
The seminal riposte to the criticisms levelled at strategic studies and the 'civilian strategists' during the 1960s.

C. Cohn, 'Sex and Death in the Rational World of Defense Intellectuals', *Signs* 12/4 (Summer, 1987).
Offers a feminist critique of strategic studies and deterrence theory.

C. S. Gray, *Strategic Studies: A Critical Assessment* **(London: Aldwych Press, 1982).**
A spirited if 'friendly' critique of the study of strategy as it developed in the post-war era.

P. Green, *Deadly Logic: The Theory of Nuclear Deterrence* **(Ohio, OH: Ohio State University Press, 1966).**
Though now somewhat dated, Green identified several issues, such as the use of euphemism and metaphor in the language of strategic studies that remain pertinent objects of criticism today.

B. S. Klein, *Strategic Studies and World Order: The Global Politics of Deterrence* **(Cambridge: Cambridge University Press, 1994).**
A broadly post-structuralist assessment of the role of strategic studies in constructing the modern West.

P. Lawrence, *Preparing for Armageddon: A Critique of Western Strategy* **(Brighton: Wheatsheaf, 1988).**
Continued the moral critique of strategic studies in the context of the 'second cold war'.

A. Rapoport, *Strategy and Conscience* **(New York: Harper and Row, 1964).**
Like Philip Green, Rapoport identified several strands of moral criticism of strategic studies that still resonate today, even if the object of his critique has evolved substantially since the time of writing.

M. Shaw, 'Strategy and Slaughter', *Review of International Studies,* **29/2 (2003).**
Offers an ardent critique of Colin S. Gray's argument for the timeless wisdom of strategy.

R. Wyn Jones, *Security, Strategy and Critical Theory* **(Boulder, CO: Lynne Rienner, 1999).**
Draws on the critical theory of the Frankfurt School and Antonio Gramsci to critique the foundational assumptions of 'traditional' strategic studies and outline a 'critical' alternative.

 # Web Links

Melbourne Business School **http://www.mbs.edu/home/jgans/mecon/value/Segment%205_3.htm** offers for the uninitiated a brief introduction to game theory, as employed during the 'Golden Age' of strategic studies.

The Campaign for Nuclear Disarmament (CND) **http://www.cnduk.org/** maintains the moral arguments for nuclear disarmament that continues to run counter to the focus on the strategic use of nuclear weapons within strategic studies, as does the Nuclear Age Peace Foundation **http://www.wagingpeace.org/index.htm**

Foreign Policy Robert S. McNamara 'Apocalypse Soon' **http://www.foreignpolicy.com/story/cms. php?story_id=2829** The former US Secretary of Defense later argued that US reliance on nuclear weapons is immoral, the latest iteration of a familiar line of critique.

Slate Website Fred Kaplan **http://www.slate.com/id/2082846/** Populist critiques of the role of strategists in formulating policy, particularly in relation to US nuclear weapons policy, are also still common.

The Practice of Strategy

COLIN S. GRAY AND JEANNIE L. JOHNSON

 Chapter Contents

Introduction: Strategic Expertise	359
Improving a Strategic Education	359
The General Theory of Strategy	363
A Call for Consummate (Re)Assessing	373
Conclusion	374

 Reader's Guide

This chapter defines the requirements of good strategy making. It begins by explaining why good strategists are hard to find and then critically examines the deficits of contemporary strategic education: insufficient attention to strategic classics and strategic history, and a pronounced bias towards American centric topics and perspectives. A lack of universal theory is identified as critical. A remedy is offered: The General Theory of Strategy. The chapter closes with a call for the regular reassessment of strategic plans and engagements, and with a strong reminder that strategy is a practical subject and knowledge from its study must be communicated to those who need it.

Introduction: Strategic Expertise

Strategic geniuses are born rather than made. It is exceedingly difficult to 'do' strategy competently. Happily, however, one need not be a strategic genius to succeed, just better in some political or military contest than the enemy's strategist. A strategist needs to be, simply, 'good enough'. That said, modern strategic studies has not performed well as an educator of would-be strategic minds. The evidence in support of this harsh judgement lies both in what is absent from the literature and in the quality of official performance. This chapter outlines the qualities a good strategist needs to be effective, and the obstacles to competent strategic performance presented by current trends in strategic studies and by real-world circumstances.

Strategic expertise is rare for at least three reasons: the position of strategist is ill-defined, the education currently on offer for would-be strategists suffers chronic, debilitating gaps and biases, and the profession has yet to come to terms with a general theory of strategy which binds together the discipline and provides structure for action.

There are professional politicians, policymakers, and professional soldiers, but there are no truly professional strategists. Strategists have to be a mixture of theorist, planner, leader, and commander, but the most effective balance among these qualities is particular to time and place. In the modern age, one might suggest that general staffs do strategy as operational plans, but they are not usually trusted to answer the 'so what?' question to their plans because doing so would cross the strategy bridge to the realm of politics.

In addition to being ill defined, the position of strategist is daunting. As has been noted by one of the authors in a previous work, the enormity and complexity of a professional strategist's task requires 'Only the most mentally stable, physically robust, best broadly educated, technically sound, and naturally intuitively gifted people' (Gray 2010: 64).

Improving a Strategic Education

Assuming a robust set of personal attributes, would-be strategists remain crippled by a faulty education; one which slights the classics of strategy and strategic history, and remains unbalanced in favour of American tasks and priorities. In our opinion, the understudied classics are located in the works of no more than eight authors written over the course of 2,500 years: Sun Tzu, Thucydides, Carl von Clausewitz, Baron Antoine-Henri de Jomini, Basil H. Liddell Hart, J. C. Wylie, Edward N. Luttwak, and Bernard Brodie.

There are three divisions in the canon of classic strategic theory. The first has three entries.

1. Carl von Clausewitz, *On War*. This is the most profound book on the theory of war and strategy ever written. It is long, philosophical, and something of a nightmare in organization. It was written between 1816 and 1831, and its argument reflects major shifts in the author's understanding, sometimes imperfectly transcribed into the text. Nonetheless, *On War* is the richest mine of strategic wisdom available.

2. Sun Tzu, *The Art of War*. As cryptic, indeed axiomatic, in style as Clausewitz is philosophical and wordy, Sun Tzu's is a brilliant terse treatise. It could be an ancient Chinese PowerPoint briefing. Unlike Clausewitz, Sun Tzu offers direct advice to help his reader be

victorious in war. Also unlike Clausewitz, Sun Tzu writes not just narrowly about war, but rather about broad relationships among war, strategy, and statecraft.

3. Thucydides' *The Peloponnesian War* is best studied in the version Thucydides, *The Landmark Thucydides: A Comprehensive Guide to 'The Peloponnesian War'*. Thucydides did not set out to write a general theory of strategy. *The Peloponnesian War*, however, contains some of the finest literary examples of grand strategic reasoning ever committed to paper, as well as richly detailed cases of military strategy. The reader receives a general strategic education from the superb description and analysis in historical context.

The second division of classical strategists has four members.

4. Baron Antoine-Henri de Jomini, *The Art of War*. Jomini is undervalued today, so far has his mantle of authority slipped from his paramount position in the middle of the nineteenth century. He was probably the most perceptive interpreter of Napoleon's way of warfare. Although his *The Art of War* is flawed and certainly dated in much of its detailed advice, it is nonetheless populated with significant insights into war as a whole, warfare, strategy, operational art, tactics, technology, and logistics. It deserves to be read, albeit with care, by strategists today.

5. Basil H. Liddell Hart, *Strategy: The Indirect Approach* is a work of great breadth and depth, marred principally by the author's determination to sell the 'indirect approach' as the magical elixir that delivers success reliably. Despite defying easy definition, the indirect approach is a valid and important idea. However, since it can have no meaning other than being whatever the enemy does not expect (i.e. the direct approach), it cannot serve as the all-context key to victory as its prophet claims; its logic is fatally circular.

6. Edward N. Luttwak, *Strategy: The Logic of War and Peace* is very recent, but it has undeniable classic features. The author treats the several levels of war systematically, emphasizing the pervasiveness of paradox and irony as inherent features of strategy. Furthermore, Luttwak's insight that there is no natural harmony among policy, strategy, operations, and tactics, though hardly original, nonetheless is both profound and of huge practical significance.

7. J. C. Wylie, *Military Strategy: A General Theory of Power Control* is probably the most competent, and notwithstanding its wonderful brevity, the deepest work on the general theory of strategy written in the twentieth century. Following Clausewitz, Wylie wisely insists that the purpose of war is to gain some measure of control over the enemy.

The third division has only one entry:

8. Bernard Brodie, as revealed in two of his books, *Strategy in the Missile Age*, and *War and Politics*, deserves inclusion as a member of the highly exclusive category of great theorists of strategy. Although nearly all of the Brodie canon was focused on American defence problems in the emerging nuclear and missile ages, his strategic theoretical range was extensive and his judgements were profound. We predict that he will merit reading a century from now, a judgement that confers at least candidate classic status among the great strategic thinkers.

A study of the strategic classics must be married to a study of strategic history. If practising strategists are ignorant of history, they are marooned on a very small island of expertise—their understanding of the present—surrounded by a vast ocean of ignorance about the past and the future. Since we cannot know anything in detail about the future, and the present is inherently transient, we need to extract whatever is extractable from our all too rich strategic history. Contexts change their character, but our 'present' has a plethora of antecedents. The Romans knew about counterinsurgency operations and counterterrorism, and so did Alexander.

The dangers of an ahistorical mindset are worthy of emphasis. Ignorant of history, the strategist will see the ever-changing present as a succession of surprises even though strategic history is a truly grand narrative showing more continuities than discontinuities. It is poor history that leads people to invent allegedly great discontinuities: the nuclear age, the cold war, post 9/11, and now 'the return of geopolitics' or 'power politics' (as if there could be any other kind!). A mind without stores of historical past will fail to see patterns and will be tempted to treat current events as singular, or unprecedented, or to pin the cause of modern happenings on particular national traits: 'Is this Russian aggression, or do all great powers typically expect to dominate their neighbourhoods?' The well-educated strategist does not need to pose this question.

History's 'ages', 'eras', 'turning points', 'tipping points', 'revolutions', 'strategic moments', and the like, are generally scholars' inventions, leaving a strategist who fails to earn his own studied interpretation of history easy prey for half-baked ideas and dodgy history (e.g. 'fourth-generation warfare', 'the Pentagon's new map', 'effects-based operations') (Hammas 2004; Barnett 2004; Anderson 2009: 78–81). The three leading thrust points of modern strategic studies—deterrence, limited war, and arms control—were all promoted, though not invented, in the mid-to-late 1950s by brilliant minds undisturbed by much grasp of history. Modern strategic theory was designed as a potent exercise in rational choice. Most of the contestably arrogant theory developed in the 1950s and 1960s was dangerously wrong, in substantial part because it could not accommodate the abundant evidence supplied by history concerning the role of contingency, especially human contingency.

Ideally, the good strategist must be a *shrewd* historian. At the least, the strategist has to know enough history to make shrewd use of the work of historians. Although history is the only strategic evidence we have, the merits and credibility of its recorders is eminently arguable. The challenge is to draw strategic lessons from history without being led astray by the inventions of hindsight. Historical perspective is desirable, but it is not virus-free. Hindsight is a curse as well as a blessing. It all but encourages us to misinterpret the past. All history is made by people *at the time—their* perspective really mattered, and matters to us in trying to understand 'why?' Empathy for historical figures is essential, but difficult to achieve. *We* in the twenty-first century now know that the cold war was a 'long peace', but in the 1950s and 1960s those of us who were there did not know that. Were the 1930s 'the path to war'?—well, obviously yes, but they did not seem that way to a lot of people at the time. In retrospect the cold war nuclear arms race was an absurdity. So why did clever and generally prudent people allow it to happen? Could it have been arrested in its military and political tracks? If so, when, how, and by whom?

Many people fail to appreciate that history, which begins today if one is looking backwards, is the only evidence we have; all else is speculation. Napoleon said there are two sources of education for a general, his own experience and the experience of other generals

(Chandler 1988: 81). The history-averse 'presentist' is likely to discover that his own life experience provides unduly thin pickings as an education for action. The more historical evidence one acquires, the better educated a consumer of history he or she ought to be.

Ahistoricism is made all the more dangerous when combined with national bias. Modern strategic studies have been largely Western, most especially American, in source, focus, and therefore outlook. The American character of modern strategic studies has been inevitable and unstoppable, even had anyone wanted to stop it. Strategic pondering needs problems to ponder and, unsurprisingly for a superpower, the United States has had more ponder-worthy strategic problems than have most polities. In addition, the openness of American society and the constitutionally mandated decentralization of the federal government has meant that opportunity knocked for different types of armchair strategists. US officialdom is willing to share its secrets with those scholars who show promise of being helpful. By contrast, Britain is more like the former USSR in this regard, as are nearly all polities.

There are baser reasons for the continuing US domination of strategic studies. These include monetary and career incentives, the opportunity for influence, and their rarity elsewhere in the world. It is a minor paradox: you can only really 'do' strategic studies professionally in the United States, because only there can you float, career-wise, among academia, think tank, industry, and government while holding a security clearance—the ticket that allows access to the inner circles of government. However, to be a player you must address current US issues as defined by US officials—typically the only ones fundable by US foundations—which may well limit the integrity of your scholarship. Even the true policy-relevant potential of your scholarship may be damaged, because you have had to buy your ticket to play as a licensed strategic thinker by using the coin of self-restraint in logic and imagination.

The leading topics, therefore, of modern strategic studies are the issues faced by the American superpower, as the officials of that superpower defined them. This has inevitably meant an overemphasis on some issues to the neglect of others. For instance, for most of the modern period, irregular warfare was not regarded by the profession's leaders, or their US government, as serious business. Nuclear proliferation, counterinsurgency, and counterterrorism, were marginal concerns to the nuclear-focused folk who did the 'big important stuff'. Ironically, as history's revenge, in official estimation today it is nuclear matters (except the essentially hopeless quest for nuclear non-proliferation) that are marginal to the strategic studies profession. On a more macro scale, some matters of general theory continue to receive insufficient attention, including analyses of military doctrine, command, logistics, and civil-military relations.

Perhaps more seriously, the US-coloured thread which weaves through the bulk of the strategic literature results in a distinct ethnocentrism. America is an amazingly open society and government structure, but its strategic studies are essentially impregnable to alien strategic world views. There is nothing wrong per se with a focus upon the leading global player, but the relentlessly American character of modern and contemporary strategic studies all but mandates that we do a poor job of understanding other cultures and traditions. Even if we only want to kill opponents, as opposed to bending their will by persuasion, a lack of understanding is apt to be a major handicap. Most polities in the world have strategic narratives of their own that are different from the American-centred view of the world (see Box 19.1). A strategic studies profession largely owned or rented by the United States cannot help

BOX 19.1 Alternate Strategic Narratives

The Russian worldview has been largely shaped by its 'geography, by a long history of "tribal" conflicts under the Mongols, [by] the expansion and rule of a multiethnic empire, and by a deep authoritarianism' (Ermarth 2009: 86–7). Fritz Ermarth argues that this helps explain Russians' comfort with martial values and their emphasis on mass in defence matters. Technological advances, he argues, are sought after as 'mass multipliers', not as a means of fighting well with fewer men.

Sarah Chayes describes aspects of identity and warfare practised in Afghanistan:

> It is a state founded not on a set of thoughts held in common and articulated through texts and institu-
> tions, but rather a state founded on the strategic nature of its territory—the crux between empires. It is
> a state founded on a fluid and tenuous interaction between collective structures, structures of nation, of
> tribe, of family, and a highly developed sense of freedom, a violent aversion to submission.
>
> (2007: 101)

Chayes argues that Afghans grudgingly gather into a nation from time to time, but tribal ties never lose their pre-eminence. Therefore, when the national government comes under attack, Afghans are quick to dissolve it 'and run like water between the fingers of their would-be conquerors' (2007: 68).

Greg Giles outlines aspects of Iranian strategic perspective that would be alien to most Western observers:

> Shi'a attitudes toward war are less goal-oriented than western concepts. As evidenced by Khomeini's
> conduct of the 8-year war with Iraq, struggle and adversity are to be endured as a sign of commitment
> to the true faith. Defeat is not necessarily equated with failure. This emphasis on continuing the struggle
> against oppression and injustice rather than on achieving 'victory' is seen as producing a high tolerance
> of pain in Iran.
>
> (2003: 147)

but be poorly equipped to cope with events shaped in large part by the beliefs and choices of those educated, possibly traumatized and otherwise scarred, by vastly un-American perspectives.

Key points

- Competent professional strategists are hard to come by.
- The position of strategist is ill-defined and daunting.
- Modern strategic studies has done a poor job of educating those interested in the trade. Its deficits include insufficient attention to the classics and strategic history as well as a pronounced bias towards American issues and security concerns.

The General Theory of Strategy

Perhaps the most important gap in a strategic education and the most serious hindrance to achieving comprehensive strategic effect is the lack of a general theory of strategy. Because the human race, always self-organizing by community, has an eternal strategic history, that is to say a history shaped, or at the least influenced, by force, there always will be a demand for strategic study. A country or other security community may either decide not, or be unable, to 'do' strategy. Such a country, however, will perform strategically, regardless of its ability to do strategy purposefully. Often polities decide on policy, then decide on action, but neglect to tie the two realms together. The purpose of the strategist is to bridge this gap by being well armed with the general theory of strategy from which today's operational strategies are fundamentally derived. Modern strategic studies must make a convincing case to would-be strategists that their plans and conduct as planners and commanders depends upon a general theory of strategy and that military doctrines about contemporary 'best practice' should derive from that theory.

A single general theory of strategy must pertain to all periods, types of warfare, technologies, and belligerents. If you are confused or uncertain about what is, and what is not 'strategic', you are unlikely to speak with authority, or even just plausibly, about 'strategic studies'. The central assumption of a general theory of strategy is that the core components of Strategy *writ large* remain constant. Each core component must be considered in the process of creating individual strategies adapted to the needs of a particular time and place. In sum: sound strategies will claim universal strategic theory as one parent, and the particular demands of the contemporary military and political context as the other. The core components of the General Theory of Strategy are outlined in Box 19.2 and then described in detail (Gray 1999, Gray 2010).

Understanding the Nature and Character of Strategy

1. Defining Strategic Terms

A conversation about strategic theory cannot begin without some agreement on the use of terms. As described above, Strategy is here assumed to have a constant nature. Strate*gies*, on the other hand, have been variously labelled as direct or indirect, sequential or cumulative, attritional or manoeuvrist-annihilating, persisting or raiding (expeditionary), coercive or brute force, offensive or defensive, symmetrical or asymmetrical, or a complex combination of other asserted labels (Gray 2010: 65).

Other terms in frequent use include **grand strategy**: the orchestration and employment of any or all the assets of a security community (a wide, rather comprehensive list), including its military instrument, for political purposes. **Military strategy** comprises the direction and use made of force and the threat of force for political purposes. Implicit in the above two definitions is the assumption that someone, a professional strategist we advocate, must consciously and competently bind the coercive elements of the state to its stated political purposes. This engineer of strategy must build and maintain a **strategy bridge** that connects the realm of military power to that of political statecraft (Gray 2010: 28-29). As we go on to describe, this bridge is trafficked by persons with institutional ties of distinctive variety and preferences. Being able to communicate effectively with each and march them to common cause presents the would-be strategist with an heroic challenge.

2. Strategy is a Political instrument

Military institutions fight, but political institutions declare war. Politics, therefore, must be understood in all its Byzantine forms. The political ends that justify organized violence are in fact negotiated commodities influenced by key actors, domestic pressures, election cycles,

---

BOX 19.2 The General Theory of Strategy

Understanding the Nature and Character of Strategy

1. Defining Strategic Terms: Grand Strategy, Military Strategy, Strategy Bridge
2. Strategy is a political instrument
3. Strategy is adversarial
4. Strategy is subject to the human condition
5. Strategy may produce ironic effects

Making Strategies

6. Seven contexts:
   - Political
   - Sociocultural
   - Economic
   - Technological
   - Military
   - Geographical
   - Historical

Executing Strategies

7. Difficulties and friction
8. Time
9. Logistics
10. Information and intelligence
11. Military doctrine
12. Strategists and the Strategy Bridge

---

bureaucratic infighting, and by foreign incentives. Strategies function with, if not principally for, political consequences. Therefore, strategy should be made with an eye steadily fixed on political considerations. Today's wars are scrutinized through moral, cultural, and legal public lenses attuned in ways absent prior to the mid-nineteenth century. The result is that even sound military strategies risk failure if not backed by strong domestic support.

3. **Strategy is Adversarial**

The immediate purpose of strategy is to constrict an enemy's choices and exploit these for political purpose. There is no point in constructing strategies without a concrete adversary. Without an obvious foe, strategists must select from among plausible adversaries, treat these as sentient, wilful actors in a contest of domination, and plan towards their defeat. Too often imagined adversaries are treated as static entities, likely to respond along rational and predictable pathways. A strategist would do well to keep in mind paradoxical and ironic aspects of strategy: what works well today frequently does not work well tomorrow—and it does not work well tomorrow in good part because it worked well today. Adversaries, if they are at all willing to learn, will make sure of this. The game of war is played against an intelligent, motivated, and dissembling foe, not an inert victim.

4. Strategy is Subject to the Human Condition

Strategies are made and carried out by *people*. The well-educated strategist will consider both human nature—the instincts, spirit, and limitations of mortal frame shared by humans as a species—as well as the individual idiosyncrasies of great men and women who may play pivotal roles in the shaping of history. Strategists have personalities that are the products of their biology and life experience. When adversarial actors are treated as rational choice automatons, the planner is also likely to underrate the role of contingency. Eccentric action is always possible.

5. Strategy May Produce Ironic Effects

History provides us with a long legacy of strategies resulting in unintended consequences—explicit ironies of the political aims intended. Strategic annals are likely to recount that the US invasion of Iraq, in the name of defeating terrorism, may have had the opposite effect—inspiring and even enabling Islamist terrorism to reach new heights.

Making Strategies

6. Seven Contexts

The General Theory of Strategy advises that the particular details of each newly crafted strategy should be constructed from its political, sociocultural, economic, technological, military, geographical, and historical contexts (Gray 2010: 38–9). Strategies are both *derived from* and *executed within* each of these contexts. Humans, with all of their idiosyncrasies and foibles, add an extra dose of contingency into each contextual category.

Political

'Politics' is a handy label for the often complex process of negotiation and dialogue between and among a strategy's stakeholders, both civilian and military, domestic and allied. Strategy is inescapably a negotiated product consistently revised by changing circumstances on the home front or developments on the battlefield. A political context stretches the breadth of the security-related decision-making process: the internal machinations of relevant bureaucracies, their negotiations with relevant policymakers, the input and influence of pressure groups and popular opinion, the political conditions of the adversary, and the myriad political pressures external to the state.

Keeping the strategy bridge in good repair requires that the strategist have a nuanced understanding of each key political player and be able to induce cooperative, complementary behaviour toward the nation's political ends. This coordination challenge on the home front is likely to prove more difficult than direct military defeat of an adversary. Without conscious strategic coordination, however, a politico/military quest may remain rudderless, riding waves of immediate institutional interest and short-term tactical advantage—a strategic style that has produced many of history's ironic, even disastrous, strategic effects.

Sociocultural

Sociocultural influences produce the strategists who craft policy and the national populace to whom they must answer; it is an essential and vastly understudied component in the orchestration of war. Culture is admittedly complex and difficult to capture in theory and even more in practice. Polities as well as individuals may possess multiple cultures. That said, in order to function in a less than chaotic way, groups must agree upon a baseline of acceptable and unacceptable activities (an ethical code), usually supported by a sense of group identity and a set of beliefs about how the world works.

Even the most talented strategists may not be able to change strategically unhelpful cultural inclinations within their home polity, but an understanding of these vulnerabilities may at the very least aid in guarding against them and playing to strengths. Conversely, understanding the culturally nuanced habits (customs) of an adversary does not guarantee predictive power over his next move, but may help the strategist narrow the field of most likely behaviours and help him anticipate strategic vulnerabilities born of cultural preference.

This sort of serious study of culture and society has not typically been the forte of modern strategic studies. Current counterinsurgency efforts have highlighted this deficit. Success in people-centric warfare requires a sound knowledge of the roles, institutions, communication patterns, and social hierarchy of the society in which you are engaged. Advantage in any sort of conflict is aided by an understanding of the locus of social authority, how it is established and communicated, and what can be done to undermine the popular legitimacy of a society's war-making institutions (see Box 19.3).

Strategy is formed and executed in a social, value laden environment. Perhaps because ethics and values are so deeply internalized, this aspect of the sociocultural context is conspicuously missing from classic discussions of warfare. Only when group ethics are compromised, as in the Abu Ghraib scandal, do communities tend to verbalize, or perhaps even recognize, their ethical statutes. It is moral beings, however, who construct strategy and their respective value sets cannot be omitted from consideration. Evolution of effectiveness of strategies will be subjected to value-laden assessments of the conflict: by participants, domestic and global observers, and the adversary. Exposure of ethical violations is near certain to reduce morale among troops and diminish support for the war effort at home.

BOX 19.3

[W]hen security communities exercise strategic choice they do so not with a completely open, or blank, mind on strategic ideas, but rather with values, attitudes and preferences through which they filter new data, and in terms of which they judge among alternative courses of action.

Gray (1999: 29)

Economic

The genius of the strategist will always be bounded by the amount of resources at hand. Economics and logistics may be the tedium of warfare, but those who plan without a keen eye to either will pay a heavy price. Indeed, historian Sir Michael Howard offers the opinion that '[t]he strategy adopted is always more likely to be dictated more by the availability of means than by the nature of ends' (Howard 1991: 32).

Technological

The technology possessed by the belligerents involved may not directly determine the outcome, but neither can it be dismissed as an unimportant element for strategy. Technology may award one side strong logistical advantage. The human requirement is unarguably 'different for the warrior who must dispatch his enemy within arm's length, as extended by an edged or pointed weapon, and the "warrior" who "wields" a keyboard to dispatch an unmanned cruise missile to its target' (Gray 1999: 37). Technological advantage can prove decisive, but it may also backfire. A superpower sitting on technological superiority may become overconfident and lazy in 'knowing' potential enemies. History has demonstrated that strategies devised by a technologically disadvantaged, but strategically cunning, foe can win the day. The morale of troops is more likely to prove decisive than is the quality of their weaponry, which is not to deny that the latter can harm the former.

Military

Recruiting, training, and arming forces are the purview of military administrations. These institutions transform society's resources into military instruments. Since the war for which you are best prepared tends to be the one you would prefer to fight, military administrations may have significant influence on the type of warfare waged and in which theatres' operations are conducted. The clever strategist must be acutely aware of the distinctions between, and embedded preferences of service cultures, and the impact these will have on the execution of security policy.

Political and military command can play a harmful role when incompetent, or be recorded in the annals of history as paramount when superb. Leadership in war has dominated the literature on military history. Our modern fascination with, and often overdeveloped confidence in, technology, however, threatens to diminish an emphasis on the skills of the leaders behind the weapons, as well as the willingness of troops to fight and risk death and injury.

Geographical

The geography of war has expanded beyond the traditional domains of land and sea. Today's theatres include air and space and the ever-increasing reach of cyber connections. The role played by terrain, climate, and distance may be determined by the extent to which they can be trumped by technology. Military might, however, is never as fungible as its wielders would like. Long-range weapon systems that can traverse thousands of miles and strike with surgical accuracy may not, in fact, diminish the salience of geography. These long-range stand-off weapons may be irrelevant when conflicts are waged in urban settings, tribal lands, or any other setting in which nominally powerful weapons are either ethically or practically unfit for battle.

Any geography—land, space, cyberspace, sea, or air that presents a vulnerability to the adversary is likely to be exploited. The advantage gained there, however, must answer to an essential element of ground truth: 'Every specific strategy, no matter how particular to armed forces, specialized for, say, air or space warfare, has to contribute to a total strategic effect upon the land, the only geography suitable for human habitation' (Gray 2010: 40).

Historical

Fate assigns a strategy's historical context in the stream of time. Prevailing notions of best practice are typically a result of recent military experiences—victorious or traumatic. Battlefield wisdom held in the minds of today's commanding generals, combined with hindsight notions of the nation's proudest military ventures produce what is believed to be the range of admissible strategic choices. A strategist cannot help but be influenced by the tenor of the time in which he resides, but can manage wider perspective and surer footing by acquiring a deeper foundation of strategic history than that possessed by his contemporaries.

Executing Strategies

7. Difficulties and Friction

Key to strategy is a sound understanding that friction, chance, and uncertainty (Clausewitz 1976: 85–6) inevitably play a significant role. Untimely rainfall, plans falling into the hands of the enemy, or cultural missteps that inspire a local blood feud, may strip away the fortunes of an otherwise successful contender. All rational choice, planning, and training, is subject to the dynamics of a battlespace rife with uncertainty. Once the enemy is engaged, the foreseeable future is discovered not to be so. The inevitability of friction, however, should not inhibit a strategist from careful and multivariate planning. Friction should be treated as an assumed variable, contingency plans put in place, and flexible response considered the norm.

8. Time

Because humans tend to assume that time is even-handed to all parties, it is often ignored as a component of strategy; but time is not even-handed. Lengthy wars may advantage irregular forces and enervate professional militaries that are hostage to budget cycles and impatient domestic opinion. Western societies who define success through results-oriented metrics and deadlines are vulnerable to opponents who do not. Time, to reinforce the cliché, may cost advanced militaries inordinate amounts of money and nothing less than political defeat.

9. Logistics

Scholars often forget that the process of applying elegant strategic ideas is unromantically bureaucratic. When theorists debate strategic concepts, they are prone to assume logistical feasibility. This may be a vast assumption. If a fighting force cannot be effectively supplied, and moved, it cannot fight. It cannot prevail. The organization of strategic initiatives includes staffing and coordinating, costing and reviewing, overseeing and providing feedback. This must be delegated. Singular strategic geniuses cannot, and should not be allowed to do it all themselves, lest we be entirely captive to the vagaries of one human's motivations and capability. This requires a military administration that aspires to, and attains, logistical excellence.

10. Information and Intelligence

The value of information and intelligence is weighed largely by its contribution to achieving strategic surprise. It is a rather curious feature of strategic history that given the substantial effort applied to crafting deception strategies aimed at surprising the enemy, rather little attention is devoted to the subject of how, precisely, one *benefits* from surprise and takes full strategic advantage of it.

In this area as well as others the information and intelligence front has a spotty record. Recent Western engagement in irregular conflicts, where populations variously hide, abet, or oust militants from their midst, has inspired a rededication to refining intelligence gathered through human and technological means and improving what have traditionally been rather simplistic and ineffective information campaigns. Western militaries have not, traditionally, been very good at recording and building on lessons learned in the information aspect of warfare, and thus force themselves to learn from raw experience lessons their grandfathers might have supplied from the past.

11. Military Doctrine

Civilian and military scholars write strategic theory. These ideas are transformed by military administrations into doctrine, the purpose of which is to identify best current practice concerning 'what to think and how to do it'. When constructed top-down, in this fashion, doctrine may prove a rather unreliable guide for actual military behaviour, serving rather as an icon, an idealized version of how the organization aims to perform, or representing a top-down attempt to move an otherwise tradition-bound institution in a new direction.

In ideal form, strategic ideas and the attendant doctrine are objectively tied to security realities. In practice, widely accepted military doctrine, often distinct to the particular services, is more often than not a detailed legitimization of a preferred way of fighting: whether this is a good fit with the current threat environment or not. Jointness (cross-service cooperation) often loses in this battle—with doctrine being crafted and pursued for the purposes and futures of individual services rather than as an attempt to operate in complementary strategic fashion.

Given these realities, it may be that the most important role played by a strategist in the formation of doctrine is not recommending the particulars of operational or tactical approach, but rather orchestrating and streamlining the *process* of strategic planning, ensuring that players are not engaging in cross-purposes and enabling comprehensive strategic effect. In an orderly, if fictional to this point, strategic universe, the general theory of strategy would educate the writers of doctrine and inspire the pens of disparate security institutions to scribe complementary means towards common ends. In the non-fictional universe it is as well to understand that the doctrine that is followed is the doctrine that is believed, not necessarily the one that is written.

12. Strategists and the Strategy Bridge

The last point of The General Theory risks stating the obvious: strategy must be planned and coordinated by a competent strategist. A good strategist has to be a theorist, a planner, and sometimes a commander. At the risk of redundancy, we emphasize again: the task of a strategist is formidable in the extreme. Even a sound education may only bring partial success to the profession. Strategy is an art, not a science, requiring physical and moral fortitude, exceptionally good judgement, and more than one's share of luck: none of which is enhanced by formal education. Training and command experience fare no better as preparatory ground. Each can prove a false friend when confidently misapplied to the next war. Given the awesome challenges to sound strategic conduct, it is not hard to see why few people can qualify as competent strategists. That said, it may be worth sounding a hopeful note: Box 19.4 highlights five strategists worthy of acclaim.

A strategist's maintenance of the strategy bridge requires a personality that can tolerate, if not connect to, lead players on both sides of the river. The character traits that make a successful politician may pose an uneasy contrast to those that define a soldier's soldier. The potential for friction is enormous. Not only must an adept strategist be able to manage a rather strong set of contrasting personalities, he must be able to carry communications effectively between them.

Strategic studies cannot hold itself hostage to official clients who may not 'get it', who may not really understand what it means to 'do strategy'. More often than not, policymakers will be insufficiently educated in the general theory of strategy to recognize good strategy from bad. The truth is, the pragmatic clients of strategic studies are not interested in the nature of war, they need to know what to do *now*. Scholarly students of strategy usually do work irrelevant to the immediate needs of the state, which means that their products have to be placed in a current context before they can contribute to security *now*. The now is always moving; the longer-term view of the scholar never arrives. Policymakers and soldiers live in the now, and a professional strategic advisor or executive must learn how to deliver his advice in a way that answers the questions sitting in their inboxes. If strategic advice is not accessible it cannot be useful.

These components, or dimensions, of a universal theory of strategy are not strictly rank ordered in relative importance, nor are they meant to be mutually exclusive. They overlap and influence one another. Moreover, the significance of each must vary from historical context to context. The aspect of strategy most decisive for one battle may certainly be trumped by its fellow in another. The purposes of defining the essential components of strategy are to put defensible parameters around the strategist's field, and to identify a knowledge base convertible into practical advice for the problems of the day. General strategic theory hitches contemporary strategic issues to a common post, and supplies reins to the strategist who may otherwise ride from one conflict to the next without direction or basic understanding of the nature of war.

BOX 19.4 Five Good (Enough) Strategists

Strategic competence, even genius, reveals itself on a spectrum of better to worse, not simply in two categories, 'good' and 'bad'. Nevertheless, many strategists in history, meaning people in roles that required them to think and behave strategically, did perform quite clearly on average far more towards the 'good' rather than the 'bad' end of the competence spectrum, or vice versa. Even superior strategists had days of poor performance; a highly gifted strategist can be defeated by a yet more highly gifted strategist in the enemy's camp. Circumstances, contexts, contributed hugely to the ability of the strategist to demonstrate their gifts. A strategist as planner or commander needs only to be good enough, not perfect; and many a poor strategist has been rescued by the willingness of his troops to fight.

Given the heavy focus in this chapter upon the strategist as conceptualizer, it might be helpful to balance the account by citing five outstanding examples of planners and commanders—individuals who clearly were 'good enough' strategists.

Alexander, rightly termed the Great, (356–323 BC), was probably the finest strategist of all time. He was obliged by culture and circumstance to play all strategic roles personally: head of state and policymaker, heroic leader/warrior (a role required of a Macedonian head of state), grand strategist, and military strategist. Alexander's vast empire was acquired and briefly secured not only on the battlefield, but also by prudent grand strategy, wise military choices, cunning diplomacy, and intensely personal leadership of all kinds. He was never defeated in the course of his short, bloody career (Lonsdale 2007).

Ulysses S. Grant (1822–1885) and *Robert E. Lee* (1807–1870), respectively by 1864 the commanders-in-chief of the Union and Confederate armies in America, were both outstanding strategists. The battlefield generalship of both has been controversial among scholars. Both have been criticized for their willingness to accept eye-wateringly heavy casualties, often suffered in frontal assaults against recently much improved small arms, and somewhat modernized artillery, of the day. As matters of sound strategic judgement, Grant and Lee had no superior option other than to seek decision by battle. Both waged an offensive style of warfare brilliantly: Lee to compensate for material and human shortages; Grant for the purpose of exploiting the Union's human and logistical advantages (Keegan 1987; Reid 2005; Glatthaar 2008).

In its war with the Irish Republican Army (IRA) from 1919–1921, Britain was both fortunate and unfortunate in the person of the leader of its enemy, *Michael Collins* (1890–1922). Collins, nominally only the IRA's Director of Intelligence, proved a formidable foe. A graduate of a British internment camp as a consequence of his participation in the strategically absurd, though spiritually uplifting, 1916 Dublin Rising, Collins decided that he would try to win a war for Irish independence, not simply make the traditional futile blood sacrifice (e.g. 1916). He largely taught himself by hard experience how to wage the only kind of warfare that the outnumbered and outgunned IRA could win, that of an irregular kind (guerrilla and terroristic). Collins proved a master strategist for irregular conflict. For most of the war he out-generalled the British by a wide margin, even though by mid-1921 he was in effect defeated militarily. He understood that above all else terrorism and guerrilla warfare were political theatre. Collins waged a struggle against British political will by challenging British values. When he judged that the gun had won all that it could win, he made peace with a British government that was seeking an exit from most of Ireland. The British were fortunate in having to deal with so pragmatic and far-sighted an Irish leader and military leader-commander as Collins. Many Irishmen were not as realistic as Collins in his willingness to accept a compromise settlement in 1921 (Townshend 1975; Foy 2006).

Field Marshal Sir Alan Brooke [usually Alanbrooke] (1883–1963) was Britain's Chief of the Imperial General Staff (CIGS) from December 1941 until 1946. His statue outside the British Ministry of Defence proclaims on its plinth, 'Master of Strategy'. Following a distinguished, if brief, record of senior battlefield command (most especially as commander of II Corps in the Dunkirk Campaign of 1940), Alanbrooke rose to head the Army and then to chair the British Chiefs of Staff Committee. Perhaps even more important than the high quality of most of his own strategic judgements on the conduct of the war, his primary duties were to hold a daily running dialogue—frequently animated—with his charismatic and forceful political master, Winston Churchill. He also managed grand strategic relations with Britain's US ally. Given that the British strategic, and therefore political, hand, became weaker and weaker vis-à-vis the US as well as the USSR from 1942 to 1945, Alanbrooke needed all his gifts and education as a master of strategy (Roberts 2008).

Key points

- Due to the inevitability of conflict between human societies, the need for strategy is permanent. Polities that fail to construct and follow a deliberate strategy will nonetheless act to strategic effect.

- Strategic studies must provide would-be strategists with a general theory of strategy. This construct defines the field of a strategist and identifies the inherent and enduring components of strategy regardless of type of conflict.

- Contemporary strategies should draw upon The General Theory of Strategy as one parent and the current socio/political, military context as the other.

- A comprehensive understanding of The General Theory of Strategy illuminates the daunting nature of the challenge that the strategist strives to meet.

- Strategic competence can, and has been achieved as manifest by five sound strategists highlighted here.

- Policymakers are not often attuned to the theory or practice of strategy. It is the job of a professional strategist to explain the utility of the chosen strategy to those who must enact it.

- The elements of strategic theory proffered here are not listed by priority or importance. The aspect of strategy that requires the most attention and resource will be dictated by the specific contexts of the day.

A Call for Consummate (Re)Assessing

Given the limits of human wisdom and the role of contingency, no contemporary strategy, no matter how tightly married to a sound understanding of general theory, will have achieved a perfect score in strategic effect. A good strategist is obliged consistently to reassess her strategies, processes, strategic education, and traffic management on the strategy bridge in order to increase strategic prowess.

Assessment of any particular modern or historical strategy presents its own challenges. Every assessment is a judgement-set made by particularly encultured persons *today*. Our current context(s) shape or drive how we judge the past. A reassessment of the Second World War may speak volumes about the world today, but rather less about 1939–1945. Despite inherent subjectivity, consistent reassessment of our own and others' strategies has value. There is a chance that it may improve self-awareness of bias, identify errors, allow suggestions for improvement, and educate the strategist with knowledge for its own sake. After all, the strategist is a scholar; one of his or her roles is to search for truth.

With that in mind we suggest that an educated strategist needs to be armed with nine fundamental questions:

1. What is it all about? (i.e. what are the stakes at hand?)

2. What strategic effect are we having?

3. Is the strategy selected tailored to meet our political objectives?

4. What are the probable limits of our power as a basket of complementary agencies of influence, and in our endeavour to control the enemy's will?

5. How might the enemy strive to thwart us?

6. What are our alternative courses of action or inaction? What are their prospective costs and benefits?

7. How robust is our home front?

8. Does the strategy we prefer today draw prudently and honestly upon the strategic education that history provides?

9. What have we overlooked? (Gray 2010: 16–17; Crowl 1987: 39–48)

The good strategist needs to be a sceptic, not a cynic, though the latter attitude would often be excusable. He has to be ready to question official arguments, demands, decisions, and performance. Above all else, he has to remember at all times the core of his duties. The good strategist is locked into an adversarial project in which the enemy always has a vote. This the strategist must counter by delivering the compound of consequences that we know as 'strategic effect' from the world of operations and tactics, and thereby secure some control over the will and ability of the enemy to resist. This, in the proverbial nutshell, is what strategy and the strategist's duty is all about.

Key points

- Strategic reassessment will always suffer from the cultural and time-driven bias of the reassessor, but must be conducted despite its flaws if we hope to identify errors and improve performance.

- The questions that drive a reassessment should examine the extent to which our strategy has, and will continue to, enable achievement of political objectives. This assessment must include the likely moves of the adversary as well as the disposition of our domestic population.

- The essential role of the strategist is to deliver the sort of strategic effect that will collapse the enemy's will to resist.

 ## Conclusion

Even the most accomplished strategist is likely to perform in ways that are context-bound, rendered imperfect by bias as well as by ignorance. It does not follow, however, that strategic studies are harmful or unnecessary. Rather, they are essential, even though they can only be performed by flawed people working through somewhat dysfunctional institutions. This is who we are and how we have to work—period.

The only way forward is to continue to practise the virtues of good strategic studies, to take seriously the application of universal theory, and to require more rigour and breadth in the studies we produce. Our trade has timeless relevance, but statesmen can, and have, from time to time and place to place, chosen to ignore it. Should the position of professional strategist ever emerge within the polities of power, that rank will have been earned by virtue of a sound understanding of the belligerent past and the ability to make its lessons practicable to those crafting the future.

Questions

1. What factors have inhibited the rise of professional strategists?

2. Where is current strategic education most in need of improvement?

3. What cautions ought to be kept in mind when reading strategic history? Are records of ancient conflicts relevant to military matters today?

4. Why are 'modern strategic studies' and 'American strategic studies' nearly synonymous?

5. What are the dangers posed by an overwhelmingly American perspective in strategic studies?

6. What is the purpose of a universal theory of strategy? What issues must it address?

7. What material, political, organizational, geographical, or even accidental factors may inhibit strategic genius? How does human contingency play a role?

8. Why might the talents of some of the most gifted strategists in history be lost on the casual observer? What are the most pronounced achievements of Alexander? How does he compare with a modern strategist like Collins?

9. Describe the bridge a strategist must build between the political and military worlds. What are the difficulties in doing so? What tasks must be performed? What skills are required?

10. What are the objectives of a rigorous reassessment of strategy? What factors must be considered?

 Further Reading

B. Brodie, *Strategy in the Missile Age* (Princeton, NJ: Princeton University Press, 1959).
Brodie's is certainly a period piece, but is also much more than that. As the doyen of American strategic thinkers of the nuclear age he provides vital historical context to the nuclear-centred practical concerns of the late 1950s.

B. Brodie, *War and Politics* (New York: Macmillan, 1973).
Brodie (1973) is a late career work (he died in 1978) that is all about the practice of strategy through the twentieth century. Because his career began before 1945, his writings had a personal historical depth that most of his professional peers lacked.

C. von Clausewitz, *On War*, translated by Michael Howard and Peter Paret (Princeton, NJ: Princeton University Press, 1976).
Clausewitz is the foundation text for the conceptual education necessary if one is to understand, let alone practice, war and strategy.

C. S. Gray, *The Strategy Bridge* (Oxford: Oxford University Press, 2010).
Gray explains that the sole purpose and therefore value of strategic theory is to assist strategic practice. The 'good enough' practicing strategist needs to be an educated strategist.

A. H. de Jomini, *The Art of War* (1838; London: Greenhill Books, 1992).
Jomini is a valuable complement, and occasional corrective, to Clausewitz, particularly in his (Jomini's) detailed treatment of doing strategy and operations. The details are dated, of course, but most of the concerns generically are not.

B. H. Liddell Hart, *Strategy: The Indirect Approach* (1941; London: Faber and Faber, 1967).
Liddell Hart provides important insight into why and how strategy has been practised, set usefully in the context of historical experience, though admittedly an experience contestably interpreted.

E. N. Luttwak, *Strategy: The Logic of War and Peace*, revised edn (Cambridge, MA: Harvard University Press, 2001).

Luttwak offers insights on the nature of strategy that are quite original, if not always sound (e.g. he mistakes irony for paradox). His argument is powerful and obliges the reader to grapple with the practical implications of the nature and structure of strategy (with its different levels).

J. A. Olsen, and Colin S. Gray (eds) *The Practice of Strategy: From Alexander the Great to the Present* (Oxford: Oxford University Press, 2011).

Olsen and Gray show from historical experience how the theory and practice of strategy have always been interdependent.

Sun Tzu, *The Art of War*, edited and translated by Ralph D. Sawyer (*c*.490 BC) (Boulder CO, Westview Press, 1994).

Sun Tzu offers direct advice for all time on the practice of statecraft and strategy, as well as on the qualities needed for competent generalship.

Thucydides, *The Landmark Thucydides: A Comprehensive Guide to 'The Peloponnesian War'*, Robert B. Strassler (ed.), revised from translation by Richard Crawley (*c*.400 BC) (New York: The Free Press, 1996).

Thucydides tells the story of a very great war, but also, indirectly, his narrative offers a master-class on the practice of grand strategy.

J. C. Wylie, *Military Strategy: A General Theory of Power Control* (1967; Annapolis, MD: Naval Institute Press, 1989).

Wylie uses theory to make sense of the practice and malpractice of modern strategy. He is terse, clear, and anchored firmly in experience, some of it his own.

 ## Web Links

US Department of Defense **http://www.defense.gov/**. This site offers links to each of the US armed services, providing some insight into their distinctive roles and perceptions of the current threat environment.

Clausewitz **http://www.clausewitz.com/index.htm** The Clausewitz homepage introduces students to the writings of the Great Prussian himself and provides links to the most recent scholarly work on Clausewitzian topics.

This Sun Tzu Art of War page **http://suntzusaid.com/** provides students with a translation of Sun Tzu's work as well as a paragraph-by-paragraph commentary.

Muir S. Fairchild Research Information Center **http://www.au.af.mil/au/aul/bibs/great/great.htm**. This link provides bibliographies on great warriors, thinkers, and leaders. Available on their list are resources for Clausewitz, Jomini, Sun Tzu, Liddell Hart, Brodie, Ulysses S. Grant, and Robert E. Lee.

20 Does Strategic Studies have a Future?

LAWRENCE FREEDMAN

Chapter Contents

Introduction: The Development of Strategic Studies	378
In and Out of the Cold War	379
Strategy and the Crisis in Social Science	382
The Academic and Policy Worlds	384
Realism: Old and New	386
The Study of Armed Force	388
Conclusion: Does Strategic Studies Have a Future?	390

Reader's Guide

This concluding chapter considers whether strategic studies has a future as an area of academic study. It charts the rise and fall of the subject in the universities and suggests reasons why it should be revived and how this might be achieved. The chapter starts by looking at the early development of strategic studies. Strategic studies was largely undertaken outside the universities and was initially influenced by the physical sciences and engineering. Even as traditional military patterns of thought appeared inadequate in the thermonuclear age, academics still found it difficult to impose a scholarly framework for the subject that could survive shifts in policy. By the end of the cold war, strategic studies was essentially a broad enquiry, drawing on a range of expertise. With the end of the cold war, the big issues that had animated the study of military strategy subsided and some questioned the continued relevance of the topic. There was a risk that strategic studies would be caught between the scholarly virtues and disciplinary organization required by the universities and the pressures and urgency of strategic practice, which is inherently interdisciplinary. Realism, the intellectual basis of strategic studies, has also been challenged for being simplistic, for making exaggerated claims for its objectivity, and for disregarding domestic and transnational factors. Furthermore, some view realism as being preoccupied with armed force to the exclusion of peaceful means of exerting influence and resolving disputes, to the point of legitimizing armed force as an acceptable instrument of policy.

A way forward is suggested based on the idea that the course of history can be altered by the choices made by individuals, groups, and governments. These decisions provide the subject matter for strategic studies. They do not need to be choices made only by states nor only about the use of armed force. Armed forces, however, provide the starkest choices that can be confronted and so provide a natural starting point for any attempt to create a general theory of strategy, while organized violence poses a series of challenges that deserves special study.

Introduction: The Development of Strategic Studies

Initially strategic studies developed outside the universities. Before the cold war there were military theorists and commentators, such as John 'Boney' Fuller and Basil Liddell Hart in Britain, who often had substantial practical experience of the subject but who wrote largely for a popular and a professional audience rather than an academic one. Their subject matter was similar to that of later strategic studies, and those that survived into the nuclear age fitted in perfectly well with the new milieu. There was some pioneering activity in the universities after the First World War with the moves to establish the scientific study of international affairs as a contribution to the avoidance of future wars. Many of those in this field had an interest in military matters although few claimed expertise in how best to fight wars, and, as we will discuss, the bias in the discipline was to some extent antistrategic.

The special flavour of strategic studies after the Second world War came from those who had been working in the physical sciences and engineering rather than the social sciences and humanities, many with their consciences stung and their policy interest engaged through the Manhattan Project. Those who had worked on operational problems from convoy protection to choosing targets for air raids had firm views about how the conduct of war could no longer be left to what they often took to be the rather primitive, intuitive forms of reasoning of the professional military. The conviction that civilians had critical contributions to make to strategic policy grew as traditional military patterns of thought appeared to be quite inadequate in the thermonuclear age. The combination of the arms race and the cold war created the conditions for the growth of a substantial research-led policy community outside the universities—new government agencies, congressional committees, think tanks and 'beltway bandits'.

This created a market for professionally trained civilian strategists that university departments might attempt to fill. It also meant that academics were never able to impose a scholarly framework for the subject that could independently survive shifts in the policy framework. Few really tried to do so. From the start it was the salience of the policy issues rather than intellectual curiosity that led to the growth of the strategic studies community. The universities were certainly not hostile to policy-led research. The cold war coincided with the expansion of the universities throughout the Western world—not only in size but also in the range of their activities. They took in subjects that were often practical in nature and moved well beyond established disciplinary boundaries. If gender and the media could become appropriate subjects for university departments, then it would have been surprising if questions of armed force had escaped the net. More seriously, those making the case for higher education were pleased to have examples of contributions to national strength. When the universities went to the US Congress for more funds after the Soviet Union had apparently rushed ahead in the technological race in October 1957 with the launch of the world's first artificial satellite (Sputnik 1) their case was made in the name of national security. Many academics thrilled to a potential role in a wider public debate, even if this meant enduring snide remarks about abstract theorizing removed from real life, and certainty that their weightier tomes would be left unread while their short, snappy opinion pieces might reach presidents and prime ministers. Academic exponents of strategic studies might have had much more training in the use of evidence and sophisticated forms of analysis but they could still drift easily into advocacy, preferring popular and professional audiences to the dustier academic conferences.

Little attempt was made to use the cold war opportunities to establish strategic studies as an academic subject. No core curriculum was developed, and there was probably only a brief period in the early 1960s, the end of what was later described as the 'golden age', when there was a serious body of literature with which everyone in the field was reasonably familiar. There was not even a consensus on how academic work in this area should be described. The policy influence was always apparent. 'Military studies' appeared too technical and narrow, redolent of map-reading and staff exercises, and contradicted the factors that had shaped the civilian role in strategic policy: the prejudice against professional military thought; the democratic conviction that at any rate the military sphere should be subordinated to the civil: and the Clausewitzian presumption that if, as the master insisted, war is concerned with the pursuit of politics by other means, then military means could only be properly understood by reference to political purposes.

In and Out of the Cold War

But what political purposes? As, at least at the governmental level, the ends of policy seemed somewhat fixed during the cold war, the focus was very much on means. The contest between liberal capitalist and state socialist forms of government was inescapable and was not seriously up for debate in Western countries. The central problem of policy was about how, if at all, political benefit might be extracted from a nuclear arsenal without triggering a cataclysmic conflagration? Any benefit would have to be deterrent because once the weapons were used the consequences were bound to be catastrophic. But if use led to catastrophe, then how could nuclear threats be made to work for the sake of deterrence, and what options would be available should deterrence fail? How could credibility be injected into preposterous posturing? The conundrums and paradoxes of nuclear deterrence drew in academic interest. This could be done not only by exploring ways of reinforcing deterrence, thereby avoiding war, but also by evaluating the other policy instruments that might reduce dependence upon this high-risk approach. They became interested in particular in arms control as a form of cooperative management of the strategic relationship between the two superpowers. Over time this had an important consequence in that it encouraged a perspective that went beyond the purely national to the systemic. If rational Soviet policies were as important as rational American policies, then American policy should be designed to coax out of Moscow a more rational Soviet policy.

The changes in the character and tempo of the cold war naturally influenced strategic studies. After the Berlin and Cuban crises of the early 1960s, further development of the purer theories of deterrence seemed less important. Academics began to find a role in questioning official policy and warning of the limits to deterrence, the distorting effects of domestic and organizational politics on crisis management and the perils of misperception. The second-order technical studies sought to offer ways out of practical difficulties experienced in arms control negotiations. A further development came as it was recognized that too much of the 'golden age' literature had taken the political context for granted, or had at least failed to appreciate the dynamic consequences of the upheavals in the third world. After Vietnam these aspects of strategy were much harder to ignore. To understand the conditions in which armed forces might be used, or at least threatened, it was necessary to delve into a diverse range of regions. It seemed more important to draw attention to the complexities of the Middle East or Central America than to think up fancy but safe ways to threaten Armageddon. Furthermore, as even official deterrence policies moved to reduce their nuclear bias and strengthen their conventional elements, professional military knowledge and experience appeared much more relevant. So, well before the end of the cold war, the field of strategic studies (now often known as security studies) had become much more diffuse. There was no recognized academic discipline; only a broad area of study, coming under a variety of headings (peace, war, defence, security, strategy, arms control). The only unifying factor was that the interest lay beyond practical matters concerned with the actual employment of armed force to the political purposes for which it might be employed and the political measures that might be adopted either to prevent this employment or to bring it to an end.

In these circumstances it was inevitable that those working in the universities would have to follow the shifts in focus in the wider policy debate. Given the sort of upheavals associated with the end of the cold war and its aftermath this was no small matter. When the policy issues of the day moved from such topics as great power confrontation and nuclear arms control to at first intra-state wars and humanitarian intervention and later on to terrorism and counterinsurgency, then quite different skills might be needed. To deal with the old agenda one might hope for scholars with a grasp of traditional statecraft, a knowledge of the political thinking at the highest levels of the world's key capitals, sensitivity to alliance relations, and a technical understanding of the properties of the critical weapons systems and how they might be employed. Add in such questions as the management of defence budgets and the intricacies of arms control negotiations and it can soon be seen that during the cold war years strategic studies had to draw on a great variety of types of expertise.

Then out goes the cold war and in comes ethnic conflict, carrying with it vast quantities of anthropological and sociological literature, combined with a necessity to follow political developments in small and weak states, whose leading lights are not themselves plugged in to the international policy circuit, dirty little militia wars and microscopic terrorist cells, problems of humanitarian intervention and social and economic reconstruction as ways of preventing, resolving, and recovering from conflicts, and large issues of forms of Islam and whether Western democracy can be exported. Some argued for an even more complete shift away from the traditional agenda, insisting that the staples of conflict and violence must give way to, or at least accommodate, the vital factors of environment and economics. A hypothetical university department set up to address strategic studies during the cold war would find that the original interdisciplinary requirements—polymathic enough—were suddenly expanded to absurd lengths.

Not surprisingly, academics often appeared to be as uncertain about the future of the international system and how to handle the new agenda as were the policymakers. It became even more difficult to give confident advice in the form of three crisp bullet points. Policy-makers became impatient with those qualities that academics believe to be those most valuable: long-term thinking, stretching the bounds of the possible and taking complexity as a challenge rather than an excuse for not going into too much detail. Academics in the strategic/security studies field could see their funding in decline and their best work crowded out by partisan clamour, parochial agency interest and the more sensationalist fare on offer.

While the pull from the policy world was to go for the simple, snappy, and the short-term, the push from the academic world was almost exactly in the opposite direction. The study of international relations, established to address the problem of war, sought to gain respectability by acquiring all the attributes of a proper discipline, including a preoccupa-tion with theory and methodology. Academic advancement had come to depend on 'con-spicuous scholarship'—publishing in the right journals, linking relatively innocuous case studies to great theoretical issues and, through extensive footnotes, demonstrating a capac-ity to reference (though not necessarily to read) all potentially relevant literature. To those for whom language itself had become an ideological battlefield, and all empiricism suspect, policy relevance signified the antithesis of sound scholarship and certainly not its highest aspiration.

As the empirical side of the business has become much more challenging and the profes-sional imperatives more theoretical, academic strategic studies lacked replenishment. Young academics were discouraged from entering into the increasingly time-consuming business of making sense of contemporary affairs—getting to know foreign countries, exploring their history, establishing networks of contacts, and following the intricate twists and turns of pol-icy debates and military decisions. Often filling the gap were journalists, reflecting their pro-fessional inclination to seek out unique sources and interview the key players, and a lack of interest in theory. For example, journalists rather than academics wrote most of the memo-rable, and reliable, accounts of the Iraq and Afghanistan Wars. At the same time, those less interested in telling stories and more concerned to influence policy, possibly by becoming policymakers themselves, gravitated to the think tanks, where they could produce serious and often quite technical studies addressing critical issues. Think tanks, however, had their own problems, such as the need to satisfy funders through constant attention to the news agenda or else the promotion of a particular worldview. Without the continuity provided by teaching programmes, and the recruitment opportunities that come with doctoral students and post-doctoral fellows, critical mass could be hard to sustain.

The problem, therefore, notably but not uniquely in the United States, was that the chal-lenge of making sense of contemporary international conflict and the determination to turn international relations into either a pseudo-science or a critical discourse led the universities to opt out of strategic studies. In their different ways journalists and think-tankers could fill some of the gaps, but their interests and contributions were likely to be more fleeting. Their roles overlapped with that of the universities but they were not the same. At their best, uni-versities could offer durable departments with their own intellectual traditions, opportuni-ties for independent research, a tolerance of the sort of eccentricity and playfulness that could lead to real innovation, a capacity to see the bigger picture, an ability to draw on wider theories, and the constant refreshment that came from encounters with fresh generations of students.

Strategy and the Crisis in Social Science

The study of strategy posed a further and particular challenge to the social sciences. It tended to adopt the perspective of individual actors within the system, as they try to make sense of their environment and shape it to their needs as best they can. Much social science theorizing necessarily seeks to reduce the importance of human agency—by looking for patterns and regularities in areas which we might have thought in our naivety to be governed by choice. Deliberate political change is still inadequately studied in political theory except in a rather cynical way. There is no point in studying strategy unless one believes that the course of history can be altered by the choices made by individuals, even if not always in the ways they would wish. Those who believe that the analysis of politics and international relations requires attempts to identify long historical cycles, or universal laws of political life, or invariable patterns of behaviour, or structural determinants of actions that leave little scope for local decision are unlikely to find strategy particularly interesting or even relevant. Instead of finding anomalous behaviour intriguing they may find it irritating because it undermines the predictive power of their models.

Strategy is important only if it is believed that individuals, groups, and governments face real choices and that the reasoning which informs these choices is worthy of careful examination. By focusing on actors within the system and their sense of their own interests and aspirations, strategic studies must be seditious. It encourages the analysis of those situations where order is absent or elsewhere; disorder is encouraged by those who believe that it will be to the advantage of those on whose behalf they are acting.

This appreciation—almost celebration—of choice is essential to the study of strategy. Strategy is undertaken in the conviction that it is possible to manipulate and shape one's environment rather than simply become the victim of forces beyond one's control. For this reason, students of strategy are naturally political voyeurs, observing the choices of others with a discerning eye, whether or not they have sympathy with their ultimate aims.

Therefore it might be argued that there is no reason in principle why strategic studies, defined as an intellectual approach to certain types of problems, rather than a field of study, could not become more prominent in academic life. Indeed we know this to be the case. There are now far more courses about strategy in management departments than in international

BOX 20.1 Similarities and Differences between the Ideas of Clausewitz and Sun Tzu

The extent of the cultural and historical gaps separating Sun Tzu's *The Art of War* and Clausewitz's *On War*, not to mention the apparently contradictory nature of their most well-known dicta, has encouraged the a priori assumption that Sun Tzu and Clausewitz espouse essentially antagonistic theories. However, closer scrutiny reveals that while a number of differences exist, so do many similarities and complementary ideas.

The main points on which Sun Tzu and Clausewitz disagree concern the value of intelligence, the utility of deception, the feasibility of surprise attack, and the possibility of reliably forecasting and controlling the course of events on the battlefield. On the qualities requisite for a military commander, though, they agree in principle but differ in emphasis: Sun Tzu relies chiefly on the master of war's skill in making calculated, rational choices, while Clausewitz considers the military genius's artistic intuition to be the critical factor. Finally they hold similar views on the primacy of politics in war; the need to preserve the professional autonomy of the military in action; the overall importance of numerical superiority; and the folly of not securing victory as rapidly and decisively as possible once war has become inevitable.

Handel (1996)

relations departments, although unfortunately this development has encouraged the rather loose view of strategy as being concerned with more visionary planning or the management of large organizations in uncertain environments. Nonetheless, the classical military strategists—Sun Tzu more than Clausewitz—loom large in the management literature, far more so than the business strategists loom in the military literature. Furthermore, many of the more formal methodologies, of which the most famous remains game theory, developed in the late 1950s with nuclear deterrence in mind, have become even more influential in economics and management studies (see Box 20.1).

This has returned to political science departments as rational choice theory, although in a form that often appears to confirm the old jibe that political science is an area of study that in failing to achieve science avoids that dangerous subject, politics. It offers undoubted analytical rigour, a shared starting point for numerous lines of enquiry and considerable theoretical promise. The problem is that the methodology can be off-putting and restrictive, readily and usefully applied to only a limited number of types of choices. It copes poorly with complexity, as well as requiring bold assumptions about what it means to be rational. This is especially disconcerting when studying armed conflict, famed for its tendency to irrationality and the imperfection of available information (pushed by Clausewitz to the centre of his theory with his stress on friction and the fog of war). Game theory provided an important means of thinking through the alternative options that presented themselves to policymakers in the nuclear age, and in particular the need to recognize the incentives for cooperation in the midst of antagonism, but it could never capture the range of factors that would shape the critical decisions. Moreover, even in economics, where rational choice theory has a much more natural home, there has been a move, in behavioural economics, towards integrating the insights from psychology and accepting that rationality is always bounded and that individual actions can rarely be understood outside their social context.

Key points

- Strategic studies, with its focus on the importance of deliberate political choice, poses problems for the social sciences, which emphasize wider patterns of behaviour and the limited opportunities for achieving change.

- Strategists are 'voyeurs', scrutinizing the choices made by others concerned with difficult decisions about the role of armed force.

- Strategic studies can be seen as an intellectual approach to specific problems rather than a distinct field of study.

The Academic and Policy Worlds

The challenge is therefore more than how to re-engage with the policy world. The relationship between academics and policymakers is bound to be fraught with ethical and practical difficulties. The need for access and the desire for influence must be balanced against the risk that critical faculties might be blunted and intellectual integrity corrupted in the search for preferment. The academic should be under no obligation to become a practitioner. In terms of defining a field of study the vantage point of a student of strategy is quite different from that of a practitioner. When the former tries to second-guess the latter in an effort to display some superior wisdom, then it might well deserve to be treated with contempt. The most helpful role remains that which can be properly described as 'academic' (even though in the policy world this is all too often synonymous with irrelevant). Unless the academic has special and relevant expertise, for example in the politics of a particular region, then the main task may be to conceptualize and contextualize rather than provide specific guidance. If it is done well the practitioner should be able to recognize the relevance for whatever may be the problem at hand.

The stressed and busy practitioner might complain that, however subtle the analysis, academic work is unlikely to be addressing the current crisis or the next policy priority in the form in which it is being faced. Compared with academic specialists, the practitioner must range far and wide because of the nature of the judgements to be made, often in a hurry. It may be necessary to address the efficiency of various forms of coercion as well as inducements, and in so doing to draw on views about human nature under stress, problems of organization of large groups of people on the move, negotiating techniques, visions of a good society, and standards of ethical conduct. Consider a general entering into battle. He must consider:

- politics (how best to define the goal of the campaign, the importance of keeping allies sweet, what the people back home will stand),

- engineering (how well the weapons work, are likely to work in practice, possible modifications to suit local conditions, ensuring that they are properly maintained),

- sociology (the likely cohesion of the enemy force under fire),

- psychology (how to motivate his own men),

- geography (the possible impact of terrain on particular tactics),
- history (what other generals got away with in similar circumstances),
- economics (the rate at which he dare expend material on specific targets).

Note that all these considerations apply only to getting the best out of one's own side. Add the need to think about an enemy and even more types of issue have to be factored into the strategic deliberations.

Furthermore, practitioners expect to be judged by results. They will therefore tend to rely on what works for them. This may be intuition and hunch, or lessons drawn from searing experience or remembered bits of history. These may be relied upon in preference to excellent information sources and exemplary staff work. When matters are finely balanced but a decision still has to be taken, a feeling about the issue may be as good a guide as any. This may strike an academic as being wholly inappropriate or based on disgracefully exaggerated generalizations. Certainly the results from such approaches can be very poor, but whether a proper academic methodology would do any better is a moot point when there is no time for long projects and there can be little tolerance of too many caveats. Wise strategists may research their decisions as much as possible, but time often precludes further deliberation. When a general is wondering whether an enemy formation might break in the face of a sudden attack, he is not going to be impressed if he is told that more research is needed or that his working hypothesis is inherently untestable. Once a fateful decision has been taken, an open mind becomes a luxury because any reappraisal may result in confused orders and demoralization.

Strategic practice, as opposed to the theory, demands risk-taking on behalf of a wider constituency, normally with the lives of service personnel and possibly with whole societies, and this brings with it certain responsibilities. It involves mobilizing human and material resources according to a developed plan against anticipated opposition and in pursuit of stated objectives. If the objectives are misplaced, the plan misconceived, or the resources unavailable or poorly mobilized, then the strategy will fail and this will be the strategist's responsibility. It is this sense of being tested by practice and judged by results that gives strategic reasoning its edge. The unaccountable academic should properly feel a degree of humility when advising on such matters. To a far greater sense than academics might like to admit the practice of strategy may depend more on character and political acumen than research.

This may help explain why the study of strategy is accommodated only with difficulty in academic life. As practice it provides opportunity for chance and irrationality to hold sway. The purist might be appalled at the arbitrary mixture of politics, sociology, economics, psychology, and history that regularly influence decisions in crisis and combat, never mind the great contributions made by intuition and hunch. Yet the fact that reality rarely shows respect for disciplinary boundaries might give the academic pause for thought, as might evidence of the extent to which carefully qualified propositions, excessively crafted formulations, and a reluctance to pronounce until all possible avenues of research have been exhausted can get in the way of clear thinking.

Effective policy outside academia draws on a range of considerations that within academia are each confined to its own disciplinary box. Within the universities, intellectual progress is assumed to depend on commonly accepted methodologies being rigorously applied within a known conceptual framework to produce results able to withstand peer review. The process is watched over sternly by professional associations and journal editors—the 'gatekeepers'. They ensure that standards are maintained so that progress can be measured. Without the disciplinary boxes it could well be that teaching and research would become unmanageable. Nonetheless, disciplinary boundaries are often artificial, and sustained through jargon that excludes the uninitiated. Indeed academics often develop particular strategies to sustain these disciplinary boundaries and to fight off intellectual intruders. Yet many of the most important academic cleavages cut across these boundaries. Fads and fashions—from rational actor theory to deconstructionism—migrate easily. Often the most innovative and influential figures are those who refuse to be confined by the established boundaries, but are happy to borrow from others. Imaginative academic administrators often ignore them. In universities as in other organizations the closer one gets to particular decisions the more complex and multifaceted they appear. Practical problems can rarely be encapsulated in the terms of a single discipline. Life is interdisciplinary.

Key points

- Tensions inevitably exist between the academic and policy worlds with their different responsibilities.
- 'Practitioners' often complain about the irrelevance of academic studies to immediate problems they face.
- Strategic reality is wide ranging and interdisciplinary and does not fit neatly into the narrow focus of most university departments.

Realism: Old and New

A starting point for a revival of strategy might be to return to the realist tradition. Contemporary students of politics and international relations often criticize this tradition as being simplistic and obsolescent, bound up with the assumption that the only choices that matter are those that states make about military power. There are three aspects to the critique: an epistemological challenge to what is taken to be exaggerated claims for objectivity as if this is the only true reflection of 'reality'; the disregard of domestic and transnational factors; and the preoccupation with armed force to the exclusion of peaceful means of exerting influence and resolving disputes. This latter complaint can be taken further and developed into a charge that the realists legitimize armed force as an acceptable instrument of policy. This charge at the level of basic morality is directly related to the first, apparently more scholastic, complaint about objectivity. The realists might claim that they do no more than attempt to make sense of the world as they find it while their critics suggest that the very language and concepts they use encourages a very particular and dangerous view of the world. In recent years this critique has become more subdued as many leading realists have warned about the dangers of imprudent commitments in support of idealistic commitments to promote freedom and democracy while neglecting questions of order and stability. Realism tends to be conservative, not neo-conservative.

A defence of strategic studies does not require a defence of realism, however much the two have been linked in the past. There are, however, elements of the realist tradition that are worth preserving while other aspects need updating. An approach to political analysis that prided itself on coming to terms with the world as it was rather than as idealists would like it to be is now supposed to depend on a dubious claim that key international events can largely be explained by the structurally defined means by which states must safeguard their security. There is room for a non-dogmatic realism that would acknowledge the significance of non-state actors, the impact of social, economic, cultural, and local political factors on state behaviour, the importance of values and mental constructs, and can be sensitive to the epistemological issues raised by presumptions of objectivity. If practitioners of international politics now talk regularly about issues of identity, norms, and globalization, then they are part of international reality. To be powerful was often described within the realist tradition in terms of possessing substantial assets—so much wealth or military capabilities. Yet poor strategy can see these squandered or trivialized, while good strategy can extract substantial political effects from meagre resources. In this sense strategy is essentially an art, less about applying power and more about creating it in the first place. This requires a much more subtle view of power, as existing only within political relationships, manifest as actors are able to alter the behaviour of others according to their own preferences.

The constructivist position, which is now emerging as a safe haven for those troubled by structural realism, while leery about following postmodernist theory into a deconstructed, relativist mire, stresses the importance of the interaction between the way we describe the world and act within it. This can represent a real advance on the tendency within the realist tradition to think of power as a measurable resource. This leads to a view of strategy as no more than a mechanical matter of expending these resources in the pursuit of clearly defined objectives. Put this way, it can appear as almost a science, opening up possibilities for prediction. The practical strategist is more likely, however, to be, perhaps unwittingly, something of a constructivist. Effective strategy requires a clear sense of the dynamic relationship between ends and means, knowing that how ends are defined in the first place is critical to whether available means will be adequate. The ability to emerge victorious out of a conflict may depend on sensitivity as to what the opponent may think are his vulnerabilities or what your side can be persuaded is an area of comparative advantage. Vital judgements—such as finding the optimum balance among broadening a coalition to maximize the isolation of the opponent, the limited time available for coalition formation, the goals that will have to be dropped to bring in the most reluctant, the extra obligations that might have to be accepted, the otherwise neutral opinions that might be offended—turn on the way we understand the workings of our own and other political systems.

Key points

- Despite critiques of realism, there are elements of this school of thought that remain very useful in the study of strategy, while there are other elements that can be brought up to date.

- A case can be made for a non-dogmatic realism, which provides a more subtle approach to the role of power in international politics than the neo-realist approach, which emphasizes the structural constraints on state behaviour.

- Newer constructivist approaches also help to focus attention on the important dynamic relationship between ends and means, which is crucial in the outcome of any conflict.

The Study of Armed Force

A new realism should therefore have no trouble looking beyond what makes states secure and more towards what makes individuals and particular groups secure. It must also admit that the business of states, once almost completely bound up with security, now takes in a wide range of economic, social, and environmental issues. From this it follows that the course and character of all conflicts, and the role to be played by armed force, must be reappraised. Strong rates of economic growth and forms of interdependence may well reduce tensions between states and create a stake in peaceful coexistence. Equally, financial crises can create intense forms of stress and reignite nationalist urges. Environmental disasters can undermine the credibility of the state apparatus so that it becomes vulnerable to other types of challenges. Changes in family structures and social mores may affect attitudes to violence, and so on. As has become painfully apparent over the past two decades, proposals to discard the traditional focus on organized violence turned out to be premature. When governments are determined to resort to force it is as well that they understand their chosen instrument.

Strategy is more ubiquitous than violence. It is present wherever there is politics, which is in all human institutions, evident in any move to mobilize support, sideline opponents and so on. The study of strategy does not depend on the possibility of a violent aspect to human affairs. Nonetheless it can still be argued that this possibility can have an important impact on attempts to develop general theories of strategy, capable of addressing all manner of political situations. If strategy is about choice then armed force provides some of the most perplexing and starkest choices that can be confronted. At these points of choice can be observed clashes between conflicting interests and values, the rough impact of brute force and the more subtle effects achieved by guile and wiles. It is the case that most political objectives can be met without the use or threatened use of violence. There are other sources of power. However, physical violence is the ultimate and, if available, can overwhelm all others. The threat posed is one that no individual or group or state can ignore because it challenges their whole existence. It is one that is only likely to be made when basic values are at stake. Situations involving the purposive use of violence are likely to stand out from the run of the mill activities at both the national and international levels. By their nature they concentrate minds on fundamentals. Ethically and politically they require exceptional justification. For all these reasons they provide a natural starting point for any attempt to build up a general theory of strategy.

This is not the same, however, as arguing that formulations developed with armed force in mind can serve a variety of purposes. For example politicians may dramatize the more troublesome social problems by calling for 'wars' against them (on drugs, cancer, etc.) and suggest that strong generalship is needed for them to be defeated. This is perhaps what happened with the 'war on terror', when a rhetorical device urging a determined effort to deal with an undoubted scourge was taken too literally. The unreflective application of the war analogy can hinder understanding by attempting to squeeze quite different types of issues into an inappropriate conceptual framework geared to military threats. In the case of drugs, for example, it may have some relevance to confrontations with Third World drug cartels but less so with attempts to make sense of patterns of consumption. Equally the notions of 'economic security' can encourage a confrontational approach to trade policy and 'environmental security' a search for explanations based on hostile actions rather than natural causes or everyday economic activity. Even more difficult is a term such as 'internal security' which might once have referred to the ability of states to deny armed groups, whether criminal or political, the ability to challenge their authority, but which now takes in anything to do with the control of borders, including economic migration or the smuggling of contraband. This has become particularly evident with the 'war on terror'. Treating it as a traditional war, against an implacable enemy determined to use every means at its disposal, has encouraged a 'whatever it takes' attitude, aimed at eliminating the enemy, and has discouraged more political approaches, designed to marginalize radicals.

A different approach would be to acknowledge that the characters and competencies of states have been subject to many changes while asserting that an enduring feature remains the aspiration to define and dominate the means of legitimate violence within territorial borders. The challenges can come from other states, or from within states in the form of secessionists or revolutionaries or elitist conspirators, or from non-state actors in the form of drug cartels and gangsters, religious sects, and minority political movements. This continues to provide a relatively sharp focus for strategic studies and provides some compensation for an unavoidably wide context.

There is no reason in principle why the strategic imagination should not be directed towards improving the human condition through finding ways to restrict and progressively reduce the role of armed force. Much strategic studies activity has been about the peaceful settlement of disputes, arms control, and generally supporting the work of the United Nations. Major international negotiations require as much of a strategic sensibility as do major wars. Yet, and this may only be a matter of temperament, there does tend to be a dark side to the strategic imagination that picks up intimations of disorder at times of stability, that senses the fragility of human institutions even while striving to reinforce them, that cannot stop thinking of war while promoting peace. This dark side may explain the accusations of allowing armed force far more prominence than it deserves. The defence is that constant consideration of the potential for instability and conflict can help prevent it from being realized. Moreover, if the strategic imagination fails to be able to generate scenarios for war, except by combining in an unlikely and tenuous fashion a series of gloomy hypotheses, then that itself is a positive sign.

Key points

- A new realism requires a broader focus than in the past to understand the nature of present-day conflicts, but care must be taken not to overlook the traditional role of armed force.

- Strategy is present wherever there is politics, and although political ends can be met without violence, force often remains the ultimate arbiter of political disputes.

- Despite attempts to apply the 'war' analogy ever more widely, strategic studies remains a subject that focuses on the role of armed force both in peacetime and in war.

Conclusion: Does Strategic Studies Have a Future?

Karl Marx once observed that men make their own history but not in the circumstances of their own choosing. The study of strategy should help with the understanding of how men (and women) go about history-making and in so doing reshape the circumstances that they face. These circumstances include many others engaged in their own history-making. I have argued that this activist view with its stress on choice and power is distinctive and cannot be confined within the boundaries of a specific academic discipline. It needs to be asserted against those who are more determinist in their outlook or transfixed by patterns and cycles in human behaviour or see the exercise of power as a failure of social institutions rather than part of their natural condition. I have further argued that the study of strategy can benefit from being pushed to extremes, by looking at those circumstances in which the prospect or actuality of organized violence looms large. There is a further benefit in that as we have not yet succeeded in banishing armed force from human affairs there are many extreme situations to be faced.

These extreme situations provide an agenda for policymakers that students of strategy may feel well placed to address. Upon this may depend the future of strategic studies in terms of academic organization. This will be testing in a number of respects. First, they will only be able to sustain any claim of relevance if they have kept in touch with the range of possible situations that might tend to extremes. This range has expanded, as it has taken in the many problems of weak states and the challenges posed by radical Islamist movements, but at the same time the most extreme situations, that is, major wars among the great powers, still appear unlikely. The tumultuous decade of the 2000s has demonstrated the need for an approach that combines general understanding of strategic behaviour with the specifics of a set of conflicts which are individually complicated. Second, with an agenda that is becoming both more diffuse and in certain respects less pressing, there may be less coherence to strategic studies. Third, there will remain a need for caution and humility. There is an enormous gulf between offering advice and taking responsibility for decisions with potentially severe consequences, normally taken in imperfect conditions in terms of what is known and the time for deliberation. Fourth, for all these reasons it must never be forgotten that strategy is an art and not a science.

 ## Questions

1. What were the implications of the early development of strategic studies?
2. What role does realism play in strategic studies?
3. What is meant by the term 'the golden age of strategic studies'?
4. How did the cold war affect the development of the study of strategy?
5. To what extent did the end of the cold war alter the agenda of strategic studies?
6. Can the academic study of strategy help the 'practitioner' of strategy?
7. What challenges does strategic studies pose for the social sciences?
8. Does strategic studies have to be bound to the 'realist tradition' in the study of politics?
9. What is the future of strategic studies according to the author?
10. Do you agree with this view?

 ## Further Reading

L. Freedman, *The Evolution of Nuclear Strategy*, 3rd edn (New York: St Martin's Press, 2004) deals with the history of all aspects of nuclear strategy.

L Freedman, *The Transformation of Strategic Affairs*, (London: Routledge, 2006) covers recent debates.

Colin Gray *Modern Strategy* (Oxford: Oxford University Press, 1999) offers a modern Clausewitzian approach.

Michael I. Handel, *Masters of War: Classical Strategic Thought* (London: Frank Cass, 1996) covers Clausewitz and Sun Tzu.

Beatrice Heuiser, *The Evolution of Strategy: Thinking War from Antiquity to the Present,* (New York: Cambridge University Press, 2010) is an impressive history of the development of strategic thought.

P. Paret (ed.), *Makers of Modern Strategy: From Machiavelli to the Nuclear Age* (Princeton, NJ: Princeton University Press, 1986) provides the best overall coverage of strategic studies.

 ## Web Links

International Institute for Strategic Studies: **http://www.iiss.org/** The website of the International Institute for Strategic Studies provides political-military strategic assessments through expert commentary, strategic dossiers, a database on Armed Conflict, and publications such as the journal *Survival* and *The Military Balance*, a comprehensive annual review of defence capabilities and developments.

Royal United Service Institute: **http://www.rusi.org/** The London-based Royal United Services Institute think tank offers defence and security-focused commentary and analysis.

United States Army War College, Strategic Studies Institute: **http://www.strategicstudiesinstitute. army.mil/** This Institute provides strategic research and analysis for the United States military, particularly the Army, and a broader community of strategic analysts.

Institute for Security Studies: **http://www.iss.co.za/** The Institute for Security Studies is a think tank working on security issues in Africa, with a particular focus on conflict and human security.

Notes

Chapter 2

1.   I am extremely grateful to Dr Larry D. Miller of the United States Army War College for pointing out an error of interpretation on this point in an earlier version of this chapter.

Chapter 7

1.   The conventional version of the JSF is expected to have a combat radius of less than 600 miles—a figure which requires some scrutiny, since real combat radii have been known to be less than those of stated number. Lockheed Martin Corp., 'F-35 Lightning II: The Future is Flying'. n.d. Accessed at http://www.lockheedmartin.com/data/assets/aeronautics/products/f35/A07-20536AF-35Broc.pdf

2.   This problem became more difficult as the South Vietnamese—lacking American mass, fire control, and air power—took over the war. See David Ewing Ott, Field Artillery, 1954–1973, Vietnam Studies (Washington, DC: Department of the Army, 1975), p. 226. The Soviet M1954(M-46)130mm gun has a range of 27.5km; the M-114 155mm howitzer a range of 14.6km. Of course, many different artillery pieces were used by both sides. http://en.wikipedia.org/wiki/130_mm_towed_field_gun_M1954_(M-46) and http://en.wikipedia.org/wiki/M144_155_mm_howitzer

3.   The T-10 parachute is a 1950s era modification of versions (the T-7, introduced in 1944) which in turn go back to the Second World War: it is an unsteerable chute, and is supposed to be replaced soon. One problem is that a chute designed for soldiers weighing some 250lb with equipment may now weigh as much as 150lb more. Special forces use much more sophisticated steerable parachutes. See, *inter alia* http://www.globalsecurity.org/military/systems/aircraft/systems/t-10.htm

Chapter 8

1.   All statements of facts or opinion are those of the author and do not reflect the official positions or views of the US Government or any US Government agency.

2.   The work of Richards Heuer (1999) has significantly advanced analysts' understanding of their cognitive limitations; the development of structured analytic techniques has continued both in intelligence training courses as well as other research institutions.

Chapter 10

1.   The author wishes to acknowledge the contribution of Professor Colin S. Gray to this work, which is based on a co-authored chapter that appeared in an earlier version of this textbook.

Chapter 11

1.   Quoted in Robert G. Joseph and John F. Reichart, *Deterrence and Defense in a Nuclear, Biological, and Chemical Environment*, Occasional Paper of the Center for Counterproliferation Research (Washington, DC:National Defense University, 1995), 4.

2.   The text of Aspin's speech can be accessed at http://www.fas.org/irp/offdocs/pdd18.htm

3.   The British Foreign Secretary, Jack Straw, for example, told the House of Commons that 'we never, ever, said that there was an imminent threat,' and claimed that instead he had merely said there was a 'clear and present danger.' See House of Commons *Official Report*, 22 October 2003, Column 677. In Washington, Defense Secretary, Donald Rumsfeld told an interviewer 'You and a few other critics are the only people I've heard use the phrase immediate threat. I didn't, the President didn't. And it's become kind of folklore that that's what happened.'

Chapter 14

1.   The authors thank the participants in the Monterey Strategy Seminar at the Center for Contemporary Conflict for their many helpful comments and criticisms.

2.   Taken from remarks by the President on Weapons of Mass Destruction Proliferation, Ft. Lesley J. McNair, National Defense University, 11 February 2004.

3.   Even here it is not clear that modern technology has made possible destruction of a new order of magnitude. After taking into account economic growth and the increased density of commerce over time, we cannot say whether the London bombings of 2005 had a larger impact than IRA attacks in earlier periods, or than attacks with dynamite did during the late 1800s.

4.   Note that cost estimated regarding the 9/11 attacks exclude the voluntary and self-imposed costs of invading Iraq, a state opposed to the movement that committed the 9/11 attacks.

5.   Excludes attacks in Iraq which occurred in context of a civil war. Based on the Global Terrorism Dataset (GTD) and RAND/MIPT dataset. Accessed 13 December 2008.

6.   Ironically, Soviet military leaders often stated how difficult it was to predict what the United States would do because they so often violated their own doctrine. Now the tables are turned and it is the United States that finds it difficult, if not impossible, to predict the actions of terrorist organizations that follow no set doctrine.

7.   Learn more about the National Exercise Program, how exercises are constructed, executed, and evaluated, from the Homeland Security Exercise and Evaluation Program at https://hseep.dhs.gov/pages/1001_HSEEP7.aspx

8.   2005 Nunn-Lugar Report, available at the website of Senator Lugar, at http://lugar.senate.gov/nunnlugar/reports/pdf/2005report.pdf

9.   Government Accountability Office (2003), *Nuclear Security: NNSA Needs to Better Manage Its Safeguards and Security Program* (Washington, DC), GAO-03-471.

10.   US Department of Homeland Security (2003), *Characteristics and Common Vulnerabilities Report for Chemical Facilities* (Washington, DC), version 1, revision 1.

11.   Department of Justice, Office of the Inspector General, *A Review of the FBI's Handling of Intelligence Information Related to the September 11 Attacks* (Washington, DC: Office of the Inspector General, November 2004; redacted and unclassified: released publicly June 2005).

12.   The search term 'Topoff' returns 31 hits in major United States newspapers on Lexis/Nexis for 2005, and only 4 hits for 2007. None of the 2007 hits entail lengthy stories.

Bibliography

Abadie, A. and J. Gardeazabal (2004) *Terrorism and the World Economy*. Cambridge, MA: Center for International Development.

Abrahms, M. (2004) 'Are Terrorists Really Rational? The Palestinian Example', *Orbis* 48/3, 533–49.

—— (2006) 'Why Terrorism Does Not Work', *International Security* 31/2, (Fall) 42–78.

Adamsky, D. (2010) *Culture of Military Innovation: The Impact of Cultural Factors on the Revolution in Military Affairs in Russia, the US, and Israel*. Palo Alto, CA: Stanford University Press.

Addington, Larry, H. (1994) *The Patterns of War since the Eighteenth Century*, 2nd edn. Bloomington, IN: Indiana University Press.

Adefuye, A. (1992) *Culture and Foreign Policy: The Nigerian Example*. Lagos: Nigerian Institute of International Affairs.

al-Zawahiri, A. (2001) *Knights Under the Prophet's Banner*. Available at http://www.fas.org/irp/world/para/ayman_bk.html

—— (2005) 'Letter from al-Zawahiri to Zarqawi', translated by the The Foreign Broadcast Information Service, October.

Allison, G. (2004) *Nuclear Terrorism: The Ultimate Preventable Catastrophe*. New York: Times Books.

Almond, Gabriel and Sidney Verba (1965) *The Civic Culture: Political Attitudes and Democracy in Five Nations*. Boston, MA: Little, Brown & Co.

American Society of International Law (1994) *United States: Administration Policy on Reforming Multilateral Peace Operations*. Washington, DC: American Society of International Law.

Anderson, William F. (2009) 'Effects-based Operations: Combat Proven', *Joint Force Quarterly* 52 (1st quarter).

Angell, N. (1914) *The Great Illusion*. London: Heinemann.

Annan, Kofi (1999) *Statement on receiving the report of the Independent Inquiry into the Actions of the United Nations during the 1994 Genocide in Rwanda*. 16 December. Available at http://www.un.org/News/ossg/sgsm_rwanda.htm

Anthony, I. and A. D. Rotfeld (eds) (2001) *A Future Arms Control Agenda*. Oxford: Oxford University Press.

Archer, Christon, John Ferris, Holger Herwig and Tim Travers (2002) *A World History of Warfare*. Lincoln, NE: University of Nebraska Press.

Ardrey, R. (1966) *The Territorial Imperative*. New York: Atheneum.

Arend, A. C. and R. J. Beck (1993) *International Law and the Use of Force: Beyond the Charter Paradigm*. London: Routledge.

Arkin, W. M. (1998) *The Internet and Strategic Studies*. Washington, DC: SAIS, Center for Strategic Education.

Arquilla, J. and D. Ronfeldt (eds) (1997) *In Athena's Camp: Preparing for Conflict in the Information Age*. Santa Monica, CA: RAND

—— (2001) *Networks and Netwars*. Santa Monica, CA: RAND. http://www.rand.org/publications/MR/MR1382/

Aussaresses, P. (2005) *The Battle of the Casbah: Terrorism and Counter-Terrorism in Algeria, 1955–1957*. New York: Enigma.

Bacevich, A. J. (1986) *The Pentomic Era: The US Army between Korea and Vietnam*. Washington, DC: National Defense University Press.

Ball, Desmond (ed.) (1993) *Strategic Culture in the Asia-Pacific Region (with Some Implications for Regional Security Cooperation)*. Canberra: Strategic and Defence Studies Centre, Australian National University.

Banchoff, Thomas (1999) *The German Problem Transformed: Institutions, Politics and Foreign Policy, 1945–1995*. Ann Arbor, MI: University of Michigan Press.

Banerjee, Sanjoy (1997) 'The Cultural Logic of National Identity Formation: Contending Discourses in Late Colonial India'. In Valerie M. Hudson (ed.) *Culture and Foreign Policy*. Boulder, CO: Lynne Rienner.

Barkawi, T. (1998) 'Strategy as a Vocation: Weber, Morgenthau and Modern Strategic Studies', *Review of International Studies* 24, 159–84.

—— and M. Laffey (2006) 'The postcolonial moment in security studies', *Review of International Studies*, 32/4, 329–52.

Barnaby, F. (2004) *How to Build a Nuclear Bomb: And Other Weapons of Mass Destruction*. New York: Nation Books.

Barnes, R. (2005) 'Of Vanishing Points and Paradoxes: Terrorism and International Humanitarian Law'. In R. Burchill, N. D. White, and J. Morris (eds) *International Conflict and Security Law: Essays in Memory of Hilaire McCoubery*. Cambridge: Cambridge University Press.

Barnett, Thomas P. M. (2004) *The Pentagon's New Map: War and Peace in the Twenty-first Century*. New York: Berkeley Books.

Baylis, John (2001) 'The Continuing Relevance of Strategic Studies in the Post-Cold War Era', *Defence Studies* 1/2, 1–14.

——, S. Smith and P. Owens (2005) *The Globalization of World Politics: An Introduction to International Relations*, 6th edn. Oxford: Oxford University Press.

—— Ken Booth, John Garnett and Phil Williams (1987) *Contemporary Strategy*. New York: Holmes & Meier.

BBC (2005) 'IAEA urged to refer Tehran to the UN', BBC news 19 September 2005. Available at http://www.bbc.news.co.ik/I.hi/world/middle_east/4259018.stm

BBC (2009) 'Stakes High for Obama on Iran', BBC news 15 January 2009. Available at http://www.bbc.news.co.ik/I.hi/world/middle_east/7829313.stm

Beam, L. (1992) *Leaderless Resistance*. Available at http://www.crusader.net/texts/bt/bt04.html

Beaufre Andre (1965a) *An Introduction to Strategy*. London: Faber & Faber.

—— (1965b) *Deterrence and Strategy*. London: Faber & Faber.

Bellamy, Alex J., Paul Williams and Stuart Griffin (2010) *Understanding Peacekeeping*. 2nd edn. Cambridge: Polity.

Benjamin, D. and S. Simon (2005) *The Next Attack*. New York: Times Books.

Benedict, Ruth (1946) *The Chrysanthemum and the Sword*. Boston, MA: Houghton Mifflin.

Berdal, M. and M. Serrano (eds) (2002) *Transnational Organized Crime and International Security*. Boulder, CO: Lynne Rienner.

Berntsen, G. and R. Pezzullo (2006) *Jawbreaker: The Attack on Bin Laden and Al-Qaeda: A Personal Account by the CIA's Key Field Commander*. New York, NY: Crown Publishers.

Bergen, John D. (1986) *Military Communications: A Test for Technology*. Washington, DC: Center of Military History.

Berger, Thomas U. (1998) *Cultures of Antimilitarism: National Security in Germany and Japan*. Baltimore, MD: Johns Hopkins University Press.

Bernstein, P. (2008) 'International Partnerships to Combat Weapons of Mass Destruction', Occasional Papers 6. National Defense University Center for the Study of Weapons of Mass Destruction, Washington DC.

Best, Geoffrey (1982) *War and Society in Revolutionary Europe, 1770–1870*. London: Fontana.

Betts, Richard K. (1997) 'Should Strategic Studies Survive?', *World Politics* 50/1 October, 7–33.

—— (1998).'The New Threat of Mass Destruction', *Foreign Affairs* 77/1.

—— (2007) *Enemies of Intelligence: Knowledge and Power in American National Security*. New York: Columbia University Press.

Betz, D. J., and T. C. Stevens (2012) *Cyberspace and the State: Towards a Strategy for Cyberpower*. Abingdon, Oxon: Routledge.

Beyerchen, Alan (1996) 'From Radio to Radar: Interwar Military Adaptation to Technological Change in Germany, the United Kingdom and the United States'. In Williamson Murray and Allan R. Millett (eds) *Military Innovation in the Interwar Period*. Cambridge: Cambridge University Press.

Biddle, Stephen (2002) *Afghanistan and the Future of Warfare: Implications for Army and Defense Policy*. Carlisle, PA: US Army War College Strategic Studies Institute.

—— (2003a) 'Afghanistan and the Future of Warfare', *Foreign Affairs*, 82/2, 31–46.

—— (2003b) Operation Iraqi Freedom: Outside Perspectives. Testimony before the House Armed Services Committee, 21 October.

—— (2004) *Military Power: Explaining Victory and Defeat in Modern Battle*. Princeton, NJ: Princeton University Press.

—— (2005) *American Grand Strategy After 9/11: An Assessment*. Carlisle, PA: US Army War Studies Strategic Studies Institute. Available at http://www.strategicstudiesinstitute.army.mil/pubs/display.cfm?pubID=603

Black, Jeremy (2001) *War*. London: Continuum.

—— (2002) *Warfare in the Western World, 1882–1975*. Chesham: Acumen.

Blair, D. (2009) *Remarks of Director of National Intelligence*, Commonwealth Club of San Francisco, 15 September at: http://www.dni.gov/speeches/20090915_speech.pdf

Blomberg, S., G. Hess and A. Orphanides (2004) 'The Macroeconomic Consequences of Terrorism', Working Paper No. 1151. Munich: CESIFO.

Booth, Ken (1979) *Strategy and Ethnocentrism*. London: Croom Helm.

—— (1981) *Strategy and Ethnocentrism*. New York: Holmes and Meier.

—— (1997) 'Security and Self: Reflections of a Fallen Realist'. In Keith Krause and Michael C. Williams (eds) *Critical Security Studies: Concepts and Cases*. London: UCL Press.

—— (2005) 'Beyond Critical Security Studies'. In Ken Booth (ed.) *Critical Security Studies and World Politics*. Boulder, CO: Lynne Rienner.

—— and Herring, E. (1994) *Keyguide to Information Sources in Strategic Studies*. London: Mansell 1994.

—— and Russell Trood (eds) (1999) *Strategic Culture in the Asia-Pacific*. New York: Macmillan.

Boulding, K. (1956) *The Image*. Ann Arbor, MI: University of Michigan Press.

Brenner, S. W. (2009) *Cyberthreats: The Emerging Fault Lines of the Nation State*. New York: Oxford University Press.

Brent, J. and V. P. Naumov (2003) *Stalin's Last Crime: The Plot Against the Jewish Doctors, 1948–1953*. New York: Perennial.

Breuning, M. (1997) 'Culture, History, Role: Belgian and Dutch Axioms and Foreign Assistance Policy'. In Valerie M. Hudson (ed.) *Culture and Foreign Policy*. Boulder, CO: Lynne Rienner Publishers.

Brodie, Bernard (1946) *The Absolute Weapon*. Harcourt, Brace & Co.

—— (1959) *Strategy in the Missile Age*. Princeton, NJ: Princeton University Press.

—— (1973) *War and Politics*. London: Cassell; New York: Macmillan.

Brownlie, I. (1963) *International Law and the Use of Force by States*. Oxford: Clarendon Press.

—— (1990) *Principles of Public International Law*. Oxford: Oxford University Press.

Bull, H. (1961) *The Control of the Arms Race*. London: Weidenfeld & Nicolson.

—— (1968) 'Strategic Studies and its Critics', *World Politics* 20/4, 593–605.

—— (1977) *The Anarchical Society: A Study of Order in World Politics*. London: Macmillan.

Bunn, E. (2007) 'Can Deterrence Be Tailored?', *Strategic Forum*. Paper No. 225. Institute for National Security Studies. Washington, DC: National Defense University.

Burchill, S., R. Devetak, Andrew Linklater, Matthew Patterson, C. Reus-Smit and J. True (2005) *Theories of International Relations*, 3rd edn. London: Macmillan.

Burkard, S., D. Howlett, H. Müller and B. Tertrais (2005) 'Effective Non-Proliferation: The European Union and the 2005 NPT Review Conference'. Chaillot Paper No. 72. Paris: EU-ISS.

Butcher, Martin (2003) *What Wrongs Our Arms May Do: The Role of Nuclear Weapons in Counterproliferation*. Washington, DC: Physicians for Social Responsibility. Available at http://www.psr.org/documents/psr_doc_0/ program_4/PSRwhatwrong03.pdf

Butterfield, H. (1952) *History and Human Relations*. London: Collins.

—— and M. Wight (1966) *Diplomatic Investigations*. London: Allen & Unwin.

Buzan, B. and E. Herring (1998) *The Arms Dynamic in World Politics*. London: Lynne Rienner.

—— and L. Hansen (2009) *The Evolution of International Security*. Cambridge: Cambridge University Press.

Byers, M. (2000) *The Role of Law in International Politics: Essays in International Relations and International Law*. Oxford: Oxford University Press.

—— (2004) 'Agreeing to Disagree: Security Council Resolution 1441 and International Ambiguity', *Global Governance* 10/2, 165–86.

Byman, Daniel A. and Matthew C. Waxman (2000) 'Kosovo and the Great Air Power Debate', *International Security* 24/4 (Spring).

Caldicott, H. (1986) *Missile Envy: The Arms Race and Nuclear War*. Toronto: Bantam.

Callwell, C. E. (1899) *Small Wars: Their Principles and Practice*. London: Her Majesty's Stationery Office.

Calvert, John (2004) 'The Mythic Foundations of Radical Islam', *Orbis* (Winter).

Carr, E. H. (1942) *Conditions of Peace*. London: Macmillan & Co.

—— (1946) *The Twenty Years' Crisis 1919–1939*, 2nd edn. London: Macmillan.

Carr, J. (2010) *Inside Cyber Warfare*. Sebastopol, CA: O'Reilly Media.

Carter, Ashton and L. Celeste Johnson (2001) 'Beyond the Counterproliferation Initiative'. In Henry Sokolski and James Ludes, *Twenty-First Century Weapons Proliferation*. London: Frank Cass.

Cartwright, Gen. J. E., USMC (n.d.) 'Memorandum for Chiefs of the Military Services, Commanders of the Combatant Commands, Directors of the Joint Staff Directorates. Subject: Joint Terminology for Cyberspace Operations.' Washington, DC: The Vice-Chairman of the Joint Chiefs of Staff.

Carvin, S. (2008) 'Linking Purpose and Tactics: America and the Reconsideration of the Laws of War During the 1990s', *International Studies Perspective* 9/2, 128–43.

Cashman, G. (1993) *What Causes War? An Introduction to Conflict*. New York: Lexington Books.

Castells, M. (1998) *The End of Millennium, iii. The Information Age, Economy, Society and Culture*. Oxford: Blackwell.

Cebrowski, Arthur and John Garstka (1998) 'Network-Centric Warfare: Its Origin and Future', *U.S. Naval Institute Proceedings* 124/1, 29.

Center for the Study of Intelligence (2004) *Intelligence and Policy: The Evolving Relationship, Roundtable Report*, 10 November. Washington, DC: Georgetown University.

Cerny, P. (1986) 'Globalization and the Disarticulation of Political Power: Towards a New Middle Ages', *Civil Wars* 1/1, 65–102.

Cha, Victor D. (2000) 'Globalization and the Study of International Security', *Journal of Peace Research* 37/3, 391–403.

Chandler, D. G. (ed.) (1988) *The Military Maxims of Napoleon*, translated by George C. D'Aguilar. New York: Macmillan.

Chayes, Sarah (2007) *The Punishment of Virtue*. London: Portobello Books.

Chivers, C. J. (2010) *The Gun*. New York: Simon & Schuster.

Churchill, Winston (1926) *The World Crisis, 1911–1914*. New York: Charles Scribner's Sons.

Cimbala, Stephen J. (1997) *The Politics of Warfare: The Great Powers in the Twentieth Century*. University Park, PA: Pennsylvania State University Press.

Cirincione, Joseph, Jon B. Wolfsthal and Miriam Rajkumar (2005) *Deadly Arsenals: Nuclear, Biological and Chemical Threats*, 2nd edn. Washington, DC: Carnegie Endowment for International Peace.

Clapham, C. (1998) 'Being Peacekept'. In O. Furley and R. May (eds.), *Peacekeeping in Africa*. Aldershot: Ashgate. 303–19.

Clarke, Arthur C. (1970) 'Superiority'. In Arthur C. Clarke, *Expedition to Earth*. New York: Harcourt, Brace & World.

Clarke, R. A. and R. K. Knake (2010) *Cyber War: The Next Threat to National Security and What to Do About It*. New York: Ecco.

Claude, I. L. ([1832] 1962) *Power and International Relations*. New York: Random House.

Clausewitz, Carl von (1976) *On War*, translated and edited by Michael Howard and Peter Paret. Princeton, NJ: Princeton University Press.

—— (1982) *On War*, abridged edn. London: Routledge.

—— (1982) *On War*. Harmondsworth: Penguin.

—— (1989) *On War*, edited and translated by Michael Howard and Peter Paret. Princeton, NJ: Princeton University Press.

—— (1993) *On War*, edited and translated by Michael Howard and Peter Paret. London: Everyman's Library.

Cline, L. (2005) *Psuedo Operations and Counterinsurgency: Lessons from Other Countries*. Carlisle, PA: Strategic Studies Institute. Available at http://www.strategicstudies-institute.army.mil/pubs/display.cfm? PubID 607

Clutterbuck, R. (1990) *Terrorism and Guerrilla Warfare: Forecasts and Remedies*. London: Routledge.

Cohen, Eliot A. (1996) 'A Revolution in Warfare', *Foreign Affairs* 75/2 March/April, 37–54.

Cohen, Stephen (2002) *India, Emerging Power*. Washington, DC: Brookings Institution Press.

Cohn, Carol (1987) 'Sex and Death in the Rational World of Defense Intellectuals', *Signs: Journal of Women in Culture and Society* 12/4, 687–718.

—— (1993) 'Wars, Wimps, and Women: Talking Gender and Thinking War'. In Miriam Cooke and Angela Woollacott (eds) *Gendering War Talk*. Princeton NJ: Princeton University Press.

Collins, A. (1998) 'GRIT, Gorbachev and the End of the Cold War', *Review of International Studies* 24/2, April.

Congressional Budget Office (2005) *Federal Funding for Homeland Security: An Update*. Available at http://www.cbo.gov/ftpdocs/65xx/doc6566/7-20-Homeland Security.pdf Accessed 10 December.

Cordesman, Anthony H. (2002) *The Lessons of Afghanistan, Warfighting, Intelligence, Force Transformation, Counterproliferation and Arms Control*. Washington, DC: Center for Strategic and International Studies.

—— (2003a) *The 'Instant Lessons' of the Iraq War, Main Report, Seventh Working Draft*. Washington, DC: CSIS.

—— (2003b) *The Iraq War: Strategy, Tactics and Military Lessons*. Washington, DC: Center for Strategic and International Studies.

—— (2004) *The War After the War: Strategic Lessons of Iraq and Afghanistan*. Washington, DC: Center for Strategic and International Studies.

Cornish, Paul and Geoffrey Edwards (2001) 'Beyond the EU/NATO Dichotomy: The Beginnings of a European Strategic Culture', *International Affairs*, 77/3, 587.

—— and —— (2005) 'The Strategic Culture of the European Union: A Progress Report', *International Affairs*, 81/4.

Creveld, Martin van (1989) *Technology and War from 2000 BC to the Present*. New York: Free Press.

—— (1991) *The Transformation of War*. New York: Free Press.

Croft, S. (1996) *Strategies of Arms Control: A History and Typology*. Manchester: Manchester University Press.

Cronin, Audrey Kurth (2002/3) 'Behind the Curve: Globalization and International Terrorism', *International Security* 27/3 (Winter), 30–58.

—— (2011) *How Terrorism Ends: Understanding the Decline and Demise of Terrorist Campaigns*. Princeton, NJ: Princeton University Press.

Crowl, Philip A. (1987) 'The Strategist's Short Catechism: Six Questions without Answers'. In George Edward Thibault, (ed.) *Dimensions of Military Strategy*. Washington, DC: US Government Printing Office for National Defense University.

Cruz, Consuelo (2000) 'Identity and Persuasion: How Nations Remember their Pasts and Make their Futures', *World Politics* 52/3, 278.

Daalder, I. and T. Terry (eds) (1993) *Rethinking the Unthinkable: New Directions in Nuclear Arms Control.* London: Frank Cass.

Danchev, A. (1999) 'Liddell Hart and the Direct Approach', *The Journal of Military History* 63/2, 313–37.

Davidson Smith, G. (1990) *Combating Terrorism.* London: Routledge.

Davis, Zachary S. (1994) *US Counterproliferation Policy: Issues for Congress. CRS Report for Congress.* Washington, DC: Congressional Research Service.

Dawkins, R. (1976) *The Selfish Gene.* Oxford: Oxford University Press.

De Vol, R. and P. Wong (2005) *Economic Impacts of Katrina.* Santa Monica, CA: Milken Institute.

Debray, R. (1968) *Revolution in the Revolution: Armed Struggle and Political Struggle in Latin America.* London: Pelican.

Demchak, C. C. (2011) *Wars of Disruption and Resilience: Cybered Conflict, Power, and National Security.* Athens, GA: The University of Georgia Press.

Denning, D. (1999) *Information Warfare and Security.* New York: ACM Press.

Department of the Army (1994) *US Army Field Manual 100-23: Peace Operations.* Washington, DC.

—— (2007) *FM 3-24, Counterinsurgency Field Manual.* Chicago: University of Chicago Press.

Department of Defense Directive 3000.07 (2008) *Irregular Warfare* (IW).

Department of Homeland Security (2007a) *After Action Quick Look Report.* Available at http://www.fema.gov/pdf/media/2008/t4_after%20action_report.pdf Accessed 21 September 2008.

—— (2007b) TOPOFF 4 Frequently Asked Questions. Available at http://www.dhs.gov/xprepresp/training/gc_1179422026237.shtm

Department of Justice (2004) *A Review of the FBI's Handling of Intelligence Information Related to the September 11 Attacks.* Washington, DC: Office of the Inspector General, November, redacted and unclassified: released publicly June 2005.

Department of the Army (1994) *US Army Field Manual 100-23: Peace Operations.* Washington, DC: Department of the Army.

—— (2007) *FM 3-24, Counterinsurgency Field Manual.* Chicago, IL: University of Chicago Press.

Deptula, David A. (2001) *Effects-Based Operations: Change in the Nature of Warfare.* Arlington, VA: Aerospace Education Foundation.

Desch, Michael C. (1998) 'Culture Clash: Assessing the Importance of Ideas in Security Studies', *International Security* 23/1 (Summer).

Diehl, Paul F. and Nils Petter Gleditsch (2000) *Environmental Conflict: An Anthology.* Boulder, CO: Westview.

Director of National Intelligence (2005) *The National Intelligence Strategy of the United States: Transformation Through Integration and Innovation.* Washington, DC: Director of National Intelligence.

—— (2007) *The 100 Day Plan: Integration and Collaboration.* Washington, DC: Director of National Intelligence.

—— (2009) *National Intelligence Strategy.* August at: http://www.nytimes.com/2011/09/30/business/global/germany-parliament-votes-to-expand-euro-bailout-fund.html?_r=1

—— (2010) *News Release.* NR-21-10, 28 October.

Dixon, C. A. and O. Heilbrunn (1962) *Communist Guerrilla Warfare.* New York: Praeger.

Dobbie, Charles (1994) 'A Concept for Post-Cold War Peacekeeping', *Survival* 36/3 (Autumn).

Douhet, Giulio (1983) *The Command of the Air,* translated by Dino Ferrari. Washington, DC: New York, Coward-McCann; previously published New York, 1942.

Doyle, M. W. (1983) 'Kant, Liberal Legacies and Foreign Affairs', *Philosophy and Public Affairs,* 12.

—— (1986) 'Liberalism and World Politics', *American Political Science Review* 80.

Dueck, Colin (2004) 'The Grand Strategy of the United States, 2000–2004', *Review of International Studies* 30/4 October.

Duffield, John S. (1999a) *World Power Forsaken: Political Culture, International Institutions and German Security Policy after Unification.* Stanford, CA: Stanford University Press.

—— (1999b) 'Political Culture and State Behavior', *International Organization* 53/4, 765–804.

Duffy, H. (2005) *The 'War on Terror' and the Framework of International Law.* Cambridge: Cambridge University Press.

Dunn, D. J. (1991) 'Peace Research Versus Strategic Studies'. In Ken Booth (ed.) *New Thinking About Strategy and International Security.* London: Harper Collins.

Earle, E. (1943) *Makers of Modern Strategy: Military Thought from Machiavelli to Hitler.* Princeton, NJ: Princeton University Press.

Ebel, Roland H., Raymond Taras and James D. Cochrane (1991) *Political Culture and Foreign Policy in Latin America: Case Studies from the Circum-Caribbean.* Albany, NY: State University of New York.

Eckstein, Harry (1998) 'A Culturalist Theory of Political Change', *American Political Science Review* 82, 790–802.

Eden, Lynn (2004) *Whole World on Fire: Organizations, Knowledge, and Nuclear Weapons Devastation*. Ithaca, NY: Cornell University Press.

Ellis, Jason (2003) 'The Best Defence: Counterproliferation and US National Security', *Washington Quarterly*, 26/2.

Enders, W. and T. Sandler (2004). 'What do we Know about the Substitution Effect in Transnational Terrorism?' In A. Silke and Gilardi (eds) *Terrorism Research*. London: Frank Cass.

Ermarth, Fritz (2009) 'Russian Strategic Culture in Flux: Back to the Future?' In J. L. Johnson, K. M. Kartchner, and J. A. Larsen (eds) *Strategic Culture and Weapons of Mass Destruction: Culturally Based Insights into Comparative National Security Policymaking*. London: Palgrave Macmillan.

European Union (2003) *A Secure Europe in a Better World: European Security Strategy*. Available at http://ue.eu.int/uedocs/cmsUpload/78367.pdf

Fall, B. B. (1998) 'The Theory and Practice of Insurgency and Counterinsurgency', *Naval War College Review* 15/1, 46–57.

Farrell, Theo (2001) 'Transnational Norms and Military Development: Constructing Ireland's Professional Army', *European Journal of International Relations* 7/1, 63–102.

—— and Terry Terrif (eds) (2001) *The Sources of Military Change: Culture, Politics, Technology*. Boulder, CO: Lynne Rienner.

Feinstein, L. and A-M. Slaughter (2004) 'A Duty to Prevent', *Foreign Affairs* 83/1, 136–50.

Feldman, Shai (1982) 'The Bombing of Osiraq: Revisited', *International Security* 7/2 (Autumn).

Feng, Huiyun (2009) 'A Dragon on Defense: Explaining China's Strategic Culture'. In J. L. Johnson, K. M. Kartchner, and J. A. Larsen (eds) *Strategic Culture and Weapons of Mass Destruction: Culturally Based Insights into Comparative National Security Policymaking*. London: Palgrave Macmillan.

Ferris, John (2004a) 'A New American Way of War? C4ISR, Intelligence and IO in Operation Iraqi Freedom, a Preliminary Assessment', *Intelligence and National Security*, 14/1.

—— (2004b) 'Netcentric Warfare and Information Operations: Revolution in the RMA?', *Intelligence and National Security*, 14/3.

Findlay, Trevor (2002) *The Use of Force in UN Peace Operations*. Oxford: Oxford University Press.

Fleck, D. (ed.) (2008) *The Handbook of International Humanitarian Law*. 2nd edn, Oxford: Oxford University Press.

Florida International University (2010) *Comparative Strategic Cultures Project*. Applied Research Center. http://strategicculture.fiu.edu/Studies.aspx

Flynn, F. (2007) *America the Vulnerable and The Edge of Disaster: Rebuilding a Resilient Nation*. London: Random House.

Flynn, M., M. Pottinger, and P Batchelor et al. (2010) *Fixing Intel: A Blueprint for Making Intelligence Relevant in Afghanistan*. Washington: Center for New American Security, January, at: http://www.cnas.org/files/documents/publications/AfghanIntel_Flynn_Jan2010_code507_voices.pdf

Flynn, S. (2004) *America the Vulnerable: How Our Government is Failing to Protect us from Terrorism*. New York: Harper Collins.

—— (2007) *The Edge of Disaster: Rebuilding a Resilient Nation*. New York: Random House.

Fontenot, Gregory, E. J. Degen and David Tohn (2004) *On Point: The United States Army in Operation Iraqi Freedom*. Fort Leavenworth, KS: US Army Training and Doctrine Command.

Forester, C. S. (1943) *The Ship*. Boston, MA: Little, Brown & Co.

Forsythe, D. (2008) 'The United States and International Humanitarian Law', *Journal of Human Rights* 7/1 (Spring), 25–33.

Fortna, V.P. (2003) 'Inside and Out: Peacekeeping and the Duration of Peace after Civil and Interstate Wars', *International Studies Review* 5/4, 97–114.

—— (2008) *Does Peacekeeping Work? Shaping Belligerents' Choices After Civil War*. Princeton, NJ: Princeton University Press.

—— and L.M. Howard (2008) 'Pitfalls and Prospects in the Peacekeeping Literature', *Annual Review of Political Science* 11: 283–301.

Foy, Michael T. (2006) *Michael Collins' Intelligence War: The Struggle between the British and the IRA, 1919–1921*. Stroud, UK: Sutton Publishing.

Franck, T. M. (1990) *The Power of Legitimacy among Nations*. Oxford: Oxford University Press.

—— (2001) 'Terrorism and the Right to Self-Defense', *American Journal of International Law* 95/4, 839–43.

—— and N. S. Rodley (1973) 'After Bangladesh: The Law of Humanitarian Intervention by Force', *American Journal of International Law* 67/2, 275–305.

Freedman, Lawrence (1981) *The Evolution of Nuclear Strategy*. New York: St Martin's Press.

—— (1986) 'The First Two Generations of Nuclear Strategists'. In Peter Paret (ed.) *Makers of Modern Strategy: From Machiavelli to the Nuclear Age*. Oxford: Clarendon Press.

—— (2000) 'Victims and Victors: Reflections on the Kosovo War', *Review of International Studies*, 26/3 (July).

—— (2003) 'Prevention, Not Preemption', *Washington Quarterly*, 26/2.

—— (2004) *Deterrence*. Cambridge: Polity Press.

—— (2004) *The Evolution of Nuclear Strategy*, 3rd edn. New York: St Martin's Press.

—— (2006) *The Transformation of Strategic Affairs*, London: Routledge.

Freud, S. (1932) 'Why War?'. In *The Standard Edition of the Complete Psychological Writings of Sigmund Freud*, xxii, 197–215. London: Hogarth Press.

—— (1968).'Why War?'. In L. Bramson and G. W. Geothals, *War: Studies from Psychology, Sociology, Anthropology*. New York and London: Basic Books.

Friedman, Norman (2000) *Seapower and Space: From the Dawn of the Missile Age to Net-Centric Warfare*. Annapolis, MD: Naval Institute Press.

—— (2003) *Terrorism, Afghanistan and America's New Way of War*. Washington, DC: US Naval Institute Press.

Friedman, T. (2002) *Longitudes and Attitudes: Exploring the World After September 11*. New York: Farrar Straus & Giroux.

Fukuyama, Francis (1999) 'Second Thoughts', *The National Interest* 56 (Summer), 16–33.

Fuller, J. F. C. (1926) *The Foundations of the Science of War*. London: Hutchinson.

—— (1932) *The Dragon's Teeth; A Study of War and Peace*. London: Constable.

—— (1942) *Machine Warfare; An Enquiry into the Influences of Mechanics on the Art of War*. London: Hutchinson.

—— (1945) *Armament and History; A Study of the Influence of Armament on History from the Dawn of Classical Warfare to the Second World War*. New York: Charles Scribner's Sons.

Gaddis, John Lewis (1986) 'The Long Peace: Elements of Stability in the Postwar International System', *International Security*, 10/4.

Galula, David (1964) *Counterinsurgency Warfare*. New York: Praeger.

Ganor, B. (2005) *The Counter-Terrorism Puzzle: A Guide for Decision Makers*. New Brunswick, NJ: Transaction.

Garnett, J. C. (1987) 'Strategic Studies and its Assumptions'. In John Baylis, Ken Booth, John Garnett and Phil Williams, *Contemporary Strategy: Theories and Policies*, 2nd edn. London: Croom Helm.

Gat, A. (1992) *The Development of Military Thought: The Nineteenth Century*. Oxford: Oxford University Press.

—— (1993) *Clausewitz and the Enlightenment: The Origins of Modern Military Thought*. Oxford: Oxford University Press.

Gates, David (2003) *Sky Wars: A History of Military Aerospace Power*. London: Reaktion Books.

Geertz, Clifford (1973) *The Interpretation of Cultures*. New York: Basic Books.

George, A.L. (2003) 'The Need for Influence Theory and Actor-Specific Behavioral Models of Adversaries'. In Barry R. Schneider and Jerrold M. Post (eds) *Know Thy Enemy: Profiles of Adversary Leaders and Their Strategic Cultures*. Alabama, GA: US Air Force Counterproliferation Center.

George, R. Z. and J. Bruce (eds) (2008) *Analyzing Intelligence: Origins, Obstacles, and Innovations*. Washington, DC: Georgetown University Press.

Gibson, W. (1984) *Neuromancer*. New York: Ace Books.

Giles, G. F. (2003) 'The Crucible of Radical Islam: Iran's Leaders and Strategic Culture'. In Barry R. Schneider and Jerrold M. Post (eds) *Know Thy Enemy: Profiles of Adversary Leaders and Their Strategic Cultures*. Alabama, GA: US Air Force Counterproliferation Center.

Glatthaar, Joseph T. (2008) *General Lee's Army: From Victory to Collapse*. New York: The Free Press.

Gleditsch, Nils Petter (2012) 'Whither the Weather? Climate Change and Conflict', *Journal of Peace Research*. 49/1, 3–9.

Glenn, J. (2009) 'Realism versus Strategic Culture: Competition and Collaboration?' *International Studies Review* 11, 523–51.

Glenn, John, Darryl Howlett, and Stuart Poore (eds) (2004) *Neorealism versus Strategic Culture*. London: Ashgate.

Goldman, Emily O. (2003) 'Introduction: Security in the Information Age'. In E. O. Goldman (ed.) National Security in the Information Age, special issue, *Contemporary Security Policy*, 24/1, 1.

Goldstone, Jack A. (2002) 'Population and Security: How Demographic Change can Lead to Violent Conflict', *Journal of International Affairs* 56/1, 3–22.

Goodrich, L. M. and E. Hambro (1949) *Charter of the United Nations: Commentary and Documents*. Boston, MA: World Peace Foundation.

Gordon, M. (1990) 'Generals Favor "No Holds Barred" by U.S. if Iraq Attacks the Saudis', *The New York Times* 25 August.

Gorman, S. (2011) 'Drones Evolve Into Weapon in Age of Terror: Intelligence Services Overcome Philosophical, Legal Misgivings Over Targeted Killings', *Wall Sreet Journal*, 8 September.

Gottman, J. (1948) 'Bugeaud, Gallieni, Lyautey: The Development of French Colonial Warfare'. In E. M. Earle (ed.) *Makers of Modern Strategy: Military Thought from Machiavelli to Hitler*. Princeton, NJ: Princeton University Press.

Government Accountability Office (2003) *Nuclear Security: NNSA Needs to Better Manage its Safeguards and Security Program*, GAO-03-471. Washington, DC: Government Accountability Office.

—— (2005) *Terrorist Financing: Better Strategic Planning Needed to Coordinate U.S. Efforts to Deliver Counter-Terrorism Financing Training and Technical Assistance Abroad*, GAO-06-19. Washington, DC: Government Accountability Office.

Gowans, A. L. (1914) *Selections from Treitschke's Lectures on Politics*. London and Glasgow: Gowans & Gray.

Graeger, Nina and Halvard Leira (2005) 'Norwegian Strategic Culture after World War II: From a Local to a Global Perspective', *Cooperation and Conflict* 40/1, 45-66.

Grant, Greg (2005) 'Network Centric: Blind Spot', *Defense News* 12 September, 1.

Gray, C. (2002) 'From Unity to Polarization: International Law and the Use of Force against Iraq', *European Journal of International Law* 13/1, 1-19.

Gray, Christine (2008) *International Law and the Use of Force*, 3rd edn. Oxford: Oxford University Press.

Gray, C. S. (1981) 'National Style in Strategy: The American Example', *International Security*, 6/2 (Fall), 35-7.

—— (1982a) *Strategic Studies and Public Policy: The American Experience*. Lexington, KY: The University Press of Kentucky.

—— (1982b) *Strategic Studies: A Critical Assessment*. London: Aldwych Press.

—— (1986) *Nuclear Strategy and National Style*. Lanham, MD: Hamilton Press.

—— (1992) *House of Cards: Why Arms Control Must Fail*. Ithaca, NY: Cornell University Press.

—— (1997) 'The American Revolution in Military Affairs: An Interim Assessment', *The Occasional*. Strategic and Combat Studies Institute, Wiltshire, UK, 28.

—— (1999a) *Modern Strategy*. Oxford: Oxford University Press.

—— (1999b) *The Second Nuclear Age*. Boulder, CO: Lynne Rienner.

—— (2002) *Strategy for Chaos: Revolutions in Military Affairs and the Evidence of History*. London: Frank Cass.

—— (2003) *Strategy for Chaos: Revolutions in Military Affairs and the Evidence of History*. London: Frank Cass.

—— (2010) *The Strategy Bridge*. Oxford: Oxford University Press.

—— and K. B. Payne (1980) 'Victory is Possible', *Foreign Policy* 39, 14-27.

Green, J. (1986) *The A–Z of Nuclear Jargon*. New York: Routledge.

Green, Philip (1966) *Deadly Logic: The Theory of Nuclear Deterrence*. Columbus, OH: Ohio State University Press.

Greig J. M. and P. F. Diehl (2005) 'The Peacekeeping-Peacemaking Dilemma', *International Studies Quarterly* 49/4, 621-45.

Griffith, Samuel (1961) *Mao Tse-Tung on Guerrilla Warfare*. New York: Praeger.

Guardian, The (2009) 'US fears that Iran has the Capability to build a nucler bomb', 2 March.

Guevara, C. (1997) *Guerrilla Warfare*, 3rd edn. Wilmington, DE: Scholarly Resources.

Gwynn, Charles W. (1934) *Imperial Policing*. London: Macmillan & Co.

Hagood, Jonathan (2007) 'Towards a Policy of Nuclear Dissuasion: How Can Dissuasion Improve U.S. National Security?' In Owen C. W. Price and Jenifer Mackby (eds) *Debating 21st Century Nuclear Issues*. Washington, DC: Center for Strategic and International Studies.

Hamilton (1992) *Parliamentary Debate*. Available at: http://www.parliament.the-stationary-office.co.uk/pa/cmigg/2g3/cmhansrd/1992-06-29/writtens-6.html

Hammes, T. X. (2004) *The Sling and the Stone: On War in the 21st Century*. St Paul, MI: Zenith Press.

Handel, Michael I. (1994) 'The Evolution of Israeli Strategy: The Psychology of Insecurity and the Quest for Absolute Security'. In Williamson Murray, MacGregor Knox and Alvin Bernstein (eds) *The Making of Strategy: Rulers, Wars and States*. Cambridge: Cambridge University Press.

—— (1996) *Masters of War: Classical Strategic Thought*. London: Frank Cass.

—— (2001) *Masters of War: Classical Strategic Thought*, 3rd edn. London: Frank Cass.

Hanson, Victor Davis (2001) *Carnage and Culture: Landmark Battles in the Rise of Western Power*. New York: Anchor Books.

Hays, Peter L., Brenda J. Vallance and Alan R. Van Tassell (eds) (2000) *Spacepower for a New Millennium: Space and US National Security*. New York: McGraw-Hill.

Heikka, Henrikki (2005) 'Republican Realism: Finnish Strategic Culture in Historical Perspective', *Cooperation and Conflict* 40/1, 91-119.

Henkin, L. (1968) *How Nations Behave: Law and Foreign Policy*. New York: Columbia University Press.

Herring, Eric (ed.) (2000) *Preventing the Use of Weapons of Mass Destruction*. London: Frank Cass.

Herzog, A. (1963) *The War–Peace Establishment*. London: Harper & Row.

Heuer, R. (1999) *Psychology of Intelligence Analysis*. Washington, DC: Center for the Study of Intelligence.

Heuiser, Beatrice (2010) *The Evolution of Strategy: Thinking War from Antiquity to the Present*. New York: Cambridge University Press.

Hoffer, E. (1952) *The True Believer: Thoughts on the Nature of Mass Movements*. London: Secker & Warburg.

Hoffman, B. (2006) *Inside Terrorism*. New York: Columbia University Press.

Holbrooke, R. (1999) 'No Media—No War', *Index on Censorship* 28/3, 20.

Holsti, O. (1976) 'Foreign Policy Formation Viewed Cognitively'. In R Axelrod (ed.) *Structure of Decision*. Princeton, NJ: Princeton University Press.

Homer-Dixon, Thomas F. (1991) 'On the Threshold: Environmental Changes as Causes of Acute Conflict', *International Security* 16/2 (Fall), 76–116.

Honig, Jan Willem (2001) 'Avoiding War, Inviting Defeat: The Srebrenica Crisis, July 1995', *Journal of Contingencies and Crisis Management* 9/4, 201.

Horowitz, D. L. (1985) *Ethnic Groups in Conflict*. Berkeley, Los Angeles, London: University of California Press.

Howard, Michael (1976) *War in European History*. Oxford: Oxford University Press.

—— (1991) 'British Grand Strategy in World War 1'. In Paul Kennedy, (ed.), *Grand Strategies in War and Peace*. New Haven, CT: Yale University Press.

—— (1991) 'Clausewitz, Man of the Year', *New York Times* 28 January, A17.

Howarth, David (1974) *Sovereign of the Seas: The Story of British Sea Power*. London: Collins.

Howlett, Darryl and John Glenn (2005) 'Epilogue: Nordic Strategic Culture', *Cooperation and Conflict* 40/1.

HPSCI (House Permanent Select Committee on Intelligence) (2006) *IC21: The Intelligence Community in the 21st Century*, Staff Study.

Hudson, Valerie M. (ed.) (1997) *Culture and Foreign Policy*. Boulder, CO: Lynne Rienner.

Hughes, Christopher W. (2004) 'Japan's Re-emergence as a "Normal" Military Power', *Adelphi Paper* 368.

Hughes, Thomas P. (1998) *Rescuing Prometheus*. New York: Pantheon Books.

Hughes, Wayne (1986) *Fleet Tactics: Theory and Practice*. Annapolis, MD: Naval Institute Press.

Huntington, S. (1993a) 'The Clash of Civilizations', *Foreign Affairs* 72/3.

—— (1993b) 'Response: If Not Civilizations, What? Paradigms of the Post-Cold War World', *Foreign Affairs* 72/5.

—— (1996) *The Clash of Civilizations: Remaking of World Order*. New York: Simon & Schuster.

Hurd, I. (1999) 'Legitimacy and Authority in International Politics', *International Organization* 53/2, 379–408.

Hurd, D., Malcolm Rifkind, David Owen and George Robertson (2008) 'Stop Worrying and Learn to Ditch the Bomb', *The Times* 30 June. Available at http://www.timesonline.co.uk/tol/comment/columnists/guest_contributors/article4237387.ece

Hyde-Price, A. (2004) 'European Security, Strategic Culture and the Use of Force', *European Security* 13/1, 323–43.

Hymans, J. E. C. (2006) *The Psychology of Nuclear Proliferation: Identity, Emotions, and Foreign Policy*. Cambridge: Cambridge University Press.

IHS Jane's Defense & Security Intelligence & Analysis (various publications).

Independent, The (2000) 'UN must Rethink its Peacekeeping Role, says Annan', *Independent* 29 May. Available at http://www.independent.co.uk/news/world/africa/un-must-rethink-its-peacekeeping-role-says-annan-715960.html

International Institute for Strategic Studies (2012) *The Military Balance*. London: IISS and Routledge.

Iraqi WMD Commission (2005) *Commission on the Intelligence Capabilities of the United States Regarding Weapons of Mass Destruction, Report to the President*, 31 March.

Isaacson, W. (1999) 'Madeline's War', *Time* 17 May.

Jackson, R. H. (1993) *Quasi-States: Sovereignty, International Relations and the Third World*. Cambridge: Cambridge University Press.

Janda, L. (1995) Shutting the Gates of Mercy: The American Origins of Total War, 1860–1880', *Journal of Military History* 59/1:15.

Jansen, J. (1997) *The Dual Nature of Islamic Fundamentalism*. Ithaca, NY: Cornell University Press.

Jenkins, B. M. (1987) 'Will Terrorists Go Nuclear?'. In W. Laqueur and Y. Alexander (eds) *The Terrorism Reader: A Historical Anthology*. New York: Meridian.

—— (2008) *Will Terrorists Go Nuclear?* New York: Prometheus.

Jervis, Robert (1976) *Perception and Misperception in International Politics*. Princeton, NJ: Princeton University Press.

—— (1979) 'Deterrence Theory Revisited', *World Politics* 31/2, 289–324.

—— (2010) *Why Intelligence Fails: Lessons from the Iranian Revolution and the Iraq War*. Ithaca NY: Cornell University Press.

Johnson, Jeanie L., K. M. Kartchner, and J. A. Larsen (eds) (2009) *Strategic Culture and Weapons of Mass Destruction: Culturally Based Insights into Comparative National Security Policymaking*. London: Palgrave Macmillan.

Johnson, L. and J. Wirtz (2008) *Intelligence and National Security: The Secret World of Spies: An Anthology.* Los Angeles, CA: Roxbury Publishing Company.

Johnston, Alastair Iain (1995) *Cultural Realism: Strategic Culture and Grand Strategy in Chinese History.* Princeton, NJ: Princeton University Press.

Jomini, de, Antoine-Henri ([1838] 1992) *The Art of War.* London: Greenhill Books.

Jones, Archer (1987) *The Art of War in the Western World.* Chicago, IL: University of Illinois Press.

Joseph, Robert G. and John F. Reichart (1995) *Deterrence and Defence in a Nuclear, Biological, and Chemical Environment.* Occasional Paper of the Center for Counterproliferation Research. Washington, DC: National Defense University.

Juperman, Alan J. (2000) 'Rwanda in Retrospect', *Foreign Affairs* 79/1 (January/February).

Kahn, H. (1960) *On Thermonuclear War.* Princeton, NJ: Princeton University Press.

——(1962) *Thinking About the Unthinkable.* New York: Horizon Press.

Kaldor, M. (1999) *New and Old Wars: Organized Violence in a Global Era.* Cambridge: Polity Press.

Kalyvas, S. (2006) *The Logic of Violence in Civil War.* Cambridge: Cambridge University Press.

Kaplan, D. E. (2005a) 'Hearts, Minds and Dollars', *US News and World Report* 25 April.

——(2005b) 'The New Business of Terror', *US News and World Report* 5 December.

Kaplan, E. et al. (2005) 'What Happened to Suicide Bombings in Israel? Insights from a Terror Stock Model', *Studies in Conflict and Terrorism* 28, 225–35.

Kaplan, F. (1983) *The Wizards of Armageddon.* Stanford, CA: Stanford University Press.

Karatzogianni, Athina (2004) 'The Politics of 'Cyberconflict', *Journal of Politics* 24/1, 46–55.

Karp, A. (2006) 'The New Indeterminacy of Deterrence and Missile Defence'. In Ian Kenyon and John Simpson (eds) *Deterrence in the New Global Security Environment.* London: Routledge.

Kartchner, K. M. (2009) 'Strategic Culture and WMD Decision Making'. In Jeannie L. Johnson, Kerry M. Kartchner, and Jeffrey Larsen (eds) *Strategic Culture and Weapons of Mass Destruction: Culturally Based Insights into Comparative National Security Policymaking.* New York: Palgrave Macmillan.

Katzenbach, Jr., E. J. and G. Z. Hanrahan (1962) 'The Revolutionary Strategy of Mao Tse-Tung', in F. M. Osanka (ed.) *Modern Guerrilla Warfare: Fighting Communist Guerrilla Movements, 1941-1961.* New York: Free Press.

Katzenstein, P. J. (ed.) (1996) *The Culture of National Security: Norms and Identity in World Politics.* New York: Columbia University Press.

Keegan, John (1987) *The Mask of Command.* New York: Viking Penguin.

——(1993) *A History of Warfare.* New York: Knopf.

——(2004) *The Iraq War.* New York: Knopf.

Kegley, C. W. and E. R. Wittkopf (1997) *World Politics: Trends and Transformation.* New York: St Martins Press.

Kent, Sherman (1966) *Strategic Intelligence for an American World Policy.* Princeton University Press.

Kenyon, I. and J. Simpson (eds) (2006) *Deterrence in the New Global Security Environment.* London: Routledge.

Keohane, Robert O. (2001) *International Institutions and State Power: Essays in International Relations Theory.* San Francisco, CA: Westview Press.

——(2002) *Power and Governance in a Partially Globalizing World.* New York: Routledge.

——and Joseph S. Nye (2001) *Power and Interdependence,* 3rd edn. New York: Longman; originally Reading, MA [1989]: Addison-Wesley.

Kerr, R. et al. (2005) 'Intelligence and Analysis on Iraq: Issues for the Intelligence Community', *Studies in Intelligence* 49/3.

Kier, Elizabeth (1995) 'Culture and Military Doctrine: France between the Wars', *International Security* 19/14, 65–94.

Kievet, James and Steven Metz (1994) *The Revolution in Military Affairs and Conflict Short of War.* Carlisle, PA: US Army War College Strategic Studies Institute.

Kilcullen, D. (2009) *The Accidental Guerrilla: Fighting Small Wars in the Midst of a Big One.* Oxford: Oxford University Press.

Kipp, Jacob, Lester Grau, Karl Prinslow, and Captain Don Smith (2006) 'The Human Terrain System: A CORDS for the 21st Century', *Military Review*, September/October, 8-15.

Kiras, James D. (2005) 'Terrorism and Globalization'. In John Baylis, Steve Smith and Patricia Owens (eds) *The Globalization of World Politics: An Introduction to International Relations,* 5th edn. Oxford: Oxford University Press.

Kissinger, H. A. (1957) *Nuclear Weapons and Foreign Policy.* New York: Harper & Row.

Kitson, Frank (1977) *Bunch of Five.* London: Faber & Faber.

Klare, M. (2001) 'The New Geography of Conflict', *Foreign Affairs* 80/3, 49–61.

Klein, Bradley S. (1994) *Strategic Studies and World Order: The Global Politics of Deterrence.* Cambridge: Cambridge University Press.

Klein, Yitzak (1991) 'A Theory of Strategic Culture', *Comparative Strategy* 10/1, 3–23.

Klonis, N. I. (pseud.) (1972) *Guerrilla Warfare*. New York: Robert Speller & Sons.

Knopf, Jeffrey (2010) 'The Fourth Wave in Deterrence Research', *Contemporary Security Policy* 31(1): 1–33.

Kosal, M. (2005) *Terrorist Incidents Targeting Industrial Chemical Facilities: Strategic Motivations and International Repercussions*. Stanford, CA: Center for International Security and Cooperation, unpublished manuscript.

Kramer, F. D., S. H. Starr, and L. K. Wentz (eds), (2009) *Cyberpower and National Security*. Washington, DC: Potomac Books.

Krause, K. and M. C. Williams (eds) (1997) *Critical Security Studies: Concepts and Cases*. London: UCL Press.

Krepinevich Andrew F. (1994) 'Cavalry to Computer: The Pattern of Military Revolution', *The National Interest* (Fall), 30–42.

Kritsiotis, D. (2004) 'Arguments of Mass Confusion', *European Journal of International Law* 15/2, 233–78.

Kuehl, D. T. (2009) 'From Cyberspace to Cyberpower: Defining the Problem'. In F. D. Kramer, S. H. Starr and L. K. Wentz (eds) *Cyberpower and National Security*. Washington, DC: Potomac Books.

Kuhn, K. (1987) 'Responsibility for Military Conduct and Respect for International Humanitarian Law', Dissemination, ICRC.

Kupchan, C. (1994) *The Case for Collective Security*. Ann Arbor, MI: University of Michigan Press.

Kydd, A. H. and B. F. Walter (2006) 'The Strategies of Terrorism', *International Security* 31/1 (Summer): 46–80.

Ladis, Nikolaos (2003) 'Assessing Greek Strategic Thought and Practice: Insights from the Strategic Culture Approach'. Doctoral dissertation, University of Southampton.

Langewiesche, W. (2007) *The Atomic Bazaar: The Rise of the Nuclear Poor*. New York: Farrar, Straus and Giroux.

Lantis, Jeffrey S. (2002) *Strategic Dilemmas and the Evolution of German Foreign Policy since Unification*. Westport, CN: Praeger.

—— (2005) 'American Strategic Culture and Transatlantic Security Ties'. In Kerry Longhurst and Marcin Zaborowski, *Controversies in Politics* 24/1, 46–55.

—— (2009) 'Strategic Culture and Tailored Deterrence: Bridging the Gap Between Theory and Practice', *Contemporary Security Policy* 30/3.

Laqueur, W. (1996).'Postmodern Terrorism', *Foreign Affairs*, 75/5, 24–37.

—— (1999) *The New Terrorism: Fanaticism and the Arms of Mass Destruction*. New York: Oxford University Press.

Larsen, Jeffrey A. (1997) 'NATO Counterproliferation Policy: A Case Study in Alliance Politics', INSS Occasional Paper 17. Denver, CO: USAF Institute for National Security Studies. Available at http://www.usafa.af.mil/df/inss/OCP/ocp17.pdf

—— and James J. Wirtz ed. (2009) *Arms Control and Cooperative Security*. London: Lynne Rienner.

Lauterpacht, H. (1952) 'The Revision of the Law of War', *British Yearbook of International Law* 29, 360–82.

Lavoy, Peter, Scott Sagan and James Wirtz (eds) (2000) *Planning the Unthinkable: How New Powers Will Use Nuclear, Biological, and Chemical, Weapons*. Ithaca, NY: Cornell University Press.

Lawrence, P. (1988) *Preparing for Armageddon: A Critique of Western Strategy*. Brighton: Wheatsheaf.

Lawrence, T. E. (1920) 'The Evolution of a Revolt', *The Army Quarterly* 1/1, 55–69.

—— (1935) *Seven Pillars of Wisdom: A Triumph*. London: Jonathan Cape.

Le Bon, G. (1897) *The Crowd: A Study of the Popular Mind*, 2nd edn. London: Fisher Unwin.

Leavenworth, K. S. (2004) US Army Training and Doctrine Command.

Lee, Steven P. (1996) *Morality, Prudence, and Nuclear Weapons*. Cambridge: Cambridge University Press.

Legro, Jeffrey W. (1996) 'Culture and Preferences in the International Cooperation Two-step', *American Political Science Review* 90/1, 118–37.

Levy, M. (1995) 'Is the Environment a National Security Issue?', *International Security* 20/2, 35–62.

Levy, J. S. and W. R. Thompson (2010) *The Causes of War*. Chichester: Wiley-Blackwell.

Lia, B. and T. Hegghammer (2004) 'Jihadi Strategic Studies: The Alleged Al Qaida Policy Study Preceding the Madrid Bombings', *Studies in Conflict and Terrorism* 27, 355–75.

Libicki, M. C. (2007) *Conquest in Cyberspace: National Security and Information Warfare*. Cambridge: Cambridge University Press.

Liddell Hart, Basil H. ([1941] 1967) *Strategy: The Indirect Approach*. London: Faber & Faber.

Lind, Jennifer M. (2004) 'Pacifism or Passing the Buck? Testing Theories of Japan's Security Policy', *International Security* 29/1 (Summer).

Lindley-French (2002) 'In the Shade of Locarno? Why European Defence is Failing', *International Affairs* 78/4, 789.

Litwak, Robert (2003) 'The New Calculus of Pre-emption', *Survival* 44/4.

Lockhart, Charles (1999) 'Cultural Contributions to Explaining Institutional Form, Political Change and Rational Decisions', *Comparative Political Studies* 32/7, 862–93.

Long, J. M. (2009) 'Strategic Culture, Al-Qaeda, and Weapons of Mass Destruction'. In J. L. Johnson, K. M. Kartchner and J. A. Larsen (eds) *Strategic Culture and Weapons of Mass Destruction: Culturally Based Insights into Comparative National Security Policymaking*. London: Palgrave Macmillan.

Longhurst, Kerry (2005) *Germany and the Use of Force: The Evolution of German Security Policy 1990–2003*. Manchester: Manchester University Press.

—— and Marcin Zaborowski (eds) (2005) *Old Europe, New Europe and the Transatlantic Security Agenda*. London: Routledge.

Lonsdale, David J. (2004) *The Nature of War in the Information Age: Clausewitzian Future*. London: Frank Cass.

—— (2007) *Alexander the Great: Lessons in Strategy*. Abingdon, UK: Routledge.

Looney, R. E. (2005) 'The Business of Insurgency: The Expansion of Iraq's Shadow Economy', *The National Interest* 81 (Fall), 117–21.

Lorenz, K. (1966) *On Aggression*. New York: Harcourt, Brace & World.

—— (1976) *On Aggression*. New York: Bantam.

Lowenthal, M. (2011) *Intelligence: From Secrets to Policy*. 5th edn. Washington, DC: CQ Press.

Luttwak, Edward (2001) *Strategy: The Logic of War and Peace*, revised and enlarged edn, Cambridge, MA: Belknap Press.

Lynn, John (2003) *Battle: A History of Combat and Culture*. Boulder, CO: Westview Press.

McConnell, M. (2008) 'Remarks By Director Mike McConnell to the US Geospatial Intelligence Foundation (USGIF) GEOINT 2008 Symposium', 30 October.

—— (2010) 'To win the cyber-war, look to the Cold War,' *The Washington Post*, 28 February. Available at http://www.washingtonpost.com/wp-dyn/content/article/2010/02/25/AR2010022502493.html

McCoubrey, H. (1998) *International Humanitarian Law*, 2nd edn. Aldershot: Dartmouth.

McCuen, John (1966) *The Art of Counter-Revolutionary Warfare*. Harrisburg, PA: Stackpole.

McGoldrick, D., Rowe, P. and Donnelly, E. (eds) (2004) *The Permanent International Court: Legal and Policy Issues*. Oxford: Hart Publishing.

MacKenzie, Donald (1990) *Inventing Accuracy: An Historical Sociology of Nuclear Missile Guidance*. Cambridge, MA: MIT University Press.

McMillan, Joseph (2005). 'Treating Terrorist Groups as Armed Bands: The Strategic Implications'. In Jason S. Purcell and Joshua D. Weintraub (eds) *Topics in Terrorism: Toward a Transatlantic Consensus on the Nature of the Threat*. Washington, DC: Atlantic Council of the United States.

McNeil, William H. (1982) *The Pursuit of Power*. Oxford: Basil Blackwell.

Mahan, Alfred (1890) *The Influence of Seapower on History, 1660–1783*, Boston, MA: Little, Brown & Co.

Mahnken, Thomas G. (2001) 'Counterproliferation: A Critical Appraisal'. In Henry Sokolski and James M. Ludes (eds) *Twenty-First Century Weapons Proliferation: Are we Ready?* London: Frank Cass.

—— (2009) 'US Strategic and Organizational Subcultures'. In J. L. Johnson, K. M. Kartchner, and J. A. Larsen (eds) *Strategic Culture and Weapons of Mass Destruction: Culturally Based Insights into Comparative National Security Policymaking*. London: Palgrave Macmillan.

—— (2011) 'Cyberwar and Cyber Warfare'. In Kristin M. Lord and Travis Sharp, (eds) *America's Cyber Future: Security and Prosperity in the Information Age*. Washington, D.C.: Center for a New American Security.

—— and J. A. Maiolo (2008) *Strategic Studies: A Reader* (Abingdon: Routledge).

Malici, Akan (2006) 'Germans as Venutians: The Culture of German Foreign Policy Behavior', *Foreign Policy Analysis* 2/1 (January).

Marighella, Carlos (1969) *Minimanual of the Urban Guerrilla*. Available at http://www.baader-meinhof.com/index.htm

Mattern, Janice Bially (2005) *Ordering International Politics: Identity, Crisis, and Representational Force*. London: Routledge.

Matthew, Richard A., Jon Barnett, Bryan McDonald and Karen L. O'Brien (eds) (2010) *Global Environmental Change and Human Security*. Cambridge, Massachusetts: MIT Press.

Matthews, K. (1996) *The Gulf Conflict and International Relations*. London: Routledge.

Mazaar, M. (2010) 'The Open-source Century: Information, Knowledge, and Intelligence in the 21st Century', *World Politics Review*, 28 September, at: http://www.worldpoliticsreview.com/articles/6535/the-open-source-century-information-knowledge-and-intelligence-in-the-21st-century

Medina, C. (2008) 'The New Analysis'. In R. George and J. Bruce, *Analyzing Intelligence: Origins, Obstacles, and Innovations*. Washington, DC: Georgetown University Press.

Meilinger, P. (2008) 'Clausewitz's Bad Advice', *Armed Forces Journal International* August.

Meron, T. (2006) *The Humanization of International Law*. Leiden: Martinus Nijhoff.

Messenger, Charles (1976) *The Art of Blitzkreig*. London: Ian Allen Ltd.

Meyer, Christoph O. (2004) *Theorising European Strategic Culture: Between Convergence and the Persistence of National Diversity*. Centre for European Policy Studies, Working Document 204 (June), http://www.ceps.be

Miller, D. (1998) *The Cold War: A Military History*. New York: St Martin's Press.

Milliken, J. (1999) 'The Study of Discourse in International Relations', *European Journal of International Relations* 5(2), 225–54.

Minear, L. and T. G. Weiss (1995) *Mercy under Fire: War and the Global Humanitarian Community*. Boulder, CO: Westview Press.

Miskimmon, A. (2004) 'Continuity in the Face of Upheaval—British Strategic Culture and the Impact of the Blair Government', *European Security* 13(3), 273–99.

Mitra, Subrata Kumar (2002) 'Emerging Major Powers and the International System (An Indian View)'. In Alistair Dally and Rosalind Bourke (eds) *Conflict, the State and Aerospace Power*. Canberra: RAAF Aerospace Centre.

Moir, L. (2002), *The Law of Internal Armed Conflict*, Oxford: Oxford University Press.

Moran, Daniel (2006) *Wars of National Liberation*. Washington, DC: Smithsonian Books.

—— and J. A. Russell (eds) (2009) *Energy Security and Global Politics: The Militarization of Resource Management*. New York: Routledge.

Morgan, P. (2003) *Deterrence Now*. Cambridge: Cambridge University Press.

Morris, Justin C. (2005) 'Normative Innovation and the Great Powers'. In A. Bellamy (ed.) *International Society and its Critics*. Oxford: Oxford University Press.

—— and N. J. Wheeler (2007) 'The Security Council's Crisis of Legitimacy and the Use of Force', *International Politics* 44/2/3, 214–32.

—— and —— (2012) 'Human Welfare in a World of States: Reassessing the Balance of Responsibility', in J. Connelly and J. Hayward (eds), *The Withering of the Welfare State: Regression*. London: Palgrave Macmillan.

Moskos, Charles C., John Allen Williams and David R. Segal (eds) (2000) *The Postmodern Military: Armed Forces after the Cold War*. New York: Oxford University Press.

Müller, Harald and Mitchell Reiss (1995) 'Counterproliferation: Putting Old Wine in New Bottles', *Washington Quarterly* (Spring).

—— David Fisher and Wolfgang Kötter (1994) *Nuclear Non-Proliferation and Global Order*. New York: Oxford University Press.

Munck, R. (2000) 'Deconstructing Terror: Insurgency, Repression and Peace'. In R. Munck and P. L. de Silva (eds) *Postmodern Insurgencies: Political Violence, Identity Formation and Peacemaking in Comparative Perspective*. New York: St Martin's Press.

Munkler, Herfield (2005) *The New Wars*. Cambridge: Polity Press, Cambridge: Polity Press.

Murray, Williamson, Macgregor Knox and Alvin Bernstein (eds) (1994) *The Making of Strategy: Rulers, States, and War*. Cambridge: Cambridge University Press.

——(1997) 'Thinking about Revolutions in Military Affairs,' *Joint Force Quarterly*, 71.

—— and Robert Scales (2003) *The Iraq War: A Military History*. Cambridge, MA: Harvard University Press.

Mutimer, D. (2000) *The Weapons State: Proliferation and the Framing of Security*. Boulder, CO: Lynne Rienner.

Nadelmann, E. (1993) *Cops across Borders*. State College, PA: Penn State University Press.

Naim, Moises (2005) *Illicit: How Smugglers, Traffickers and Copycats are Hijacking the Global Economy*. New York: Doubleday.

Nasution, A. H. (1965) *Fundamentals of Guerrilla Warfare*. New York: Praeger

National Intelligence Council (2004) *Mapping the Global Future*. Washington, DC: Government Printing Office.

National Resources Defense Council http://www.nrdc.org/nuclear/nudb/datab19.asp

Negroponte, J. (2006) The Science and Technology Challenge. Remarks of the Director of National Intelligence at the Woodrow Wilson International Center for Scholars, 25 September.

Nelson, K. L. and S. C. Olin, Jr. (1979) *Why War: Ideology, Theory, and History*. Berkeley and Los Angeles, CA: University of California Press.

Newman, R. (1961) Review in *Scientific American* 204/3, 197.

Newmann, Iver B. and Heikka, Hennikki (2005) 'Grand Strategy, Strategic Culture, Practice: The Social Roots of Nordic Defense', *Cooperation and Conflict* 40, 5–23.

Niebuhr, R. (1932) *Moral Man and Immoral Society: A Study in Ethics and Politics*. New York and London: Charles Scribner's Sons.

Nietzsche, F. (1996) *Beyond Good and Evil*, translated by W. Kaufmann. New York: Random House.

Nofi, A. A. (1982) 'Clausewitz on War', *Strategy and Tactics*, 91, 16.

Nye, Jr., Joseph S. (1986) *Nuclear Ethics*. London: Macmillan.

——. (1988) *Nuclear Ethics*. New York: Free Press.

—— (2011) *The Future of Power*. New York: Public Affairs.

O'Connell, M. E. (2002) 'The Myth of Preemptive Self-Defense', *American Society of International Law*. Available at http://www.asil.org/taskforce/oconnell.pdf

O'Connell, Robert L. (1989) *Of Arms and Men: A History of War, Weapons and Aggression*. Oxford: Oxford University Press.

O'Hanlon, Michael E. (2000) *Technological Change and the Future of Warfare*. Washington, DC: Brookings Institution Press.

Olsen, J. A., and Colin S Gray (eds) (2011) *The Practice of Strategy: From Alexander the Great to the Present*. Oxford: Oxford University Press.

Olson, W. C., D. S. Mclellan and F. A. Sondermann (1983) *The Theory and Practice of International Relations*, 6th edn. Englewood Cliffs, NJ: Prentice Hall.

O'Neill, Bard (1990) *Insurgency and Terrorism: Inside Modern Revolutionary Warfare*. Washington, DC: Brassey's.

Oppel, R. (2007) 'Foreign Fighters in Iraq Are Tied to Allies of US,' *New York Times*, 22 November.

Orme, J. (1997).'The Utility of Force in a World of Scarcity', *International Security* 22/3, 136–67.

Osgood, R. E. (1962) *An Alternative to War and Surrender*. Chicago, IL: Chicago University Press.

—— (1962) *NATO: The Entangling Alliance*. Chicago, IL: University of Chicago Press.

O'Tuathail, G. (1996) *Critical Geopolitics: The Politics of Writing Global Space*. London: Routledge.

Owens, William A. (1995) *High Seas: The Naval Passage to an Uncharted World*. Annapolis, MD: Naval Institute Press.

—— K. W. Dam, and H. S. Lin (eds.), (2009) *Technology, Policy, Law, and Ethics Regarding US Acquisition and Use of Cyberattack Capabilities*. Washington, D.C., The National Academies Press.

—— and Edward Offley (2000) *Lifting the Fog of War*. New York: Farrar, Straus, & Giroux.

Paddon, E. (2011) 'Partnering for Peace: Implications and Dilemmas', *International Peacekeeping* 18/5, 518–35.

Paget, Julian (1967) *Counter-Insurgency Fighting*. London: Faber & Faber.

Pape, R. (2005) *Dying to Win: The Strategic Logic of Suicide Terrorism*. New York: Random House.

Paret, P. (ed.) (1986) *Makers of Modern Strategy: From Machiavelli to the Nuclear Age*. Princeton, NJ: Princeton University Press.

Paris, Roland (2004) *At War's End: Building Peace After Civil Conflict*. Cambridge: Cambridge University Press.

Parsons, T. (1951) *The Social System*. London: Routledge and Kegan Paul.

Payne, Keith B. (1996) *Deterrence in the Second Nuclear Age*. Lexington, KY: University Press of Kentucky.

—— (2001) *The Fallacies of Cold War Deterrence and a New Direction*. Lexington, KY: University Press of Kentucky.

—— (2002) 'Deterrence: Theory and Practice'. In J. Baylis, E. Cohen, C. S. Gray, and J. W. Wirtz (eds) *Strategy in the Contemporary World: An Introduction to Strategic Studies* Oxford: Oxford University Press.

—— (2007) 'Deterring Iran: The Values at Stake and the Acceptable Risks'. In P. Clawson and M. Eisenstadt (eds) *Deterring the Ayatollahs: Complications in Applying Cold War Strategy to Iran*. Policy Focus No. 72. Washington, DC: The Washington Institute for Near East Policy.

—— (2008) *The Great American Gamble: Deterrence Theory and Practice from the Cold War to the Twenty-first Century*. Fairfax, VA: National Institute Press.

Pelfrey, W. (2005) 'The Cycle of Preparedness: Establishing a Framework to Prepare for Terrorist Threats', *Journal of Homeland Security and Emergency Management* 2/1.

Peoples, Columba (2007) 'Technology and Politics in the Missile Defence Debate: Traditional, Radical, and Critical Approaches', *Global Change, Peace and Security* 19/3, 265–80.

Perkovich, George (2004) 'The Nuclear and Security Balance'. In F. R. Frankel and H. Harding (eds) *The India–China Relationship*. New York: Columbia University Press.

—— Jessica Tuchman Matthews, Joseph Cirincione, Rose Gottemoeller and Jon B. Wolfsthal (2005) *Universal Compliance: A Strategy for Nuclear Security*. Washington, DC: Carnegie Endowment for International Peace.

Peters, R. (1994) 'The New Warrior Class', *Parameters* 24/2, 16–26.

Petroski, Henry (1982) *To Engineer is Human: The Role of Failure in Successful Design*. New York: Random House.

—— (1992) *The Evolution of Useful Things*. New York: Vintage Books.

Pictet, J. (1985) *Development and Principles of International Humanitarian Law*. The Hague: Martinus Nijhoff.

Pillar, P. (2006) 'Intelligence, Policy, and the War in Iraq', *Foreign Affairs* (March/April).

——(2011) *Intelligence and US Foreign Policy: Iraq, 9/11 and Misguided Reform*. New York: Columbia University Press.

Pollack, Kenneth M. (2002) *Arabs at War: Military Effectiveness, 1948–1991*. Lincoln, NE: University of Nebraska Press.

Poore, Stuart (2004) 'Strategic Culture'. In John Glenn, Darryl Howlett and Stuart Poore, *Neorealism versus Strategic Culture*. Aldershot: Ashgate.

Porch, Douglas ([2000] 2001) *Wars of Empire*. London: Cassell.

Pouligny, B. (2006) *Peace Operations Seen From Below: UN Missions and Local People*. Bloomfield, CT: Kumarian.

Preston, Richard A. and Sidney F. Wise (1970) *Men in Arms: A History of Warfare and its Interrelationship with Western Society*, 2nd edn, 104–5. New York: Praeger.

Pye, Lucian (1985) *Asian Power and Politics: The Cultural Dimension of Authority*. Cambridge, MA.: Harvard University Press.

Quester, G. (1977) *Offense and Defense in the International System*. New York: John Wiley and Sons.

——(1984).'War and Peace: Necessary and Sufficient Conditions'. In R. O. Matthews, A. G. Rubinoff and J. G. Stein (eds) *International Conflict and Conflict Management*. Scarborough, Ontario: Prentice-Hall.

Qurashi, A. (2002) 'Al-Qa'ida and the Art of War', *Al-Ansar* www-text in Arabic, FBIS document ID GMP20020220000183[0].

Raine, L. P. and F. J. Cilluffo (eds) (1994) *Global Organized Crime: The New Empire of Evil*. Washington, DC: Center for Strategic and International Studies.

Ralph, J. (2007) *Defending the Society of States: Why America Opposes the International Criminal Court and its Vision of World Society*. Oxford: Oxford University Press.

Rapoport, Anatol (1964) *Strategy and Conscience*. New York: Schocken Books / Harper & Row.

——(1965) 'The Sources of Anguish', *Bulletin of Atomic Scientists* 21/10 (December).

Rassmussen, M. (2005) '"What's the use of it?", Danish Strategic Culture and the Utility of Armed Force', *Cooperation and Conflict* 40, 67–89.

Rattray, Gregory J. (2001) *Strategic Warfare in Cyberspace*. Cambridge, Massachusetts: MIT Press.

——(2002) 'The Cyberterrorism Threat'. In Russell D. Howard and Reid L. Sawyer (eds) *Terrorism and Counterterrorism: Understanding the New Security Environment*. Guildford, CT: McGraw-Hill.

Raudzens, George (1990) 'War-Winning Weapons: The Measurement of Technological Determinism in Military History', *Journal of Military History* 54 (October), 403–33.

Rauschning, H. (1939) *Germany's Revolution of Destruction*, translated by E. W. Dickes. London: Heinemann.

Record, Jeffrey (2003) *Bounding the Global War on Terrorism*. Carlisle, PA: Army War College.

——(2004) *Dark Victory: America's Second War Against Iraq*. Washington, DC: US Naval Institute Press.

Reid, Brian Holden (2005) *Robert E. Lee, Icon for a Nation*. London: Weidenfeld and Nicolson.

Reus-Smit, C. (2004) *The Politics of International Law*. Cambridge: Cambridge University Press.

——(2007) 'International Crises of Legitimacy', *International Politics* 44/2/3, 157–74.

Ricks, T. (2006) *Fiasco: The American Military Adventure in Iraq*. New York: Penguin.

Roberts, Andrew (2008) *Masters and Commanders: How Roosevelt, Churchill, Marshall, and Alanbrooke Won the War in the West*. London: Allen Lane.

Robertson, S. (2000) 'Experimentation and Innovation in the Canadian Armed Forces', *Canadian Military Journal*, 64.

Robinson, L. (2008) *Tell Me How this Ends: General David Petraeus and the Search for a Way Out of Iraq*. New York: Public Affairs.

Robinson, P., N. de Lee, and D. Carrick (eds) (2008) *Ethics Education in the Military*. Aldershot: Ashgate.

Rose, M. (1995) 'A Year in Bosnia: What has been Achieved', *RUSI* 140/3, 23.

Rosen, Stephen (1996) *Societies and Military Power*. Ithaca, NY: Cornell Studies in Security Affairs.

——(1995) 'Military Effectiveness: Why Society Matters', *International Security* 1914, 5–31.

——(2005) *War and Human Nature*. Princeton, NJ: Princeton University Press.

Rosenau, J. N. (1990) *Turbulence in World Politics*. Princeton, NJ: Princeton University Press.

Rousseau, J. J. ([1754] 1993) 'A Discourse on the Origin of Inequality'. In G. D. H. Cole (ed.) *The Social Contract and Discourses*. London: J. M. Dent.

Rumsfeld, D. (2003) *Memo on Global War on Terrorism*. Available at http://www.usatoday.com/ news/washington/ executive/rumsfeld-memo.htm

Russell, R. B. (1958) *A History of the United Nations Charter*. Washington DC: Brookings Institute.

Rynning, S. (2003) 'The European Union: Towards a Strategic Culture?', *Security Dialogue* 34/4 (December).

Sagan, S. (2005) 'Learning from Failure or Failure to Learn: Lessons from Past Nuclear Security Events'. Paper presented to the IAEA International Conference on Nuclear Security, 16 March.

Sageman, M. (2004) *Understanding Terror Networks*. Philadelphia, PA: University of Pennsylvania Press.

—— (2007) *Leaderless Jihad: Terror Networks in the Twenty-First Century*. Philadelphia, PA: University of Pennsylvania Press.

Samore, Gary (2003) 'The Korean Nuclear Crisis', *Survival* 45/1.

Sarkesian, S. C. (ed.) (1972) *The Military-Industrial Complex: A Reassessment*. Beverly Hills, CA: Sage.

Sassòli, M. (2004) 'The Status of Persons Held in Guantanamo under International Humanitarian Law', *Journal of International Criminal Justice*, 2/1 (March), 96–106.

Schabas, W. A. (2004) *An Introduction to the International Criminal Court*, 2nd edn. Cambridge: Cambridge University Press.

Schell, J. (1982) *The Fate of the Earth*. London: Picador.

—— (1984) *The Abolition*. New York: Knopf.

Schelling, Thomas C. (1963) *Strategy of Conflict*. New York: Oxford University Press.

—— and M. Halperin (1985) *Strategy and Arms Control*. Washington, DC: Pergamon-Brassey's.

Schmid, A. P. and A. J. Jongman (1988) *Political Terrorism: A New Guide to Actors, Authors, Concepts, Data Bases, Theories and Literature*. New Brunswick, NJ: Transaction Books.

Schmitt, B., Darryl Howlett, John Simpson, Harald Müller and Bruno Tertrais (2005) *Effective Non-proliferation: The European Union and the 2005 NTPT Review Conference*. Chaillot Paper 77. Brussels: EU Institute for Security Studies.

Schwartau, W. (1996) *Information Warfare*, 2nd edn. New York: Thunder's Mouth Press.

Schwartz, Stephen I. (1998) *Atomic Audit: The Costs and Consequences of US Nuclear Weapons since 1940*. Washington, DC: Brookings Institution.

—— (2003) *China's Use of Military Force: Beyond the Great Wall and the Long March*. Cambridge: Cambridge University Press.

Schwartzstein, Stuart J. D. (ed.) (1996) *The Information Revolution and National Security: Dimensions and Directions*. Washington, DC: Center for Strategic and International Studies.

—— (1998) *Cybercrime, Cyberterrorism and Cyberwarfare: Averting an Electronic Waterloo*.

Washington, DC: Center for Strategic and International Studies.

Scobell, Andrew (2002) *China and Strategic Culture*. Carlisle, PA: US Army War College, Strategic Studies Institute, May.

Sepp, K., R. Kiper, J. Schroder and C. Briscoe (2004) *Weapon of Choice: U.S. Army Special Operations in Afghanistan*. Fort Leavenworth, KS: US Army Command and General Staff College Press.

Shaw, M. (2003) 'Strategy and Slaughter', *Review of International Studies* 29/2, 269–77.

Shaw, R. P. and Y. Wong (1985) *Genetic Seeds of Warfare: Evolution, Nationalism and Patriotism*. London: Unwin Hyman.

Shawcross, William (2000) *Deliver us from Evil: Warlords and Peacekeepers in a World of Endless Conflict*. London: Bloomsbury.

Shay, Jonathan (1994) *Achilles in Vietnam: Combat Trauma and the Undoing of Character*. New York: Simon & Schuster.

Sheldon, John B. (2011) 'Stuxnet and Cyberpower in War,' *World Politics Review*. Available at http://www.worldpoliticsreview.com/articles/8570/stuxnet-and-cyberpower-in-war

Shultz, G., William Perry, Henry Kissinger and Sam Nunn (2008) 'Toward a Nuclear Weapon-free World', *Wall Street Journal* 15 January A 15. Available at http://online.wsj.com/public/article_print/SB120036422673589947.html

Sims, J. and B. Gerber (eds) (2005) *Transforming US Intelligence*. Washington, DC: Georgetown University Press.

Singer, M. and A. Wildavsky (1993) *The Real World Order: Zones of Peace/Zones of Turmoil*. Chatham House, NJ: Chatham House Publishers.

Singer, P. W. (2009) *Wired for War: The Robotics Revolution and Conflict in the 21st Century*. New York: Penguin.

Sloan, Elinor (2002) *The Revolution in Military Affairs*. Montreal: McGill-Queen's Press.

Smith, H. (2005) *On Clausewitz: A Study of Military and Political Ideas*. New York: Palgrave Macmillan.

Smith, Sir R. (2006) *The Utility of Force: The Art of War in the Modern World*. London: Penguin.

Smith, S., K. Booth, and M. Zalewski (eds) (1996) *International Theory: Positivism and Beyond*. Cambridge: Cambridge University Press.

Snyder, Jack (1977) *The Soviet Strategic Culture: Implications for Nuclear Options*, R-2154-AF. Santa Monica, CA: Rand Corporation.

—— (2002) 'Anarchy and Culture: Insights from the Anthropology of War', *International Organization* 56/1 (Winter).

Sokolski, Henry (2001) *Best of Intentions: America's Campaign Against Strategic Weapons Proliferation.* London: Praeger.

—— and James Ludes (2001) *Twenty-First Century Weapons Proliferation.* London: Frank Cass.

Spanier, J. W. and J. L. Nogee (1962) *The Politics of Disarmament: A Study of Soviet–American Gamesmanship.* New York: Praeger.

Stedman, Stephen John (1997) 'Spoiler Problems in Peace Processes', *International Security* 22/2 (Fall).

Stewart R. (2011) 'What Can Afghanistan and Bosnia Teach Us About Libya?' *The Guardian*, 7 October. Available at http://www.guardian.co.uk/world/2011/oct/08/libya-intervention-rory-stewart

Stolfi, R. H. S. (1970) 'Equipment for Victory in France in 1940', *History* 55.

Stone, P. (2003).'Iraq–al-Qaeda Link Weak Say Former Bush Officials', *National Journal* (8 August).

Stout, M. Huckabey, J., Schindler, J. and Lacey, J. (2008) *The Terrorist Perspectives Project: Strategic and Operational Views of Al Qaida and Associated Movements.* Annapolis, MD: Naval Institute Press.

Strachan, Hew (1988) *European Armies and the Conduct of War.* London: Routledge.

Strachan, H. (2005) 'The Lost Meaning of Strategy', *Survival* 47/3, (Autumn).

Suganami, H. (1996) *On the Causes of War.* Oxford: Clarendon Press.

Sun Tzu (1963) *The Art of War*, translated by Samuel B. Griffith. Oxford: Oxford University Press.

—— (1993) *The Art of War*, translated by Roger Ames. New York: Ballentine Books.

—— (1993) *The Art of War.* Courier Dover Publications, New York.

—— (1994) *The Art of War*, edited and translated by Ralph D. Sawyer (*c.*490 BC) (Boulder CO, Westview Press.

Swidler, Ann (1986) 'Culture in Action: Symbols and Strategies', *American Sociological Review* 51/2, 73.

Taber, R. (1970) *The War of the Flea: Guerrilla Warfare Theory and Practice.* London: Paladin.

Tannenwald, Nina (1999) 'The Nuclear Taboo: The United States and the Normative Basis of Nuclear Non-Use', *International Organization* 53/3, 83–114.

—— (2005) 'Stigmatizing the Bomb: Origins of the Nuclear Taboo', *International Security* 29/4, 5–49.

Technology Review (2004) 'We got Nothing until they Slammed into us', November, 38.

Terrif, Terry, Aaron Karp and Regina Karp (eds) (2006) *The Right War? The Fourth Generation Warfare Debate.* London: Routledge.

Tharoor, Shashi (1995–6) 'Should United Nations Peacekeeping Go "Back to Basics"', *Survival* 37/4 (Winter).

Thompson, K. (1960) 'Moral Purpose in Foreign Policy: Realities and Illusions', *Social Research* 27/3.

Thompson, Michael, Richard Ellis and Aaron Wildavsky (1990) *Cultural Theory.* Boulder, CO: Westview Press.

Thompson, R. (1966) *Defeating Communist Insurgency: Experiences from Malaya and Vietnam.* London: Chatto & Windus.

Thornton, E. P. (1981). 'A Letter to America', *The Nation* 232, 24 January.

Thucydides ([*c.*400 BC] 1996) *The Landmark Thucydides: A Comprehensive Guide to 'The Peloponnesian War'.* Robert B. Strassler (ed.), revised from translation by Richard Crawley. New York: The Free Press.

Till, Geoffrey (2004) *Seapower: A Guide for the Twenty-first Century.* London: Frank Cass.

Toffler, Alvin and Heidi (1993) *War and Antiwar: Survival at the Dawn of the 21st Century.* Boston, MA: Little, Brown & Co.

Townshend, Charles (1975) *The British Campaign in Ireland, 1919–1921: The Development of Political and Military Policies.* Oxford: Oxford University Press.

Transnational Organized Crime (1998) 'Special Issue: The United States International Crime Control Strategy', 4/1.

Treverton, G. (2001) *Reshaping National Intelligence for an Age of Information.* Cambridge: Cambridge University Press.

——. (2003a) 'Intelligence: The Achilles Heel of the Bush Doctrine', *Arms Control Today* 33/6, July/August.

——. (2003b) *Reshaping National Intelligence for an Age of Information.* Cambridge: Cambridge University Press.

Trinquier, R. (1964) *Modern Warfare: A French View of Counterinsurgency.* New York: Praeger.

Tse-Tung, Mao (1961) *Mao Tse-Tung on Guerrilla Warfare.* New York: Praeger.

—— (1966) *Selected Military Writings of Mao Tse-Tung.* Peking: Foreign Languages Press.

—— (1967) *Selected Military Writings of Mao Tse-Tung*, 2nd edn. Peking: Foreign Language Press.

United Nations (1992) *An Agenda for Peace. Preventive Diplomacy, Peacemaking and Peacekeeping. Report of the Secretary-General Pursuant to the Statement Adopted by the Summit Meeting of the Security Council on 31 January 1992.* New York: United Nations. Available at http://www.unh.org/Docs/SG/agpeace.html

—— (2000) Resolution 1296. Available at http://daccessdds.un.org/doc/UNDOC/GEN/Noo/399/03/PDF/Noo39903.pdf?OpenElement

—— Peacekeeping (2011), 'Background Note: United Nations Peacekeeping'. Available at www.un.org/en/peacekeeping/documents/backgroundnote.pdf

—— (2011) 'World Population to reach 10 Billion by 2100 if Fertility in all Countries Converges to Replacement Level', May 3, United Nations Press Release http://esa.un.org/wpp/Other-Information/Press_Release_WPP2010.pdf

—— Security Council Department of Public Information (2011) 'Security Council Approves "No-Fly Zone" over Libya, Authorizing 'All Necessary Measures' to Protect Civilians, by Vote of 10 in Favour with 5 Abstentions,' SC/10200, 17 March. Available at http://www.un.org/News/Press/docs/2011/sc10200.doc.htm

—— Blue Book Series. New York: United Nations.

—— (1945) Charter of the United Nations. New York: United Nations. Available at http://www.un.org/en/documents/charter

—— (1949) The Geneva Convention. New York: United Nations. Available at http://www.unhchr.ch/html/menu3/b/91.htm

UK Army Field Manual (1995) Wider Peacekeeping. London: HMSO.

US Army/Marine Corps (2007) Principles of Counterinsurgency from FM 3-24, Counterinsurgency Field Manual. Chicago: University of Chicago Press.

US Army Military History Institute (2002) Operation Enduring Freedom, Strategic Studies Institute Research Collection, Tape 032602a, CPT H. et al.; Memorandum for the Record, CPT H. int., 2 July 2002.

—— (2003) Operation Enduring Freedom, Strategic Studies Institute Research Collection, Tape 042403a2sb St Col al Saadi int.

US Department of Homeland Security (2003) Characteristics and Common Vulnerabilities Report for Chemical Facilities, version 1, revision 1. Washington, DC: US Department of Homeland Security.

US Department of Justice (2005) Office of the Inspector General, A Review of the FBI's Handling of Intelligence Information Related to the September 11 Attacks. Washington. DC: Office of the Inspector General, November 2004; redacted and unclassified: released publicly June .

US Joint Chiefs of Staff (2004) Joint Doctrine for Combating Weapons of Mass Destruction. Washington, DC: Department of Defense.

—— (2011) The National Military Strategy of the United States of America: Redefining America's Military Leadership. Washington, DC: Joint Chiefs of Staff.

US Joint Forces Command (2001) A Concept for Rapid Decisive Operations. Norfolk, VA: Joint Forces Command J9 Joint Futures Lab.

United States Strategic Command (2004) Strategic Deterrence Joint Operating Concept, Version 1.0. Offut Air Force Base, NE: U.S. Strategic Command.

United States White House (2002) The National Security Strategy of the United States of America. Available at http://www.white-house.gov/nsc/nss.pdf

Vasconcelos, Alvaro D. (2009) What Ambitions for European Defence in 2020? Paris: European Union Institute for Security Studies.

Vickers, Michael (1996) Warfare in 2020: A Primer. Washington, DC: Center for Strategic and Budgetary Assessments.

Von Hippel, Karin (2000) Democracy by Force: US Intervention in the Post-Cold War World. Cambridge: Cambridge University Press.

Wæver, O. and B. Buzan (2010) 'After the Return to Theory: The Past Present, and Future of Security Studies'. In A. Collins (ed.) Contemporary Security Studies, 463–83. Oxford: Oxford University Press.

Walker, William (2011) A Perpetual Menace: Nuclear Weapons and International Order. London: Routledge.

Wallace, W. (1996) 'Truth and Power, Monks and Technocrats: Theory and Practice in International Relations', Review of International Studies 22/3, 301–21.

Walt, S.M. (1991) 'The Renaissance of Security Studies', International Studies Quarterly 35, 211–39.

Waltz, K. N. (1959) Man, the State, and War. New York: Columbia University Press.

—— (1962) 'Kant Liberalism and War', American Political Science Review 56/2, 331–40.

Waltzer, Michael (1978) Just and Unjust Wars. London: Allen Lane.

Warner, M. (2002) 'Wanted: A Defintion of Intelligence', Studies in Intelligence 46/3, 21.

Weigley, Russell (1988) 'Political and Strategic Dimensions to Military Effectiveness'. In Allan R. Millett and Williamson Murray (eds) Military Effectiveness, vol. 3. The Second World War. Boston, MA: Allen & Unwin.

—— (1991) The Age of Battles: The Quest for Decisive Warfare. Bloomington, IN: Indiana University Press.

Weinberger, Sharon (2008) 'The Pentagon's Culture Wars,' Nature 455(2), 583–5.

Weiss, Thomas and Cindy Collins (2000) Humanitarian Challenges and Intervention: World Politics and the Dilemmas of Help. Boulder, CO: Westview Press.

Weller, Marc (2000) 'The US, Iraq and the Use of Force in a Unipolar World', Survival 41/4.

—— (2012) Iraq and the Use of Force in International Law. Oxford: Oxford University Press.

Welsh, J. (ed.) (2004) Humanitarian Intervention and International Relations. Oxford: Oxford University Press.

Weltman, John J. (1995) *World Politics and the Evolution of War*. Baltimore, MD and London: Johns Hopkins University Press.

Wendt, A. (1992) 'Anarchy is what States Make of it: The Social Construction of Power Politics', *International Organization*, 46/2, 391–426.

—— (1995) 'Constructing International Politics', *International Security* 20/1, 73–4.

—— (1999) *Social Theory of International Politics*. Cambridge: Cambridge University Press.

Wheeler, Nicholas J. (1999) 'Humanitarian Intervention in World Politics'. In John Baylis and Steve Smith (eds) *The Globalization of World Politics*. Oxford: Oxford University Press.

—— (2000) *Saving Strangers: Humanitarian Intervention in International Society*. Oxford: Oxford University Press.

—— and Alex Bellamy (2005).'Humanitarian Intervention and World Politics'. In John Baylis and Steve Smith (eds) *The Globalization of World Politics*. Oxford: Oxford University Press.

White, N. D. (1997) *Keeping the Peace*. Manchester: Manchester University Press.

Wheeler-Bennett, J. (1935) *The Pipe Dream of Peace: The Story of the Collapse of Disarmament*. New York: Morrow.

White House (1993) *Gulf War Air Power Survey*. Washington, DC: Government Printing Office.

—— (2000) *A National Security Strategy for a Global Age*. Washington, DC: Government Printing Office.

—— (2002) *National Strategy to Combat Weapons of Mass Destruction*. Washington, DC: Government Printing Office.

—— (2003) *National Strategy for Combating Terrorism*. Washington, DC: Government Printing Office.

—— (2006) *National Strategy for Combating Terrorism*, 2nd edn. Washington, DC: Government Printing Office.

Wilkinson, P. (1986) *Terrorism and the Liberal State*. London: Macmillan.

—— (2001) *Terrorism and Democracy: The Liberal State Response*. London: Frank Cass.

Williams, M. (1993) 'Neorealism and the Future of Strategy', *Review of International Studies* 19/2, 103–21.

Wilson, E. O. (1978) *On Human Nature*. Cambridge, MA: Harvard University Press.

Wilson, H. W. (1928) *The War Guilt*. London: Sampson Low.

Wilson, R. W. (2000) 'The Many Voices of Political Culture: Assessing Different Approaches', *World Politics* 52/2, 246–73.

Wohlstetter, Roberta (1962) *Pearl Harbor: Warning and Decision*. Stanford University Press.

Woodbury, G. L. (2004) Recommendations for Homeland Security Organizational Approaches at the State Government Level. Monterey: Naval Postgraduate School, Master's thesis.

Woolsey, J. (1998) Testimony to the Committee on National Security, US House of Representatives, 12 February.

Wright, Gordon (1968) *The Ordeal of Total War 1939–1945*. New York: Harper & Row.

Wright, M. C. (1956) *The Power Elite*. London: Oxford University Press.

Wylie, J. (1989) *Military Strategy: A General Theory of Power Control*. Annapolis, MD: Naval Institute Press.

Wyn Jones, Richard (1999) *Security, Strategy and Critical Theory*. Boulder, CO: Lynne Rienner.

Yin, T. (2011) '"Anything But Bush?": The Obama Administration and Guantanamo Bay', *Harvard Journal of Law and Public Policy*, 34/2, 453–92.

Zaborowski, Marcin (2004) 'From America's Protégé to Constructive European: Polish Security Policy in the Twenty-first Century', Occasional Paper No. 56, European Union Institute for Security Studies.

Zenko M. (2011) 'Libya: "Justifications" for Involvement', website of the Council on Foreign Relations, posted 24 June. Available at http://blogs.cfr.org/zenko/2011/06/24/libya-justifications-for-intervention/

Index

Abadie, A. 270
abstractionists 346, 347
Abu Ghraib prison 64, 367
academia
   development of strategic
      studies 343, 378–83, 384–6
   future of strategic studies 390
academic approach in strategic
      studies 6
Adefuye, A. 93
adversarial nature of strategy
      365–6
Afghanistan
   counterinsurgency
      strategies 165, 167
   irregular warfare 179, 181, 182,
      186, 187
   peace operations 291, 299
   revolution in military affairs 235
   September 11 attacks 69
   Soviet invasion 56, 163, 179
   strategic culture 89
   strategic narrative 363
   Taliban 174, 248, 249–55,
      259–60, 263, 264
   US military transformation 248,
      249–55, 263–4
   weak states' forces 234
African Union, peace
      operations 290, 291
aid agencies 296
Aideed, General Mohammed
      Farah 62, 289, 296, 297
AIDS 335, 337
air warfare
   evolution of modern warfare 50,
      53–4
   geography and strategy 116–17,
      123, 124–7
   peace operations 298–9
   power 231, 237–8, 239,
      240, 242
   revolution in military
      affairs 236–7
   technology 141–2
   USA 298
aircraft carriers 54
al-Qaeda
   demographics 329
   high and low politics 324–5
   homeland security 272, 278
   intelligence 156, 166

irregular warfare 174, 181,
      182–3, 186, 187, 188, 190,
      191, 192
   strategic culture 90
   strategic plan 269, 270
   strategic studies 12
   strategic surprise 161–2
   strategic theory 62, 69, 73
   US military transformation 249,
      250–3, 260, 264
   WMDs 218
   see also September 11 terrorist
      attacks
Alai, Haji Gul 253
Alanbrooke, Field Marshal Sir 372
Albright, Madeline 64
Alexander the Great 372
Algerian insurgency 187
Almond, Gabriel 78, 79
American Anthropological
      Association 89
American Civil War 45, 46–7
American War of Independence 63
amnesty 188
Amnesty International 111
amphibious operations 54
anarchy
   classical realist tradition 8
   Hobbesian 26, 35
   international 25–6
animal behaviourism 29–30
Annan, Kofi 290
anthrax 191, 216
Anti-Ballistic Missile (ABM)
      Treaty 204, 218
antimatter bombs 209
Arab–Israeli conflict 55, 147
Arab League 108
Arab Revolt 179
Arab Spring
   intelligence 166
   internal and inter-state
      conflicts 35
   nuclear weapons 211
   power 244
   social media 271
Ardrey, Robert 28
Argentina
   Falklands war 24, 31–2
   Great Paraguayan War 47
Armée Liberation Nationale 187
armies see land warfare

arms control 214, 224–7
   cold war 214–17
   definitions 215
   historical context 361
   post-cold war era 218–20
   treaties 206
arms races
   as cause of war 23
   technology 142–3
ARPANET 143
artificial intelligence 148
Arusha Accords 290
Asahara, Shoko 192
Aspin, Les 221, 222
assertive disarmament 207
Atlantic Charter 183
Atta, General Muhammad 252
attrition versus manoeuvre 119
Aum Shinrikyo 191, 192, 272
Australia
   power 234, 239
   strategic culture 81
Austro–Prussian War 46
avian influenza 336, 338
al-Awlaki, Anwar 191

Bader Meinhoff Gang 272
Baldwin, Stanley 125
Balkanization 36
ballistic missile defences
      (BMD) 204, 210, 216–17
ballistic missiles 199, 201, 210, 216–17
al-Bana, Hasan 73
Bangladesh, peace operations 290
Baring, Sir Evelyn 33
Barkawi, Tarak 350, 351
Basque separatists 270
Beaufre, Andre 4, 5
Belarus, nuclear weapons 196
Belgium, peace operations 290
Berenhorst, Georg Heinrich von 43
Berger, Thomas 85
Bethmann-Hollweg, Theobald
      von 103
Betts, Richard K. 6, 13, 73, 220
   intelligence 163
Betz, David J. 306, 307
Biddle, Stephen 6, 282
Bin Laden, Osama
   elimination 156, 166
   intelligence 156, 166

Bin Laden, Osama (*continued*)
  irregular warfare 181, 190, 192
  US military transformation 252,
    253, 254
biodiversity, threats to 330
biological warfare 130, 191, 216,
    218, 219, 220
  economic costs 292
  see also weapons of mass
    destruction
Biological Weapons Convention
    (BWC)/Biological and
    Toxin Weapons Convention
    (BTWC) 216, 218, 219, 225
biotechnologies 148
Black September 269, 270
Blair, Dennis 167
Blair, Tony 25
blitzkrieg 51, 53
Blomberg, S. 270
body bags effect 294
Boer Wars 47
Bolivia, irregular warfare 180
bombs
  antimatter 209
  technology 142, 145
Booth, Ken 79–80, 347–8, 349, 350
border security 274, 276–7
Bosnia
  new world order 233
  peace operation 288–90, 291,
    293, 296
    air power 298
    media 293
  strategic culture 86
  technology 139
Boulding, Kenneth 30
Boutros-Ghali, Boutros 289
bovine spongiform
    encephalopathy 337
Brahimi Report 291
Brazil
  cyberpower 315
  Great Paraguayan War 47
  irregular warfare 178, 181
  power 243
Breuning, M. 82
bridge, strategy 364, 371
Brodie, Bernard 2, 6, 10, 343, 360
  and criticisms of 346
  intelligence 157
  nuclear weapons 198
  strategic theory 5–6, 61
Bull, Hedley 37
  arms control and
    disarmament 215
  and criticisms of 342, 345–6,
    347, 350, 351
Bunn, Elaine 92

bureaucratization, and evolution of
    modern warfare 40
Bush, George H. W. 294
Bush, George W.
  Guantanamo Bay 111
  homeland security 268
  intelligence 161–2, 164, 165
  Iraq War 25
  September 11 terrorist
    attacks 161–2, 164
  strategic culture 85
  WMDs 222, 224
Butcher, Martin 222
Butterfield, Herbert 7, 32
Buzan, B. 13, 216, 343

Callwell, C. E. 46
Calvert, John 81–2
Campaign for Nuclear
    Disarmament (CND) 349
Canada, power 234, 239
Carr, E. H. 21
Carr, Jeffrey 305
Carter, Jimmy 217
Cartwright, General James E. 305
Cashman, Greg 31
Castro, Fidel 177
causes of war 19–23, 34–8
  efficient and permissive 24–7
  frustration explanations 30
  group explanations 33–4
  human nature explanations
    28–34
  immediate and underlying 23–4
  misperception explanations
    30–3
  necessary and sufficient 27
Cebrowski, Vice Admiral Arthur
    K. 72
censorship 51
centralization, and evolution of
    modern warfare 40
centre of gravity, enemy's 67
Cha, Victor 90
Chamberlain, Neville 24, 31
character of strategy, understanding
    the 364–6
Chayes, Sarah 363
Chechnya 145, 147, 179, 192, 292
chemical warfare 191, 216, 218,
    219, 220
  economic costs 271
  homeland security 278
  US stockpile, elimination of 333
  see also weapons of mass
    destruction
Chemical Weapons Convention
    (CWC) 218, 219

China
  army 231, 242
  cyberpower 315
  humanitarian intervention 293
  irregular warfare 180
  Korean War 67
  Kosovo Embassy, bombing
    of 298
  military expenditure 140, 242
  nuclear weapons 196, 200, 203,
    205, 210
    arms control 215
    nuclear testing 215
    strategic culture 93
  power 231, 234, 239, 240, 241,
    242, 243–4
  revolution in military affairs 140
  strategic culture 84, 85, 93
  Syrian war 108–9
  systems integration 143
  UN Security Council 293
cholera 336
Churchill, Winston 31, 152
Cimbala, Stephen 329
civil wars
  causes 34–6
  evolution of modern warfare 56
civilian technologies 143–4
civilians
  military human resources
    challenges 146
  peace operations 296
  as strategists 342–5, 387–9
  targeting of 50, 52
civilizations, conflicts between 36
classical realist tradition 7–9
Clausewitz, Carl von 359
  and criticisms of 352
  cyberwar 311
  dimensions of strategy 7
  evolution of modern warfare 40,
    43–4, 48
  geography and strategy 116
  imperfect information 383
  intelligence 152, 162
  international law 104, 105
  intra-state conflict 12
  irregular warfare 174, 179, 190,
    193
  law as political instrument 62
  strategic culture 78, 82
  strategic theory 61, 63, 64, 65–9,
    72, 73, 74
  strategy defined 4, 5, 11
  and Sun Tzu, ideas compared 70,
    71, 383
  technology 140
climate, and strategic culture
    80–1

Clinton, Bill
humanitarian interventions 294
peace operations 289
WMDs 218, 221, 223
close combat
Afghanistan 251-4
Iraq 255-7
CNN effect, humanitarian
intervention 293-4
Cochrane, James 84
Cohen, Eliot 298
Cohn, Carol 353-4
cold war 55-6, 232
environmental damage 333-4
high and low politics 324
humanitarian intervention 287
intelligence 157-9
nuclear weapons 23, 196,
198-201, 204
arms control 214-17, 224-5
space war 128
strategic culture 79, 81
strategic studies 2-3, 379-82
Collins, Michael 372
colonial warfare 46
Columb, Admiral 48
Columbia, insurgency 177
command, control, communications,
computers, intelligence,
surveillance, and
reconnaissance (C4ISR)
235, 236, 239
commercial technology, rise
of 143-4
commons issues 329-32
communications
evolution of modern warfare 45
and frequency of terror 271-2
homeland security 268
low politics 324
power and warfare 238-9
revolutionary insurgency 120
compartmentation in
intelligence 162
Comprehensive Test Ban Treaty
(CTBT) 218, 226, 227
Condorcet, M. 326
Confucius 29
Congo, peacekeeping 288, 290
conscription 41, 51, 119
constructivism 387
strategic culture 83-4
contexts for strategy 366-9
contract law 98
Convention on the Prohibition
of Anti-Personnel
Landmines 111
Cooperative Threat Reduction
Programme 226

Corbett, Sir Julian 48
Cornish, Paul 89
corps system, and evolution of
modern warfare 42
cosmopolitanism 86
Costa Mendez, Dr Nicanor 32
counterespionage 153, 156
counterforce threats 198
counterinsurgency and
counterterrorism 184-9, 269
geography and strategy 120
intelligence 161-2, 165, 275, 276
practice of strategy 362, 367
principles, prerequisites, and
laws 185-6
strategic culture 89
US military transformation 248
see also homeland security
counterintelligence 153, 156
counterproliferation 202, 205-7,
210, 220-2
challenges 222-3
emergence 222
Counterproliferation Initiative
(CPI) 221, 222
counter-revolution 235-7
counterterrorism see counterinsurgency and counterterrorism
countervalue threats 198
covert action 156
credibility
cyber deterrence 313
nuclear weapons 199
Creveld, Martin van 137, 329
Crimean War 46
critical security studies 349
criticisms of strategic studies 9-13,
341-2, 356-7
approaches 348-54
continuing debate? 355-6
'Golden Age' 342-5
strategists' responses 345-8
crowd psychology 33
cruise missiles 201
Cruz, Consuelo 88
Cuban missile crisis
arms control 214, 215
strategic surprise 161, 162, 163-4
Cuban revolution 177
culture
political 78-9
strategic see strategic culture
cyber-attacks see cyberwar and
cyber-attacks
cyber deterrence 313-14
cyber security 312-14
cyberwar and cyber-attacks
129-30, 148, 191-2,
311-15, 317

Arab-Israeli conflict 147
challenges and unknowns 314
change in the character of
war? 316
cyber security 312-14
definitions 307-8
homeland security 278
power 239
strategic theory 73
see also cyberpower; cyberspace
cyberpower 303-4, 308, 317-19
attributes 310
definitions 304-8
new dimension for conflict
311-15
recasting of international
politics 315-16
revolution in military
affairs? 315-17
see also cyberwar and
cyber-attacks; cyberspace
cyberspace 303, 308, 317
characteristics 309-10
definitions 304-6, 308
global commons 310-11
infosphere 309
layers 306
revolution in military
affairs? 315, 316
see also cyberwar and
cyber-attacks; cyberpower
Cyprus 179

Darfur 290, 291
Dawkins, Richard 22, 29
DDT 135
Debray, Regis 180
decapitation strikes 201
deception
cyberpower 316
intelligence 152, 156, 162, 164
peace operations 297
power 239
Sun Tzu 71
decolonization 232, 233
defence intellectuals 351
defence organizations, and strategic
culture 81
defencism 86
deforestation 339
Dek, Kapil 57
Demchak, Chris C. 307, 308
democracy
causes of war 34
and demographics 329
evolution of modern warfare 40
nuclear weapons 203
technology 144, 145

demographics of global
politics 327–9
Denmark, strategic culture 85, 86
Denning, Dorothy 305
denuclearization 202, 207
depleted uranium (DU) 332
desertion from armies 41
deterrence
cyber 313–14
historical context 361
nuclear see nuclear deterrence
Deutsch, Karl 344, 347
diarrhoeal diseases 336
diplomacy, WMDs 223–4
disarmament 214–15
assertive 207
denuclearization 202, 207
see also arms control
disarming strikes 201
disease 135, 334–8
displacement 30
Dobbie, Colonel Charles 288
Dr Strangelove 343
Dostum, General Abdul Rashid 252
Douhet, Giulio 53, 125, 126
Doyle, Michael 34
'drones' 156
drugs, war on 326, 389
Du Teil, Jean 42
Duffield, John S. 86–7
Dutch Republic 41
Dymond, Jonathan 29
dysentery 336

Earle, Edward Mead 62
East Timor 87, 183
Ebel, Roland 84
Eckstein, Harry 84
Economic Community of West
African States Ceasefire
Monitoring Group
(ECOMOG) 291–2
economic costs
of homeland security 276, 277
of war 35, 237, 241–2, 270–1
cyberpower 316
economic disruption 278
economic sanctions 107
economic security 389
economic sensitivities and
vulnerabilities 338
economic warfare 122–3
economics and the practice of
strategy 368
Eden, Anthony 24
Eden, Lynn 88
education, strategic 359–63
Edwards, Geoffrey 89

Egypt
Israel, wars with
blitzkrieg 53
Yom Kippur War 161, 162
power 244
Einstein, Albert 28
Eisenhower, Dwight D. 152, 162,
296
electromagnetic spectrum
(EMS) 306, 309
Electronic Numerical Integrator and
Computer 304
Ellis, Richard 87
'end of history' 3
energy security 338
England see United Kingdom/Great
Britain/England
England, Gordon 305
entente cordiale 23
environmental damage 325, 327,
330, 332–4
environmental security 389
EOKA 179
eradication, irregular warfare
188–9
Ermarth, Fritz 86, 363
Estonia, Soviet war memorial 82
ethics see morality and ethics
ethnic conflict 12
causes 35–6
focus of strategic studies 380
ethnocentrism
criticisms of strategic studies 347
practice of strategy 362–3
strategic culture 80
European Security Strategy
(ESS) 88–9
European Union (EU)
Iraq War 106
strategic culture 88–90
evolution of modern warfare
39–40
industrialization of war 44–7
Napoleonic legacy 40–4
naval warfare 47–9
nuclear weapons and
revolutionary warfare 55–6
postmodern war 56–8
total war 49–54
executing strategies 369–71

Falklands war 24, 31–2
Fall, Bernard 176–7
fallout 201
Farrell, Theo 82–3
feminism 353
Feng, Huiyun 85
Finland, strategic culture 81, 85

First World War
air power 125
immediate and underlying
causes 23–4, 270
international law 103
naval warfare 48–9
power 232
technology 141
total warfare 50, 51, 52, 53, 54
fissile material 198
Fissile Material Cut-off Treaty
(FMCT) 226, 227
Flynn, S. 277
foco, theory of the 180
force, use of
and international law 102–5
in peace operations 288, 292
Forester, C. S. 135–6
fossil fuel depletion, as potential
cause of war 35
Foster, Gregory D. 4, 5
fourth generation warfare
(4GW) 189–90
France
Algerian insurgency 187
conscription 41, 119
entente cordiale 23
evolution of modern
warfare 41–4, 45, 46, 47
industrialization 45, 46
Napoleonic legacy 41–3
naval warfare 47
Libyan intervention 108
naval warfare 122
nuclear weapons 196, 200, 203,
205
arms control 215
nuclear testing 215
peace operations 290, 296
power 234, 239, 241, 242
Second World War
causes 31
liberation 296
total warfare 51
strategic culture 84
Franco–Austrian War 46
Franco–Prussian War 45, 46
Franklin, Benjamin 326
Franz Ferdinand, Archduke 23–4,
270
Freedman, Lawrence 92
Freud, Sigmund 28
friction 69, 73
and practice of strategy 369
Friedman, Thomas 270, 271
frustration explanation of war 30
Fuerzas Armadas Revolucionarias
de Colombia Ejército del
Pueblo (FARC) 177

Fukuyama, Francis 3
full force protection 298
Fuller, Major General J. F. C. 133,
    136, 378
future of strategic studies 377–8,
    390–1
    academic and policy
        worlds 384–6
    armed force, study of 388–90
    cold war, in and out of
        the 379–82
    development of strategic
        studies 378–9
    realism 386–7
    social science, crisis in 382–4

Gaddafi, Muammar
    NATO's intervention in
        Libya 297, 298
    overthrow 34–5
Galtieri, President 32
Galula, David 185
game theory 343, 345, 346, 383
Gardeazabal, J. 270
Garnett, J. C. 11
Garstka, John J. 72
Gaulle, Charles de 53
Gaza, Israel–Hamas conflict
    (2008) 35, 244
Geertz, Clifford 78
general theory of strategy 363–73,
    388
    classics of 359–61
    components 365
Geneva Conventions 109–10
Geneva law 109, 110
Geneva Protocol, biological
    weapons 219
geography and strategy 115, 130–1
    air power 124–7
    cyberspace war 129–30
    irregular warfare 179, 181, 182,
        186, 187
    land warfare 117–21
    lay of the land 116–17
    maritime strategy 121–4
    practice of strategy 368–9
    space war 128–9
    strategic culture 80–1
    US military transformation 251
George, Alexander 92
Georgia
    conflict with Russia (2008) 35,
        64, 234, 293
    geography 251
Germany
    First World War 48–9, 50
    irregular warfare 180

power 239
Second World War
    causes 31, 32, 33
    naval warfare 122
    total warfare 51–3
    strategic culture 84, 86, 88
Giap, General Vo Nguyen 180
Gibson, William 304
Giles, Gregory 92, 363
global economic crisis 166
    as potential cause of war 35
    sensitivities and
        vulnerabilities 338
Global Initiative to Combat Nuclear
    Terrorism 226
global issues, intelligence
    166–7
Global Nuclear Energy
    Partnership 226
global positioning system 137
global security 12
globalization, and strategic
    culture 90
Godwin, William 326
Goethe, Johann Wolfgang von 43
goodwill see public opinion
Gorbachev, Mikhail 159
governments, strategists' advice
    for 10–11
grand strategy 4, 364
Grant, Ulysses S. 372
gravity, enemy's centre of 67
Gray, Colin S.
    and criticisms of 346–7, 348,
        350, 355
    dimensions of strategy 7
    Napoleonic warfare 43
    practice of strategy 367
    strategic culture 79
    strategic studies in the
        academy 10
Great Britain see United Kingdom/
    Great Britain/England
Great Paraguayan War 47
Greece
    armies in classical Greece 231
    strategic culture 82
Green, Philip 9, 10, 343–4, 345,
    346, 347, 352–3
Griffith, Brigadier General Samuel
    B. 184
Grimslay, Mark 4, 5
Grivas-Dighenis, George 179
group explanations of war
    33–4
Guantanamo Bay 111
Guderian, Heinz 53
guerrilla warfare see irregular
    warfare

Guevara, Ernesto 'Che' 175, 181,
    182, 190
    foco, theory of the 180
Guibert, Jacques Antoine Hippolyte,
    Comte de 41
Gulf war (Operation Desert Storm)
    air power 298
    causes 24, 25, 31
    humanitarian intervention 34
    Kurds 292
    oil 330
    strategic theory 67, 68
    technology 136, 137, 139,
        141–2, 143
    WMDs 220, 244
Gulf War Syndrome 337
gunboat diplomacy 123–4, 236
Gwynn, Charles W. 185

Habr Gidr 62
Habyarimana, President 290
hackers and hacktivism 307
Hague Conventions 109
Hague law 109–10
Haiti 293
Hamas 273
    conflict with Israel (Gaza
        2008) 35
    power 244
Hamilton, Archie 332
Hansen, L. 13
Hardin, Garrett 329
Harland, Gordon 7–8
Hegel, G. W. F. 21
Henkin, Louis 97, 99
Henry IV 37
hepatitis B 336
hepatitis C 336
Herring, Eric 216, 349
Hess, G. 270
Hezbollah
    conflict with Israel 35, 144
    irregular warfare 176
    power 244
    technology 143
hidden targets, finding
    (Afghanistan) 250–1
historian, strategist as shrewd
    361–2
historical context, and practice of
    strategy 369
history, 'end of' 3
Hitler, Adolf
    causes of Second World War 24,
        31, 32, 33
    intelligence 162
    total warfare 51
HIV 335

Hobbes, Thomas 7
   anarchy 26, 35
Hoffer, Eric 33
homeland defense 269
homeland security 267–8, 282–5
   new threat? 268–73
   preparations 273–81
   small-N problem 273–4
Homer-Dixon, Thomas 325
Horner, Lieutenant General
      Charles A. 64
Howard, Sir Michael 7, 351, 368
Hudson, Valerie 83
human intelligence (HUMINT) 154,
      155, 160
human nature 7–8
   explanations of war 21–2, 28–34
   practice of strategy 366
Human Rights Watch 111
Human Terrain System (HTS) 89
humanitarian intervention 34,
      286–8, 300–2
   disease 337
   permissive causes of war 25
   politics 292–5
   problems and prospects 300
   tsunami (2004) 124, 326
humanitarian law, international
      (IHL) 109–12
Huntington, Samuel 36, 189
Hurd, Douglas 226
Hurd, Ian 99, 100
Hutus 290
Hyde-Price, Adrian 91
Hymans, Jacques 87
hyperpower 233–5

ideas, war of 282
identity politics 57
imagery intelligence (IMINT) 155
imagination, strategic 389
impartiality, and peace
      operations 292
improvised explosive devices
      (IEDs) 145
India
   cyberpower 315
   Mumbai attacks (2008) 184, 191
   nuclear weapons 196, 203, 205,
      210, 211, 215, 218, 227
   power 239–40, 241, 242, 243
   strategic culture 84
Indo-China war 34
Indonesia
   cyberwar 191
   East Timor 87, 183
Industrial Revolution 122
industrialization of war 40, 44–7

influenza 334, 336
information glut 165–6
information technology 143, 146–7
   intelligence 165–6
   irregular warfare 191–2
   social media 271
   see also cyberpower
information warfare 129–30
infosphere 309
institutions
   classical realist tradition 8–9
   low politics 324
   power 232
   preparation for war 368
insurgency 173–4, 192–4
   counterinsurgency 184–9
   definitions 174–6
   now and in the future 189–92
   theory and practice 176–83
   see also irregular warfare
intelligence 151–2, 168–9
   analysis 154–5
   Clausewitz 71
   collection 154, 155
   community, evolution 159–60
   definitions 153
   as enabler of US strategy
      153–60
   failures, inevitability of 163
   homeland security 274, 275–6,
      282
   Mao 71–2
   nature of 153–7
   peace operations 297
   post-9/11 164–7
   practice of strategy 370
   space war 128–9
   special intelligence missions 156
   strategic surprise 160–4
   Sun Tzu 70–1
Intelligence Reform and Terrorism
      Prevention Act 2004 (IRTPA,
      USA) 164–5
intercontinental ballistic missiles
      (ICBMs) 199, 210
Intermediate Nuclear Force (INF)
      Agreement 217
internal security 389
internal wars see civil wars
International Atomic Energy Agency
      (IAEA) 198, 208, 219
   Iran 224
   Iraq 206, 220
International Court of Justice
      (ICJ) 98
International Criminal Court
      (ICC) 98, 111–12, 291
international humanitarian law
      (IHL) 109–12

international law see law,
      international
International Peace Research
      Institute, Oslo (PRIO) 325
international relations 349, 381,
      382–3
   post-positivist turn 349
   strategic culture 81
Internet 304
   cyberspace war see cyberwar and
      cyber-attacks
   intelligence 154, 166
   low politics 324
Iran
   intelligence 160
   irregular warfare 181
   new world order 233
   nuclear weapons 200, 202, 203,
      206, 210, 211, 216, 225, 227
      assertive disarmament 207
      diplomatic option 223, 224
      strategic culture 91, 92
      Stuxnet attack 130, 148, 311,
         312, 314
   power 241, 244
   strategic narrative 363
   war with Iraq 25
Iraq
   Abu Ghraib prison 64, 367
   army 63, 140, 141
   Ba'ath Party, overthrow and
      banning of 63, 68, 248, 262
   counterinsurgency strate-
      gies 165
   geography 251
   invasion of Kuwait 24, 25, 31, 68
      international law 101
   irregular warfare 67, 181, 186,
      187, 190
   jihad, popular support and
      negative measures 183
   Kurds 292
   new world order 233
   revolution in military af-
      fairs 235–6
   strategic culture 89
   US military transformation
      255–63
   war with Iran 25
   WMDs 206, 207, 220, 222, 223,
      225
   intelligence 159–60, 163, 164
   see also Gulf War; Iraq War
Iraq War
   causes 25, 31
   friction 69
   humanitarian issues 34, 299
   intelligence failures 71
   international law 106, 108, 111

irregular warfare 63, 67, 179
land warfare 117
media 147
power 238, 239
strategic theory 68
technology 139, 144-5
unintended consequences 366
US military transformation 248,
249, 255-64
WMDs 222, 225
ironic effects resulting from
strategy 366
irregular warfare 173-4, 192-4
colonial warfare 46
counterinsurgency and
counterterrorism 184-9
definitions 174-6
Napoleonic legacy 42
now and in the future
189-92
power 245
practice of strategy 362, 367
technology 145
see also insurgency; terrorism
Islamic extremism
homeland security 269, 270,
272, 282
irregular warfare 174, 190
strategic theory 62
unintended consequences of
strategy 366
see also al-Qaeda; Taliban
isolation, irregular warfare 187
Israel
cyberwar 312, 314
Egypt, wars with 53
Hamas conflict (Gaza 2008) 35,
244
Hezbollah conflict 35, 144,
244
media 147
nuclear weapons 196, 205, 207,
208, 216, 227
Osirak attack 223
Palestine 269-70
targeted killings 272
power 232, 234, 237, 244
strategic culture 81
Syria attack 225
technology 134, 143, 145
Yom Kippur War 161, 162
nuclear weapons 208
Italy
causes of Second World War 31
Red Brigade 269

Jackson, Robert 104
Jansen, Johannes 174

Japan
power 232, 234, 238, 240, 241,
242, 243, 244
Second World War 52, 53, 78
strategic culture 78, 84, 85, 86,
87, 88
systems integration 143
Jemaah Islamiyah 273
Jervis, Robert 30, 347, 348
jet engines 143
jet fuel, jettisoning of 332
Jeune Ecole 48, 49
jihadists
Iraq, popular support and
negative measures 183
strategic theory 70, 72
Johnson, Jeannie 77
Johnston, Alastair Iain 80, 83-4
Johnston Atoll Chemical Agent Disposal System (JACADS) 333
Joint Strike Fighters (JSFs) 134
Jomini, Baron Antoine-Henri de 48,
360
Jordan
irregular warfare 181
power 244
journalists, strategic studies 381
jus ad bellum 102-3, 105-9
jus in bello 102, 103, 105, 109-12
justice, pursuit of 37-8

Kagame, Paul 290
Kahn, Herman 2, 6, 343, 344
and criticisms of 346, 352
game theory 345
intelligence 157
moral issues 9
parody 343
Kant, Immanuel 342
Kartchner, Kerry 77, 91, 93
Karzai, Hamid 252
Katzenstein, Peter J. 13
Kautilya, Vishnugupta Chanakya 82
Kazakhstan, nuclear weapons 196
Keegan, John 72
Kellogg-Briand Pact 206
Kennan, George 157
Kennedy, John F. 161, 164
Kent, Sherman 153, 157,
158, 163
Kenyon, Ian 91
Keohane, Robert 113, 338
Khan, A. Q. 202
Khomeini, Ayatollah 363
Kier, Elizabeth 84
Kim Jong-Il 92
Kipp, Jacob 89
Kiras, James 90

Kissinger, Henry 2, 6
intelligence 159
strategy 5
WMDs 226
Kitchener, Lord 136
Kitson, Frank 185
Klare, Michael 330
Klein, Bradley S. 12-13, 349-51,
354
Knopf, Jeffrey 91
Kony, Joseph 299
Korean War
China's entry 67
land warfare 117
limited warfare 55-6
US losses 68
Kosal, M. 278
Kosovo War
humanitarian intervention 291,
292, 293
air power 298-9
public opinion 297, 298
power 238
revolution in military affairs 235
strategic theory 64
technology 139
Kubrick, Stanley 343
Kuehl, Daniel T. 306, 307
Kuhn, Colonel Klaus 104
Kupchan, Charles 88
Kuwait
air power 298-9
Iraqi invasion 24, 25, 31, 68
international law 101
liberation 296

Laffey, M. 350
land warfare
evolution of modern warfare
industrialization of war 44-7
Napoleonic legacy 41-3
geography 116-21
manoeuvre versus attrition 119
power 231, 238, 239, 242
revolution in military affairs
236-7
language of strategic studies 352-4
Larsen, Jeffrey 77
Lauterpacht, Sir Hersch 97, 102
law, international 96, 112-14, 238
breaches 101-2
classical realist tradition 8-9
coercion, self-interest, and
legitimacy 99-101
efficacy 97-8
force, use of 102-5
jus ad bellum 105-9
jus in bello 109-12

law, international (*continued*)
  obedience, reasons for 98–102
  peace operations 291
  perception–reality gap 97–8
law enforcement, homeland
      security 275–6
Lawrence, P. 349
Lawrence, T. E. 175, 179
Le Bon, G. 33
League of Nations 9
Lebanon
  Israel versus Hezbollah
      conflict 35, 144, 244
  technology 143
Lee, Robert E. 372
Lee, Steven P. 10
legitimacy, irregular warfare 181–3
Legro, Jeffrey 84
Lévi-Strauss, Claude 78
Levy, J. S. 35
Levy, Marc 325
Liberation Tamil Tigers of Eelam
      (LTTE) 177
Liberia 291–2
Libicki, Martin C. 305, 306
Libya
  nuclear weapons 202
  war (2011)
    causes 25, 34–5
    humanitarian intervention 291,
        297, 298, 299
    intelligence 166
    international law 108
    power 234
Liddell Hart, Basil H. 360, 378
  blitzkrieg 53
  strategic theory 70
  strategy defined 4, 5
  war as political instrument 62
Lindley-French, Julian 89–90
Lisbon Treaty (2009) 89, 90
location, irregular warfare 184–6
Lockerbie bombing 189
logistics, and the practice of
      strategy 368, 369–70
Long, Mark 90
longbows 137
Lord's Resistance Army 299
Lorenz, Konrad 28
Louis XVI 41
Ludendorf, Erich 52
Luttwak, Edward N. 360
Lyautey, Marshal 188
Lyme disease 337

McConnell, Vice-Admiral Mike
      307
McCoubrey, Hilaire 98

machine guns 45
Mackinder, Sir Halford 48
mad cow disease 337
Mahan, Alfred Thayer 47–8, 121–2,
      350
Mahnken, Thomas 85
making strategies 366–9
malaria 336
malicious software (malware) 312,
      314
  Stuxnet attack 130, 148, 191,
      311, 312, 314
Malthus, Thomas Robert 325,
      326
management studies 382–3
manoeuvre versus attrition 119
Mao Tse-tung
  irregular warfare 180, 182, 190
    stages of insurgency 177, 178
    'Three Rules and Eight
        Remarks' 181, 182
  strategic theory 70, 71–2, 73
Marighella, Carlos 178, 180, 181,
      182
maritime strategy *see* naval warfare
      and maritime strategy
Marshall, Andrew 57
Marx, Karl 390
Marxist terrorist groups 180
Matthews, Ken 97
Mead, Margaret 78
measles 337
media 35
  global coverage 166
  humanitarian intervention 293,
      294
  international law 111
  technology 147
megacities 328
Meilinger, Philip 72
Meyer, Christoph 89
Middle East War (Six-Day War) 161
military administrations, and
      practice of strategy 368
military balances 239–41
military culture 84
military doctrine, and practice of
      strategy 370–1
military revolutions 57
military science 6
military strategy 364
military studies 379
mindset problem, intelligence 162,
      163
misperception explanations of
      war 30–3
Montecucolli, Raimondo de 118
Montesquieu, Baron de la Brède
      et de 41

morality and ethics
  classical realist tradition 8–9
  practice of strategy 367
  strategic studies 9–10
    criticisms 343–4, 345, 348–9,
        352
Morgenthau, Hans 8
Morocco, irregular warfare 188
Moscow Treaty (Strategic Of-
      fensive Reductions Treaty,
      SORT) 206, 218, 227
Müller, Harald 221, 224
multiple independently targ-
      etable re-entry vehicles
      (MIRVs) 199, 217
Murray, Williamson 4, 5, 57
muskets 136, 137
Mussolini, Benito 31
mutual assured destruction
      (MAD) 204, 210, 348
myths, and strategic culture 81–2

Naji, Abu Bakr 73
nanotechnologies 148, 165–6, 227
Napoleon Bonaparte
  evolution of modern war-
      fare 40–4, 47
  experience, sources of 361
  intelligence 152
  naval warfare 122
  technology 136
Narodna Odbrana 270
Nasser, Gamal Abdel 24
Nasution, Abdul Haris 181
nation-building 81
National Intelligence Estimates,
      USA 158
national liberation, wars of 174
nationalism 40, 51
NATO *see* North Atlantic Treaty
      Organization
nature of strategy, understanding
      the 364–6
naval warfare and maritime strategy
  and air power 123
  evolution of modern
      warfare 47–9, 53
  geography and strategy 116–17,
      121–4
  power 231, 238, 239, 240, 242
  revolution in military
      affairs 236–7
Negroponte, John 166
neo-institutionalists 324
neo-traditionalists 346
net-centric warfare (NCW) 235,
      236
netspeed 310

'New Abolitionists' 226
new agenda for security and
        strategy 323-5, 339-40
    commons issues 329-32
    conceptual framework 325-7
    cyberpower 311-15
    demographics of global poli-
        tics 327-9
    disease 334-8
    environmental damage 332-4
    sensitivities and
        vulnerabilities 338-9
New START treaty 206, 210,
        227
new world orders 232-4
Newman, J. R. 9
Niebuhr, Rheinold
    causes of war 30, 33
    morality 8
Nietzsche, Friedrich 33
Nigeria, strategic culture 93
Nixon, Richard 159
Nogee, Joseph 215
non-governmental organizations
        (NGOs)
    international law 111
    low politics 324
non-proliferation, nuclear
        weapons 205-7, 210,
        215-16, 225, 226
Non-Proliferation Treaty
        (NPT) 205-6, 215-16, 218,
        219, 223, 225, 227
'New Abolitionists' 226
norms, and strategic culture
        82-3
North Atlantic Treaty Organization
        (NATO)
    Afghanistan 299
    air power 298-9
    expansion plans 218
    humanitarian intervention 291,
        293, 298
        Bosnia 289
        Kosovo 64, 297, 298-9
        Libya 297, 298
    strategic studies' role 351
North Korea
    intelligence 160
    nuclear weapons 196, 200, 202,
        203, 205, 206-7, 209, 210,
        211, 216, 225, 227
        assertive disarmament 207
        diplomatic option 223-4
        strategic culture 91, 92
    peacekeeping 288
    power 234, 239, 243
    strategic culture 86, 91, 92
Norway, strategic culture 81, 85

nuclear deterrence 22, 196,
        198-209, 210
    criticisms of strategic
        studies 344-5, 347-8, 350-1
    evolution of modern warfare 55,
        56
    focus of strategic studies 379-80
    language of strategic studies 352
    moral issues 9
    strategic culture 79-80, 91-2
Nuclear Freeze movement 349
nuclear powers, growth in the
        number of 196
Nuclear Security Summit
        (2010) 226
nuclear taboo 207-8, 209
nuclear weapons 195-7, 209-12,
        216, 219, 220
    air power 125
    arms control treaties 206
    cold war 214-17
        residual role 218
    criticisms of strategic
        studies 342, 343-9
    deterrence see nuclear
        deterrence
    development of strategic
        studies 2, 3, 343
    diplomatic option 223-4
    environmental damage 333
    evolution of modern warfare 51,
        52, 55-6
    First Nuclear Age 197-200
    focus of strategic studies 379-80
    force levels worldwide 200
    language of strategic studies 352-4
    moral issues 9
    practice of strategy 362
    Second Nuclear Age
        adapting to the 205-9
        risks 200-5
    Stuxnet attack 130, 148, 311,
        312, 314
    technology 137
    terminology 201
    testing 215
    unstable nuclear states 203
    see also weapons of mass
        destruction
Nunn, Sam 226
Nunn-Lugar Cooperative Threat
        Reduction Program 277
Nuremberg Tribunals 110
Nye, Joseph 10, 307, 338

O'Brian, Patrick 136
Obama, Barack
    Guantanamo Bay 111

intelligence 166
    peace operations 299
        Libya 297, 299
    WMDs 224, 226, 228
Ogarkov, Nikolai 139
oil 35, 257, 258, 259, 330
    peak 338
Omar, Mullah Muhammad 252
Open Skies agreement 214
open source intelligence
        (OPINT) 154, 155
Organization for the Prohibition
        of Chemical Weapons
        (OPCW) 218, 219, 225
organizational culture 84, 88
Orphanides, A. 270
Osgood, Robert 4, 5
Owen, David 226
Owens, Admiral William A. 72,
        139-40

Paixans, General 47
Pakistan
    nuclear weapons 196, 202, 203,
        205, 209, 211, 218, 227
    power 239-40, 243
Palestine 269-70, 272
parachute operations 54, 137-8
Paraguay 47
Parsons, Talcott 78, 79
Partial Test Ban Treaty 215, 324
Pauling, Linus 37
Payne, Keith 91, 348
peace 26, 37-8
peace dividend 3
peace operations 286-92, 300-2
    military character 295-9
    problems and prospects 300
peacekeeping 287-92
Pentagon attack see September 11
        terrorist attacks
Perkovich, George 223
Perry, William 226
Petroski, Henry 133
Philippines
    geography 251
    irregular warfare 189
pillage 41, 42
poison gas 50
Poland, strategic culture 93
policy advocacy by strategists
        10-11, 351-2
policy world 384-6
political culture 78-9
political mobilization, and
        transnational norms 83
political structure, and strategic
        culture 81

politics
  high and low 324–5, 327, 338
  of humanitarian interven-
      tion 292–5
  and practice of strategy 364–5,
      366–7
  recasting of international politics
      by cyberpower 315–16
  strategic studies 382, 383
Popular Front for the Liberation of
    Palestine (PFLP) 269–70
population growth 325–6, 327–9
postmodern war 56–8
power and war 2, 230, 242–6
  arms 241
  arts of war 237–9
  classical realist tradition 8
  cyberpower see cyberpower
  future for power relations 243
  history 231–2
  and hyperpower 234–5
  intricacies 232
  military balances 239–41
  new world orders 232–4
  revolution and counter-
      revolution 235–7
  world on the scales 241–2
practice of strategy 358, 374–6
  consummate (re)assessor 373–4
  general theory 363–73
  improving a strategic
      education 359–63
  strategic expertise 359
pre-emptive and preventive
    strategies
  homeland security 279–81
  intelligence 165
  WMDs 222, 223
Princip, Gavrillo 270
Proliferation Security Initiative
    (PSI) 207, 223, 226
propaganda 129
  irregular warfare 187
  power 239
  total warfare 51
Prussia
  evolution of modern warfare 43,
      44, 45, 46
  power 232
psychological causes of war 30–1
psychological dimensions of military
    technology 136, 137
psychological warfare
  irregular warfare 188
  power 239
public opinion
  humanitarian intervention
      293–4
  irregular warfare 179–80, 182–3

land warfare 117
peace operations 297–9
Pye, Lucian 78

al-Qadhafi, Muammar
  NATO's intervention in
      Libya 297, 298
  overthrow 34–5
al-Quarashi, Abu' Ubayd 73

radar 51
radio technology 135
radiological weapons 216
  see also weapons of mass
      destruction
Raglan, Lord 136
railways, and evolution of modern
    warfare 44–5, 46, 139
Rapoport, Anatol 11, 343–5,
    346
rational choice theory 383
Rattray, Gregory J. 305
Reagan, Ronald
  arms control 217
  and criticisms of 348, 349
  intelligence 159
realism 2–3
  classical realist tradition 7–9
  international law 97, 99
  low politics 324
  old and new 386–8
  reconstructive critique of
      strategy 346
Red Cross 110
refugees, and disease 337
Reiss, Mitchell 221
religion
  as cause of war 36
  irregular warfare 190
  see also Islamic extremism
repeating weapons 45
reputational benefits of obeying the
    law 100
research and development 143,
    144
resources
  practice of strategy 368
  strategic culture 80–1
respiratory infections 336
Revere, Paul 152
revolutionary warfare
  evolution of modern
      warfare 55–6
  geography and strategy
      120
revolutions in military affairs
    (RMAs) 57, 235–7

arts of war 237
criticisms of strategic studies 352
cyberpower 315–17
technology and warfare 138–46
ricin 216
Rifkind, Malcolm 226
rifled weapons 45, 46, 136, 139
Robertson, George 226
Robinson, Linda 67
robotics 148
rogue states 221
roles, state 82
Rosen, Stephen Peter 80, 84
Rote Armee Faktion 180
Rousseau, Jean-Jacques
  causes of war 25, 26, 29
  evolution of modern warfare 41
Rumsfeld, Donald 272
Russia
  Chechnya 145, 147, 179, 292
  environmental problems
      333–4
  Georgia 35, 64, 234, 293
  humanitarian intervention 293
  power 234, 241, 242, 243, 244
  strategic culture 86, 91
  Syrian war 108–9
  systems integration 143
  technology 145
  UN Security Council 293
  WMDs 227
  worldview 363
  see also Soviet Union
Russo–Japanese War 47
Rwanda 147, 233, 288–9, 290–1
Rwandan Patriotic Front (RPF) 290
Rynning, Sten 90, 91

Sadat, Anwar 162
Saddam Hussein
  causes of Gulf wars 24, 31
  government as hub of power 67
  insurgency 63, 67
  overthrow 68
  US military transformation 255,
      259, 262, 263, 264
  WMD capabilities 159–60, 164
St Petersburg Declaration 109
Saint Pierre, Abbé de 342
Samore, Gary 224
Saneyuki, Akiyama 48
sarin 272
SARS 336, 338
satellites 128–9
  civilian 144
  navigation 137
Saudi Arabia, power 244
Saxe, Maurice de 42

Schelling, Thomas C. 2, 6, 91, 343
  and criticisms of 346
  game theory 345
Schiller, Johann Christoph Friedrich
    von 43
Schwartau, Winn 305
Schwartzkopf, General
    Norman 296
scientific approach in strategic
    studies 6, 10
scientific method, and evolution of
    modern warfare 40
Scobell, Andrew 85
scorched earth, Iraq 255, 257–9,
    263
Second World War
  air power 125, 141, 142
  causes 23, 24, 31, 32, 33
  intelligence 152, 160, 161, 162
  international law 105
  irregular warfare 188
  naval warfare 49, 122
  nuclear weapons 51, 52, 55,
    197, 198
  Pearl Harbor attack 160, 161
  political culture 78
  power 232
  strategic culture 84
  strategic surprise 160, 161, 162
  technology 141, 142
  total warfare 40, 51–4, 55
security studies 3–4, 380
  critical 349
  and strategic studies, relationship
    between 13–14
self-defence, anticipatory 106
sensitivities 338–9
September 11 terrorist attacks 4
  economic costs 271
  homeland security 268
  international law 106
  power and war 233
  rational calculus of war 69
  strategic culture 85
  strategic surprise 161–2
Serbia 293
  cyberwar 191
severe acute respiratory syndrome
    (SARS) 336, 338
Shaw, M. 355
Sherman, General William
    Tecumseh 46
Shirzai, Gul Agha 252
Shultz, George 226
Sierra Leone 296
signal-to-noise ratio,
    intelligence 275
signals intelligence (SIGINT) 154,
    155

Simpson, John 91
Singapore, power 234
Six-Day War 167
small-N problem 273–4, 280
smallpox 216, 334
Smith, Hugh 65
Smith, General Sir Rupert 35, 174,
    289
Snyder, Glenn 345, 346
Snyder, Jack 79, 80
social engineering 30
social learning, and transnational
    norms 83
social media 271
social psychology, causes of war 30,
    33–4
social science, crisis in 382–4
societal security 12
society, and practice of strat-
    egy 367
Somalia 62
  geography 251
  hijacking of ships 175
  humanitarian intervention 68,
    288–9, 296, 297, 326
  media 147
  irregular warfare 190, 192
South Africa, nuclear weapons 196,
    202
South Korea, power 234, 242, 243
Soviet Union
  Afghanistan war 56, 163, 179
  cold war 3, 55, 232–3
    arms control 214–15, 216–17
    arms race 23
    nuclear weapons 196,
      198–201, 203, 204, 206
    space war 128
  collapse 3
  Cuban missile crisis 161, 162,
    163–4
  intelligence 158–9, 162–3, 166
  nuclear weapons 196, 197,
      198–201, 203, 204, 205, 206
    arms control 214–15, 216–17,
      218
    arsenal reduction 208
    nuclear deterrence and
      strategic culture 79
  power 232–3, 241, 244
  practice of strategy 362
  technology 139
space-based sensing 143
space command and control
    systems 143
space war 128–9, 148
Spain, terrorism 270
Spanier, John 215
Special Forces, power 238

special intelligence missions 156
Sri Lanka, insurgency 177
stability and support operations
    (SASO) 248
Stalin, Joseph 162
state-centric approach to world
    politics 12
stealth technology 135, 139
Stevens, Tim C. 306, 307
Strategic Arms Limitation Treaties
    (SALT I and II) 216–17, 218
Strategic Arms Reduction Talks
    (START I, II, and New
    START) 206, 210, 227
strategic culture 76–8, 93–5
  case studies 85–6
  as cause of war 36
  constructivism 83–4
  continuity versus change 84–7
  definitions 80
  irregular warfare 188, 189–90
  keepers of strategic culture 87–8
  non-state, state and
    multi-state 88–90
  and nuclear deterrence 79–80
  practice of strategy 367
  sources 80–3
  WMDs 90–2
strategic education 359–63
strategic imagination 389
strategic nuclear weapons 198–9
Strategic Offensive Reductions
    Treaty (SORT, Moscow
    Treaty) 206, 218, 227
strategic preferences 70
strategic studies 2–7
  in the academy 10
  classical realist tradition 7–9
  criticisms see criticisms of
    strategic studies
  development 378–9
  future see future of strategic
    studies
  'Golden Age' 342–5
  language of 352–4
  relevance 355
  and security studies, relationship
    between 13–14
  world according to 349–51
strategic surprise see surprise,
    strategic
strategic terms, defining 364
strategic theory 60–1, 74
  Clausewitz's On War 65–9
  enduring relevance of
    strategy 72–4
  logic of strategy 61–5
  Sun Tzu, Mao and the
    jihadists 70–2

strategists *see* practice of strategy
strategy
    definitions 5
    ends of 351–2
    enduring relevance 72–4
    general theory *see* general theory
        of strategy
    logic 61–5
    practice *see* practice of strategy
strategy bridge 364, 371
structured analytic techniques 163
Stuxnet attack 130, 148, 191, 311,
        312, 314
sublimation 30
submarine-launched ballistic mis-
        siles (SLBMs) 199, 210
submarines 49, 50, 51, 53, 54
Sudan
    geography 251
    irregular warfare 192
Suez crisis 24
Suganami, Hidemi 22–3, 24, 33
suicide terrorism 271
Sun Tzu 359–60
    barbarity, unnecessary 105
    and Clausewitz, ideas
        compared 70, 71, 383
    intelligence 152, 168
    strategic culture 78, 82
    strategic theory 61, 63, 70–1, 72,
        73, 74
    war as political instrument 62
Sundarji, General 220
supply issues
    for armies, and evolution of
        modern warfare 41,
        42, 45
    irregular warfare 187
support, irregular warfare 179–81
    popular *see* public opinion
'surging', intelligence agencies
        167
al-Suri, Abu Musab 73
surprise, strategic
    causes and correctives 160–4
    and peace operations 297
Sweden, strategic culture 85–6
Swidler, Ann 79, 87
symbols, and strategic culture 81,
        82
Syria
    international law 108–9
    Israel's 2007 attack 225
    nuclear weapons 202
    power 244
    technology 143
    Yom Kippur War 161
systems analysis 343, 345, 346
systems integration 143

Taber, Robert 174, 188, 190
tactical nuclear weapons
        (TNWs) 198
tailored deterrence 91–2
Taiwan
    Haitian presidential
        inauguration 293
    power 240, 244
Taliban
    irregular warfare 174, 182, 192
    nuclear weapons 203
    technology 139
    US military transformation 248,
        249–55, 259–60, 263, 264
Tamil Tigers 177
tanks
    evolution of modern warfare 50,
        51, 53
    M1A2 and Merkava com-
        pared 134
    technology 134, 135, 138
Taras, Raymond 84
Taylor, A. J. P. 31
TeAmZ USA 191
technology and warfare 132,
        148–50
    air power 125
    challenges of the new
        technology 146–7
    cyberpower *see* cyberpower
    economics 237, 241–2
    evolution of modern warfare 40,
        44, 45
    naval warfare 47, 48
    total warfare 50, 51–2, 53
    future 147–8
    intelligence 165–6
    irregular warfare 174, 188, 191–2
    language of strategic studies 354
    mapping military
        technology 136–8
    political reform 271
    and power 243
    practice of strategy 368
    revolution in military af-
        fairs 138–46, 237
    revolutionary insurgency 120
    strategic culture 81, 90
    strategic theory 72
    technophiles and
        technophobes 133
    terrorism 270
    US military transformation 248,
        259–60
    ways of thinking about 133–6
telegraphs 45, 139
Templar, Sir Gerald 187
Terriff, Terry 82
terror, war on 389

terrorism 173–4, 192–4, 269–71
    counterterrorism 184–9
    definitions 174–6
    homeland security 268–73,
        282–3
        small-N problem 273–4
        US preparations 274–81
    now and in the future
        189–92
    theory and practice 176–83
    transnational 269
    see also irregular warfare
Thatcher, Margaret 24
thermal imaging devices 138
thermonuclear weapons 197–8
think tanks 343, 381
Thompson, Kenneth 25
Thompson, Michael 87
Thompson, Robert 184, 185
Thompson, W. R. 35
Thornton, E. P. 10
Thucydides 8, 78, 82, 360
time
    irregular warfare 177–8
    practice of strategy 369
torpedoes 49
total war 40, 49–55
tragedy of the commons 329, 330
transformation theory *see* United
        States of America: military
        transformation
transformed forces 236, 237–8
transistors 143
transnational terrorism 269
Treitschke, H. von 21
Treverton, Gregory 167
Trotsky, Leon 10
tsunami (2004), humanitarian
        relief 124, 326
tuberculosis 336
Turkey
    defence expenditure 140
    power 238, 239, 244
Tutsis 290

Ukraine, nuclear weapons 196
understanding the nature and
        character of strategy
        364–6
UNESCO, 'Peace Through
        Understanding' motto 32
unintended consequences of strat-
        egy 366
United Kingdom/Great Britain/
        England
    air power 125
    American War of
        Independence 63

Cyprus 179
entente cordiale 23
evolution of modern warfare
    army, limitations on 41
    naval warfare 47, 48
    total warfare 50, 51
Falklands war 24, 31–2
First World War 50
Gulf War 25, 31, 141–2
Iraq War 111
Libyan intervention 108
naval warfare 122
nuclear weapons 196, 200, 203,
    205
    testing 215
peace operations 288, 296
power 234, 239, 241, 242
practice of strategy 362
Second World War
    causes 31, 33
    total warfare 51, 53
technology 141–2
United Nations Security
    Council 108, 109
United Nations
Charter 183
    jus ad bellum 105–9
classical realist tradition 9
General Assembly 98
humanitarian intervention 300
    permissive causes of war 25
    Security Council politics 292–3
peace operations 287–91, 292,
    295–6, 300
    Bosnia 289–90, 296
    Libya 297
    Rwanda 290–1
    Somalia 62, 297, 289, 326
Security Council (UNSC)
    cold war 287
    humanitarian
        intervention 292–3
    international law 98, 170–9
    Libya 297
    peace operations 287–8, 291,
        295, 297
support 389
WMDs
    arms control 226
    counterproliferation 222–3
    defined 216
    Iran 224
    Iraq 220
United States of America
Afghanistan
    casualties 299
    military transformation 49–55
    technology 139
air power 298

American-centric paradigm in
    strategic studies 362–3
American Civil War 45, 46–7
American War of
    Independence 63
army deployment 117
Board of National Estimates 158
Central Intelligence Agency
    (CIA) 154, 155, 156, 159,
    160, 165
chemical weapons stockpile
    destroyed 333
cold war 3, 55, 232–3
    arms control 214–15, 216–17
    arms race 23
    nuclear weapons 196,
        198–201, 203, 204, 206
    space war 128
cyberpower 311, 312
Defense Intelligence Agency 159
Director of National Intelli-
    gence 158, 160, 165
environmental problems 333
Guantanamo Bay 111
Gulf War
    causes 25, 31
    strategic theory 67, 68
    technology 136, 137
homeland security 267–8,
    270–1, 282–3
    Department of Homeland
        Security 160, 165
    National Exercise
        Program 275, 276, 281,
        282, 283
    National Planning
        Scenarios 278
    new threat? 268–73
    Northern Command
        (NORTHCOM) 276–7
    preparations 273–81
    small-N problem 273–4
    TOPOFF series 276, 277, 278,
        280, 282, 283
Human Terrain System (HTS) 89
humanitarian intervention 294
    Bosnia 293
    Rwanda 290
    Somalia 68, 147, 289, 293,
        294, 296
intelligence and strategy 152–68
Iraq War
    casualties 299
    causes 25, 31
    international law 106, 108, 111
    military transformation
        255–63
    revolution in military
        affairs 235–6

strategic theory 68
    technology 139, 144–6
irregular warfare 174, 192–3
    counterterrorism
        measures 186, 188
    Lockerbie bombing 189
Korean War 55–6, 68
manoeuvre warfare 119
military transformation 247–9,
    263–6
    Afghanistan 249–55
    Iraq 255–63
National Geo-spatial Intelligence
    Agency 154
National Reconnaissance
    Office 154
National Security Agency 154
navy 123
    Cooperative Engagement
        Capability 143
    nuclear weapons 196, 197,
        198–201, 203, 204, 205,
        206, 210
    arms control 214–15, 216–17,
        218, 226, 227
    arsenal reduction 208
    assertive disarmament 207
peace operations 288, 290–1
    full force protection 298
    Libya 108, 297
power 234–5, 242, 243, 244–5
    arts of war 237–9
    military balances 239, 240,
        241
    new world order 232–4
    revolution in military
        affairs 235–7
revolution in military affairs 57,
    235–7
Second World War 54
strategic culture 79, 85
strategic surprise 160–4
strategic theory 63, 64
systems integration 143
tailored deterrence 92
technology 133, 134, 136, 138,
    139–40, 144–5
    military transformation 248
    quality versus quantity 141
    speciation of weapons 141,
        142, 143
United Nations Security
    Council 108, 109
Vietnam War 55, 56
WMDs 220–4, 226
Universal Adversary (UA)
    279–80
unmanned airborne vehicles (UAVs,
    'drones') 156

uranium, depleted (UA) 332
urban warfare 238
    US military transformation 251,
        255-7, 260-3
utopian thinkers 3

Verba, Sidney 78, 79
Vietnam, power 238
Vietnam War
    intelligence 159
    irregular warfare 179, 180, 186,
        188
    land warfare 117, 119
    limited warfare 55, 56
    strategic theory 63, 67
vitamin deficiency 37
Von Maltzen 48
Von Moltke, Field Marshal Count
    H. 4, 5
vulnerabilities 338-9

Wæver, O. 343
Wallace, W. 36
Waltz, Kenneth 25, 29, 30
Walzer, Michael 10
warfare
    air see air warfare
    biological see biological warfare
    causes see causes of war
    chemical see chemical warfare
    coming change in the character
        of? 316-17
    criticisms of strategic studies 12
    cyberspace see cyberspace war
    economic costs 35, 270-1
        cyberpower 316
    evolution see evolution of mod-
        ern warfare
    friction 69, 73
    geography see geography and
        strategy
    international law 102-12
    irregular see irregular warfare
    land see land warfare
    limited versus unlimited 67-8, 361
    nature of 66-7
    naval see naval warfare and
        maritime strategy

nuclear see nuclear weapons
    as political instrument 62
    power see power and war
    preparation for 368
    rational calculus of 68-9
    space see space war
    strategic theory see strategic
        theory
    study 21-8
        difficulties 22-3
    technology see technology and
        warfare
    virtues 21
    'within' and 'beyond' states
        34-6
warrior cultures 190, 192, 329
Washington, George 152
water scarcity 330
weak states 234
weapons
    air power 125, 126
    environmental damage 332-3
    evolution of modern warfare 44,
        45, 46
    of mass destruction see
        weapons of mass
        destruction
    nuclear see nuclear weapons
    power 241
    space war 128
    speciation 141-3
    technology 135, 136, 137, 138,
        141-3
weapons of mass destruction
    (WMDs) 213-14,
        227-9
    arms control 224-7
        cold war 214-17
        definitions 216
        post-cold war era
            218-20
    counterproliferation 220-2
        challenges 222-3
    counterterrorism 165
    definitions 216
    diplomatic option 223-4
    homeland security 277-8
    international regimes 219
    irregular warfare 191, 192
    and power 244, 245

strategic culture 90-2
    technology 145
    see also biological warfare;
        chemical warfare; nuclear
        weapons
Weber, Max 79
Weigley, Robert 72-3
Wells, H. G. 125
Wendt, Alexander 83
Wikileaks controversy 156
Wildavsky, Aaron 87
Wilson, Edward 28
Wilson, R. W. 87
Wilson, Woodrow 29
Wohlstetter, Albert 2, 6, 343
Wohlstetter, Robert 160
women, and evolution of modern
        warfare 51
Woolsey, James 220
World Trade Center attack see
        September 11 terrorist
        attacks
World War I see First World War
World War II see Second World
        War
Wylie, J. C. 5, 360
Wyn Jones, Richard 352, 354

Yeltsin, Boris 218
Yemen, irregular warfare 188
Yom Kippur war
    infrared projectors 138
    nuclear weapons 208
    strategic surprise 161, 162
Yoshida Doctrine 85
youth bulges 328
Yugoslavia, former
    humanitarian intervention 34
    strategic culture 86
    technology 143
    tribunals 291

Zaborowski, Marcin 93
al-Zarqawi, Abu Musab 183
al-Zawahiri, Ayman 64, 174, 183,
        269, 272, 278
Zenko, Micah 297
Zia, General Mohammed 253